Macroeconomics

Macroeconomics

A European Text

Second Edition

Michael Burda and
Charles Wyplosz

OXFORD UNIVERSITY PRESS

1997

For Maike and Maxwell

A la Dame de Taulignan et ses enfants

Oxford University Press, Great Clarendon Street, Oxford OX2 6DP

Oxford New York

Athens Auckland Bangkok Bogota Bombay
Buenos Aires Calcutta Cape Town Dar es Salaam
Delhi Florence Hong Kong Istanbul Karachi
Kuala Lumpur Madras Madrid Melbourne
Mexico City Nairobi Paris Singapore
Taipei Tokyo Toronto

and associated companies in
Berlin Ibadan

Oxford is a trade mark of Oxford University Press

Published in the United States
by Oxford University Press Inc., New York

British Library Cataloguing in Publication Data
Data available

Library of Congress Cataloging in Publication Data
Burda, Michael C.
    Macroeconomics : a European text / Michael Burda and Charles
Wyplosz. — 2nd ed.
    Includes bibliographical references and index.
    1. Macroeconomics. 2. Europe—Economic conditions. I. Wyplosz.
Charles. II. Title
HB172.5.B87 1997 339—dc20 96–24643

ISBN 0–19–877469–9
ISBN 0–19–877468–0 (pbk)

10 9 8 7 6 5 4 3 2 1

Typeset by Graphicraft Typesetters Ltd., Hong Kong
Printed by Mateu Cromo, Spain

Preface to the Second Edition

Second editions usually track first ones quite closely, and ours is no exception. Why tinker with a winning formula? Our 'European text' has been a successful recipe, and has been widely adopted across Europe, in the original English as well as in French, German, Italian, Spanish, and Polish translations. (Russian and Ukrainian are on the way!). Over the past three years, a number of motivated colleagues and students came to us with constructive criticisms and suggestions. We have freely used their advice where possible and wound up revising a number of chapters more thoroughly than is commonly the case; those suggestions we didn't adopt in the end were those that would have increased the length of the book, something we wanted to avoid. (In fact this book is longer because of typesetting improvement, designed to make the book easier to read.)

So what is new in the second edition?

First, we have produced two new chapters. Chapter 10 appears at the junction between the building blocks of macroeconomics (microfoundations, partial equilibrium analyses of goods, money, and labour markets) and what was traditional macro of earlier decades (IS–LM, neoclassical synthesis with short-run nominal rigidities). It presents a general macroeconomic equilibrium emphasizing the role of assumptions about wage and price rigidity, including both the classical and Keynesian models in the same structure (IS, LM, labour, and production).[1] It is a concession to demands—which we had rejected earlier—to set up the closed economy version of the IS–LM framework before going full speed into the more elaborate and complex Mundell–Fleming formulation. We think the current setup will give the student more breathing room to master this important material.

The second major addition, Chapter 14, presents business cycles in theory and practice. It serves several purposes. To begin with, it gives the teacher an excellent opportunity to apply the efficient but complex AS–AD framework to an important set of macro issues: the characteristics, causes, and effects of the cycle. Second, many teachers were looking for a descriptive treatment of the cycle and the long tradition of theories that have sought to explain it. A somewhat smaller, but active, subset sought a more balanced exposition of the real business cycle theory than is found in most undergraduate macroeconomics textbooks. Finally, we wanted to present the students with what for us was a surprisingly robust set of stylized facts about business cycles across countries and especially in Europe. In the process we rediscovered the old and useful

---

[1] The inspiration is Patinkin's (1956) synthesis and Sargent's (1987) advanced text.

'reference cycle' approach pioneered half a century ago by Burns and Mitchell at the National Bureau of Economic Research. In doing so we have given teachers and students considerable ammunition for animated discussions over the 'correct' theory of the cycle, which we agnostically leave open.

Second, all chapters have been revised, some significantly. In the quest for more logical continuity, we inverted the order of the labour and growth chapters and rewrote them to account for this change. Chapter 7 has been scaled down—we removed the imports/exports approach to the real exchange rate and trade balance, leaving to a box the discussion that probably belongs in a course on international trade. Chapters 10–12 (now 11–13) have been polished up, while Chapter 17 (supply side) has received a section on the European unemployment problem, relieving the earlier labour market chapter of its considerable institutional burden. Material from the two omitted chapters (LDC debt and Eastern Europe) have been blended into the main text; the debt crisis is no longer 'hot' for the moment, while central and eastern Europe looks increasingly like 'normal' macroeconomies. The book contains a number of new, improved, and updated mathematical appendices.

Third, we have updated and streamlined tables, figures, boxes, and exercises. Practical information provided in our book is highly valued by instructors, yet too much data can clutter the presentation. We have tried to accommodate this desire for less 'busy-ness' in the layout, while adding some new examples and updating older ones. We have suppressed a number of exercises which were rightfully considered too difficult or orthogonal to the important issues, while adding new ones which draw material from current issues and problems. Overall, our publisher has made a real effort to bring more space and fresh air to the textbook. While there may be more pages, they are easier to read, and, most importantly for the students, there is no more material.

To the instructor

As with the first edition, the text begins with microfoundations and moves towards more 'standard' macroeconomic approaches. While our own experience has convinced us that this is a superior pedagogical approach, we are aware that some instructors prefer to deal with microfoundations after students have acquired a feel for the 'big picture'. We have tried to make the book open for reading in a different order than is currently structured. In particular, we would like to suggest the following two possible alternative 'tracks' for courses too short to cover the core of the book—Chapters 1–14:

Aggregate demand/ business cycles track	Neoclassical/ microfoundations track
Chapter 1	Chapter 1
Chapter 2	Chapter 2
Chapter 3	Chapter 3
Chapter 8	Chapter 4
Chapter 9	Chapter 5
Chapter 11	Chapter 6
Chapter 12	Chapter 8
Chapter 13	Chapter 9
Chapter 14	Chapter 10
Chapter 5	Chapter 12
Chapter 6	Chapter 13
Chapter 7	Chapter 14

Acknowledgements

The second edition owes a great deal to the many colleagues who have taken the time to let us know of their reactions. We have not always followed their suggestions, but we have certainly listened very carefully.

Major changes have been undertaken following extensive exchanges with Jean-Pierre Danthine (University of Lausanne), Antonio Fatas (INSEAD), Michael Funke (Hamburg University), Alistair Milne (University of Surrey), and Anders Vredin (Stockholm School of Economics).

Very useful comments and suggestions which have also shaped the revisions were provided by Hans Aage (Roskilde University), Roger Backhouse (University of Birmingham), Antonio Barbosa (Universidade Nova de Lisboa), Guiseppe Bertola (Universita Turin), Mark de Broeck (KU Leuven), Manuel Correla de Pinho (University of Porto), Stefan Gerlach (BIS), Nathalie Gilson (Facultés Catholiques de Mons), Francis X. Hof (Technische Universität Wien), Jesper Jespersen (Roskilde University), Thorolfur Matthiasson (University of Iceland), Andrew Oswald (Oxford), and Heiki Taimio (University of Joensuu). In addition, we have used some exercises generously offered to us by Morten Skak (Odense University).

The following have generously helped with data collection: Benoit Coeuré (INSEE), Francesco Papadia (Bank of Italy), Pierre Sicsic (Banque de France), Jorg Elmeskov (OECD). Institutional (not proprietary) information on the Bundesbank was provided by Karen Cabos and Otmar Issing.

Our publisher has shown understanding as successive deadlines were transgressed; we appreciate the trust and encouragement from Andrew Schuller and Tracy Mawson. Graduate students Antje Mertens, Stefan Profit, Manfred Königstein, and especially Mark Weder should be thanked for their careful reading of draft chapters as well as constructive comments. Michaela Kleber and Gitte Aabo also provided useful comments at the development stages of the second edition.

A number of research assistants have helped us update the data and produce new tables and figures; we acknowledge the dedicated efforts of Matthas Almus, Ulrike Handtke, Matthew Hansen, and Astrid Knott. Finally, we are indebted to our secretaries Brigitte Pernet in Fontainebleau, Laurence Péricard in Geneva, and especially Claudia Keidel in Berlin.

Contents

Part V: Inflation and Business Cycles

Part VI: Macroeconomic Policy

Part VII: Financial Markets and the Exchange Rate

Detailed Contents

Part II: The Real Macroeconomy

3. Intertemporal Budget Constraints   45

Part VI: Macroeconomic Policy

Introduction to Macroeconomics

This part sets the scene. Chapter 1 explains the object and methods of macro-economics, its history and usefulness, and its controversies. It provides a large number of essential definitions and offers a preview of what is to follow. Chapter 2 presents the national income accounts, which describe the inner relationships of the economy's activity, as well as the balance of payments, which summarizes an economy's dealings with the rest of the world.

1

What is Macroeconomics?

1.1. Overview

Not a day passes when we don't hear about unemployment, inflation, economic growth, stock markets, interest rates, or foreign exchange rates. We hear and read so much about these phenomena because, directly or indirectly, they affect our well-being. It is perhaps mostly for this reason that macroeconomics, the study of economy-wide phenomena, is so exciting. More than just headlines, however, macroeconomics is a fascinating intellectual adventure. The breadth of issues it covers is evidence enough of its inherent complexity, yet, simple economic reasoning can take us a long way. And it is often surprising how well a few simple ideas fit complex situations.

Macroeconomics can also be useful. The economic well-being of poor and wealthy households alike are affected by movements in interest rates or the rate of inflation. Businesses stand to gain or lose considerable amounts of money when their economic environment changes, regardless of how well they manage their affairs. Being prepared for such changes in fortunes can have considerable value—in Europe for example, where dismissing employees and closing factories can be especially costly. Macroeconomics is relevant to voters who wonder what their governments are up to, or to consumers who care about interest and exchange rates. It is useful to governments as it may help avoid some of the miseries that have plagued mankind, such as deep recessions and hyperinflations which can tear at a society's social fabric.

1.1.1. Income and Economic Growth

One of the most important economic measures of a nation's well-being is its output and income deriving from market activities. The next chapter presents details on a measure of such activities, the **gross domestic product (GDP)**. GDP increases when more is produced and earned within a nation's boundaries. Figure 1.1(*a*) displays the evolution of GDP for France, Germany, and the UK since 1900. In all cases, a positive long-run general tendency or **trend** dominates shorter-run fluctuations. Especially in the last few decades, the underlying trend rate of growth has been fairly stable. This point is supported by part (*b*) of the figure, in which the data are plotted on a logarithmic scale on the vertical axis, so that the slope of the curve

is a measure of the growth rate. A constant growth rate per annum would yield a straight line.[1]

For the large majority of countries, this trend growth in total output reflects remarkable increases in living standards. Table 1.1 shows that per capita or average income has increased by a factor of 4 in Belgium since 1900, by a factor of 7 in Sweden, and by a factor of 14 in Japan. In contrast, real income per capita rose by only 70% over the same period in India and by only 10% in Bangladesh. Needless to say, some countries have faced serious setbacks, such as wars and famines, while others grew rapidly initially but then slowed down.

Economic growth is one of the most exciting issues in macroeconomics. There are many reasons for economies to grow, and they are reviewed in Chapter 5. One of them is population increase, since more people can produce more output. Another is the accumulation of means of production: plant and equipment, roads, communication networks, and other forms of infrastructure make workers more productive. Most important is the development and harnessing of knowledge to economic ends. For example, the sharp acceleration of scientific discoveries towards the end of the eighteenth century is sometimes associated with the onset of the industrial revolution.

A second important message contained in Figure 1.1 is that the real output of economies tends to fluctuate around its trend. In Figure 1.2, we demonstrate this point by plotting quarterly data (sampled every quarter, meaning three months) of the GDP for the UK. Successive periods of fast growth and consolidation are called **business cycles**. One important challenge of macroeconomics is to explain these deviations of GDP from its underlying trend: why they occur and persist over a few years, and what can be done, if anything, to avoid the disruptions that are associated with them. This is the common thread of Parts III, IV, and V of this book.

1.1.2. Fluctuations in Economic Activity and Unemployment

One important phenomenon associated with cyclical fluctuations is **unemployment**, the fact that people

---

[1] For mathematically inclined readers, if $x(t)$ grows at the constant rate g, $(1/x)dx/dt = g$, so that $x(t) = A\exp(gt)$ or $\ln x(t) = \ln A + gt$, where A is a constant and t stands for time.

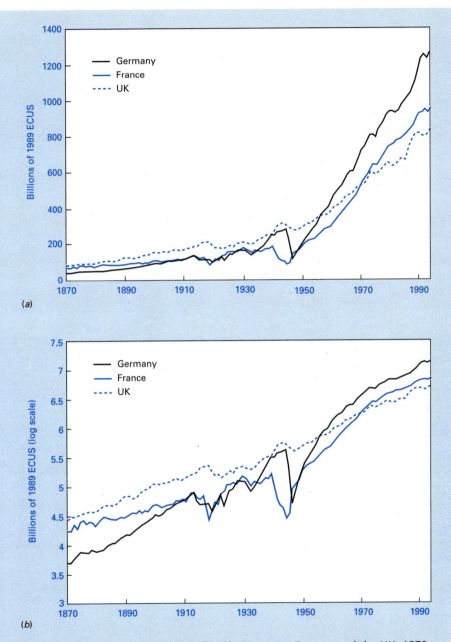

(a)

(b)

Figure 1.1. Gross Domestic Product (GDP), Germany, France, and the UK, 1870–1994

The movements of real product and income of the three economies here have been dominated by positive economic growth. Growth is exponential, implying that the level of output is rising by ever-larger increments each year. When the data are displayed on a logarithmic scale instead (part *b*), equal distances on the vertical axis represent increments of equal percentage size, so the slope of the curve is the rate of growth.

Source: Maddison (1991); IMF

Table 1.1. Real Income per capita
(GNP, 1980 $US)

	1900	1913	1929	1950	1987	1992	Av. growth rate (%)
Austria	1,651	1,985	2,118	2,123	8,792	10,000	2.0
Belgium	2,126	2,406	2,882	3,114	8,769	10,185	1.7
Canada	1,808	2,773	3,286	4,882	12,702	12,635	2.1
Denmark	1,732	2,246	2,913	3,895	9,949	10,423	2.0
Finland	1,024	1,295	1,667	2,610	9,500	9,050	2.4
France	1,600	1,934	2,629	2,941	9,475	10,385	2.1
Germany	1,558	1,907	2,153	2,508	9,964	11,350	2.2
Italy	1,343	1,773	2,089	2,323	9,024	10,129	2.2
Japan	677	795	1,162	1,116	9,756	11,833	3.2
Netherlands	2,146	2,400	3,373	3,554	9,197	10,323	1.7
Sweden	1,482	1,792	2,242	3,898	10,328	10,312	2.1
Switzerland	2,077	2,474	3,672	5,256	11,907	12,233	1.9
UK	2,798	3,065	3,200	4,171	9,178	9,650	1.4
USA	2,911	3,772	4,909	6,697	13,550	14,229	1.7
Bangladesh	349	371	372	331	375	451	0.3
India	378	399	403	359	662	756	0.8
South Korea	549	610	749	564	4,143	5,970	2.7
Argentina	1,284	1,770	2,036	2,314	3,302	2,714	0.8
Mexico	649	822	835	1,169	2,667	3,172	1.7
USSR[a]	797	973	1,044	2,265	5,948	6,301	2.4

[a] Soviet data were notoriously unreliable and optimistic. We present them to show the approximate performance of the most important economy of the ex-communist world.

Sources: Maddison (1991); Heston and Summers (Penn); World Tables Mark 5.6a

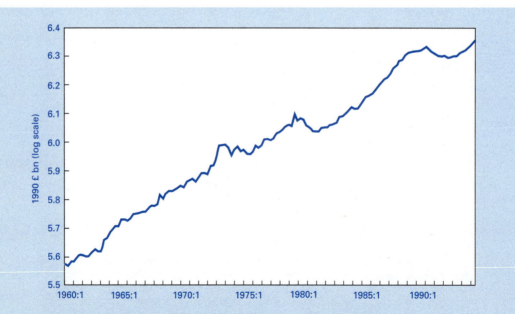

Figure 1.2. Quarterly Gross Domestic Product, UK, 1960:1–1994:2

With quarterly data, fluctuations of economic activity around trend become more apparent.

Sources: IMF; OECD

seeking jobs cannot get them. Unemployment exists even in economies that are growing rapidly. Chapter 6 is devoted entirely to studying this 'scourge' of advanced economies. To measure unemployment, we usually relate it to the size of the total **labour force**. The labour force consists of those individuals who are either working or are actively looking for a job. In comparison with the total population, it leaves out young people who are not yet working, the old who are retired, and those who do not wish to work. The **unemployment rate** is the ratio of the number of unemployed workers to the size of the labour force.

Table 1.2 presents the **correlation coefficient** between GDP growth and the rate of unemployment. The correlation coefficient is a statistical measure of how closely the two variables move together. The fact that it is negative means that, in periods of expansion when the GNP is growing rapidly, unemployment tends to be falling, and that it rises in periods of slow growth. This inverse relationship between output growth and unemployment is called **Okun's Law**.[2] The law is not perfect—if it were, the correlation coefficient would be −1. This illustrates how economic 'laws' are usually approximations to reality, and not reality itself.

There are many reasons why we should be concerned about unemployment. First, it represents a loss of output and income as workers stay idle. Second, even with well developed and efficient unemployment assistance programmes, unemployed workers may experience emotional stress and their skills may deteriorate. Even if they are not measurable, the social and psychological costs of unemployment are high for the affected individuals and for society as a whole. At the same time, unemployment is known to exert down-ward pressure on labour costs, which may eventually encourage firms to hire additional personnel. Thus, equilibrating mechanisms are at work which run from unemployment to wage moderation to job creation.

1.1.3. Factors of Production and Income Distribution

Total national income is created by work effort combined with equipment. (Land and other inputs also matter, but in a much smaller proportion.) **Labour** and **capital** are the technical names given to these two main **factors of production**, or inputs necessary for the generation of goods and services. The distribution of total income between these two factors of production is, of course, a deep political issue, but one with important economic aspects as well. Understandably, wage-earners wish to enlarge their share of the pie. Figure 1.3 shows the share of income in manufacturing that goes to labour, the **labour share**. It also plots the evolution the stock market **index** over time. An index is a number whose value does not have a meaning *per se*, but is set to take a simple value (e.g. 1 or 100) on a particular date for easy comparison. In stock markets, companies are traded and valued on the basis of their profitability. The figure shows an inverse relationship between the labour share and the stock price index. When the share of income going to labour is high, less is available for the firms' owners, and stock prices are depressed. In Chapter 4 we will see that depressed stock prices may adversely affect the accumulation of productive equipment and, ultimately, the growth and size of the economic pie itself.

1.1.4. Inflation

The **inflation rate** measures the rate of change of the average level of prices. The price level is usually measured as a price index, the price of goods in terms of money. Inflation is usually quoted in percentages per year, even when it is measured more frequently, such as every quarter or every month. Most of the time, inflation is low or moderate at rates ranging from just above 0% to 4% or 6%. In the 1970s many European countries experienced double-digit inflation, with rates rising to 10%, 20%, or more. In a number of countries, for example in Latin America, inflation rates of several hundred per cent were quite common, and some remain so. When inflation is very high it is usually measured on a monthly basis; the term **hyperinfla-**

Table 1.2. Okun's Law

	Correlation coefficient[a]
Germany	−0.71
UK	−0.63
Italy	−0.18
Sweden	−0.70

[a] Correlation coefficient between change in unemployment rate and growth rate of real GNP, 1965–93.

Sources: IMF; OECD

[2] Named after the late US economist Arthur Okun, who found that a 1% decrease in the US unemployment rate was associated with a roughly 3% increase in economic growth. Although this relationship varies across countries and time periods, it is a useful element in the macroeconomist's toolbox.

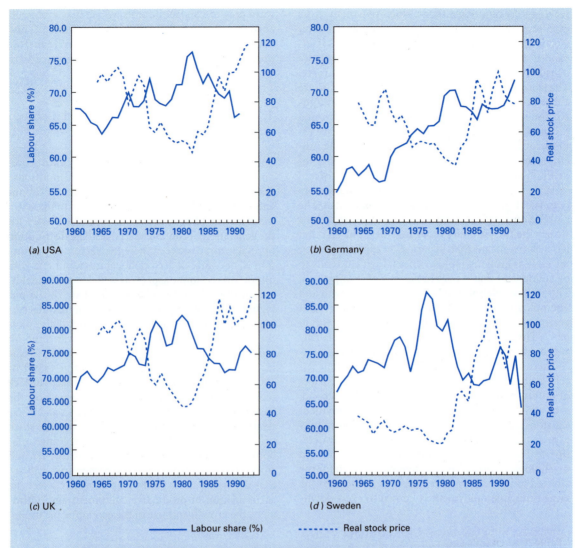

Figure 1.3. Labour Share of Income in Manufacturing and Stock Prices, Four Countries, 1960–1993

Labour and capital share the fruits of the economic activity of a nation. The labour share is the fraction accruing to workers in the form of wages and other compensation. The valuation of firm assets reflected in stock prices is negatively associated with the labour share.

Sources: OECD; IMF; US Department of Labor

tion describes situations when this monthly inflation rate exceeds 50%. A sign of exceptional economic distress, hyperinflation was observed in Central Europe in the early 1920s, in Latin America in the 1980s, and in Poland and the USSR in the twilight of their communist regimes in the late 1980s/early 1990s.

In normal times, inflation is related to the business cycle. Figure 1.4 shows how the rate of inflation changes when the rate of capacity utilization varies.

The rate of **capacity utilization** is a measure of how fully companies employ their plants and equipment, and it serves as a good indicator of cyclical conditions. The inflation rate is generally **procyclical**: it rises in periods of high growth and declines in periods of slow growth or stagnation. In contrast, the behaviour of unemployment is **countercyclical**. The behaviour of inflation is investigated in Parts IV and V of this book.

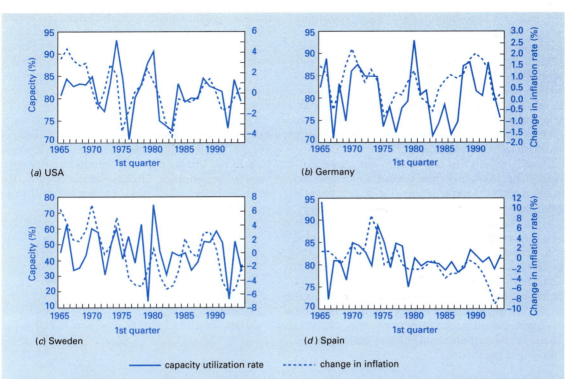

Figure 1.4. Capacity Utilization Rates and Inflation, Four Countries, 1965–1994

When measures of the utilization of capacity indicate a high level of employment in facto-ries, the rate of inflation tends to increase. Conversely, low levels of activity are accompanied with falling inflation.

Sources: IMF; OECD *Main Economic Indicators*

1.1.5. Financial Markets and the Real Economy

Financial markets play a central role in modern economies and are of major interest in macroeco-nomics. In conjunction with banks, financial markets collect resources from households in the form of savings and lend them out. They provide a means for trading currencies, stocks, and bonds. One specific feature of these markets is the extreme volatility of their prices. One measure of volatility is the **coefficient of variation**, which is the variability of some quantity measured as a fraction of its average value.[3] Table 1.3 compares the coefficients of variation of financial market prices (stocks, exchange rates, interest rates) with the coefficients of variation of macroeconomic variables such as the GDP, the price level, and **invest-ment**. The rate of investment measures the speed at

Table 1.3. Quarterly Variability of Macro-economic Variables as Measured by their Coefficients of Variation[a]

	France	Germany	UK
Real GDP growth	1.20	1.38	1.94
Inflation rate	0.57	0.51	0.64
Change in stock prices	8.03	8.66	4.37
Change in value of currency[b]	−7.35	2.31	−6.94
Nominal interest rate	0.27	0.40	0.28
Investment ratio	0.09	0.10	0.07

[a] Standard deviation divided by the mean over the sample (1970:1–1994:4).
[b] (1975:1–1994:4)

Sources: IMF; OECD

---

[3] Technically, the coefficient of variation is the standard devia-tion of a variable divided by its mean.

which firms acquire the physical means of production, as a percentage of GDP.

Several conclusions may be drawn from the table. First, financial variables are generally the most volatile of macroeconomic variables. Second, growth rates tend to be more volatile than either interest rates or the investment ratio. Third, the rate of inflation is considerably less volatile than the rate of economic growth. Chapter 10 shows that price rigidity can explain why short-run economic fluctuations occur.

Physical investment is related to financial conditions. In fact, it is one channel through which financial markets affect the **real economy**. The real economy is contrasted with the financial or **monetary economy**: the former concerns the production and consumption of goods and services, and the incomes associated with productive activities; the latter deals with trade in assets, i.e. monetary and financial instruments. Chapter 10 draws the first linkages between real and monetary spheres of the macroeconomy, while Chapter 11 directly addresses the short-run determination of output, interest rates, and exchange rates. Chapters 12 and 13 take up the issues of inflation, exchange rates, and output together.

1.1.6. Openness

Most countries are closely integrated with the rest of the world. They engage in trade, exporting and importing goods and services. The advanced economies are also linked together by trade in financial assets. As a consequence, events in one country can have large effects on other countries. In financial markets, this is illustrated by the rapidity with which they react to each other. It is not a new phenomenon, however: at the turn of the century, trade was already very developed, even if means of communication were considerably slower. Chapter 20 provides a brief historical overview, and Chapter 21 applies those lessons to the current macroeconomic future of Europe.

One measure of a country's openness, or exposure to the influences of the rest of the world, is the ratio of its exports to its GNP. Table 1.4 presents a selection of such ratios. Smaller countries tend to be more open than larger countries. The smaller the country, the more likely that it will specialize in some goods and import the others.

Table 1.4. Ratio of Exports to GDP, 1994

	%
Belgium[a]	69.6
Denmark	34.9
Ethiopia	11.2
India[b]	9.6
Italy	23.0
Japan	9.5
Luxemburg[a]	89.0
Netherlands	51.6
Poland[b]	19.8
Spain	22.3
USA	10.7

[a] 1993 [b] 1992

Source: *IFS Yearbook 1995*

1.2. Macroeconomics as a Discipline

1.2.1. The Genesis of Macroeconomics

Why do we observe cyclical fluctuations in the level of activity, for example the movements of GNP around its trend as in Figures 1.1 and 1.2? Why is unemployment generally countercyclical while changes in inflation seem to be procyclical? It is only recently that economics has concerned itself with such questions. For a long time it was believed that, as a good approximation at least, properly functioning markets would deliver the best possible outcome, and that there was no point in looking into their aggregate behaviour. This principle was called *laissez-faire*. Laissez-faire was opposed by proponents of **interventionism**, who advocated government support for particular markets and industries, including subsidies and protection from foreign competition.

This does not mean that the business cycle was ignored. In fact, a number of cycles were studied and identified, from inventory cycles of one or two years' duration to the Kondratieff cycles lasting roughly half a century. Such cycles were seen as the cumulative outcomes of disturbances such as discoveries, inventions, exceptionally good or bad crops, wrong bets by firms on goods that customers want to buy, or even changing tastes of consumers at home and abroad.

Inflation was seen as the consequence of rapidly growing money stocks, first because of gold discoveries, then because of reckless paper money creation by central banks. As will be seen in Chapter 14, much of this wisdom remains valid today. Yet the Great Depression of the 1930s, which sent millions into unemployment and misery, seemed too severe to be simply bad luck. Reflecting upon the Great Depression in 1936, British economist John Maynard Keynes published *The General Theory of Employment, Interest and Money*, a book that launched the study of macroeconomics. Keynes stressed the role of aggregate demand in macroeconomic fluctuations. His followers later persuaded policy-makers to engage in **aggregate demand management**, that is, to manipulate government demand in order to smooth out fluctuations, mainly to avoid protracted recessions.

An evaluation of the success of demand management policies—which is the subject of Chapters 15 and 16—is not conclusive. There have been both benefits and costs. Since the Second World War, the amplitude of the business cycle seems to have diminished considerably, as can be seen in Figure 1.1. While earlier generations assumed that favourable periods of growth were inevitably followed by periods of declining activity, today we worry mostly about slowdowns of growth. At the same time, economists have also begun to think hard about the supply side—meaning the productive capacity of an economy—and more efficient utilization of labour and capital resources. This applies especially to unemployment, which is a big problem in Europe. These topics are the subject of Chapter 17.

Another remarkable change in the behaviour of the postwar economy concerns the general **price level**, or the cost of goods in terms of money. Up until the Second World War, prices were as likely to rise as they were to fall, as can be seen from Figure 1.5. Apart from war periods, the price level was in fact trendless. Over long periods, say twenty or fifty years, the cost of living, a measure of the average price level, was essentially constant. These two observations show that the world is different today. One interpretation of the postwar era—a controversial one, as we shall see—is that macroeconomics has led to more stable growth rates at the cost of inflation.

1.2.2. Macroeconomics and Microeconomics

Logically, the macroeconomy is just the sum of hundreds or thousands of markets, each of which is explained by microeconomic principles. Microeconomics is devoted to the study of prices of individual goods and of the markets where these goods are produced and sold. Why do we need two separate disciplines? To a great extent they are linked. Microeconomics is dedicated to the analysis of market behaviour of individuals. Macroeconomics is concerned with collective behaviour, the outcome of individual decisions taken without full knowledge of what others do. Keynes stressed the notion of **co-ordination failures**, which arise in decentralized markets as illustrated in the following example.

A consumer wants to purchase a car, but his income is insufficient for him to do so. A car manufacturer could actually hire him to build cars, and with his salary he would then be able to buy one. That one sale, however, would not suffice to pay his salary, so other buyers would need to be found. In order to generate sufficient demand for his employment, several other individuals would need to be hired under similar arrangements, perhaps in different industries. A considerable amount of co-ordination among producers and consumers would be required for this to occur. In principle, prices and markets should fulfil this co-ordinating role. If for some reason they fail to do so, there may be many such consumers wishing to buy goods and willing to work to produce them, but this potential may not be realized and we may have both recession (fewer sales) and unemployment (fewer jobs). Even if market forces tend to correct this imbalance (which they eventually do), the period of time necessary may be long enough to involve significant social costs.

Macroeconomics started with the idea that prices and markets do not continuously resolve all the co-ordination requirements of a modern economy. As micro-economics has moved in this direction too, the sharp distinction between the two fields has been eroded. Modern macroeconomics starts from sound microeconomic principles, and we follow this approach in the early chapters. We then focus on market failures to study business cycles and what can be done about them.

1.2.3. Macroeconomics and Economic Policy

Early macroeconomics argued that governments have the means and the duty to correct market failures. The experiences of the past decades have shown that governments too may fail. Indeed, one major dividing line among macroeconomists is between those who most fear market failures and those who most fear government failures. Yet, in nearly every country, governments are held responsible for the good health of the macroeconomy. At election times incumbent governments are judged, first among many other issues, on

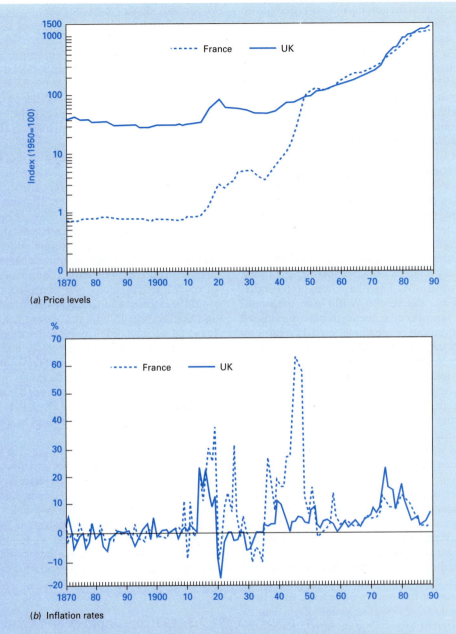

Figure 1.5. Price Levels and Inflation Rates, France and the UK, 1870–1990

Until the outbreak of the First World War, the price level was stable, and inflation was close to zero on average. Since the Second World War, the price level has risen secularly, meaning that average inflation has been positive.

Source: Maddison (1991)

their economic performance. Box 1.1 shows that most governments that failed to deliver low levels of unemployment and inflation have not been re-elected. This attitudinal change explains why we sometimes refer to the birth of macroeconomics as the **Keynesian revolution**. It also shows why the study of macroeconomics is so intertwined with policy and indeed with politics. Part V is devoted to these issues.

BOX 1.1. ECONOMICS AND POLITICS

Inflation and unemployment are often called the two evils of macroeconomics. They are also two measures of national performance which the public understands and can easily monitor. These two rates have been added together to obtain what is called the **misery index**. The index itself has no scientific basis, yet it seems to contain information about the political fortunes of governments: when the index is rising, incumbents tend to be thrown out of office. In many countries, both unemployment and inflation rose around 1973–4, and yet again around 1979–80. Each time, the rise of the misery index was largely related to the sharp increase in oil prices—the so-called oil shocks. The governments at the time were saddled with the blame: in 1974 Giscard d'Estaing displaced the Gaullist government; in Holland, the left replaced the Liberals. Later, the conservative CDU/CSU replaced the SPD in 1982 as reaction to a sharp increase in the misery index; similarly, in Holland, the Liberals regained control of the government in Holland, while in 1982 the Socialists under François Mitterand triumphed in France. Many associate the fall of Margaret Thatcher in 1990—although the Conservative government survived—with a sharp increase in the misery index at the time. The links between economics and elections is one of the subjects of Chapter 16.

1.2.4. Demand and Supply Sides

In its most concentrated form, macroeconomics boils down to the separation of all phenomena into two categories: those that affect the demand for goods and services, and those that affect the supply of those goods and services. This fundamental distinction corresponds to a sharp separation between various types of policy pursued by governments as well as types of disturbance to the economic environment.

The **demand side** relates to spending decisions by **economic agents**, or decision-makers in an economy —households, firms, and government agencies, both at home and abroad. The principle of aggregate demand management policies is that the government can take actions to offset or smooth out those of private agents—firms and households—in order to dampen or eliminate fluctuations in total spending. The idea is to take the edge off recessions as well as booms. Two traditional demand management instruments are fiscal and monetary policy. **Fiscal policy** manipulates the government expenditure or taxes in an attempt to affect the volume of national spending. This subject is studied in detail in Chapter 15. **Monetary policy** is directed at influencing interest and exchange rates, and more generally at conditions on financial markets and their links with the real economy. Chapters 8 and 9 provide an in-depth analysis.

The **supply side** relates to the productive potential of the economy. The choice of hours worked by households, the productivity of their labour, and in general the efficiency with which resources are allocated in generating a nation's output all influence an economy's aggregate supply. Accordingly, supply-side policies represent the government's effort to increase the economy's overall efficiency. In part, this effort is about cutting down government-induced inefficiencies, which were introduced before the importance of the supply side was understood, or as the result of successful lobbying by interest groups. Unemployment policy—designed to fight the scourge of market economies—occupies a key role in the supply side. Chapter 17 explores these issues and shows how the government can improve or worsen the economic climate.

1.3. The Methodology of Macroeconomics

1.3.1. What is to be Explained?

Macroeconomics is concerned with aggregate activity, the level of unemployment, interest rates, inflation, wages, the exchange rate, and the balance of payments with other countries. As Figure 1.6 shows, the variables to be explained using economic principles are called **endogenous** variables. The other variables—those we do not try to explain but take as given—are called **exogenous** variables. Examples of variables considered exogenous are policy instruments (the tools of fiscal and monetary policies), economic conditions abroad (foreign levels of activity and interest rates), the price of oil on international markets,

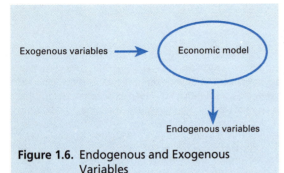

Figure 1.6. Endogenous and Exogenous Variables

Endogenous variables are the object of analysis in an economic model. Exogenous variables are determined outside the economic model. The weather, political decisions, and the onset of time are examples of variables usually considered exogenous.

and sometimes domestic social conditions such as trade union militancy. The goal is to explain the evolution of endogenous variables by the behaviour of exogenous variables.

The distinction between endogenous and exogenous variables is somewhat arbitrary. Many exogenous variables are not strictly independent of the endogenous variables. For example, fiscal and monetary policy decisions are often responses to the course of inflation or unemployment. While it is convenient to take policy variables as exogenous, it is sometimes illuminating to endogenize them. Chapter 16 takes some steps in this direction.

1.3.2. Theory and Realism

Macroeconomics proceeds by making simplifying assumptions. We never literally believe in our assumptions, but we need them in order to see through the vast complexity of an economy. This is why the distinction between endogenous and exogenous variables is artificial. Truly exogenous variables are few: two examples are climatic conditions (and even these may be affected by economic events, such as the greenhouse effect) and scientific discoveries and inventions (which also may result from economic decisions). The task of systematically linking the behaviour of endogenous variables to changes in exogenous variables is accomplished by specifying relationships between all the variables of interest.

All these relationships, when brought together, constitute a *theory*. Almost by definition, theory departs from realism. If the real world could be understood without simplifying assumptions, theories would be unnecessary. The problem is not with economics, it is with the world's inherent complexity. Intellectual progress is made by weeding out those assumptions and theories that lead us to false conclusions. As time passes, some theories prove to be unfounded, while others gain acceptability. This process is long and complex, and far from complete. Because macroeconomics is a young discipline, a number of controversies continue to dominate academic discussion, and this aspect is discussed in Section 1.4 below.

1.3.3. Positive and Normative Analysis

Macroeconomic analysis and policy are closely linked. Because a number of exogenous variables are under the control of government, it makes sense to ask what is good and what is bad policy. At its best, macroeconomics can explain the economy; for example, it can link particular events to exogenous events or policy decisions. This is **positive economics**: it refrains from value judgements. **Normative economics** takes a further step and passes judgement or makes policy recommendations. In so doing, it must specify what criteria are used in arriving at particular conclusions. This inevitably implies a value judgement. Economists generally like to make policy recommendations. As long as they reveal their criteria, this is part of their professional activity. In this text however we will generally refrain from normative economics.[4] We believe that many readers will use their own knowledge to indulge in the normative side of macroeconomics: this is what makes it fun.

1.3.4. Testing Theories: The Role of Data

The generally accepted way of evaluating theories is to submit them to scientific tests. In macroeconomics, this means looking at the facts, i.e. at data. This is easier said than done, and there are a number of unusual difficulties. First, data correspond to sometimes elusive concepts, as Chapter 2 illustrates. Second, constructing aggregate data implies enquiring

---

[4] It is a fact that 'social conscience' motivates many to study economics. Much like medical doctors who want to cure the sick, economists are often eager to provide relief to the disadvantaged and suffering.

into the behaviour of millions of individuals, who sometimes have good or bad reasons to misrepresent the truth. Third, economics shares the predicament common to other social sciences that experimentation is not really possible—when observed, people often change their behaviour. More importantly, no macroeconomist would wish to start a hyperinflation just to test a theory. Finally, many important variables simply are not observable. This is the case of expectations, for example. Macroeconomists are forced to conduct empirical tests with the data that they have. They develop statistical techniques, often sophisticated ones, to deal with observation and measurement errors. They refine the techniques they use to gather and analyse data. This allows the elimination of some theories and the modification of others. The surviving theories will be those that withstand the test of time in this scientific process.

1.3.5. Macroeconomic Modelling and Forecasting

Economists are always being asked to make forecasts. Governments, international organizations, and large financial institutions employ large teams of economists to prepare them. If macroeconomics were to be judged by the performance of forecasts, the verdict would not be unkind. The respectable track record of forecasters has however been sullied by some large historical errors. Box 1.2 illustrates this fact by examining the accuracy of forecasts for the year 1991.

There are several reasons why economic forecasting is inherently difficult. First and foremost, even an excellent understanding of an economy's structure—how its endogenous variables interact—does not preclude misjudging changes in exogenous variables. A

BOX 1.2. FORECASTING: THE DIFFICULT YEAR 1991

The year 1991 was a year in which forecasts went significantly wrong. Economists systematically overpredicted both growth and inflation. It was an unusual year for two reasons. First, totally unexpected events occurred in Eastern Europe. In particular, the astonishingly swift unification of Germany could not have been anticipated. Its implications also took time to be understood, if only because the German government's reaction has been shaped gradually. Second, firms and consumers grew pessimistic over the course of 1990, which led them to reduce consumption and investment spending. This may have been related to Iraq's invasion of Kuwait and the impending conflict there, another unanticipated event. Table 1.5 shows the forecasts and the actual outcomes.

Table 1.5. Forecasts and Outcomes, 1991 (%)

	Belgium	Germany	Spain	France	Italy	UK	USA
GNP growth rate							
Forecast (May 1990)	2.5	3.7	3.6	3.2	2.8	2.4	2.3
Forecast (June 1991)	2.3	2.8	3.0	1.5	1.8	2.3	0.0
Actual outcome	1.4	3.2	2.5	1.4	1.0	−1.9	−0.5
Inflation rate							
Forecast (May 1990)	2.7	3.0	6.1	3.0	5.0	5.1	4.6
Forecast (June 1991)	3.8	3.5	6.0	3.0	6.3	6.5	4.5
Actual outcome	3.2	3.5	5.9	3.2	6.5	5.9	4.2

Sources: March 1990 forecast: *European Economy*, suppl. A, April–May 1991; June 1991 forecast: *European Economy*, suppl. A, June 1991. GNP data are taken from OECD, *Economic Outlook*, Dec. 1991; CPI from OECD, *Economic Outlook*, Dec. 1992

good example of this was the oil price increase of 1973, or the Gulf War of 1991. Second, expectations—which are volatile in nature—wield an important influence over the economy. Governments sometimes react to their own forecasts by implementing policies that invalidate those forecasts. Political changes occur quickly and can disrupt the economic environment. Finally, it takes time—often several months—to know what has really happened at any given point, so forecasts are always based on provisional information which becomes more precise only with time.

Most forecasts are generated by computer-based models. These models resemble those that we present in this book. They are made of hundreds, sometimes thousands, of equations. Constructing these equations is a long and difficult task. The exogenous variables must be guessed by forecasters before they can ask their computers for an answer. This introduces many margins of error. The models can never be fully reliable, and the exogenous variables may be difficult to pinpoint. For these reasons, the forecasters themselves take their results with a grain of salt, and often, when the outcome is not completely satisfactory, may 'drop in' their own subjective factor to the results.

1.4. Preview of the Book

1.4.1. Structure

The book proceeds in steps. Parts I–IV build up an understanding of the measurement and the behaviour of the underlying economy. Part I is concerned mostly with defining terms and constructing a macroeconomic vocabulary. Part II elaborates the behaviour of the real economy. It focuses on the motivations of consumers and producers, abstracting from the influences of money and financial aspects of the economy. Part III studies money and its central role in macroeconomics, as well as the financial system that creates it. Part IV studies macroeconomic equilibrium in the short, medium, and long run. Part IV examines inflation and its evolution, and pins down its determinants over a longer horizon. It introduces a framework for thinking about inflation and the business cycle. Part V then uses this framework to explore policy issues facing governments: fiscal policy, demand management, and supply policy.

The focus then shifts to more specialized topics in macroeconomics. Part VI deals with financial markets, with emphasis on foreign exchange rates. Finally, Part VII considers how macroeconomic principles are used to approach some of the most pressing economic issues for Europe: the international monetary system, and the evolution of Europe from the European Monetary System to monetary union.

1.4.2. Controversies and Consensus

Economists often make a bad name for themselves by quarrelling in public. This is intellectually healthy, but highly misleading for laymen whose opinions are often based on accounts in the popular press. Disagreements bear on what most outsiders will see as finer points, if not outright hair-splitting. It is unfortunate that some of these disagreements have important policy implications. We present some—but by no means all—of the disagreements along the way, leaving readers free to judge for themselves. Yet we do not dwell upon them. Because there is so much that is not controversial, that it is best first to understand where the consensus lies.

Almost from the beginning, macroeconomics has been divided into two main schools of thought. Keynesians (and their neo-Keynesian heirs) and Monetarists (and neo-Monetarists)[5] continue to pursue the old debate between *laissez-faire* and interventionism. Keynesians are often characterized by the view that markets are imperfect and that governments have some informational advantage; they believe in active policy interventions. Monetarists see politics and the power of bureaucracies as barriers to government attempts to deal successfully with market failures, which they see as of lesser importance. Given these premises,

---

[5] These are not exclusive labels. In the USA, where most of the debate takes place, reference is sometimes made to salt-water and clear-water macroeconomists. Salt-water economists defend the Keynesian legacy from universities located on the two seaboards (Harvard, MIT, Yale, Stanford, Berkeley). Clear-water economists, most often associated with the Monetarist legacy, hail from universities located near the Great Lakes, e.g. Chicago, Rochester, or Minnesota. In Europe, these controversies are less evident: national traditions tend to make British or French economists more Keynesian and German or Swedish economists more Monetarist. But in each instance, there are as many exceptions as examples of the rule.

each school uses theories and data to build and support its case.

1.4.3. Rigour and Intuition

The only possible scientific approach to the complexities of the real world is the rigour of reasoning. However, to be useful, macroeconomics must be versatile and easily put to work when we want to understand particular events. This is why a great deal of macroeconomics simply amounts to accumulating intuition about particular phenomena. Our objective is, therefore, to leave readers with an intuitive understanding of how the economy functions. We do this by trying to draw robust yet simple conclusions from the various and often intricate principles presented. Such intuition is never completely rigorous, but can be useful in practice. Rigour plays its crucial role in reminding us when intuition is correct, and when it should be used with caution.

1.4.4. Data and Institutions

Macroeconomics is fascinating because it tells us a great deal about the world in which we live. It is not merely a set of abstract principles with interesting logical properties. Many assumptions and results will look odd at first sight. Yet, they are chosen because they are efficient in capturing key aspects of the real world. This is why at each important step we pause to look at facts. Facts can be data or particular episodes. Studying them carefully shows how theories work and shapes our understanding of macroeconomic phenomena. It broadens our knowledge of important events that have shaped the lives of millions of people. Whether or not history repeats itself remains an open question; in any case, we can learn a great deal from it.

On the other hand, a graph or a table is no substitute for more rigorous analysis of the data. Merely demonstrating that two economic variables move closely together is a far cry from proving that one causes the other. Our motive in using data to illustrate economic phenomena is to give readers a feel for economics itself. At the end of each chapter we give a list of suggested reading—which is by no means meant to be exhaustive—for those who want to learn more about the theory and practice of macroeconomics.

Finally, good economic theories must be valid under different conditions. At the same time, the response of different countries to exogenous economic stimuli are often shaped by their particular economic and political institutions. These include their form of government, the existence of labour unions and employers' associations, and differing forms of regulation. There is a great deal of controversy about both the relevance of these institutions to macroeconomic outcomes and their economic exogeneity—that is, whether they too respond to economic stimuli and evolve over time. The interplay of macroeconomic principles and institutions is an essential part of a proper understanding of the field, and this is why we spend a lot of time reviewing them. The economics of these institutions is, however, far beyond the level of this textbook.

1.4.5. Europe

Our textbook bears the subtitle 'A European Text'. Does this mean that we think that macroeconomics in Europe is fundamentally different from macroeconomics elsewhere, say in the USA, Japan, or Latin America? Most certainly not! On the contrary, in this book we represent the view that macroeconomics is sufficiently *global* in scope to apply to economies around the world. This includes the transforming economies of Central and Eastern Europe as well as the newly developing economies of southern and eastern Asia. On the other hand, we do wish to send a more subtle signal: we believe strongly that European economies have important distinguishing features that make them hard to study through the lens of, say, the leading textbooks from North America.

There is much in Europe that warrants such a European emphasis. Rather than a collection of states under a central government, Europe is a mosaic of nation-states, each with a sovereign macroeconomic policy-maker, but also with distinct preferences and endowments. Surely, the completion of the Single European Market and the accession of Austria, Finland, and Sweden to the European Union, as well as the clear move of the ex-communist economies in the heart of Europe towards market systems, will increase the pressure towards integration. Most important, the increasing likelihood of a common currency by the end of this century will have far-reaching macroeconomic consequences for all countries on the Continent, whether they are in the Union or not. Throughout the book, and especially in Chapter 21, we try to make this important point felt.

Key Concepts

- macroeconomics
- gross national product (GNP)
- trend
- economic growth
- business cycle
- unemployment
- labour force
- unemployment rate
- correlation coefficient
- Okun's Law
- labour
- capital
- factors of production
- labour share
- index number
- inflation
- hyperinflation
- capacity utilization

- procyclical and countercyclical
- investment ratio
- real economy
- *laissez-faire* versus interventionism
- aggregate demand management
- price level
- co-ordination failure
- Keynesian revolution
- misery index
- demand side
- economic agents
- fiscal policy
- monetary policy
- supply side
- endogenous
- exogenous
- normative and positive economics

Suggested Further Reading

On economics as a science, and the process of scientific discovery, see:

Friedman, Milton (1953), 'The Methodology of Positive Economics', in his *Essays in Positive Economics*, University of Chicago Press.

Kuhn, Thomas S. (1982), *The Structure of Scientific Revolutions*, University of Chicago Press.

On the state of macroeconomics and its controversies, see:

Greenwald, Bruce C., and Stiglitz, Joseph E. (1988), 'Examining Alternative Macroeconomic Theories', *Brookings Papers on Economic Activity*, 1: 207–70.

Mankiw, N. G. (1990), 'A Quick Refresher Course in Macroeconomics', *Journal of Economic Literature*, 28: 1645–60.

Solow, Robert M. (1980), 'On Theories of Unemployment', *American Economic Review*, 70: 1–11.

2

Macroeconomic Accounts

Facts and theories meet in analysis. The combination of the two is essential if economics is to progress, since it is neither a pure subject, like mathematics, of which one does not ask that the theories should be applicable to actual phenomena, nor is it a collection of facts, like the objects on a junk heap, of which one does not ask how they are related.

Richard Stone

2.1. Overview

This chapter provides a description of the macroeconomy and a definition of the more frequently used concepts—for example the gross domestic product or GDP, which were referred to only casually in Chapter 1. The national income accounts, which are produced by each country according to internationally accepted norms, provide the yardstick by which we can measure economic performance. This chapter presents **accounting identities**; that is, it describes how macroeconomic magnitudes relate to each other *by definition*. Later chapters will use macroeconomic analysis to explain behavioural relationships among these magnitudes.

The distinction between description (this chapter) and analysis (the rest of the book) can be illustrated by an example from biology. That living organisms consist of a collection of different cells is a biological description; how these cells function and affect each other constitutes the analysis. In a similar way, decomposing gross domestic product into its components provides a rich insight into macroeconomics; looking at the external accounts shows how one country is linked with the rest of the world. The analysis will have to wait until subsequent chapters.

2.2. Gross Domestic Product (GDP)

2.2.1. Three Definitions of Gross Domestic Product (GDP)

The **gross domestic product** (GDP) is defined for a particular geographic area—usually a country, but possibly a region or a city, or a group of countries such as the European Community (EC). It is also defined over a time interval, usually a year or a quarter; this is because the GDP is a **flow variable**, much like the amount of water flowing down a river. Flow variables contain a time dimension, and therefore differ from **stock variables**, such as the amount of water retained by a dam, which are always defined at a particular point in time.[1]

[1] Another example of a stock variable is a company's *balance sheet*, which measures its financial state at a single point in time, say 31 December; in contrast, an *income statement* records the profit or loss attributed to the firm over a time period, say 1 January to 31 December, and is a flow variable.

A country's GDP is a measure of its productive activity. One way of measuring productive capacity is simply by the production and final sale of goods and services. This provides the first definition:

Definition 1: GDP = $\sum$ net final sales within a geographic location.

This definition specifically refers to **final sales**. Final sales correspond to sales of goods and services to the consumer or firm that will ultimately use them. For example, the purchase of a loaf of bread or a motor car by a household or of a machine tool by a manufacturing firm is a final sale. In contrast, a car sold to a dealer which is subsequently resold during the measurement period is not: rather, it is counted as an **intermediate sale**. Intermediate sales refer to goods or services purchased and used for the production of other goods and services. This would include the sale

BOX 2.1. VALUE ADDED: AN EXAMPLE

Suppose a keg of beer was produced and sold for final consumption at the price of ECU 100. For this to occur, a brewery bought barley from a farmer, paying ECU 10, energy with a value of ECU 20, and a keg at a cost of ECU 5. (For simplicity, the intermediate inputs of the farmer, energy producer, and keg manufacturer are ignored.) The beer is actually sold to a wholesaler for ECU 80, so the brewery's own contribution to value added per keg is ECU 45, which is used to cover labour costs (wages and salaries as well as social security contributions) of ECU 35 and ECU 5 in taxes. The remaining ECU 5 are the brewer's profits. The wholesaler sells the keg for ECU 90 to the retailer, so his value added is ECU 10; by selling the keg for ECU 100, the retailer also generates ECU 10 of value added. Summing up, the final price can be broken down into value added at each stage of production and delivery of the final good:

Value added contributed by the:

Farmer	ECU	10
Energy producer		20
Keg manufacturer		5
Brewery		45
Wholesaler		10
Retailer		10
		___
Sum:	ECU	100

of wheat to the bakery, bread to a restaurant, or tyres to a motor car manufacturer. Intermediate sales are excluded from GDP to avoid double counting, for example including the sale of bread twice in the case of a baker selling bread to a grocery shop. For that reason, GDP should never be confused with total turnover or total sales of an economy. For consistency, exports are counted as final sales regardless of how the foreigners use them, and imports are always subtracted from final sales.

A second definition of GDP recognizes that final sales represent an increase in the value of goods and services sold in the economy during the measurement period. This increase is called **value added**:

Definition 2: GDP = $\sum$ value added occurring within a given geographic location.

A firm creates value added by transforming raw materials and unfinished goods into products it can sell in the market place. The firm's value added is the difference between its sales (turnover) and the costs of raw materials, unfinished goods, and imports from abroad. If the firm produces intermediate goods, its sales are costs to its customers, who produce, and the value added that it created will not be counted twice. When the final consumer purchases a good or a service in the market, the price includes all the value added created at each stage in the production process, hence the consistency between Definitions 1 and 2. Box 2.1 illustrates how productive activities contribute to a country's total value added.

The value added produced within an economy is the source of income for factors of production employed by the firm. The activities for which wage-earners, stockholders, and other factors of production are compensated correspond to their contribution to increasing the value of goods and services in the course of their economic activities. Without value added it would not be possible to pay wages, salaries, interest, and profits. This provides the third and final definition of GDP:

Definition 3: GDP = $\sum$ factor incomes earned from economic activities occurring within a geographic location.

GDP is thus the sum of all incomes earned within a country's borders—by residents and non-residents alike. To produce goods and services, firms use factors of production: workers' time, talents, and efforts; equipment; land; buildings. These factors of production are supplied ultimately by households. Because one person's spending must be someone else's income, the third definition of GDP is also consistent with the first.

GDP statistics are quoted daily in the financial and political press. The GDP is generally considered to be

BOX 2.2. WHAT GDP MEASURES

Because it concerns only recorded market transactions, the GDP is an imperfect measure of economic well-being. A number of activities are not recorded, either because they are not carried out through legal channels or because they do not correspond to market activities, like growing vegetables in the garden. Furthermore, goods and services are measured by their sale prices: two identical goods may enter the GDP differently if one of them is sold at a discount. Finally, it is not a measure of happiness: painful expenses (having a tooth removed, for example) enter the GDP in the same way as pleasurable ones. When someone dies, GDP rises: the funeral service, the hospital expenses, and the execution of the will by lawyers and bankers all represent additional final sales of the goods and services that result. Pollution and other forms of environmental damage are ignored in the GDP, since they are not traded in the market.

Services enter the GDP exactly like goods. Services include medical doctors' fees or an estate agent's commission when an existing house is sold. In the latter case, if the house's value has increased since it was purchased, the previous owner enjoys a capital gain, but this form of income does not enter GDP.[2] Used-goods sales, such as cars or antique furniture, do not enter the GDP either. Such transactions represent a transfer of ownership rather than production; these goods entered GDP when first sold. Sales by retailers from inventory accumulated in earlier periods actually reduce GDP, as they represent a depletion of stocks.

Public services are part of GDP, even if they are not really sold. Their price is simply measured by their cost of production. For example, public education enters GDP as the sum of teachers' salaries, operating costs such as electricity or heating costs, and equipment including rents. The national defence enters the GDP as total expenditure on armed forces.

---

the most important indicator of an economy's health, and its evolution is closely watched by managers, economists, and politicians. Yet the definition of GDP contains a fair amount of arbitrariness, and it is open to debate whether every positive movement in GDP constitutes an improvement in national well-being. More details on this controversial issue are provided in Box 2.2.

2.2.2. Gross National Product (GNP)

Once agreed upon, geographical boundaries are unambiguous. Economic boundaries are more subtle. In particular, should one define a country by the location of its economic activity, or by the activities of its residents, wherever such activities may be taking place? The GDP follows the first approach: it is the value added produced by all factors of production within some well defined geographic location, including factors owned by foreign residents. For example, if a French company owns a German subsidiary, income received from German operations is considered as German GDP. The Italian living in Como who commutes to his job to Lugano contributes to the GDP of his workplace (Switzerland), not his resident country (Italy).

Unlike the location-based GDP concept, the **gross national product** (GNP) is *ownership-based*. It is the value added that is generated by all factors of production, owned by residents both at home and abroad. It includes value added or income earned abroad and repatriated by residents.

Table 2.1 compares GDP and GNP for several countries. In general, the difference between GDP and GNP is small and evolves slowly over time, but there are interesting exceptions. Because of the large number of Swiss-owned multinational companies, Switzerland

---

[2] From an economic point of view, this capital gain should probably be included. On the other hand, many such capital gains will cancel against other capital losses, at least among residents. The rest may be very difficult to measure, especially when they are unrealized, i.e. merely accrued but not yet converted into money by sale.

Table 2.1. Nominal GDPs and GNPs in 1993

	GDP (ECU bn)	GNP (ECU bn)	Difference GNP/GDP (%)
Belgium	180.0	180.8	0.5
Denmark	115.0	111.3	–3.3
Germany	1473.4	1467.8	–0.4
Ireland	40.4	35.7	–11.5
Kuwait	19.1	22.7	18.5
Pakistan	41.3	41.8	1.3
Switzerland	198.0	206.2	4.1
Turkey	83.7	86.5	3.3

Source: IMF

earns a significant proportion of its income in activities abroad. Its GNP exceeds its GDP by about 4%. Pakistan too has a GNP bigger than its GDP because a large number of its residents work abroad on a temporary basis and remit labour income to the home country; through these activities, Pakistanis may own significant assets abroad and derive income from them. A more spectacular example is Kuwait, which has used its oil income over the years to acquire wealth abroad; as a result of its high investment income, its GNP exceeds its GDP by roughly 20%. In contrast, the GNPs of Denmark and Ireland are smaller than their GDPs, because these countries are home to many subsidiaries of foreign multinational corporations, are hosts to large numbers of temporary foreign workers, or pay interest to foreigners on debt held abroad.

In recent years more and more countries have begun to stress GDP over GNP statistics, presumably because GNP is less reliable. It may swing radically from quarter to quarter as large multinationals repatriate income for reasons having little to do with value added during the period. The two measures are often used interchangeably, although the distinction can have considerable economic significance. For the rest of this chapter we shall treat GNP and GDP as the same—effectively assuming that net factor income from abroad is zero. In Chapter 3, however, the emphasis will shift to GDP, which is a better indicator of domestic output and production.

2.2.3. Real versus Nominal, Deflators versus Price Indices

2.2.3.1. Real and nominal GDP

Now that we understand how GDP data are constructed, we can see how statisticians have solved one of the first problems we encountered at school: adding apples and oranges. The solution is to use prices to convert volumes (the numbers of apples and oranges) into values (sales of apples and oranges).

Suppose an economy produces these two goods and requires no imports. Multiplying the quantities of apples and oranges sold, Q^a and Q^o, by their respective prices, P^a and P^o, yields the **nominal GDP**, or GDP at current prices:

$$(2.1) \qquad GDP = P^a Q^a + P^o Q^o.$$

If the price of oranges increases from one year to the next, the GDP rises even if the volume of final sales remains unchanged. An increase in nominal GDP can

result from either higher prices or more output. To separate the effects of output and price movements, we distinguish between nominal and **real GDP**. Whereas nominal GDP is computed as in (2.1) using the actual selling prices, real GDP is computed by using prices observed in some predetermined base year.[3] Increases in real GDP correspond to increases in physical output. In our example, if prices of apples and oranges were P_0^a and P_0^o in the base year, the real GDP in year t, when net final sales of apples and oranges are Q_t^a and Q_t^o, is:

$$(2.2) \qquad Real\ GDP_t = P_0^a Q_t^a + P_0^o Q_t^o.$$

This distinction is very general and applies to all macroeconomic variables: nominal variables represent values at current prices; real variables represent volumes at constant prices. As an example, Table 2.2

Table 2.2. Growth Rates of Nominal GDP, Real GDP, and GDP Deflator: Germany, 1975–1993

	Growth rate (% per annum) in:		
	Nominal GDP	Real GDP	GDP deflator
1975	4.3	−1.3	5.6
1976	8.7	5.2	3.6
1977	6.5	2.8	3.7
1978	7.1	3.0	4.2
1979	7.9	4.1	3.7
1980	5.8	1.0	4.9
1981	4.2	0.1	4.1
1982	3.4	−0.9	4.3
1983	4.9	1.7	3.2
1984	4.8	2.8	2.0
1985	4.0	2.0	2.0
1986	5.4	2.3	3.1
1987	3.3	1.5	1.9
1988	5.2	3.7	1.5
1989	5.9	3.6	2.4
1990	8.7	5.5	3.1
1991	8.7	4.9	3.8
1992	6.1	1.7	4.3
1993	1.4	−1.7	3.1

Source: German Council of Economic Advisors Annual Report 1994/95

---

[3] Problems arise when new goods are introduced, or existing goods improve in quality. National income accountants have devised procedures to deal with such effects.

BOX 2.3. PRICE DEFLATORS AND PRICE INDICES

The price index closest to the GDP deflator is the producer price index (PPI), with fixed weights corresponding to a basket representative of national production. Similarly, the CPI is closely tracked by the consumption deflator, the ratio of nominal and real aggregate consumption. Fixed-weight indices such as the CPI and the PPI are examples of a fixed-weight, or **Laspeyres index**. The consumption deflator, which is based on the actual share of goods in the corresponding year's consumption, is called a variable weight or **Paasche index**. The CPI and the consumption deflator include goods and services produced abroad and imported, while the PPI and the GDP deflator do not, but these latter measures include goods and services locally produced and exported. Figure 2.1 suggests a growing divergence between the PPI and the CPI in Italy over the 1980s. The reason is that imported goods prices increased by less than those of domestically produced goods.

Other frequently used deflators are related to exports, imports, investment goods, and government purchases. The wholesale price index (WPI) measures the average price of goods at the wholesale stage, and various commodity price indices track the evolution of raw materials prices. The dizzying diversity of indices and deflators simply reflects the fact that there is no absolute 'average' price. Different price levels are used for different purposes. For example, wage-earners wish to tie their wages to their cost of living; in this case, the relevant index is the CPI or the consumption deflator. In the case of Italy, linking wages to the CPI rather than to the PPI resulted in higher profits for firms whose incomes are better described by the PPI. Because the CPI and other Laspeyres indices are easy to compute, they tend to be used most often in practice.

---

reports growth rates of nominal and real GDP for Germany.

2.2.3.2. Price deflators and indices

The distinction between nominal and real GDP can be used as a measure of the general price level, or the price of goods in terms of money. The rate of increase in this measure can therefore serve as a measure of inflation. The **GDP deflator**, which is one way of measuring the price level, is defined as the ratio of nominal to real GDP:

$$(2.3) \qquad \text{GDP deflator} = \frac{\text{Nominal GDP}}{\text{Real GDP}}.$$

The rate of increase in the GDP deflator can be approximated by the formula:

$$(2.4) \quad \text{GDP deflator inflation} = \text{Nominal GDP growth rate} - \text{real GDP growth rate}.$$

For example, Table 2.2 shows that in 1993 the nominal GNP of Germany rose by 1.4% while the real GNP fell by 1.7%. On average, therefore, prices rose by roughly 3.1%.[4]

In the chosen base year, nominal and real GDP coincide and the GDP deflator equals 1.0. (Sometimes it is multiplied by 100 for ease of comparison over the years.) It can be thought of as an average of all prices of final goods in terms of money, where each price is implicitly weighted by the proportion of the corresponding good in the GDP. As these proportions change over the years, so do the weights.

An alternative measure of inflation is based on an average of prices with fixed weights, called a **price index**. A basket of goods is selected and the amount of each good, or category of goods, in the basket is used to weight the corresponding prices. An example is the **consumer price index (CPI)**. This is based on a basket of goods consumed by an 'average citizen'. Box 2.3 presents some frequently used deflators and indices. Figure 2.1 shows the growth rates of the GDP deflator and of the CPI in Italy. Differences between the two measures of inflation are usually not very important but they can be significant—for example, when the price of imports changed sharply as in 1981 and 1986.

2.2.4. Measuring and Interpreting GDP and GNP

Although the concepts of GDP and GNP are straightforward to define, they are costly and difficult to

---

[4] To see why this formula is an approximation, suppose real GDP increased at rate g and inflation at rate π. The rate of nominal growth must be $(1 + g)(1 + \pi) - 1 = g + \pi + g\pi$. For g and π small, $g\pi \cong 0$, so the rate of growth of nominal GDP is approximately $g + \pi$.

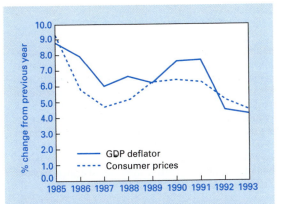

Figure 2.1. GDP Deflator and the Consumer Price Index Inflation Rates: Italy

Both the GDP deflator and the consumer price index (CPI) measure the price level, or the price of goods in terms of money. They are used to compute an economy's inflation rate. The figure shows that both inflation rates tend to move together over time. The underlying price levels, however, can diverge.

Sources: OECD *Economic Outlook*, Dec. 1994, June 1995; *International Financial Statistics Yearbook*, 1994

measure. Governments generally are responsible for constructing these data, but are often forced to cut corners to save money. Often the statistical offices turn to their own sources of information. One natural source is the tax authorities. Firms report sales (first definition of GDP), individuals report incomes (third definition), and in most countries (all EC countries, but not the USA) value added taxes (VAT) are collected by intermediate and final sellers who then report their value added as they pay the tax (second definition).

The fact that GDP figures are collected through tax returns immediately raises concern about the quality of the data. Both individuals and firms may be less than candid about their finances to the fiscal authorities. What is not reported is sometimes referred to as the **underground economy**, which can be fairly large, as described in Box 2.4.

The amount of information required to construct the national accounts is enormous, and errors in collecting and adding up the numbers are inevitable.[5] For that reason, too, aggregate data can never be fully precise and complete. Furthermore, data from tax returns

are processed with considerable delay. Usually at the end of the first month of each quarter, figures for the preceding quarter are released. Box 2.5 explains how such flash estimates are produced and updated several times over the following years. The inaccuracy of these estimates is unsettling because they are frequently used by governments when setting policy, by investors assessing the value of their assets, and by firms deciding on hiring or firing workers and on acquiring equipment. This is why other indicators are often used to supplement the GDP and GNP figures.[6] It is also why analysts tend to concentrate on growth *rates* rather than *levels*. As long as the distortions do not change much over time, measured GDP and GNP growth rates are fairly accurate.

It is tempting to compare GDPs across countries. Most often we look at GDP per capita, or the average income earned within a country's boundaries. Data like those reported in Table 2.1 must be regarded with caution, however. First, GDP is a measure of *income*, not wealth. Income is a flow, while wealth is the stock of assets accumulated over longer periods of time. For example, the average income earned in the UK is lower than that of Abu Dhabi; yet average British wealth is likely to be much higher, as Britain has been accumulating wealth for centuries, in the form of private assets (e.g. houses, factories, jewels, stocks) and national assets (e.g. the London Bridge, the paintings in the British Museum, the roads and telecommunication networks, and much more).

The second caveat is that in many less developed countries (LDCs) a large number of transactions are not recorded. For example, most food can be produced within the extended family (a non-market activity), or exchanged for other food (a non-reported market activity). Very low reported per capita income levels in LDCs underestimate true value added and income.

Finally, GDPs are measured in the country's local monetary unit, or currency. They must be converted into a common currency using a rate of exchange. In Table 2.5 we use the European currency unit (ECU) for this purpose.[7] Exchange rate fluctuations may alter the valuation of a country's GDP in another currency quite dramatically. For example, the table shows a decline in US GDP between 1985 and 1993; this corresponds to a drop in the value of the dollar against the ECU over that period.

---

[5] This is why in practice data from the three definitions are compared and used to reduce inconsistencies.

[6] Ch. 14 provides a description of the most frequently used indicators.

[7] The ECU is not a real currency. Rather, it is a unit of account for intra-EC transactions and is worth roughly $1.25 in 1996. Ch. 21 provides a detailed explanation.

BOX 2.4. THE UNDERGROUND ECONOMY

Who hasn't taken advantage of a carpenter's, car mechanic's, or painter's offer to do some work 'without a receipt'? Agents engage in the underground, or informal economy for straightforward reasons. First, they want to avoid taxes (the value-added tax, employment and social security charges, profit taxes). Another reason is that criminal activities, such as drug-dealing, prostitution, or racketeering, are obviously better kept underground.

How large is the underground economy? By definition, its size is unknown, but national income statisticians often attempt to guess its importance. Table 2.3 presents some estimates based on a variety of methods. The first column is based on household electricity consumption, which is higher in economies where unreported market activity is more significant.[8] The second approach also relies on the amount of large-denomination currency in circulation: underground transactions do not use bank accounts and profits are held in large bills. Tax investigators use much information of this kind to track down unreported incomes, and their findings provide another way of estimating the size of the underground economy. The last column shows the 'consensus' of a large number of studies.

Table 2.3. Estimates of the Size of the Underground Economy (% of GDP)

Country	Method 1[a]	Method 2[b]	Range of alternative studies[c]
Australia	7	8	
Austria	11	12	
Belgium	17	18	
Canada	11	12	3–8
Denmark	16	17	
Finland	11	12	
France	6	6	4
Germany	11	12	4–24
Greece	20	20	
Ireland	21	22	
Italy	16	17	6–24
Japan	3	4	
Netherlands	8	9	5–22
Norway	5	6	6–16
Portugal	13	14	
Spain	21	22	
Sweden	7	7	4–17
UK	10	11	2–15
USA	10	11	2–26
Hungary	31	30	
Poland	35	n.a.	
Czechoslovakia	34	n.a.	

[a] Method 1 based on household electricity consumption.
[b] Method 2 based on cash in circulation.
[c] Range of studies based on a number of different methodologies.

Sources: Lackó (1995); *Economie et Statistiques*, November 1989

[8] More generally, the sale of intermediate inputs related to final production is often used to indicate underground economy activities. For example, a wide discrepancy exists between the purchase of construction materials and reported construction activity.

BOX 2.5. HOW NATIONAL ACCOUNTS ESTIMATES VARY OVER TIME

Because governments, firms, and investors require timely information about the economy, national statistical institutes in advanced economies have devised ways of quickly producing preliminary estimates of GDP and GNP. The procedure is based on the knowledge that the value added of, for example, the 100 largest corporations represents a given proportion of GDP. If the proportion were 10%, as these firms fill in VAT tax reports or respond to specially designed questionnaires, multiplying by 10 their combined value added provides a rough early estimate of GDP. A few months later, revised estimates can be based on data provided by a larger sample of firms. Waiting still longer will allow the incorporation of estimates based on an early and partial analysis of tax returns. Detailed analysis of all tax returns data—using procedures to reconcile differences between measures based on the three definitions—lead to a final figure. Table 2.4 shows successive estimates of 1986 French GNP. The first estimate, published six months after year end, fell short of the latest figure by more than 1%! This may not seem like much, but it amounts to a full 15% difference for the actual growth rate recorded that year (7.5%).

Table 2.4. Various Estimates of French GNP for 1986

Date of publication	GNP (bns of current FF)	% difference from previous year	% difference from June 1987
June 1987	5015.9	—	
Sept. 1988	5034.9	+0.4	0.4
Sept. 1988	5052.5	+0.3	0.7
June 1990	5069.3	+0.3	1.1

Source: *Bulletin Trimestriel de la Banque de France*, various issues

2.3. Flows of Incomes and Expenditures

2.3.1. The Circular Flow Diagram

Let us assume that net income earned by residents from foreign sources is zero, so GNP is equal to GDP. Each individual's expenditure necessarily contributes to some other individual's income. The simplified **circular flow** diagram represented in Figure 2.2 is based on this simple truth and goes a long way in tracking the functioning of an economy. Based on the first two definitions of GDP, it shows how income from sales goes from firms to individuals and back to the market place. The GDP appears in the left part of the figure. It represents the final net sales of firms.[9]

What do firms do with their receipts? To find out we move clockwise. The government, represented by the circle inside the circular flow, takes (in taxes of all sorts) and gives (in the form of various transfers), and it takes more than it gives. The difference between taxes and transfers is called **net taxes** and is represented by *T*. What is left of GDP after these taxes and transfers is **private income**.

Once they have paid wages and salaries, other production costs and taxes,[10] firms can either save their income or distribute it to their owners. Households receive income as employees or as shareholders. They can either spend it on *consumption* or save it. Merging firms and households into the private sector, the flow diagram shows how aggregate private savings (*S*) are deposited with the financial sector. The financial sector includes banks, financial institutions, and stock markets whose function is to collect savings and channel them to firms seeking to invest, that is to purchase productive equipment. This activity, called **financial intermediation**, is represented by the right-lower circle. In the aggregate, the private sector uses its **savings**—what it does not consume—to finance the

---

[9] Technically it also includes the 'sales' of households' labour and capital abroad, as well as the 'sales' of the self-employed.

[10] The other production costs are mainly land and buildings, financial costs (borrowing from banks and bondholders), and raw materials and intermediate goods which, for the country as a whole, are imported.

Table 2.5. GDPs per capita in 1985 and 1993

	1985	1993
	ECUs	
Australia	13,356	13,734
Austria	11,310	19,363
Belgium	10,706	17,874
China	357	388
Denmark	15,012	22,254
Finland	14,327	16,246
France	12,537	18,548
Germany	13,431	22,413
Greece	4,401	6,101
Iceland	15,804	19,284
Ireland	7,027	11,350
Italy	9,916	17,166
Japan	14,584	28,874
Netherlands	11,699	17,421
Norway	18,394	20,382
Poland	2,506	1,905
Portugal	2,741	6,594
Spain	5,644	10,426
Sweden	15,899	18,174
Switzerland	18,816	28,790
UK	10,722	13,868
USA	22,218	21,121

Source: IMF

acquisition of new productive equipment by firms. Productive equipment is referred to as physical **capital**, and purchases of new equipment is called **investment**. The excess of private saving over investment $(S - I)$ is called net private saving. It can be positive or negative. Firms and households spend their income—part of it borrowed—to consume (C) and to invest (I).[11]

To private sector expenditures on goods and services $(C + I)$ the government adds its own demand (G). Governments purchase goods (roads, military equipment, newly built buildings, and stationery for the bureaucracy) and services (of civil servants and other employees). In addition, governments distribute various subsidies to firms and households, and pay interest on the public debt. Total national spending, sometimes called **absorption**, is the sum $(C + I + G)$

[11] It is important to stress the difference of this terminology from that often used in the business or popular press, in which 'investment' includes the acquisition of existing assets or financial instruments. Although these assets are often issued by firms to finance the purchase of productive equipment, their simple acquisition or sale does not give rise to what is called 'investment' in economics, i.e. the creation of new productive capacity.

of private and public spending on goods and services. Part of absorption includes the purchase of imported goods and services (Z). This is shown as the branch going into the left-most circle which represents the rest of the world; it should not be thought of merely as merchandise purchases, but as covering all kinds of services, including labour and capital services. Similarly, while some domestic income thus leaks abroad, foreigners buy domestically produced goods and services, the country's exports (X). Netting these two flows with the rest of the world gives net exports $(X - Z)$. Net exports, which can be positive or negative, further increase the total demand for domestic production.

The sum of absorption and net exports represents the total final sales that occur within the geographic area, in other words the GDP. The circular flow of income is closed. This circularity is the essence of economic activity: we (collectively) earn to (collectively) spend.

2.3.2. Summary of the Flow Diagram

The flow diagram can be summarized using the two first definitions of GDP, which is represented by the symbol Y. As net final sales, the GDP is broken down into four main categories: sales of consumption goods and services (C), sales of investment goods and additions to stocks (I), sales to the government (G), and sales to the rest of the world (X). Since part of domestic income leaks abroad to pay for imported goods, imports (Z) must be subtracted, giving the first decomposition of GDP (details are provided in Box 2.6):

$$(2.5) \qquad Y = C + I + G + X - Z.$$

The flow diagram also shows how GDP can be viewed as net incomes earned by factors of production (or by residents, on the GNP definition). What does the private sector do with this income? The three possibilities are given by the right-hand side of the flow diagram: they pay taxes net of transfers (T), they save (S), and they consume (C). Hence the second decomposition:

$$(2.6) \qquad Y = C + S + T.$$

Table 2.6 presents these various components as a percentage of GDP for a few countries. Consumption typically amounts to 50%–65% of GDP. The 'size of government' is often measured by the share of its expenditures, the sum of purchases and transfers, or the share of gross taxes. It varies considerably, even among advanced economies. Scandinavian countries have large public sectors. When total spending is

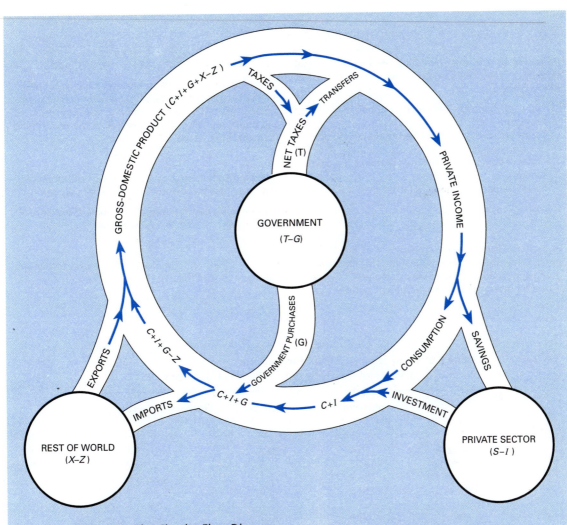

Figure 2.2. The Circular Flow Diagram

The lower left part of the wheel represents sales of domestically produced goods and services, the sum of consumption spending (C), investment spending (I), government purchases (G), and exports (X) less imports (Z). In the upper left part of the wheel this is interpreted as income to residents. This income is taxed by the government, which also pays out various transfers. What is left, private income, may be saved (S) or spent (C). The private sector borrows to invest in productive equipment (I). The balance S – I is the private sector's net saving behaviour. The balance T – G is the public sector borrowing requirement. X – Z represent the country's net exports.

considered, including transfers, the government often 'captures' more than half of GDP: many goods and services that are privately produced elsewhere are delivered freely as public goods in northern Europe; these include medical services, schools, child care, and public transport.

The investment rate—defined in Chapter 1 as the ratio of investment to GDP—varies between 15% and

25%. Because investment corresponds to the accumulation of productive equipment, it can affect future economic growth. Countries with low investment rates, like the USA and the UK, have indeed grown more slowly than Germany, Italy, or Japan although it is still premature to draw conclusions from this fact. In addition, not all public spending is collective consumption. Governments also invest. Infrastructure

BOX 2.6. ALTERNATIVE DECOMPOSITIONS OF GDP

Definition 1 states that the GDP is the sum of net final sales by residents. We can distinguish among four types of final sales:

- sales of domestic consumption goods to domestic consumers, C^d
- sales of domestically produced equipment to domestic firms including inventory accumulation, I^d
- sales of domestically produced goods to the government, G^d
- sales to foreign customers, i.e. exports, X;

so that GDP is:

$$Y = C^d + I^d + G^d + X.$$

Households, firms, and the government all purchase imports. Total consumption C is the sum of locally produced goods and services C^d and of imported ones C^z. The same is true for investments and government outlays:

$$C = C^d + C^z, \qquad I = I^d + I^z, \qquad G = G^d + G^z.$$

Consumption of domestic goods by residents is the difference between their total consumption and their spending on imports ($C^d = C - C^z$), and similarly for investment and public spending. This gives (2.5) in the text, noting that total imports are:

$$Z = C^z + I^z + G^z.$$

Following Definition 2 of GDP, the sum of households' and firms' incomes, income is disposed as follows:

— households pay net taxes T^h, consume C, and save S^h
— firms pay net taxes T^f, and save S^f.

So

$$Y = C + T^h + S^h + T^f + S^f.$$

Since $S = S^h + S^f$ and $T = T^h + T^f$, the second accounting definition of GDP follows:

$$Y = C + S + T.$$

Table 2.6. Components of GDP: Expenditure
(average of quarterly data 1970–1994, as % of GDP)

	Consumption (C)	Investment (I)	Government purchases (G)
Australia	59.4	24.2	16.4
Germany	54.5	21.8	19.7
France	59.3	22.7	18.6
UK	59.5	18.0	22.6
Italy	62.1	22.7	16.4
Japan	59.9	30.8	9.5
Canada	59.0	19.9	21.0
Switzerland	62.2	25.6	13.3
USA	65.6	15.7	19.4

Source: OECD *National Accounts*

equipment (roads, bridges, public utilities, telecommunications) is often publicly owned, built, and operated.

The GDP and its decomposition reveal flows of incomes and spending derived from the production of goods and services. This is what is sometimes called the real side of an economy. Part of these flows leak out to the financial side as corporate and household savings; others leak out to the government as a surplus (or, if the net leakage is negative, a deficit); others to foreigners as net exports. Over time, they accumulate into stocks of assets or liabilities. How the financial side of the economy functions, and how the real and financial sides are linked, is studied in Part III of this book.

2.3.3. More Detail

While GDP or GNP represents the collective income earned within a nation's boundaries, not all of it ends up in the hands of individuals. What households actually receive to spend or save is called **personal**

Table 2.7. GNP and Personal Disposable Income, 1992 (ECU bn)

Country	GNP	Personal disposable income	
		Level	% of GNP
France	1009.3	764.8	75.8
Germany	1395.2	951.8	68.2
Sweden	184.8	134.6	72.8
Switzerland	193.1	138.2	71.6
UK	818.3	633.2	77.4
USA	4646.7	3468.5	74.6

Sources: OECD *National Income Accounts*; IMF

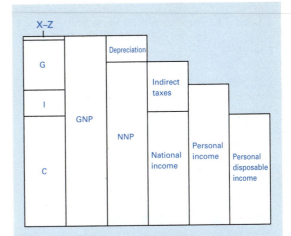

Figure 2.3. From Expenditure to Income to Personal Disposable Income

Depreciation is stripped away from GNP to obtain net national product (NNP). Indirect taxes are removed from, and firm subsidies added to, NNP, yielding national income at factor prices (NI). After this, national income is distributed: firms' savings (retained earnings), corporate taxes, and contributions to social security are subtracted from national income, and what remains is paid to households as various forms of income. The government also transfers income to households (social security, unemployment insurance, etc.). This results in personal income (PI). After income taxes and some miscellaneous fees, we are left with personal disposable income (PDI), that is, resources available to households for spending or saving.

disposable income. Table 2.7 shows that some 30%–40% of GNP does not reach individual households. It either goes to the government (net taxes) or is saved by firms (retained earnings).

Figure 2.3 starts with GNP and, moving right, decomposes it by its ultimate recipient. The first item is **depreciation**: in the process of producing GNP, productive equipment is subjected to wear and tear and obsolescence. Properly measured, this depreciation should be subtracted from GNP to give a clearer picture of the output that is actually available as income. Subtracting depreciation from GNP gives us the **net national product (NNP)**.[12] Moving further to the right, national income is what is left for firms once indirect taxes are paid out. Indirect taxes vary from country to country, and include the value added tax (VAT) and excise taxes (on petrol, tobacco, alcohol). They are collected by sellers on behalf of the government.

After indirect taxes, firms dispose of the value added they generate in four ways. First, they pay wages and salaries and other compensation to their employees. This includes contributions to social insurance. Second, they pay interest to bondholders and banks. Third, they pay corporate or business income taxes. What remains is profits to the firms' owners, or shareholders. These profits are either distributed as dividends or held back as retained earnings, sometimes called net corporate saving.[13]

To summarize, what is not paid as corporate taxes

or saved by firms accrues to households as employees, owners, or rentiers. When government transfers (e.g. unemployment benefits, disability payments, health care reimbursements, family allowances) are added to labour incomes and distributed profits, the result is personal income. Households cannot freely dispose of their personal income: they must first pay personal income taxes, as well as non-tax payments like parking fines and other governmental fees. What is left for consumption and saving is personal disposable income.

2.3.4. A Key Accounting Identity

The two decompositions of GDP, (2.5) and (2.6), are accounting identities: they hold by definition. Therefore it is always the case that:

$$C + S + T = C + I + G + X - Z.$$

---

[12] In practice, financial accounting of depreciation is determined by tax regulations. Firms are allowed to subtract from their revenues a given proportion of the book value of equipment for computing taxable profits. It may under- or overstate actual economic depreciation by a wide margin.

[13] Adding net corporate savings to depreciation gives gross corporate savings. It represents the resources that firms set aside to strengthen their financial position, and to replace used equipment.

Table 2.8. The Accounting Identity in 1987 (% of GNP/GDP)

	S – I	T – G	CA
USA	−1.1	−2.4	−3.5
Japan	2.9	0.7	3.6
EC	4.2	−3.5	0.7
Belgium	9.0	−7.1	1.9
Denmark	−5.4	2.5	−2.9
France	1.4	−1.9	−0.5
Germany	5.9	−1.9	4.0
Italy	10.9	−11.1	−0.2
Netherlands	7.9	−6.5	1.4
Spain	3.2	−3.2	−0.0
Sweden	−4.9	4.2	−0.7
UK	0.4	−1.3	−0.9

Source: OECD *Economic Outlook*

Consumption C appears on both sides of this equality and can be eliminated. When this is done and terms are rearranged, the two accounting identities yield a third one:

$$(2.7) \qquad (S - I) + (T - G) = (X - Z).$$

Parentheses highlight the fact that the corresponding expressions appear in Figure 2.2 as net flows to the private sector (household and business), government, and the rest of the world, respectively. Each of the three net flows can be thought of as a form of saving, a leakage out of (if positive), or an injection into (if negative), the flow of income and expenditure. The identity says that there can be no net leakage. If $S > I$, the private sector as a whole is a net saver. If $S < I$, the private sector is a net borrower. Similarly, if $T > G$ the government is saving, and if $G > T$ it is borrowing by issuing public debt to domestic or foreign residents. In Section 2.4 it is shown why positive net exports ($X > Z$) imply that the country as a whole is saving, accumulating claims on the rest of the world, while negative net exports imply that the country is borrowing. When this account includes exports or imports of all goods and services, it is called the **current account**.

Table 2.8 presents the accounting identity (2.7) for several countries in 1987. In the USA the private sector is close to balance and we observe the matching 'twin deficits' in net exports and the budget. The US external deficit seems related to the budget deficits of the Reagan administration in the early 1980s. Given their sizes (their combined GNPs represent 61% of

world GNP), the USA, Japan, and the EC come close to representing the whole world. The US external deficit must be approximately matched by external surpluses in Japan and the EC. Indeed, while the EC is in external balance in 1987, Japan has a surplus which matches the US deficit.

2.3.5. Identities versus Economics

The identity (2.7) implies that all goods and services produced must be purchased, or that the demand for goods and services must equal the supply. For example, if private savings in a country exceed private investment ($S > I$), either net exports must be positive or the government budget must be in deficit, or both. Without knowing more, it is impossible to know whether (1) the government deficit is at the origin of positive net private savings, (2) an export boom is generating income that is simply saved by residents, or (3) a fall in domestic investment spending induces a domestic recession which reduces both imports and tax revenues, leading to current account surplus and/or budget deficit. This is the difference between measuring data and interpreting them. This is also the difference between accounting and economics. The identity (2.7) is not only a requirement that accounts be correctly measured: as a market equilibrium condition, it also implies that some adjustment mechanism is at work.

The 1987 situation depicted in Table 2.8 illustrates this point. A Japanese net export surplus is matched by an excess of private savings over investment. The USA complained that its own external deficit was the result of what it perceived as an exogenous Japanese external surplus. The USA laid the blame on excessive saving (low total spending) and insufficient investment spendng in Japan. The Japanese countered that their external surplus and savings were largely an endogenous response to the US budget and external deficit. For the EC as a whole, the excess of savings over investment was mirrored in the average budget deficit. Within the EC the situation varied considerably, with some countries running large deficits and others large surpluses. As a whole, the Europeans blamed America's twin deficits for pushing interest rates up and discouraging investment worldwide, siding on this issue with Japan. They also complained that weak demand in Japan had depressed world incomes, thus siding with the USA. Both Japan and the USA thought the Europeans should put their house in order and cut their own budget deficits.

There is an element of truth in each of these assertions: what separates them out is the assumptions about what is exogenous—the US and EC budget deficits, or weak Japanese demand. Sorting out and assessing these arguments will require a lot more information, as well as some macroeconomic theory.

2.4. Balance of Payments

The **balance of payments** records all transactions between a country and the rest of the world. The presentation in Table 2.9 separates out international transactions on goods and services (upper part) from

---

Table 2.9. Balance of Payments

1. Exports of Goods
2. Imports of Goods

---

3. **Merchandise Trade Balance = (1) – (2)**
4. Exports of Services
5. Imports of Services
6. Net Royalties
7. Net Investment Income

---

8. **Invisible Balance = (4) – (5) + (6) + (7)**
9.   Balance on Goods and Services = (3) + (8)
10. Net Foreign Workers' Remittances
11. Net International Aid

---

12. **Unilateral Transfers = (10) + (11)**
13.   Current Account Balance (CA) = (3) + (8) + (12)
14. Gross Inward Direct Investment
15. Gross Outward Direct Investment
16. Gross Inward Portfolio Investment
17. Gross Outward Portfolio Investment

---

18. **Long-Term Capital Account Balance**
    = (14) – (15) + (16) – (17)
19. Short-Term Inward Capital Flows
20. Short-Term Outward Capital Flows

---

21. **Short-Term Capital Account Balance**
    = (19) – (20)
22.   Capital Account Balance (KA) = (18) + (21)
23. Errors and Omissions
24.   Overall Balance = (13) + (22)

---

25. **Balance on Official Intervention Account (net sales of foreign exchange) (OFF)**

Memo: Balance of Payments: *CA + KA + OFF = 0*

financial transactions (lower part). The balance of payments must obey rules of 'double-entry bookkeeping', meaning that every transaction gets recorded twice: once in the account that is being transacted, and once in the account that paid for it. Rather than going into the accounting details, we shall simply formulate the following simple rule: transactions involving *outflows of our money* should be regarded as deficit (−) items; items leading to *inflows of our money* are considered as surplus (+) items. The rest will become clear as we move along.

2.4.1. Commercial Transactions

The first accounts to consider in Table 2.9 record exports and imports of goods, imports entered with a minus sign. The net result is the **merchandise trade balance**. The balance of trade on goods and services is equal to the merchandise trade balance plus the balance on **invisibles**, which include investment income, royalties, and other services. The most important item is the **current account**, which was mentioned previously. It can be obtained by adding to the balance of goods and services the balance of unilateral transfers, that is payments not related to commercial or financial transactions (public transfers, foreign aid, payments to and from the EC budget, and what guest workers remit to their home countries). All current account items may be broadly interpreted as transactions describing sales and purchases of goods and services, including the services of foreign workers, capital, and know-how, or the goodwill of countries receiving aid. This is one interpretation of net exports $(X - Z)$ in the previous sections, although not the one used by national statistical agencies.

The importance of the current account is best seen by returning to the GDP decomposition. When GDP and GNP are equal and unrequited transfers are zero, the current account can be simply expressed as $CA = X - Z$ or

$$(2.8) \qquad CA = Y - (C + I + G) = Y - A,$$

where $A = C + I + G$ has already been defined as absorption, or total domestic spending on goods and services, both domestic and foreign. By definition, the current account is the excess of income (GNP) over spending. It signals whether the country is a net borrower or a net lender. When a country earns more than it spends $(CA = Y - A > 0)$, it is a net lender *vis-à-vis* the rest of the world. Conversely, a country running a

current account deficit spends more than it earns $(CA < 0$ and $A > Y)$ and must match the difference by borrowing abroad.

Table 2.10 provides a few illustrative examples. Turkish citizens working as guest workers abroad contribute to the balance of payments of Turkey through positive unilateral transfers. Since many Turkish workers live in Germany, there must be a negative counterpart in the German balance on unilateral transfer with Turkey. France and Germany stand in contrast. France sually has a trade deficit, while Germany normally exhibits a trade surplus. These imbalances are often matched by an invisibles surplus in France and deficit in Germany, reflecting the countries' comparative advantages. The UK usually enjoys a surplus of invisibles owing to its specialization in insurance and financial services; France owes its invisibles surplus to its tourist industry.

2.4.2. Financial Transactions

The rest of the balance of payments describes financial, or capital, account transactions. Current account surpluses must be matched by net outflows of financial capital because the country is lending to the rest of the world, or, put differently, is acquiring assets abroad. Current account deficits imply borrowing from abroad, so financial capital is flowing into the country. Accordingly, the remainder of the balance of payments, representing financial transactions, must be equal to, and of opposite sign to, the current account. This is merely an implication of double-entry accounting. Any transaction must have its counterpart of opposite sign: exports (a plus entry in the current account) imply income from abroad, which must be sent back either through imports (a minus entry in the current account) or lending, i.e. saving (a minus entry in the capital account). This is why all items in the balance of payments must add up to zero.

There are two main distinctions among financial transactions. The first concerns private and official accounts. The balance of purchases of foreign assets by private domestic residents is called the **capital account**. The official interventions account summarizes the dealings of the monetary authorities. If this account is in surplus, residents have sold more assets to foreigners then they have purchased. Monetary authorities are public agencies which—among other tasks discussed in Chapters 8 and 9—buy and sell foreign money in exchange for local money. These actions are

Table 2.10. Balance of Payments, Various Countries, 1992 ($US bn)

	Bolivia	France	Italy	Sweden	Turkey	UK	Germany
Trade balance	−0.43	1.75	3.08	6.72	−8.19	−23.42	32.76
Invisible balance	−0.14	20.81	−3.75	−2.81	4.82	6.27	−33.71
Unilateral transfers	0.24	−8.50	−5.66	−2.60	4.05	−9.10	−32.04
Current account	−0.53	4.33	−27.90	−8.78	−0.94	−17.85	−22.15
Long-term capital	0.28	−44.15	19.06	9.83	0.45	10.45	27.74
Short-term capital	0.09	24.60	−7.14	0.63	3.19	−12.17	35.90
Errors and omissions	0.03	2.10	−8.00	5.26	−1.22	12.14	1.51
Change in official reserves[a]	0.12	13.09	23.99	−6.95	−1.48	7.35	−43.00

[a] An increase in foreign reserves is represented by a positive entry, corresponding to a deficit on the *OFF* account (see text).

Source: IMF

called **foreign exchange market interventions**. When a monetary authority buys back its own currency, it spends some of the foreign currencies that it holds, which are called **foreign exchange reserves**. This is reported with a plus sign, to reflect that domestic money is flowing in.[14] Selling official foreign exchange reserves is one way of financing a current account deficit (much as an individual would sell off some assets to meet an excess of spending over income). Another possibility is for the private sector to sell off its foreign assets or to borrow abroad. The distinction between private and official financing is taken up in Section 2.4.4.

The second distinction is between long-term and short-term capital transactions. Long-term accounts concern the sales or purchases of assets of more than one year to maturity. Examples are foreign direct investment, acquisition of foreign companies, portfolio investment, or the establishment of subsidiaries abroad. Short-term transactions involving assets of less than one year of maturity—including bank accounts—are often associated with 'hot money', motivated by the expectation of quick returns rather than by long-term business strategies.

2.4.3. Errors and Omissions

There is a final item in Table 2.9, 'Errors and Omissions', which requires some explanation. By definition, the total of the balance of payments should be zero:

$$(2.9) \qquad \underset{\substack{\text{current} \\ \text{account}}}{CA} + \underset{\substack{\text{capital} \\ \text{account}}}{KA} + \underset{\substack{\text{official} \\ \text{interventions}}}{OFF} = 0.$$

While accounting guarantees the consistency of current and capital accounts in theory, the nature of data gathering for payments statistics virtually guarantees discrepancies. Trade data originate with customs authorities. Financial data come from the banking system, since international transactions are mediated by financial organizations. Official interventions, of course, are known by the monetary authorities, which are often responsible for collecting the data and producing the balance of payments accounts. In practice, relationship (2.9) never holds when data are actually collected, hence the need for an additional account called 'Errors and Omissions': this balancing item is necessary to arrive at zero at the bottom of the table. While there are genuine mistakes—the sheer volume of data to be treated is an invitation for errors—there may be fewer innocent 'omissions'.[15]

Table 2.10 shows some sizeable deficits or errors and omissions in Italy and Turkey; these might reflect savings illegally exported. Large positive entries might indicate uninvoiced or under-invoiced exports or overinvoiced imports. In the late 1980s the UK experienced a widening of its Errors and Omissions account as deregulation of London financial markets led to an increasing volume of undetected capital inflows. Finally, one cannot help but suspect that Bolivia's role in the world drug trade influences the evolution of its errors and omissions account.

---

[14] Note that this follows the rule of thumb mentioned above for thinking about the sign of an entry in the balance of payments: ask yourself whether it means that domestic money comes in (a plus) or goes out (a minus).

[15] Normally, the sum of the current accounts of all countries in the world should equal zero. In fact, it is systematically negative, as receipts are 'omitted' more often than expenditures.

2.4.4. The Meaning of the Accounts

A current account imbalance must be matched one for one by either the private capital account or official interventions by the monetary authorities. What difference does it make? A country running a current account surplus is receiving more payments from abroad than it disburses. If the private capital account is in balance, more domestic money must be flowing in than is leaving the country. This is possible only if someone makes up the difference. In fact, the imbalance between inflows and outflows translates into excess demand for the domestic currency on exchange markets worldwide. This demand tends to appreciate, or increase the value of, the domestic currency.[16] If the monetary authorities want to avoid such an appreciation, they must relieve the pressure by selling the 'missing' domestic currency—hence a minus entry in the official capital account (OFF) in (2.9)—against foreign currencies. The country's current account surplus takes the form of an acquisition of foreign exchange reserves. This can be thought of as an official loan to foreign monetary authorities.[17]

Suppose the central bank refused to intervene (OFF = 0). In this case the domestic currency would be in short supply on world markets and would tend to appreciate in value. The exchange rate appreciation works towards reducing the current account surplus as domestic goods become more expensive and foreign goods become cheaper, and prompts capital out-

flows as residents find it profitable to acquire cheap foreign assets. In the accounting identity (2.9); either the current account surplus disappears or the private capital account is negative. Similarly, a current account deficit can be financed privately (a positive capital account), publicly (a sales of foreign exchange reserves), or both.

The monetary authorities determine if, and to what extent, a current account imbalance translates into a change in the exchange rate. At one extreme, the monetary authorities may be committed to maintaining a fixed exchange rate—as within the European Monetary System—and they must intervene. If they do so, they must purchase or sell foreign exchange to whatever extent necessary. At the other extreme, the monetary authorities never intervene and the exchange rate is determined solely by the market. This is why the sum of the current and capital accounts (including errors and omissions) attracts special attention: it is the negative of the interventions by the monetary authorities and reveals their behaviour. It is sometimes called the balance of payments (BoP):[18] ignoring error and omissions,

$$(2.10) \qquad \text{BoP} = \text{CA} + \text{KA} = -\text{OFF}.$$

A balance of payments surplus means that the authorities have acquired foreign exchange reserves. Put differently, they have sold the domestic currency to match an excess demand for the domestic currency, thus preventing or reducing pressure for an exchange rate appreciation (OFF < O). A balance of payments deficit corresponds to a loss of reserves as the monetary authorities buy back the domestic currency to prevent a depreciation (OFF > O).

---

[16] Later chapters develop this in greater detail. A currency *appreciates* when its value in terms of other currencies increases. Conversely, if its value decreases, we speak of a *depreciation*.

[17] Indeed, if the Bundesbank, the monetary authority of Germany, buys US dollars, it is accepting claims on the US Federal Reserve, the monetary authority of the USA. This is, technically and in practice, a loan. Much more will be said about these operations in Chs. 8, 9, and 20.

[18] Strictly speaking, this is incorrect, because the balance of payments, which refers to the entire sum of international payments, is always zero.

2.5. Summary

1. The gross domestic product (GDP) can be defined in three equivalent ways: as the flow of final sales, the flow of factor incomes, or the flow of value added.

2. Because nominal GDP measures final sales at market prices, an increase in the price level leads to an increase in GDP even if quantities sold are constant. Real GDP is computed by pricing current output with constant prices, corresponding to a chosen base year.

3. The GDP deflator is the ratio of nominal to real GDP. It is one measure of the price level. Inflation is approximately equal to the difference between the nominal and real GDP growth rates. Price indices use constant-weights baskets of goods and services, and may also be used to compute inflation rates.

4. The location of factors of production defines the gross domestic product (GDP). Alternatively, ownership of factors of production defines the GNP. Net factor income earned abroad by labour and foreign investment enters the GNP, not the GDP, while net income earned by foreign-owned factors operating locally enters the GDP, not the GNP.

5. Measurement of GDP is imperfect, costly, and time-consuming. A large amount of economic activity is unmeasured, such as household services and the underground economy. Yet year-on-year comparisons, such as annual growth rates, are less affected by measurement problems.

6. GDP is equal to the sum of consumption, investment, government spending, and the current account ($Y = C + I + G + CA$). At the same time, GDP is equal to consumption, plus private sector savings, plus net taxes (gross taxes less public transfers received by the private sector) ($Y = C + S + T$). It follows as an identity that the current account surplus is equal to the surplus of the government plus the surplus of the private sector ($CA = (T - G) + (S - I)$).

7. The balance of payments is a record of current account transactions and their financial counterparts, the capital account. The current account is the sum of the merchandise, invisibles, and transfer accounts; any surplus or deficit must be matched by an equal and opposite sum of private long-term capital, short-term capital, errors and omissions, and official intervention accounts.

8. When the monetary authorities undertake to maintain the value of their country's exchange rate, they must intervene on exchange rate markets to match any possible balance of payments imbalance. Conversely, the exchange rate floats freely when the monetary authorities refrain from intervening; then all adjustment for balance of payments equilibrium occurs within the private sector, as a result of changes in the market-determined exchange rate.

Key Concepts

- accounting identities
- gross domestic product (GDP)
- flows and stocks
- final sales
- intermediate sales
- factors of production
- value added

- underground economy
- nominal and real GDP
- GDP deflator
- consumer price index (CPI)
- gross national product (GNP)
- circular flow
- net taxes

- private income
- consumption
- financial intermediation
- physical capital
- investment
- saving, net private saving
- absorption
- net exports
- real and financial sides of the economy
- depreciation

- net national product
- personal disposable income
- current account
- balance of payments
- merchandise trade balance
- invisibles
- capital account, private versus official, short-term versus long-term
- foreign exchange market intervention
- foreign exchange reserves

Exercises: Theory

1. You are given the following data:

GNP	5000
depreciation	500
before-tax corporate profits	1000
social security contributions	700
transfers to households and firms	1000
net interest to foreigners	200
proprietary income	70
net corporate saving	600
indirect taxes	1000
subsidies to enterprises	400
fines and fees	100
net remittances to rest of world	500
corporate taxes	100
consolidated government deficit	100
personal taxes	1500
household savings	200
investment expenditure	1200

Compute: NNP, national income, personal income, personal disposable income, consumption, government purchases, GDP, the current account balance. State your assumptions clearly.

2. The flow descripton of GDP presented considers that all produced goods, final and intermediary, are sold. In fact, some are stocked as additions to inventories. How do national accounts treat changes in inventories?

3. Governments often run a budget deficit, so they have to borrow. How could Figure 2.2 be amended to represent borrowing at home, and abroad?

4. In Figure 2.2, locate the NNP and describe firms' provisions for depreciation.

5. What happens to GDP when the owner of a small firm marries his secretary and stops paying for her work, which she continues to perform?

6. 'Services do not contribute to GDP as much as industry because industry produces tangible goods.' Comment.

7. I bought my house for ECU 80,000. I just sold it for ECU 110,000, and the estate agent received a 10% commission from the buyer. What is the effect on GDP?

8. Suppose that parking violation fines have increased by ECU 1 million this year as the police have hired additional personnel (previously unemployed) at an annual cost of ECU 300,000. What is the effect on GDP? Would the answer change if the new personnel were previously receiving ECU 300,000 worth of unemployment benefits?

9. GDP is often criticized as a measure of well-being, particularly because many goods are not priced in the market, especially public goods. Give some examples of how one could improve or adjust GDP to account for this problem.

10. A number of countries include housing mortgage payments in the CPI. Economists contend that this does not make any sense. What is your view?

Exercises: Applications

1. Suppose you have the following data on prices and quantities:

Prices (ECU)			
	Apples	Pears	Petrol
1993	1.0	2.0	5.0
1994	1.0	3.0	6.0
Quantities			
	Apples	Pears	Petrol
1993	300	100	50
1994	400	150	40

(a) If the economy produced all three (and only these three) goods, compute the nominal GDP in both periods, and real GDP at 1990 prices. What is the rate of inflation in 1991, as measured by the change in the GNP deflator?

(b) Suppose a CPI is constructed using weights corresponding to quantities produced in 1990. What is the rate of inflation measured by the CPI?

2. Suppose that the petrol in the previous question is imported. How do your answers change?

3. According to Table 2.4, the CPI and the GNP deflator behaved quite differently in Germany during 1979–81 and 1985–6. How could you explain this divergence? If you were a union negotiator, on which index would you choose to base your wage demands? If you represented the employers' association?

4. How would the following transactions be recorded in the French balance of payments?

   - A French resident buys a Volkswagen produced in Wolfsburg, Germany.
   - A French resident purchases a house in Switzerland.
   - A French national living in Switzerland buys a house in Switzerland.
   - A French resident builds a house in Italy, paying Italian residents to do the job.
   - A German banker sends his daughter at the Sorbonne a wire transfer in French francs.
   - The same German banker wires money to his bank account in Paris.
   - A Tunisian worker in Marseilles sends money to his family in Tunis.
   - Peugeot SA, a French concern, pays dividends to a resident of Finland.
   - Profits of Owen Corning, a US company, are reinvested in capacity expansion of a factory in Fontainebleau, France.
   - Banque de France sells pesetas to prevent the price of pesetas in francs from rising above its maximum allowable rate in Paris.
   - A French resident of Colmar, a town in Alsace near the German border, smuggles home a stereo purchased in Freiburg (Germany).

5. Over the past five years taxes were about 60% of GDP in Sweden. Yet disposable income over the past five years also amounted to 60% of GDP. How can these numbers be reconciled?

6. In 1985 the sum of all balances on current account of the world amounted to about $100 billion. How can you explain this?

7. Suppose you know that two fishing villages have identical GNPs and identical fishing fleets. However, one is situated on the sea coast, the other on a freshwater lake. Is the GNP or the NNP a better measure of economic welfare of the two communities? (Hint: think of depreciation!)

8. Table 2.8 shows that in Belgium and Italy net private saving is positive and very large. How can you explain this fact? To whom are households and firms lending?

9. 'Commuters reduce the GDP because they send home a large fraction of their earnings.' Comment.

10. 'Legalizing drugs would increase the GDP and tax receipts, but worsen the balance of payments.' Comment.

Suggested Further Reading

Internationally standardized macroeconomic data are published by:

The International Monetary Fund in *International Financial Statistics* (monthly), and *World Economic Outlook* (twice a year).

The Organisation for Economic Cooperation and Development (OECD) in *National Income Accounts*, *Main Economic Indicators*, and *Employment Outlook* (annual with monthly updates), and *OECD Economic Outlook* (twice a year). The OECD also publishes a yearly *Country Report* on each of its member countries—the major industrialized countries.

The United Nations in its *Annual Yearbook*.

On Europe, the Commission of the European Communities publishes *Eurostat* and a bimonthly review, *European Economy*.

The World Bank specializes in less developed countries and publishes annually, among others, the *World Debt Tables*.

Each country has its own reporting system, with the central bank often publishing balance of payments data. Examples of such publications are:

Annual Abstract of Statistics, Central Statistics Office, London

Bank of England Quarterly Bulletin

Bulletin de la Banque de Belgique

Bulletin Trimestriel de la Banque de France

Economie et Statistiques, Institut National de la Statistique et des Etudes Economiques, Paris

Monthly Report of the Deutsche Bundesbank, Frankfurt

PART II

The Real Macroeconomy

The analysis begins here. Part II focuses exclusively on the real side of the macroeconomy, the demand for and production of goods and services, leaving aside the monetary sphere, the nominal side. It is concerned with the behaviour of households, firms, and the government, and studies how these interact in various markets. We start with the study of spending decisions by households, firms, and governments. This opens the way to analysis of the production side, starting with growth, the most fundamental issue, which distinguishes poor from rich countries. Then, we look at a very special market, the labour market: the supply of labour by households, the demand by firms, and how they interact. The last chapter introduces the real exchange rate. Later on we shall interpret this part as describing the long run. Having the long run clearly set up will prove to be a useful beacon once we deal with the messier short run.

3

Intertemporal Budget Constraints

The future influences the present as much as the past.

Nietzsche

3.1. Overview

The circular flow diagram of the last chapter summarized income and spending flows of the three main aggregated sectors of economic activity: the private sector, the government, and the rest of the world. Each of these sectors has a net financing balance. If investment exceeds private savings, the private sector is borrowing. If the government's spending exceeds its revenues, then it is borrowing as well. If both private and public sectors of a nation are in deficit, the nation as a whole is borrowing, meaning that the current account is also in deficit. If this is the case, the rest of the world is running a surplus with that nation. Alternatively a government deficit could be offset entirely by net private savings, leaving the current account unaffected.

By borrowing and lending, economic agents can shift resources between the present and the future. Borrowing brings forward resources for use today, implying less spending in the future. Lending allows agents to defer current resources to some later date. As a result, these activities link the present and the future: liabilities must be eventually repaid, while accumu-

lated assets will eventually be spent. The ability to borrow and lend depends on expectations of future conditions. Because they are a central and pervasive feature of economic life, it is natural to begin Part II with a careful study of the **intertemporal budget constraints** that agents face. This chapter describes the constraints of all three sectors and shows how they relate to each other.

Modern macroeconomics stresses the importance of expectations of the future for current behaviour. For example, if Spanish or former East German workers expect their incomes to grow rapidly, despite currently low levels, it may make sense for them to borrow now and raise their current standards of living instead of waiting. In contrast, the lucky winner of a lottery will want to save a large fraction of the gain because it is unlikely to occur again. Investment decisions by firms are also similar to a gamble on future demand. Not the present, not the past, but expectations of the future exert the greatest influence on firms' capital budgeting decisions.

3.2. Thinking about the Future

3.2.1. The Future Has a Price

It is a basic economic principle that anything of value must have a price. This includes money and goods delivered at future dates, and specialized markets exist for the sole purpose of pricing future outcomes. London's Commodity Futures, New York's Mercantile Exchange, and many other such markets deal in contracts for future delivery of primary commodities in specific volume and quality—appropriately called futures. The most obvious example is the market for financial resources. Almost all economies have some form of

market for loans, in which the interest rate—the price for borrowing resources to be repaid in the future—is determined. More advanced countries have stock markets in which the values of firms are assessed, primarily on the basis of expected future earnings (profits).

Microeconomic principles may be extended usefully to analysing how the future is priced. There is a direct parallel between *intertemporal* consumption choices (between present and future goods) and *intratemporal* consumption choices (among goods at a particular point in time). For simplicity, microeconomic analysis of consumer behaviour often assumes that the

BOX 3.1. EXPECTATIONS

In order to formalize expectations, it is necessary to recognize explicitly the existence of uncertainty. We consider a random variable x_t in period t and denote the current expectation of its value in time $t+1$ as $_t x_{t+1}$.

Rational expectations asserts that differences between a variable's expectation and its realization are unpredictable:

$$x_{t+1} - {}_t x_{t+1} = \varepsilon_{t+1},$$

where ε is a purely random forecast error, sometimes called white noise.[1] If ε is equal to zero each period, we simply have the case of perfect foresight.

Adaptive expectations assumes that agents gradually correct their mistakes. According to this view, if they underestimated an economic variable last time, they raise their expectation; if they overestimated it, they reduce their forecast:

$$_t x_{t+1} - {}_{t-1} x_t = \alpha(x_t - {}_{t-1} x_t),$$

where α measures the extent to which agents adjust their expectations for past mistakes. While making sense, this trial-and-error process implies that agents accumulate knowledge only from their past experience. Static expectations, in which agents expect no change at all, can be seen as the special case $\alpha = 0$, whereas myopic expectations ($\alpha = 1$) implies that agents' forecasts are equal to last period's realized value.

An alternative assumption is that agents form extrapolative expectations of the future as a continuation of past trends:

$$_t x_{t+1} = x_t + \beta(x_t - x_{t-1}),$$

where β is the extent to which agents expect past trends to continue in the future.

---

budget is exhausted among available goods on the basis of their relative prices and consumer preferences. The same principle should apply to intertemporal decisions: when consumers choose between consuming goods now and consuming them in the future, they effectively decide whether to save or to borrow.

Not only do rational households plan spending over time, they also take into account—and possibly decide on—future incomes and resources. Similarly, firms must forecast the profitability of plant and equipment in which they invest. In the end, the income of firms is income of the households that own them.

3.2.2. The Rational Expectations Hypothesis

Because agents are so concerned with the future, we must think seriously about the way they form expectations about it. This book takes the view that agents' forecasts are correct on average. This working assumption is called the **rational expectations hypothesis**. It does not imply that individual agents forecast the future perfectly; it does imply that they do not make systematic mistakes. Alternative assumptions about expectations are presented formally in Box 3.1. These

alternatives to rational expectations rule out forward-looking behaviour, or assume that agents do not use all the available information about the future. The rational expectations hypothesis takes the opposite position, assuming that agents do use all available information, and use it in a skilled enough way to be right, on average.

This book adopts the rational expectations hypothesis for two reasons. The first is internal consistency. Economics is based on the hypothesis that agents behave rationally. If we accept this as a description of consumption and production, why not about expectations formation? Second, while rational expectations may seem unrealistic—surely ordinary people are not well informed enough to behave that way—alternatives are no closer to realism, for they assert that agents can be systematically wrong. If economic actors make systematic errors and suffer losses as a consequence, they will take steps to avoid such errors in the future.

In fact, it is usually sufficient for rational expectations to hold for the economy if a few well-informed agents behave in this way. If unions act on behalf of their members, it suffices that *their* expectations be correct on average. In financial markets, all that is required is that a number of professional traders be well informed with sufficient resources at their disposal. If they perceive that prices are too low compared with their valuation, they will buy, forcing prices upwards; if prices are too high to be consistent with their expectations, they will sell. Less well informed customers end up accepting the market prices because they are on average right, even if never quite right.

---

[1] A more formal description is that $_{t-1} x_t$ is the mathematical expectation of x_t based on all information I_{t-1} available at time $t-1$: $_{t-1} x_t = E(x_t \mid I_{t-1})$.

3.2.3. The Parable of Robinson Crusoe

The analysis of private sector behaviour proceeds in two steps. This chapter establishes an intertemporal budget constraint facing households, firms, the government, and the nation as a whole. Chapter 4 will use these constraints to study the actual behaviour of economic agents. Because there are millions of agents, a difficulty arises: how can we account for so many actions? One simplifying assumption is that, as a first approximation, all consumers and firms are alike. This step is by no means absurd; at the macroeconomic level, agents face common average price levels, interest rates, and macroeconomic conditions. The simplification allows us to study the behaviour of just one consumer and one firm as the average behaviour of the economy. The representative consumer and a representative firm should be understood as a parable, a way of capturing key insights about reality. A long tradition in economics proceeds by describing the situation of Robinson Crusoe, stranded on an island and forced to fend for himself.[2]

Time is of the essence in macroeconomics. We will capture the intertemporal aspects of Crusoe's economic environment in a simple way. It is convenient to collapse time into two periods, 'today' and 'tomorrow', where tomorrow is a metaphor for the future. Effectively, the day after tomorrow Crusoe is rescued, so he need no longer concern himself with the economics of his island.

3.3. The Household's Intertemporal Budget Constraint

3.3.1. Consumption and Intertemporal Trade

Robinson Crusoe was forced to survive using a single available resource, coconuts. In fact, we initially imagine that the island does not even have coconut trees: rather, the coconuts simply wash up on the beach. The number of coconuts that he (rationally) expects to have today and tomorrow is called his **endowment**.[3] It is exogenous because, until Robinson learns how to plant coconuts, he has no choice but to consume what nature gives him. His endowment of coconuts today (Y_1) and coconuts tomorrow (Y_2) is represented as point A in Figure 3.1. Since the coconuts are perishable, Crusoe's consumption of coconuts could also be represented by point A, in the event he did nothing to change his situation. This point is sometimes called the **autarky** point. A household or a country operates in autarky when it does not trade with the rest of the world.

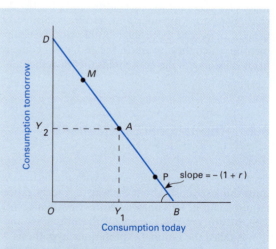

Figure 3.1. Endowment, Wealth, and Consumption

Endowment available today and tomorrow determines wealth and available consumption choices along the budget line *BD*. The same level of wealth (*OB*) can be achieved by professional athletes (point *P*) and university students (point *M*).

---

[2] The two-period parable—based on the classic novel by Daniel Defoe (1660–1731)—is the workhorse of modern economic analysis and is attributable to the American economist Irving Fisher (1867–1947).

[3] Two caveats apply. First, we assume that there is no uncertainty and that Crusoe has a perfect foresight with respect to the future. Perfect foresight is the equivalent of rational expectations when there is no uncertainty. Second, we consider that Crusoe has little else to do with his time so that coconuts can be gathered at no personal cost. Ch. 6 considers the important case when Crusoe enjoys leisure and puts a price on working (picking up coconuts).

If, however, there is a not-too-distant island, trade is possible. Because Crusoe's coconuts are just as good as his neighbours', one might think that there is no reason to trade.[4] That is not correct. Crusoe may well be interested in **intertemporal trade**, or trade across time. He might lend his neighbours some coconuts today if he expects to find only a few tomorrow. On the contrary, if today's 'harvest' is abnormally low, he may borrow coconuts now and repay later when times are better.

3.3.2. The Real Interest Rate

Crusoe and his neighbours must agree on the terms of repayment: how much should he pay (or receive) tomorrow for one coconut borrowed (lent) today? These terms are the **real interest rate**. If the neighbours are already conducting intertemporal trade among themselves, and are willing to offer him the same rate of interest, then from Crusoe's point of view the interest rate, denoted by r, is exogenous. If he lends 100 coconuts today, he will receive $100(1 + r)$ coconuts tomorrow. Equivalently, to receive 100 coconuts tomorrow he must save $100/(1 + r)$ coconuts today; a coconut tomorrow is worth $1/(1 + r)$ coconuts today. This is called the **intertemporal price**, the price of tomorrow's consumption in terms of today's consumption. It says that goods tomorrow are less valuable than goods today, and this is why the real interest rate r is positive. The real interest rate measures the cost of waiting. Valuing future goods in terms of goods today (here, dividing by the interest factor 1 plus the real interest rate) is called **discounting**. Box 3.2 presents this important concept more generally. It can be used for example to explain the inverse relationship between bond prices and interest rates.

Intertemporal trade allows Crusoe to choose consumption combinations represented by the line BD in Figure 3.1. This line must go through endowment point A, since he can always choose not to trade at all. At point B Crusoe forgoes consumption tomorrow completely: he borrows against his future endowment Y_2, receives $Y_2/(1 + r)$ coconuts, and consumes $Y_1 + Y_2/(1 + r)$ coconuts today. At point D he fasts today, and lends all his current endowment Y_1 in order

to consume $Y_1(1 + r) + Y_2$ coconuts tomorrow. This shows that the slope of the line, called the budget line, is $-(1 + r)$.[5] If the rate of interest increases, the budget line becomes steeper: for a given amount of saving today, more will be available tomorrow.

3.3.3. Wealth and Present Discounted Values

If Crusoe consumes C_1 in the first period and his income 'from nature' is Y_1, his saving is $Y_1 - C_1$. If $Y_1 - C_1$ is positive, he is lending; if $Y_1 - C_1$ is negative, he is borrowing. In the second period, his consumption C_2 will equal the sum of income Y_2 plus $(1 + r)(Y_1 - C_1)$, the interest and principal on his savings in period 2. (If saving was negative in the first period, this means paying back principal plus interest.) Formally, we have

$$(3.1) \qquad C_2 = Y_2 + (Y_1 - C_1)(1 + r).$$

This is simply a restatement of Crusoe's **intertemporal budget constraint**. It can be rearranged as

$$(3.2) \qquad C_1 + \frac{C_2}{1 + r} = Y_1 + \frac{Y_2}{1 + r}.$$

The left-hand side is the **present discounted value** of consumption: it is the sum of today's and tomorrow's consumption valued in terms of goods today. The right-hand side is equal to the present discounted value of income (his endowment). It is the maximum consumption that Crusoe could enjoy today given his resources today and tomorrow, and is represented by point B in Figure 3.1. OB is the present discounted value of Crusoe's total endowment, or his total wealth represented by the symbol Ω:

$$(3.3) \qquad \Omega = Y_1 + \frac{Y_2}{1 + r}.$$

The pattern of consumption over both periods can be sustained by individuals with very different income profiles. It doesn't matter whether Crusoe is a university student with low current and high future income, as represented by point M in Figure 3.1, or a

---

[4] In a more involved parable, Robinson's coconuts might be sufficiently different from those of the neighbouring natives—and vice versa—to make *intra*temporal trade possible. We will put aside this possibility for later chapters.

[5] The slope is the ratio OD/OB. From the text we know that $OD/OB = [Y_1(1 + r) + Y_2]/[Y_1 + Y_2/(1 + r)] = 1 + r$. The slope is negative because the budget constraint is downward-sloping.

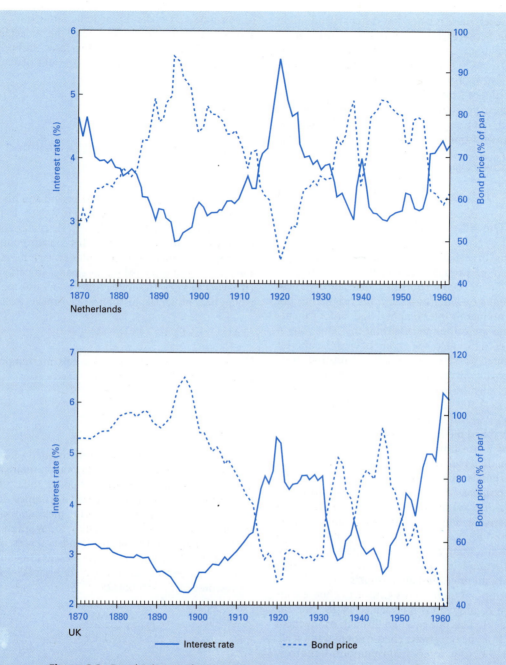

Figure 3.2. Bond Prices and Interest Rates

Bond prices and interest rates move inversely. Increases in interest rates decrease the present value of future coupon payments and the value of bonds. Put differently, the price of the bond for a given stream of coupon payments determines the rate of interest.

Source: Homer (1963)

BOX 3.2. DISCOUNTING AND BOND PRICES

Discounting is used in economics and finance to evaluate the value of future incomes or expenditures in terms of resources today. It is frequently used to value financial assets. Discounting asks: what is the amount required today, given an interest rate, to generate some payment or payments in the future?

Consider the simplest case of a bond which pays ECU 100 in one year's time. (This type of bond is called a *pure discount* bond.) If the interest rate is 5%, what is the value of this bond today? It is the amount invested now that yields 100 next year. If that amount is B, then it must be true that

$$B(1 + 0.05) = 100,$$

so $B = 95.24$. We can ask how much this bond would be worth if it were a two-year discount bond instead:

$$B(1 + 0.05)^2 = 100,$$

so that now $B = 90.70$. The further in the future the payback is, the more heavily any amount is discounted.

Consider any stream of payments a_t in a future year t. Generalizing, the present value of period $t = n$ payment is $a_n/(1 + r)^n$, and the present value of the whole stream of future incomes $t = 1, \ldots, n$, discounting at rate r, is:

$$\frac{a_1}{1 + r} + \frac{a_2}{(1 + r)^2} + \frac{a_3}{(1 + r)^3} + \ldots + \frac{a_n}{(1 + r)^n}.$$

A simple example is the case of a consol, a bond that promises to pay a fixed amount for ever. The price of a consol p is simply the present discounted value of its payments:

$$p = \frac{a}{1 + r} + \frac{a}{(1 + r)^2} + \frac{a}{(1 + r)^3} + \ldots + \frac{a}{(1 + r)^n} + \ldots = \frac{a}{r}.$$

This shows that the price of a consol is inversely related to the interest rate. Other bonds have a finite maturity so the formula is more complicated, but the general principle remains that higher real interest rates imply lower bond prices. This is illustrated in Figure 3.2.

---

professional athlete with high current and low future income (point P). As long as these points are on the same intertemporal budget constraint, the present discounted value of income is the same and intertemporal trade allows income to be shifted across time by borrowing and lending.[6]

If Crusoe has initial tradable wealth B_0 (an initial cache of coconuts), his wealth will increase by this amount and the budget constraint will be modified as follows:[7]

$$(3.4) \qquad C_1 + \frac{C_2}{1 + r} = Y_1 + \frac{Y_2}{1 + r} + B_0.$$

Naturally, this means that he can consume more in both periods. If he started with a debt, then B_0 is negative and he will have to consume less in order to repay the debt with interest. In general, total wealth is the sum of inherited wealth or indebtedness B_0 and of the present value of income. This is shown in Figure 3.3, where the inherited wealth or indebtedness is added

to the present value of income. At a given real interest rate, it implies shifting the budget line BD to $B'D'$ or $B''D''$.

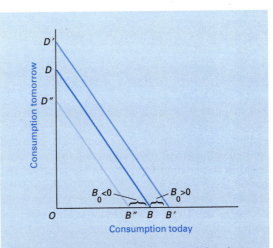

Figure 3.3. Inheriting Wealth or Indebtedness

When some wealth $B_0 > 0$ is left over from previous periods, the budget line shifts from BD to $B'D'$. If debt $B_0 < 0$ is inherited instead, the budget line is $B''D''$. The lines are parallel because the real interest rate is unchanged.

---

[6] The ability to borrow fully against future income may be questioned when future income is uncertain. This objection is valid. Uncertainty not only leads individuals to be more cautious, but also may make lenders more reluctant to extend credit.

[7] This is obtained by noting that today's available resources are $Y + B_0$ so that (3.2) is changed to $C_2 = Y_2 + (Y_1 + B_0 - C_1)(1 + r)$.

3.4. The Firm and the Private Sector's Intertemporal Budget Constraint

3.4.1. Firms and the Investment Decision

So far the endowment has been considered exogenous. In fact, income mostly comes from carefully chosen productive activities. Production normally requires that some current endowment be diverted from consumption and used to acquire productive capital. Crusoe could plant coconuts today which would grow into trees bearing coconuts tomorrow. Naturally, once planted, a coconut cannot be consumed: it is useful only for its future production. The use of valuable resources to produce more goods later is called **investment** or **fixed capital formation**.[8] Indeed, a large quantity of goods—plant and equipment—have no consumption value whatsoever; they are designed solely to make future production possible.

Like consumption, the investment decision has a fundamental intertemporal aspect. Firms decide to accumulate capital when it is profitable to do so, and profitability depends on expected future outcomes. In order to finance their investments, firms obtain resources from the capital market (stock exchanges, bond markets, or banks) or use their own funds (retained earnings).

3.4.2. The Production Function

The investment decision depends upon the amount of output that can be produced with the available equipment (the number of coconuts to be obtained from planting a tree). The **production function** $F(K)$ captures this relationship between capital input and output and is depicted in Figure 3.4. The shape of the curve implies that, as more capital is accumulated, the additional or marginal yield declines. That marginal output decreases when more input is put in place is called the principle of **diminishing marginal productivity**.[9] The reason behind this principle is that, given

the existing amount of labour used to man the equipment (here, Crusoe's time), adding new equipment is less and less effective in raising output.

3.4.3. The Cost of Investment

Starting with no capital stock (there were no coconut trees on the island), today's investment represents the total stock of capital available for production tomorrow. (Box 3.3 considers the more realistic case when previously accumulated capital already exists.) Crusoe understands that he can either invest K in productive equipment, or lend K to his neighbours. In the first case, he will have an output $F(K)$ tomorrow. In the second case, he will receive an income $K(1 + r)$. The real interest rate represents the **opportunity cost** of the resources used in investment. Because of the option of lending at rate r, the investment must yield at least $1 + r$ to be worth undertaking.[10]

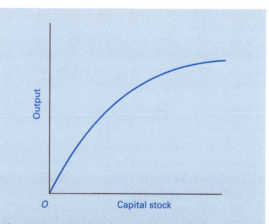

Figure 3.4. The Production Function

As more input is added, output increases, but at a decreasing rate. This is the principle of declining marginal productivity.

---

[8] Ch. 2 stresses the distinction between the acquisition of productive equipment—investment—and the acquisition of existing assets. Savings can take the form of purchasing either existing or newly created assets.

[9] Mathematically, this can be expressed as $F'(K) > 0$, $F''(K) < 0$.

[10] Alternatively, Crusoe could borrow coconuts for investment purposes. The interest rate then is the cost of investment. This is discussed in S. 3.4.4 and in Box 3.4.

BOX 3.3. GROSS INVESTMENT, DEPRECIATION, AND THE CAPITAL STOCK

When previously accumulated capital exists, the situation is somewhat more involved than in the case of Crusoe's bare island. The stock of capital may differ in the future from the accumulated stock K_1 in two ways. First, new capital I_1 may be invested. Second, depreciation may re-move some of the value of the capital stock. Depreciation occurs because of wear and tear or obsolescence. It is a proportion δ of the capital stock. The new capital stock is:

$$K_2 = K_1 + I_1 - \delta K_1$$
new capital stock = old capital + gross investment − depreciation
$$= (1 - \delta)K_1 + I_1.$$

The change in the capital stock, $\Delta K = K_2 - K_1$, is the difference between gross investment and depreciation of previously accumulated capital. For the capital stock to grow, fresh investment must exceed depreciation.

Figure 3.5 shows the opportunity cost $K(1 + r)$ as the ray OR. As long as the amount of output exceeds the cost, the technology is sufficiently productive and investment is worthwhile. At point A, investment just covers its cost, there is no economic profit. To the right of A, investment uses up more resources than it produces. Positive economic profits occur only to the left of A.

Changes in the interest rate can change the set of investment levels that are productive. If the rate of interest were to increase, the OR line would rotate upward, pushing point A to the left, reducing the return from any investment level, and thus narrowing the range of productive investments. Another angle on the problem is to compute the net return V from investing K. It is the difference between the present value of output tomorrow and investment today:[11]

$$(3.5) \qquad V = \frac{F(K)}{1 + r} - K.$$

Investment is carried out only if it has a positive present value, that is if $V > 0$ or if $F(K) > K(1 + r)$. Figure 3.6 illustrates a case when the technology is not

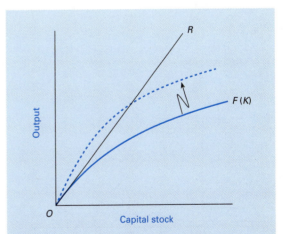

Figure 3.6. Unproductive Technology

Given the interest rate, no firm will operate with a production function $F(K)$. Technological innovation may occur and open up profit opportunities.

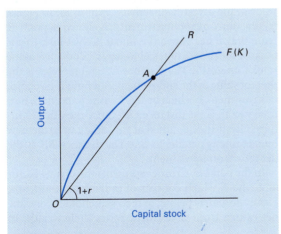

Figure 3.5. Productive Technology

The cost of borrowing to finance investment is given by OR. As long as output exceeds the cost of borrowing, the technology is productive and the producer makes profit. Beyond A, she makes losses.

[11] The trees are assumed not to have resale value; they die after the second period. If they didn't, one would need to add back the resale value of the depreciated trees in the second period, which would increase the value of the investment activity. This modification is described in detail in the next chapter.

productive enough given the real interest rate. In that case it does not pay to invest: it is more profitable to lend at the rate r. It would require either an improvement in technology (for the production function schedule to shift upward) or a lowering of the interest rate for investment to be worthwhile.

3.4.4. The Intertemporal Budget Constraint of the Consolidated Private Sector

The budget constraint of Section 3.3 takes endowments as given. Once investment and production are taken into account, income tomorrow is no longer simply given by nature. The budget constraint now depends on the amount that is invested and on its profitability. As long as it is profitable, investment increases wealth. Figure 3.7 shows how this happens. Starting from point A, Crusoe can save either by lending to his neighbours or by investing an amount I_1 up to Y_1. If all his savings are invested, the capital stock available for tomorrow's output production is the difference between today's endowment Y_1 and consumption C_1:

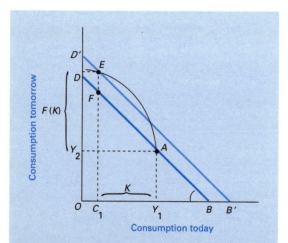

Figure 3.7. Investment Increases Wealth

Investing K in the productive technology allows a household to improve its wealth over and above that corresponding to the initial endowment A. Here wealth increases by BB' as FE additional goods become available in the second period.

$$(3.6) \qquad K = I_1 = Y_1 - C_1.$$

The more he invests—the more we move to the left—the larger will be tomorrow's production. This is why the production function is now the mirror image of the one shown in Figure 3.6: as we move leftward from the endowment point A, investment increases and tomorrow's output becomes larger. Tomorrow's income is the sum of the endowment Y_2 (the coconuts lying on the beach) plus output $F(K)$:

$$(3.7) \qquad C_2 = Y_2 + F(K).$$

The intertemporal budget constraint determines the present value of consumption $C_1 + C_2/(1 + r)$. With $C_1 = Y_1 - I_1$ given by (3.6) and C_2 given by (3.7), the present value of consumption is equal to wealth Ω:

$$(3.8) \qquad C_1 + \frac{C_2}{1 + r} = \Omega,$$

where wealth is now expressed as

$$(3.9) \qquad \Omega = Y_1 - I_1 + \frac{Y_2}{1 + r} + \frac{F(K)}{1 + r}$$

$$= Y_1 + \frac{Y_2}{1 + r} + \frac{F(K)}{1 + r} - I_1.$$

| Total wealth | = | endowment | + | net return on investment |

Wealth now consists of two parts. The first part is the present value of the endowment as before in (3.3). The second part is the increase in wealth by V, the net value of the investment activity, as in (3.5). In Figure 3.7 the outcome of investment I_1 is shown as point E. Note that E lies above the initial budget line; this is because the production technology is productive at the rate of interest r. The distance OB still represents the present value of the endowment. But now, for a choice of investment I_1 which brings Crusoe to point E, new total wealth is the distance OB'. Since the value of future output is discounted at the same rate r, the new budget line is parallel to BD. The distance BB' is the net return on investment.[12]

In the parable, Crusoe represents the private sector as a whole, which consists of individuals and firms. Firms ultimately belong to their shareholders, and the net return from investment raises their wealth. In

[12] Note that the production schedule cuts the new budget line $B'D'$, suggesting that this result might be improved by investing a little bit less than I_1. Ch. 4 shows that, when Crusoe behaves optimally, he will invest to push out his new budget line as far as possible.

BOX 3.4. THE MODIGLIANI–MILLER THEOREM

One of the implications of the consolidation of household and firm accounts is that households ultimately own the firms and that the activity of firms affects the value of household wealth. In practice, firms may be owned directly by households (we speak of stocks or shares in the firm, or equity ownership), or firms may borrow resources with a promise to repay in the future (they issue debt). Shareholders are therefore called **residual claimants**, since they have a claim to whatever remains after firms have incurred their costs, serviced their debt (outstanding bonds and borrowing from banks), and paid taxes. Similarly, if a firm is declared bankrupt, those who have lent to the firm (bondholders, banks, and other creditors) have priority over equity holders. Under ideal conditions, it does not matter whether a firm uses debt or equity to finance an investment project. This is the Modigliani-Miller Theorem.[13]

In the same vein, there is no difference between firms' savings and household savings lent to firms, at least to first approximation. Firms' savings amount to retaining earnings instead of distributing them to shareholders. In that case, shareholders are entitled to the future earnings generated by non-distributed profits. The number of shares does not change but each share is worth more. In the second case, the shareholders provide the firm with additional resources in return for future earnings associated with the new investment: they now hold more shares but the value of each share remains approximately unchanged. In both cases, for a given investment project, the shareholders' wealth is the same. In the first case, they implicitly lend to the firm the equivalent of undistributed earnings.

Thus, the firm is a 'veil' which acts on behalf of its shareholders. It is irrelevant whether the firm or the shareholders do the saving. In practice, the relative shares of saving by firms and households vary considerably from one country to another (Figure 3.8). But when household and corporate savings are added up, national patterns appear more similar. For example, the bulk of saving is done by firms in Italy and Japan. The opposite holds in Germany and the UK. One reason for this variation is the difference in the tax treatment of dividends, retained earnings, and capital gains. When the capital gains associated with retained earnings are taxed less heavily than dividend income, for example, shareholders are better off when firms save on their behalf.

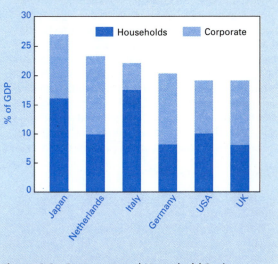

Figure 3.8. Corporate and Household Saving, 1981–1987

Total saving rates differ across countries, but not as much as the share of saving of the corporate and household sectors. Tax treatment of income from saving largely explains the latter difference.

Source: Dean *et al*. (1989)

---

effect, the firm is simply a veil. It should be valued as the present value of net income from all its activities. If shareholders anticipate that a firm will become more profitable in the future—because of a technological advance, as represented by the shift in Figure 3.6—then net expected returns rise and they are richer. This wealth gain takes the form of an increase in the value of the firm. In the real world, this would be reflected in the value of a firm on the stock market.

Does it matter how this increase in wealth occurs—whether firms borrow to finance the investment or use their own savings? In Crusoe's world the answer is simple: it doesn't. This is easy to see from Figure 3.7: if borrowed coconuts can be planted, Crusoe could bring forward the present value of his endowment to point *B*. Yet as long as he invests as in Figure 3.7, the value of his wealth is the same! It does not matter whether a firm uses debt (borrowing) or equity (own saved funds) to finance the investment plans. This result, known as the **Modigliani–Miller Theorem**, is discussed in more detail in Box 3.4.

---

[13] It is named after the two Nobel Prize laureates, Franco Modigliani of MIT and Merton Miller of the University of Chicago.

3.5. Public and Private Budget Constraints

3.5.1. The Public Budget Constraint

There was no government on Robinson Crusoe's island. In the real world, there is a public sector which taxes, purchases, and transfers incomes. A government is little different from other economic agents. It can borrow and lend, and then repay its debt with interest or be repaid by its debtors.[14] Within the two-period framework, the government spends G_1 and G_2 today and tomorrow, and raises net taxes, T_1 and T_2. Because they are a central component of the intertemporal budget constraint, we shall henceforth separate out interest payments from T for the rest of this book.[15]

Suppose there is no initial debt. If Crusoe's government spends more than its income today, then $G_1 - T_1 > 0$ and it borrows today. Tomorrow's taxes must cover both tomorrow's spending and the debt service:

$$(3.10) \qquad T_2 = G_2 + (G_1 - T_1)(1 + r_G),$$

where r_G is the rate of interest at which the government can borrow or lend.

If the government runs a surplus today, $G_1 - T_1$ is negative and tomorrow's taxes T_2 can be less than tomorrow's spending. This is the government's intertemporal budget constraint, similar to the household budget constraint (3.2). It may also be rewritten in present-value terms:

$$(3.11) \qquad G_1 + \frac{G_2}{1 + r_G} = T_1 + \frac{T_2}{1 + r_G}.$$

Defining D_0 as the debt inherited from the previous period, today's budget deficit can be separated into two parts: the **primary deficit**, which is the amount by which non-interest expenditures exceed revenues, and net interest payments:

$$\text{Total deficit} = \underbrace{(G_1 - T_1)}_{\substack{\text{primary} \\ \text{deficit}}} + \underbrace{r_G D_0}_{\substack{\text{debt} \\ \text{service}}}.$$

Then the government budget constraint can be rewritten in terms of primary budget deficits:

$$(3.12) \qquad D_0 + (G_1 - T_1) + \frac{G_2 - T_2}{1 + r_G} = 0.$$

The sum of the initial debt and of the present value of primary budget deficits must be zero. The constraint is illustrated in Figure 3.9 for the case where $D_0 = 0$. In that case, the budget line passes through the origin because the government has no initial debt or assets, and the slope of the line is $-(1 + r_G)$. Then a budget deficit (surplus) today must be matched by a budget surplus (deficit) tomorrow:

$$(3.13) \qquad (G_1 - T_1) + \frac{G_2 - T_2}{1 + r_G} = 0.$$

Do governments actually respect their budget constraints? To be sure, there are spectacular examples of government defaults, or repudiation of past debts. Most were associated with sharp political upheavals: the turbulent years of the French revolution, the October 1917 revolution in Russia, the end of the Weimar

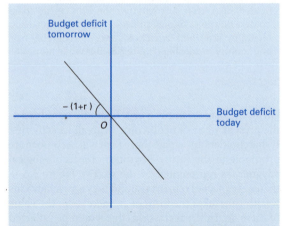

Figure 3.9. The Government Budget Line

A deficit today must be matched by a budget surplus tomorrow, or vice versa, if the government is to obey its intertemporal budget constraint.

---

[14] The rationale for governments and their economic activities is developed in Chs. 15 and 16. A key difference with the private sector is that governments can legally default on their debt obligations, since they define what is legal. Governments that default explicitly on the national debt are relatively rare. However, governments may use their right to create money to effectively diminish the real value of their obligations. Since we consider here only the real economy, this issue is taken up in Chs. 9 and 15.

[15] It should be stressed that G represents government purchases of goods and services and should be distinguished from total government outlays, which include transfer payments. In our notation, transfer payments are deducted from taxes to give net taxes, T.

Republic in 1933, Castro's revolution in Cuba.[16] In most cases, however, it is politically difficult for a government to default.

The logic of this argument implies that primary deficits now require primary surpluses later, and conversely. Given spending plans, lower taxes today are followed by higher taxes tomorrow. Alternatively, for a given path of taxes, more spending today requires spending cuts tomorrow. How long does 'today' last before a government is hit 'tomorrow' by the budget constraint? Governments that start with little debt can run deficits for many years.[17] Figure 3.10 presents examples of primary budget balances relative to the size of the economy (GDP). Some countries (the USA, the UK) show a succession of moderate primary deficits and surpluses. In other cases (Belgium, Denmark, Ireland) deficits have been sustained over many years, yet eventually the budget constraint has prevailed and the primary budgets have been corrected, sometimes moving into spectacular surpluses.

3.5.2. The Consolidated Public and Private Budget Constraint

Just as the corporate veil was pierced when we consolidated the household and firm budget constraints, might it not be the case that the private sector also sees through the public sector veil? Could the private sector understand that it ultimately pays the taxes anyway? Ignoring the existence of firms, the budget constraints of the private and public sectors are recalled:

$$(3.14) \qquad C_1 + \frac{C_2}{1+r} = Y_1 - T_1 + \frac{Y_2 - T_2}{1+r}$$

$$(3.15) \qquad G_1 + \frac{G_2}{1+r_G} = T_1 + \frac{T_2}{1+r_G}.$$

Note that the government and the private sector do not necessarily face the same interest rates when they engage in borrowing or lending activities: the government sector borrows and lends at rate r_G, the private sector at rate r. Starting with the case where the interest rates are the same ($r = r_G$), adding up the private

and public budget constraints gives the following expression:

$$(3.16) \qquad C_1 + \frac{C_2}{1+r} = (Y_1 - G_1) + \frac{Y_2 - G_2}{1+r}.$$

This looks very much like the private sector budget constraint (3.14), except that taxes have been replaced by public spending. There are three ways of interpreting this important result. First, as seen by reorganizing (3.16), total national spending—the sum of private and public spending on goods and services—cannot exceed the country's wealth. The country can borrow or lend abroad, but it must respect the nation's budget constraint:

$$(3.17) \qquad \underbrace{(C_1 + G_1) + \frac{C_2 + G_2}{1+r}}_{\substack{\text{present value of} \\ \text{total domestic spending}}} = \underbrace{Y_1 + \frac{Y_2}{1+r}}_{\substack{\text{present value of} \\ \text{domestic incomes}}}.$$

3.5.3. Ricardian Equivalence: the Benchmark Case

Equation (3.16) has a second interpretation. Private sector wealth is the difference, in present-value terms, between private endowments and public spending. It is as if the government simply confiscates the resources corresponding to its expenditures, and the private sector takes the remainder. Given public spending decisions, taxes can be levied today or tomorrow: the time profile of taxation has no effect on private wealth.

The result, that the private sector fully internalizes the public sector budget's constraint, is known as the **Ricardian equivalence proposition**.[18] In Figure 3.11, point A represents Crusoe's endowment measured before taxes. Once public spending is taken into account as in (3.16), the private endowment is represented by point A'. The government reduces Crusoe's private wealth by an amount represented by the distance BB', which is either the present value of taxes or the present value of public spending. (The two are equal because of the government budget constraint (3.15).) Public spending can be financed either by current taxes or by borrowing. If the government reduces taxes today without changing its expenditures, it borrows today and will raise taxes tomorrow. For the private sector, this means more net-of-tax income today and less tomorrow. As long as the public and private

---

[16] The public debt must be carefully distinguished from the external debt, although in some instances the public debt is held by foreigners and represents the bulk of the external debt. This chapter assumes that the public debt is held by domestic residents. The case of the external debts is the subject matter of S. 3.6.

[17] Ch. 15 provides discussion and data on the stock of public debt, which in some countries (Belgium, Ireland, Italy) exceeds annual GDP.

[18] Named after English economist David Ricardo (1772–1823), who first formulated this idea, only to dismiss it as unlikely. The idea has been revived and championed by Harvard economist Robert Barro.

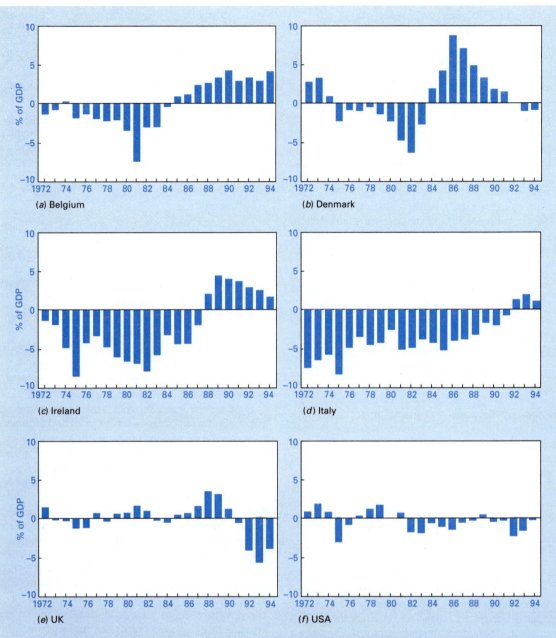

Figure 3.10. Primary Budget Surpluses, Six Countries, 1972–1994

Over time, primary budget balances must add up, in present-value terms, to initial public debt. Some governments maintain near-primary budget balances. Those that have allowed deficits to cumulate into large indebtedness eventually have to run surpluses.

Source: OECD, *Economic Outlook*

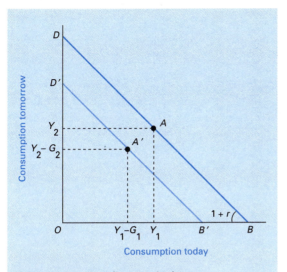

Figure 3.11. Ricardian Equivalence

The government's spending and taxing activities reduce private wealth. Given government purchases, the precise scheduling of taxes does not matter.

sectors borrow and lend at the same rate ($r = r_G$), these intertemporal shifts are equivalent and the public borrowing can be matched one for one by private saving along the same private budget line.

The third interpretation of (3.16) concerns private wealth. When a government borrows to cover its deficit, it issues bonds which are a promise to repay interest and principal. Do households that own the debt consider it as part of their wealth? In this interpretation, they do not: government's indebtedness does not appear as part of private wealth in the right-hand side of (3.16). The reason is that the private sector pierces the veil of government: it recognizes that the government's promises to pay—the principal and interest on public debt—is matched by taxes levied to service the debt. Public bonds are an asset to households which is exactly offset by the value of their future tax liabilities. Ricardian equivalence asserts that government debt does not represent net wealth to the aggregate private sector.

3.5.4. Where Ricardian Equivalence Can Fail

This section considers the many assumptions, implicit or explicit, required to reach the Ricardian equivalence result. It should become clear that, in fact, budget

deficits probably do matter, and that at least some fraction of public debt is regarded by the private sector as wealth.[19]

3.5.4.1. Mortal or new citizens

The Ricardian equivalence proposition is, in the first instance, a proposition concerning aggregate budget constraints. Thus, the mere fact that citizens are not all alike does not imply that the aggregate household sector can escape the implications of equations (3.14)–(3.15). Even if some citizens hold the public debt and others do not, *aggregate* future tax burden will be the same.

On the other hand, citizens are certainly mortal. If they are not alive in period 2, they will not fully incorporate the intertemporal budget constraint of the government into their own budget constraints. If the current private sector fails to factor in *all* future tax liabilities, it is possible that government debt represents private wealth to some agents, and bond-financed deficits increase their wealth.

3.5.4.2. Different interest rates

It has been explicitly assumed that the government and the private sector face the same interest rate as they engage in financial trade ($r = r_G$). How realistic is this assumption? In Table 3.1 two categories of borrowing rate are displayed. Treasury bond rates represent the cost of borrowing faced by the public sector. The corporate bond rate is the interest rate charged by the bond market for firms with the best credit rating; most private borrowers face significantly higher rates (by some 1%–2% more for businesses, and much more for households). In most cases, private borrowing rates exceed the comparable public borrowing rate. This is probably because the government is considered less risky.

When $r > r_G$, combining the private and public budget constraints (3.14) and (3.15) yields, instead of (3.16),[20]

---

[19] Other potential failures of the Ricardian equivalence proposition are related to the behaviour of agents under uncertainty, and go beyond the scope of this book.

[20] To see this, multiply both sides of (3.15) by $(1 + r_G)/(1 + r)$, and rewrite as

$$G_1 + \frac{G_2}{1 + r} + \frac{r_G - r}{1 + r}G_1 = T_1 + \frac{T_2}{1 + r} + \frac{r_G - r}{1 + r}T_1$$

so that

$$T_1 + \frac{T_2}{1 + r} = G_1 + \frac{G_2}{1 + r} + \frac{r_G - r}{1 + r}(G_1 - T_1).$$

Substitution in (3.14) yields (3.18).

Table 3.1. Public and Private Borrowing Rates, February 1995: Long-Term Bonds (% per annum)

Country	Treasury bonds	Corporate bonds
Belgium	6.83	7.33
Canada	7.54	8.80
France	7.17	7.60
Germany (West)	6.35	5.86
Italy	11.51	10.09
Netherlands	6.37	6.62
Spain	10.55	11.18
Sweden	8.99	10.04
Switzerland	4.06	4.10

Source: The Economist, 4 November 1995

$$(3.18) \quad C_1 + \frac{C_2}{1+r} = (Y_1 - G_1) + \frac{Y_2 - G_2}{1+r}$$
$$+ \left[\frac{r - r_G}{1+r}\right](G_1 - T_1).$$

The left-hand side is the private sector's present value of consumption, discounted at the rate of interest at which private citizens can engage in intertemporal trade. It therefore also represents private wealth. When $r > r_G$, a fraction of the deficit $G_1 - T_1$, which is public borrowing in period 1, enters private sector wealth, the right-hand side of (3.18). A tax cut under these conditions is equivalent to the government subsidizing the private sector by 'lending' the tax reduction today and demanding repayment tomorrow—through taxes—at a lower interest rate. The government gives the private sector access to a lower interest rate, which raises its wealth.[21]

This is illustrated in Figure 3.12. Crusoe's after-tax endowment is at point A. Discounted at the private rate of interest r, Crusoe's wealth is OB. When the government reduces taxes today it increases the private sector endowment by the same amount. However, taxes will have to be raised next period by an amount dictated by the government budget constraint, corresponding to the lower public sector borrowing

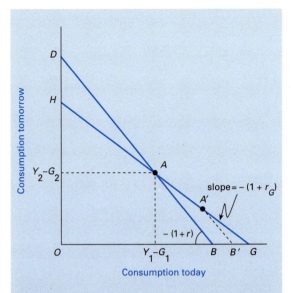

Figure 3.12. Lower Government Interest Rate

When the government can borrow at the rate r_G (along GH), lower than the rate r that the private sector faces, a reduction in today's taxes raises the private sector wealth by BB', as its post-tax endowment changes from point A to point A'.

rate r_G. This is why the new post-tax-cut endowment point A' lies on line GH, which is flatter than the private sector budget line BD. Private wealth discounted at the private discount rate r is measured by OB', which is clearly larger than OB. The difference, BB', represents the last term in (3.18), the present value of the wealth gain that accrues to the public when the government borrows on its behalf.

3.5.4.3. Restrictions on borrowing

Many households cannot borrow as much as future expected income would justify. Borrowers may be unable to convince lenders—typically banks—of their creditworthiness. At the same time, lenders do not have the means of fully investigating customers' statements on a credit application form. In addition, future incomes are never really certain; so lending to households is often risky. Borrowing rates exceed lending rates to compensate for this risk. In the worst case, no lending is extended and individuals are credit-rationed. The case of credit rationing is represented in Figure 3.13. With a net private endowment repre-

---

[21] Contrary to appearances, there is no 'free lunch' here: the government is simply borrowing on better terms than the private sector can. In doing so, it effects a transfer from lenders to the beneficiaries of the tax cut, who experience an increase in the present value of their resources. In reality, lenders could be foreigners, but are more likely to be wealthier residents.

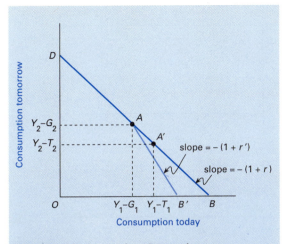

Figure 3.13. Borrowing Constraints

When the household cannot borrow at all, its budget line is restricted to the segment *AD*, because it cannot consume today more than what is left of the endowment after public spending ($Y_1 - G_1$). If the government reduces taxes and borrows instead (abroad), the household's borrowing line extends to the segment *A'D*. When borrowing constraints take the form of a higher private borrowing rate *r'*, the budget line is the kinked line *B'AD*. A budget deficit at *A'* relaxes the private household's budget constraint.

3.5.4.4. Distortionary taxation and unemployed resources

Ricardian equivalence also fails to hold because taxes are distortionary. People change their behaviour in response to taxes. For example, taxation on labour income or wages may lead some to work less, and this will reduce output. In the parable of Crusoe, the endowments of coconuts are exogenous, so increasing taxes on them does not affect their supply. In the real world, taxes can reduce wealth because they reduce output.[22] This is especially important in the presence of under-utilized resources. If a tax cut increases the level of economic activity and generates additional income, then the associated fiscal deficit will be associated with higher wealth.

3.5.4.5. Evidence[23]

Ricardian equivalence has several controversial implications. The first is that, given present and future public spending (G), it does not matter how and when taxes are levied to satisfy the public sector budget constraint. The second implication is that an increase in the budget deficit brought about by tax reductions will be offset one for one by an increase in private saving, leaving total national spending unchanged. In that case, and this is the third implication, the current account, which is the nation's total saving, should be unrelated to the budget deficit.[24] Finally, the real interest rate—which we will later see balances the demand for and the supply of saving—should not be affected by changes in the budget deficit if the private sector fully offsets the saving behaviour of the government.

Given the list of assumptions presented in the previous sections, it seems quite unlikely that Ricardian equivalence will hold fully in practice.[25] Yet the surprise is that there are indications that the private sector sometimes offsets government budgetary actions. For example, most OECD countries experienced a decrease in public saving (an increase in budget deficits) in the 1980s. This decrease was due primarily to changes in

sented by point *A*, the agent can only move along her budget line on the segment *AD*. The segment *AB* is not attainable through private borrowing. If the government runs a deficit today, the agent may reach point *A'* as she consumes $Y_1 - T_1$, which is larger than $Y_1 - G_1$ since $T_1 < G_1$.

Most often individuals face higher and rising costs of borrowing as the lending bank or agent (a pawn shop, the Mafia, or notaries in France) demands higher interest to compensate for additional risk. The situation is similar to the case studied in the previous section and is also illustrated in Figure 3.13. When lending, the constrained agent can move along *AD*, but for borrowing she now moves along *AB'*. The budget line is now kinked at the endowment point. In this case, public debt contributes to citizens' wealth, and the time profile of taxes affects the private sector budget constraint. At point *A'* the constrained citizen is better off than anywhere along *AB'*. As in the previous section, the government borrows on behalf of its citizens, increasing the wealth of those who cannot borrow on those terms.

[22] These responses are discussed in detail in Ch. 17.
[23] An overview of the debate and existing evidence can be found in the symposium published in the Spring 1989 issue of the *Journal of Economic Perspectives*.
[24] The equality between the current account and national saving is established in Ch. 2 and further elaborated in S. 3.6.
[25] Its main advocate, Robert Barro, concludes his overview of the evidence as follows: 'I have argued that empirical findings . . . tend mainly to support the Ricardian viewpoint. However, the empirical analysis involves substantial problems about data . . . and the results are sometimes inconclusive' (Barro, 1989).

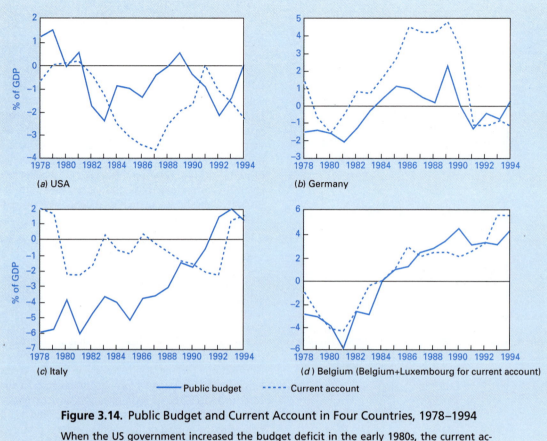

Figure 3.14. Public Budget and Current Account in Four Countries, 1978–1994

When the US government increased the budget deficit in the early 1980s, the current account worsened in parallel.

Source: OECD, *Economic Outlook*

tax revenue so the observed decline in national saving would seem to contradict the Ricardian equivalence. Yet, with the exception of Germany, private saving rose, partially offsetting public behaviour. In the UK, private saving actually more than offset the decline in public saving. The private sector may well view at least some of the government's indebtedness as its own. Short-run evidence is often less favourable to Ricardian equivalence, possibly because it takes time for the private sector to decide whether fiscal actions are permanent—and require offsetting action—or temporary—and can be ignored as a first approximation.[26]

Figure 3.14 provides evidence from four countries. Two are relatively highly indebted as a percentage of GDP (Belgium and Italy) and two are not (USA and Germany). If the movements observed in the deficit are occurring because of an intertemporal reallocation of taxes, then the USA, Belgium, and Germany do not support the Ricardian equivalence hypothesis. In the USA, parallel increases in public and external deficits in the first half of the 1980s, associated with large tax cuts during that period, indicate no offsetting action by the private sector. German unification is also evidence for the twin deficit logic. Since government

[26] Testing of the Ricardian equivalence principle is difficult because it relies critically on expectations that are not observable. For example, a tax cut combined with a future reduction in government purchases raises private wealth. This is due not to the tax cut, but to the expected spending cut (G_2 in (3.15) declines). If instead

the tax cut is expected to be reversed with no reduction in public spending, private wealth remains unchanged under the Ricardian equivalence principle. In both cases, what is observed is the reduction in taxes today. The difference is expected future public spending and taxes.

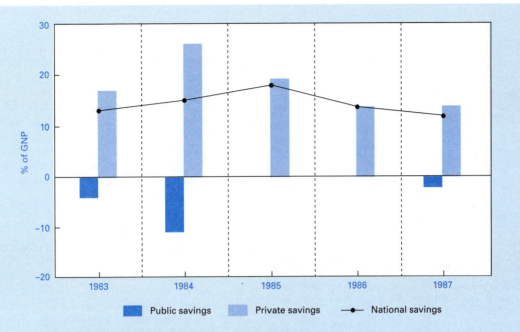

Figure 3.15. Israel's Fiscal Stabilization, 1983–1987

In the mid-1980s the Israeli government took explicit measures to close its budget deficit. As public savings increased, private savings declined, almost fully offsetting the effect on total national saving.

Source: Barro (1989)

spending *rose* as a consequence, the behaviour of the current account seems to violate the Ricardian logic.

Italy, on the other hand, is an economy where the recent past may lend support to the Ricardian hypothesis. It is well known that a very large fraction of the Italian national debt is held by Italian households, and it seems that the recent behaviour of the deficit shows little correlation with total national savings. Another good example is the Israeli experience in the mid-1980s (Figure 3.15).

3.6. The Current Account and the Budget Constraint of the Nation

3.6.1. The Primary Current Account

The budget constraint of the nation shown in (3.17) results from the consolidation of the budget constraints of the private and public sectors. The country's net saving *vis-à-vis* the rest of world occurs through the balance on the current account. Much like the public sector budget surplus, it can be decomposed into a **primary current account** (PCA) and net external investment income, rF:

$$(3.19) \qquad CA = PCA + rF,$$

where F represents the country's net asset position *vis-à-vis* the rest of the world, and r, as before, is the

Table 3.2. Net External Asset Positions (% of GNP)

	1970	1980	1987	1992
Austria	−2.4	−5.9	4.4	3.5
France	5.7	12.4	6.2	2.6
Germany (West)	8.8	6.2	15.8	17.6
Greece	−5.3	−16.4	−43.4	−32.1
Iraq	27.0	3.4	2.9	—
Israel	−13.1	−56.8	−57.4	−17.6
Italy	−4.8	7.3	−4.1	−8.1
Japan	9.3	3.5	13.6	20.0
Portugal	25.6	−4.5	−25.4	−14.0
Singapore	30.0	13.8	−26.6	8.8
Spain	−11.8	−9.0	−1.0	−12.4
UK	7.0	7.2	24.5	5.2
USA	5.8	4.0	−8.2	−12.7

Sources: Estimates reported in Sinn (1990) for 1970, 1980, and 1987; 1992 estimated by authors using IMF current account data.

average real interest rate paid on F. Net investment income is positive when the country holds more assets than liabilities, or negative, in the case of an indebted country. Table 3.2 provides a few estimates of net national asset positions. While most countries have small net positions, and only a few have sizeable positive positions, several countries are highly indebted. In examining Table 3.2, one should remember that the value of net foreign assets differs from domestic wealth, which includes the capital stock, land and buildings, and natural resources.

In the two-period framework, ignoring any initial asset position, the budget constraint of the nation requires that the present value of country's primary current accounts equal zero:

$$(3.20) \qquad PCA_1 + \frac{PCA_2}{1+r} = 0.$$

Primary current account deficits in the first period must be repaid by primary current surpluses (in present value) in the second. Symmetrically, surpluses in the first period enable a nation to spend more than it produces in the future. It would seem wasteful for a country eventually not to take advantage of this fact; otherwise it is literally giving away resources for claims on the rest of the world which it will never use.

Condition (3.20) can be suitably modified if there is an initial net asset position F_0:

$$(3.21) \qquad PCA_1 + \frac{PCA_2}{1+r} = -(1+r)F_0.$$

If a country has net wealth at the beginning of period 1 (F_0 is positive), it can draw on its external assets plus interest to run future current account deficits in present-value terms. If there is external debt (F_0 is negative) the present value of current accounts must be positive, by an amount sufficient to repay the external debt. In practice, it is the magnitude of the cumulated stock of external assets that determines the payback burdens of a country. This is illustrated in Figure 3.16, which shows how large external imbalances are eventually corrected.

3.6.2. A Caveat: Sovereign Borrowing

Even though the consolidation of private and public sectors in Table 3.2 is possible in theory, it is useful in practice to distinguish between international borrowing by private entities and **sovereign borrowing**, or international borrowing by national governments. Although the intertemporal budget constraint still holds, sovereign borrowing is special. Unlike private lending within a country, enforcement of sovereign loan contracts is legally impossible. In effect, a sovereign borrower can walk away from its debt. This fundamental difference shapes perceived lending strategies and realized outcomes. As a result, much of this debt may be to official lenders, i.e. international organizations like the World Bank and the IMF, or to governments (sometimes called sovereign lenders).

Another reason to exercise caution when consolidating assets into 'international investment positions' is the fact that the government may not be able count the assets of the private sector as its own. In fact, it may be quite difficult for a highly indebted government to get at private sector assets—it may do so by taxes or even confiscation, but this may cause private agents to engage in **capital flight**, transferring their resources abroad. Box 3.5 provides some interesting details on this important phenomenon.

3.6.3. GDP, GNP, and the Current Account

Let us now assume—an assumption that we will maintain for the rest of this book—that net foreign labour income, foreign remittances, and foreign aid transfers are zero. In this case, the only difference between GDP

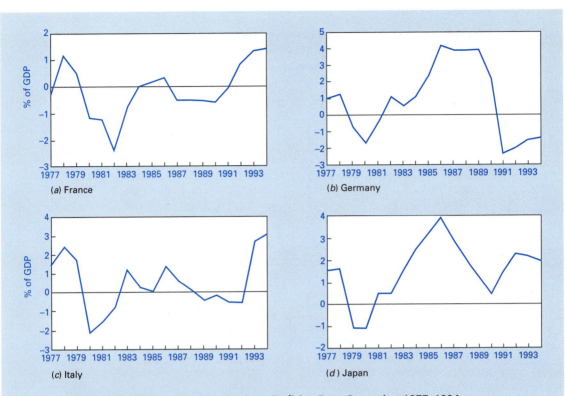

Figure 3.16. Primary Current Account Deficits, Four Countries, 1977–1994

The present value of a country's primary deficits (resp. surpluses) cannot exceed its initial net asset (resp. liability) position. Countries that run a string of large deficits eventually run surpluses, and conversely.

Sources: OECD, *Economic Outlook*; IMF

BOX 3.5. CAPITAL FLIGHT

The magnitude of financial assets spirited away by residents to foreign countries, called capital flight, is not known with certainty. This is especially true in countries where such actions are illegal and show up only in the errors and omissions of the balance of payments. Some estimates are shown in Table 3.3. They reveal the astonishing fact that many highly indebted countries have sizeable *private* assets abroad.

Capital can leave the country in many ways. The most common and troublesome way is through the conversion of domestic money into foreign exchange, which is either hoarded or (most often) deposited abroad. It remains there for a number of reasons: fear of taxation to service foreign debt, exchange rate risk, future restrictions on capital, or political instability.

In several of the countries cited in the table, merely repatriating domestically owned foreign assets would solve the debt problem. Since confiscating these assets is impossible and probably undesirable, stopping and reversing capital flight requires that uncertainty—fears of asset holders—be eliminated. Often the credible removal of market regulations and a sound and fair tax system can coax funds home by offering capital owners a high rate of return.

Table 3.3. Capital Flight, Various Countries, 1989

	Flight of capital assets (1987 $US bn)	As % of long-term public and publicly guaranteed foreign debt
Argentina	46	111
Bolivia	2	178
Brazil	31	46
Chile	2	17
Columbia	7	103
Ecuador	7	115
Côte d'Ivoire	0	0
Mexico	84	114
Morocco	3	54
Nigeria	20	136
Peru	2	27
Philippines	23	188
Uruguay	4	159
Venezuela	58	240
Yugoslavia	6	79
Total	295	103

Source: Bulow and Rogoff (1990)

and GNP is net investment income, and GNP, GDP, and the current account can be related in the following way:

$$(3.22) \quad GNP = Y = C + I + G + CA$$
$$= C + I + G + PCA + rF_0$$
$$= GDP + rF_0.$$

The principle that the present discounted value (PDV) of primary current accounts matches the country's net external position F_0 then implies that the present value of domestic spending cannot exceed that of domestic production plus initial assets:

$$(3.23) \quad C_1 + I_1 + G_1 + \frac{C_2 + I_2 + G_2}{1 + r}$$

present value of total domestic spending

$$= GDP_1 + \frac{GDP_2}{1 + r} + F_0,$$

present value of gross domestic products

value of initial assets (net investment position)

where we allow for the possibility that investment takes place in the second period, for completeness.

3.7. Summary

1. Because households may borrow or lend, their budget constraint is fundamentally intertemporal. It incorporates all current and future spending on the one hand, and all current and future income on the other. Future spending and incomes are discounted using the interest rate at which households can borrow or lend.

2. Wealth is the sum of the present value of current and future income and inherited assets less debts. The intertemporal budget constraint requires that the present value of spending be less than, or equal to, wealth. It applies to all economic agents, households, firms, the public sector, and the nation as a whole.

3. When firms invest, they forgo—on behalf of their shareholders—current consumption for future output. The profitability of investment depends both on the technology and on the rate of interest. The rate of interest is the opportunity cost of capital that investors apply to investment projects because it is available on other assets.

4. Budget constraints can be added together, or consolidated. Consolidating the households' and the firms' budget constraints gives the budget constraint of the private sector. As a first approximation, corporations are a veil: they provide their owners or shareholders with a means of increasing their wealth.

5. The public sector intertemporal budget constraint implies that, for a given time profile of government purchases, tax reductions today imply tax increases later on, and conversely. Alternatively, given a tax profile, more government spending today implies less spending later on, and conversely.

6. The Ricardian equivalence proposition asserts that the private sector internalizes the public sector budget constraint. Public debt is not considered as private wealth, and the time profile of taxes does not affect the private sector budget constraint. As the private sector can freely borrow at the same rate as the government, public dissaving (saving) is matched one for one by private saving (dissaving): the private sector pierces the veil of the government budget to keep total national saving unchanged.

7. Ricardian equivalence is unlikely to hold for several reasons. For example, individuals may expect that some current public debt will be repaid after they die; also, private interest rates typically exceed the rate at which the government borrows. Many households face borrowing constraints. Taxes may change the endowment available to the government to tax. Yet there is some evidence that the private sector may internalize part of government debt.

8. The national budget constraint is the consolidation of the private and public sector budget constraints. It states that the present value of primary current account deficits cannot exceed the nation's net external wealth. It also implies that, all things being equal, higher primary current account deficits today will require primary current account surpluses in the future.

9. Although it must also obey an intertemporal budget constraint, sovereign borrowing by a nation may differ from private international borrowing by its residents. One difference is that the assets of defaulting governments are hard to seize.

Key Concepts

- **intertemporal budget constraint**
- **rational expectations hypothesis**
- **endowment**
- **autarky**
- **intertemporal trade, intertemporal price**
- **real interest rate**
- **discounting, discount factor, and present discounted value**
- **budget line**
- **fixed capital formation (investment)**
- **production function**
- wealth
- diminishing marginal productivity
- opportunity cost
- gross/net investment
- primary government budget surplus or deficit
- borrowing constraints
- Ricardian equivalence proposition
- primary current account
- sovereign borrowing
- capital flight

Exercises: Theory

1. Review the reasons why rational expectations are assumed in economic models. Under which conditions can static expectations be rational? [*Harder.*] Under which conditions can extrapolative expectations be rational?

2. Derive the intertemporal budget constraint of a household which starts out with inheritance B_0 by writing down the flow income/spending constraints for periods 1 and 2, and then consolidating.

3. Suppose that Crusoe cannot trade with neighbours, but also that coconuts no longer spoil completely, so he can store them for consumption tomorrow. Suppose that 10% of the stored coconuts are lost because of spoilage. Represent this situation graphically.

4. Suppose Crusoe were able to plant more than Y_1 coconuts by planting those borrowed from the capital market (i.e. importing capital goods). Would this increase his wealth? What is the maximum that he could plant?

5. Draw the government budget line in Figure 3.9. when there is an initial public debt D_0.

6. In the text, Robinson Crusoe does not want to leave any wealth beyond tomorrow, presumably because he knows he will be rescued. The situation would be different

if he wanted to leave his friend Friday a gift of fixed amount B_2 in the second period. (B_2 might also be thought of as a bequest.) Write down Crusoe's budget constraint and represent it graphically.

7. Under which conditions does Ricardian equivalence occur? Which conditions seem more likely to be violated? Can you imagine conditions under which government debt is actually perceived as a net liability by some households?

8. Derive the Ricardian equivalence result when investment is possible, and taxation remains lump-sum; that is, when T_1 and T_2 are both independent of the level of economic activity. Suppose now that the government finances its need to spend G_1 and G_2 only by taxing capital. Does your answer change?

9. Now suppose the government can finance its spending only by a first-period lump-sum tax T_1 or by taxing second-period production at rate τ; i.e. $T_2 = \tau F(K)$. Write down the budget constraint of the government and derive the household's wealth. Do you think the path of taxes will matter? Why or why not?

10. Derive a household's budget constraint for n periods, when exogenous income in each period is Y_t, $t = 1, \ldots, n$. Then let n go to infinity: there are now two solvency constraints to find (see Appendix).

Exercises: Applications

1. If a firm decides not to distribute dividends to its shareholders, its share price often increases. Why? Are the shareholders necessarily wealthier?

2. What is the present value for Crusoe of 100 coconuts tomorrow if the real rate of interest is (a) 5%? (b) 10%?

3. A country's endowment over two periods is 1000 today and 1800 tomorrow. The real interest rate is 3%. Draw the budget line. What is the largest debt that it can incur today? How does your answer change if the real interest rate is 8% instead?

4. In the case of exercise 3 above, suppose that the country consumes the same amount today and tomorrow. How much can it consume with (a) a 3% interest rate? (b) an 8% interest rate? Is there an interest rate at which it would still consume the same amount in both periods and yet run a current surplus today?

5. The real interest rate is 10%. What is the value of a new firm which invests ECU 100,000 and expects to have returns net of costs of ECU 40,000 next year, ECU 52,000 the year after, ECU 56,000 the third year, and then to close down with equipment valued at zero? How does your answer change if the equipment is instead sold for ECU 20,000?

6. Suppose a newly elected government expects to last two 'periods' and promises to leave the national debt *unchanged* when it leaves office. It inherits a national debt of ECU 100 billion. Expenditures in the current year are ECU 10 billion, while net tax revenues are ECU 9 billion. The interest rate is 5%. What will be the primary surplus in the second period necessary for the government to keep its promise?

7. Table 3.2 shows that the net external asset position of the UK increased considerably over the 1980s. How could that be related to the discovery of oil in the North Sea? (*Hint*: draw a budget line with no inherited wealth, and then consider the case of inherited wealth.)

8. Up until the mid-1980s, many countries imposed ceilings on the amount of credit available. As a result, many households could not borrow at all. Deregulation has removed these ceilings and households are now freer to borrow. Has their wealth increased? What if, as a result of more competition, the real interest rate declines?

9. In many countries *chain letters* are common. Under this scheme, a recipient of the letter must send a fixed amount of money to the name at the top of a list, add his own to the bottom, and then send the same letter out to 10 (new) people. When the recipient's name reaches the top of the list, he is promised a large sum of money. Do such schemes violate a budget constraint? Why do you think they are illegal?

10. In Figure 3.16 Germany's current account has declined dramatically since 1989. Many have blamed this development on the reunification of Germany. How might you explain this, appealing to equation (3.22)? How sustainable would a deficit be, in light of the data in Table 3.2?

Suggested Further Reading

The two-period framework is used to interpret actual economic conditions in:

Sachs, Jeffrey (1981), 'The Current Account and Macroeconomic Adjustment in the 1970s', *Brookings Papers on Economic Activity*, 1: 201–68.

The Ricardian proposition is examined by several authors in the *Journal of Economic Perspectives*, 3 (1989): 37–54, and in

Seater, John (1993), 'Ricardian Equivalence', *Journal of Economic Literature*, 31: 142–90.

Appendix: Budget Constraints over Many Periods

This appendix provides a formal treatment and a generalization of the two-period analysis of intertemporal budget contraints in the main text.

Households (without investment)

At the end of period t, the household receives income Y_t and consumes C_t. If $B_{t-1} \neq 0$ is inherited net financial wealth and r is the (constant) real interest rate, the change in wealth is given by

(A3.1) $$B_t - B_{t-1} = Y_t - C_t + rB_{t-1}$$

or

$$B_{t-1} = \frac{B_t - Y_t + C_t}{1 + r}.$$

But this must also hold for $t + 1$:

(A3.2) $$B_t = \frac{B_{t+1} - Y_{t+1} + C_{t+1}}{1 + r},$$

so, by substitution,

$$B_{t-1} = \frac{C_t - Y_t}{1 + r} + \frac{C_{t+1} - Y_{t+1}}{(1 + r)^2} + \frac{B_{t+1}}{(1 + r)^2}.$$

Successive iteration yields

(A3.3) $$B_{t-1} = \frac{C_t - Y_t}{1 + r} + \frac{C_{t+1} - Y_{t+1}}{(1 + r)^2} + \ldots + \frac{B_{t+n}}{(1 + r)^{n+1}}.$$

Attention is drawn to the last term, which is the present value of agent's net assets in period $t + n$. As n goes to infinity, one would expect that the household would have to repay its debt—to transfer resources equal in present value to its initial debt. (Households cannot repay their debt by borrowing for ever.) In terms of the model of the main text, this is like the condition that no net or positive asset position remains after period 2. With an infinite horizon, this requirement can be written as[27]

(A3.4) $$\lim_{n \to \infty} \frac{B_{t+n}}{(1 + r)^{n+1}} \geq 0.$$

At the same time, it makes little sense to go to 'the end' with unspent wealth; this would imply forgone consumption possibilities. As long as this can be ruled out, the inequality

[27] This condition is sometimes called a 'no-Ponzi' condition, named after Charles Ponzi, an Italian immigrant to the USA who for a time could promise abnormally high rates of interest by paying off old investors with money borrowed from new ones. When the scheme finally collapsed, thousands of investors had lost their life fortunes. Ponzi went to jail, and died there.

of (A3.4) can be replaced by an equality. Now we find the infinite-horizon equivalent of (3.4) in the main text, for period $t = 1$:

(A3.5) $$\sum_{i=1}^{\infty} \frac{C_i}{(1 + r)^{i-1}} = (1 + r)B_0 + \sum_{i=1}^{\infty} \frac{Y_i}{(1 + r)^{i-1}},$$

which says that the present value of consumption is equal to household's wealth, the sum of inherited financial wealth B_0, plus interest on that wealth rB_0, plus the present discounted value of income.

Firms (with investment)

The firm makes a net cash flow in period t Π_t of

(A3.6) $$\Pi_t = F(K_{t-1}) - I_t,$$

which is paid at the end of the period. Thus, today's value of the firm can be decomposed as this period's profit plus the present value of the firm next period:

(A3.7) $$V_t = \frac{\Pi_t}{1 + r} + \frac{V_{t+1}}{(1 + r)^2}.$$

Iterating on this expression gives

(A3.8) $$V_t = \frac{\Pi_t}{1 + r} + \frac{\Pi_{t+1}}{(1 + r)^2} + \frac{\Pi_{t+2}}{(1 + r)^3} + \ldots + \frac{V_{t+n}}{(1 + r)^{n+1}}.$$

As n goes to infinity, the firm cannot have a negative present value—it would be bankrupt. Nor does it make sense for the owners to reach 'the end' with unspent residual wealth. So we have the following transversality condition:

(A3.9) $$\lim_{n \to \infty} \frac{V_{t+n}}{(1 + r)^{n+1}} = 0.$$

Therefore, the value of the firm at the end of period $t = 1$ is the present discounted value of its profits:

$$V_t = \sum_{i=1}^{\infty} \frac{\Pi_i}{(1 + r)^{i-1}}.$$

The Private Sector (with investment)

In each period, households that own the firm split total income between consumption C and investment I:

(A3.10) $$Y_t + F(K_{t-1}) = C_t + I_t.$$

Assume that capital depreciates completely each period. The present value of consumption is at most the present discounted value of available resources—the sum of endowment Y_t and net output of the firm $F(K_{t-1})$ less investment I_t. In present value terms, this can be written as

$$(A3.11) \quad \sum_{i=1}^{\infty} \frac{C_i}{(1+r)^{i-1}} = (1+r)B_0 + \sum_{i=1}^{\infty} \frac{Y_i + F(K_{i-1}) - I_i}{(1+r)^{i-1}}$$

$$= (1+r)B_0 + \sum_{i=1}^{\infty} \frac{Y_i}{(1+r)^{i-1}} + V_1.$$

The present value of consumption is bounded by wealth, the sum of inherited assets, the present value of endowment, and the value of the firm. This left-hand side of (A3.11) corresponds to Ω defined in the text for the two-period model.

Government

The same reasoning applies to the government as to households. The result is a condition that prohibits net public debt in 'the end' and requires that the present value of taxes must equal the initial debt and the present value of spending:

$$(A3.12) \qquad \lim_{n \to \infty} \frac{D_{t+n}}{(1+r_G)^{n+1}} = 0.$$

It is possible to derive the infinite period equivalent of (3.11):

$$(A3.13) \quad \sum_{i=1}^{\infty} \frac{T_i}{(1+r_G)^{i-1}} = (1+r)D_0 + \sum_{i=1}^{\infty} \frac{G_i}{(1+r_G)^{i-1}},$$

where G and T occur at the end of the period.

The Public and Private Sectors

With taxes T_t in each period, the private sector's budget constraint (A3.11) becomes

$$(A3.14) \quad \sum_{i=1}^{\infty} \frac{C_i}{(1+r)^{i-1}} = (1+r)B_0 + \sum_{i=1}^{\infty} \frac{(Y_i - T_i)}{(1+r)^{i-1}} + V_1.$$

When all the taxes remain lump-sum and government and private sector borrow and lend at the same rate ($r = r_G$), (A3.11) and (A3.13) can be combined to yield

$$(A3.15) \quad \Omega = \sum_{i=1}^{\infty} \frac{C_i}{(1+r)^{i-1}}$$

$$= (1+r)(B_0 - D_0) + \sum_{i=1}^{\infty} \frac{(Y_i - G_i)}{(1+r)^{i-1}} + V_1.$$

Since there is only one 'representative agent' in the economy, $B_0 - D_0$ can be thought of as the nation's inherited external investment position (net foreign assets/liabilities), which is the sum of private assets (B_0) and government assets ($-D_0$).

4

Private Sector Demand: Consumption, Investment, and the Current Account

All production is for the purpose of ultimately satisfying a consumer.

J. M. Keynes

4.1. Overview

When defined as final goods expenditures, the GDP consists of consumption, investment, government purchases, and the net exports of goods and (non-interest-bearing) services. These components represent demands for goods and services by various sectors—households, firms, the government, and foreigners.

This chapter focuses on the private elements of aggregate spending: consumption and investment. Table 4.1 shows that the variability of these components is quite different, suggesting that they are driven by different motives; private consumption seems more stable and investment more volatile. The chapter uses economic theory to explain the private components of aggregate demand. The point of departure is microeconomics, which assumes that people are rational, or that they strive to do the best they can given their available resources and opportunities. This rational or *optimizing* behaviour is the cornerstone of modern economic analysis. Although it is sometimes understood as implying extraordinary intelligence or the ability to perform elaborate calculations, optimizing behaviour simply means that agents, possibly through trial and error, behave in some consistent fashion.[1] The parable of a representative consumer and a representative firm is used to establish the fundamental determinants of consumption and investment decisions.

The challenge is to use microeconomic principles to provide an accurate description of the macroeconomy: does its behaviour roughly correspond to that of a representative agent? As it turns out, the answer is largely affirmative. This chapter derives the **consumption function** and the **investment function**, two key building blocks of macroeconomic analysis. In turn, these functions have important implications for the way we think about the primary current account.

Table 4.1. Coefficient of Variation of GDP by Expenditure, 1970–1994 (average of quarterly data)

	Consumption (C/Y)	Investment (I/Y)	Government purchases (G/Y)
Australia	0.022	0.082	0.060
Germany	0.019	0.100	0.050
France	0.019	0.087	0.034
UK	0.042	0.070	0.060
Italy	0.035	0.108	0.027
Japan	0.025	0.069	0.063
Canada	0.017	0.092	0.050
Switzerland	0.025	0.098	0.060
USA	0.023	0.061	0.065

Source: OECD, *National Accounts*, authors' calculations

4.2. Consumption

To a good approximation, consumption is spending by households.[2] Put in relation to their disposable income, consumption can be thought as the opposite to household saving. The decision to consume is a decision not to save, and saving is a decision to postpone consumption. It is fundamentally intertemporal: now or later, which is better? *Micro*economics focuses on how households decide *what* to consume, e.g. apples or oranges. For *macro*economics, the emphasis is on *when* to consume. For this reason, we make the simplifying assumption that there is only one good to consume (Robinson Crusoe's coconuts) and the focus is the choice between now and later.[3]

4.2.1. Optimal Consumption

As Robinson Crusoe considers consuming the coconuts that he finds on the beach, he realizes that he can borrow or lend some of them through intertemporal trade with his neighbours. In fact, he may choose any combination of consumption today and consumption tomorrow as long as he remains on, or inside, his budget constraint. His choice depends on his preferences, which are described in Figure 4.1 by **indifference curves**. Each curve corresponds to a given level of **utility**, or well-being. A particular indifference curve represents combinations of consumption today and consumption tomorrow that leave Crusoe indifferent.

Higher indifference curves correspond to higher levels of utility.

Two central aspects of indifference curves are their slope and their curvature. For a particular consumption combination, the slope of an indifference curve depicts Crusoe's willingness to swap consumption tomorrow for consumption today, holding utility constant. Where the curve is steep, for example, he is willing to give up a lot of future consumption to increase today's consumption. A flat curve indicates reluctance to give up consumption tomorrow for consumption today. The second aspect, the curvature, shows the rate at which slope changes along a given *IC*. As Figure 4.1 shows, the willingness to substitute consumption intertemporally generally depends on the relative abundance of consumption in the two periods. In the normal case presented in panel (*a*), moving along an indifference curve upwards and to the left, Crusoe is less and less willing to give up coconuts today as the expected consumption of coconuts tomorrow grows larger and larger. Box 4.1 provides more details on the phenomenon of intertemporal substitution.

Naturally, Crusoe wants to consume as much as possible in both periods, but he is restricted by his intertemporal budget, which is the straight line in Figure 4.2. The best that he can do is point *R*, where the highest possible indifference curve just touches the budget line. A more desirable indifference curve like *IC*₃ is beyond his means, as it lies above his budget line. He can afford the utility level corresponding to *IC*₁ because this curve cuts the budget line, but can acquire the higher utility associated with *IC*₂, which is tangent to his budget line. Box 4.1 provides a more detailed interpretation.

When Crusoe is on his budget line, he spends his total wealth (*OB*) in the course of the two periods:

$$(4.1) \qquad C_1 + \frac{C_2}{1+r} = Y_1 + \frac{Y_2}{1+r} = \Omega.$$

If he can borrow or lend as much as he wants at the going interest rate, his consumption pattern over time depends only on the present *value* of his income—his budget constraint—and not on the particular *timing* of his income. In Figure 4.2, a 'student Crusoe' (with endowment *M*) borrows because his current income

---

[1] Introspection often makes us sceptical about such assumptions. Who hasn't given in to the temptation of buying a pastry when not really hungry or a stereo system when short of cash? Such departures from rationality are in fact infrequent enough to be outweighed by a majority of well-thought-out decisions. This is why rationality in economics is the right way to approximate reality.

[2] Naturally there are some exceptions. For example, when a household purchases a newly constructed house in the measurement period, this expenditure is not counted as consumption, but rather as investment (see S. 4.3). Similarly, when a household engaged in a private business purchases a computer or a stereo system for the office, this is excluded from consumption. Businesses do not generally consume; their expenditures on consumption goods are generally counted as intermediate expenditures.

[3] It matters if oranges are imported while apples are produced at home, however. This affects the current account and brings in the exchange rate. For this reason, Ch. 7 returns to the issue and considers two goods.

BOX 4.1. INDIFFERENCE CURVES AND INTERTEMPORAL SUBSTITUTION

A 'normal' indifference curve is shown in panel (a) of Figure 4.1. The slope of the indifference curve shows how many units of goods tomorrow we are willing to give up for an additional unit of goods today. Along a given indifference curve, moving to the right, today's consumption increases while tomorrow's declines. The curve becomes flatter because we are willing to give up increasingly less consumption tomorrow for consumption today. The opposite occurs as we move up and to the left. The **marginal rate of intertemporal substitution** is represented by the slope of the curve.

The curvature of the indifference curve captures how readily the consumer substitutes consumption across time. In Figure 4.1, panel (a) describes the normal situation, and panels (b) and (c) represent two opposite extremes. In case (b) there is no substitutability at all: the consumer is better off only if consumption is increased in fixed proportion in both periods. Case (c) depicts the case where

the marginal rate of substitution is constant: the consumer is always willing to substitute the same amount of consumption today for consumption tomorrow.

A key feature of point R in Figure 4.2 is that the marginal rate of substitution is just equal to the slope of the budget line, or $1 + r$. To see why, suppose that Crusoe is on his budget constraint but has a marginal rate of substitution of 1; he is willing to exchange one coconut today for one tomorrow. By lending 1 today, he gets $(1 + r)$ tomorrow, and can make himself better off, i.e. moving towards point R. If he goes too far, the marginal rate of substitution will exceed $(1 + r)$; he will then prefer to shift consumption back to the present and can increase his utility by doing so. Only when the marginal rate of substitution is equal to the intertemporal price of consumption has Crusoe exhausted the gains from intertemporal trade.

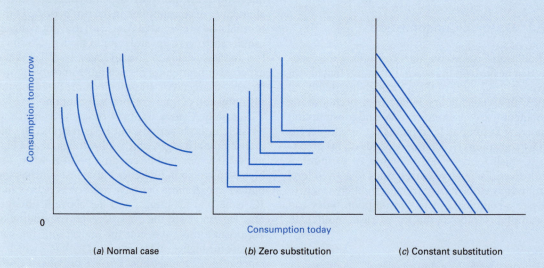

(a) Normal case   (b) Zero substitution   (c) Constant substitution

Figure 4.1. Indifference Curves

Along any indifference curve, utility is constant. In panel (a), consumption tomorrow can be substituted smoothly for consumption today, but, as consumption today increases, at a decreasing rate. In (b), the consumer can be made better off only by increasing consumption today and tomorrow in fixed proportions. In (c), consumption today and consumption tomorrow are always substituted at the same rate. In all cases, indifference curves further up in the north-east direction correspond to higher utility levels.

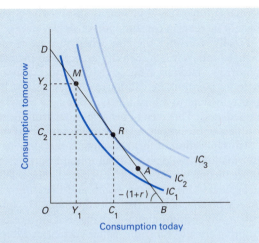

Figure 4.2. Optimal Consumption

The budget line shows how much can be consumed today and tomorrow for given endowment (represented by point M) and real interest rate (the slope). Optimal consumption is achieved at point R. In this case the consumer borrows today $C_1 - Y_1$ and repays $Y_2 - C_2$ tomorrow. Consumption at R is also possible for an individual with endowment A, who lends today and dissaves tomorrow.

Y_1 is low relatively to his future income Y_2, while a 'professional athlete Crusoe' (endowment point A) with high current and low future income will save. Since both individuals lie on the same budget line, they have the same wealth OB. If both have identical tastes as described by their indifference curves, saving and borrowing allows them to have identical consumption patterns. The associated principles of life-cycle and permanent income consumption are presented in Box 4.2.

4.2.2. Implications

4.2.2.1. Permanent versus temporary changes in income

How does Robinson Crusoe respond to a temporary increase in income? Imagine that today's harvest is unusually plentiful, rising to Y_1' in Figure 4.4, while next period's harvest Y_2 is expected to remain unchanged. For simplicity, the figure represents the case where, initially, consumption was exactly matching income in both periods so that there was no need to borrow or lend (points A and R overlap). The endowment point now shifts from A to A', on the new budget

---

BOX 4.2. PERMANENT INCOME AND LIFE CYCLE[4]

Most individuals or households do not expect a constant flow of income over their lifetimes. Typically, young people earn less than older people. The principle of optimal consumption implies that they should borrow when young and repay debts or even save when older in order to *smooth* the time profile of consumption.

Figure 4.3 displays a typical pattern of rising expected income and shows how **life-cycle consumption** would be chosen. To maintain a constant flow of consumption, the individual spends each year an amount corresponding to his or her **permanent income**. Permanent income is that income which, if constant, would deliver the same present value of income as the actual expected income path. It is a good measure of sustainable consumption over the time horizon of an individual.

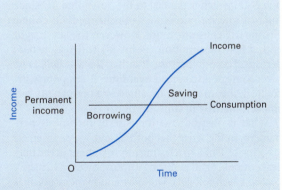

Figure 4.3. Life-Cycle Consumption

When income is expected to increase over a lifetime, consumption smoothing implies borrowing when young and paying back when older.

---

[4] The permanent income hypothesis was developed in the late 1950s by Chicago economist Milton Friedman and was cited as his main contribution when he was awarded the Nobel Prize. The life-cycle theory of consumption was also recognized by the Nobel Prize committee as an important contribution of MIT economist Franco Modigliani.

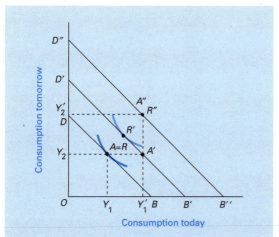

Figure 4.4. Temporary and Permanent Income Changes

The shift from *A* to *A'* describes a temporary increase in income. Consumption rises both today and tomorrow. (The household moves from *R* to *R'*.) Part of today's income windfall is saved to sustain higher spending tomorrow. The shift to point *A''* represents a permanent increase in income. It does not require consumption smoothing through saving or borrowing. The best course of action is permanently to increase consumption (to point *R''*).

line $B'D'$, which is parallel to the initial line BD since the real interest rate remains unchanged. Of course Crusoe will consume more. However, the key insight is that his consumption (point R') will rise in *both* periods. Today it increases less than the windfall, as he saves some of it to spread over time. A temporary increase in income is accompanied by a permanent, but smaller, increase in consumption.

What if, instead, the increase in income is permanent, in the sense that both Y_1 and Y_2 rise by equal amounts? (Think of a lasting improvement in the harvest outlook, or an enduring improvement in Crusoe's coconut technology!) The new endowment point is A'' and the corresponding budget line is $B''D''$. Optimal consumption moves to point R''. As a first approximation, points A'' and R'' coincide and consumption rises in both periods.[5] Being equally better off in both periods, Crusoe sees no reason to save or borrow. A permanent increase in income is absorbed in a permanent increase in consumption of similar size.

Finally, consider the case when income is unchanged today, but is correctly expected to increase tomorrow. If Robinson knows that his future crop will be more plentiful, he will borrow today against his future income to afford a better standard of living immediately. This type of behaviour, far from being thriftless or incautious, actually makes him better off.

An implication of this reasoning is that only new information should alter consumption behaviour. If future incomes are correctly anticipated, they will be incorporated into current wealth and therefore will already be affecting current consumption. The only reason why consumption will change is if unexpected disturbances affect income, either current or future, so that wealth is changed. Since all that is known of the future is already taken into account in the evaluation of wealth, only true surprises can alter wealth and therefore consumption. Put differently, changes in consumption must be unpredictable. This is known as the **random walk** theory of consumption, because changes in consumption should be random.[6]

4.2.2.2. Consumption smoothing and the current account

The common theme behind the three cases examined above is that people generally dislike highly variable consumption patterns. When faced with a temporary change in income, rational consumers save or borrow to spread the effects on consumption over time. In bad times, this may take the form of dissaving (spending from accumulated savings) or borrowing (from the bank, from relatives, or using a credit card). In good times, consumers accumulate assets or repay their debts. This phenomenon is known as **consumption smoothing**. It explains why consumption is less variable than GDP in Table 4.1, and is in general the most stable component of aggregate demand.

This does not mean that consumption is *always* more stable than GDP. Since the evolution of actual GDP is a mixture of permanent and temporary disturbances, consumption will on average reflect the nature of this mixture, responding more to permanent than to temporary changes. Indeed, there are times

---

[5] This is only an approximation. Impatient consumers may bring forward some of tomorrow's windfall, whereas more patient agents would save some of today's windfall for tomorrow's consumption.

[6] The random walk theory of consumption was formulated by Robert Hall of Stanford University. It is surprisingly difficult to reject empirically.

BOX 4.3. BOOM AND BUST IN THE UK: 1988–1993

In the late 1980s the UK went through its worst recession since the Second World War. Figure 4.5 shows that the real GDP growth started to decline in 1988, and turned negative in late 1990. It is only at the end of 1992 that growth was positive again. There is very little evidence that consumption was being smoothed during this period. Were UK consumers busy disproving economic principles? A more likely interpretation runs as follows. Banking reform in the mid-1980s introduced competition among financial institutions to offer consumer loans to the public. This led to the consumption boom of 1987–8. By then, it became clear that loans would have to be re-paid and that the boom could not continue. Anticipating bad times, consumers cut down on spending.

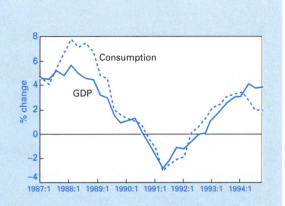

Figure 4.5. Real GDP and Consumption Growth in the UK, 1987–1994

The 1988–92 recession in the UK appears to have been prompted, at least in part, by a sharp decline in spending by consumers.

Source: OECD *National Accounts*

---

when consumption is more unstable than GDP. A good example is the case when income is expected to fall in the future: consumption spending declines immediately while income is still stable. The subsequent fall in GDP is then frequently seen as being caused by the consumption shortfall, while in fact it is simply the correctly anticipated consequence. Box 4.3 presents an example where consumption seems to have preceded GDP when the UK was entering into a recession.

Consumption smoothing is possible because Crusoe borrows when facing a temporary loss of income today or a windfall tomorrow, and saves when benefiting from a temporary gain or expected future bad times. Saving and borrowing play the role of a buffer in the presence of transitory income disturbances. Moving from a particular individual to the country as a whole, the logic remains the same but the mechanics are slightly trickier. When Mr Crusoe lends to fellow resident Mr Friday, there is no change in aggregate saving. At the country level, net borrowing or lending can only be *vis-à-vis* the rest of the world: saving or borrowing takes place through the primary current account.

The consequence of aggregate consumption smoothing, therefore, is temporary imbalances in the primary current account. Recall from (3.22) that the primary current account is GDP less domestic spending:

$$(4.2) \qquad PCA = Y - (C + I + G).$$

If GDP declines while investment and public spending remain unchanged, consumption smoothing implies a worsening PCA. Similarly, a temporary increase in GDP would lead to a temporary surplus. For most countries, primary current accounts are typically small and oscillate around zero. To some extent these may be regarded as an optimal response to temporary shifts in incomes. Figure 3.16 provides evidence that this is true. A specific example reviewed in Box 4.4 is the reaction to the oil price increases that occurred in the 1970s.

4.2.2.3. Consumption and the real interest rate

When the real interest rate rises, the rewards to savings rise. Put differently, the price of consumption tomorrow in terms of consumption today declines. Will saving always increase and consumption always decline? The question is harder to answer than it first

BOX 4.4. OIL SHOCKS AND EC CURRENT ACCOUNTS

Oil prices have increased abruptly three times in the past quarter-century. At the end of 1973 they quadrupled. They doubled in several instalments over 1979–80, and increased by 50% in 1990, after a marked decline in 1986 (see Figure 4.6). For most European countries which are heavily dependent on oil for their energy needs, an oil shock can be thought of as a reduction in income.[7] Even if the price increase is permanent, the short-run impact is larger than in the long run because conservation can attenuate this effect over time. Oil-importing (exporting) countries should respond by running current account deficits (surpluses). Figure 4.7 shows that Europe, comprising mostly oil-importing countries, underwent a current account deficit after each shock, and a surplus after the counter-shock of 1986. Yet some European countries are energy-exporters and benefit from oil shocks. This is the case of the Netherlands, which exports natural gas, since the price of gas moves with that of oil. The Dutch current account stands in sharp contrast with that of most countries in Europe, which are heavy importers of oil. After each shock, these current accounts appear to be the mirror image of each other.

Figure 4.6. Real Price of Crude Oil, 1965–1994

The real price of oil is computed as the ratio of the US dollar price of crude oil to the consumer price index of all industrialized countries.

Source: IMF

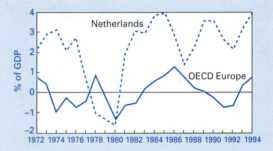

Figure 4.7. Current Accounts: Europe and the Netherlands, 1972–1994

As an importer of oil, Europe suffered an income loss at the time of the oil shocks. Consumption smoothing calls for temporary borrowing now (current account deficit) and repayment later (current account surplus). The Netherlands, a gas exporter, experienced a temporary windfall which was saved abroad through current account surpluses.

Sources: OECD *Economic Outlook*; IMF

---

appears. Figure 4.8 shows that the effect on consumption today depends on whether Crusoe is a net borrower (e.g. a student) or a net lender (e.g. a professional athlete). Since endowments today and tomorrow are unchanged in both panels of the figure, the budget line rotates around point *A*. Optimal consumption shifts from point *R* to point *R'*. Net lenders gain from higher interest rates, moving to a higher indifference curve and consuming more in both periods. The current consumption of borrowers, in contrast, generally declines. The borrower who faces higher interest costs is in the opposite situation, as he must devote more resources to debt service. He borrows less and may even reduce tomorrow's consumption. We say that increases in interest rates have important redistributive effects between borrowers and lenders.

The effect of the interest rate on consumption is ambiguous because it works through two channels. First, it increases the cost of goods today compared with those tomorrow. An increase in the interest rate

---

[7] At the time it was not obvious whether these shocks were temporary or permanent. Fig. 4.6 strongly suggests that they were temporary, but back in the mid-1970s or early 1980s Fig. 4.6 was not available, and the oil price increase was often regarded as permanent. Milton Friedman was a lone voice in the wilderness when he wrote in 1975: 'Almost regardless of our energy policy, the OPEC cartel will break down. That is assured by a worldwide reduction in crude-oil consumption and expansion in alternative supplies in response to high prices. The only question is how long it will take' (*Newsweek*, 17 Feb. 1975).

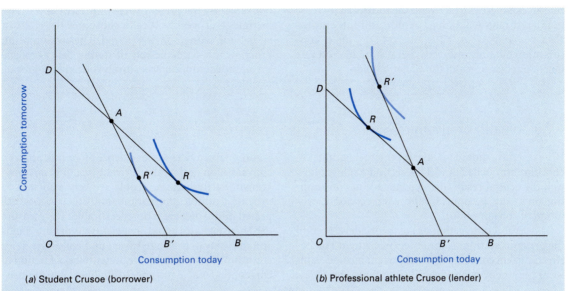

(a) Student Crusoe (borrower) (b) Professional athlete Crusoe (lender)

Figure 4.8. The Effect of an Increase in the Interest Rate

As the interest rate increases, the budget line becomes steeper and rotates about the endowment point A. The response of the consumer depends on whether she is a borrower or a lender. The borrower (a) will tend to consume less today because the interest rate at which resources are brought forward has increased. The lender (b) consumes more today, since the same amount of lending can increase the amount of consumption possible tomorrow without reducing today's.

makes the budget constraint steeper, since it determines the slope of the intertemporal budget constraint. Second, it reduces the value of wealth Ω, which is the present discounted value of all income.

To separate these effects fully, it is useful to consider the effect of an interest rate increase *holding wealth constant*. Figure 4.9 shows that, even holding

wealth constant at its original value, an increase in interest rates may either reduce or increase consumption today. In the example shown, there is no net effect on consumption today. At the same time, both consumers in Figure 4.8 experience a decline in wealth (from OB to OB'), because future income is discounted at a higher interest rate. Because *all* households have

Figure 4.9. An Increase in the Interest Rate, Holding Wealth Constant

For the university student (borrower) in Figure 4.8, an increase in the interest rate rotates the budget line around point A, leading to less consumption today. Holding wealth constant, however, the net effect on current consumption is ambiguous, bringing the consumer to point R″. In contrast, an increase in the interest rate unambiguously reduces wealth, and thereby consumption. A similar, weaker effect can be shown for the professional athlete (lender).

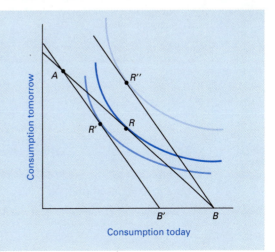

resources expected to arrive in the future, an increase in interest rates will reduce wealth, and this effect is always *unambiguous*. Thus, interest rates affect consumption but only indirectly, because an interest rate increase reduces wealth for *all* households.

4.2.3. Wealth or Income?

How seriously should we take the microeconomics of consumption behaviour? This section explores how well the central result, the dependence of consumption on wealth, accounts for the macroeconomic evolution of consumption.

The central implication of the theory developed in the previous sections is the absence of a tight link between current consumption and current income. Consumption today is not determined by income today,

but rather by the present value of present and future incomes—or wealth. Wealth subsumes the effect of all income changes in any period. The **consumption function** is a symbolic way of stating that aggregate private consumption is positively related to aggregate wealth Ω:

$$(4.3) \qquad C = C(\Omega).$$
$$_{+}$$

Figure 4.10 provides some evidence of the link between consumption and wealth. Private wealth is not well-known. Partly because people are very reluctant to provide truthful information about their assets, expected future income is not measurable. The measure used here includes liquid financial assets of households and the value of their fixed assets and real estate. Both consumption and wealth are presented as a fraction of current disposable income. In all four countries con-

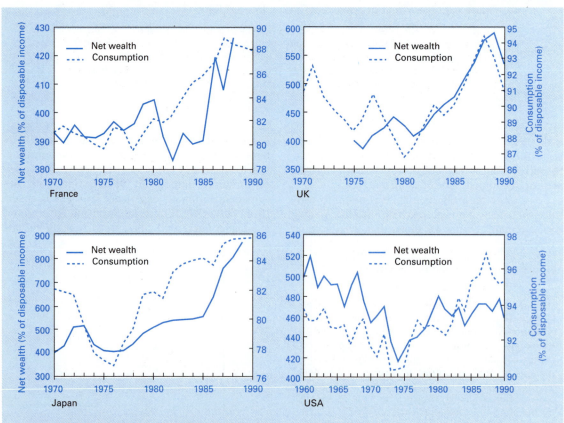

Figure 4.10. Consumption and Wealth

The link between consumption and wealth is quite strong, but far from perfect.

Source: OECD

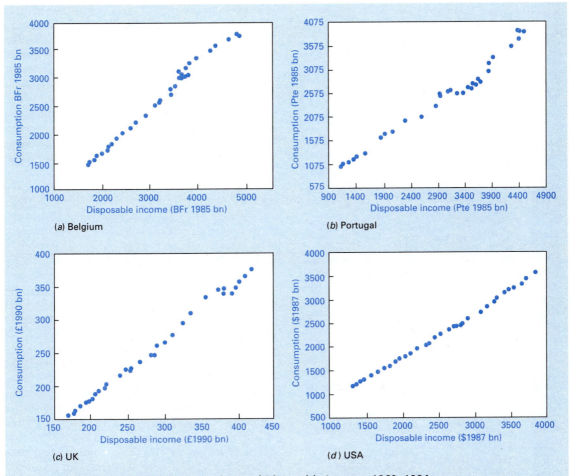

Figure 4.11. Real Consumption and Disposable Income, 1960–1994

The positive link between consumption and disposable income is robust, with noticeable deviations.

Source: OECD, *Economic Outlook*

sidered, consumption and wealth move together, but the link is far from perfect.

An old tradition in macroeconomics which can be traced back to Keynes relates aggregate consumption to disposable income Y^d, which is roughly GDP less net taxes. Figure 4.11 shows that the link is strong, and in some cases stronger than that between consumption and wealth. One possible explanation is related to the fact that income consists of both permanent and temporary components. Income and wealth may grow in tandem so that the observed consumption–income relationship may reflect a common dependence on wealth.

A more fundamental explanation is related to a household's ability to borrow and lend. The Crusoe parable assumes that every household can borrow freely at a given interest rate. This might be the case if present and future incomes of individual households—against which borrowing is pledged—were known with certainty to lenders. In real life, banks and other lending intermediaries cannot know the repayment prospects of all individual borrowers with certainty. A common banking practice is to demand collateral—the borrower pledges tangible wealth such as a house in case of non-payment. This option is not available to all households. Banks charge higher interest

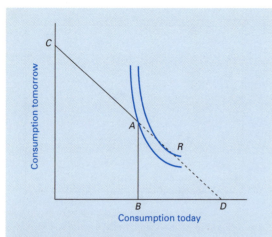

Figure 4.12. Credit Constraints

If Crusoe cannot borrow, his budget constraint shrinks from *CD* to *CA*. He would like to be at point *R*, however, borrowing today and paying back tomorrow. The best outcome for him under the circumstances is to consume at point *A*, with consumption equal to income both today and tomorrow.

rates to customers who appear riskier and sometimes refuse to lend at any rate, or place ceilings on the amount that can be borrowed. Consumers who cannot obtain credit in spite of future earnings potential are said to be **credit-rationed**.

In the presence of credit rationing, spending is constrained by current disposable income, not wealth.[8] This is shown in Figure 4.12, which uses Figure 3.13 as its point of departure. Here Robinson Crusoe is completely prevented from borrowing. His consumption possibilities are limited to the kinked line *CAB*. In particular, he cannot reach the segment *AD* of his intertemporal budget constraint and thus his preferred consumption pattern *R* is not possible. In that case, the best option for him is to be at point *A*,

---

[8] Ch. 3 provides a detailed treatment of interest rates and credit rationing. It also shows that with credit rationing, Ricardian equivalence will not hold for those who would like to borrow, so that current taxes affect current consumption as well, hence the relevance of disposable income as opposed to GDP.

where he consumes exactly his income in both periods. If a significant proportion of households is rationed in credit markets, disposable income also will influence consumption, along with wealth, which matters for non-rationed households. Box 4.5 illustrates the importance of national borrowing constraints in the early phase of the process of economic transformation in Eastern Europe. But even in advanced countries, credit rationing affects a substantial proportion of households. It is therefore not surprising to observe the tight link between consumption and disposable income in Figure 4.11.

4.2.4. The Consumption Function

Let us now summarize the results set out thus far. Consumption is driven primarily by wealth, and wealth is based on current and discounted future incomes of households. In practice, many people are unable to borrow even though their expected future income is higher. For them, disposable income is the effective determinant of consumption. This, along with the fact that income and wealth tend to grow together, means that consumption seems to be better explained by disposable income. In fact, both matter, as can be seen from the example in Box 4.5 and as is apparent in Figure 4.11. We saw from the discussion in Section 4.2.2 that the real interest rate also affects consumption, but its direct role is ambiguous. In all likelihood, a negative effect of interest rates on consumption is most likely to occur indirectly through wealth: a rise in interest rates reduces wealth and consumption. In the end, the consumption function that links consumption to its determinants can be written as

$$(4.4) \qquad C = C(\Omega, Y^d).$$
$$\qquad\qquad\qquad\quad + \quad +$$

This is the fundamental formulation that will be used in the rest of this textbook.

BOX 4.5. CURRENT INCOME AND SPENDING IN EAST GERMANY AND POLAND

The swift conversion of East Germany (the former German Democratic Republic) and Poland to market-based economies in 1990 provides a unique example of an anticipated increase in permanent income. In both countries, the adoption of market-based institutions implied that income levels would eventually reach Western Europe's. The transition to a market economy however is painful, possibly leading to an initial fall in income as inefficient production capacity is shut down and workers change occupations and industries. While current observable income falls, wealth is rising because future incomes are so much larger than before. Faced with an expected windfall, optimal consumption rises, both now and in the future. Actual current consumption can increase only if people are able to borrow. As part of German unification, the citizens of the Eastern Länder had access to a well-

developed domestic financial market. For the former East Germany, borrowing 'abroad' meant becoming customers of West German banks, or recipients of credits or grants from the government. On the other hand, Poland started with a large external debt preventing its government from further borrowing, and its citizens and firms certainly did not have access to foreign bank credit despite high growth. Figure 4.13 shows the dramatic difference. In East Germany after 1990, while GDP fell, private consumption rose to nearly equal all of GDP. Public spending and private investment also rose, bringing the current account deficit to nearly 100% of GDP. In credit-constrained Poland, on the other side, spending followed income. Because of its large external debt, Poland actually had to run a primary surplus. In contrast, East Germany's large external debt was assumed by West Germany.

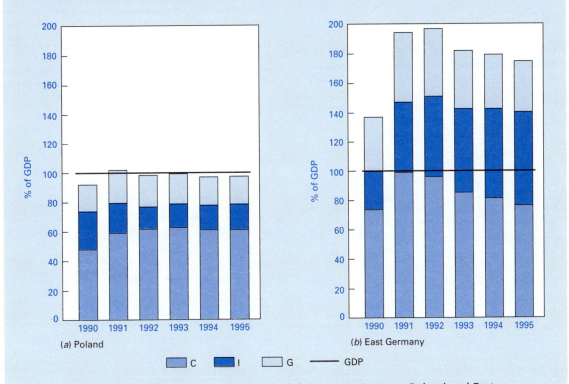

(a) Poland

(b) East Germany

C   I   G   —— GDP

Figure 4.13. GDP, Domestic Demand and the Current Account: Poland and East Germany

Spending in East Germany rose after unification as firms, citizens, and authorities were able to borrow against higher expected future income. There is no link between consumption and spending as 'foreign' borrowing is almost as large as income. In Poland, which has similar long-run growth prospects, spending follows income because of the impossibility of borrowing large amounts abroad.

Sources: DIW Wochenbericht; World Bank; CSO; DGII

4.3. Investment

The second category of private spending decisions which we would like to explain is investment. Investment goods are not intended for consumption. They include machine tools, computers, office furniture, land-moving equipment, buses, and construction of new factory buildings, as well as increases in inventories to be sold at a future date. All these goods have the common trait that they enable the production of goods and services in the future. The decision to invest is therefore an intertemporal decision which is best analysed using microeconomic principles.

4.3.1. The Optimal Capital Stock

The amount of output that can be produced by a representative firm is described by the production function $Y = F(K)$, which gives output of coconuts Y

available tomorrow when Crusoe plants K coconuts today on his bare desert island. The production function is depicted in panel (*a*) of Figure 4.14.[9] A related concept is the **marginal productivity of capital (MPK)**. This is the amount of extra output that can be obtained when an additional unit of capital is installed ($\Delta Y/\Delta K$), and can be measured as the slope of the production function.[10] Because of the principle of declin-

---

[9] This paragraph summarizes the exposition of the firm's budget constraint in S. 3.4 of Ch. 3.

[10] To see why, imagine a point on the curve. An increase ΔK in the stock of capital is represented as a horizontal move from the initial point. How much output ΔY is available? It is measured as the vertical distance which brings us back to the production function. The ratio $\Delta Y/\Delta K$ is the slope of the line connecting the point of departure and the point of arrival back on the production function. As the initial step ΔK is made shorter, this slope becomes the slope of the curve itself. (Formally, the line becomes tangent to the curve.)

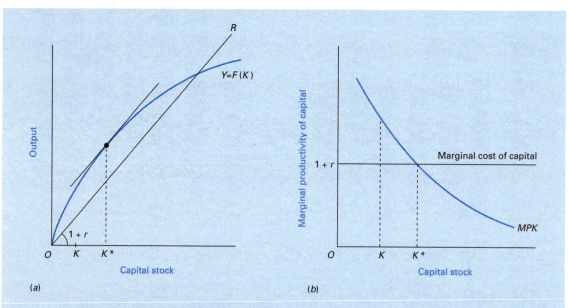

Figure 4.14. The Optimal Capital Stock

The optimal stock of capital K^* is achieved when the firm's production function is farthest from the line *OR*, which represents the cost of capital. There the marginal productivity of capital is equal to its marginal cost (MPK = 1 + *r*). Investment is the difference between the desired capital stock K^* and the previously accumulated capital stock K.

ing marginal productivity, the MPK declines as more capital is put in place, as is shown in panel (b).

Investment costs resources. First, it involves an outlay for the investment good itself, which is lost afterwards since Crusoe abandons his coconut grove upon rescue. If the investment is financed by borrowing, the **marginal cost** of investment will be $(1 + r)$. If the investment is financed by resources that could instead be invested in financial assets, the **opportunity cost** of the investment is $(1 + r)$. In any case, the ray OR in panel (a) represents the total cost, $(1 + r)K$, of capital installed today and productive tomorrow: it is the sum of the principal and the interest charged. (The cost of equipment here is unity because it takes one coconut to start a tree.) The marginal cost of capital, or the cost of one incremental unit of productive capacity, is simply $(1 + r)$. It is represented in panel (b) by a horizontal line. The firm's profit in the second period is the difference between what it produces and the cost of production:

$$(4.5) \qquad \text{Profit} = F(K) - K(1 + r).$$

In panel (a), this is measured as the vertical distance between the curve depicting the production function and the ray OR. To maximize profit, the manager chooses the **optimal capital stock** K^* such that the distance between the two schedules is as large as possible. This occurs where the slope of the production schedule (given by its tangent) is equal to the slope of the cost-of-capital schedule OR. Then the marginal productivity of capital (MPK) is equal to the marginal, or opportunity, cost $1 + r$. (Box 4.6 provides an extension of this result.)

$$(4.6) \qquad \underset{\substack{\text{marginal productivity} \\ \text{of capital}}}{MPK} = \underset{\substack{\text{marginal cost} \\ \text{of capital}}}{1 + r}.$$

In Figure 4.14(b), the optimal capital stock K^* corresponds to the intersection of the MPK and marginal cost curves.

If each and every firm behaves optimally, the same principles can be applied to the economy as a whole. Two conclusions follow. First, the optimal capital stock depends positively on the expected effectiveness of the available technology. An improvement in technology

---

BOX 4.6. LOOKING BEYOND THE NEXT PERIOD AND TAKING ACCOUNT OF CAPITAL DEPRECIATION

The two-period approach continued here from Chapter 3 implicitly assumes that when Crusoe is rescued at the end of the second period he abandons his capital stock. But what if he sells it to Friday, who chooses to stay on the island? If there is a 'resale market', the results will change in an important way. When stating, as in (4.6), that the marginal cost of capital equals its marginal product, we need to include the resale value of capital as part of the firm's income. For simplicity, suppose the price of trees is equal to one (coconut). Then the optimal condition is

$$(4.8) \qquad \underset{\substack{\text{marginal product}}}{MPK} + \underset{\substack{\text{resale value}}}{1} = \underset{\substack{\text{marginal cost}}}{1 + r}.$$

The cost of capital is 1, the same as the value of output since these are all coconuts. This condition can be rewritten more simply as:

$$(4.9) \qquad MPK = r.$$

The marginal product of capital need only be equal to the real interest rate, rather than $1 + r$, because Crusoe needed to recoup the principal of his investment. In practice, firms can usually resell their equipment at some price,

so they will require a lower productivity because they take into account the value of their equipment. So equation (4.9) rather than (4.6) is more likely to be relevant in practice. It is important to note that this does not invalidate the investment function (4.7).

But the story continues: an additional element of realism recognizes that installed capital is being worn out over time, or becomes economically obsolete. The decaying of equipment can be captured by a **rate of depreciation** δ. Tomorrow's value of today's capital is not 1 but $1 - \delta$. Taking this into account, (4.8) becomes

$$(4.10) \qquad \underset{\substack{\text{marginal product}}}{MPK} + \underset{\substack{\text{resale value}}}{1 - \delta} = \underset{\substack{\text{marginal cost}}}{1 + r}$$

which can be simplified as

$$(4.11) \qquad MPK = r + \delta.$$

Here the marginal or **user cost of capital** is equal to the sum of the interest rate r and the rate of depreciation δ. Depreciation can be thought of as an additional cost of capital. From (4.11) the original case can be regarded a special case in which depreciation is complete ($\delta = 1$).

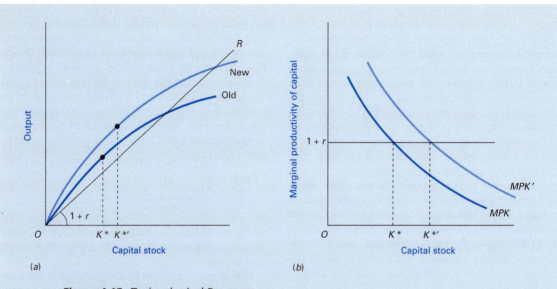

Figure 4.15. Technological Progress

Technological progress makes more output possible with the same stock of capital. In panel (a) the production schedule shifts upward. In panel (b) the MPK schedule moves up to the right. The optimal stock of capital is now *K**', larger than initial *K**.

or technological progress means that more output can be produced with the same capital stock. In Figure 4.14, the production function in panel (*a*) and the MPK schedule in panel (*b*) both shift upward. The optimal stock of capital increases from *K** to *K**'. Second, the optimal capital stock depends negatively on the real interest rate. If the real interest rate increases, the cost schedule *OR* rotates counter-clockwise in Figure 4.15(*a*) and the marginal cost schedule shifts upward in panel (*b*). The intuition behind this important result is that, for a given state of technology, higher opportunity costs of capital reduce the amount of capital that can be employed and still be more profitable than simply 'lending' the resources in the financial markets.

for capital lost through physical or economic depreciation.[11] In Figure 4.14, we can find the optimal stock of capital *K** and the stock of capital inherited from past investment *K*—perhaps there were already some coconut trees around when Crusoe came to his island. Ignoring depreciation, optimal investment is simply the difference *K** − *K*. It can be seen that, given the accumulated stock of capital so far and the rate of depreciation, the determinants of optimal investment are the same as those of the optimal stock of capital. An increase in the real interest rate which lowers the optimal stock of capital also lowers optimal investment, since the pre-existing capital stock and the rate of depreciation remain unchanged. Accordingly, the investment function could be expressed as

$$(4.7) \qquad I = I(r).$$

4.3.2. Investment and the Real Interest Rate

Investment is carried out for two purposes: to bring the capital stock to its desired level, and to make up

[11] From Box 3.3 we know that $\Delta K = I - \delta K$, where ΔK is the increase in the stock of capital, δ is the rate of depreciation, and therefore δK is the amount of capital that was used up. This decomposition can be rewritten as $I = \Delta K + \delta K$, which shows that I—gross investment—must cover ΔK—net investment—as well as replacing depreciated capital.

4.3.3. The Accelerator Principle

In contrast to Crusoe's treeless island, in the real world some capital stock already exists. It could be expected that, in order for the capital stock to reach its optimal level derived in Section 4.3.1, investment would have to move in roughly the same proportion. This idea gives rise to a simple way of thinking about investment. Suppose the optimal capital stock is proportional to the expected output level:

$$(4.12) \qquad K_2^* = vY_2,$$

which can be justified both theoretically and empirically.[12] Then, when firms invest to keep the capital stock at its optimal level, an increase of GDP from Y_1 to Y_2 requires a change from $K_1^* = vY_1$ to $K_2^* = vY_2$. Ignoring depreciation, this means an investment of:

$$(4.13) \qquad I_1 = K_2^* - K_1^* = v(Y_2 - Y_1) = v\Delta Y_2.$$

This relationship captures the **accelerator principle**. Any expected increase in real GDP requires a matching increase in the capital stock. In practice, the capital–output ratio v is between 2 and 3. (Annual GDP represents between one-third and one-half of the installed capital stock.) GDP movements therefore are associated with much larger changes (an 'acceleration') in investment.[13] This provides one reason why investment is more volatile than GDP: it is based on expectations of the future. In the following sections we will develop this idea in greater detail.

4.3.4. Investment and Tobin's q

Why do observers of the economic scene continuously monitor the evolution of stock markets? Prices of shares often move in erratic ways which may not seem particularly related to economic activity. In fact, stock prices are intimately related to macroeconomics. Aggregate economic activity affects stock prices, and stock prices are important determinants of aggregate economic activity. One important link is via wealth: when stock prices rise, shareholders become richer and spend more. Another link, which is our focus here, is investment.

Shares in publicly traded companies are titles of ownership. They represent claims on firms' present and future profits. Profits are the difference between firms' sales and their costs, which are mostly wages when the economy as a whole is considered. Share prices can be thought of as the market's best estimate of the value of those present and future profits. This value may differ from the price of the capital goods which constitute the firm itself, which is sometimes called the replacement cost of a firm's capital stock.

For a number of reasons, it is likely that the market value of a firm will differ from the replacement cost of its physical capital. One such reason is the existence of intangible assets. The value of the firm may be enhanced by such factors as its know-how, its network of distributors and retailers, its reputation among customers, etc. A more important reason, from the point of view of macroeconomics, is the fact that 'Rome wasn't built in a day'. Establishing a new firm from scratch requires time and resources. These costs are greater, the more rapidly an investment project is undertaken. To summarize this, we define a ratio, called **Tobin's q**, which is defined as follows:[14]

$$(4.14) \qquad \text{Tobin's } q$$
$$= \frac{\text{market value of installed capital}}{\text{replacement cost of installed capital}}.$$

The numerator of Tobin's q is the firm's value as priced on the stock market, the total value of all existing shares. The denominator is the amount that would have to be spent to replace the capital goods incorporated in existing firms.

The **q-theory of investment** relates the behaviour of aggregate investment to Tobin's q. When Tobin's q is greater than unity, installed capital is more valuable than what it cost to purchase it, and investment is positive. For example, a Tobin's q of 1.2 would imply that a firm that spends 100 on investment increases its market value by 120. It gives a value to 20 to uninstalled equipment. Given the principle of declining marginal productivity, investment reduces the return on the capital over time and therefore reduces Tobin's q.

---

[12] The long-run stability of the capital–output ratio is stressed in Ch. 5. Consider the case of the Cobb–Douglas production function $Y = AK^\alpha$. Here marginal productivity is $MPK = \partial Y/\partial K = \alpha AK^{\alpha-1} = \alpha Y/K$. The optimal capital stock is K^* such that $MPK = 1 + r$, so $\alpha Y/K^* = 1 + r$, and $K^* = \alpha Y/(1 + r)$. Setting $v = \alpha/(1 + r)$ gives (4.12).

[13] To account for depreciation, (4.22) is simply changed to $I_1 = v\Delta Y + \delta K_1$. The same conclusions apply.

[14] It is named after US economist and Nobel laureate James Tobin, who in 1969 pointed out the relevance of the ratio of market valuation of the firm's stock market to the replacement value of the firm's capital stock. In the meantime, more sophisticated analyses have shown the conditions under which this average q concept is equal to the marginal concept presented in the text. For our purposes, we will simply assume that these conditions are met.

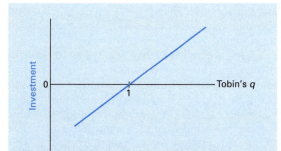

Figure 4.16. The q-theory of investment

When Tobin's q is larger than 1, it pays for firms to invest. When Tobin's q is less than 1, there is no incentive to invest, but rather an incentive to disinvest, or to dismantle or abandon productive capacity.

Firms will continue to invest until Tobin's q has returned to unity. Alternatively, when q is lower than 1, selling off equipment at replacement cost would be profitable for the firm's shareholders, so investment should be negative. If installed equipment cannot be resold, at least investment should stop and the capital stock be allowed to decline through depreciation. The dependence of investment on Tobin's q is displayed in Figure 4.16.

How is the q-theory related to material covered in the previous section, which showed that the interest rate is a key determinant of investment? The market values firms by discounting future earnings using the real interest rate. Any increase in the rate leads to heavier discounting and therefore to a decline in stock prices. Thus, the negative effect of the real interest rate on investment is actually incorporated into Tobin's q. In addition to the interest rate, Tobin's q incorporates two other factors in the investment decision. First, gains in productivity of capital raise future income, and thereby increase share prices and q. Second, q incorporates the role of expectations. Inevitably, investment is a bet on the future: firms buy equipment now to produce output for several years under uncertain conditions. How they will be able to take advantage of the equipment is not known when the investment occurs. Uncertainty ranges from the general economic situation, to competition in domestic and foreign markets, to the evolution of technology and even political developments. All these aspects are continuously evaluated by the stock markets. Forward-looking share prices are volatile because these factors are volatile, and in the end this explains why investment is the most

volatile component of GDP. This dependence on fleeting expectations led Keynes to assert that volatile patterns of investment reflect the **animal spirits** of entrepreneurs, that is, their expectations of the future profitability of investment. It is exactly this volatility that is evident for all countries in Table 4.1. Figure 4.17 shows that Tobin's q typically leads investment.[15] The link is quite strong, with a variable but relatively short lag. Yet not all companies are publicly traded; in fact, most firms are too small to issue shares, and many larger ones are reluctant to 'go public'. It is often cheaper for firms to draw on their own savings (retained earnings) because profits are usually taxed less when reinvested than when distributed. Some firms prefer to finance investment by borrowing rather than by issuing shares; especially in continental Europe, bank lending plays an important if not dominant role. For these firms, Tobin's q still adequately measures the incentive to invest: it reflects both expected profitability—the numerator—and the real cost of borrowing through the discount factor and the cost of capital—the denominator.

Tobin's q explains why there is a link between national stock markets and the state of the national economy. The economic function of stock exchanges is to evaluate the future profitability of firms and to place a value today for the whole stream of future earnings from capital ownership. For the macroeconomy as a whole, average stock prices represent the value of the capital stock in place. Financial markets also assess the degree of riskiness related to unavoidable uncertainty, and this is factored into share prices.[16] Present and especially future economic conditions affect stock prices. Conversely, we should expect stock markets to affect economic conditions since stock prices influence investment through Tobin's q.

4.3.5. The Microeconomic Foundations of Tobin's q[17]

4.3.5.1. Installation costs

We have now seen two reasons for a firm to invest. The first one is to reach the optimal stock of capital.

---

[15] As in the text, the rate of investment is the ratio of investment to the capital stock (I/K).

[16] Ch. 18 presents a description and analysis of financial markets.

[17] This section is a more advanced presentation of the q-theory of investment based on the notion of installation costs. It shows the similarity with the reasoning used to establish the optimal stock of capital. It can be skipped without any loss of continuity. The Appendix presents a formal analysis.

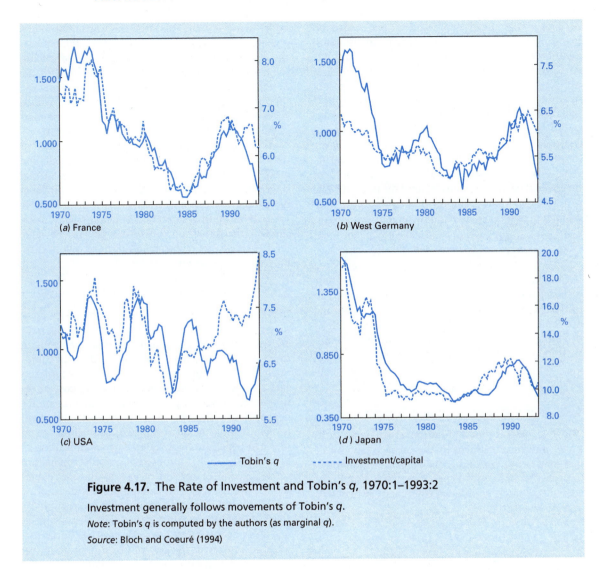

Figure 4.17. The Rate of Investment and Tobin's *q*, 1970:1–1993:2

Investment generally follows movements of Tobin's *q*.

Note: Tobin's *q* is computed by the authors (as marginal *q*).

Source: Bloch and Coeuré (1994)

The second one is to take advantage of the difference between the value of installed capital and its replacement cost. We would expect firms to seize such opportunities quickly. In practice, however, firms do not adjust the capital stock instantaneously to its optimal level. For this reason *q* can differ systematically from unity for a long time. One reason for this is that firms face **installation costs** in addition to the direct costs considered so far.

The idea behind installation costs is simple. With adequate resources, it could have been possible to dig the Eurotunnel in just six months. Doing so, however, would have been enormously 'costly' in many ways, so it was completed over several years instead. Intui-

tively, the bigger the investment per unit of time, the more costly it is to install it. Examples of installation costs include the fact that each addition of new equipment in a factory disrupts existing production and that workers must be trained to operate new equipment.

Installation costs are thus one way of explaining why Tobin's *q* is not always equal to unity. In their absence, firms would always immediately bring capital to its optimal stock level, equating marginal productivity and marginal cost as in equation (4.6), which can be rewritten as

$$(4.15) \qquad \frac{MPK}{1+r} = 1.$$

$MPK/(1 + r)$ is the present value of the return on investment: it is next period's return on the latest addition of capital discounted back to today.[18] It must be equal to the marginal cost of equipment which is unity. When installation is costly, however, the cost of investing is not just the price of equipment: it now includes an additional cost, the marginal cost of installing new equipment, ϕ. This installation cost can be thought of as equipment which is 'eaten up' in the installation process. Furthermore, ϕ is an increasing function of the investment undertaken.[19] The optimal investment decision is to invest until the present value of the MPK of new equipment is equal to the augmented marginal cost of equipment:

$$(4.16) \qquad \frac{MPK}{1 + r} = 1 + \phi.$$

Comparing (4.13) and (4.14), we see that the effect of installation costs is to raise the MPK required to justify the investment. This can be achieved by aiming at a capital stock lower than K^*, given the principle of declining marginal productivity. Because installation costs increase with the size of investment, firms break the path towards K^* into smaller steps which entail smaller costs.

4.3.5.2. Installation costs and Tobin's q

The stock market should value the return on an additional unit of investment by the present value of its marginal return, $MPK/(1 + r)$. In the case of Robinson Crusoe, the replacement cost of capital is simply the cost of coconuts (uninstalled equipment) which is 1. Tobin's q is therefore[20]

$$(4.17) \qquad q = \left(\frac{MPK}{1 + r} \right) \bigg/ 1.$$

Equation (4.5) establishes the link between the two investment principles. The optimal capital stock of capital is reached when (4.6) is satisfied, that is when Tobin's q is equal to 1. When q is above 1, the MPK is

larger than $1 + r$ and investment is warranted. When q is lower than 1, the MPK is low given the replacement cost of physical capital. The principle of declining marginal productivity indicates that the MPK can be raised by reducing the stock of capital; firms will then sell or scrap equipment and investment will be negative. If technological progress increases the marginal product of capital, it will raise Tobin's q.

As new capital is put in place, the MPK declines, as does q. Investment becomes smaller and installation costs ϕ decline until they become negligible. At that stage $q = 1$, $MPK = 1 + r$, and the stock of capital is at its optimal level. Installation costs cause firms to move towards the optimal capital stock incrementally; along the way the return on investment in present-value terms exceeds the replacement, or user, cost of capital.[21] Box 4.7 provides more details.

4.3.5.3. The geometry of installation costs

Installation costs have two particular properties. First, they increase with the size of the investment. Big steps are more than proportionally more expensive than small ones. Second, they are transitory. Once the equipment is in place, the only relevant cost is the interest rate and depreciation—the opportunity cost of resources employed in production. Figure 4.18 modifies panel (b) of Figure 4.15 two ways. First, investment is measured on the horizontal axis as the investment rate I/K, which probably gives a better indication of the intensity of disruptions giving rise to installation costs.[22] Second, on the vertical axis, marginal costs and returns are expressed in today's present discounted values. The marginal cost of capital in present value is always 1, because one unit of capital implies giving up one unit of consumption good today. The horizontal schedule represents the cost of investment in the absence of installation costs. With installation costs, the cost of investment exceeds the cost of capital. The more equipment is put in place, the higher is the marginal cost; hence the upward-sloping marginal cost of investment curve. The marginal return on investment is $MPK/(1 + r)$; it is downward sloping because of the principle of declining marginal productivity.

Firms invest until the marginal cost equals the

---

[18] Here we consider just two periods, so 'tomorrow' is a shorthand for the indefinite future. The proper formulation is the present discounted value of all future MPKs.

[19] For example, the investment costs associated with a 10% increase in the capital stock are associated with four times the costs implied by a 5% increase.

[20] We have cheated a bit here. The definition of Tobin's q is based on the market value of firms, while what matters in theory is the *marginal* return on investment. The market value of firms depends on the *average* return on all capital, not just the latest addition. We overlook the difference between these two definitions of average and marginal q.

[21] Another approach, pioneered by Professors Finn Kydland of Texas and Edward Prescott of Minnesota, stresses that it takes time to design, acquire, and put in place new equipment. The implications are similar to those of installation costs.

[22] In the absence of depreciation, $I/K = \Delta K/K$. Focusing on the investment rate is justified by the idea that a given amount of investment is more disruptive in a small firm (or economy) than in a large one.

BOX 4.7. THE USER COST OF CAPITAL AND THE PRICE OF INVESTMENT GOODS

In Robinson Crusoe's world, coconuts were used for both consumption and investment. In the real world, investment and consumption goods are different and have different prices. This complicates slightly, but does not invalidate, the main line of reasoning. Let p^K be the relative price of investment goods, defined as P^K/P, where P is the ECU price of consumption goods and P^K the ECU price of capital goods. If p^K is constant, profit for the firm expressed in units of the consumption good is:

$$(4.18) \qquad \text{Profit} = \frac{F(K)}{1+r} - p^K K.$$

Comparing this expression to (4.5), the optimal stock of capital fulfils a slightly modified version of (4.6):

$$(4.19) \qquad MPK = p^K(1+r),$$

and the definition of Tobin's q becomes

$$(4.20) \qquad q = \frac{MPK/(1+r)}{p^K}.$$

The only difference is that Tobin's q now compares the marginal product of capital with its replacement cost, the price of investment goods. With installation costs, optimal investment must obey

$$(4.21) \qquad MPK/(1+r) \quad = \quad (1+\phi)p^K$$
$$\text{present value of MPK} \quad \text{marginal cost of capital}$$

or, in terms of Tobin's q,

$$(4.22) \qquad q = \frac{MPK/(1+r)}{p^K} = (1+\phi).$$

The analysis can be extended in a straightforward way to several periods and to allow the price of investment goods to vary over time. If Crusoe buys investment goods at p_1^K and sells back $(1-\delta)$ at price p_2^K, he would maximize

$$(4.18') \qquad \text{Profit} = \frac{F(K)}{1+r} - p_1^K K + \frac{(1-\delta)p_2^K K}{1+r}$$

and optimal capital stock would satisfy

$$(4.19') \qquad MPK = (1+r)p_1^K - (1-\delta)p_2^K$$
$$= [(1+r) - (1-\delta)(1+\pi^K)]p_1^K,$$

where π^K is the rate of change in the price of capital goods ($p_2^K/p_1^K - 1$). For small r, δ, and π^K, this can be approximated by

$$MPK \approx (r + \delta + \pi^K)p_1^K.$$

The right hand side is a measure of the **user cost of capital** which incorporates the possibility that the relative price of investment goods may change over time.

---

marginal return at point A in panel (a) of Figure 4.18, where the two curves intersect. The value of an additional unit of capital installed,—Tobin's q— exceeds the replacement cost of capital. Without installation costs, the firm would choose point B instead and invest more. It may be surprising that the marginal return is higher with than without installation costs. Rather than reducing the long-term profitability of investment, installation costs simply induce firms to invest at a slower rate. In the long run, firms achieve the same desired capital stock as in the absence of adjustment costs.

Panel (b) shows how the investment rate moves over time. With q above 1, investment first occurs at rate $(I/K)_1$ corresponding to point A. Each MPK schedule is drawn for a given stock of already installed capital. Moving along the schedule, we find the profitability of further additions to the existing capital stock.

Once the capital stock has increased as a result of investment, however, these additions become less productive—because of the principle of declining marginal productivity. So, as further investment accumulates, the MPK schedule shifts downwards, in the figure

from MPK_1 to MPK_2.[23] As long as Tobin's q is greater than unity investment continues, but at declining rates, here at rate $(I/K)_2$ corresponding to point B. The process will continue until q is driven down to 1 and the capital stock has reached its long-run, optimal level.

4.3.6. The Investment Function

The **investment function** is the relationship summarizing compactly all the ideas that have been developed until now. First, investment is inversely related to the interest rate. Essentially, this is because buying equipment amounts to using resources—either by borrowing or by using previously accumulated savings—that could be used elsewhere. The real interest rate is the opportunity cost of those resources. Higher interest rates imply lower investment spending.

The accelerator mechanism is based on the

---

[23] The observant student will note that for linear curves, and in the absence of depreciation, the intercept of each successive MPK curve with the vertical axis is determined by the value of q in the preceding period.

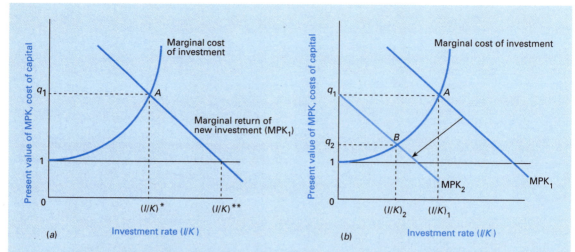

Figure 4.18. Tobin's q

In panel (a) profits are maximized at point A, where the marginal return of investment in present-value terms is equal to its marginal cost. The marginal cost of capital is 1 (unit of forgone consumption). The optimum rate of investment is $(I/K)^{**}$. Tobin's q corresponds to point A: it is the ratio of the marginal return on new investment to the cost of new capital. In the absence of installation costs (point B), the optimum rate of investment $(I/K)^*$ brings the capital stock immediately to its optimum level. In panel (b) investment starts at point A as before. With a higher stock of capital, the MPK then declines as represented by the shift from MPK_1 to MPK_2. With Tobin's q still above unity, investment continues but at the lower rate $(I/K)_2$. The process continues until q is equal to 1, and no further investment is warranted.

hypothesis that the relationship between the capital stock and output is relatively stable. Anticipated future increases in output require an increase in the stock of capital. Since the rate of proportionality is greater than 1, increases in output lead to magnified increases in investment expenditures. Not only can this explain the volatility of investment, but it also reinforces the familiar idea that the future matters for current decisions.

The fact that some firms finance their expenditures by issuing shares on the stock market implies that stock prices will be positively associated with investment. High stock prices mean that the market places a high value on installed capital, so firms can raise more resources per share issued, and this encourages investment. This effect is the essence of Tobin's q. Tobin's q also incorporates some, but not all, of the effect of real interest rates on investment, because a higher interest rate discounts more heavily future profits and reduces q. Many firms raise money not on the stock market, but by issuing bonds or borrowing from banks. Thus, aggregate investment will depend negatively on interest rates, holding q constant.

In theory, Tobin's q should contain all information necessary to infer the profitability of investment, subsuming the other two arguments r and ΔY. In practice, however, Tobin's q is measured using stock prices, while many firms finance investment through other channels than the stock market. The need for more capital as GDP grows (the accelerator effect) should also raise q as it increases future profits. As with households, however, many firms are rationed on the credit market so that income is directly used to finance spending on productive equipment. An increase in current, as well as future, GDP will positively affect expenditure on investment.

These results can be summarized by the following **investment function**, which will be used repeatedly throughout the book:

$$(4.23) \qquad I = I(r, \Delta Y, q).$$
$${-} \quad {+} \quad {+}$$

Investment depends negatively on the real interest rate r, positively on the change in GDP, and positively on Tobin's q.

4.4. Private Demand and the Primary Current Account

From Chapter 3, we know that the primary current account (PCA) is the difference between net output (GDP net of interest payments on the country's asset position *vis-à-vis* the rest of the world) and absorption (total domestic spending):

$$(4.24) \qquad PCA = \underset{\text{GDP}}{Y} - \underset{\text{absorption}}{(C + I + \overline{G})}.$$

The PCA has a useful interpretation: it is the residual amount of GDP not absorbed domestically.

Previous sections established the consumption and investment functions, which relate private spending to a number of determinants. For given GDP,[24] increases in domestic spending will reduce the primary current account. All other things equal, increases in private wealth, Tobin's q, and public spending $\overline{G}$ have negative effects on the primary current account; on the other hand, a higher real interest rate, which depresses investment spending, and increased taxes, which reduce private consumption, both improve the primary current account. Box 4.8 shows, as an example, how Spain's current account reacted to an investment boom in the 1980s.

[24] In Ch. 10 GDP is made endogenous and is further studied in chapters that follow.

BOX 4.8. THE SPANISH CURRENT ACCOUNT

Spain's surge of domestic spending, after joining the EC in 1986 and following several years of post-Franco industrial restructuring, illustrates well the current account effect of domestic demand. Table 4.2 shows that the current account's swing from a surplus in 1985–6 to a deficit in 1990 amounted to about 4.5% of GDP. Much of this can be tracked down to the boom in non-residential investment. A natural interpretation of the events is that, instead of financing the investment boom by reducing domestic consumption, Spain turned to the world markets to obtain resources: it borrowed from the rest of the world by running a current account deficit. In doing so, Spanish consumers could, for a time, smooth their consumption patterns.

Table 4.2. Spain in the 1980s

	1980–4	1985	1986	1987	1988	1989	1990
Annual % growth in:							
GDP	1.1	2.5	3.8	5.6	5.2	4.8	3.7
Investment	−2.1	4.1	10.0	14.0	14.0	13.7	6.8
Residential	−3.9	−1.5	2.0	6.2	11.2	2.3	3.7
Non-residential	−3.5	0.5	14.2	21.0	14.1	15.6	3.9
Consumption	0.0	2.4	4.1	5.8	4.7	5.5	3.7
Current account (% of GDP)	−1.5	1.7	1.7	0.0	−1.1	−2.9	−3.4

Source: OECD

4.5. Summary

1. Rational consumers attempt to smooth consumption over time, borrowing in bad years, saving in good ones. Consumption is driven primarily by wealth, the present discounted value of current and future incomes, and initial net asset holdings. Over a life cycle, income typically increases. To smooth out consumption, agents typically borrow when young and pay back later.

2. Individual consumption smoothing means that, in the aggregate, temporary disturbances are met by current account imbalances (national saving or dissaving) to reduce the need to adjust consumption abruptly. In contrast, permanent disturbances lead to immediate consumption adjustment rather than to borrowing or lending.

3. Financial market imperfections, arising from uncertainty about future incomes and the inability of banks to assess individual future prospects, prevent households from borrowing against future expected income. As a result, current disposable income also affects aggregate consumption.

4. The effect of changes in the real interest rate on current consumption is ambiguous. Lenders tend to increase, while borrowers decrease, consumption in response to increases in the interest rate. In the aggregate, however, higher interest rates are likely to reduce consumption by reducing wealth.

5. The consumption function relates aggregate consumption to wealth (positively) and disposable income (positively).

6. The optimal capital stock equates the marginal productivity of capital to the marginal cost of capital. The optimal capital stock increases when the real interest rate declines and when technological gains raise the marginal productivity of capital.

7. Investment over and above capital depreciation increases the capital stock. As the optimal capital stock, investment is driven by the real interest rate.

8. The accelerator mechanism links investment to changes in output. This is both a mechanical relationship (in the long run the capital output ratio is constant) and a symptom of credit-rationing.

9. The ratio of the market value of installed capital to the replacement cost of installed capital is called Tobin's q. It is an approximation of the ratio of the present discounted value of the marginal return of investment to the marginal cost of capital. This ratio is equal to unity when the capital stock has reached its optimal level. When Tobin's q is larger than unity, the capital stock is below its optimal level and firms benefit from further investment.

10. The market value of installed capital, the numerator in Tobin's q, is priced in the stock market. In setting this price, stock markets look ahead. The forward-looking nature of Tobin's q mirrors how firms take into account expected future earnings when they make investment decisions.

11. Because of various installation costs, firms do not acquire their optimal capital stock immediately. Rather, they spread investment over time, gradually bringing capital up to the optimal level.

12. The present discounted return to investment exceeds the marginal cost of capital to compensate for installation costs. Investment proceeds until the present value of its return, at the margin, equals the marginal cost of investment, the sum of borrowing and installation costs.

13. The investment function states that aggregate investment depends upon: (i) the real interest rate (negatively); (ii) Tobin's q (positively); (iii) GDP growth (positively).

14. The primary current account is the excess of net income over total spending. Given GDP, increases in aggregate spending worsen the primary current account.

Key Concepts

- preferences
- indifference curves
- utility
- marginal rate of intertemporal substitution
- life-cycle consumption
- permanent income
- permanent and transitory disturbances
- consumption smoothing
- random walk
- consumption function
- credit-rationing

- marginal productivity of capital (MPK)
- marginal cost of capital
- optimal capital stock
- opportunity cost of investment
- capital depreciation
- user cost of capital
- accelerator principle
- Tobin's q
- q-theory of investment
- animal spirits
- installation costs
- investment function

Exercises: Theory

1. What are the effects on current and future consumption of an income windfall expected in the future? Show your reasoning graphically.

2. Two consumers have the same endowment today and tomorrow and face the same real interest rate. Represent graphically the fact that one is more impatient than the other. What does this imply for consumption and saving?

3. Should a temporary increase in taxes to finance a temporary increase in public spending reduce the current account deficit? What about a permanent increase in both taxes and public spending?

4. Holding public spending unchanged, what is the effect of a future increase in consumption taxes on current consumption?

5. Consider the case of a household that is unable to borrow. What is the effect on its consumption pattern (i) of a fall in real interest rates? (ii) Of an increase in real interest rates? (*Hint*: see Chapter 3.)

6. Show, using Figure 4.12, the effect of an increase in interest rates on the optimal capital stock.

7. Optimal investment is determined by the real interest rate, *given* the stock of capital accumulated in the past K_0 and the rate of depreciation δ. What is the effect of a higher K_0 on I? The effect of a higher δ?

8. What would be the effect on stock prices of a reduction in installation costs? Would the optimal capital stock be affected?

9. Suppose a major technological innovation improves the economy-wide future productivity of capital. What would be the expected effect on stock prices?

10. In the Crusoe parable, assume that coconuts rot away at the rate $0 < \delta < 1$ and that both planting and intertemporal trade with the natives is impossible (because of bad weather, perhaps). Will Crusoe still save under these conditions? More generally, what are the implications of negative interest rates for Crusoe's consumption and investment behaviour?

11. In Figure 4.4 it is assumed that initially there is no borrowing or lending.

    (*a*) If the consumer was initially a net borrower, what is the effect of (i) a temporary increase in income? (ii) a permanent increase? Contrast your results with the case treated in the text.

    (*b*) Apply the same question for the case where the consumer was initially a net lender.

12. Show that a net lender is better off (i.e. utility increases) following an increase in the real interest rate. Might it also be possible for a net borrower to be better off?

Exercises: Applications

1. Consider a household whose income is 1000 today and 1500 tomorrow.

   (a) If the real interest rate is 5%, what is its wealth (i) in terms of today's consumption? (ii) in terms of tomorrow's consumption? Compute the household's permanent income (see Box 4.2).

   (b) If today's income unexpectedly increases by 200, what is the change in the permanent income?

   (c) If income goes up by 200 permanently, what is the effect on permanent income?

   (d) Answer the same questions with a 10% real interest rate.

2. There is evidence that spending on durable goods increases faster than spending on nondurables during a temporary boom expansion. Can you give some economic reasons why? (*Hint*: think of durable goods expenditure as a form of saving.)

3. There is evidence that elderly people continue to accumulate wealth, even after retirement. Is this consistent with our theory of consumption? How might this discrepancy be explained?

4. Imagine a highly indebted country which can no longer borrow abroad, such as many Latin American countries in the 1980s or Poland and Russia in the 1990s. What could be the effects of an increase in worldwide real interest rates on these countries' income and consumption levels?

5. It is often the case that poorer countries save less than richer countries. They also have a higher proportion of young people. Use the theory of life-cycle consumption to explain this fact.

6. In the 1980s world real interest rates increased sharply. Consumption decreased in many economies as a result, even in some that were net creditors to the rest of the world. Can consumption theory explain this?

7. In the late 1980s, a major deregulation of financial markets occurred in the UK. As a result, many consumers became eligible for credit who normally would not have been. What was the effect on the British current account, and why? Could this effect be permanent?

8. When Norway discovered oil under the North Sea in the early 1980s, its current account went into large deficit for a few years. Give two (good) reasons why that should happen.

9. A great deal of debate has arisen in Germany on the financing of the expenditure necessary to improve the much neglected infrastructure in its new eastern states. One side favours increased taxes, which would fall largely on households. The other side favours an increased budget deficit. Which side is right? How important

to your answer is your assumption of whether the spending increase is permanent or temporary?

10. The following data are the consumption (C) and current account (CA) data (in millions of dinars) of Kuwait immediately following the oil shock of 1973–4:

CA	1972	1973	1974	1975	1976
C	427	439	563	756	1027
CA	701	798	2711	1899	1742

Source: IMF

In the years following the OPEC price increase, some observers attributed the 'slow' rate of consumption growth and the ballooning current account to 'the inability of the Kuwaiti economy to absorb such a large increase in wealth'. Can you think of another interpretation? What might explain why other countries (Algeria or Nigeria for example) experienced prolonged current account deficits?

Suggested Further Reading

Some of the classic readings on consumption and investment are:

Ando, Albert, and Modigliani, Franco (1963), 'The "Life-Cycle" Hypothesis of Saving: Aggregate Implications and Tests', *American Economic Review*, 53: 55–84.

Friedman, Milton (1957), *A Theory of the Consumption Function*, Princeton University Press.

Hall, Robert (1978), 'Stochastic Implications of the Life-Cycle–Permanent Income Hypothesis: Theory and Evidence', *Journal of Political Economy*, 86: 971–88.

For a more advanced treatment, see

Blanchard, Olivier and Fischer, Stanley (1989), *Lectures on Macroeconomics*. Cambridge, Mass.: MIT Press.

Romer, David (1996), *Macroeconomics*. New York: McGraw-Hill.

Tobin, James (1969), 'A General Equilibrium Approach to Monetary Theory', *Journal of Money, Credit and Banking*, 1: 15–29.

Some applications to policy issues:

Börsch-Supan, Axel (1991), 'Aging Population: Problems and Policy Options in the US and Germany', *Economic Policy*, 12: 103–40.

Hayashi, Fumio (1986), 'Why is Japan's Saving Rate so Apparently High?' *NBER Macroeconomics Annual*, pp. 147–210.

Summers, Lawrence H. (1981), 'Taxation and Corporate Investment: a q-Theory Approach', *Brookings Papers on Economic Activity*, 1: 67–140.

Ueda, Kazuo (1988), 'Perspectives on the Japanese Current Account Surplus', *NBER Macroeconomics Annual*, pp. 217–55.

Appendix: Consumption, Investment, and Tobin's q

Consumption: Two Periods

We describe the preferences with a utility function over consumption in both periods: $U(C_1, C_2)$. To make things simpler, we assume that the utility function is time-separable, i.e. that the utility in each period is independent of consumption in the other:

$$(A4.1) \qquad U(C_1, C_2) = u(C_1) + \frac{u(C_2)}{1 + \rho},$$

where $u(C_i)$ is the one-period utility of consumption in period $i = 1, 2$ ($u'>0$, $u'' < 0$) and ρ is called the subjective rate of time preference, with ρ strictly positive. Denoting wealth by $\Omega = Y_1 + Y_2/(1 + r)$, the budget constraint is

$$(A4.2) \qquad C_1 + \frac{C_2}{1 + r} = \Omega.$$

Substituting C_1 from (A4.2) into (A4.1), we maximize $U(C_1, C_2)$ and obtain the first-order condition

$$(A4.3) \qquad (1 + \rho)\frac{u'(C_1)}{u'(C_2)} = 1 + r.$$

Equation (A4.3) implies that the marginal rate of substitution of goods in period 2 for goods in period 1 is equal to the corresponding economic rate of transformation (the gross interest rate $1 + r$).

Several implications follow from (A4.3). Since $u'' < 0$, u' is a decreasing function of C. If r rises, $u'(C_1)$ must increase relatively to $u'(C_2)$, so C_1 must fall relatively to C_2. Intuitively, the price of period 2 consumption relative to that of period 1 consumption ($1/(1 + r)$) falls, making C_1 more expensive. Second, an increase in impatience (ρ increases) produces the opposite effect. Third, if $r = \rho$, consumption is perfectly smoothed out—that is, $C_1 = C_2$. This is so because the return on waiting (measured by the real interest rate, i.e. the cost of consuming now) is exactly compensated by impatience.

In order to derive the level of consumption today, more information is required (i.e. the functional form taken by the utility function). Yet it is possible, by total differentiation of (A4.3), to obtain a number of comparative-statics results as follows. The total differential of (A4.3) yields

$$(A4.4) \qquad [(1 + \rho)u''(C_1) + (1 + r)^2 u''(C_2)]dC_1$$
$$= (1 + r)^2 u''(C_2)d\Omega + [u'(C_2)$$
$$+ (1 + r)(\Omega - C_1)u''(C_2)]dr,$$

which, setting $dr = 0$, gives the effect of wealth on consumption as

$$(A4.5) \qquad \frac{dC_1}{d\Omega}\bigg|_{dr=0} = \frac{(1 + r)^2 u''(C_2)}{(1 + \rho)u''(C_1) + (1 + r)^2 u''(C_2)},$$

which is unambiguously positive. A corresponding expression can be derived for C_2.

The effect of an increase in the interest rate on C_1 can likewise be derived from (A4.4), setting instead $d\Omega = 0$:

$$(A4.6) \qquad \frac{dC_1}{dr}\bigg|_{d\Omega=0} = \frac{u''(C_2) + (1 + r)(\Omega - C_1)u''(C_2)}{(1 + \rho)u''(C_1) + (1 + r)^2 u''(C_2)}.$$

This expression, in contrast to (A4.5), cannot be signed unambiguously. One can however rewrite the right-hand side of (A4.6) as

$$(A4.7) \qquad \frac{u'(C_2)}{(1 + \rho)u''(C_1) + (1 + r)^2 u''(C_2)} +$$
$$\frac{(1 + r)(\Omega - C_1)u''(C_2)}{(1 + \rho)u''(C_1) + (1 + r)^2 u''(C_2)}.$$

Multiply numerator and denominator of the first term by $(1 + r)^2 u''(C_2)$ and substitute (A4.5) to obtain

$$(A4.8) \qquad \frac{u'(C_2)}{(1 + r)^2 u''(C_2)}\frac{dC_1}{d\Omega} + \frac{(\Omega - C_1)}{(1 + r)}\frac{dC_1}{d\Omega}.$$

Finally, define the elasticity of intertemporal substitution as[25]

$$(A4.9) \qquad \sigma = \frac{-u'(C_2)}{u''(C_2)C_2}.$$

Using this definition, rewrite (A4.8) as

$$(A4.10) \qquad \frac{dC_1}{dr}\bigg|_{d\Omega=0} = \left[\frac{\Omega - C_1}{1 + r} - \frac{\sigma C_2}{(1 + r)^2}\right]\frac{dC_1}{d\Omega}$$
$$= \frac{(1 - \sigma)(\Omega - C_1)}{1 + r}\frac{dC_1}{d\Omega},$$

so that $dC_1/dr\,|_{d\Omega=0} < 0$ for $\sigma > 1$, and $dC_1/dr|_{d\Omega=0} > 0$ for $\sigma < 1$. *Holding total wealth* Ω *constant, the effect of an interest rate increase depends on the elasticity of substitution; it is negative for a high elasticity of substitution ($\sigma > 1$) and positive for a low value ($\sigma < 1$).*[26] This corresponds to the discussion in Section 4.2.4 in the main text. On the other hand, the total effect on consumption consists of (A4.10) plus the wealth effect of an interest rate increase, which is always negative since $d\Omega/dr < 0$; so

$$(A4.11) \qquad \frac{dC_1}{dr} = \frac{dC_1}{d\Omega}\bigg|_{d\Omega=0} + \frac{dC_1}{d\Omega}\frac{d\Omega}{dr}.$$
$$\qquad\qquad\qquad (?) \qquad\qquad (-)$$

[25] See Blanchard and Fischer (1989: 40). The parameter σ can be thought of as the inverse of the elasticity of marginal utility of consumption $-[u''(C_2)C_2]/u'(C_2)$.

[26] In the case of unit elasticity—the case of log utility, or $U(C) = \log(C)$—the net effect is zero.

Investment: Two Periods

Robinson Crusoe decides how many coconuts (I_1) to plant, given that when he does so installation costs him $I_1 \Phi(I_1/K_1)$ coconuts in addition to the K_1 trees that already exist. We assume that $\Phi' > 0$, $\Phi'' > 0$ (installation costs are convex, i.e. they increase more than proportionately), and that $\Phi(0) = \Phi'(0) = 0$ (no costs are incurred when no investment is undertaken). Capital stock in the second period will be, in the absence of depreciation, $K_2 = K_1 + I_1$. If Y_i represents his period i endowment, the budget constraint is

$$(A4.12) \quad C_1 + \frac{C_2}{1+r} = Y_1 + \frac{Y_2}{1+r} + \frac{F(K_1+I_1)}{1+r} - I_1 - I_1\Phi\left(\frac{I_1}{K_1}\right).$$

Crusoe must decide how many coconuts to plant. He chooses I_1 in order to maximize his wealth, i.e. the right-hand side of (A4.12). This means that the consumption decision, which was covered above, is separated from the investment decision. The first-order condition[27] for investment is:

$$(A4.13) \quad \frac{F'(K_2)}{1+r} = 1 + \Phi\left(\frac{I_1}{K_1}\right) + \left(\frac{I_1}{K_1}\right)\Phi'\left(\frac{I_1}{K_1}\right).$$

Now define q as follows:

$$(A4.14) \quad q_1 = 1 + \left(\frac{I_1}{K_1}\right)\Phi'\left(\frac{I_1}{K_1}\right) + \Phi\left(\frac{I_1}{K_1}\right).$$

It is the marginal cost of investment. By (A4.13), q_1 is also equal to $F'(K_2)/(1 + r)$, the present value of next period's MPK, net of installation costs. This is Tobin's q. Define the function $\Psi(I_1/K_1)$ as

$$(A4.15) \quad \Psi\left(\frac{I_1}{K_1}\right) = \left(\frac{I_1}{K_1}\right)\Phi'\left(\frac{I_1}{K_1}\right) + \Phi\left(\frac{I_1}{K_1}\right).$$

The function $\Psi(I_1/K_1)$ is increasing when $\Phi'(I_1/K_1) > 0$ and $\Phi''(I_1/K_1) > 0$. In addition, $\Psi(0) = 0$. Then (A4.14) becomes $\Psi(I_1/K_1) = q_1 - 1$, which can be inverted to give

$$(A4.16) \quad I_1 = K_1\Psi^{-1}(q_1 - 1),$$

where Ψ^{-1} is the inverse function of Ψ. As $\Psi^{-1}(0) = 0$, no investment occurs when $q_1 = 1$. Since Ψ is increasing in I_1/K_1, Ψ^{-1} is increasing in q_1 and the firm invests when $q_1 > 1$.

Investment: the Infinite-Horizon Case

The two-period case can be extended to the more general case of an infinite horizon by reasoning recursively. Π_t is the firm's profit in period t:

$$(A4.17) \quad \Pi_t = F(K_t) - I_t - I_t\Phi(I_t/K_t),$$

where $\Phi(I/K)$ is the installation of investment. Capital accumulates as follows:

---

[27] The second-order condition $F''(K_2)/(1 + r) - \phi''(I_1/K_1)K_1 < 0$ is assumed to be satisfied.

$$(A4.18) \quad K_{t+1} = (1 - \delta)K_t + I_t,$$

where δ is the rate of capital depreciation. From period t onwards, the firm chooses its planned investment to maximize the present value V_t of its profits

$$V_t = \sum_{i=0}^{\infty} \frac{\Pi_{t+i}}{(1+r)^i}$$

under the constraint (A4.17). The Lagrangean of this problem in period t can be written as

$$(A4.19) \quad \mathcal{L}_t = \sum_{i=0}^{\infty} \frac{\Pi_{t+i}}{(1+r)^i}$$
$$- \sum_{i=0}^{\infty} \frac{q_{t+i}}{(1+r)^i}[K_{t+i+1} - (1 - \delta)K_{t+i} - I_{t+i}],$$

where q_{t+i} is the Lagrange multiplier in period $t + i$. It has the interpretation of the shadow price of an additional unit of capital when the firm is behaving optimally. The necessary first-order conditions for an optimum are $\forall i = 0, 1, \ldots$

$$(A4.20)$$
$$\frac{\partial \mathcal{L}_t}{\partial I_{t+i}} = \frac{-1 - \Phi(I_{t+i}/K_{t+i}) - (I_{t+i}/K_{t+i})\Phi'(I_{t+i}/K_{t+i}) + q_{t+i}}{(1+r)^i}$$
$$= 0,$$

and

$$(A4.21) \quad \frac{\partial \mathcal{L}_t}{\partial K_{t+i}} = \frac{\partial \Pi_{t+i}/\partial K_{t+i}}{(1+r)^i} + \frac{(1 - \delta)q_{t+i}}{(1+r)^i} - \frac{q_{t+i-1}}{(1+r)^{i-1}}$$
$$= 0.$$

From (A4.20), the optimal investment can be derived, conditional on the inherited capital stock, as

$$(A4.22) \quad q_{t+i} - 1 = \Phi(I_{t+i}/K_{t+i}) + \frac{I_{t+i}}{K_{t+i}}\Phi'(I_{t+i}/K_{t+i}).$$

Define $\Psi(I_{t+i}/K_{t+i}) = \Phi(I_{t+i}/K_{t+i}) + (I_{t+i}/K_{t+i})\Phi'(I_{t+i}/K_{t+i})$, and invert (A4.22) to get

$$(A4.23) \quad I_{t+i}/K_{t+i} = \Psi^{-1}(q_{t+i} - 1),$$

which is a positive function of q in each period. Recursive substitution of (A4.21) yields, for any T,

$$(A4.24) \quad q_t = \left[\frac{1-\delta}{1+r}\right]^T q_{t+T} + (1+r)^{-1}\sum_{i=0}^{\infty} \Pi'_{t+i}\left[\frac{1-\delta}{1+r}\right]^i,$$

where $\Pi'_{t+i} = [F'(K_{t+i}) - \Phi(\cdot) - \Phi'(\cdot)]$ is shorthand for the marginal net productivity of investment. If we impose the side condition that q_t not grow too fast, or

$$(A4.25) \quad \lim_{t\to\infty}\left[\frac{1-\delta}{1+r}\right]^T q_{t+T} = 0,$$

then we obtain

$$(A4.26) \quad q_t = (1+r)^{-1}\sum_{i=0}^{\infty}\left[\frac{1-\delta}{1+r}\right]^i \Pi'_{t+i}.$$

Equation (4.24) gives the value of q for an infinite horizon. As in the main text, it is the present discounted value of future net marginal products of investment. With capital depreciation at rate δ, however, positive replacement investment occurs only if $q > 1$ in the long run with K constant. More precisely, combining (A4.17) and (A4.21) plus $K_t = K_{t+1} = K = I/\delta$ requires $\delta = \Phi'^{-1}(q_{t+i} - 1)$, so it must be that $q > 1$.

5

Equilibrium Output and Growth

The consequences for human welfare involved in questions like these are simply staggering:
Once one starts to think about them, it is hard to think about anything else.

R. E. Lucas, Jr

5.1. Overview

It seems an almost immutable law of nature that economies grow. Over decades and centuries, more goods are produced and standards of living improve. Despite setbacks arising from wars, natural disasters, or epidemics, **economic growth** has been responsible for staggering changes in standards of living over the long run. Table 5.1 shows the evolution of GDP per capita, the usual measure of standard of living, in Western Europe and China over the past six centuries. On this measure, standards of living increased by a factor of 33 in Western Europe compared with 4.7 in China, the most advanced economy at the outset of this period. Such enormous changes are the result of small, annual steps; in advanced economies, roughly 2%–4% per year. Apparently minor differences should not be taken lightly: a difference in GDP growth of 2% between two identical nations compounds into a 49% difference in GDP levels after 20 years, and a 170% difference after half a century.

Table 5.1 raises a host of intriguing questions. Is economic growth a universal phenomenon? Why are national growth rates so similar? Why do some countries exhibit periods of spectacular growth, as in the case of Japan in the period 1950–73 and the USA in 1820–70, and periods of stagnation, as in China until very recently? Is there a tendency for growth rates to converge, so that periods of above-average growth compensate for periods of below-average growth? What does this imply for the underlying levels of GDP per capita? These questions are among the most important ones in economics, for growth determines the wealth and poverty of nations.

There are four main reasons why economies grow. First, the lesson of Chapter 4 is that savings makes investment in productive equipment possible, and this accumulates over time as increases in the physical capital stock. More capital enables a given number of workers to produce more. Second, the work-force of a nation tends to increase, so more workers are able to produce more. In Europe, indigenous population growth has given way to immigration and the entry of a higher proportion of women into the labour force. A third factor is **technological progress**: as knowledge accumulates and techniques improve, workers and the machines they work with become more productive. Finally, productivity itself may be influenced by the size of the economy or the behaviour of agents. Because these four explanations are not mutually exclusive, this chapter develops a framework that incorporates all four, and shows how they can complement each other.

5.2. Equilibrium Output: Statics and Dynamics

The ancient Greek philosopher Zeno theorized that the trajectory of a fast-moving arrow could be decomposed into a succession of instantaneous positions. Much like Zeno's arrow, economic growth can be seen as a succession of instantaneous motionless equilibria. It is useful to begin our analysis of growth with a careful study of such instantaneous short-run equilibria, in which the supply of labour and capital are given and so therefore are the level of output and the income of factors; over time, the size of the labour force changes and capital is accumulated. This section starts with a characterization of the short-term equilibrium, bringing together results from previous chapters. Next, it shows how long-run growth is explained by a succession of short-term equilibria in which more inputs become available and technology improves.

Table 5.1. The Growth Phenomenon
(a) GDP per capita in Western Europe and China, 1400–1989 (1985 $US)

	1400	1820	1950	1989
Western Europe[a]	430	1,034	4,902	14,413
China	500	500	454	2,361

(b) Average Annual Real GDP Growth Rates, 1820–1989

	1820–70	1870–1913	1913–50	1950–73	1973–89	1820–1989
Belgium	2.2	2.0	1.0	4.1	2.1	2.2
Denmark	1.9	2.7	2.5	3.8	1.7	2.5
Finland	1.6	2.7	2.7	4.9	3.1	2.7
France	1.2	1.5	1.1	5.0	2.3	1.9
Germany	1.6	2.8	1.3	5.9	2.1	2.5
Italy	1.2	1.9	1.5	5.6	2.9	2.2
Nether.	1.8	2.3	2.4	4.7	2.0	2.5
Norway	1.8	2.1	2.9	4.1	4.0	2.7
Sweden	1.6	2.2	2.7	4.0	2.0	2.4
Switzerland	N.A.	2.1	2.6	4.5	1.3	N.A.
UK	2.0	1.9	1.3	3.0	2.0	2.0
Japan	0.3	2.3	2.2	9.3	3.9	2.8
USA	4.5	3.9	2.8	3.6	2.7	3.7

[a] 'Western Europe' includes its 'offshoots': Australia, Canada, and the USA.

Source: Maddison (1991)

5.2.1. Static General Equilibrium

5.2.1.1. The aggregate production function

The **aggregate production function** describes how an economy's capital stock K and employed labour L produce the total output of an economy, or its GDP:

(5.1) $$Y = F(K, L).$$
$$\quad\quad\quad + \;\; +$$

The production function (5.1) has properties similar to those introduced in previous chapters. The main difference is that it is a function of two inputs—labour and capital—rather than a single one. The production function is a simplification but also a very powerful short-cut. Figure 5.1 plots an example. The height (output produced) is a function of the level of inputs employed. Holding one input constant and increasing the other results in more output (hence

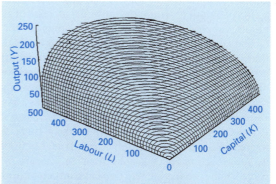

Figure 5.1. The Production Function

The production function relates inputs—capital K and employment (man-hours) L—to output Y on the vertical scale.

BOX 5.1. A FORMAL TREATMENT OF THE PRODUCTION FUNCTION

Formally, the marginal productivities of labour and capital are the partial derivatives of the production function with respect to labour and capital:

$$MPL(K, L) = \frac{\partial F(K, L)}{\partial L} = F_L(K, L),$$

$$MPK(K, L) = \frac{\partial F(K, L)}{\partial K} = F_K(K, L),$$

where *MPL* and *MPK* are functions of both *K* and *L*. The assumption that more inputs result in more output means that $F_K > 0$, $F_L > 0$. That marginal productivity is decreasing in those inputs can be expressed mathematically by

$$\frac{\partial MPL(K, L)}{\partial L} = \frac{\partial F_L}{\partial L} = F_{LL} < 0$$

$$\frac{\partial MPK(K, L)}{\partial K} = \frac{\partial F_K}{\partial K} = F_{KK} < 0.$$

It is usually also assumed that increasing the level of one factor increases the productivity of the other; that is, $F_{KL} > 0$.[1]

Constant returns occur when multiplying both inputs by some constant *t* (e.g. $t = 2$ when they are doubled), increases output by the same proportion:

$$F(tK, tL) = tF(K, L).$$

More generally, functions are said to be homogeneous of degree *n* if for any positive constant *t* the following condition holds: $F(tK, tL) = t^n F(K, L)$. The case $n = 1$, which is called linear homogeneous, corresponds to constant returns to scale. If $n > 1$, returns are increasing; and if $n < 1$, returns are decreasing. One important feature of the linear homogeneous production function is given by Euler's theorem:[2]

$$F(K, L) = KF_K(K, L) + LF_L(K, L).$$

If inputs are paid their marginal product, only in the case of constant returns to scale will the sum of the factor incomes (*wL* and *rK*, respectively) exactly equal total output. Under increasing returns, factor payments exceed output, while there is a residual leftover when returns are decreasing.[3]

---

the plus signs underneath *K* and *L* in (5.1)), but in declining amounts. This is the law of **diminishing marginal productivity** already encountered in Chapters 3 and 4. More formal aspects of the production function can be found in Box 5.1.

5.2.1.2. Returns to scale

Diminishing marginal productivity must be distinguished from **returns to scale**, which describes the reaction of output to an equiproportional increase of all inputs. Suppose, for example, that the inputs of capital and labour were both doubled. If output doubles, the production function is said to have **constant returns to scale**. If output more than doubles, we observe **increasing returns to scale**, while **decreasing returns** occur when output increases by less than 100%. The arguments presented in Box 5.2 suggest that decreasing returns to scale are unlikely. Increasing returns, in contrast, cannot be ruled out, but until we reach Section 5.5 constant returns to scale are assumed. If the production function has constant returns to scale, output per hour of work—the **output–labour ratio** (*Y*/*L*)—depends only on capital per hour of work—the **capital–labour ratio** (*K*/*L*). The produc-

tion function can be written in the following *intensive form:*[4]

(5.2) $\quad y = f(k) \qquad$ where $y = Y/L$ and $k = K/L$.

5.2.1.3. General equilibrium

We shall consider an economy consisting of many firms, each of which is assumed to maximize its profits. To do so, it will hire capital and labour to the point where the marginal contributions of these production factors to profits just equal their marginal costs. For the case of capital, we saw in the previous chapter that

---

[2] *Proof:* start with the definition of returns to scale: $F(tK, tL) = t^n F(K, L)$. Differentiate both sides with respect to *t*, then set $t = 1$ to get: $KF_K(K, L) + LF_L(K, L) = nF(K, L)$. Euler's theorem corresponds to the case $n = 1$.

[3] This is because, for functions with increasing returns to scale, any weighted average of marginal productivities exceeds the corresponding weighted average of average productivities. The left-hand side of the last formula derived in the previous footnote represents the remuneration of the factors of production when they are paid their marginal productivity. The right-hand side is larger than $F(K, L)$ when $n > 1$, and smaller when $n < 1$.

[4] If $Y = F(K, L)$ has constant returns, then $tY = F(tK, tL)$ where $t > 0$. Let $t = 1/L$. This gives $y = F(k, 1)$, which we rename as $f(k)$. The intensive production function $f(k)$ is so called because it expresses output produced per unit of labour (*y*) as a function of the capital intensity of production (*k*).

[1] See theoretical exercise 9.

BOX 5.2. THE REPLICATION PRINCIPLE

It might seem that only a careful study of how firms and corporations operate will tell us whether returns to scale are increasing, decreasing, or constant. While there is evidence that constant returns to scale characterize most industries, the replication principle is often invoked to rule out the possibility of decreasing returns to scale. At the enterprise level, decreasing returns are plausible because, as the scale expands (say, doubles), congestion on the shop-floor increases, distances between services increase, management talent per employee becomes stretched, and there is possibly less cohesion within the work-force. The replication principle notes that, in the presence of decreasing returns to scale in a given plant, it is always possible to do just as well by building a new plant with exactly the same characteristics as the existing one. Doing so would imply a simultaneous doubling of inputs and outputs, and hence constant returns to scale. Replication thus guarantees that decreasing returns can be avoided when and if they set in. If this is true for every firm, it should also apply to a country as a whole.

On the other hand, returns to scale can be increasing. For example, a second plant might benefit from the existence of the first one because bulk deliveries of inputs or outputs are more efficient. In addition, some services may be common to both plants, such as marketing, research and development, or management time. Many inputs—designs or basic research—are freely available to all firms after they are developed; a doubling of total designs in the economy implies a doubling of designs available to each firm in the economy.

the optimal capital stock will equate the marginal productivity of capital (MPK) to the cost of capital, which is exogenously determined by world capital markets at $\bar{r}$. While we will not study labour markets in detail until Chapter 6, the same logic applies to this factor of production: firms will employ labour to the point at which the marginal productivity of labour (MPL) is equal to the real wage w (the nominal wage in ECUs divided by the price index for consumption goods). Formally, these conditions for profit maximization can be written as

$$(5.3) \qquad \bar{r} = MPK \qquad w = MPL.$$

Equations (5.3) give rise to aggregate demand curves for labour and capital, and these curves are displayed in Figure 5.2. Since the production function obeys the law of diminishing marginal productivity, MPK and MPL fall when more capital and labour, respectively, are used. At the same time, increasing one input makes the other more productive. The MPK shifts upward when more units of labour are employed. Similarly, the MPL is higher, the more equipment is employed:

$$(5.4) \quad \bar{r} = MPK\,(K, L) \qquad w = MPL\,(K, L).$$
$$\qquad\qquad\quad -\ + \qquad\qquad\qquad +\ -$$

The two input markets, therefore, are not independent of one another. A change in the capital stock changes labour demand and a change in employment affects the demand for capital. This interdependence means that the outcomes of both markets are determined simultaneously. This is called **general equilibrium.**

Each market is in **partial equilibrium** when demand equals supply. In Figure 5.2, the supply of capital is given by past accumulation (investment) so that its supply is given and described by the vertical schedule corresponding to $\bar{K}$. The marginal product of capital is equal to its opportunity cost, $\bar{r}$. Households' supply of labour is, for the moment, assumed to be given to the economy. It is characterized by a vertical schedule in panel (b).[5] Equilibrium in the labour market determines employment $\bar{L}$ and the real wage rate $\bar{w}$. The figure describes a situation of general equilibrium because the MPK and MPL schedules are drawn for, respectively, the equilibrium levels of labour and capital, $\bar{L}$ and $\bar{K}$.[6]

The production function $Y = F(K, L)$ says that, if the input of factors increases, the real GDP will also increase. Economic growth occurs when both markets move from one equilibrium to another, because of increases in capital and labour or because of technological progress. The following sections explain how this happens.

5.2.2. Capital Accumulation and the World Interest Rate

Capital accumulation is perhaps the most obvious source of economic growth. In a country small enough not to affect the world interest rate, investment and

---

[5] The labour supply curve is drawn vertically in Fig. 5.2. In Ch. 6, we will see that the aggregate supply of labour, through the behaviour of either households or labour unions, could be upward-sloping, or even backward-bending.

[6] Two exercises at the end of the chapter consider the case when we do not start from a situation of general equilibrium.

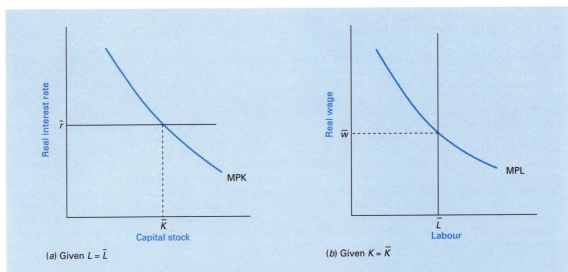

Figure 5.2. Static General Equilibrium

The world real interest rate $\bar{r}$ determines the economy's capital stock $\bar{K}$. Labour market equilibrium occurs in the right panel at real wage $\bar{w}$ and an employment level $\bar{L}$. For this to be a general equilibrium, the MPK schedule must correspond to employment L and the MPL schedule in panel (b) to capital stock $\bar{K}$.

saving are two disconnected decisions, because the investment decision depends only on the world rate of interest and the state of technology. Figure 5.3 illustrates the effect of a reduction in world interest rates. As its cost is reduced, more capital is accumulated at point A' in panel (a). With a higher capital stock, the MPL schedule shifts upward in panel (b): point A' shows that, when the supply of labour is given, a lowering of the exogenous real interest rate is associated with higher real wages.

Out-of-equilibrium conditions refer to situations such as a war, which destroys part of the capital stock, or to a country that is not yet developed enough to have accumulated all the productive equipment it desires. In Figure 5.3 the economy is at point A'', with the same MPK schedule. (Labour supply is unchanged.) The return to equilibrium point A means a period of catching-up, as both the stock of capital and output rise faster than when in equilibrium.

For a small open country, the world interest rate can be taken as given. Yet the question arises: How is the world interest rate determined? Figure 5.4 shows that world preferences and technology are the central determinants. *Technology* determines the means by which goods today can be transformed into goods tomorrow. The amount of capital accumulated in the past is represented by point A. It can be consumed

today, or used in the production of goods tomorrow according to the production schedule AB, given the world labour force.[7] Two polar cases illustrate the saving decision. If all is consumed today—consumption takes place at point A—there will be no production and nothing available for consumption tomorrow. If there is no consumption today, all is invested: tomorrow's consumption is given by point B.

World *preferences* are described by the usual indifference curves. As a whole, the world cannot lend or borrow, so production and consumption cannot be separated over time except by investing in production. Under these conditions, world equilibrium occurs at the tangency point E with the single indifference curve shown. The slope of FG, the tangent line common to the production and indifference schedules, determines the world interest rate. If patience of the world's households increases, the indifference curve becomes flatter and the world interest rate declines. In contrast, productivity gains make the production function steeper and result in a higher world real interest rate. This is necessary to increase desired savings by households.

---

[7] The principle behind this schedule is developed in Ch. 3 (Fig. 3.7).

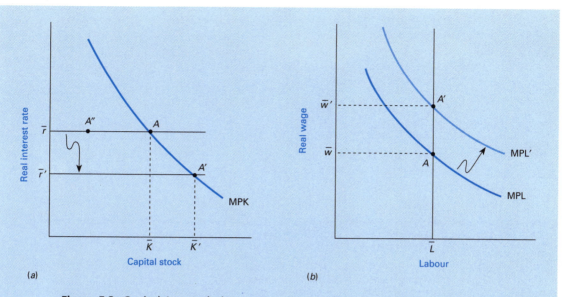

Figure 5.3. Capital Accumulation

Given the world real interest rate, capital is accumulated to point *A*. This implies the MPL schedule in panel (*b*) and real wage $\bar{w}$. The effect of a lower world real rate of interest is represented by point *A'* in panel (*a*). The higher capital stock shifts the MPL schedule to MPL', raising real wages in the process. At points out of equilibrium, such as *A"* with interest rate $\bar{r}$ and $\bar{K}' < \bar{K}$, accumulation would occur up to *A*.

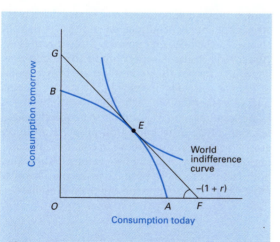

Figure 5.4. The World Interest Rate in Equilibrium

The curve *AB* describes how existing resources can be used today for producing more goods tomorrow. Since the world as whole cannot be saving or dissaving, equilibrium must occur along *AB*. The best outcome is at point *E*, where a world indifference curve is tangent to *AB*. The tangent through *E* determines the world real rate of interest.

5.2.3. Growth in Labour Supply

The production function predicts that an increase in the supply of labour (through demographic changes, immigration, or increased labour force participation) should also be a source of economic growth. In Figure 5.5 we show the effects of an exogenous increase in the supply of labour, represented in panel (*b*) as a shift from $\bar{L}$ to $\bar{L}'$. Given the MPL, real wages must indeed fall. But this is only a partial equilibrium effect. With more labour in use, the MPK schedule in panel (*a*) shifts upwards and new capital is installed. With more capital in place, the MPL schedule in panel (*b*) shifts upwards as well. Increased labour supply is indeed a source of growth and capital accumulation. Under constant returns, equilibrium (point *B'*)—which requires some time to be achieved—will be characterized by wages at the same level as before. Because labour and capital have both increased, equilibrium output also increases.

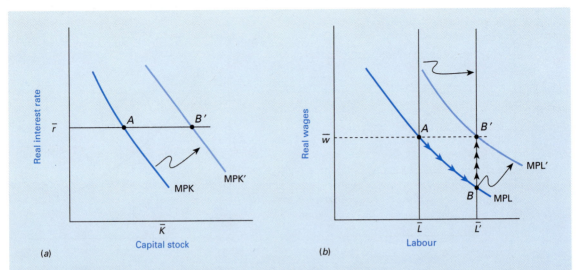

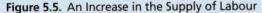

Figure 5.5. An Increase in the Supply of Labour

After an exogenous increase in labour supply from $\bar{L}$ to $\bar{L}'$ shown in panel (*b*), a partial equilibrium occurs at point *B* and real wages decline. However, the MPK schedule in panel (*a*) shifts upward as a consequence. As more capital is accumulated, there is a further shift to MPL' in panel (*b*). In the new equilibrium, income and capital have increased. Under constant returns, real wages return to their original level.

5.2.4. Technological Change

Improvements in technology—**technological progress** —constitute a third source of growth. It will prove convenient to give an explicit role to technological change by introducing a factor called **total factor productivity** and represented by the term *A* in the aggregate production function:

$$(5.5) \qquad Y = AF(K, L).$$

The term *A* captures the idea of technological progress. If *A* increases over time, with $F(K, L)$ unchanged, the same combination of capital and labour delivers increasing quantities of output. In Figure 5.6, both MPK and MPL schedules shift upward. More capital is accumulated because it is more productive (point *A'* in panel (*a*)), output rises, and wages are higher (point *A'* in panel (*b*)). The increase in the stock of capital further pushes the MPL schedule upward, with still higher wages at point *A''*. Contrary to frequently voiced fears, this type of technological progress produces growth without hurting labour in equilibrium. Equilibrium output increases for two reasons: first, because both factors are more productive; second, because more capital has been installed in the meantime.

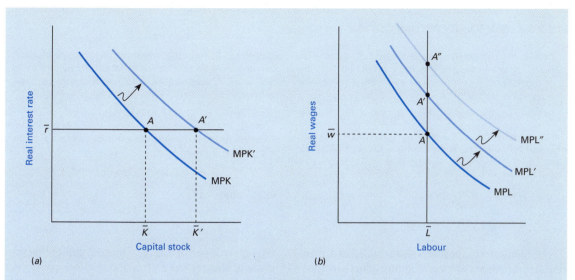

Figure 5.6. An Improvement in Productivity

An increase in total factor productivity shifts the production function depicted in Figure 5.1 upward for any level of inputs. It thereby shifts both marginal productivity schedules to MPK′ and MPL′ respectively. At unchanged world interest rates, capital rises as shown in panel (a) by the move from A to A′. This higher capital stock further shifts the MPL schedule to MPL″ in panel (b). Overall, capital, output, and real wages rise.

5.3. Accounting for the Sources of Economic Growth

5.3.1. The Solow Decomposition

The last section discussed several factors that might be responsible for economic growth; it might be useful to know the contributions of each. Denoting the steady-state growth rate of real GDP ($\Delta Y/Y$) by g, a little bit of algebra (see Box 5.3) results in the so-called **Solow decomposition:**[8]

$$(5.6) \quad g = \frac{\Delta Y}{Y} = \frac{\Delta A}{A} + \alpha\frac{\Delta K}{K} + (1-\alpha)\frac{\Delta L}{L}.$$

$$\underset{\substack{\text{growth} \\ \text{rate}}}{} \quad \underset{\substack{\text{rate of} \\ \text{technological} \\ \text{change}}}{} \quad \underset{\substack{\text{rate of} \\ \text{capital} \\ \text{accumulation}}}{} \quad \underset{\substack{\text{growth rate of} \\ \text{labour inputs}}}{}$$

Equation (5.6) decomposes growth into three components. First, technological progress is captured by the rate of increase of total factor productivity $\Delta A/A$. Second, capital accumulation contributes to growth in proportion to its income share in GDP, denoted by α. Third, increases in the labour force also raise output in proportion to its share $(1-\alpha)$ in GDP.

While labour and capital inputs, and their shares in GDP, are measurable, the growth of total factor productivity $a = \Delta A/A$ is not observable. The Solow decomposition, however, also gives us a convenient definition of total factor productivity growth: it is a weighted average of capital and labour (average) productivities growth rates:

$$(5.7) \quad a = \alpha\left(\frac{\Delta Y}{Y} - \frac{\Delta K}{K}\right) + (1-\alpha)\left(\frac{\Delta Y}{Y} - \frac{\Delta L}{L}\right).$$

[8] Robert Solow, MIT economist and Nobel Prize winner, pioneered the study of economic growth in the 1950s. Much of what follows is often referred to as the Solow growth model.

BOX 5.3. THE SOLOW DECOMPOSITION

The Solow decomposition can be derived by studying the origins of small changes in output produced with the aggregate production function $Y = AF(K, L)$, which can be approximated as:[9]

$$\Delta Y = \Delta A \cdot F(K, L) + MPK \cdot \Delta K + MPL \cdot \Delta L,$$

and where $MPK = A\Delta F/\Delta K$ is the marginal product of capital and $MPL = A\Delta F/\Delta L$ is the marginal product of labour. Dividing both sides by $Y = AF(K, L)$, and rearranging, results in

$$g = \Delta Y/Y = a + (MPK \cdot K/Y)(\Delta K/K) + (MPL \cdot L/Y)(\Delta L/L).$$

To derive (5.6), note that when the factors of production are paid their respective marginal productivities, as in (5.3), $w = MPL$ and $r = MPK$. It follows that share of capital in GDP is

$$\alpha = rK/Y = MPK \cdot K/Y.$$

Since the production function exhibits constant returns to scale, the share of labour is $1 - \alpha$:

$$1 - \alpha = wL/Y = MPL \cdot L/Y,$$

which delivers (5.6).

The Solow decomposition also establishes a theoretical link between average labour productivity (output per man-hour) and capital per man-hour. Subtracting the rate of growth of labour inputs $\Delta L/L$ from both sides of (5.7) gives

$$(5.8) \qquad \frac{\Delta Y}{Y} - \frac{\Delta L}{L} = a + \alpha \left(\frac{\Delta K}{K} - \frac{\Delta L}{L} \right),$$

or:[10]

$$\frac{\Delta(Y/L)}{Y/L} = a + \alpha \frac{\Delta(K/L)}{K/L}.$$

Ignoring long-term trends in hours per worker and labour force participation, this relationship implies that GDP per capita grows with the rate of technological change ($\Delta A/A$) and with the growth rate of capital per capita.

5.3.2. The Contribution of Capital and Labour

5.3.2.1. Capital input

Except for periods of wartime destruction, productive capital has generally grown faster than employed labour. Yet there are important differences across countries, and over time in the same country. Since these differences are mirrored in GDP growth rates, investment occupies centre stage in analyses of a coun-

try's growth performance. Table 5.2 shows that, because of war-related destruction and low investment during the Great Depression, capital stock grew slowly during the first half of the century. A catch-up occurred after the Second World War.

5.3.2.2. Labour input

The most appropriate measure of labour input is total number of hours worked. For several reasons, growth in population or the number of employees does not necessarily translate into increased man-hours. Even if unemployment is ignored, the number of employed people at work differs from the size of the population, and the relationship between employment and hours worked is constantly changing. People live longer, study longer, and retire earlier. At the same time, women have increased their labour force participation over the past three decades.[11]

Table 5.3 shows that these effects have roughly cancelled each other out as employment and population

Table 5.2. Productive Capital Stock, 1913–1987 (average annual growth rates)

	1913–50	1950–73	1973–87
France	1.21	6.37	3.69
Germany	1.06	7.71	2.68
Netherlands	2.43	6.89	2.16
UK	1.55	5.70	2.25
Japan	3.59	10.21	6.65
USA	1.69	3.84	2.59

Source: Maddison (1991)

---

[9] This equation can be derived exactly using calculus. Simply differentiate the constant returns production function $Y = AF(K, L)$ totally, divide by Y, and substitute for the factor shares, assuming that factor prices (wage and interest rate respectively) equal marginal products.

[10] Recall that the growth rate of a ratio is approximately equal to the difference between the growth rate of the numerator and the growth rate of the denominator.

[11] The economics of these phenomena will be discussed in Ch. 6.

Table 5.3. Population, Employment, and Hours Worked, 1900–1987 (average annual growth rates)

Country	Population	Employment[a]	Hours worked per person[a]
Australia	1.7	1.8	−0.6
Austria	0.3	0.2	−0.6
Belgium	0.4	0.3	−0.8
Canada	1.8	2.0	−0.5
Denmark	0.8	1.1	−0.5
Finland	0.7	0.9	−0.6
France	0.4	0.1	−0.7
Germany	0.7	0.7	−0.6
Italy	0.6	0.6	−0.6
Japan	1.2	1.0	−0.3
Netherlands	1.2	1.2	−0.6
Norway	0.7	1.0	−0.7
Sweden	0.6	0.7	−0.7
Switzerland	0.8	0.8	−0.5
UK	0.4	0.5	−0.7
USA	1.3	1.6	−0.6

[a] 1900–86

Source: Maddison (1989)

Table 5.4. The Solow Decomposition, 1913–1987[a] (average annual growth rates)

	France	Germany	Japan	Netherlands	UK	USA
GNP	2.6	2.8	4.7	3.0	1.9	3.0
Contribution of inputs	1.1	1.4	3.0	2.0	1.2	2.0
Residual	1.5	1.4	1.7	1.0	0.7	1.0

[a] An adjustment is made to account for the modernization of productive capital.

Source: Authors' calculation from data in Maddison (1991)

size have increased by similar amounts. Second, employment and the number of hours worked may grow at different rates. Table 5.3 also documents a sharp decline in the number of hours worked per person as people put in shorter days, shorter weeks, and fewer weeks per year. Indeed, the number of man-hours has grown much more slowly than population and employment, even declining in Austria, Belgium, France, and the UK. Overall, European labour input has increased between nil and 0.3%, while immigration lifted it well above 1% in North America and Australia. The

dramatic decline in hours worked per person (an average annual reduction of 0.6% per year means a total reduction of 68% over the period 1900–86) is a central feature of the growth process. As societies have become richer, demand for leisure has increased.[12] In the UK, for example, the average number of hours worked per year has declined from 2725 in 1900 to 1511 in 1986.

5.3.3. The Solow Residual

Table 5.4 applies the Solow decomposition to several countries to account for the evolution of real GDP. As

[12] The demand for leisure and the possibility of declining working hours per person are discussed in Ch. 6.

BOX 5.4. THE PRODUCTIVITY GROWTH SLOWDOWN

Table 5.5 displays trends in total factor productivity growth over the past few decades. A remarkable development across the world, which began in the mid-1970s, was a systematic **productivity growth slowdown**. This development surprised many observers, who thought that technological change had in fact accelerated, noting spectacular developments in electronics, information processing, biotechnology, etc. One reason for the slowdown might be the two oil price increases of 1973/4 and 1979/80, which reduced the productivity of existing energy-intensive equipment and methods of production. Another explanation links it to the ensuing slowdown in investment. Still another explanation might be the compositional effects of labour supply as women joined the labour force. Finally, the industrial economies saw a significant development of the service or tertiary sector during this period, ranging from dry cleaning to management consulting, which tend to be labour-intensive and characterized by less productivity growth.

Table 5.5. Total Factor Productivity Growth, 1913–1987 (% per annum)

	1913–50	1950–73	1973–87
France	0.57	1.79	0.61
Germany	0.17	2.14	0.50
Japan	0.14	1.20	0.20
Netherlands	0.12	0.83	0.54
UK	0.35	0.73	0.73
USA	0.83	0.77	0.10

Source: Maddison (1991)

the table shows, labour and capital growth can account for only a fraction of total economic growth. The unexplained remainder—called the **Solow residual**—represents between one-third and one-half of GDP growth. The Solow residual can be thought of as the increase in total factor productivity, and is often interpreted as a measure of technological progress. Using this accounting procedure, it appears that total factor productivity has slowed down after 1973, an important evolution which is presented in Box 5.4.

Growth accounting is a useful first step: it shows where growth originates. It does not, however, explain the behaviour of labour, capital, and productivity. In the next section we shall develop a model which is designed to explain economic growth, appropriately called the **Solow growth model**.

5.4. Balanced Growth and the Solow Growth Model

According to Solow decomposition, some countries may grow rapidly as they use capital more intensively; others may have fast-growing populations; still others may have rapid rates of total factor productivity growth. At this stage it is useful to let the facts guide the theory. Indeed, while most economic variables tend to increase without bound, some ratios seem to be stationary, or to hover around a horizontal trend. Paths characterized by such stable ratios are called **balanced growth** paths. Focusing on balanced growth paths considerably narrows down the analysis because it points towards stable relationships or regularities in the data and challenges theory to provide explanations for them.

5.4.1. Some Regularities about Long-Run Growth

In 1961, the British economist Nicholas Kaldor identified several regularities, or **stylized facts**, about

Table 5.6. Growth in Capital and Output per Man-hour, 1913–1987[a] (average annual growth rates)

	1913–50		1950–73		1973–87	
	Y/L	K/L	Y/L	K/L	Y/L	K/L
France	1.9	2.0	5.0	6.3	3.2	4.7
Germany	1.0	0.8	5.9	7.7	2.6	3.4
Japan	1.8	3.2	7.6	8.7	3.5	6.1
UK	1.6	1.8	3.2	5.9	2.3	2.8
USA	2.4	1.3	2.5	2.7	1.0	1.1

[a] Labour is measured in man-hours.

Source: Maddison (1991)

growth in the advanced economies.[13] First, Kaldor noted that labour input measured in man-hours (L) grows more slowly than capital and output. Put differently, the ratios of capital and output to labour (K/L and Y/L) have increased secularly. Table 5.6 displays the growth rates of output and capital per man-hour since the early twentieth century.

Kaldor's second observation was that the ratio of capital to output (K/Y) shows no systematic trend, or that the rate of growth of the capital stock and output seem to track each other. The behaviour of the capital–output ratio is shown in Table 5.7. While the capital–output ratios (K/Y) differed considerably across the industrialized countries a century ago, they seem to have converged to a common level in the past few decades. There are two possible reasons for this fact. First, the countries that started with much lower capital–output ratios (Japan, the UK) might not have been in general equilibrium. Second, it takes a very long time to reach full general equilibrium because capital accumulation is a slow process.

Another interesting set of regularities identified by Kaldor concerns the remuneration of factors and their shares in national income. For example, despite high variability, the rate of profit on capital and the real interest rate have no discernible trend, as is apparent from Figure 5.7. This contrasts sharply with real wages, which follow a secular rising trend also visible in Table 6.1. Secular increases in labour productivity—an implication of the trend increase in the ratios of output

[13] Kaldor (1961: 177–222).

and capital to labour (Y/L and K/L)—are translated into higher real wages and increasing living standards.

Remarkably, despite the secular growth of wages and the constancy of the real rate of interest, the distribution of income between capital and labour has been relatively stable. The shares of capital and labour incomes in national product (rK/Y and wL/Y) fluctuate about a horizontal trend. This is consistent with a constant capital–output ratio (K/Y) and a constant return on capital (r) since the capital share (rK/Y) is just the product of the two. Noting that the wage share wL/Y is the ratio of the real wage to average labour productivity $w/(Y/L)$ provides another way of looking at this regularity. If wages keep up with productivity, the wage share, and its complement the capital share, will be trendless, as indeed Figure 1.3 suggests. Within countries, the 1970s were marked by a general increase in labour shares, a trend that was sharply reversed in the 1980s. One production function (5.1) capable of satisfying these conditions is the **Cobb–Douglas production function**, which is discussed in Box 5.5.

Table 5.7. Capital–Output Ratios (K/Y), 1913–1987

	1913	1950	1973	1987
France	1.64	1.68	1.75	2.41
Germany	2.25	2.07	2.39	2.99
Japan	1.01	1.80	1.73	2.77
UK	1.03	1.10	1.73	2.02
USA	2.91	2.26	2.07	2.30

Source: Maddison (1991)

5.4.2. Implications of Balanced Paths for Steady-State Growth

The stylized facts suggest that a realistic way of studying growth is to consider paths along which capital and output grow at the same rate. These are called **balanced growth paths**. If the economy were to remain on its balanced growth path for a long time, most variables would increase smoothly. Such a smooth path is called a **steady state**. The analysis of steady states starts with the Solow decomposition of the aggregate production function $Y = AF(K, L)$, which takes the following form:

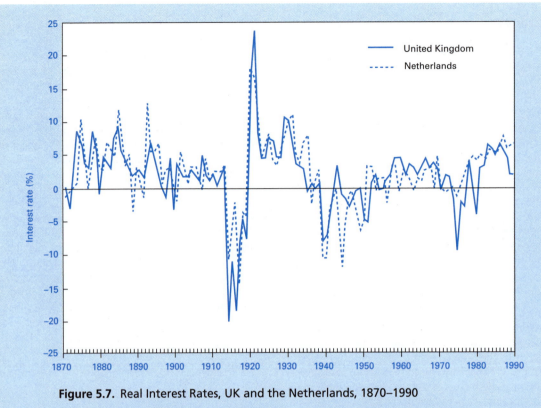

Figure 5.7. Real Interest Rates, UK and the Netherlands, 1870–1990

Over longer periods, real interest rates fluctuate around a horizontal trend.

Sources: IMF; Homer (1963); Maddison (1991)

BOX 5.5. THE COBB–DOUGLAS PRODUCTION FUNCTION

The most widely used and convenient formalization of the relationship between capital, labour, and output is the Cobb–Douglas production function. It is named after the two Americans, Professor Charles Cobb, a mathematician at Amherst College, and Paul Douglas, an economics professor from the University of Chicago, although several European economists—Wicksteed, Wicksell, and Walras—had used it earlier without giving it a name. The function has the form

$$Y = AK^{\alpha}L^{1-\alpha},$$

where α is a constant between 0 and 1, and the constant A represents the state of technology. The most noteworthy property of this function is that the elasticity of output with respect to either input is constant. In addi-

tion, the Cobb–Douglas production function has three important properties:

1. It has constant returns to scale. When written in intensive (per-man-hour) form, it is

$$y = Ak^{\alpha} \quad \text{with } y = Y/L \text{ and } k = K/L.$$

2. The marginal products of capital and labour are a multiple of *average* products Y/K and Y/L:

$$MPK = \partial Y/\partial K = \alpha AK^{\alpha-1}L^{1-\alpha} = \alpha Y/K$$
$$MPL = \partial Y/\partial L = (1-\alpha)AK^{\alpha}L^{-\alpha} = (1-\alpha)Y/L.$$

3. When factors are paid their marginal product, the labour and capital income shares are constant, or

$$(MPK \times K)/Y = \alpha.$$
$$(MPL \times L)/Y = 1 - \alpha.$$

(5.6) $g = \dfrac{\Delta Y}{Y} = \dfrac{\Delta A}{A} + \alpha \dfrac{\Delta K}{K} + (1 - \alpha)\dfrac{\Delta L}{L}.$

For the time being, both technological progress (measured by the rate of growth of total factor productivity $a = \Delta A/A$) and the increase in labour supply ($n = \Delta L/L$) are assumed exogenous.[14] Along a balanced growth path, the growth rate of GDP (g) and the rate of capital accumulation ($\Delta K/K$) are equal, which, together with (5.6), implies

(5.9) $g = n + \dfrac{a}{1 - \alpha}.$

In a balanced-growth steady state, the growth rate of output is explained by just two exogenous factors: the rate of growth of labour input, and technological progress measured by total factor productivity growth.[15]

5.4.3. Savings and Per Capita Growth

The Solow decomposition implied that capital accumulation—and therefore saving—was an important determinant of the economy's growth performance. Once we restrict ourselves to balanced growth paths, however, this insight disappears, as growth depends only on technological progress and population increase. When the rates of labour force participation and unemployment are constant, the rate of growth of the population is the same as the rate of growth of employment. Equation (5.9) therefore implies that

(5.10) $\dfrac{\Delta(Y/L)}{Y/L} = g - n = \dfrac{a}{1 - \alpha},$

or that per capita growth is driven only by technological progress.

Equation (5.10) contains the curious implication that along balanced growth paths savings have no effect on growth. To see this, we consider a production function in Figure 5.8, which relates production per capita ($y = Y/L$) to capital per capita ($k = K/L$). This is the production function in its intensive form $y = Af(k)$ introduced in (5.2). Per capita output increases

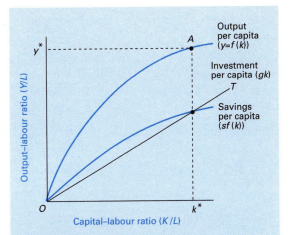

Figure 5.8. The Steady State without Technical Progress

Per capita savings is given by $sf(k)$, the savings rate times per capita income. Investment per capita is the amount of investment needed to sustain the capital–labour ratio along a balanced growth path. This is given by gk, the line OT. In the absence of technical progress, $g = n$. The steady state is given by the intersection of OT with the savings function, and capital per capita is k^* and per capita output y^*.

with per capita capital, although at a decreasing rate owing to the declining marginal productivity of capital.

The next step is to understand how the capital stock evolves. Note that the nation's budget constraint implies that there can be no permanent current account imbalance. Ignoring net foreign asset income, in the steady state total savings equals investment I. We assume that the private sector—households and firms—save a fixed proportion s of their real income:[16]

(5.11) $S = sY.$

Ignoring the depreciation of capital, the increase in the capital stock ΔK equals the sum of public and private savings, so $\Delta K = I = S$.

Since saving is a fixed proportion of output, per capita saving is given by a schedule that lies below the production function. In the steady state under balanced growth, investment keeps the capital stock growing at the same rate as output. This means that, in per

---

[14] Exogenous does not necessarily mean constant. The analysis that follows does not preclude changes in the growth rates of overall productivity and labour input as long as these changes are not systematically related to the growth process itself.

[15] As α, the income share of capital, is smaller than 1 (usually between 0.25 and 0.5), the weight on technical progress will be larger than 1 (from 1.33 to 2).

[16] The assumption that $S = sY$ can be linked to saving behaviour is described in S. 5.2.2. It is not generally the case that optimal saving is consistent with such a simple rule, but the second stylized fact warrants the short-cut.

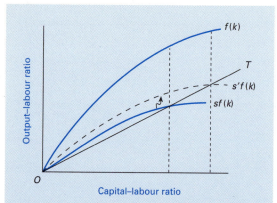

Figure 5.9. An Increase in the Savings Rate

An increase in the savings rate raises capital intensity and per capita income. In the absence of technical progress, growth continues to equal the rate of population growth.

capita terms, investment is just proportional to the capital stock:[17]

$$(5.12) \qquad \frac{I}{L} = gk.$$

This relationship is represented in Figure 5.8 by the investment line. The intersection of the saving and investment schedules determines the steady-state capital intensity k^* and per capita output y^*. When there is no technological progress ($a = \Delta A/A = 0$), there is no steady-state growth and the economy is stationary.

When the savings rate increases from s to s', the savings function shifts upwards as shown in Figure 5.9. Per capita capital stock and output per capita are both higher, indicating more capital-intensive production, but the growth rate itself remains unchanged, as is clear from (5.9) and (5.10). Only technological progress (shifts in the production function) affects per capita growth. *In the Solow model of economic growth, a higher saving rate only raises the capital–output ratio, the capital intensity of production. The saving rate s, and the rate of capital accumulation, do not affect the steady-state growth rate of the economy.*

This characterization of the steady state along balanced growth paths is contradicted by a strong positive association in the data between investment and

growth. Figure 5.10 shows the strength of this relationship. One possible interpretation is that few countries have reached their steady state. Off equilibrium, as at point A'' in Figure 5.3, a country is in the process of catching up, and this process may be a very long one. Under this interpretation, fast-growing economies need a high rate of capital accumulation to move in the direction of point A in Figure 5.8.[18]

5.4.4. The Golden Rule

Even if the savings rate does not affect growth, it does affect output per hour worked and per capita income. This raises the question of how much saving is desirable: how much income should be saved to reach the highest possible level of per capita consumption (public and private) in the steady state, given the rate of population growth and the state of technology? Recalling that per capita consumption is what is left of GDP after putting aside the savings needed to finance steady-state investment, we have, in per capita terms,[19]

$$(5.13) \qquad c = y - gk.$$

In Figure 5.11 per capita consumption is measured as the vertical distance between per capita output and the investment per capita schedule. The highest consumption level corresponds to the capital stock k^{**}, where the slope of the production function is parallel to the investment schedule.[20] The marginal productivity of capital is equal to the growth rate, i.e. the slope of the investment line,

$$(5.14) \qquad MPK = g.$$

This is known as the **golden rule**. If the capital–labour ratio exceeds k^{**}, too much capital has been accumulated. This situation of **dynamic inefficiency** means that, by reducing savings now, an economy can consume more today *and* in the future. Dynamically inefficient economies simply invest too much and consume too little. To the left of k^{**}, steady-state income and consumption may be raised by saving more temporarily. The economy is called **dynamically efficient** because it faces a valid trade-off between the current

---

[17] This follows from the fact that the investment rate is equal to the economy's growth rate: $I/K = \Delta K/K = g$. Dividing by L gives per capita investment: $I/L = (I/K)(K/L) = gk$. In the presence of capital depreciation, $I = \Delta K + \delta K$ where δ is the rate of depreciation, and $I/L = (g + \delta)k$. Investment must be higher to keep capital growing at the rate g because a proportion δ is depreciated.

[18] An alternative interpretation is that investment might actually affect the rate of technical progress (a), a possibility taken up in S. 5.5.4.

[19] If we overlook the current account, the national income identity can be written $Y = C + I$, where $C = C^P + G$ denotes the sum of private and public consumption. Since $I = \Delta K$, we have $Y = C + \Delta K$, and in per capita terms (5.14).

[20] The appendix provides a formal derivation of k^{**}.

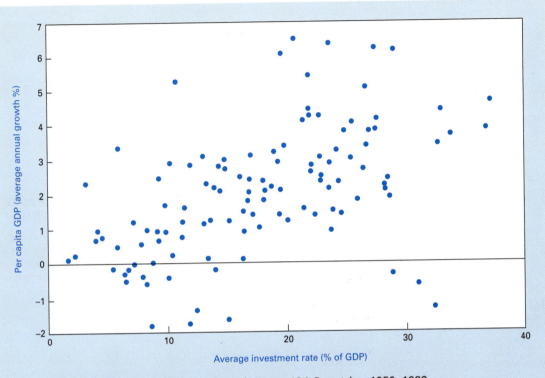

Figure 5.10. Investment and Growth Rates, 124 Countries, 1950–1988

For a sample of 124 countries over the period 1950–88, the correlation coefficient between investment and GDP growth rates is 0.51.

Source: Summers and Heston (1991)

generation, which could give up some consumption, and future generations, which would benefit from the resulting additional capital and income. Box 5.6 argues that dynamic inefficiency may have characterized the communist economies of Central and Eastern Europe.

5.4.5. Growth and the Current Account

Implicitly, the previous sections have considered the whole world as a single economy, assuming that capital is fully mobile, and is installed wherever it is most profitable. This might seem appropriate for advanced and highly integrated economies. Countries with low rates of saving should import savings from abroad to finance the accumulation of capital until their MPK is brought down to the world level. Conversely, countries with high saving rates should export their savings to capital-poor and high-MPK countries. Current

account deficits or surpluses would simply match any discrepancy between a country's savings and the investment level required to bring the domestic capital stock to the level where its marginal product is the same as elsewhere. In principle, this should be independent of a nation's consumption, which depends on wealth (present *and* future resources).

Yet a stylized fact of growth is that national saving and investment rates move together tightly, either over time or across countries. Figure 5.12 shows that countries that save more tend to invest more.[21] This fact, which contradicts the view that investment and saving should be disconnected, is called the Feldstein–Horioka puzzle.[22] The puzzle is deepened by the fact

[21] The correlation between saving and investment rates in Fig. 5.12 is 0.82, which is quite high. Some of the few interesting cases that diverge from the rule are the object of Ex. 2 in the theory section.

[22] Martin Feldstein is an economist at Harvard University and Charles Horioka, a former student of Feldstein, is working in Japan. They pointed out the high degree of correlation between saving and investment in a celebrated article (Feldstein and Horioka 1980).

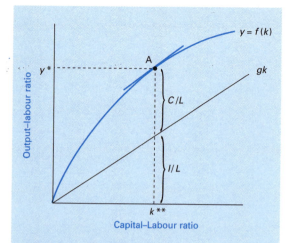

Figure 5.11. The Golden Rule

Per capita consumption is the vertical distance between the per capita production function and the investment line *gk*. It is at a maximum at point *A* corresponding to k^{**}, where the slope of the production function, the marginal productivity of capital, is equal to the slope of the investment line, the growth rate.

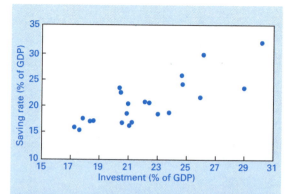

Figure 5.12. Investment and Savings Rates, 22 Countries, average 1980–1992

While investment and savings rates differ considerably from country to country, the two rates are highly correlated across countries. Countries that save a large fraction of their income tend to invest a large fraction as well.

Sources: OECD *Economic Outlook*; IMF

BOX 5.6. DYNAMIC INEFFICIENCY IN CENTRALLY PLANNED ECONOMIES

It is difficult to identify dynamically inefficient economies. This is because it is necessary to estimate the marginal product of capital, among other things. In general, however, studies conducted on data from OECD countries generally cannot reject that most industrial economies are dynamically efficient. This means that, while these economies are not at golden rule levels of capital intensity, they would not be able to reach this level without loss of welfare. That is to say, the marginal product of capital was considerably higher than the population growth rate.

Before their transformation to market economies in the early 1990s, centrally planned economies might have met the conditions for dynamic inefficiency. Under communism, party officials often proudly touted the fulfilment of production targets, especially for investment and intermediate goods; yet the consequence was rarely seen in overall standards of living. The reason for this might be that these economies may have overinvested to the point of dynamic inefficiency in the period 1950–80. As documented in Table 5.8, they diverted large amounts of resources to investment, although consumer goods were in short supply.

Table 5.8. Investment Ratios in Europe, 1989 (% of GDP or NMP)[a]

	%		%
Bulgaria	34.4	Belgium	19.5
Czechoslovakia	32.5	France	20.5
German Democratic Republic	27.0	West Germany	20.7
Hungary	28.7	Italy	20.1
Poland	26.0	UK	18.8
Italy	29.3	Spain	20.6

[a] Centrally planned economies measured not the GDP but net market product or NMP, which excluded certain types of services that are normally counted in GDP.

Source: Begg *et al.* (1990)

that saving and investment were less correlated in the early part of the twentieth century among the industrialized countries, and that this correlation is lower in the LDCs than in the advanced countries.

The high correlation of domestic saving and investment across countries has several interpretations. One is that capital is not really mobile internationally, so that each country must finance its own capital accumulation. There may also be costs to moving resources across national boundaries. Another interpretation is that investment opportunities around the world are really not uncorrelated: when an investment boom occurs in one country it occurs in others as well. Another possibility is that governments care about the

current account and adjust their own saving and investment behaviour to that of the private sector to keep total saving and investment more or less balanced. Conversely, in the spirit of Ricardian equivalence, it might be that the private sector at large adjusts its saving and investment behaviour to the government's so as to avoid accumulating net external positions.

Although explaining it remains controversial, the Feldstein–Horioka puzzle in Figure 5.12 remains an important fact. It suggests that ultimately, while a nation can use its current account to smooth consumption, foreign borrowing is not a long-term source of resources for expanding the nation's capital stock.

5.5. Sources of Sustained Growth and Interpretations of Technological Change

We are now in a position to answer the question posed at the beginning of the chapter: What are the sources of growth observed in the world today? The analysis up to this point has offered us two explanations. The first is that countries grow because increases in physical capital per capita lead to growth in income per capita. We saw in Section 5.3 that this explains only a fraction of the growth actually observed across the world: the other explanation is that total factor productivity increases (and the Solow residual rises). In this section we show just how far these two can go. In doing so, we push to the frontiers of research in this area.

5.5.1. Exogenous Technical Change and the Convergence Hypothesis

The standard interpretation of technical change is that it is the result of exogenous advances in knowledge. Since knowledge is relatively costless to import, all countries should attain eventually the same 'A' term in their production functions. This implies a 'catching-up' process by which poorer countries acquire techniques and learn over time how to use them effectively. Moreover, the positive correlation between investment and growth observed in Section 5.4.3 can also be explained if there is a 'catching-up' process under way. If technology is equally available in all countries

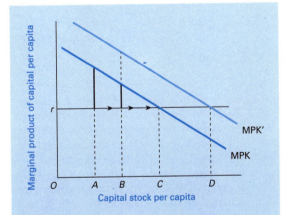

Figure 5.13. Convergence and Economic Growth in Theory

If two countries operate with the same production function and have the same savings rate, the law of declining marginal product of capital implies that the poorer country should grow faster than the richer one. Here growth is determined by increases in the capital stock per capita over time (along the horizontal axis). Along the convergence path to point *C*, a poorer country starting with capital stock per capita *OA* should grow faster than a richer country with *OB*. If country *B* has a more productive technology or invests more, it may grow faster as it approaches its higher level of steady-state income.

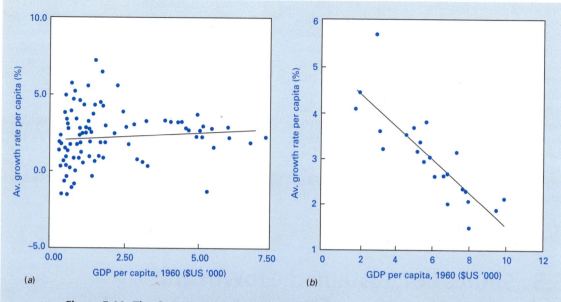

Figure 5.14. The Convergence Hypothesis in Reality

Panel (*a*) shows no relationship between the per capita growth rate between 1960 and 1985 and initial per capita GNP, for a sample of 98 countries. Poor countries do not seem to catch up. However, when the sample is restricted to 23 OECD countries, as in panel (*b*), the convergence hypothesis is supported.

Sources: Barro (1991); Summers and Heston (1991)

and capital is mobile, capital–labour ratios (*k*) and MPKs should in theory be equalized everywhere. Countries with low capital–labour ratios have high marginal products of capital and should attract foreign investment. Even if this process takes time, a process of convergence should be observed towards the same per capita GDP. Countries that start from a low per capita GDP should grow faster to catch up with the richer countries.

This convergence process can be understood using a modified version of Figure 5.3 written in per capita terms in Figure 5.13. For a given production function, those countries with the least capital per head will have the highest marginal product, and also the highest average product from capital. Additional units of capital will lead to the fastest growth in these countries. In the figure, the speed of growth will be positively related to the height of the distance between the marginal product of capital curve and the interest rate.

This implication that countries with lower capital stocks and initial incomes should grow faster is called the **convergence hypothesis**. It can be tested using actual data from the world's economies. Figure 5.14(*a*)

plots the average growth rate over the period 1960–85 of 98 countries against their initial (1960) per capita GDP. The central prediction of the convergence hypothesis, a negative association between these two variables, finds little support in the panel (*a*) of the figure. However, panel (*b*), which presents the same data for the advanced countries alone, leads to a different conclusion: there, convergence seems to be taking place. Thus, standards of living in the wealthier countries are converging, but some poorer countries seem to be 'stuck' in a **poverty trap**, with low GNP per capita and low growth. The exogenous interpretation of technological change is hard-pressed to explain such poverty traps.

The Solow decomposition leads to an analysis that does well in explaining most of the stylized facts. This analysis rests on the assumption that technological change that occurs exogenously can nevertheless be observed through the growth residual *a*. As such it is tautological: the residual is what is needed to fit the facts in the decomposition. An explanation of technological progress is needed. The following discussion explores some interpretations of technological change.

5.5.2. Human Capital

The first interpretation of a concerns the evolution of human capital. Human capital is the education, training, or work experience acquired by individuals. Its accumulation is very similar to that of physical capital. Investment in human capital is costly, so individuals balance costs and returns from this activity—the present discounted value of higher wages, net of taxes. Human capital (denoted H) can be considered another factor of production, alongside physical capital and labour. Labour measures the *number* of hours of work effort, independent of its quality. If the true production function is instead $Y = AF(K, H, L)$, then the Solow decomposition can be extended in the following fashion:

$$(5.15) \quad g = \frac{\Delta A}{A} + \alpha\frac{\Delta K}{K} + \beta\frac{\Delta L}{L} + \gamma\frac{\Delta H}{H}.$$

Constant returns to scale in human capital, physical capital, and labour correspond to the case where $\alpha + \beta + \gamma = 1$.

Introducing human capital provides an attractive interpretation of the mysterious rate of technological change. With $a' = \Delta A/A + \gamma\Delta H/H$, (5.15) resembles the initial decomposition (5.6): the residual a' also includes the rate at which human capital is accumulated. The more a country saves to invest in human capital accumulation, the faster it will grow.

Human capital provides an interpretation of both the lack of convergence between rich and poor countries and the link between growth, investment, and saving. If we rewrite (5.15) as

$$(5.16) \quad (g - n) - \gamma\left(\frac{\Delta H}{H} - n\right) = \alpha\frac{\Delta K}{K} - n,$$

adjusted per
capita growth

it appears that, in per capita terms, growth adjusted for the accumulation of human capital depends on capital accumulation, that is on investment and saving. Figure 5.15 displays the same countries as Figure 5.14, but the vertical axis now represents per capita GDP growth adjusted for human capital accumulation, as in the modified Solow decomposition (5.15). 'Adjusted' convergence now seems to be underway, but what prevents the poor countries from catching up in terms of per capita GDP is insufficient human capital accumulation. In contrast to physical capital, human capital is not mobile enough and lacks a functioning world market. Box 5.7 further elaborates on

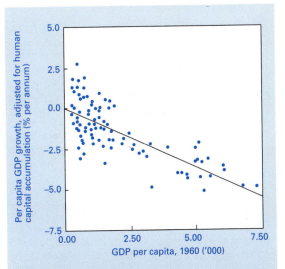

Figure 5.15. The Convergence Hypothesis with Adjustment for Human Capital

When the per capita growth rate is corrected for investment in human capital, convergence occurs among the 98 countries plotted in the figure. The barrier to convergence appears to be insufficient investment in human capital among the poorer countries.

Source: Barro (1991)

this important observation. If over time the poorer countries manage to accumulate human capital, they must eventually converge. While this is under way, convergence—and growth—will be faster the more is saved and invested in both human and physical capital.

5.5.3. Public Infrastructure

A very similar analysis applies to public infrastructure. Public infrastructure refers to roads, bridges, highways, dams, airports, sanitation facilities, hospitals, and other forms of productive capital that are usually supplied by the government. Like human capital, public infrastructure can be incorporated into the aggregate production function and can help explain part of the Solow residual.[23] Like human capital, public infrastructure is financed by (public) saving and is most

---

[23] Formally, just replace H in (5.15) and (5.16) by a term measuring infrastructure.

BOX 5.7. PHYSICAL AND HUMAN CAPITAL ACCUMULATION[24]

GDP per capita in the EC countries is 5–6 times that in India, and 10–15 times higher than in some African nations. If all countries had access to similar production technologies (similar production functions), the return on investment should be higher in countries that have very low capital–labour ratios, as shown in Table 5.9. Why is convergence occurring so slowly, if at all? Why should investment occur at all in rich countries while the marginal product of capital is in principle so high in the poor countries?

One answer is that the capital–labour ratio is an imperfect indicator of productivity. If the aggregate production function includes human capital, $Y = F(K, L, H)$, the marginal productivity of capital may also be a positive function of the aggregate human capital stock. Table 5.9, which illustrates the wide disparity of investment in human capital around the world, suggests that a combination of low capital–labour ratios *and* a low human capital stock may explain why the MPK is not higher in poor countries. In terms of Figure 5.13, high-human-capital nations would have an MPL curve lying above that of a low-human-capital economy. One way to measure investment in human capital is to look at education levels. Table 5.10

shows that, among the east Asian economies, both literacy and high educational achievement are associated with high growth rates.

Table 5.9. Average Investment in Human Capital, 1960–1985

	Capital–labour ratio	Investment in human capital[a]
Algeria	49	4.5
Argentina	2878	5.0
Côte d'Ivoire	42	2.3
Guatemala	975	2.4
India	396	5.1
Italy	8515	7.1

[a] Investment in human capital is measured as the percentage of working-age population in secondary school.

Sources: Summers and Heston (1991); Mankiw *et al.* (1990)

Table 5.10. Human Capital Indicators and Growth in Asian Economies, 1960–1992

	Primary enrolment ratio, 1960	Secondary enrolment ratio, 1960	Literacy rate, 1960	Average per capita growth rate, 1960–92 (% per annum)
Hong Kong	0.87	0.24	0.70	6.4
India	0.67	0.06	0.39	1.6
Japan	1.03	0.74	0.98	5.2
South Korea	0.94	0.27	0.71	6.7
Malaysia	0.96	0.19	0.53	4.5
Singapore	1.11	0.32	0.50	6.6
Taiwan	0.96	0.28	0.54	6.0
Thailand	0.83	0.12	0.68	4.6

Sources: Heston and Summers (1988) and Barro and Wolf (1989); Penn World Table (Mark 5.6a)

often not traded on world markets so that insufficient accumulation may occur in particular countries and can explain the lack of convergence among nations. The early actions of the German government after its reunification with the former GDR is a prime example of the importance of this type of capital (see Box 5.8).

5.5.4. Endogenous Growth[25]

If technological change is endogenous, convergence among nations' per capita incomes need never occur. In the case of **endogenous growth**, government policies can affect growth rates in both positive and negative directions.

---

[24] The material in this box is based on an argument presented by Lucas (1990).

[25] This section presents more advanced material and newer, still unconfirmed, theories.

BOX 5.8. REBUILDING EAST GERMANY AFTER REUNIFICATION

In the summer of 1990, the economic condition of the German Democratic Republic looked abysmal. The communist regime had clearly spent too much on supervising people and not enough on supervising the state of its infrastructure, which was in a shambles. Roads had not been repaired for decades. An estimated 45% of the equipment in the postal and communications network was more than 20 years old. East Germans by best estimates had fewer than half the telephones per capita as West Germans in 1989, and those they had did not work very well. Water was not potable, the air was polluted, and so on. It has been estimated that bringing East Germany up to the infrastructure level of the West will cost roughly ECU 500 billion. This poor infrastructure is often cited as one key reason why foreign and West German firms were slow to invest initially, and why such great sums are being spent to rectify the situation. The productivity of all factors of production is simply less when infrastructure is poor.

In the meantime much investment has occurred. Table 5.11 shows the extent to which investment has taken place; roughly 40%–45% of gross domestic product of the former East Germany has been invested in new plant, equipment, and housing. To a great extent, this investment has been subsidized by the government, while a large part of it represents infrastructure investment. In the meantime more telephones have been installed in Eastern Germany since unification than had ever been installed up to 1989. Eastern Germany was able to finance this by breaking the Feldstein–Horioka puzzle, running current account deficits of almost 100% of GDP.

Table 5.11. Investment in Eastern Germany after Unification, 1991–1994

	DM 1991 bn		% of Eastern German GDP	
	1991:2	1994:2	1991:2	1994:2
Consumption	45.5	50.0	106.1	87.0
Investment plus Inventory Accumulation *of which*:	18.8	38.3	43.8	66.6
Equipment	10.2	14.2	23.8	24.7
Government Purchases	20.3	22.6	47.3	39.3
Gross Domestic Product	42.9	57.5	100.0	100.0
Current Account[a]	−41.7	−53.4	−97.2	−93.7

[a] More accurately, the balance of exports of goods and services produced in East Germany over imports (German: *Außenbeitrag*)

Source: DIW *Wochenbericht*, various issues

5.5.4.1. Increasing returns to scale

All the analysis so far has assumed constant returns to scale in production. Yet, while decreasing returns are ruled out by the replication principle, increasing returns to scale are plausible and raise the intriguing possibility that growth might proceed on its own strength, even in the absence of technological progress. Suppose that, in addition to constant returns to scale in physical capital and labour, there is constant returns to scale in the accumulation of human capital *alone*. Consequently, as more human capital is accumulated, its marginal productivity does not decline: it remains constant. There is no reason to refrain from accumulating human capital for ever at any rate. When a country saves and invests more in human capital, it does not face declining returns and can grow faster even in the steady state. Technological progress is endogenous to saving, and so is steady-state growth. Not only do countries no longer need to converge, they may well continue to *diverge*. This fascinating possibility remains to be confirmed. If true, it suggests an important role for saving and for policies designed to increase saving and investment in human capital, such as education and research and development.

5.5.4.2. Externalities

In the presence of increasing returns, paying all factors their marginal productivity more than exhausts total income derived from production. (Box 5.1 provides details.) One way for a firm to survive under such

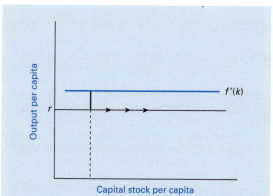

Figure 5.16. Endogenous Growth

If the accumulation of capital per head does not depress the marginal product of capital, the economy will continue to have incentives to invest. Such a situation can give rise to endogenous growth.

conditions is to benefit from positive **externalities**. An externality arises when one agent's actions have an implication, positive or negative, on other agents' well-being and behaviour, yet there can be no market price reward. One example is the presence in an area of a large industrial network of contacts and exchanges of information. Each single firm benefits at no cost from this network externality: it is a 'free' factor of production. Education and public infrastructure are other examples of externalities with potentially important implications for growth.

The best-known example of positive externalities is the development and proliferation of knowledge. Knowledge differs from human capital: it is not part of one particular individual or generation, and does not disappear when its creator does. Unless a civilization is destroyed, the stock of accumulated ideas, designs, and innovations is unlikely to decline. While particular innovations are exogenous—they occur randomly, often by luck—research and development is very similar to investment in productive equipment. If this activity operates under constant returns to scale, it will grow indefinitely, providing society as a whole with the externality that it generates.

5.6. Summary

1. The economy's productive capacity is defined by the aggregate production function, defined over capital and labour inputs.

2. With constant returns to scale in the production function, the marginal productivities of capital and labour are declining. The demand for capital and labour will be such that their marginal productivities equal their marginal costs. In the short run, the stock of capital is given by past accumulation. General equilibrium occurs when labour employed is such that the MPK is equal to the world real rate of interest, while the real wage is equal to the MPL at the chosen capital stock.

3. Over time, the stock of capital is changing as a result of saving and investment. This results in changing demand for labour and rising real wages. In principle, saving and investment decisions are disconnected: saving is driven by intertemporal consumption smoothing, and investment by the difference between the MPK and the opportunity cost of capital, the interest rate.

4. There are three main sources of growth: increases in the availability of labour, capital accumulation, and technological change. The Solow decomposition captures the two first sources of growth and isolates the third as a residual. In practice, this residual accounts for between one-third and one-half of growth.

5. Some stylized facts can guide the search for theory. Output and capital grow at about the same rate, and faster than labour (man-hours). While real wages have grown steadily, the rate of profit and capital and labour shares remain stable over the long run, despite short-run fluctuations.

6. Balanced growth paths are characterized by a steady capital–output ratio. Steady states are a convenient way of describing the broad long-run features of the growth phenomenon. In practice, economies are never on their steady-state path, but are generally moving towards it.

7. Along a balanced growth path, an increase in GDP can be entirely explained by the rate of population growth and by exogenous technological progress. The rate of growth of the third factor in the Solow decomposition—capital—is the same as the growth rate of output. Its level—more precisely, the ratio of capital to output or of capital to labour—is determined by the saving rate.

8. Saving does not affect the growth rate of the economy along balanced growth paths. Yet a higher saving rate raises the steady-state capital intensity of the economy. Off balanced growth paths, the saving rate therefore can influence the speed at which the economy grows, all other things being equal.

9. If more saving means more capital and output per capita, an optimal saving rate can be defined. The golden rule states that steady-state per capita consumption is highest when the MPK is equal to the economy's growth rate.

10. If saving exceeds its golden rule rate, the economy is dynamically inefficient: all generations could be made better off by consuming more, now and for ever. In the opposite case, the economy is efficient because it is impossible to make all generations better off. Raising the capital–labour ratio requires sacrifices by the current generation for the benefit of successive generations.

11. In an open economy it is possible, in principle, to escape the savings–investment link by borrowing abroad. Yet, there is still a strong correlation between investment and saving across countries.

12. The lack of clear convergence of growth rates and levels of per capita income in the community of nations, as well as the effect of saving on growth, suggest either that the process of convergence is slow or that technological progress may be endogenous and specific to each country.

13. An important source of growth appears to be human capital. Because there is no organized international market for human capital, different countries may save and accumulate human capital at different rates. This is a major reason why convergence does not occur.

14. Increasing returns to scale and externalities may also explain the absence of convergence and the role of saving. Knowledge, human capital, and public infrastructure are possible factors that generate externalities. Policies designed to increase their accumulation may be desirable.

Key Concepts

- economic growth
- technological progress
- aggregate production function
- diminishing marginal productivity
- returns to scale (constant, increasing, decreasing)
- output–labour ratio
- capital–labour ratio
- general and partial equilibrium
- capital accumulation
- out-of-equilibrium conditions
- total factor productivity
- Solow decomposition, Solow residual
- productivity growth slowdown
- balanced growth paths
- stylized facts
- steady state
- golden rule
- dynamic inefficiency/efficiency
- Feldstein–Horioka puzzle
- human capital
- Cobb–Douglas production function
- convergence hypothesis
- poverty trap
- endogenous growth
- externalities

Exercises: Theory

1. Suppose that an influx of migrants increases the labour supply by 20%, which continues to be inelastically supplied. Show diagrammatically the general equilibrium outcome.

2. Suppose an economy sustains the destruction of half its capital stock as the result of a war. In terms of Figure 5.2, describe the general equilibrium outcome.

3. Show in Figure 5.2 the general equilibrium effect of technological regress, that is, a decline in A.

4. Suppose the aggregate production function is given by $Y = \sqrt{KL}$. Does it have increasing, decreasing, or constant returns to scale? (*Mathematical hint*: What are the marginal products of capital and labour, respectively?)

5. Suppose that capital depreciates at rate δ. Find the balanced growth path relationship between the capital–output ratio, the savings rate s, and the rate of GDP growth g.

6. What is the golden rule of capital accumulation if capital depreciates at rate δ? What happens to the golden rule per capita capital stock as δ increases?

7. Using Figure 5.8, show graphically the effect of technological progress, that is, a one-off increase in A.

8. Infrastructure can be considered as another factor of production, along with capital, labour, and human capital. What would be the corresponding Solow decomposition if infrastructure were considered explicitly?

9. (*Hard, mathematical*) Show that Euler's theorem implies that marginal productivity of one input increases when use of the other one is raised, or that[26]

$$\partial F_K / \partial L = \partial F_L / \partial K = F_{KL} > 0.$$

Exercises: Applications

1. In Table 5.7 it is seen that during the postwar period both output and capital per capita have grown faster in France than in the USA. In addition, capital has grown faster than output in France, and at about the same rate in the USA. How can this be explained?

2. Two outliers in Figure 5.12 are Ireland and Switzerland, where saving and investment rates differ markedly. What facts about these countries might explain this divergence?

3. Eastern Europe has a high-quality labour force, but has embarked on economic transformation with an inadequate capital stock. What are the implications for the marginal product of capital in Eastern Europe? What is the implication for capital accumulation and growth in Western Europe?

4. How might your answer to the previous question be affected by the Feldstein–Horioka puzzle?

5. The rate of population growth has been assumed exogenous. Yet, fertility tends to be inversely related to per capita income; that is, households in wealthier countries tend to have fewer children. What can be the reason(s)? What does this imply for convergence?

6. Consider a country with zero technological progress and $K/Y = 3$. Its population grows at the rate of 2% per year and the share of capital in income is 0.25. What is the rate of growth of its GDP *per capita* if the saving rate is 20%? If it is 30%? How do your answers change if depreciation occurs at a rate of 0.05% per year?

---

[26] Answer: taking the derivative of F with respect to L gives $F_L = \partial F/\partial L = \partial(KF_K + LF_L)/\partial L = KF_{KL} + F_L + LF_{LL}$.

Hence $KF_{KL} + LF_{LL} = 0$. Since K and L are positive and F_{LL} is negative, F_{KL} must be positive.

7. Suppose the aggregate production function is $Y = \sqrt{HKL}$, where H measures input of human capital. Suppose further that the capital–labour ratio is identical in Sri Lanka and Egypt, but that H is twice as high in Egypt as in Sri Lanka. What is the ratio of the marginal product of capital in the two countries? What is the ratio of the marginal product of human capital? If you wish, you may evaluate (H, K, L) as $(2, 200, 200)$ and $(1, 100, 100)$.

8. Suppose K/Y is constant at 2. What is the investment–output ratio consistent with 5% real growth (*a*) if the rate of depreciation is 5%? (*b*) if growth is 7%?

9. 'Curtailing migration will keep labour in short supply and thereby keep real wages high.' Comment.

10. It is often contended that the loss of highly skilled workers from developing countries through migration retards economic growth. Explain how this might be true, drawing on the ideas presented in Section 5.5.

Suggested Further Reading

Two classics are:

Maddison, Angus (1982), *Phases of Economic Development*, Oxford University Press.
Solow, Robert M. (1970), *Growth Theory: An Exposition*, Oxford University Press.

Some of the newer ideas in economic growth have been explored in:

Mankiw, N. Greg, Romer, David, and Weil, David (1992), 'A Contribution to the Empirics of Economic Growth', *Quarterly Journal of Economics*, 57: 407–38.
Romer, Paul (1987), 'Crazy Explanations for the Productivity Slowdown', in S. Fischer (ed.), *NBER Macroeconomic Annual 1987*, 163–210.
Solow, Robert M. (1994), 'Perspectives on Growth Theory', *Journal of Economic Perspectives*, 8: 45–54.

Also see the 'Symposium on New Growth Theory' in the *Journal of Economic Perspectives*, 8(1): 3–72, 1994 (articles by Paul Romer, Gene Grossman and Elhanan Helpman, Robert Solow, Howard Pack).

For a perspective on capital accumulation in Europe, West and East, see:

Bean, Charles (1989), 'Capital Shortages and Persistent Unemployment', *Economic Policy*, 8: 11–54.
Begg, David, Danthine, Jean-Pierre, Giavazzi, Francesco, and Wyplosz, Charles (1990), 'The East, the Deutschmark, and EMU', in *Monitoring European Integration: The Impact of Eastern Europe*, Centre for Economic Policy Research, London.

Appendix: The Modified Solow Growth Model, Conditional Convergence, and the Golden Rule

The Basic Model and Equilibrium

The following is a brief mathematical exposition of the most commonly studied version of the growth model analysed in the text. Advanced textbooks, such as Barro and Sala-i-Martin (1995) or Romer (1996), provide details.

Production is given by the constant returns to scale production function

(A5.1)
$$Y = F(K, AL),$$

with the characteristics discussed in Box 5.2. Technical progress, or growth in A, is labour-augmenting; it increases effectiveness of labour input. It grows at constant rate a. By the constant returns to scale property, we can write

(A5.2)
$$y = f(k),$$

where $y = Y/AL$ and $k = K/AL$. Notice that the intensive form is defined in terms of capital per *effective* unit of labour. (Sometimes the term 'efficiency units' of labour is used.) The source of growth in this model is increases in k over time, given by

(A5.3)
$$\frac{dk}{dt} = \frac{(1/AL)dK}{dt} - \frac{(K/AL^2)dL}{dt} - \frac{(K/A^2L)dA}{dt}$$
$$= \left[\frac{(1/K)dK}{dt} - \frac{(1/L)dL}{dt} - \frac{(1/A)dA}{dt}\right]k$$
$$= \left[\frac{(1/K)dK}{dt} - n - a\right]k;$$

or, in terms of growth rates, the growth rate of the capital stock in per capita effective labour terms is the gross growth rate of the capital stock minus the growth rate of the labour force (n), minus the rate of exogenous technical progress (a):

(A5.4)
$$\frac{(1/k)dk}{dt} = \frac{(1/K)dK}{dt} - n - a.$$

In the Solow model, the capital stock increases because households save a constant fraction s of their income Y; it decreases at the same time by depreciation at rate δ, so

$$\frac{dK}{dt} = sF(K, AL) - \delta K,$$

or, dividing by AL and substituting,

(A5.5)
$$\frac{(1/AL)dK}{dt} = \frac{k(1/K)dK}{dt} = sf(k) - \delta k.$$

Now substitute (A5.5) into (A5.3) to obtain

(A5.6)
$$\frac{dk}{dt} = \left[\frac{sf(k)}{k} - a - \delta - n\right]k = sf(k) - (a + \delta + n)k.$$

This equation is sometimes called the fundamental equation of the Solow growth model. It completely describes the dynamics of the capital stock, and thereby of output as well.

The steady-state equilibrium in the Solow growth model is characterized by $dk/dt = 0$. Define k^* as the value of k that solves this condition, and let y^* be the output per efficiency unit of labour which corresponds to k^*; that is, $y^* = f(k^*)$. Then

(A5.7)
$$sf(k^*) = (a + \delta + n)k^*.$$

The equilibrium is shown as the intersection of the savings curve $sf(k^*)$ and the investment requirement line (the ray given by $(a + \delta + n)k$) at point E in Figure A5.1. As long as the economy lies to the left of point E, positive capital accumulation and growth will take place (per efficiency unit of labour), whereas an economy lying to the right of point E will have falling k and y.

Convergence near the steady state

We now use the Solow model to study the approximate growth behaviour of the economy in the neighbourhood of the steady state. The growth rate of y, $(1/y)dy/dt$, can be written as

$$\frac{(1/y)dy}{dt} = \frac{d \ln y}{dt} = \frac{d \ln(f(k))}{dt} = (1/y)f'(k)\frac{dk}{dt}$$
$$= \left(\frac{1}{y}\right)f'(k)[sf(k) - (a + \delta + n)k].$$

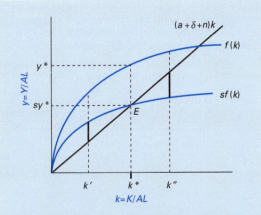

Figure A5.1. The Modified Solow Growth Model

Assuming that $f(k)$ can be inverted, we can write k as a function of y, $k = k(y)$, so

(A5.8) $$(1/y)\frac{dy}{dt} = G(y),$$

where the function

$$G(y) \equiv sf'(k(y)) - (a + \delta + n)\frac{f'(k(y))k(y)}{y}.$$

By definition of this function, $G(y^*) = 0$. Take a first-order Taylor approximation around $G(y^*)$ to obtain

$$\frac{d\ln y}{dt} = G'(y^*)(y - y^*)$$

$$= \left[sf''k' - (\alpha + \delta + n)\left(f''k'k + f'k' - \frac{f'k}{y^*} \right) \right]\frac{y - y^*}{y^*}.$$

Since $k'(y) = 1/f'(y)$ and $(y - y^*)/y^* \approx \ln y - \ln y^*$, we can rewrite

$$\frac{d\ln y}{dt}$$
$$= \left[\frac{sf'' - (\alpha + \delta + n)(f''k + f' - f'^2 k/y^*)}{f'} \right](\ln y - \ln y^*),$$

or, defining $\alpha_K = f'k/y$ as the income share of capital in national output at the steady state y^*,

$$\frac{d\ln y}{dt} = \left\{ \frac{f''}{f'}[sy^* - (a + \delta + n)k^*] \right.$$
$$\left. - (1 - \alpha_K)(a + \delta + n) \right\}(\ln y - \ln y^*).$$

Using (A5.7), this last expression can be rewritten as

(A5.9) $$\frac{d\ln y}{dt} = \lambda(\ln y^* - \ln y),$$

where $\lambda \equiv (1 - \alpha_K)(a + \delta + n)$. The parameter λ, which is positive, can be thought of as the 'speed of convergence', or the rate at which the gap $\ln y^* - \ln y$ is closed; when $y^* > y$, y is growing. The solution of the differential equation (A5.9) is

$$\ln y(t) = \ln y(0)e^{-\lambda t} + \ln y^*(1 - e^{-\lambda t}),$$

where $y(0)$ is the initial per capita GDP level and y^* is as before the corresponding steady-state value. Using the fact that $(y - y^*)/y^* \approx \ln y - \ln y^*$, this can be approximated by

(A5.10) $$y(t) = y(0)e^{-\lambda t} + y^*(1 - e^{-\lambda t}).$$

Note that $y(t)$ is a weighted average of the initial condition $y(0)$ and the steady-state $y(\infty) = y^*$.

Golden Rule Per Capita Capital Stock, Savings Rate, and Output

At each instant, effective per capita consumption is c, which in a closed economy without a government is given by $f(k) - (a + \delta + n)k$, or that output which is not diverted to capital formation. To find the characteristics of the steady-state path with the highest per capita consumption level, it is necessary to find the value k^{**} that solves the following problem:

$$\max_k c = f(k) - (a + \delta + n)k,$$

subject to a side condition that k is non-negative.[27] The first-order condition for an optimum is

(A5.11) $$f'(k^*) = (a + \delta + n).$$

(The second-order condition for a maximum is fulfilled as long as $f'' < 0$, which is assumed.) The intuition of (A5.11) is that consumption is maximized when the marginal consumption made possible by a higher level of capital intensity (the left-hand side) is equal to the 'cost' or the steady-state investment necessary to maintain that intensity (the right-hand side) or the sum of the growth rate of technical efficiency (A), the depreciation rate, and the population growth rate.

From (A5.7), the savings rate corresponding to k^{**} can be found to be

(A5.12) $$s^{**} = \frac{f'(k^{**})k^{**}}{f(k^{**})}.$$

Equation (A5.12) implies that per capita steady-state consumption is maximized when the savings rate is equal to the income share of capital, assuming that labour and capital are traded under conditions of perfect competition and receive their marginal products.[28] Finally, output is given by

(A5.12) $$y^{**} = f(k^{**}) = \frac{(a + \delta + n)k^{**}}{s^{**}}.$$

---

[27] Technical note: usually this problem, as well as those involving the uniqueness of the equilibrium, can be ruled out by the conditions $\lim_{k \to 0} f'(k) = \infty$, $\lim_{k \to \infty} f'(k) = 0$, as well as $k(0) = 0$.

[28] To see this, note that $s = F_K(K/AL, 1)(K/AL)/F(K/AL, 1) = F_K(K/AL, 1)K/F(K, AL) = F_K(K, AL)K/F(K, AL)$. The last step follows from the fact that F is homogeneous of degree 1, and that first partial derivatives of F are therefore homogeneous of degree 0.

6

Labour Markets and Equilibrium Unemployment

Labour is the source of all value.

Karl Marx

In our present day complicated economic life we are likely to be confused by the many industrial operations and money transactions. But net income remains exactly what it was to primitive Robinson Crusoe on his island—the enjoyment from eating the berries we pick, so to speak, less the discomfort or the labor of picking them.

Irving Fisher

6.1. Overview

In the last chapter, available output was determined by the endowment of capital and technical sophistication. The supply of labour was simply taken as given, regardless of the wage or other variables. At any moment of time, therefore, the economy relied on what history had left, i.e. capital, labour, and knowledge. In practice, however, income is not derived just from fixed endowments. Even in storybooks, life is not so simple: Robinson Crusoe had to expend time and effort to gather and transport the fruits that he would eventually consume. Indeed, most people are able to choose whether or not they will work, and sometimes how much they will work or at least how much effort they will put in their work. Households work so that they can consume, but they also desire to spend some time *not* working, which is called **leisure** or free time. The *supply* of labour is presented as a trade-off between consumption and leisure. Labour must also be in *demand*. For that, it must have value to firms. How the markets value labour and how demand and supply interact is the subject matter of this chapter.

This chapter deals with an important market. Marx had a point when he viewed labour as the most important factor of production. Everything we use stems from labour. Raw materials are drawn from the earth by human hands; equipment used in this process is produced from labour and previously manufactured equipment, itself the output of labourers and capital in a more distant past. Even the knowledge embodied in people—sometimes called 'human capital'—comes from our own efforts at mastering skills and techniques, as well as the time our teachers spend in trying to educate us.

As before, we begin the analysis by studying the behaviour of a representative household that supplies labour. Next, we look at demand by a representative firm. This naturally leads into the standard confrontation of demand and supply. Yet, the labour market is not a standard 'market'. Workers are not identical, and the quality of labour services is difficult to ascertain and harder to monitor. Unlike machines or raw materials, workers can decide whether they would like to work for a particular employer and under which conditions to render labour services. In fact, the employment relationship involves explicit and implicit contractual arrangements with durable features such as personal bonds or firm-specific competence and knowledge. The labour market is also characterized by unique institutions, such as labour law or collective bargaining, and is the object of complex legal and customary rules. Finally, the labour market is a dynamic market, with suppliers of labour entering and exiting unemployment at a remarkable rate. We show how these interactions help understand the concept of equilibrium unemployment, which may differ from actual unemployment.

6.2. Demand and Supply in the Labour Market

6.2.1. Labour Supply and the Labour–Leisure Trade-off

In order to consume, most households need income. In modern societies, earning income means working, or supplying labour to firms in return for a wage or salary. Supplying labour is something that millions of families do every day. Labour has a cost too: every hour worked is an hour less of free time. Because households value both consumption and leisure, they balance the two, just as they balance consumption of goods today against saving and goods tomorrow. As we focus on the **consumption–leisure trade-off**, we ignore the intertemporal aspects which were considered in Chapters 3, 4, and 5. In the now-familiar parable, Robinson Crusoe in this chapter is assumed to consume all that he earns during each period.

6.2.1.1. Preferences

Crusoe's preferences with regard to consumption and leisure are shown in Figure 6.1 using indifference

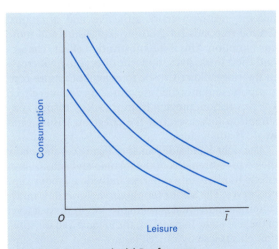

Figure 6.1. Household Preferences

An indifference curve shows the rate at which a representative household substitutes consumption for leisure, holding utility constant. Higher curves correspond to higher levels of utility. The maximum amount of time available is $\bar{\ell}$ hours.

curves.[1] Each indifference curve shows how readily Crusoe substitutes consumption for leisure, holding constant his level of utility or satisfaction. The shape of the indifference curves reflects a decreasing marginal rate of substitution: the greater a household's consumption relative to its leisure, the more consumption it is willing to give up for an additional unit of leisure, or the higher is the marginal rate of substitution of consumption for leisure. As always, higher indifference curves correspond to higher levels of utility.

6.2.1.2. The budget constraint

Crusoe's 'budget constraint' is fixed by the total amount of time, denoted $\bar{\ell}$, available over any given period (a day, a month, a year, or more). Time is a scarce resource and it has a price. The price of an hour of leisure is its opportunity cost: how much can be earned from working instead. Equivalently, the price of leisure is measured in terms of the consumption goods that cannot be consumed for lack of earned income: the price of leisure is then called the **real (consumption) wage**. In practice, it is measured as the ratio of nominal wages (W) to the consumer price index (P).

With $\bar{\ell}$ hours at his disposal and facing an hourly real wage $w = W/P$, the value of Crusoe's total time endowment in terms of consumption is $\bar{\ell}w$. The budget constraint states that this endowment can be allocated between consumption, with value C, and ℓ hours of leisure, with value ℓw.[2]

$$(6.1) \qquad \bar{\ell}w = \ell w + C.$$

Alternatively, the budget constraint can be expressed in terms of 'cash flow' (more accurately, coconut flow). When Crusoe spends ℓ hours of leisure, he works $\bar{\ell} - \ell$ hours and earns $w(\bar{\ell} - \ell)$ coconuts. Since Crusoe does not save, this income $w(\bar{\ell} - \ell)$ is spent on consumption; so

$$(6.2) \qquad w(\bar{\ell} - \ell) = C,$$

which is the same as (6.1). The budget constraint is shown in Figure 6.2 as AB. Its negative slope ($-w$)

---

[1] This is the same idea as in Ch. 4, except that here we look at two 'goods' in a given period, rather than at different points in time.

[2] The nominal budget constraint is $\bar{\ell}W = \ell W + PC$. To write it in terms of consumption goods as in (6.1), we simply divide by P, the price of consumption goods.

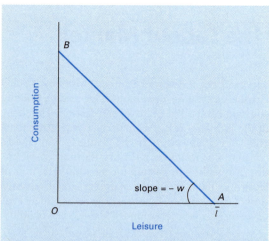

Figure 6.2. The Household Budget Constraint

The household has $\bar{\ell}$ hours at its disposal (measured by the distance *OA*) for either leisure or work. For every unit of leisure that it gives up, it can earn a quantity *w* of consumption goods. The real wage *w* determines the slope of the budget line *AB*.

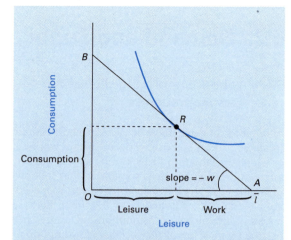

Figure 6.3. Optimal Choice

Given the budget constraint, the highest possible utility is achieved at point *R*, where an indifference curve is tangent to the budget line.

measures the trade-off of consumption for leisure offered by the market: how much consumption must be given up to get an additional unit of leisure. The distance *OA* is Crusoe's endowment of time, or the fixed number of hours he has at his disposal. The distance *OB* measures the value of that endowment in terms of consumption goods. It is the total amount of consumption attainable when leisure is zero. If Crusoe had inherited some initial wealth, the budget constraint would be shifted vertically by that amount, which he could consume without having to work at all. If the real wage changes, the budget line rotates around point *A*, which measures his time endowment $\bar{\ell}$. With a wage increase, for example, more consumption can be afforded (*OB* increases) and the budget line rotates clockwise. If instead the real wage falls, *OB* declines, and the line turns in a counter-clockwise direction.

6.2.1.3. Optimal choice: the individual labour supply schedule

Crusoe maximizes his utility by choosing the highest possible indifference curve without violating his budget constraint. This is achieved at point *R* in Figure 6.3, where the indifference curve is tangent to the budget line. At this point, given the going market wage *w*, he cannot make himself better off by further trading leisure against consumption: the marginal rate of

substitution of consumption for leisure and the wage are equal.

In the first panel of Figure 6.4, an increase in the real wage changes Crusoe's consumption–leisure choice from *R* to *R′*. It is useful to distinguish two effects. First, Crusoe faces a higher opportunity cost of leisure in terms of consumption goods. Work has become relatively more attractive and a rational Crusoe responds by choosing less leisure and more consumption. This is the **substitution effect**. The second effect works in the opposite direction. An increase in the wage allows Crusoe to enjoy both more consumption and more leisure: this is the **income effect**. For this reason, moving from *R* to *R′*, Crusoe's consumption increases, but the effect on leisure (and work) is ambiguous.

The right-hand side panels of Figure 6.4 show how the relative strengths of the income and substitution effects translate into different individual **labour supply curves**. The labour supply curve shows how much labour an individual is willing to supply at each level of the real wage. In panel (*a*) the income and substitution effects exactly cancel: leisure—and labour supply—remain unchanged. This is the 'benchmark' case where labour supply is inelastic, or unresponsive to the real wage. If the substitution effect predominates, Crusoe responds to higher real wages by reducing his leisure time: labour supply is elastic (panel (*b*)). In panel (*c*) the income effect dominates: both consumption and leisure increase. In this case labour supply is

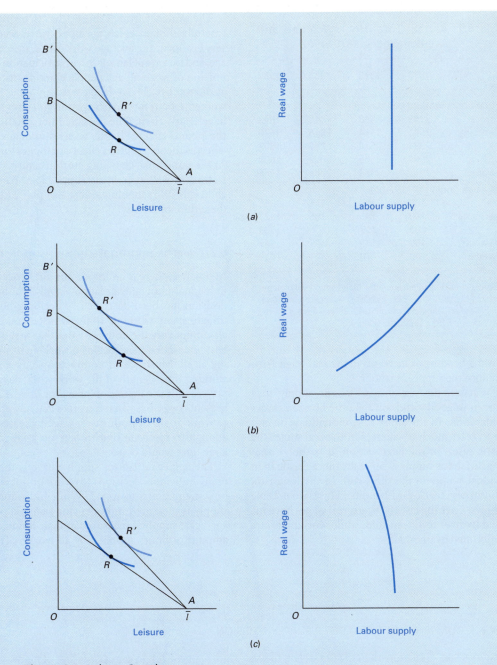

Figure 6.4. Labour Supply

When the real wage increases, the budget line rotates around point *A* (the endowment of time remains unchanged) and becomes steeper, because a unit of leisure is exchanged for more units of consumption. This allows both consumption and leisure to increase at the same time (income effect). Because leisure is more expensive, however, some is given up (substitution effect). In case (*a*) income and substitution effects exactly cancel in the left-hand panel and labour supply, shown in the right-hand panel, is vertical. In case (*b*) the substitution effect dominates, leisure is reduced, and the labour supply schedule is upward-sloping. In case (*c*) the income effect dominates, leisure increases, and labour supply is back-ward-bending.

Table 6.1. Annual Total Hours Worked and Average Wages, 1870–1987

	1870	1913	1938	1987
Annual hours worked per person				
France	2945	2588	1848	1543
Germany	2941	2584	2316	1620
UK	2984	2624	2267	1557
USA	2964	2605	2062	1608
Sweden	2945	2588	2204	1466
Real wage (index: 1870 = 100)				
France	100	205	335	1358
Germany	100	185	285	1227
UK	100	157	256	589
USA	100	189	325	643
Sweden	100	270	521	1439

Sources: Hours worked are from Maddison (1991); wages are from Mitchell (1978, 1983) and OECD, *Main Economic Indicators*; German wage data from 1913–38 are approximated using average labour productivity growth

backward-bending as increases in the real wage actually reduce the supply of labour.

In practice, the response of labour supply to a change in wages depends on the time horizon under consideration. In the short run, individuals do not seem to react much to changes in the real wage (the inelastic case). In the next section, it is shown that aggregate labour supply is generally more elastic than individual supply in the short run. In the long run, labour supply is backward-bending. This is what Table 6.1 shows. Over the last 100 years, real wages have increased by five- to fifteen-fold, while working hours have declined by one-half.

The evidence from Table 6.1 has to be interpreted carefully, though, as labour supply varies according to sex. For men, the average work-week, the retirement age, and the **rate of labour force participation** (the proportion of working-age people working or registered as unemployed) have fallen secularly since 1900. For women, labour force participation and hours per week have clearly risen. One possible interpretation is that the income effect of higher wages dominates for men, whereas the substitution effect dominates for women. At the same time, changing customs and sociological factors, as well as publicly supplied services such as child care and schooling, must also play a key role in these developments.

6.2.1.4. The aggregate labour supply curve

In practice, there is an important difference between individual and aggregate labour supply. The individual decision has been described as deciding how much time to spend working. In many instances, individuals cannot vary the hours of work that they supply; at best, they can choose between working or not working at all. Most labour contracts specify a standard working time (length of the work-week, days of leave per year). It is a matter of 'take it or leave it'. Box 6.1 presents two cases where a worker actually prefers not to work at all. In both cases, wage increases are not enough to motivate him to take up a job, although large ones would do so.

The aggregate labour supply curve is the sum of many individual decisions (to work or not work, and how many hours to work). While individual labour supply is measured in hours (for example per year), aggregate supply is measured in **man-hours**, the total amount of hours supplied by all workers (men and

BOX 6.1. LUMPINESS IN THE LABOUR SUPPLY DECISION

In Figure 6.5(*b*), Crusoe-the-Hermit is not willing to give up much leisure (lonely contemplation) for consumption. His indifference curve is too steep (his marginal rate of substitution of consumption for leisure is too high) for him to work at all at the going wage. He chooses corner point *A*. In panel (*a*) Crusoe has to commute to get to work, which costs him a quantity *AA'* of unpaid leisure. In this example, Crusoe chooses not to work unless the wage is sufficiently high. In both cases, there is a wage rate high enough to coax Crusoe out of his decision not to work. If the actual labour force consists of a mixture of workers of the types displayed in Figures 6.4 and 6.5, an increase in real wages will bring some individuals into work, while those already working may not vary their labour supply. A flatter aggregate supply curve will emerge from vertical or near-vertical individual supply curves.

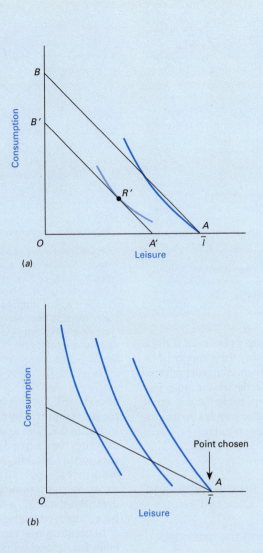

Figure 6.5. Crusoe Stays Home

Crusoe may decide not to work at all, choosing point A. In panel (a), going to work costs him AA' (time and transportation). If he stays home, only A is feasible; if he goes to work, his budget line is A'B', in which case R' is the best choice. He is better off at point A than at point R'. In panel (b), the real wage is simply too low to compensate his preference for leisure given by his indifference curves.

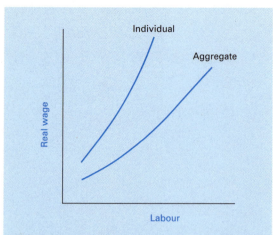

Figure 6.6. Individual and Aggregate Labour Supply

The aggregate labour supply curve is less steep than the individual one because new workers choose to enter the labour force as wages rise.

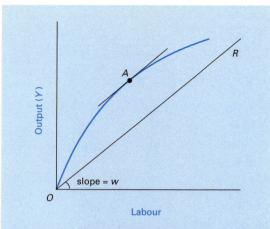

Figure 6.7. The Production Function

When more work is added, output increases but at a declining rate. This additional output is the marginal productivity of labour (MPL). The ray *OR* represents the cost of using *L* hours of work when the hourly real wage is *w*. The distance between the production curve and the cost line represents the firm's profit. It is at a maximum at point *A*, where the curve is parallel to *OR*, i.e. where MPL = *w*.

women, of course).[3] When wages rise, even if those who already work do not modify their supply of labour (the benchmark case), others who had preferred not to work now decide to join the labour force. Figure 6.6 shows how it is then possible for a steep or even vertical (inelastic) individual supply curve to co-exist with a flatter aggregate supply curve.

6.2.2. Labour Demand, Productivity, and Real Wages

6.2.2.1. Labour demand and the extended production function

The analysis of labour demand has already been discussed briefly in Chapter 5. It is virtually identical to the analysis in Chapter 4 of the optimal stock of capital, in which a representative firm takes employment as given. Here, the capital stock is given and we study the optimal demand for labour. When the capital stock is constant, the firm can change the amount of output produced by adjusting the amount of labour (man-

---

[3] Aggregate employment is sometimes measured as the number of people who have a job. Generally, we will use the first definition (man-hours), and make explicit mention when referring to the number of employed workers. Under any definition, when more workers enter the labour force, the labour supply curve shifts to the right independently of the wage level.

hours) used. The link between output *Y* and employment *L* is captured by the production function shown in Figure 6.7. The slope of the production function measures the **marginal productivity of labour** (MPL), the quantity of additional output obtained when one more unit of input (an hour) is used. The shape of the curve reflects the principle of decreasing marginal productivity; the MPL is declining as the amount of labour employed increases.

In deciding how much labour to employ, the firm looks for the highest possible profit given the hourly real wage *w*. The line *OR* represents the cost of labour to the firm: its slope is *w* since *L* hours of work cost *wL*. For each level of employment, profit is measured as the vertical distance between the curve depicting the production function and the labour cost line *OR*. It is at a maximum at point *A*, where the curve is parallel to *OR* and the MPL is equal to the real wage. If the MPL exceeds the real wage, hiring one more hour of work raises profits by MPL and costs by only *w*, implying an increase in profits. The firm would therefore hire the extra hour and would continue doing so until the MPL has declined to the point where it is equal to the real wage. In the opposite case, in which the real wage exceeds the MPL, the firm can increase its profit by reducing its demand for labour. Because

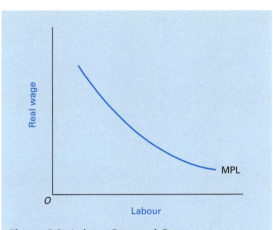

Figure 6.8. Labour Demand Curve

The firm maximizes profits when MPL = w, so its demand for labour is given by the declining marginal product of labour (MPL) curve.

it is optimal to set labour such that MPL = w, the MPL schedule in Figure 6.8 is also the **labour demand** curve.

6.2.2.2. Wage and profit shares

The portion of GDP that goes to workers is called the *wage share* and is given by wL/Y. The rest, the *profit*, or *capital share* $(1 - wL/Y)$, goes to firm owners.[4] Obviously, these two shares move in opposite directions. But what is the effect of an increase in wages on the labour share? At the given employment level L, labour costs (wL) rise because an hour of work (w) costs more. With higher wages, however, total employment (L) is reduced as firms move down their labour demand schedules. The effect on the numerator of the labour share is therefore ambiguous. At the same time, a decline in employment generally means a decline in output, and therefore a decline in the denominator. If the demand for labour is not very elastic, neither labour demand L nor output Y change much in response to an increase in the real wage. Then both total labour costs and the labour share increase, while the profit share declines.

Changes in the labour share are important for two reasons. First, the distribution of income between capital and labour has political elements that can affect the behaviour of governments. Second investment responds to profitability, which is related to the profit

share. Investment, in turn, affects growth.[5] When labour demand is rather inelastic, therefore, exogenous wage increases may reduce profitability, Tobin's q, investment, and the standard of living.

6.2.2.3. Shifts in the demand for labour

Now consider the effects of an increase in the capital stock K, which was assumed constant so far. Figure 6.9(a) shows that this normally raises MPL—the production function becomes steeper at every level of production. The labour demand curve shifts out in panel (b). A technological improvement that shifts out the production function produces a similar effect.[6] This helps account for the fact that wages have grown secularly over time.

6.2.3. Labour Market Equilibrium

We now have the building blocks for understanding the labour market: a supply curve derived from household behaviour, and a demand curve derived from firm behaviour. The interaction of supply and demand for labour is depicted in Figure 6.10. Equilibrium occurs at the intersection of the two curves (point A). At wage w^* the market clears (there is no excess demand or supply): L^* is the number of hours firms want to hire and households want to work. Both the real wage rate and employment are endogenously determined in the labour market.

This simple characterization of the labour market will serve as the benchmark for the rest of the chapter. Figure 6.11(a) provides an example of its usefulness. It depicts an increase in labour productivity, which has occurred over centuries as the result of capital accumulation and technological advances. The labour demand curve shifts outward; the supply curve is unaffected. The effect is an increase in living standards as real wages increase. If the labour supply curve is perfectly vertical, employment remains unchanged and labour income wL rises proportionally to the real wage. If the supply curve is backward-bending, employment

---

[4] This is not quite accurate: in fact, rental income, patent and royalty payments, and other minor factor incomes have been ignored.

[5] The inverse relationship between real wages and the profit share is illustrated in Ch. 1, Fig. 1.4. The link between investment and profits is studied in Ch. 4. The growth effects were analysed in Ch. 5. The Appendix presents a formalization of this section.

[6] Ch. 5 discussed technical change. An exception would be a *labour-saving* technical change, such as robots, which would reduce the demand for labour at any wage and shift back the demand for labour.

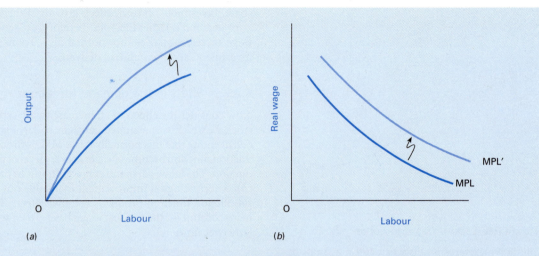

(a)   (b)

Figure 6.9. An Increase in Labour Productivity

Labour becomes more productive either because more capital is put in place or because of technological progress. In panel (a), at any level of labour input, more output is produced and the production function is everywhere steeper. The MPL increases and the demand for labour schedule shifts up in panel (b).

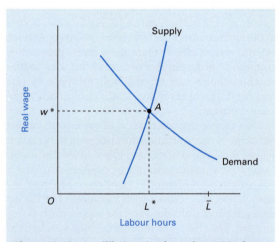

Figure 6.10. Equilibrium in the Labour Market

Labour market equilibrium occurs at point A where demand and supply are equal. The real wage w^* clears the market at employment level L^*. If total labour endowment is $\bar{L}$, the distance $(\bar{L} - L^*)$ is voluntary unemployment.

(man-hours) declines while real wages increase. Table 6.1 seems to indicate that this has been the case over the past century. The second panel of Figure 6.11 shows that an exogenous increase in the supply of la-

bour leads to an increase in employment in the short run, but also to a reduction in real wages.[7]

6.2.4. The Interpretation of Unemployment

While the supply-and-demand apparatus allows us to evaluate the effect of various changes on equilibrium employment and real wages, it is disappointing in one crucial respect. At point A in Figure 6.10, labour supplied is equal to labour demanded. Any unemployed resources correspond to voluntary decisions of households and firms. If total available labour supply is $\bar{L}$, unemployment (measured as hours of work not hired) is measured as $\bar{L} - L^*$. Since point A is on the labour supply curve, it corresponds to the optimal behaviour of households. The interpretation of Figure 6.10 is that the equilibrium real wage w^* is too low to persuade all workers to give up leisure: some may wish to work only part-time, others may not want to work at all.

It might be disturbing to think that unemployment could be chosen freely. Yet **voluntary unemployment** is an important phenomenon. It is not only the very

---

[7] Ch. 5 gives a longer-run perspective on the effects of exogenous increases in the working population.

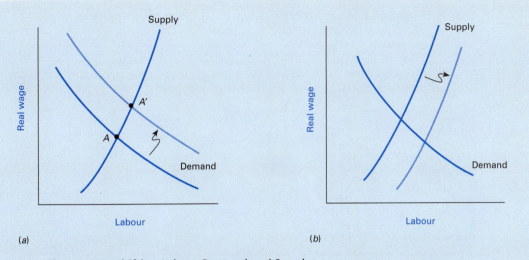

Figure 6.11. Shifting Labour Demand and Supply

When labour demand increases (panel (a)), for example because of additional capital or technological progress, the real wage and the employment level both increase. When labour supply increases instead (panel (b))—because of new entries into the labour force, for example—employment rises but the real wage declines.

wealthy who can afford not to work: those who receive an income from other sources (from a spouse or from the state, for example) may also find that the net wage they can earn does not compensate for lost leisure or nonmarket activities, including working at home or raising children. Voluntary unemployment is likely to be more widespread among low-skilled people who cannot hope to earn much, or in countries where taxes are so high that working yields little net gain.

Box 6.2 shows that it may actually be costly to take up a paid job. The most obvious costs are faced by families with children. The cost of child care—or simply the unavailability of such services—explains why two-earner families are not as common in some countries as in others. Table 6.2 presents the proportion of women of working age in the labour force, whether employed or not (the participation rate), the female unemployment rate, and the proportion of women of working age actually employed. The variation of these proportions is quite substantial across countries, and points to differences in both cultures and institutions. Female participation in the labour force is very high in countries like Denmark and Sweden, which have a highly developed and subsidized child care system.

BOX 6.2. HOW CAN A JOB COST MONEY?

The social systems of most countries share two institutional features. First, poor people receive transfers—income maintenance programmes—from the state. Second, income taxes are progressive: the rate of taxation increases as income rises. Taking up a job implies receiving a salary, but also paying taxes if the salary is high enough, and losing eligibility for income maintenance programmes. It is conceivable then that people can be financially worse off by taking a job, not to mention incurring a loss of leisure, and possibly some activity in the underground (shadow) economy. Implicitly, these people face an effective marginal tax rate—considering the overall effect of work on their income—in excess of 100%. A study in Britain in 1986 reveals that 2% of households faced a marginal tax rate of 60% and above, in some cases above 100%.

Table 6.2. Female Labour Force Participation Rates, Unemployment Rates, and Employment Ratios, 1993

	Participation rates	Unemployment rates	Employment ratios
Belgium[a]	54.1	9.5	46.4
Canada	65.3	10.5	58.4
France	59.0	13.8	50.9
Germany[b, c]	58.2	6.4	54.5
Ireland[b]	39.9	15.4	35.1
Luxemburg[b]	44.8	2.8	43.9
Netherlands[a]	55.5	7.3	50.6
Portugal	61.3	6.5	57.2
Spain	42.8	28.9	30.5
Sweden	75.7	6.6	70.7
UK	65.3	5.4	55.0
USA	69.1	6.5	64.6

[a] 1992   [b] 1991   [c] West Germany only
Source: OECD Labour Force Statistics

6.3. A Static Interpretation of Unemployment

Our first attempt at defining unemployment in the last section was somewhat unsatisfactory. Unemployment is more than simply labour voluntarily withheld from the market. The International Labour Organization (ILO) or the Organization for Economic Cooperation and Development (OECD) define an individual as unemployed if he does not have a job during the reference period *and* is actively looking for one *and* is ready to work.

The labour force is then defined as the part of the population (N) that is either working (L) or unemployed (U). The labour force mainly excludes young people in school, the retired, and those who do not wish to work. Thus we can write:

$$(6.3) \qquad \underset{\text{labour force}}{N} \; = \; \underset{\text{employment}}{L} \; + \; \underset{\text{unemployment}}{U}.$$

The rest of this chapter sets out to examine alternative reasons for unemployment as well as its implications for the well-being of society.

6.3.1. Involuntary Unemployment and Real Wage Adjustment

One interpretation of unemployment is the failure of markets to clear. In contrast with the assumption that real wages adjust to clear the labour market, Figure 6.12 considers the case where the real wage is fixed at w', which is higher than the market-clearing level w^*. At w' firms are willing to hire a quantity L' of labour, while workers supply L''. Since firms cannot be forced to hire more than they wish, actual employment is L', and $L'' - L'$ is labour supplied but not demanded by the market. If the real wage were to decline to w^*, demand would increase, supply would decrease, and full employment be restored at L^*.

In Figure 6.12, it is the failure of the real wage to decline that creates unemployment. **Involuntary unemployment** occurs when an individual is willing and able to work at the wage w' but cannot find a job, no matter how hard he or she tries. This is a key result: the existence of involuntary unemployment must be explained by **real wage rigidity**, which we examine next.

6.3.2. Collective Bargaining and Real Wage Rigidity

For sustained real wage rigidity to occur, market processes must be prevented from running their course. Somehow, involuntarily unemployed workers must be

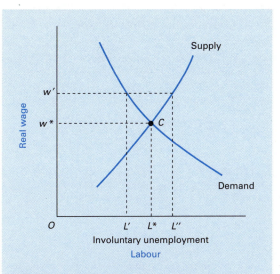

Figure 6.12. Involuntary Unemployment

At the real wage rate w' workers supply L'' of labour but firms demand, and hire, only L'. The quantity $L'' - L'$, which is supplied by households but not demanded by firms, represents involuntary unemployment. If the real wage were to adjust to the level w^*, the market would clear at point C.

unable to supply their labour services at wages below w^*, or firms must be unwilling to take up such offers, or be unable to make their own. What important institutional feature has been overlooked so far? **Labour unions** are one of the most fundamental and universal institutions that operate in modern economies. They are matched by equally powerful employers' associations, such as the CBI in the UK, the CNPF in France, the BDA in Germany, or the SAF in Sweden. The perfect-competition description of labour markets of Section 6.2 contrasts sharply with the bilateral bargaining commonly observed in Europe between employers and unions. We first characterize the economic role of trade unions to discover how unemployment can be voluntary from the perspective of trade unions and nevertheless be involuntary from the viewpoint of the individual household.[8]

6.3.2.1. Labour unions and their rationale

The employer–employee relationship has inherently conflictual aspects. One reason for this is the distribu-

tion of income; economic principles assert that income should be split according to marginal productivity, but marginal productivity is not easily measured, and economic principles are not always adhered to. Another more subtle reason is that firms need to monitor effort at work, a key element of productivity, which is under the control of each individual employee. Individual workers facing a large employer are in a poor bargaining position. They have little influence over their own wage rate and may not even feel safe discussing working conditions, fearing reprisals in the form of a salary cut or dismissal. They may also feel pressure from powerful employees to accept conditions that would not be acceptable under competitive conditions.

To resist such pressures, but especially to achieve higher pay levels and a voice in the day-to-day operation of the workplace, workers have organized themselves into trade or labour unions. As Table 6.3 shows, union organizations vary considerably from country to country. Scandinavian countries have a tradition of centralized unionization; Britain is organized according to craft; France, Italy, and Spain have unions with ties to political parties. These differences reflect social history as well as the costs and benefits associated with union membership. The costs are dues that members must pay. The benefits vary, ranging from higher wages and protection from arbitrary employer decisions to more specific advantages, including priority for certain jobs and income supplements when unions are on strike. In some countries, many advantages accrue to all workers, so there is little point in paying the union dues. This is the case in France, for example.[9] In other countries, such as Belgium and Scandinavia, unions manage funds that hand out some social benefits. In the USA, some unions even issue credit cards and provide other services to their members.

6.3.2.2. The economics of labour unions

Unions have two major economic objectives: higher real wages, and more jobs.[10] It is useful to think of their preferences in terms of indifference curves as shown in Figure 6.13. The slope of the indifference curve represents the willingness of the union leadership to trade off employment for wages. Panel (*a*) describes the average union which accepts a trade-off between employment and higher wages. A 'hard-line' union which

---

[8] It should be stressed that we limit ourselves strictly to the economic significance of trade unions. As the history of the labour movement amply demonstrates, unions have had an enormous influence on modern society which goes beyond economics.

[9] This is an example of the so-called free-rider problem. If no workers pay dues, the union disappears and no one is protected. So some workers must pay the dues for all to have a union.

[10] This is a simplification, of course. Unions care for other things too, such as safety at work, working time, workers' say in working conditions and organization.

Table 6.3. European Trade Unions: Structure and Membership, 1970 and 1988

Country	Structure and principal unions	Union density[a]	
		1970	1988
Austria	Umbrella/industrial (ÖGB)	59.8	45.7
Belgium	Party, religious (FGTB, CSC, CGSLB, CNC)	46.0	53.0
Denmark	Umbrella (LO)	60.0	73.2
Finland	Umbrella (SAK)	51.3	73.3[b]
France	Party, religious (CGT, CFDT, CFTC, GGC, FO)	22.3	12.0
West Germany	Umbrella/industrial (DGB, DAG)	33.0	33.8
Ireland	Mostly crafts in ICTU, fragmented	53.1	52.4[c]
Italy	Party, religious (CGIL, CISL, UIL)	36.9	39.6
Neth.	Party, religious (FNV, CNV, RMHP, AVC)	37.0	25.0
Norway	Umbrella (LO, AF, YS)	50.6	57.1[a]
Sweden	Umbrella (ILO, TCO, SACO/SR)	67.7	85.3
Switz.	Mostly plant-level (SGB)	30.7	26.0[b]
UK	Mostly crafts (96 in TUC, fragmented)	44.8	41.5
memo:			
USA	Mostly local plant-level (AFL–CIO)	22.8	16.4[a]

[a] Union density is the percentage of employed workers who are union members. (Unemployed workers are not counted.)
[b] 1989   [c] 1987

Sources: OECD, *Employment Outlook*, July 1991; Barnouin (1986); Roberts (1985)

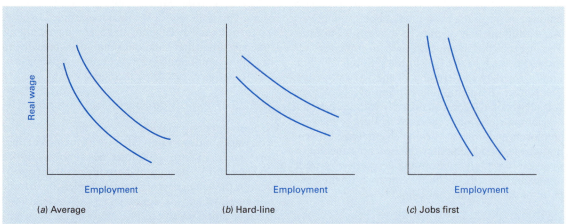

(a) Average   (b) Hard-line   (c) Jobs first

Figure 6.13. Trade Unions' Indifference Curves

When a trade union values both higher wages and more employment, its preferences are described by indifference curves. A 'hard-line' union is not willing to give up much in lower wages to raise employment. A union mainly preoccupied with employment is represented by steep indifference curves.

goes for high wages is represented in panel (*b*): here the curves are flatter as the union is not willing to give up much in terms of real wages for additional employment. A union that cares more about jobs than wages is characterized in panel (*c*) by steep indifference curves.

In contrast to Section 6.2, union indifference curves replace the representative individual's indifference curves, symbolizing the fact that the active agent in the labour market is not the individual, but his or her trade union—or, more generally, the collective bargaining process. The 'budget line' faced by the union is the demand for labour. From Section 6.2.2 we know that labour demand is given by the MPL (either a firm's

MPL, or that of an industry or the entire economy: if firms are all alike, their individual demand does not differ from the collective one defended by an employers' association).

The optimal choice for the union is the tangency point between the highest indifference curve and labour demand. When the demand for labour shifts out—as a result of capital accumulation or technological progress, for example—the succesive tangency points map out a **collective labour supply curve** as represented in Figure 6.14. The curve describes the most desired joint evolution of real wages and employment from the union's viewpoint.

The shape of the collective labour supply curve

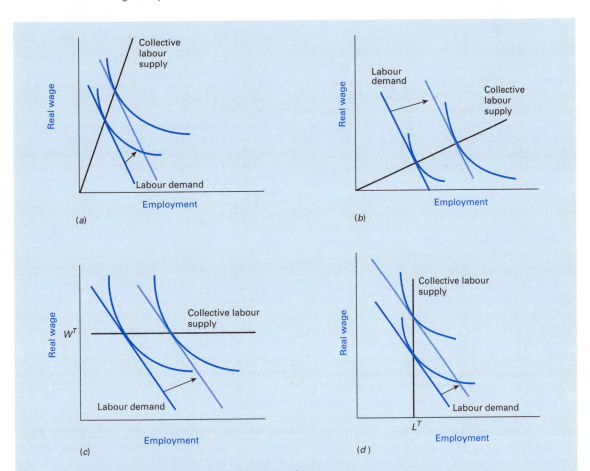

Figure 6.14. The Collective Labour Supply Curve

The collective labour supply curve is obtained by connecting the points of tangency between the indifference curves and a shifting labour demand schedule. Panels (*c*) and (*d*) respectively describe unions with a target wage level w^T and target employment level L^T. Panels (*a*) and (*d*) give rise to steep schedules, whereas (*b*) and (*c*) are associated with real wage rigidity and a more elastic supply of labour.

reflects the preferences of the union, as shown by the various panels of Figure 6.14.[11] Panel (*a*) is an example of a 'hard-line' union with a steep trade-off of wages for employment; panel (*b*) is the counter-example of a 'jobs-first' union requiring only moderate wage increases to supply more labour. Panel (*c*) shows a union with a well defined real wage target ready to accept a wide latitude of employment outcomes, yielding a flat collective labour supply curve at the target level. The other extreme is panel (*d*), which aims at a given level of employment, and is willing to set wages at whatever level is necessary to keep this group employed.[12] The appendix provides a formalization of these ideas.

6.3.2.3. Employment effects of collective bargaining

The collective labour supply curve resembles the individual supply curve of Figure 6.6, but has different origins. Collectively, through their unions, workers feel that they have more strength and accordingly aim at better outcomes. In particular, for a given amount of labour supplied, they ask for higher real wages: the union-driven collective labour supply curve lies above the individual labour supply curves. In Figure 6.15, without the union equilibrium would occur at point *B*: individuals would be willing to provide employment L_2 at wage w_2. They cannot, however, because the wage w_1 is set through negotiations between the firms and the trade union, and individuals cannot simply underbid their employed colleagues. Unemployment $(L_1' - L_1)$ is involuntary for affected individuals, but voluntary from the union's point of view.

Why do unions enforce wage rigidity apparently against the will of unemployed workers? One reason is that the leadership is elected by the employed. Unemployed workers are always a small minority of the membership, even at record high unemployment rates of 10% or even 20%. Furthermore, unemployed workers often give up their membership or lose interest in union affairs. Unions end up representing those who work, not those who are unemployed. Employed workers look for high real wages (for themselves) at the cost of some unemployment (for others). Box 6.3 illustrates how the relentless rise of unemployment in Europe after the two oil shocks can be explained by this effect.

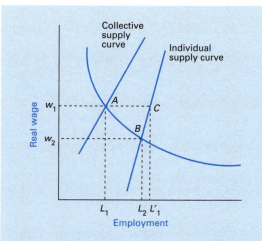

Figure 6.15. Labour Market with a Trade Union

When a labour union represents workers at wage negotiations, labour market equilibrium occurs at point *A*. If the union collective labour supply curve is above the individual labour supply curve, the real wage w_1 is higher and employment L_1 (hours or number of workers) lower than at point *B*, which would be the outcome if individuals were negotiating individually. The result is the existence of **union-voluntary, individual-involuntary unemployment** $(L_1' - L_1)$: it is the difference between actual employment L_1 and the amount of work L_1' that workers are individually willing to supply at the real wage rate w_1.

The split between unions and unemployed workers cannot go too far, though. After unemployment increased to high levels in Europe in the 1970s and 1980s, unions have become more employment-conscious and real wage growth has moderated. One reason is that members become worried that they too might become unemployed. Another is that the loss in membership revealed in Table 6.3 above has meant lower income for the union from dues as well as less overall influence.

It would be unfair to assert that unions are solely responsible for real wage rigidity. As mentioned above, employers' associations often represent the interests of firms. They provide a means for policing collective bargaining agreements reached with unions. In the end, employers' associations do not control the demand for labour: this is the prerogative of the individual companies. While it is in firms' interest to keep wages low, it is also in their interest to keep the wages of their competition high, or at least to prevent their competitors from hiring cheap labour. Thus, employers' associations also contribute to real wage rigidity.

---

[11] A technical note: this is true only for a given shift of the labour demand curve. Here we consider only parallel shifts; one could imagine however, that other types of shifts would change both the position *and* the slope of the labour demand curve.

[12] This group may be the current union members, or the subset of the membership that is employed, or some core of so-called 'insiders', those members with sufficient seniority.

BOX 6.3. THE HYSTERESIS EFFECT

The two oil shocks of the mid-1970s and early 1980s correspond to a significant inward shift of the aggregate labour demand curve in Figure 6.15, hence to less employment. If trade unions respond to a narrower membership by calling for higher wages, the collective labour supply curve shifts upward. Owing to the behaviour of the 'insiders' who have jobs, employment prospects for 'outsiders' are reduced. After the oil shocks are absorbed, the employment level is permanently reduced. That such an effect—dubbed the 'hysteresis effect'—has been observed in several European countries is suggested by the step-wise increase in the unemployment rate following each oil shock (Figure 6.16). In contrast, in the USA and Japan, where unions may have been less 'hard-line', unemployment rates increased at the time of each oil shock but then reverted towards earlier levels.

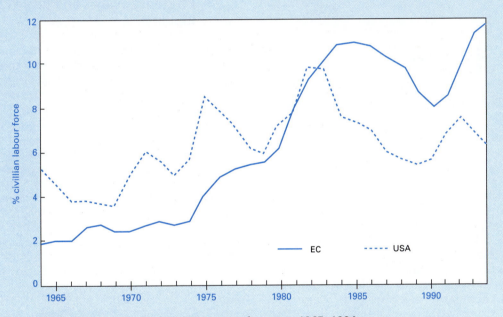

Figure 6.16. Hysteresis in EC/EU Unemployment, 1965–1994

The unemployment rate increased in both the EC/EU and the USA after the two oil shocks. In the USA the rate has since come down, to about where it was in the early 1970s. In the EC/EU, the unemployment rate seems to suffer from hysteresis, stabilizing wherever unexpected shocks move it.

Source: IMF, *World Economic Outlook*, October 1995

6.3.3. Social Minima and Real Wage Rigidity

Involuntary unemployment occurs when real wages are downwardly rigid. Beyond monopolistic behaviour by trade unions and employers' associations, several other institutional and economic factors contribute to wage rigidity. Among institutional factors frequently suspected are social minima, or minimum standards for income and earnings mandated by the government for reasons of social equity or protection.

Minimum wages prevent wages from declining below some level. Many countries legislated minimum wages long ago for a variety of reasons. One was to prevent employers with too much market power from depressing wages artificially. Another reason was to protect young people from exploitation. With schooling rudimentary and poverty endemic, for many youngsters on-the-job training was the only way to get started; unscrupulous employers would offer very low wages, sometimes below minimal survival needs. Social protection was and still is justified; but, paradoxically,

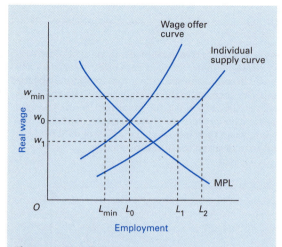

Figure 6.17. Minimum Wages

Minimum wages reduce the demand for labour below the level that would result with either union-negotiated wages or individual-supplied labour.

To serve any purpose at all, the minimum wage w_{min} must be higher than the wage w_0 that would obtain otherwise, and which is itself higher than what individuals would accept (w_1) if only to cover their part of the cost of investing in human capital. The result is unemployment ($L_2 - L_{min}$) even higher than the level ($L_1 - L_0$) implied by the union-set wage. Some evidence on the effect of minimum wages is presented in Box 6.4.

6.3.4. Efficiency Wages and Real Wage Rigidity

Another reason why real wages may not decline in the presence of involuntary unemployment is that firms do not wish to reduce them. The phenomenon is often called **efficiency wages**, and it is related to the difficulty for firms to observe work effort. By paying a worker a wage in excess of his marginal productivity, firms may attempt to elicit more work. A worker who is dismissed for lack of effort is unlikely to obtain such a good deal elsewhere, especially if dismissals are interpreted as a sign of poor work effort. Firms may also pay efficiency wages to obtain a better selection of applicants and to keep workers from quitting too often.

In capital-intensive industries, where shirking could seriously disrupt the production process and where a high-quality work-force is of primary importance, firms have a strong incentive to offer efficiency wages. In this case, the function of real wages is not just to equate demand and supply in labour markets. As a result, wages will not generally be able to satisfy both functions. Real wages will tend to be rigid and may be set above the market-clearing level, as in Figure 6.15.

youth unemployment may be exacerbated by minimum wages. Their effect is to deter firms from hiring workers whose MPL is below the minimum wage rate. Those most likely to be hurt are poorly educated young people with no job experience and older workers with obsolete skills. The effect is quite widespread, because, once a floor is set, it pushes up the lower echelons of the wage pyramid, possibly affecting better qualified workers as well. The range of qualifications for which the MPL is below the real wage is wider than just the very lowest echelons.

Figure 6.17 illustrates the effect of minimum wages.

6.4. A Dynamic Interpretation of Unemployment

6.4.1. Labour Market States and Transitions

Any person can find herself in one of three situations: employed, unemployed, or out of the labour force. Figure 6.18 displays these three states and the various flows that describe how workers shift from one situation to another. A striking aspect of labour markets in developed economies is the size of these flows. Table 6.5 shows that the flow of individuals moving into and out of unemployment per year is almost twice the stock of unemployment at any given time. In contrast to the static picture painted in Section 6.3, labour markets are remarkably dynamic, even when unemployment is high and stable.

There are three ways of becoming unemployed. First, new entrants to the labour market join the labour force before they have found a job but are unsuccessful, at least initially. Second are **separations** from jobs. Voluntary separations from the employee viewpoint (quits) account for roughly 50% to 66% of all separations from employment in the UK, and up to 70% in the USA. Yet quits rarely lead to unemployment: most workers who quit immediately take up

BOX 6.4. MINIMUM WAGES AND YOUTH UNEMPLOYMENT

It is striking that teenagers in the USA often work during the summer when their European counterparts go on vacation. One reason might be that wages that must be paid for young, unskilled labour are too high in Europe. The US minimum wage amounts to about a third of the average manufacturing wage, while in many European countries it exceeds 50%. This is one reason why filling station attendants and grocery shop assistants have all but disappeared in most European countries. Table 6.4 shows non-employment and unemployment rates for young people in a number of countries as well as the average minimum wage as a fraction of the average wage. In interpreting the table, it is important to note that Denmark exempts those below 18 from collective bargaining agreements. The UK does not have a minimum wage, and teenagers are generally not unionized.

It is especially noteworthy that in France, Belgium, the Netherlands, and Portugal, the minimum wage as a fraction of the median wage is high, meaning that a great many jobs are paid the minimum wage.

In France the minimum wage, called the SMIC (Salaire Minimum Interpersonel de Croissance), is an important element of the collective bargaining system. It is set by a council on which both the government and unions are represented. Many government employees receive the SMIC. In 1987, roughly 8% of wage-earners in industry, commerce, and services were covered by the SMIC, a much higher proportion than in the USA (less than 4%).

While the minimum wage in general has a negative effect on youth employment, it may lead to a substitution of adults for youths, at the same time increasing the employment of the former.

Table 6.4. Youth Unemployment and Minimum Wages, 1990

	Minimum wage as % of:		Nonemployment ratio[a]		Unemployment rate
	Average wage	Median wage	Age 14–19	Age 20–24	Age 20–24
Belgium	—	66	94.1	46.6	13.0
Canada	34	—	45.2	21.4	11.7
Denmark	None[b]		47.9	29.2	14.4
France	49	61	91.4	46.0	18.5
Germany	None[c]		70.2	29.0	3.8
Italy	None[c]		86.3	50.6	26.6
Netherlands	56	72	68.7	31.6	8.9
Portugal	—	74	65.7	32.1	8.6
Spain	34[d]	—	70.0	34.1	30.6
UK	None		49.3	29.3	13.1
USA	40	—	48.2	24.2	8.8

[a] The nonemployment ratio is defined as the fraction of the population in the specified age bracket that is currently not employed.
[b] Youths under 18 are exempted from union wage agreements.
[c] Union agreements restrict employment of youths in industry and many service sectors.
[d] 1990.

Sources: OECD Jobs Study (1994), Part II; S. Bazen and G. Benhayoun, 'Low Pay and Wage Regulation in the European Community', *British Journal of Industrial Relations*, 30 (1992): 623–38; Eurostat; OECD *Employment Outlook*, 1995; *Labour Force Statistics*, 1971–91

another job (transition from employment to employment) and most of those who do not get a new job leave the labour force, often for reasons of pregnancy, return to school, retirement, etc. Finally, job losers—those who are *in*voluntarily separated—tend to flow into unemployment. Job loss may occur when short-term contracts expire (common in France and Spain), factories close or relocate, or because of layoffs (more common in the USA and Denmark).

6.4.2. Stocks, Flows, and Frictional Unemployment

The fact that no two positions and no two persons are the same means that finding a job is not always easy and may take time. It requires pairing a worker and an unfilled job opening or vacancy. The matching of skills, occupation, industry, and geographical location requires a large amount of information. The more

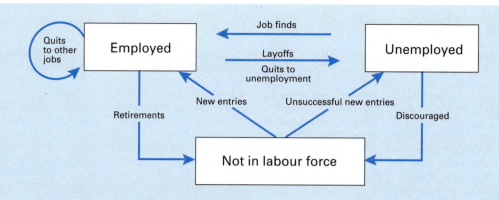

Figure 6.18. A Map of Labour Markets

Every individual is in one of three states: employed, unemployed, or out of the labour force. At any time, large numbers of workers are flowing from one state to another.

Table 6.5. Unemployment: Flows and Stocks in 1987 (millions)

	Unemployment flows		
	Into unempl.	Out of unempl.	Unemployment stocks
France	4.12	4.13	2.73
Germany	3.73	3.64	2.50
UK	3.03	3.48	2.70

Source: Burda and Wyplosz (1994)

efficient the labour markets are, the faster the match is achieved. In the mean time, **frictional unemployment** occurs. This is an unavoidable result of the dynamics of labour force movements, the normal process of job loss and creation.

In addition to the efficiency of the job matching process, frictional unemployment depends on the number of job separations and the number of vacancies. If we ignore the flows from and to 'Not in the labour force' in Figure 6.18, the number of workers who become unemployed (per month or per year) represents a fraction s, called the **separation rate**, of existing jobs (L). While unemployment rises by sL workers, it declines as unemployed workers find jobs. If we use f to denote the job **finding rate**, i.e. the fraction of the unemployed (U) who go into employment, the change in unemployment in a given period is given by

$$(6.4) \qquad \Delta U = sL - fU.$$

Frictional unemployment can be understood as the stock U_f unemployment that is expected to occur, on average, when unemployment remains steady. Equality of flows into and out of unemployment occurs when $\Delta U = 0$ in (6.4), or when

$$(6.5) \qquad U^f = \frac{s}{f}L.$$

It is convenient to express unemployment as a proportion of the labour force $N = L + U$. Then (6.5) shows that the frictional *rate* of unemployment is[13]

$$(6.6) \qquad u^f = U^f/N = \frac{s}{s+f}.$$

Both separation and finding rates can be interpreted as probabilities: the average probability s of losing a job when currently employed, and the average probability f of finding a job when unemployed.[14] Frictional unemployment is larger, the less frequent are job finds and the more frequent are job separations.

The separation rate s has two components: structural and cyclical. The structural aspect is linked to the ease with which firms dismiss workers. It is lower in countries where legal and social restrictions exist (as in most European countries) than in countries where redundancies are more acceptable (e.g. the UK and

---

[13] Since $N = L + U$ (see (6.3)), $1 = (L/N) + (U/N)$. Dividing (6.5) by N, and substituting $L/N = 1 - u$ gives (6.6).

[14] Naturally, as averages, these tend to obscure the large degree of heterogeneity: some individuals find a job readily after becoming unemployed, whereas others may have very low probabilities of exiting unemployment.

Table 6.6. Inflows into Unemployment and Unemployment Rates in the UK

	Inflow rate into unemployment (% per month)	Unemployment rate (% of relevant labour force)
By region: Britain, 1988		
South East	0.80	5.3
East Anglia	0.83	4.9
South West	1.03	6.2
West Midlands	0.97	9.0
East Midlands	0.97	7.5
Yorkshire/Humberside	1.20	9.7
North West	1.30	10.9
North	1.47	12.2
Wales	1.40	10.6
Scotland	1.50	11.7
TOTAL	1.07	8.0
By demographic group: UK, 1984		
Aged 16–19	3.33	22.1
Aged 20–24	1.33	16.9
Aged 25–54	0.74	8.8
Aged 55–64	0.47	8.3
White	0.92	10.4
Non-white	1.43	20.1
Male	0.78	11.2
Female	1.17	10.2
By skill: UK, 1984		
Professional/managerial	0.50	5.3
Clerical	0.88	8.0
Other non-manual	1.14	12.2
Skilled manual	1.02	12.6
Other manual	1.32	15.5

Source: Layard *et al.* (1991)

the USA). The cyclical aspect simply refers to the fact that during recessions the probability of losing a job rises and so, therefore, does frictional unemployment.

Table 6.6 shows that for a given country (the UK), job separation rates vary considerably across, age, region, and skill groups. Those specific labour force groups that exhibit higher separation rates of inflow into unemployment have higher frictional, and probably therefore overall, unemployment rates.

6.4.3. Job Finding and the Duration of Unemployment

The finding rate f depends on the effectiveness of the matching process. It depends on how hard unem-

ployed workers look for jobs, how many job openings are available, and how easy it is to spot an opportunity. It may also depend on incentives to remain unemployed, and unemployment insurance may therefore exert a perverse effect. Because unemployment often represents personal trauma, **unemployment benefits** or assistance respond to a widely perceived need for solidarity and social conscience. Table 6.7 shows that unemployment benefit systems vary considerably from country to country, with respect to eligibility criteria, income replacement, and the period over which they are paid.

At the same time, unemployment benefits have adverse side-effects. They may encourage unemployed workers in declining industries to wait for an unlikely recovery rather than to retrain and change sectors. They also act as a disincentive for looking for a job, or

Table 6.7. Unemployment: Conditions for Eligibility and Benefits

	Eligibility conditions[a]		Maximum duration[b]		Replacement rate[c]	
	Employment	Period	Benefit	Assistance	Single	Married
Austria	156 wks	5 yrs	30 wks	∞	41	44
Belgium	90 wks	27 mos.	∞		60	60
Denmark	(d)	3 yrs	30 mos.	∞	64	64
Finland	(d)	4 yrs	2 yrs	∞	59	59
France	12 mos.	24 mos.	30 mos.	∞	59	59
Germany	3 yrs	4 yrs	12 mos.	∞	58	58
Greece	7 mos.	12 mos.	5 mos.		50	50
Ireland	48 wks.	1 yrs	15 mos.	∞	29	43
Italy	1 yrs	2 yrs	6 mos.		15	15
Netherlands	3 yrs	5 yrs	38 mos.		70	70
Norway	(d)	2 yrs	80 wks		62	62
Spain	48 mos.	48 mos.	24 mos.		62	80
Sweden	5 mos.	12 mos.	60 wks		90	90
Switzerland	12 mos.	2 yrs	50 wks		70	70
UK	11 wks[e]	1 yrs	52 wks	∞	16	26
USA	20 wks	1 yrs	26 wks		50	50

Notes: Situation on 1 Jan. 1989 for a worker 40 years old. 'Married' refers to dependent spouse and no children.

[a] Required period of employment during a reference period for maximum duration of benefits (e.g. to qualify an Austrian worker must have been working for at least 156 wks over 5 yrs before becoming unemployed).

[b] Period of eligibility for maximum unemployment benefits and follow-up assistance.

[c] Ratio of maximum benefits to previous earning (both before tax).

[d] Denmark, Finland, and Norway use a rolling reference period system.

[e] The criterion is a level of insurance contribution amounting to about 11 wks in most cases.

∞ = indefinitely.

Source: OECD, *Employment Outlook*, July 1991

---

as an incentive for being 'choosier'.[15] If the benefits are generous, and particularly if they are long-lasting, some unemployed workers may require longer to find a job that they are willing to accept. This is especially true for low wage-earners (see Box 6.2). As can be seen in Figure 6.19, there is a tendency for people to remain unemployed longer in countries where unemployment benefits are more generous, paying more income over longer periods. As the finding rate declines, frictional unemployment rises. This confirms an uncomfortable trade-off between social concern and economic efficiency.

[15] Strictly speaking, this applies only to those who already qualify for benefits. In many European countries and the USA, prior work experience is required before one can draw unemployment insurance benefits. In this case, individuals will be more willing to accept the first job. This is often called the 'entitlement effect'.

6.5. The Equilibrium Rate of Unemployment

6.5.1. The Concept

If all unemployment were voluntary, it would hardly attract any attention. High and mostly involuntary unemployment means that labour markets do not function like other markets. A large number of imperfections, arising from both economic and institutional factors, forces us to qualify the pure-competition paradigm of Section 6.2 and to consider an alternative definition of equilibrium to the equality of demand for labour by firms and the supply of labour by households.

Labour market equilibrium occurs when the unemployment rate stabilizes. Because of imperfections, labour markets may be in equilibrium and yet unemployment may not be limited to voluntary unemploy-ment. **Equilibrium unemployment** can be viewed as the sum of frictional and structural unemployment:

(6.7)   Equilibrium unemployment
         = frictional unemployment
         + Structural unemployment.

Frictional unemployment occurs because it takes time for a match to occur between a worker seeking a job and a vacancy needing to be filled. It depends on the efficiency of the labour market, including the eagerness of both parties to find a match quickly. The frictional unemployment rate may well vary over time, not just because the market's efficiency changes but because economic conditions make it more or less likely for people to find jobs or to become unemployed.

Structural unemployment has many causes. The common thread is that the supply of labour is mediated by a number of institutions and regulations. Collective labour supply, which is brought into balance with labour demand in equilibrium, does not quite match individual supply behaviour. Some workers are involuntarily unemployed even when real wages equate the collective supply of labour with the demand of firms.

Estimates of equilibrium rates of unemployment are provided in Table 6.8. The contrast between Europe and North America is striking. The equilibrium unemployment rate was generally very low in Europe in the 1960s. Since then it has risen considerably while remaining stable in the USA. A comparison of Table 6.8 and Figure 6.16 shows that actual unemployment

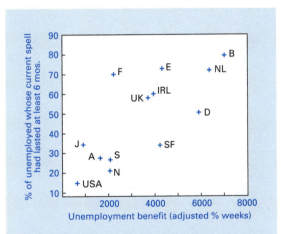

Figure 6.19. Long-term Unemployment Rates and the Generosity of Unemployment Insurance, 1985

The generosity of unemployment insurance systems is calculated as the maximum amount that someone who becomes unemployed can expect to receive. Generosity depends on the level of the benefits and on the period of time over which they are served. The diagram indicates that where the system is more generous the proportion of long-term unemployed in the total population of unemployed tends to rise.

Source: Burda (1988)

Table 6.8. Estimates of Equilibrium Rates of Unemployment

	1966–75	1976–85	1986–95
Germany	1.2	4.9	7.1
Italy	5.9	8.3	11.3
Japan	1.6[a]	2.1	2.5
Spain	2.9[b]	11.6	20.1
UK	2.6	7.1	8.4
USA	5.2	7.5	6.3

[a] 1968–75; [b] 1967–75.

Source: OECD

BOX 6.5. THE EUROPEAN WAGE SHOCK AND EUROSCLEROSIS

The 1960s witnessed an increase in trade union militancy in several European countries. The May 1968 general strike in France was soon followed by labour unrest in Italy, Belgium, and Germany. In the UK, these were the years when Marxist-led unions exerted influence on the ruling Labour Party. 'Hardline' European unions succeeded in pushing real wages higher and increasing their downward rigidity. Figure 6.20 illustrates the effects of the wage shock by providing a comparison with the USA. The persistence of high unemployment despite improved economic conditions is a consequence of the limited job creation reported in the figure. This dismal performance led to the depressing bout of 'Eurosclerosis' in the early 1980s.[16] Facing an apparently unstoppable rising tide of unemployment, many leaders simply accepted it as structural, and therefore beyond policy influence. Yet unions cannot overlook completely the plight of the unemployed. Over the latter part of the 1980s, unions gradually bowed to market pressure and in some countries, such as Mrs Thatcher's UK, to political pressure too. As real wage growth has slowed down, employment has started to grow faster, allowing a decline in the rate of unemployment.

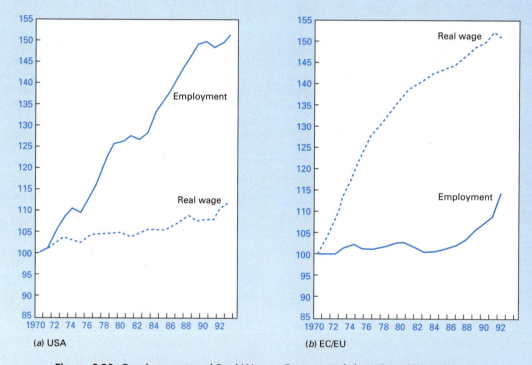

(a) USA   (b) EC/EU

Figure 6.20. Employment and Real Wages: Europe and the USA, 1970–1992

Over the period 1970–92, real wages increased by more than 50% in Europe while employment stagnated. At the same time, as real wages stagnated in the USA, employment rose by 50%. (Real wages = total compensation per employee deflated by the GDP deflator.)

Source: OECD, *The OECD Job Study* (1994)

has followed the same pattern. To begin to understand this dramatic evolution, we return to the two components of the equilibrium rate of unemployment.

[16] The term 'Eurosclerosis' was coined by German economist Herbert Giersch of the Kiel Institute of World Economics.

6.5.2. The European Experience

The evidence suggests that European unemployment rose when large numbers of workers lost their jobs at the time of the oil shocks. The expected subsequent return to pre-oil-shock levels has been thwarted in many EC countries by a fall in the finding rate, so exit from unemployment has become increasingly harder. Is the development of the social safety net to be blamed for having provided workers with the incentive to wait out their unemployment? Circumstantial evidence— for example Figure 6.20—points in that direction when based on a comparison between Europe, where the safety net has become extensive, and the USA. Yet there is some disturbing counter-evidence. The social safety net is even more developed in Sweden and Norway, where long-term unemployment has remained lower. This implies that what really matters is not the safety net itself, but the disincentives that it may generate. Unemployment benefits, for example, provide an alternative to finding a job, and help transform temporary unemployment into permanent—structural—unemployment. Long-term unemployment has become increasingly widespread, and as workers gradually lose their human capital and contact with the active labour force, they become unsuitable for any vacancy.

The strikingly different evolution of the equilibrium unemployment rate across countries also points to the importance of institutions in shaping the levels of wages. This concerns the process of wage bargaining. The comparison between the EC and the USA in Box 6.5 shows that high unemployment in the EC is related to steep real wage increases, amounting to what has been dubbed the European 'wage shock'. Labour costs consist not only of wages: labour taxes (social security and retirement contributions) have also been allowed to rise steeply. Of importance too is the regulation of the use of labour (length of the work-week, dismissal procedures, part-time work, etc.).[17]

6.5.3. Actual and Equilibrium Unemployment[18]

It can take a long time, often years, before real wages actually adjust to their long-run values shown in Figures 6.10 and 6.15. In the meantime, actual unemployment can deviate from equilibrium unemployment.

[17] Ch. 17 provides a more detailed exposition.
[18] This section briefly presents an issue to be explored at length in Ch. 12.

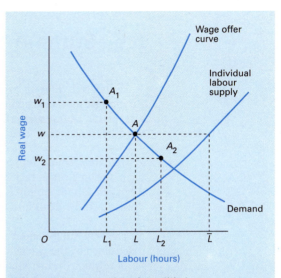

Figure 6.21. Actual and Equilibrium Employment

When unions negotiate on behalf of workers, market equilibrium occurs at point A, and equilibrium unemployment is $L - \bar{L}$. Actual employment and unemployment may differ if the real wage is slow to move to its equilibrium level w. If it is above the market equilibrium level ($w_1 > w$), firms reduce employment to L_1 and actual unemployment exceeds equilibrium unemployment. Conversely, below-equilibrium real wages ($w_2 < w$) allow firms temporarily to find a way of connecting with structurally unemployed workers willing to work at lower wages than the union-set level. The resulting unemployment rate is lower than the equilibrium level.

Actual employment is below, and actual unemployment above, equilibrium when the real wage is above the equilibrium level, as at point A_1 in Figure 6.21. When the real wage is low, firms may be able temporarily to move away from the union-set collective labour supply curve towards the individual labour supply curve (point A_2), for example by using agencies specializing in temporary jobs or overtime work. Workers may have overestimated the real wage by underestimating the rise in the price level. Firms may be willing to hire more workers at the going wage. In such situations employment is above, and unemployment below, the equilibrium level.

6.6. Summary

1. Households trade off leisure against consumption (more generally, labour income). An increase in wages can induce more labour supply if the substitution effect dominates (elastic labour supply), less labour supply if the income effect dominates (backward-bending), or no change at all (inelastic supply).

2. Individual labour supply seems to be inelastic in the short run and backward-bending in the long run as real wage gains are taken partly in the form of additional leisure. Aggregate labour supply is more responsive in the short run as real wage increases draw new individuals into the labour force.

3. The demand for labour by firms depends on its (marginal) productivity which is determined by the available technology and the capital stock. Firms hire labour to the point at which the marginal productivity of labour is equal to the real wage. The labour demand schedule is shifted outwards by an improvement in technology or an increase in the capital stock.

4. Equilibrium employment and the wage level are given by the intersection of labour demand and labour supply. Improvements in technology or increases in capital will be reflected in higher wages if labour supply is inelastic, and in higher employment if labour supply is elastic.

5. Involuntary unemployment arises when real wages do not clear the market so that not all labour supplied by households is actually hired.

6. Labour unions care about real wages and employment. In determining their target wage, given the demand for labour firms, they ask for higher real wages than if the labour market were perfectly competitive. While the resulting unemployment rate is (optimal and) voluntary for unions, it may be involuntary for individuals.

7. Very centralized or decentralized wage negotiations deliver lower real wages and less unemployment than negotiations taking place at intermediate levels of centralization (industry by industry, or by craft).

8. Because firms cannot easily monitor work effort or wish to elicit lower turnover or improve worker quality, they may offer efficiency wages. This is yet another reason why real wages may be set above market-clearing levels.

9. Labour markets are also characterized by widespread government interventions. Minimum wages, designed to protect workers, can actually cause unemployment.

10. The labour market is characterized by a considerable amount of flow between its different states (employment, unemployment, not in the labour force). Search is an important aspect and results in frictional unemployment. Alongside structural unemployment, it is a source of equilibrium unemployment.

11. Search may be more or less efficient. It is affected by government labour market policies. Unemployment benefits, designed to make unemployment more bearable, provide disincentives to quickly finding a new job, thereby increasing frictional unem-

ployment. Other programmes, such as training and relocation subsidies, reduce frictional unemployment.

12. Because of distortions and regulations, equilibrium unemployment is never zero or entirely voluntary. Individuals may be willing to work at lower wages than those prevailing in equilibrium, but they cannot underbid. This is the sense in which real wages are downwardly rigid.

13. Real wages are slow to adjust to disequilibria, if only because they fulfil many other roles. As a result, actual and equilibrium unemployment may differ for long periods of time.

Key Concepts

- leisure
- consumption–leisure trade-off
- real (consumption) wage
- income effect, substitution effect
- labour supply: individual and aggregate
- labour force
- participation rate
- man-hours
- marginal productivity of labour (MPL)
- labour demand
- wage and profit shares
- voluntary and involuntary unemployment
- real wage rigidity
- trade unions, labour unions
- collectively voluntary/individually involuntary unemployment
- collective labour supply curve
- hysteresis
- minimum wages
- efficiency wages
- unemployment benefits
- unemployment stocks and flows
- separation and separation rate
- finding rate
- frictional unemployment
- equilibrium unemployment
- structural unemployment

Exercises: Theory

1. Suppose that the household in Figure 6.3 receives an inheritance. What is the effect on its decision to work and to consume? According to this result, do rich people work more or less than poor people?

2. Suppose Robinson Crusoe is paid a higher wage ('overtime') if he works more than 8 hours a day, but only has 16 hours at his disposal.

   (a) Draw his budget constraint in this case.
   (b) Does the existence of overtime necessarily make him better off?
   (c) Show Crusoe's optimal behaviour for 'normal' indifference curves. Under which conditions will he choose to work overtime? Under which conditions will he refuse?

3. Normally Crusoe sleeps eight hours a day. Suppose it were possible for him to stay awake an extra hour per day without any impairment of his abilities. What would the effect be (a) on his consumption? (b) on the amount of leisure taken? How much would he be willing to pay for this innovation?

4. How should the equilibrium rate of unemployment respond (a) to an exogenous decrease in investment over several years? (b) to an exogenous increase in productivity? How does your answer depend on the institutions of wage determination?

5. What is the effect on the labour market of a minimum wage that is actually lower than the equilibrium wage? Show in your graphical answer the new equilibrium wage and the level of employment.

6. A new labour tax is imposed which is proportional to wages. Individuals care about after-tax wages.

   (a) Draw the old and new individual supply curves.
   (b) What is the effect on the equilibrium wage and employment levels?
   (c) What is changed if wages are set through negotiations with a trade union which also cares about after-tax wages?

7. Many countries have housing rent control; i.e. rent increases are tightly controlled below levels that would prevail in a free market. How might this affect equilibrium unemployment? (*Hint*: think about labour mobility and mismatch.)

8. What is the effect on wages, employment, and unemployment of a wave of immigration:

   (a) in the absence of minimum wage legislation?
   (b) in the presence of minimum wage legislation?

9. How should Figure 6.13 be redrawn if unemployment benefits are generally available and provide a floor under which wages cannot fall? (*Hint*: the trade union would never accept wages lower than the unemployment benefits.) What is the implication for the collective labour supply curve?

Exercises: Applications

1. One of the immediate consequences of opening the borders between East and West Germany was the potential for migration between the two regions. Because of a more productive capital stock and more know-how, wages in the West were about three times as much as those in the East. Consequently many East Germans moved to the West. What are the consequences for this migration for real wages (*a*) in West Germany? (*b*) in East Germany? (*c*) for employment in the two regions? Can you explain why West German trade unions were eager to organize their comrades in the East?

2. It is often said that unemployment insurance in Europe was always generous and thus cannot be responsible for the present high unemployment on the Continent, which has emerged only since the mid-1970s. Examples are Germany, France, and Belgium. Evaluate this statement.

3. In Japan the bonus system is widespread. Workers often receive 30% of their pay in the form of a profit-contingent payment, which can go up or down depending on the fortunes of the enterprise in which they work. What are the implications of such a system for real wage rigidity and equilibrium employment?

4. It is a fact that in fishing communities and tourist areas the average rate of unemployment over long periods of time is higher than in highly industrialized regions. How could our concept of frictional unemployment explain this fact?

5. Many newly industrializing countries, such as Korea, have underdeveloped or repressed trade union movements. These countries also have a very low wage share, and thus a high rate of return on physical capital. How might this be explained?

6. Youth employment is very low in Germany, at least in comparison with other European countries. It is often asserted that this is because training for youth is subsidized by the state. Is this a good use of public money?

7. It is often the case that unemployment benefits are paid out of a fund financed by taxes levied on the firms proportionately to their wage bill. How might this affect equilibrium unemployment?

8. It is sometimes suggested that the massive influx of women into the labour force is a cause of unemployment.

    (*a*) Draw the effect on the labour market as described by Figure 6.10. What does it mean for real wages and employment?

    (*b*) Using Chapter 4, note that more available labour raises the MPK. Assuming that, as a result of more investment, the capital stock increases: how does your answer to (*a*) change?

Suggested Further Reading

Two textbooks provide further analyses:

Ehrenberg, Ronald, and Smith, Robert (1988), *Modern Labour Economics*, 3rd edn., Scott Foresman, Glenview, Ill. and London.

Layard, Richard, Nickell, Stephen, and Jackman, Richard (1991), *Unemployment*, Oxford University Press.

High European unemployment has been studied in detail. A survey is:

Bean, Charles (1994), 'European Unemployment: a Survey', *Journal of Economic Literature*, 32: 573–619.

See also the special issue of the *Swedish Economic Policy Review*, 1 (1–2), Autumn 1994 (articles by Lars Calmfors, Jorgen Elmeskov, Charles Wyplosz, Patrick Minford, Rudiger Dornbusch, Jacques Drèze and Henri Sneessens, and Richard Jackman).

Some interesting contributions are

Bentolila, Samuel, and Dolado, Juan (1994), 'Labour Flexibility and Wages: Lessons from Spain', *Economic Policy*, 18: 53–100.

Blanchard, Olivier J., and Summers, Lawrence H. (1986), 'Hysteresis and the European Unemployment Problem', *NBER Macroeconomics Annual*, 1: 15–77.

Blanchflower, David, and Oswald, Andrew (1994), *The Wage Curve*, MIT Press, Cambridge, Mass.

Burda, Michael (1988), 'Wait Unemployment in Europe', *Economic Policy*, 7: 391–426.

Calmfors, Lars, and Driffill, John (1988), 'Bargaining Structure Corporatism and Macroeconomic Performance', *Economic Policy*, 6: 13–62.

Lindbeck, Assar (1993), *Unemployment and Macroeconomics*, MIT Press, Cambridge, Mass.

Saint-Paul, Gilles (1993), 'On the Political Economy of Labour Market Flexibility', *NBER Macroeconomic Annual*, 8: 151–86.

A controversy on the effects on minimum wages has arisen: see

Card, David, and Krueger, Alan B. (1995), *Myth and Measurement: the New Economics of the Minimum Wage*, Princeton University Press.

Machin, Steven, and Manning, Alan (1994), 'Minimum Wages, Wage Dispersion and Employment: Evidence from the UK Wage Councils', *Industrial and Labour Relations Review*, 47 (2): 319–29.

Kennan, John (1995), 'The Elusive Effects of Minimum Wages', *Journal of Economic Literature*, 33: 1949–65.

Appendix: Labour Supply and Demand, and the Collective Labour Supply Curve

Household Labour Supply

Robinson Crusoe maximizes his utility function defined over consumption C and leisure ℓ:

(A6.1) $$U = U(C, \ell),$$

subject to the budget constraint

(A6.2) $$w\bar{\ell} = w\ell + C,$$

Where w is the real (consumption) wage and $\bar{\ell}$ is Crusoe's time endowment. The first-order condition is found by substituting C from (A6.2) into (A6.1) and maximizing with respect to ℓ:

(A6.3) $$U_\ell / U_c = w.$$

The ratio of the marginal utilities *vis-à-vis* leisure (U_ℓ) and consumption (U_c) is the marginal rate of substitution and the (absolute value of the) slope of the indifference curve. This measures the ratio of the changes in leisure and consumption that keep the utility level unchanged. At the optimum, the amounts substituted are such that this ratio is equal to the real wage rate.

The individual labour supply curve is the (implicit) function household labour supply L as to real wage w defined by (A6.3):

(A6.4) $$L^{s,\text{individual}} = L^s(w),$$

where the wealth argument has been suppressed. Aggregation over many households results in

(A6.5) $$L^s = L^s(w, \bar{L}),$$

where $\bar{L}$ is the number of individuals of working age.

The Demand for Labour by Firms

Since capital is fixed, we can write the production function simply as $Y = F(\bar{K}, L) = F(L)$. Express the firm's profit in terms of units of output, or as

(A6.6) $$\Pi = F(L) - wL.$$

Choosing employment to maximize (A6.6) gives

(A6.7) $$\text{MPL} = F'(L) = w.$$

The inverse of relationship (A6.7) determines the demand for labour;

(A6.8) $$L = L(w) = F'^{-1}(w), \text{ with } L'(w) < 0.$$

Wages and the Labour Share

The wage share is $s = wL(w)/F(L)$. What is the effect of an increase in the real wage on s? Differentiating this expression yields

(A6.9) $$\frac{\partial s}{\partial w} = \frac{L}{Y}\left[1 + \frac{wL'}{L} - \frac{wF'L'}{Y}\right].$$

Define two elasticities as

η_{Lw} = elasticity of labour demand to the real wage
$$= -\frac{dL}{dw}\frac{w}{L} = -\frac{wL'}{L}$$

θ_{YL} = elasticity of output with respect to labour
$$= \frac{dY}{dL}\frac{L}{Y} = \frac{F'L}{Y}.$$

(A6.9) can be rewritten as

(A6.10) $$\frac{\partial s}{\partial w} = \frac{L}{Y}[1 - \eta_{LW}(1 - \theta_{YL})].$$

Since $F' = w$, θ_{YL} is also labour's share in value added and $(1 - \theta_{YL})$ is the profit share. Thus, the condition for the wage share to be increasing when the real wage rises is that $\eta_{Lw} < 1/(1 - \theta_{YL})$, or that the elasticity of labour demand be less than the inverse of the profit share. This is the more likely to happen the smaller is the profit share and the less elastic is the demand for labour, i.e. if the demand for labour does not decline 'too much' in response to an increase in real wages.

Collective Labour Supply

Consider a labour union that has utility given by $U(w - \bar{w}, L - \bar{L})$. In this formulation (sometimes known as a Stone–Geary specification), utility is dependent on the excess of wages and employment above exogenous reference levels, here $\bar{w}$ and $\bar{L}$. We assume that $U_w > 0$, $U_L > 0$ while $U_{ww} < 0$, $U_{LL} < 0$, and $U_{wL} > 0$. We consider only the case of a monopoly labour union, which sets the wage unilaterally.[19]

The union maximizes utility subject to the labour demand curve (A6.8), by choosing the real wage w that maximizes $U(w - \bar{w}, L(w) - \bar{L})$. The first-order condition is

(A6.11) $$\frac{U_w}{U_L} = -L'(w),$$

---

[19] For more sophisticated treatments of the collective bargaining process, which allow for bargaining between unions and employer associations, see an advanced textbook, e.g. Booth (1995).

where the derivatives are evaluated at the optimum value. Equation (A6.11) has an interpretation similar to that of (A6.3): the union picks a wage such that the marginal rate of substitution of employment for wages is equal to the slope of the labour demand curve. This corresponds to points of tangency in the various panels traced out in Figure 6.14.

We can solve this condition by considering a specific form of the utility function:[20]

$$(A6.12) \quad U(w - \bar{w}, L - \bar{L}) = [\alpha(w - \bar{w})^{1/\rho} + (1 - \alpha)(L - \bar{L})^{\delta\rho}]^{1/\rho},$$

with $1 > \rho > -\infty$. First consider the case $\gamma = \delta = 1$. It can be shown that the elasticity of substitution between adjusted employment and wages is given by $(1 - \rho)^{-1}$. As ρ approaches 0, the function assumes the form

$$(A6.13) \quad U(w - \bar{w}, L - \bar{L}) = (w - \bar{w})^{\alpha}(L - \bar{L})^{(1-\alpha)},$$

whereas the case $\rho \to -\infty$ gives

---

[20] This form exhibits constant elasticity of substitution between isoelastic functions of 'normalized' employment and wages.

$$(A6.13') \quad U(w - \bar{w}, L - \bar{L}) = \min[(w - \bar{w}), (L - \bar{L})],$$

and $\rho = 1$ yields the linear form

$$(A6.13'') \quad U(w - \bar{w}, L - \bar{L}) = \alpha(w - \bar{w}) + (1 - \alpha)(L - \bar{L}).$$

An alternative class of union preferences arises when $\rho = 1$ with γ or δ less than unity:

$$(A6.14) \quad U(w - \bar{w}, L - \bar{L}) = \alpha(w - \bar{w})^{\gamma} + (1 - \alpha)(L - \bar{L})^{\delta}.$$

Panels (a) and (b) of Figure 6.14 correspond to the case $\bar{w} = \bar{L} = 0$. The union in panel (a) places relatively high weight on wages, whereas the union in panel (b) places more weight on employment. In panels (c) and (d), the reference level for wages and employment are nonzero, and $\rho = 1$ is assumed. In (c) $\gamma = 1$, $\delta < 1$, $\bar{w} = 0$, but $\bar{L} > 0$ would lead to vertical collective labour supply curves. $\bar{L} > 0$ could be understood as the 'membership' or reference group. In panel (d), $\gamma < 1$, $\delta = 1$, $\bar{L} = 0$, but $\bar{w} > 0$; this implies a horizontal collective labour supply curve, where $\bar{w}$ can be thought of as the 'target wage' for the union.

7

The Real Exchange Rate

> Suppose a man climbs five feet up a sea wall, then climbs down 12 feet. Whether he drowns or not depends upon how high above sea-level he was when he started. The same problem arises in deciding whether currencies are under- or over-valued.
>
> *The Economist*, 26 August 1995

7.1. Overview

This chapter completes the analysis of the real macro-economy. As in Chapter 5, it examines an economy on its long-run growth path, when all markets are in equilibrium. The key difference is that the analysis is expanded to consider two goods. This important modification allows us to study **relative prices**, or prices of goods in terms of others (e.g. how many cakes can be exchanged for a car). It is relative, rather than absolute, prices that matter for decisions taken by economic agents. Previous chapters have described the crucial role played by relative prices such as the real wage (the ratio of nominal wages to a price index) or the real interest rate (the price of tomorrow's consumption in terms of today's consumption). Relative prices are the essence of a market economy.[1] They act as signals and provide incentives to producers and consumers to adapt their behaviour to changing market conditions.

The **real exchange rate** also performs this important function. The real exchange rate is the relative price of foreign goods and services in terms of domestic goods and services. It can be thought of as the **nominal exchange rate** (the price of foreign money in terms of our money) suitably adjusted for the price level at home (the price of our goods in terms of our money) and abroad (the price of foreign goods in terms of foreign money). In the end, the real exchange rate is one mechanism which helps countries meet their intertemporal budget restriction discussed in Chapter 3. Understanding what determines the real exchange rate, its effects on the economy, and how it relates to the nominal exchange rate—which is quoted daily on foreign exchange markets—is the main objective of this chapter.

The real exchange rate can be defined in a number of ways. This chapter looks at two important ones. The first is simply the ratio of prices abroad to those at home, expressed in a common currency. A second, more theoretical, definition distinguishes between those goods and services that are traded internationally and those that are produced at home and are not subject to international competition. In either case, the exchange rate has the chore of allocating goods to their best uses, and ensuring that markets clear.

7.2. The Real Exchange Rate and the Primary Current Account Function

7.2.1. The Real Exchange Rate Defined

To compare prices of goods produced at home with those of goods produced abroad, we need to express them in a common currency. For that purpose, we use the nominal exchange rate. There are two ways of quoting an exchange rate: either by the number of foreign monetary units per domestic unit (this is called **British terms**, e.g. $1.5 per £1 for Britain) or by the number of domestic monetary units per foreign unit (called **European terms**, e.g. DM2.3 per £1 for Germany). *This text adopts the convention of European terms.* Table 7.1

[1] Indeed, a crucial first step in the transformation of Eastern European countries to market economics was the freeing of prices so that they could play this fundamental role.

Table 7.1. Nominal Exchange Rates on 15 December 1995: Some Examples (European Terms)

Country where quoted (currency of quotation)	Foreign currency quoted	Exchange rate
Belgium (BF)	DM	20.56
	LIT	0.01859
France (FF)	£	7.641
	$US	4.965
Germany (DM)	FF	0.2907
	$C	1.049
Poland (New Zlt)	Kcs	0.09519
	¥	0.02480

Key to symbols: BF: Belgian Franc; DM: Deutschmark; LIT: Italian lire; £: UK pound sterling; $US: US dollar; FF: French franc; $C: Canadian dollar; Zlt: Polish zloty; Kcs: Czechoslovak crown; ¥: Japanese yen.

Source: *Financial Times*, 16/17 December 1995

provides some examples of how exchange rates are quoted in different countries.[2] An **appreciation** of a currency should be thought of as an increase in its value in terms of foreign currencies, or as the fact that less of it must be relinquished to buy one unit of foreign currency. Quoted in European terms, an appreciation of our currency is a decline in the exchange rate, since foreign currency is cheaper. Conversely, a loss of value, or a **depreciation**, would imply a rise in the exchange rate since foreign currency is dearer. For example, from the German perspective, the Deutschmark depreciates *vis-à-vis* the pound sterling when the exchange rate changes from DM 2.3/£ to DM 2.5/£.

If E denotes the exchange rate (say, Euros per $1) and P^* is the price of foreign goods expressed in foreign currency (say, $), then the domestic price of foreign goods is EP^*. Conversely, if P is the price of domestic goods in domestic currency, their price in foreign currency is P/E.[3] The real exchange rate, the relative price of foreign goods in terms of domestic goods, is

$$(7.1) \qquad \lambda = \frac{EP^*}{P}.$$

The real exchange rate can be thought of as the nominal exchange rate 'doubly deflated' by foreign and domestic goods prices. As long as goods prices P^* and P remain unchanged or move closely together, the nominal and real exchange rates move together. Nominal and real exchange rates do not always move in tandem, however, as Figure 7.1 illustrates.

If domestic and foreign price levels expressed in the same currency do not move together, the real and nominal exchange rates will move apart. For example, if foreign prices rise faster than domestic prices, the real exchange rate will depreciate if the nominal exchange rate remains constant (Switzerland in the late 1980s). Another possibility is for the nominal exchange rate to appreciate while the real exchange rate remains relatively unchanged (Japan, on average, over 1975–90). Conversely, a country with high inflation such as Italy has maintained a roughly stable real exchange rate despite a large nominal depreciation. In general, real exchange rates are more stable in the long run than in the short run, and also more stable than nominal rates in the long run. This is why it is more important to understand the fundamental determinants of the real exchange rate in the long run first, and then to study the nominal exchange rate in the short run.[4]

[2] Ch. 18 treats exchange markets and exchange rate quotations in more detail.

[3] To see this: P is measured in Euros, P^* is measured in dollars, and E is expressed in terms of Euros per dollar. Then EP^* is measured in Euros (since (Euro/$)($) = Euro), and P/E is measured in dollars.

[4] This chapter thus deals with the real exchange rate in the long run. Ch. 8 studies the nominal exchange rate in the long run and provides a full treatment of the principle of purchasing power parity. In Chs. 13 and 19 the short run is reconsidered.

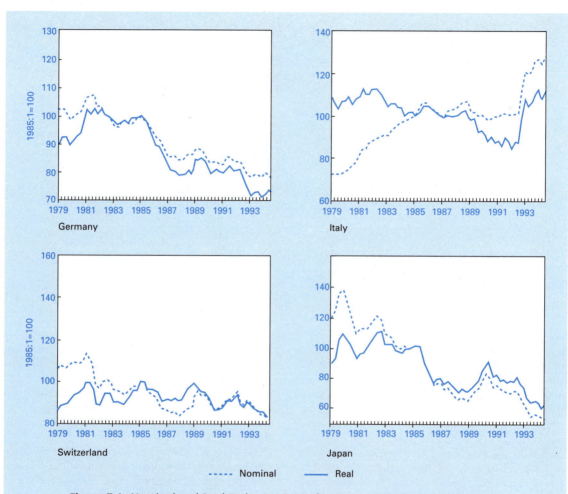

Figure 7.1. Nominal and Real Exchange Rates (European terms), Four Countries, 1979–1994

Nominal exchange rates move quickly and prices move slowly. This is why sudden movements in the nominal exchange rate are reflected in the real exchange rate. Over the longer run, different evolutions of domestic and foreign prices may break the co-movements between the two exchange rates. This is visible in the cases of Italy—where a nominal depreciation occurs alongside a higher-than-average inflation rate—and Switzerland—with a nominal appreciation alongside a lower-than-average inflation rate.

Sources: IMF; OECD

7.2.2. Measuring the Real Exchange Rate in Practice

Measuring real exchange rates in practice poses two problems. The first concerns the definition of 'foreign'. In reality, the rest of the world comprises a large number of countries which need to be aggregated in some way. The solution consists in computing P^* as a weighted average of prices in a large number of trad-

ing partner countries (ideally, all of them) and E as a corresponding weighted average of our nominal exchange rate *vis-à-vis* each of them. The weights assigned to each country are chosen to represent its importance to us. Box 7.1 explains how this averaging is accomplished. The corresponding values of E and λ which result from these calculations are called nominal and **real effective exchange rates**. These are indices—we can no longer express the nominal exchange

---

BOX 7.1. COMPUTING AND COMPARING EFFECTIVE EXCHANGE RATES[5]

Effective exchange rates are computed using a number of partner-countries. Each partner-country receives a weight typically representing its importance in trade, for example its share of our exports or our imports, or the average of both. Geometric averaging is applied to price indices in these countries and to our bilateral exchange rates *vis-à-vis* their currencies. If there are n countries and E_i is the bilateral nominal exchange rate *vis-à-vis* country i with trade weight w_i, our effective nominal exchange rate is:

$$E = (E_1)^{w_1} (E_2)^{w_2} (E_3)^{w_3} \cdots (E_n)^{w_n}.$$

where $\sum w_i = 1$. The foreign price level $P*$ is computed by applying the same weights to each partner-country's price index P_i:

$$P* = (P_1)^{w_1} (P_2)^{w_2} (P_3)^{w_3} \cdots (P_n)^{w_n}.$$

Then the effective real exchange rate is simply the average of our real exchange rates *vis-à-vis* each partner-country:

$$\lambda = \frac{EP*}{P} = \left(\frac{E_1 P_1}{P}\right)^{w_1} \left(\frac{E_2 P_2}{P}\right)^{w_2} \left(\frac{E_3 P_3}{P}\right)^{w_3} \cdots \left(\frac{E_n P_n}{P}\right)^{w_n}.$$

This formula could be applied to prices of more specific classes of goods. The *relative export price ratio* is close to the ratio of import to export prices, studied in Box 7.3 below. (It differs because it is not our imports that are used in the numerator, but 'their' exports, which includes flows to other countries in the world.) Another index frequently used is the ratio of manufacturing prices to the GDP deflator. Because the GDP deflator contains services that are not traded, this ratio is often called the *internal terms of trade*.[6] Over the past few decades for most countries, the traded—nontraded goods price ratio has been more stable. The tendency for the latter to appreciate over time is a feature common to most advanced countries. The higher volatility of the import—export price ratio reflects more directly changes in the volatile nominal exchange rate, combined with slow-moving prices. In particular, the appreciation of the US dollar over 1979–85, and its depreciation ever since, is visible, as are the oil shocks (1973–4 and 1979–80) and the 1986 counter-oil shock. Clearly, the various measures of the real exchange rate need not follow identical patterns.

---

rate in value terms—computed to take a simple value, e.g. 1 or 100, in some base year.

A second problem arises when deciding which prices to compare. A real exchange rate is the price ratio of two baskets of goods and services. Because so many baskets are possible, there is no one real exchange rate that answers all the questions one may wish to consider. Several possible definitions will be discussed later in this chapter. The ratio of traded to nontraded goods prices—sometimes called the **internal terms of trade** —is appealing because it describes best how domestic resources are allocated between sectors open to foreign competition and others that are sheltered. This decomposition, however, ignores the possibility that domestically produced traded goods might be fundamentally different from those sold by foreign countries. An alternative definition of the real exchange rate distinguishes between imports and exports, implicitly lumping together traded and nontraded goods in the export category. Box 7.1 presents two indices close to these definitions. Broader-based real exchange rates compare consumer price indices or GDP deflators. Other indices are designed to measure a country's competitiveness by focusing on production costs, chiefly labour costs (wages plus taxes that apply to labour usage).

---

[5] Nominal and real effective exchange rates are computed and published by various sources. Among them, *International Financial Statistics*, a monthly publication of the International Monetary Fund, presents a variety of real exchange rates (using GDP deflators, export prices, CPIs, labour costs) computed using a sample of 18 advanced economies; *World Financial Markets*, a monthly publication of Morgan Guarantee Trust, publishes effective rates using either a sample of 19 advanced countries or a much larger sample of advanced and less developed countries.

[6] The GDP deflator is a weighted average of traded and nontraded goods prices. If the manufactured goods represent the traded goods, then the ratio of the two prices should follow a pattern similar to the ratio of traded to nontraded prices.

7.2.3. How the Real Exchange Rate Affects the Primary Current Account

What is the link between the real exchange rate and the primary current account (PCA)? Consider, for instance, a real depreciation, or an increase in the price of foreign goods in terms of our goods. Two effects could be expected. First, on the production side, more resources will be diverted towards producing goods that can be exported, since they are cheaper for foreigners; at the same time, production of substitutes for foreign goods will also increase. These both improve the PCA. Second, on the consumption side, an increase in foreign prices will tend to reduce domestic spending on foreign goods. This too improves the PCA. The **primary current account function** formally summarizes these observations:

(7.2) $$PCA = PCA(\lambda, \dots).$$
  $+$

As usual, the plus sign indicates that the argument λ (the real exchange rate) has a positive effect on the primary current account. All other things equal (and represented by the points), a real depreciation leads to an improvement in the primary account balance—a reduction in the deficit or an increase in the surplus.[7] This function is represented by the upward-sloping schedule in Figure 7.2. The rest of this chapter analyses this dependence, a key macroeconomic relationship.

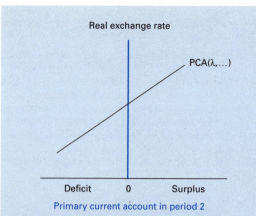

Figure 7.2. The Primary Current Account Function

The primary current account function shows the relation between the real exchange rate and the primary account balance. It is upward-sloping because a more depreciated real exchange rate, everything else unchanged, leads to an improvement in the primary current account.

7.3. The Real Exchange Rate as the Relative Price of Traded Goods

7.3.1. Traded versus Nontraded Goods

A useful way of thinking about the real exchange rate is to separate out internationally **traded goods**—which are exported or imported—and **nontraded goods**—those exclusively produced and consumed locally. Examples of goods or services that cannot be physically traded are housing, construction, and transportation. Other goods and services may not be traded because country-specific regulations limit their usefulness elsewhere or prevent their exchange. The most important obstacle to trade is transportation costs: haircuts, medical services, car repair, or cement are good examples. Many goods may be nontraded but are nevertheless tradable: if protection were removed or transportation costs were to fall, they might become traded.[8] Yet the distinction is useful, because nontraded goods do not face the same competitive pressure as traded goods.

Denoting by P^T and P^N the prices of traded and nontraded goods, measured in Euros, the relative price of traded goods in terms of nontraded goods in the same currency is

(7.3) $$\lambda = \frac{P^T}{P^N}.$$

Under pressure from world trade, the domestic price of traded goods P^T will align itself with foreign prices P^{T*} when expressed in the same currency, so $P^T = EP^{T*}$. This is an extreme way of recognizing the restrictions that international competition imposes on

---

[7] The other variables that affect the PCA are specified further in Ch. 11.

[8] Financial services were long considered a nontraded good, until the information technology revolution sharply reduced the costs of providing and transporting such services.

the domestic pricing of traded goods. It is roughly correct for 'small' countries which do not influence world prices very much. The real exchange rate as the relative price of traded goods in terms of nontraded goods can therefore be expressed as

$$(7.4) \qquad \lambda = \frac{EP^{T*}}{P^N}$$

The relative price of traded goods is our first definition of the real exchange rate. It is sometimes called the **internal terms of trade**.

7.3.2. The Production Possibilities Frontier

When resources are not wasted, producing more of one good in an economy implies producing less of the other. This trade-off is represented in Figure 7.3 by the **production possibilities frontier (PPF)**. The curve describes how much of traded (Y^T) and nontraded goods (Y^N) can be simultaneously produced, given existing resources and technology. Moving along the PPF reveals how production can be shifted from one

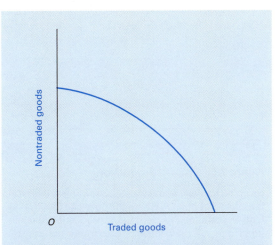

Figure 7.3. The Production Possibilities Frontier (PPF)

The production possibilities frontier (PPF) summarizes maximal combinations of different goods that an economy can produce, given its resource constraints and, perhaps, its markets institutions and regulations. Its slope is the marginal rate of transformation or, here, how many units of nontradable goods must be given up to obtain a unit of the tradable good.

sector to the other by transferring resources. Box 7.2 explains why the PPF is bowed out from the origin.[9]

There are two main reasons why the PPF shifts outward over time. First, more inputs may become available. Second, technical progress in either or both of the two sectors allows more production with the same inputs. The PPF also subsumes imperfections and distortions in goods, labour, and capital markets. For example, if a reduction in the generosity of unemployment benefits leads workers to supply more labour, such a policy would shift the PPF outwards.

For any chosen combination of production of tradable and nontradable goods, nominal GDP in Euros is given by

$$(7.5) \qquad \text{nominal GDP} = P^T Y^T + P^N Y^N.$$

The real GDP is obtained by deflating the nominal GDP. This can be done by using an aggregate price index (the GDP deflator) or else by choosing one good as **numeraire**. A numeraire is simply a good in which other goods prices are quoted. Choosing the nontraded good as numeraire, the real GDP, measured in units of nontraded goods, is obtained by dividing the nominal GDP by P^N, the price of *nontraded goods*:

$$(7.6) \qquad Y = \lambda Y^T + Y^N \qquad \text{with } \lambda = P^T/P^N.$$

A particular value of real GDP could correspond to any number of different combinations of the two goods. These combinations are shown in Figure 7.4 as the **price line** AB. A higher real GDP with the same λ corresponds to a higher price line, like $A'B'$. The slope of the price line ($-\lambda$) corresponds to the real exchange rate. The intersection with the y-axis represents the value of GDP in terms of the numeraire (nontraded goods). If the real exchange rate depreciates (the traded goods price rises relatively to the nontraded goods price), less of the more valuable traded good is needed to achieve a given real GDP and the new price line AC is steeper.

Figure 7.5 shows that the most-preferred outcome for an economy is attained at point P, where a price line is tangent to the PPF. At this point there is no incentive to shift production in favour of either of the two goods: given the relative price λ, this output mix maximizes real GDP. When relative prices change, so does the optimal output mix. For example, when the relative price of traded goods rises (a real exchange rate depreciation), the price line becomes steeper and the tangency point moves to P'. Production shifts towards the more valuable traded good and away from the less valuable nontraded good. A decline in

[9] Technically, it is said to be concave.

BOX 7.2. THE SHAPE OF THE PRODUCTION POSSIBILITIES FRONTIER

The shape of the PPF describes how an economy's available resources can be used to produce various combination of two goods. As we move down the curve to the south-east, the production of nontraded goods declines while that of traded goods increases. The negative slope simply says that we cannot produce more of one good without producing less of the other one since this requires reallocating capital and labour. The rate at which one good is 'transformed' into the other, i.e. the marginal rate of transformation, is measured by the slope of the PPF at any particular point. The steeper the slope, the more nontraded goods must be given up to produce one more traded good. The PPF is bowed-out to reflect the fact that as we keep substituting, say, giving up nontraded for traded goods, we must increasingly sacrifice more and more nontraded goods to obtain the same additional quantity of traded goods. One reason is that some factors

of production are fixed—the stock of capital at any time, management skills, land, natural resources. For example, given the stock of capital, as labour is shifted towards the traded goods sector, the MPL declines in the traded goods sector and rises in the nontraded goods sector: moving workers is increasingly costly in terms of lost nontraded output, and is less and less effective in producing more traded goods. Other reasons for decreasing returns are: labour is specialized, as some workers enjoy a comparative advantage in producing particular goods; there are costs of moving from one pattern of production to another; and technologies differ across sectors. Only if both sectors were to use the same technology, with constant returns to scale, if no particular skills were required, and if the movement of inputs across sectors were costless would the PPF be a straight line and the marginal rate of transformation be constant.[10]

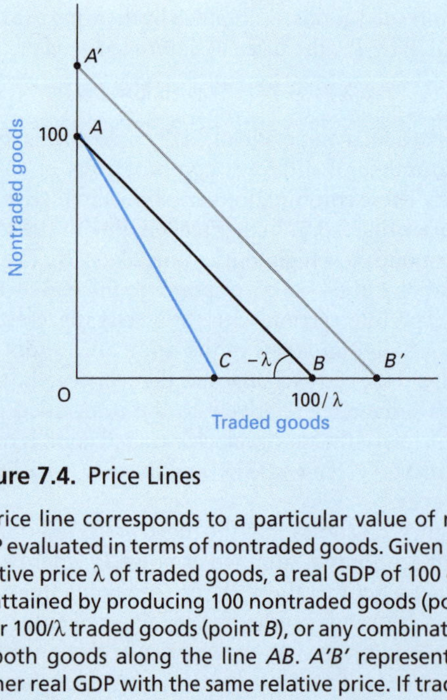

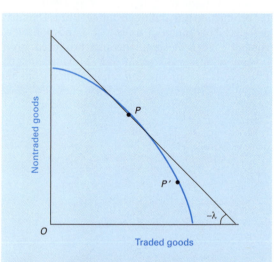

Figure 7.4. Price Lines

A price line corresponds to a particular value of real GDP evaluated in terms of nontraded goods. Given the relative price λ of traded goods, a real GDP of 100 can be attained by producing 100 nontraded goods (point A) or 100/λ traded goods (point B), or any combination of both goods along the line AB. A'B' represents a higher real GDP with the same relative price. If traded goods become more expensive (λ rises) the price line becomes steeper, with the intercept moving from point B to point C. The intersection of the price line with the y-axis (point A) is the value of total GDP.

Figure 7.5. Optimal Production

Given technology and resources, the highest real GDP is achieved at point P, where the price line (which is as high as possible) is tangent to the production possibilities frontier. If the relative price of traded goods rises, maximum GDP is reached at a point like P', where more of the more highly valued traded good is produced.

the marginal productivity of labour MPL^N, hence a loss of output of MPL^N/MPL^T. Similarly, the shift of capital would entail a loss of output of MPK^N/MPK^T. If firms are operating efficiently, these two ratios will be equal. If production exhibits constant returns and is identical in both sectors and producers face the same factor costs, they will choose the same marginal productivity and therefore the trade-off between the goods is constant: a straight line.

[10] Suppose producing an additional unit of the tradable good requires $1/MPL^T$ units of labour and $1/MPK^T$ units of capital to be shifted away from the nontraded sector. For the nontraded sector, losing $1/MPL^T$ man-hours would reduce output proportionally to

the relative price of traded goods (a real exchange rate appreciation) triggers the opposite shift of resources and production.

7.3.3. The Case of a Balanced Primary Current Account

The real exchange rate determines the optimal production mix, but what determines the real exchange rate? The answer is that the market does. Technology, resources, and consumer tastes meet each other in the market place. Technology and resources are summarized by the PPF. We need only know something about tastes and the budget constraint of consumers, and it will be possible to solve for the equilibrium relative price of traded goods. This equilibrium real exchange rate can be thought of as the rate needed to achieve equilibrium in the long run.

Figure 7.6 depicts tastes of households in the usual way. Much like the preferences between consumption today and consumption tomorrow (intertemporal choice), preferences between traded and nontraded goods (*intra*temporal choice) can be summarized by indifference curves, with the same shape for the same

reasons. And as usual, moving outward gives higher utility levels.

Free choice in the market place permits consumers to achieve the highest possible utility given the available technology and endowment of productive resources. Relative prices in equilibrium reflect the marginal rate of substitution for consumers and the marginal rate of transformation of nontraded for traded goods. In Figure 7.7 this occurs at point A, where the PPF and the indifference curves are tangent. Their common slope at the tangency point determines the corresponding price line and therefore the market-clearing price. At that relative price producers maximize value added and consumers are happy to buy both goods exactly in the proportion produced. The PPF plays a role similar to a budget line: it describes the country's existing resources, except that a relative price is needed to value these resources. The interaction between technology (the PPF) and tastes (the indifference curves) in the market place determine the equilibrium relative price.

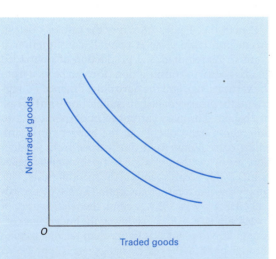

Figure 7.6. Indifference Curves

Consumers' intratemporal preferences are described by indifference curves. Each curve becomes flatter towards the right because as more traded goods are consumed the willingness to give up more nontraded goods for one more traded good declines. Curves to the northeast correspond to increasing levels of satisfaction.

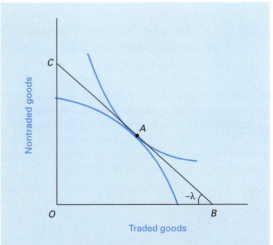

Figure 7.7. Optimal Production and Consumption

Available technology and resources constrain efficient production to points on the PPF. The highest satisfaction is attained at point A, where one indifference curve is tangent to the PPF. The common slope of the PPF and the indifference curve at this point represents the relative price that will lead markets to achieve optimality: the production mix reflects what consumers want.

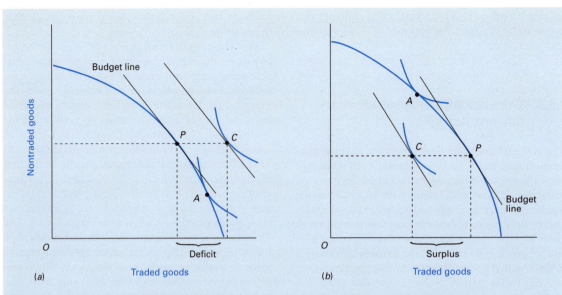

Figure 7.8. Optimal Production and Consumption with Current Account Imbalances

When the current account is not in balance, the economy's consumption of tradable goods and services will differ from its production. Panel (*a*) shows the case of a deficit when the economy consumes more tradable goods than it produces. A real depreciation towards point *A* induces additional production, and discourages consumption of the tradable goods.

7.3.4. The Case of a Nonzero Primary Current Account: the Role of the Real Exchange Rate

An important feature of Figure 7.7 is that at point *A* the primary current account is balanced. Aggregate income and total spending are equal. How should we think of PCA imbalances? Because nontraded goods are both produced and consumed locally, in equilibrium production Y^N must equal absorption A^N:

$$(7.7) \qquad Y^N = A^N.$$

For traded goods, however, production and absorption need not be equal. When spending exceeds production, for example, the difference is met through imports. Similarly, exports can absorb the difference between the local production and consumption of traded goods. The primary current account is the difference between production Y^T and spending on traded goods A^T:[11]

<hr/>

[11] Note that the PCA is expressed in units of traded goods, because net foreign assets and liabilities are most likely to be valued in terms of the goods and services that can ultimately be consumed with them. To express the PCA in terms of nontraded goods and the link with the usual accounting identity, note that $Y = Y^N + \lambda Y^T$ and $A = A^N + \lambda A^T$ so that $PCA = Y - A = \lambda(Y^T - A^T)$.

$$(7.8) \qquad PCA = (Y^T - A^T)$$

Panel (*a*) of Figure 7.8 shows the case of a deficit. Production takes place at point *P*, consumption at point *C*. As required, the production of nontraded goods is equal to consumption (this can be seen from the vertical axis), and the horizontal distance *PC* represents the primary deficit. In comparison with the case of a balanced primary current account (point *A*), two differences stand out. First, the budget constraint, which corresponds to income earned from production, lies below the price line going through tangency point *C*, which corresponds to the spending level. This simply says that total real absorption $\lambda C^T + C^N$ exceeds real GDP $Y = \lambda Y^T + Y^N$. Second, the relative price of traded goods ($\lambda = P^T/P^N$) is lower: the budget line corresponding to point *C* is flatter than the one passing through point *A*: the real exchange rate is appreciated relative to that occurring at point *A*.

It follows that a real appreciation tends to push the PCA from balance into deficit. This occurs for two reasons. First, a real appreciation raises local demand for relatively cheaper traded goods. (*C* is north-east of *A*.) Second, it provides incentives for shifting productive resources away from traded and towards better priced nontraded goods. (The economy moves along

BOX 7.3. THE REAL EXCHANGE RATE AS THE RELATIVE PRICE OF IMPORTED GOODS

The distinction between traded and nontraded goods discussed in Section 7.3 implies that trade is 'one-way'. Either a country imports (i.e. spends assets or borrows) or it exports (accumulates assets or pays down existing debt), but not both. The real world is clearly not so simple. Countries tend to specialize in goods, exporting some in order to import others. The oil shocks of the 1970s—sharp increases in oil prices while other traded goods prices remained constant—shows the limitation of the traded–nontraded goods distinction.

In addition to the ratio of foreign prices to domestic prices in the same currency, or the ratio of traded goods prices to nontraded goods prices, there is a third way to define the real exchange rate, which distinguishes between goods produced domestically and those produced abroad.[12] Let P^z be the price of imports and P^x be the price of exports, both measured in Euros. If foreign producers of imports quote prices P^{z*} in their own currency, the domestic currency price of imports is $P^z = EP^{z*}$ where E is the nominal exchange rate. The real exchange rate can be defined as

$$(7.9) \qquad \lambda = \frac{P^z}{P^x} = \frac{EP^{z*}}{P^x},$$

and the real exchange rate, once again, the nominal rate E 'doubly deflated': A real appreciation occurs when λ decreases, either because the nominal exchange rate appreciates (E declines) or because export prices increase faster than import prices.

The reciprocal of the real exchange rate is sometimes called the **terms of trade**. To distinguish it from the internal terms of trade of Section 7.3, it is sometimes called the external terms of trade. The terms of trade measures

how many foreign goods can be purchased with one unit of domestic output. When the terms of trade rise—a real appreciation—residents can receive more imports for the same quantity of exports.[13] Formally,

$$(7.10) \qquad \text{Terms of trade} = 1/\lambda = P^x/P^z.$$

The primary current account is the difference between exports and imports of goods and services. Expressed in nominal terms and in the domestic currency, it is $P^x X - P^z Z$. The real primary current account can be expressed in terms of one of the two goods, for example using exported goods as the numeraire:

$$(7.11) \qquad \text{Real PCA} = X - \left(\frac{P^z}{P^x} \right) Z$$
$$= X - \lambda Z,$$

where the real exchange rate $\lambda = P^z/P^x$.

The real exchange rate defined in this fashion works in a similar way to that of the relative price of traded goods in terms of nontraded goods. A country may produce some of the goods it imports as well as those it exports, or it may be specialized in the production of exports. If a country is small, its terms of trade will be determined by world tastes and production possibilities and will be unaffected by the amount of exports it produces (we say that the country is a price-taker). If the country is large relative to the rest of the world, an increase in export production may depress its terms of trade, leading to a real depreciation. Under these conditions, a country that attempts to meet its intertemporal budget constraint by producing more for export will have to produce greater quantities than would a simple price-taker.

---

the PPF to the north-west.) The higher consumption of nontraded goods is met by local production, while the increased demand for traded goods is satisfied by imports. Overall, the country is better off as measured by the relative position of the indifference curves going through A and C, but it lives off borrowed money or spends accumulated savings to pay for spending in excess of earnings.

Figure 7.8(b) presents the opposite case of a PCA surplus. Consumption occurs *inside* the PPF, since the surplus corresponds to income in excess of spending. This occurs if, starting from balance at point A, the real exchange rate depreciates, i.e. if the price of

tradables rises relatively to the price of nontraded goods. Productive resources are shifted towards the production of traded goods, while spending on these goods declines.

Summarizing, we have seen one of the most widely cited theoretical justifications of the upward-sloping PCA function depicted in Figure 7.2. The exchange rate affects the PCA by shifting production and spending between traded and nontraded goods in opposite directions. An alternative interpretation of the real exchange rate which allows for greater differentiation of imported and exported goods is sketched in Box 7.3.

---

[12] While beyond the level of this textbook, these ideas are available in any good book on international trade.

[13] The terms of trade thus correspond to using 'British terms' to quote the real exchange rate.

7.4. The National Intertemporal Budget Constraint and the Equilibrium Real Exchange Rate

7.4.1. The Long Run and the Primary Current Account: a Review

The national intertemporal budget constraint introduced in Chapter 3 states that a nation cannot borrow beyond its means. At the same time, accumulated assets can and should be eventually spent.[14] In present-value terms, the current and future primary current account deficits cannot exceed the initial net asset position of the country (or the surpluses must at least match the initial debt). In the simplified two-period framework, this statement was formally written as equation (3. 21):

$$(7.12) \qquad PCA_1 + \frac{PCA_2}{1 + r} \geq -(1 + r)F_0,$$

where F_0 is the net external position of the country inherited from the past at the beginning of the first period (and before interest is paid). F_0 is positive when the country is a net lender, and negative when the country is a net debtor.

As long as it meets its intertemporal budget constraint, the country is free to choose the pattern of its primary accounts over time. This degree of freedom evaporates in the second and 'last' period. Tomorrow's primary account must match the accumulated net external position. As in Chapters 3 and 4, 'tomorrow' is a metaphor for the long-run steady state in which, on average, short-run fluctuations simply cancel out. Then the PCA must be such that the country repays its accumulated debt, or spend its assets, inherited from period 1:

$$(7.13) \qquad PCA_2 = -(1 + r)F_1.$$

Put somewhat differently, period 2's (tomorrow's) primary current account surplus must at least equal, in present value, the initial net liability position $-(1 + r)F_0$ plus PCA_1, the primary surplus incurred in period 1 (today).[15]

7.4.2. Equilibrium Real Exchange Rate and Primary Current Account in the Long Run

The requirement that the long-run PCA be consistent with the country's external budget constraint is what allows us to define the **equilibrium, or long-run, real exchange rate**. The primary current account function depicted in Figure 7.2 explains how the equilibrium real exchange rate is determined. In the second period, condition (7.13) says that the primary current account is to be equal to the negative of the country's net foreign asset position, plus interest. This is shown as the vertical schedule $-(1 + r)F_1$ in Figure 7.9. If a country is indebted, then $F_1 < 0$, and the schedule $-(1 + r)F_1$ will lie to the right in the figure. If on the other hand a country is a net creditor with $F_1 > 0$, the vertical schedule will lie to the left in the figure. For the budget constraint to be satisfied in the steady state, the economy must be at the intersection of the primary current account schedule and this vertical line. At point A, the equilibrium exchange rate can be read off the vertical axis.

As it represents the long run, the equilibrium real exchange rate is not expected to be observed all the time. As the nominal exchange rate fluctuates, or depending on the evolution of inflation at home and abroad, the actual real exchange rates varies. When it is appreciated relative to its equilibrium level we say that it is **overvalued**; it is said to be **undervalued** in the opposite case. In the long run, however, it must return to its equilibrium value to ensure that the budget constraint is not violated.

$$\begin{aligned} PCA_2 &\geq -[(1 + r)^2 F_0 + PCA_1(1 + r)] \\ &= -(1 + r)[(1 + r)F_0 + PCA_1] \\ &= -(1 + r)F_1. \end{aligned}$$

The net asset position inherited in the second period (F_1) is the initial net asset position plus the period 1 primary surplus—or minus the period 1 deficit: $F_1 = (1 + r)F_0 + PCA_1$. The overall current account is what it takes to repay the debt plus interest, or to spend accumulated assets. It is the negative of the capital account, which in the second period represents the full repatriation of the investment position. In the notation used here,

$$CA_2 \quad = \quad PCA_2 + rF_1 \quad = \quad -F_2.$$

current account = primary current account + interest = −capital account.

---

[14] This section presents a review of the two-period framework developed in Ch. 3. When an infinite horizon is considered, the problem becomes somewhat more complicated; see Ch. 15 for details.

[15] Period 2's (tomorrow's) primary account surplus must at least equal, in present value, the initial net liability position $-(1 + r)F_0$ plus the primary surplus incurred in period 1 (today):

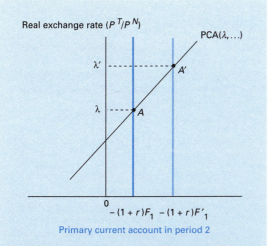

Real exchange rate (P^T/P^N)

PCA$(\lambda, \dots)$

λ' ---- A'

λ ---- A

0 $-(1+r)F_1$ $-(1+r)F'_1$

Primary current account in period 2

Figure 7.9. The Equilibrium Real Exchange Rate

Long-run equilibrium requires that the primary current account match the net asset position, inclusive of interest payments $-(1+r)F_1$. To point A corresponds the equilibrium real exchange rate λ. A less favourable net asset position $F'_1 < F_1$ means that a lower primary current account deficit (or a larger current account surplus) is necessary. The vertical schedule is shifted to the right. This requires a higher—depreciated—real exchange rate to generate a larger primary current account surplus to serve the external debt if $F_1 < 0$, or a smaller deficit as net foreign repayments are reduced if $F_1 > 0$.

Table 7.2. Price Level Comparisons, 1985 (USA = 100)

	GDP deflators		
Europe		**Asia**	
Austria	77.5	Bangladesh	22.1
Belgium	69.3	India	27.2
Denmark	84.3	Israel	67.7
France	74.0	Japan	96.6
Germany	80.0	Pakistan	26.2
Greece	58.9	Saudi Arabia	104.4
Iceland	87.4	Taiwan	68.5
Ireland	74.5	**Africa**	
Italy	68.0		
Netherlands	78.0	Chad	31.0
Norway	89.8	Egypt	84.6
Portugal	43.8	Ethiopia	30.1
Spain	55.1	Senegal	40.2
Sweden	98.8		
Switzerland	107.1	**Central and South America**	
UK	72.7		
North America and Oceania		Argentina	51.9
		Brazil	43.6
		Chile	32.8
Canada	92.6	Mexico	47.4
USA	100.0	Peru	34.0
Australia	93.2	Venezuela	67.4
New Zealand	71.7		

Source: Summers and Heston (1988)

7.4.3. Implications of the Theory

Figure 7.9 shows that a larger foreign indebtedness, F'_1 instead of F_1, implies a rightward shift of the net asset position schedule, and requires a future depreciation of the equilibrium real exchange rate. In order to satisfy its budget constraint, a country that has been borrowing abroad must generate primary current account surpluses. Productive resources have to be shifted towards the traded goods sector, and local demand must be curtailed. The market mechanism delivers this result through changes in the real exchange rate.

This result helps explain a well-known fact observed by travellers: wealthier countries are systematically more expensive than poorer ones. This fact is documented in Table 7.2, which shows the GDP deflators in various countries converted into a common currency. The GDP deflator can be seen as a weighted average of traded and nontraded goods prices. If the prices of internationally traded goods are roughly equalized in a common currency,[16] differences in average price levels reflect differences in nontraded goods prices—such as haircuts, hotel rooms, transport, and bread. The table suggests that nontraded goods are cheaper in poorer countries. Why is that so?

The first reason is demand. While the level of traded goods prices depend on global market conditions, nontraded goods prices are dictated by domestic conditions. From Chapter 4 we know that, when domestic wealth is low, spending is low. Low demand for nontraded goods in poorer countries will tend to reduce their price relative to richer countries.

The second reason is supply. Poorer countries are characterized by lower stocks of physical and/or human capital (Chapter 5), which implies low productivity in the traded goods sector. When productivity is

---

[16] The assumption that prices of internationally traded goods are equalized is sometimes called the Law of One Price. Reasons for and exceptions to this rule are developed in Ch. 8.

BOX 7.4. THE BALASSA–SAMUELSON EFFECT

The observation that price levels in wealthier countries are systematically higher than in poorer ones is known as the Balassa–Samuelson effect.[17] The effect works like this. Let the CPI be a (geometrically) weighted average of traded and nontraded goods prices, with weights a and $(1 - a)$ reflecting the shares of these goods in the consumption basket:

$$(7.14) \qquad P = (P^T)^a (P^N)^{1-a}.$$

International competition in tradable goods links the tradable goods price to the foreign tradable goods price level in terms of the domestic currency:

$$(7.15) \qquad P^T = E P^{T*}.$$

At the same time, the real wage is equal to the marginal product of labour, so

$$(7.16) \qquad \frac{W^T}{P^T} = MPL^T \quad \text{and} \quad \frac{W^{T*}}{P^{T*}} = MPL^{T*},$$

where W^T is the wage in the traded goods sector. Combining (7.14), (7.15), and (7.16) yields the condition

$$(7.17) \qquad \frac{W^T}{E W^{T*}} = \frac{MPL^T}{MPL^{T*}},$$

which connects wages in the tradable goods sector at home and abroad. Holding the exchange rate E constant, it can be seen that domestic wages are higher, the higher

is local labour productivity in the tradable sector relative to that in the rest of the world.

The next step is to recognize that labour *within a country* will move to keep wages in the tradable and non-tradable sectors close together:

$$(7.18) \qquad W = W^T = W^N \quad \text{and} \quad W^{T*} = W^{N*} = W^*.$$

But the nontradable sector real wage is equal to the MPL in the nontradable sector, so

$$(7.19) \qquad W^N = P^N MPL^N \quad \text{and} \quad W^{N*} = P^{N*} MPL^{N*}.$$

Finally, productivity in nontradables does not vary much across countries, so as a first approximation $MPL^N = MPL^{N*}$.[18] Combining this with the definition of relative price levels (7.14), the labour equalization condition (7.17), and the marginal product conditions in (7.19), we arrive at an expression for the relative price levels at home and abroad:

$$(7.20) \qquad \frac{P}{EP^*} = \frac{(P^T)^a (P^N)^{1-a}}{E(P^{T*})^a (P^{N*})^{1-a}} = \left(\frac{P^T}{EP^{T*}}\right)^a \left(\frac{P^N}{EP^{N*}}\right)^{1-a}$$
$$= \left(\frac{W}{EW^*}\right)^{1-a} = \left(\frac{MPL^T}{MPL^{T*}}\right)^{1-a},$$

which shows directly that countries with higher traded goods productivity have higher price levels, measured in the same currency.

---

low, for this sector to be competitive in world markets, wages must be commensurately low. Wages will also be low in the nontraded sector since worker mobility, customs (desire of fairness), and trade union activity typically prevent wages from differing much from one sector to another. With low wages, prices in the nontraded goods sector will therefore be lower in poorer countries, unless in that sector too productivity is lower than in wealthier countries. In practice, productivity levels in the labour-intensive nontraded goods sector differ considerably less across countries than in the capital-intensive traded goods sector: haircuts are produced with scissors all over the world. Summarizing, in poorer countries traded goods prices differ little from those in richer countries, while nontraded goods prices are lower. As a result, overall price levels in poorer countries are lower. This is

known as the **Balassa–Samuelson effect** and is presented formally in Box 7.4.

7.4.4. The Fundamental Determinants of Real Exchange Rates

The factors that drive the real exchange rate in the long run are called its fundamental determinants, or **fundamentals**. We have already seen why they must include the inherited net external position F, which determines what primary current account is compatible with obeying the nation's budget constraint. More generally, the list of fundamentals includes all those

---

[17] It is named after Hungarian-born Bela Balassa, currently at Johns Hopkins University, Baltimore, and Paul Samuelson, a Nobel Prize winner from MIT.

[18] Naturally, this is only an approximation (just like the assumption that wages are equal across sectors) which can be weakened without affecting the central conclusions. The reason often given is the relative unimportance of capital in nontradable production (as opposed to tradables).

BOX 7.5. RESOURCE WINDFALLS: THE DUTCH DISEASE

In the late 1970s, the real exchange rate of Britain appreciated by close to 50% (Figure 7.10). This dramatic change occurred after Britain discovered large reserves of oil in the North Sea. Oil production, begun at the end of the 1970s, enabled the country to be roughly self-sufficient over most of the 1980s. Britain's primary current account can be separated into two parts: the non-oil primary current account (NOPCA) and the oil current account (OCA). While the non-oil account normally depends upon Britain's real exchange rate—defined as the relative price of imports to non-oil exports—the oil current account is essentially independent of the country's exchange rate. Then the long-run condition tying down the primary account can be written as

$$PCA = NOPCA(\lambda) + OCA = -(1 + r)F_1.$$

Over just a few quarters, the oil current account moved from deficit to balance. For any value of the real exchange rate, the primary current account had significantly improved. Graphically, in Figure 7.9 the (non-oil) primary current account schedule shifted to the right, which for a given value of external net foreign assets means a real appreciation of the pound.

This was not the first instance of a resource discovery leading to a considerable appreciation. The Netherlands experienced a similar disturbance when natural gas was discovered in the 1960s. Not coincidentally, the effect of natural resource discoveries on the real exchange rate is sometimes called the **Dutch disease**. It is perceived as a disease because the real appreciation reduces a country's competitiveness and hurts domestic producers of traded goods who were competitive before the discovery. Producers have to become less competitive for the non-oil current account to worsen as required by the budget constraint. The beneficiaries are British and Dutch citizens, who as consumers enjoy an improvement in the terms of trade even if, as workers, they lose jobs in distressed sectors. When Norway also found oil in its part of the North Sea, it was able to avoid some of the more painful aspects of the Dutch disease by subsidizing the manufacturing industry (i.e. exports). The real kronor hardly appreciated (as compared with sterling). The previous relationship can be amended by separating the non-oil current account into government ($NOPCA^G$) and private ($NOPCA$) components:

$$NOPCA(\lambda) + OCA + NOPCA^G = -(1 + r)F_1.$$

If the public current account deficit matches the improvement in the oil account (so that $OCA + NOPCA^G$ remains unchanged), the real exchange rate is shielded from the Dutch disease.

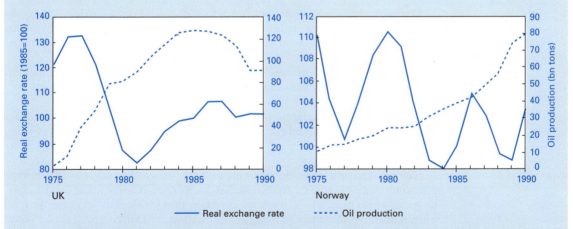

UK

Norway

———— Real exchange rate   - - - - - Oil production

Figure 7.10. Oil Production and the Real Exchange Rate, UK and Norway, 1975–1990

The exploitation of North Sea oil has been accompanied by a sharp and long-lasting—beyond an initially even sharper move—real exchange rate appreciation (a fall in the index when expressed in European terms) in the UK. Active policies have prevented, or at least delayed, the 'Dutch disease' effect in Norway.

factors that affect the primary current account and shift the primary function depicted in Figure 7.9. For example, imagine a country whose primary current account—the difference between income or output and spending—is initially incompatible with long-run equilibrium (point *A*). Gains in competitiveness which boost output, or increased domestic thriftiness which cuts spending, both improve the current account. In Figure 7.9 the PCA function line shifts to the right and the equilibrium real exchange rate appreciates. The reason is that the previously required PCA is now more than sufficient to cover the intertemporal budget constraint. Were the exchange rate to remain unchanged, the nation would accumulate unused (unspent) assets. To avoid this, the PCA must deteriorate somewhat. The exchange rate fulfils its equilibrating role by appreciating in real terms.

Thus, any change in the economy that reflects 'deep' or structural changes is likely to affect the current account and therefore the equilibrium real exchange rate. Box 7.5 presents the example of natural resource discoveries, which make countries richer. A different example is an increase in real wages, perhaps as the result of heightened union militancy. This would reduce firms' profits and capital accumulation, leading to reduced use of labour and the country's productive resources. The real exchange rate would have to depreciate to boost the country's competitiveness and re-establish the required primary current account.

In practice, disturbances large enough to produce significant short-run changes in the equilibrium real exchange rate are rather rare events. For example, to move the external net asset position by a larger fraction of GDP would require persistent current account deficits over an extended period. This is why it is often a good rule of thumb to consider that the equilibrium real exchange rate remains roughly unchanged.

7.5. Summary

1. Real exchange rates measure the price of foreign goods in terms of domestic goods. A variety of prices can be used (export price index, CPI, WPI, GDP deflator, labour costs) to 'double-deflate' the nominal exchange rate and address different questions.

2. Effective nominal and real exchange rates are weighted averages of a country's exchange rates *vis-à-vis* the rest of the world, in practice its main trading partners.

3. Regardless of the definition, the real exchange rate affects the primary current account. An increase in the real exchange rate (a depreciation) will tend to improve the primary current account.

4. Nominal exchange rates, the domestic value of foreign currency, translate foreign prices into domestic currency terms. Real exchange rates, ratios of foreign and domestic goods prices expressed in the same currency, move with nominal exchange rates when the ratio of domestic and foreign prices is constant. Differing price evolutions at home and abroad tend to break the link between nominal and real exchange rates.

5. A widely used interpretation of the real exchange rate is the relative price of traded goods in terms of nontraded goods. While the production and consumption of nontraded goods must be equal, the primary current account is the difference between the production of and spending on traded goods.

6. A real exchange rate depreciation (appreciation) improves (worsens) the primary current account by diverting resources from the nontraded (traded) to the traded (nontraded) goods sector, while consumption declines (increases).

7. The primary current account is driven in the long run by the nation's budget constraint. So the equilibrium long-run real exchange rate depends on the country's inherited net external position. Countries that accumulate large external indebtedness will tend to have depreciating real exchange rates, and countries with large external asset positions will tend to have appreciating real exchange rates.

8. Increases in wealth and productivity, especially in the traded goods sector, are associated with more appreciated real exchange rates. This explains why price levels measured in a common currency are lower in poorer countries.

9. The equilibrium real exchange rate also changes in response to disturbances that affect a country's structure: productivity, tastes, other relative prices. These are generally rare events.

Key Concepts

- relative prices
- real exchange rate
- nominal exchange rate
- European/British terms
- appreciation/depreciation
- effective exchange rates (nominal and real)
- primary current account function
- traded and nontraded goods
- production possibilities frontier (PPF)

- numeraire
- price line
- terms of trade: internal and external
- real equilibrium exchange rate
- over- and undervaluation
- Balassa–Samuelson effect
- fundamental determinants/fundamentals
- Dutch disease

Exercises: Theory

1. What happens to the real exchange rate between two countries if the price level at home doubles, all other things given? If the price of foreign goods doubles? If the nominal exchange rate doubles?

2. Are the following goods traded or nontraded? On what does your answer depend?

   (*a*) Restaurant meals
   (*b*) Banking services
   (*c*) Architectural services
   (*d*) Newspapers
   (*e*) Meat
   (*f*) Car rentals

3. Explain why the PPF may shift out. What are the effects on the real exchange rate in the traded–nontraded goods model? Does it matter for which goods the productivity increase occurs?

4. In the traded–nontraded goods decomposition, draw the price line using the traded good as numeraire. What is the effect of a real appreciation? Is the result different if we use the nontraded good as numeraire?

5. The primary current account function allows us to find the equilibrium real exchange rate graphically (Figure 7.9). Using this graphical apparatus, determine the effect of an anticipated increase in domestic productivity. (**Hint**: do not forget that wealth is the present value of income.)

6. Using Figure 7.9, argue that an increase in the real interest rate causes a real depreciation for indebted countries and a real appreciation for net lender countries.

7. Why do producers like, and consumers dislike, real depreciations?

8. A country produces two goods using only labour. Producing good A requires 10 hours of work. For good B it takes 6 hours. The labour force contributes 10,000 hours of work annually.

   (*a*) Draw the PPF.
   (*b*) Can you predict the relative price of good A in terms of good B?
   (*c*) What will the country produce if, on world markets, good A is twice as expensive as good B?
   (*d*) If the country is closed to world trade, can you predict what will be produced? At what relative price?

9. Explain why it is optimal to produce along the PPF and not inside it. Picking a point on the PPF in Figure 7.7 that is not at the tangency with the price line, explain why it is desirable to move towards the tangency point.

10. An increase in union militancy results in higher real wages in both traded and nontraded sectors, leading to involuntary unemployment.

   (*a*) What is the short-run effect on the production possibilities frontier?
   (*b*) Suppose the effect is regarded as only temporary. What is the short-run effect on the equilibrium real exchange rate? How does your answer change if the market determines that the effects are long-term?

Exercises: Applications

1. All indices are 100 in the base year. The price index of nontraded goods is 105. The effective nominal exchange rate index (European terms) is 93 and the foreign traded goods price index is 110. Compute the effective real exchange rate and the consumer price index (CPI), given that consumers on average devote 30% of their

spending to nontraded goods. What is the effect on the real exchange rate (percentage of appreciation/depreciation) and on the CPI of each of the following?

(*a*) Nontraded goods prices increase by 20%
(*b*) The effective nominal exchange rate declines to 85
(*c*) Inflation abroad is 15%
(*d*) A 10% tariff is imposed on all traded goods

2. After wars, victor-countries often exact reparations from the losers in the form of valuable resources, financial assets, or other forms of tradable wealth. What would you expect to be the effect of such action in each of the two countries? Thinking in terms of traded and nontraded goods, explain the effect on consumption, the relative price of traded goods, and production.

3. The following table gives the terms of trade of Belgium. It has been argued that this apparently permanent decline is related to the massive subsidies that went into declining industries in the 1970s. Can you explain precisely how this might have occurred? Do you think the change is permanent?

Terms of trade of Belgium (1985 = 100)

1975	1979	1981	1983	1987	1990
134.9	138.7	112.7	98.3	101.1	95.4

Source: IMF

4. The following table presents the nominal and real exchange rates for Italy: How might you explain the difference in the evolution of the two rates?

Nominal and real effective exchange rates in Italy
Indices in European terms (1985 = 100)

	1975	1985	1990
Nominal	48.0	100.0	99.4
Real	99.2	100.0	91.0

Source: IMF

5. In 1990, Czechoslovakia increased the price of US dollars in terms of crowns (the local currency) by roughly 65%. If local prices of goods in Czechoslovakia (i.e. in crowns) are held constant, what will happen to the demand for Czechoslovak exports? For imports? How can you explain the fact that the current account first worsened, then improved?

6. Use Box 7.3 to explain why OPEC member-countries would like to limit the production of oil to sustain the terms-of-trade improvement that they achieved at the time of the oil shocks.

7. The table below is comparable to Table 7.2, except that it refers to big cities. It appears that relative prices differ much more from country to country than from city to city. How can you explain the differences between the two tables? What economic forces would you expect to reduce intercity differences within a country relative to variation among countries?

Costs of living indices, 1990 (London = 100)

Europe		Asia	
Brussels, Belgium	109.7	Dacca, Bangladesh	77.4
Copenhagen, Denmark	125.5	Bombay, India	81.1
Paris, France	111.3	Tokyo, Japan	141.0
Frankfurt, Germany	110.7	Karachi, Pakistan	66.7
Stockholm, Sweden	127.2	Riyadh, Saudi Arabia	89.9
Milan, Italy	115.7	Africa	
Amsterdam, Netherlands	100.8	N'Djamena, Chad	137.3
Oslo, Norway	139.0	Dakar, Senegal	113.5
Lisbon, Portugal	90.0	North America	
Barcelona, Spain	108.9	New York	102.2
Geneva, Switzerland	123.4	Chicago	106.8
London, UK	100.0		

Source: *Financial Times*, 10 August 1990

8. When Germany was reunited in 1990, the Deutschmark became the single currency of both former countries. East Germany, though, was indebted to the rest of the world. What does this mean for the real exchange rate of the Deutschmark, now the currency of both Germanies? Does it matter if a large part of East Germany's debt is owed to West Germany?

9. What would you expect the effect of debt relief (i.e. the reduction of the debt in present-value terms) to have on the price level of a highly indebted country?

10. It is observed that fast growing countries often have more rapid *inflation* than slow growing countries. How might you explain this? (*Hint:* the Balassa–Samuelson effect.)

11. Equadoria, a highly indebted country which had suspended its debt service for many years, has now decided to repay. What should happen to:

(*a*) the ratio of its traded to nontraded goods prices?
(*b*) consumption of each category of goods?
(*c*) production of each category of goods?

12. Some countries have obtained a partial cancellation of their external debt. Using Figure 7.8, predict the effect on the ratio of traded to nontraded goods prices. (*Harder*) Using Figure 7.8, predict the effect on the production and consumption of both goods.

13. The real exchange rates of all 'transforming' countries (formerly centrally planned economies in Eastern and Central Europe) have appreciated by huge amounts after 1990—by 40% in the Czech Republic and a factor of 15 in Russia. Can you explain this general phenomenon?

PART III

Money

Until now our attention has been restricted to the real side. We have not yet recognized the existence of money and the fact that goods we buy and wages we earn are measured in units of money, or in *nominal terms*. This part completes this important oversight. It also shows that it is possible to separate out the real from the nominal side in the long run. In the shorter run, the real and monetary sectors are intertwined. This interaction—among other things—gives rise to the phenomenon of business cycles, the succession of periods of rapid economic growth and recession.

The main objective of Part III is to establish what money is, how it is created, and what role it plays in a modern, open economy. We also study how central banks operate, torn between objectives that may be at times conflicting: setting the interest rate, the exchange rate, the rate of money growth, and ultimately the rate of inflation.

8

Money and the Demand for Money

Money is not, properly speaking, one of the subjects of commerce; but only the instrument which men have agreed upon to facilitate the exchange of one commodity for another. It is none of the wheels of trade: it is the oil which renders the motion of the wheels more smooth and easy.

David Hume

The invention of a circulating medium, which supersedes the narrow, cumbrous process of barter, by facilitating transactions of every variety of importance among all sorts of people, is a grand type of advance in civilisation.

Chambers's Encyclopedia, 1870

8.1. Overview

All societies since time immemorial have used one form of money or another. Money is a very special form of wealth, or asset. Its return is typically very low—banknotes yield no interest at all—and yet it is perceived as desirable, even the ultimate form into which other assets can be transformed. The reason is that money facilitates transactions between economic agents. It is indispensable to the proper functioning of a modern economy. To be convinced of this, we need only imagine the costs a barter economy would impose on our daily lives. Yet, the definition of money is far from clear. Banknotes and coins are money. What about chequebook balances? Travellers' cheques? Savings accounts? Other financial instruments? There are indeed various forms of money, some of them even produced by different agents. This chapter therefore starts with several definitions of money. The question of the supply of money, however, is left for the next chapter.

The present chapter focuses on the demand for money. Since money is not an ideal form for holding wealth, we need to understand why it is held at all. This is the first step towards understanding money's role in the macroeconomy: its effect on prices, interest rates, and, eventually, real economic activity.

8.2. What is Money?

The definition of money has been an issue of dispute for a long time, and the difficulties have been compounded recently by the computer revolution. Once upon a time, gold, silver, and other commodities served as money. Slowly but surely, paper money (banknotes) edged out these **commodity monies**. Next came the widespread use of sight deposits. Nowadays, the speed, ease, and low cost of converting one type of asset into another have blurred conventional distinctions between money and other related forms of wealth. A proper definition must capture the enduring qualities that characterize money, while abstracting from those that are transient, arbitrary, or country-specific.

8.2.1. A Narrow Definition

Currency (banknotes and coins) is undoubtedly a form of money, even though a century ago there were doubts that these forms were as trustworthy as coins made from precious metals. Yet, the use of currency to settle transactions is relatively limited, so economic agents often use bank deposits instead. This is the rationale for a first definition of money: currency in the hands of the public (households, firms, and governments) plus sight deposits (bank accounts that are payable on demand, often called demand deposits). This **monetary aggregate** is denominated as M1. One key characteristic of M1 is that it is generally accepted as a means of payment.

$$M1 = \text{currency in circulation} + \text{sight deposits}.$$

This measure is open to different interpretations which highlight the danger of rigid definitions. For example, should travellers' cheques be counted as money? They do not fit the bureaucrat's definition, but they seem to function much like the other stuff. Some countries do include travellers' cheques in M1. What about credit cards or even prepaid telephone cards, or foreign currency, which in some countries, such as post-communist Eastern Europe, is used alongside domestic currency? Practices differ, and changing circumstances and technology will call any definition into question.

8.2.2. Broader Aggregates

Sight deposits at banks have two main characteristics: (1) cheques can be written or wire transfers can be made against them, and (2) the interest paid is either nil or lower than what other assets offer. This is why banks often offer more attractive accounts that bear interest, but cannot be drawn on with cheques. Yet such funds can often be transferred into regular sight deposits—often a phone call, or a series of keystrokes on a telephone handset (or the Minitel in France), is enough. The ease of transfer renders these assets very similar to sight deposits. This is why it is often argued that they should be included in a definition of money. This aspect gives rise to M2, a broader definition which, because each country's financial system offers

a different palette of such assets, is somewhat country-specific. Generally, however we can define

$$M2 = M1 + \text{time (or savings) deposits at banks} \\ \text{with unrestricted access.}$$

An even broader measure includes instruments such as large certificates of deposit, or time deposits with a longer-term and possibly restricted access, foreign currency deposits, and deposits with nonbank institutions. The precise meaning of 'larger' and 'longer maturity' depends on local rules and regulations. The distinction is one of degree: these instruments are less liquid, meaning that they are more costly or difficult to convert into cash or checking accounts. This is called M3:

$$M3 = M2 + \text{larger, fixed-term deposits} + \text{accounts} \\ \text{at nonbank institutions.}$$

8.2.3. Liquidity versus Yield

Beyond currency and M1, all definitions are inevitably arbitrary and vary from country to country. This is why **monetary aggregates** like those presented in Table 8.1 are not directly comparable across countries. Still, all the aggregates measure the 'liquid wealth' of the nonbanking sector. M1 is considered perfectly liquid, whereas M2 and M3 are less practical for transactions.

Beyond the definitions, differences across countries reflect the stage of development of banking services as well as national regulations. Banks and financial institutions (savings banks, unit trusts, investment

Table 8.1. Money in Five Countries, year-end 1994

		Currency	M1	M2	M3[a]
UK	(£bn)	18.7	254.9	410.5	569.6
	% GDP	2.8	38.1	61.4	85.2
France	(FF bn)	252.2	1671.9	3004.4	5226.2
	% GDP	3.4	22.7	40.7	70.8
Germany	(DM bn)	225.9	764.1	1282.7	1937.0
	% GDP	7.6	25.7	43.1	65.1
Japan	(¥ tr)	35.7	132.9	519.4	1034.9
	% GDP	7.6	28.3	110.7	220.5
USA	($ bn)	357.6	1173.7	3639.1	4331.0
	% GDP	5.3	17.4	54.0	64.3

[a] for UK, M4 is used.

Sources: IMF; various central banks' bulletins

BOX 8.1. THE VISION OF WICKSELL: A MONEYLESS SOCIETY

Once upon a time, money was gold or silver, or seashells, or large stones on South Pacific islands. Such **commodity money** has an *intrinsic* value, since it is made of goods that can be used for other purposes. These goods are 'wasted' when used as money, and this is one reason why paper and cheap metal have replaced silver or gold. A century ago, the Swedish economist Knut Wicksell went further. He asked: Why have money at all? He envisioned a central record keeper who would keep a tally of all credits and debits. Whenever an individual worked, his balance would be credited; whenever he spent, the balance would be debited. In principle, it would be possible to run a negative balance, i.e. to borrow from the system. In the end, instead of producing currency, the central bank would operate and guarantee the system and determine the value of the unit of account. At the time, Wicksell's moneyless society was dismissed as impractical science fiction.

A century later, the technical problems of establishing such a 'moneyless society' have been largely solved. Large powerful computers can keep accurate, up-to-date records and investigate the creditworthiness of households and businesses. In Swindon, a community near London, a large-scale experiment in this direction is already underway. Would there be a demand for money, as we have defined it, in a 'moneyless society'? If the system were perfect and all transactions could be recorded at point of sale, probably not. Yet the amount of trade that occurs in informal settings is still large, and often convenient. It may be a long time before the local newspaper kiosk installs such a system. More importantly, a significant portion of society may have something to hide from a system like Wicksell's. Anyone trying to evade taxes, work in the black market, or engage in other illicit activity will always desire a means of payment that is not necessarily traceable to the transacting party. Right or wrong, the very intrusiveness of Wicksell's system might be its most objectionable trait.

management firms, and life insurance companies) compete for customers' wealth. In some countries banks are able to offer interest on checking accounts; in others they have to compete through different means (free bank accounts, proximity of branches, computerized services). Competition and technical change force banks and financial institutions to invent new types of accounts that are not part of M1 but are better remunerated and yet easily transformed into a form suitable for transactions. The computer revolution has made complex transfer agreements virtually costless and has thereby rendered money definitions increasingly arbitrary. Many believe we are not so far from reinventing the moneyless society that the Swedish economist Knut Wicksell once imagined, which is described in Box 8.1. As a simplification, we will generally think of money in terms of its narrower definition, M1.

8.3. Why Is This Money?

Technology makes the search for a definition of money very difficult indeed. Perhaps it would make more sense to look for defining characteristics of money. Why is M1 money? Why do businesses and individuals use it? On the surface, both questions seem trivial. Good business sense would say that money is whatever is generally accepted in payment, and it is used because others will accept it. The reasoning is circular: money is money because it is accepted, and it is accepted because it is money! In a perplexing way, this circularity is one of money's most intrinsic and durable aspects, despite its other rapidly changing attributes over the centuries. In the end, the best definition of

money is: an asset that is generally accepted as a means of payment.[1]

8.3.1. Economic Functions of Money

An alternative, and widely used, approach is to define money by its attributes, that is by what money does

---

[1] In a way, we know about as much as a US Supreme Court Justice knew when asked to define pornography: I can't tell you what it is, but I know it when I see it.

for us and why we use it. This section presents several key ideas from this rich tradition.[2]

8.3.1.1. A medium of exchange

Money is a **medium of exchange**. People use it to settle accounts, regardless of what is being bought or sold. In a remarkably convenient way, money solves the **double coincidence of wants**. Thomas is selling apples. François is interested in purchasing some, but he is selling tomatoes which Thomas does not want to buy (he is looking for potatoes). Direct trade may not take place between the two of them. They would need to find Vittorio, who happens to be selling potatoes and is interested in buying tomatoes. Money admirably solves that problem.

8.3.1.2. A unit of account

In a moneyless or barter economy, all goods would be traded according to their relative prices (tomatoes versus apples versus potatoes versus tomatoes). As the number of goods grows, the number of relative prices rises rapidly. With two goods there is a single relative price; with three goods, there are three relative prices; with five goods, ten. If there are 50 goods, the number of relative prices rises to 1225; and so on.[3] The need for a 'common denominator' or **unit of account** is obvious. Money serves as a numeraire or a benchmark in which all other goods are priced.

8.3.1.3. A store of value and standard of deferred payment

Money is indeed an asset, and is therefore one way of holding wealth. Wealth transfers resources from the present to the future, for later consumption or further wealth accumulation. The value of money may change over time, but that is true of any other **store of value**. Similarly, money can be used as the numeraire in which debt contracts are written: it serves as a **standard of deferred payment**.

8.3.2. A Dominated Asset

Money is a **dominated asset**. It bears a lower rate of return than assets of comparable riskiness, such as

Treasury bills (short-term government bonds), which are also backed by the state. This is the cost of 'staying liquid' and is the reason for the systematic inverse relationship between liquidity and returns: the larger the yield on a monetary instrument, the more restrictions are attached to it. Examples are the need to maintain a minimum (and often substantial) balance, limitations on the minimum amount that can be settled per cheque, charges on cheque writing or transfers to other accounts, and so on. As a rule, the more liquid an asset is, the lower is its yield. Liquidity carries a price in terms of interest forgone.

8.3.3. A Public Good

The superiority of money, which compensates for its inferiority in terms of interest, is that it is a means of payment. This means that it is so generally accepted that it can be used as payment without asking. But *why* is it so generally accepted? Perhaps the following example can illustrate this very special feature of money.

Suppose a shopkeeper accepts a written promise from a trustworthy customer to pay his grocery bill at some future date. This promise, or IOU,[4] represents the shopkeeper's claims on his customer's future resources and is simply a loan. This loan has value; if the customer in question is particularly trustworthy, the shopkeeper might be able to use this IOU to pay for his own purchases. The IOU could end up held by parties completely unrelated to the shopkeeper or his customer; it might be used as *money*. For that to happen, the public will require significant information about the initial customer's creditworthiness. And yet, if they simply *assume* that the customer is creditworthy, the money could circulate as a means of payment without any difficulty. In the end, the reputation of the initial issues of the IOUs determines the acceptability of this type of money. Yet it is very unlikely that the shopkeeper himself, much less third parties, will ever know, or care to know, enough about individuals to accept their IOUs as money. Private IOUs are a victim of the phenomenon of **information asymmetry**: the fact that others know less about the customer than he himself does. As a result, if his IOUs were widely accepted, he could very well one day succumb to the temptation of issuing more IOUs than he is able to repay. Since this potential misbehaviour is easily suspected, no one will accept these IOUs.

---

[2] This tradition starts with the work of British economist William Jevons (1875).

[3] The mathematical formula for the number of relative or bilateral prices is $n(n-1)/2$, where n is the number of goods.

[4] IOU = I owe you.

BOX 8.2. PARALLEL CURRENCIES

There have been a number of episodes in history when private money has circulated alongside, or even in lieu of, fiat money created by the state. Some examples of such 'free issue' environments are Scotland in the eighteenth century, the USA in the nineteenth century, and Hong Kong today. In these episodes banknotes privately issued by local banks circulated along with gold, silver, or national banknotes. Even assuming its authenticity, however, it was often difficult for those presented with such banknotes to know their true value, since this involved information about the solvency of the bank in question, as well as what others thought of the notes. Generally, banknotes were sold at a discount from face value. (In nineteenth-century USA, it was related to the distance from the issuing bank.) Banknotes were treated as the senior debt of the issuing bank: their holders were the very first to be paid off in the event of bankruptcy. All the same, bank failures often meant that the money became worthless. It was common for 'banknote reporters' to publish regular listings of counterfeit banknotes as well as discounts or premiums in terms of gold, so that transacting parties might agree on an exchange value.

Nowadays parallel currencies are observed in countries with extreme economic instability and mistrust of the government, but they usually circulate in the form of foreign exchange rather than private issue. US dollars and Deutschmarks circulated freely in many Eastern European and Latin American countries, as well as in Israel during the hyperinflation of the early 1980s. This phenomenon of *dollarization* became very widespread in the former communist countries early on in their process of economic transformation; Table 8.2 shows the extent of currency substitution that occurred. Dollarization usually comes to an end as soon as conditions stabilize and public trust is restored.

Table 8.2. Currency Substitution in Central and Eastern Europe, 1993[a]

Albania	18	Poland	28
Bulgaria	30	Romania	35
Estonia	5	Russia	35
Latvia	25	Slovenia	42
Lithuania	25	Ukraine	28

[a] Currency substitution is defined as the ratio of foreign currency deposits to broad money.

Source: Sahay and Végh (1995)

Money is accepted either because it has intrinsic value (gold, for example), or because it is an IOU from an institution with a solid reputation. The creditworthiness of the state is essential for **fiat money**[5]—noncommodity money—to circulate. Confidence emerges as the key characteristic of money. Other institutions may attempt to acquire sufficient reputation to issue their own parallel currencies, and Box 8.2 reports on some historical experiments with them.

For IOUs to circulate in the above example, several costs are incurred. The value of the IOUs must be ascertained at each transaction, and in case of default the shopkeeper may be required to guarantee the bad debt. The safety of money is a **public good**, meaning that it is enjoyed simultaneously by different people.

The social benefit (the gains to all members of the community) from this activity exceeds its private cost (to the shopkeeper). Unfortunately, the shopkeeper cannot charge others for providing this service and so he has little incentive to supply private money, even if it is desirable from a social point of view. It is a general result that, if left to the market, public goods are undersupplied, no matter how useful they are. This is where governments have a special responsibility. Because they are easily recognized and enjoy more credibility than the average citizen, governments usually establish the monetary standard and supply the medium of exchange, sometimes declaring it to be legal tender and requiring that it be accepted in exchange for goods. In the end, this is probably the most efficient way of satisfying the definition given at the beginning of this section.

[5] Fiat comes from the Latin 'let there be', or 'let it be'.

8.4. Money: A Balance Sheet Approach

8.4.1. Consolidated Balance Sheets

Money is an asset for those who hold it. With the exception of commodity money, however, it is also someone else's liability. This can be seen by examin-ing the **balance sheets** of the banking system displayed in Figure 8.1. A balance sheet is a snapshot of an entity's financial status. **Net worth** is the difference between the value of its assets—listed on the left side of the balance sheet—and its liabilities—listed on the

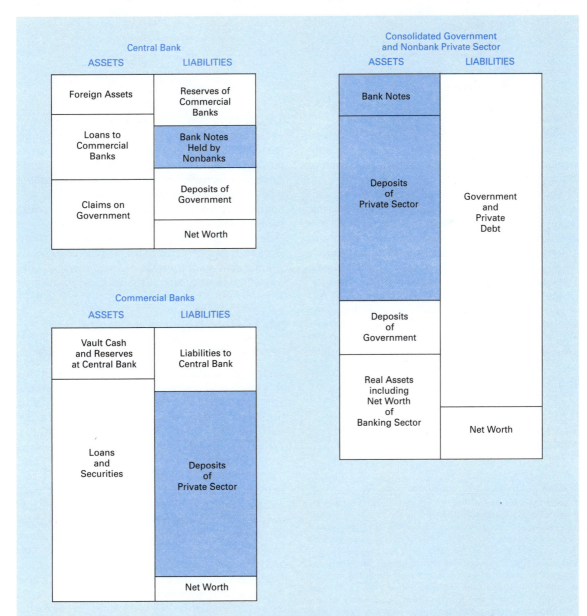

Figure 8.1. Balance Sheets of the Central Bank, the Commercial Banks, and the Nonbank Sector

Table 8.3. Assets of Central Banks in Selected Countries, year-end 1994 (ECU billion)

	Gold[a]	Foreign assets	Loans to commercial banks	Claims on gov't
Denmark	0.57	8.44	7.66	2.68
France	24.98	56.46	30.35	10.90
Germany	7.19	67.52	114.25	13.81
Italy	21.07	45.36	1.21	97.99
Norway	0.03	17.26	0.70	1.65
Sweden (1993)	0.26	18.90	0.14	10.65
UK (1993)	4.07	39.97	0.24	19.80

[a] National valuation.

Source: IMF

right side. We consider three big players: the central bank, the commercial banking sector, and the non-banking sector, which includes households, corporations, and the government.[6]

The balance sheets depicted in Figure 8.1 are *consolidated*: the assets and liabilities belonging to the same sector cancel. For example, within the nonbank sector, borrowing by the government or corporations from private citizens cancel out and do not appear. The money stock M1 is represented by the tinted area, the sum of currency held by the public and sight deposits. It is on the asset side of the nonfinancial sector.[7] It appears simultaneously as a liability of the consolidated banking sector.

8.4.2. Currency as a Liability of the Central Bank

Cash held by the public is a liability of the central bank. When central banks first began issuing paper money,

or currency, in the nineteenth century, they committed themselves to exchanging these banknotes against gold on demand. This is how the public eventually came to trust paper money and regard it as good as gold or silver. Today, the gold backing is gone, gold holdings represent a very small fraction of a central bank's assets, and silver has all but disappeared from their vaults. As Table 8.3 shows, precious metals have since been supplanted by the debt of the Treasury, the commercial banking system, or foreign central banks. These assets now constitute the 'backing' for currency.

8.4.3. Sight Deposits as a Liability of Commercial Banks

Sight deposits, the larger part of M1, are liabilities of the commercial banking sector. Figure 8.1 shows that sight deposits are backed by three types of asset. First, banks hold some currency and deposits with the central bank; both of these are the central bank's liability. (We ignore here their holdings of foreign currency.) Second, banks may own government debt. Third, banks hold debt of households and firms. If we consolidate the liabilities of the central bank and commercial banks, we arrive at M1 and the government's own deposits. Money is thus as good as the consolidated assets of the central bank and the commercial banks, and that is the indebtedness of the government and of the private sector.

This is why, in the end, modern money—in contrast to gold or silver money—ultimately rests on the trust of agents in their own economies. To bolster this trust, regulations are designed to enhance the credit-

---

[6] Here we treat the central bank as a separate entity, as it is in most industrialized countries. In some economies the central bank is under the direct control of the government and the positions are best considered as consolidated.

[7] Following common practice, we have excluded government deposits at the central bank from M1. Government accounts tend to be quite volatile and are not really under the control of the private sector. Volatility is a problem because the aggregates often move too much to be used as a gauge of monetary conditions. In some countries (for example the USA), as a result of a sharp distinction between the Treasury and the central bank, the Treasury actually refrains from using the central bank for the bulk of its transactions, preferring accounts at commercial banks.

worthiness of the banking sector. Yet, banking panics may occur in troubled times, when the value of such regulation may be called into question. Out of concern for their wealth, people withdraw their deposits to acquire foreign currencies or other nonfinancial assets such as gold or durable goods. When the chain of confidence breaks in one place, the whole fragile edifice can come tumbling down.

8.5. The Demand for Money

It is the exceptional individual indeed who derives pleasure from owning and holding money *per se*. For most households and firms, money is useful because it facilitates transactions. Since money is a dominated asset, however, most people will not hold a significant fraction of their wealth in that form. Figure 8.2 shows

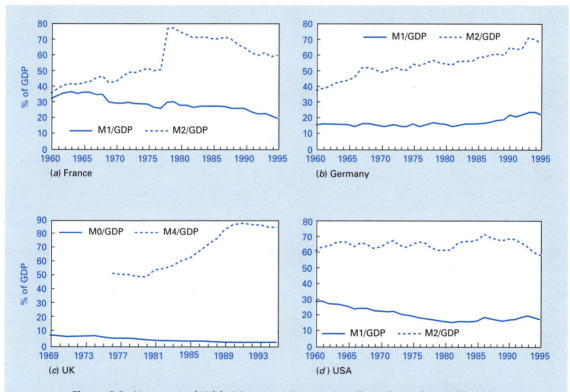

Figure 8.2. Narrow and Wide Monetary Aggregates, Four Countries, 1960–1990

Changing definitions over time and across countries makes it difficult to track down the evolution of monetary aggregates. For Britain, we show the monetary base M0, a very narrow aggregate, and M4, a very wide aggregate. In France, M2 was redefined in 1978, hence the break in the series. Possible economies of scale may encourage a downward trend in the narrow aggregates. In Germany and the UK the narrower aggregate has declined in part because depositors have shifted part of the wider aggregates into better remunerated bank accounts.

Sources: IMF; CSO (UK)

the evolution of M1 and M2, scaled by nominal output (M/PY). Because the money stocks are nominal, it is natural to measure them relative to nominal rather than real output. Recent innovations in payment technologies have provided a convenient means of shifting resources from non-interest-bearing, or low-interest, sight deposits (M1) to better remunerated accounts (M2). This may explain the upward trend in M2 although the expected downward trend in M1 is at best modest. In fact, the figure suggests that where a downward trend occurred it was reversed after 1985. Both ratios also fluctuate quite sizeably. This section is devoted to explaining these evolutions in money demand.

8.5.1. The Price Level as a Determinant of Money Demand

Money demand is largely motivated by the need to carry out transactions, that is by its command over goods and services. Money is valued for its purchasing power. The implication is that the demand for money is a demand for *real* rather than nominal balances. The real value of money can be represented as:

$$\text{Real money stock} = M/P,$$

where M is the nominal stock of money and P is the consumer price index (CPI). The real money stock remains unchanged when the nominal stock increases exactly by the same proportion as the price level. All other things being equal, if the money supply and the price level (and the nominal value of other assets in the economy) were to double, there would be no effect on the real economy. This property is called the **neutrality of money**. It has important implications in macroeconomics.[8]

8.5.2. Real Income as a Determinant of Money Demand

The main reason for holding money (M1) is to facilitate transactions. The real volume of economic activity must therefore be an important factor in determining the demand for money, and we should expect a positive relationship between real GDP and the real money stock. Is this relationship proportional? The Appendix shows that **transaction costs** (bank commissions, or time and effort spent converting money from and into other assets) lead people to use money more efficiently. If we ignore this effect, however, the demand for money should be proportional to the level of economic activity, approximated by the GDP.[9]

The elasticity of money demand with respect to GDP is defined as the percentage increase in money demand resulting from a 1% increase in the GDP.[10] If it is equal to unity, money demand is proportional to GDP. The presence of scale economies would correspond to elasticities less than unity. Table 8.4 presents elasticities of money demand for a number of countries, separating the short run (within one quarter) from the long run. For the long run, when adjustment of money balances is complete, the elasticities are as often above as they are below unity, the average being 1.2. Bearing in mind the lack of precision inherent in obtaining such estimates, it is acceptable, as a rule of thumb, to consider that money demand is about proportional to income, all other things equal.

8.5.3. Nominal Interest Rates as a Determinant of Money Demand

The **nominal interest rate** is the rate actually paid by borrowers for loans or bonds that are denominated in money terms. By contrast, real interest rates—which have been the only interest rates considered so far—would apply to loans in terms of goods, or loans based on a price index. The difference between the two interest rates is that the prices of goods typically rise because of inflation, so that repayment of loans in money rather than 'in kind' at the same interest rate would penalize the lender. Because he receives money worth less in the meantime, he will require a higher nominal interest rate as compensation: the nominal rate increases with inflation (see Section 8.7.2).

The nominal interest rate matters for the demand for money because it is the **opportunity cost** that households and firms face for holding wealth in the fallow form of money. Money bears a zero nominal interest rate—and a negative real interest rate, as explained below—which must be compared with the

---

[8] In particular, the exclusive focus on real variables in Parts I and II is justified as a description of the long run because this is when neutrality is most likely to hold. In Chapter 10 the topic of money neutrality is explained in more detail.

[9] GDP is not an ideal measure of transactions in an economy; total sales, as opposed to final sales, might be preferable.

[10] The formal definition is $\dfrac{\Delta(M/P)/(M/P)}{\Delta Y/Y}$.

Table 8.4. Elasticities of Money Demand
(effect of a 1% increase in income (GNP) or of a 1 percentage point increase in the nominal interest rate)

	Real income		Nominal interest rate	
	Short run	Long run	Short run	Long run
Belgium	0.06	0.41	−0.50	−3.57
Denmark	0.27	1.67	−0.30	−1.88
Finland	0.64	1.13	−0.77	−1.57
France	0.10	0.36	−0.19	−0.70
Germany	0.35	1.19	−0.53	−1.83
Greece	0.16	1.25	−0.13	−1.00
Ireland	0.07	1.48	−0.45	−9.00
Italy	0.11	1.88	−0.31	−5.17
Netherlands	0.41	0.71	−0.86	−1.51
Norway	0.09	1.74	−0.23	−4.60
Portugal	0.18	0.95	−0.51	−2.68
Sweden	0.49	1.40	N.A.	N.A.
Switzerland	0.04	0.36	−0.79	−7.18
UK	0.12	1.70	−0.43	−6.14
Japan	0.05	1.76	−0.44	−6.29
USA	0.06	1.18	−0.12	−2.40
Unweighted av.		1.20		−3.70

Note: The short-run effect is measured within a quarter. The long-run effect corresponds to a complete adjustment of indefinite duration. The demand concerns the real stock of money.

Source: Fair (1987)

nominal rate available for other assets. Holding money implies forgoing that nominal interest rate. It may seem negligible, but it is not. From Table 8.1, for example, we know that in 1994 M1 represented about 25% of GDP in Germany. The German interest rate was then just above 5%. Since German M1 bears negligible interest, the opportunity cost borne by money holders that year amounted to more than 1% of Germany's GDP. For large firms, which work with large cash balances, the cost is not trivial, and cash management, the art of reducing these balances, is very serious business. Table 8.4 shows estimates of the elasticity of money demand *vis-à-vis* the interest rate. The negative signs confirm that money demand declines when interest rates rise. The average long-run effect means that, when the nominal interest rate rises by one percentage point, real money demand falls by 3.7%.[11]

[11] There is a subtle difference between the income elasticity of money demand (the % effect of a 1% increase in income) and the semi-elasticity of a one-percentage-point increase in the interest rate. Formally, the elasticity of y with respect to x is $(\Delta y/y)/(\Delta x/x)$ and the semi-elasticity is $(\Delta y/y)/\Delta x$.

8.5.4. The Money Demand Function

Summarizing the previous sections, the demand for nominal money is proportional to the price level, or, equivalently, the demand for money is a demand for real money. Real money, in turn, is demanded to facilitate real transactions and therefore increases with the real GDP. Holding money, though, has a cost that is measured by the nominal interest rate. Higher interest rates discourage the holding of wealth in the form of money. On the other hand, if it is costly to turn other assets into liquidity, real money holdings are larger. The **money demand function** is a compact way of describing these various effects:

$$(8.1) \qquad M/P = L(Y, i, c),$$
$$+ \quad - \quad +$$

where M is the nominal stock of money, P is the price level, Y is real GDP, i is the nominal interest rate, and c is the average cost of converting other forms of wealth into money. The Appendix shows how (8.1) can be

BOX 8.3. THE MANY REASONS FOR HOLDING MONEY

The demand for money is explained in the text by its role in facilitating transactions. This is often called the *inventory theory of money* because it comes from the trade-off between the cost of holding that inventory—interest costs—and the transaction cost of converting interest-bearing assets into money. The inventory explanation may also be expanded to account for uncertainty and the perceived risk of being caught without liquidity in emergencies. This behaviour is dubbed the *precautionary motive* and generally predicts that the demand for money rises when economic conditions become more uncertain.

A very different approach emphasizes that money is one asset among several. The *portfolio balance view* argues that agents spread their wealth so as to diversify their assets, considering not only the returns (zero for currency, the nominal yield on bonds) but also the risk

characteristics of each asset. The corresponding demand-for-money function includes the interest rate and transaction costs as before, but instead of transactions and the real GDP it is related to wealth. One particular aspect of the portfolio approach is the *speculative motive*. In fast-moving financial markets, traders must be ready to buy or sell quickly very large amounts of assets. When interest rates are low and expected to rise, bond prices are expected to fall. (Box 3.2 explains the inverse relationship between bond prices and the interest rate.) It is then considered better to 'stay liquid', to hold more money and fewer bonds on which capital losses are possible. Conversely, when interest rates are high and expected to fall, traders want to acquire bonds and take advantage of capital gains when their prices rise: the speculative demand for money declines.

formally justified by inventory management principles. Others justifications are summarized in Box 8.3.

The effect of the price level on money demand is shown in Figure 8.3, where it is assumed, for simplicity, that real GDP is constant. Then, as long as the inflation rate ($\Delta P/P$) is constant, the real demand for money remains unchanged. Panel (*a*) shows the case of zero inflation ($\Delta P/P = 0$). The price level is constant except for one jump which is perceived by agents as unique (for example, an increase in sales tax or VAT). Panel (*b*) shows the case of a non-zero but constant inflation rate ($\Delta P/P > 0$). The real money demand is constant, but lower than with zero inflation, and the nominal money demand rises in proportion to the price level. Panel (*c*) shows the case where inflation is rising. Real money demand declines while nominal money grows increasingly faster, yet slower than the price level.

The **velocity of money** measures how many times on average a unit of money is spent during the measurement period (usually a year). It is defined as $V = PY/M$, and is the inverse of the ratio shown in Figure 8.2. For example, if $V = 3$, the money stock M is spent on average three times on the GDP, or the money stock 'turns round three times' over the year. Given the money demand function, velocity is:

$$(8.2) \qquad V = \frac{Y}{L(Y, i, c)}.$$

In the particular case where real money demand is proportional to real GDP, velocity is independent of GDP.[12] In the short run, transaction costs do not change much so that velocity simply moves as the interest rate changes. When the interest rate rises, holding money becomes more expensive and people save on cash balances; the money turns round faster, and velocity increases. Over the longer run, if transaction costs decline, people will hold less money and velocity will show a rising trend.

8.6. Equilibrium in the Money Market: the Short Run

The real money demand function is depicted in Figure 8.4. Its negative slope reflects the opportunity cost of holding money. Its position corresponds to a particular GDP level. If the GDP increases, so does the demand for money at any nominal interest rate. The schedule shifts to the right.

Chapter 9 is devoted entirely to the way central banks control the supply of money. Here we simply assume that the central bank fixes the nominal money

[12] When money demand is proportional to real GDP, it can be rewritten as $L(Y, i, c) = Y l(i, c)$ and $V = Y/Y l(i, c) = 1/l(i, c)$.

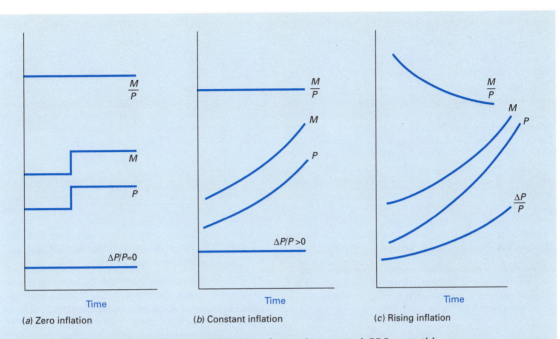

(a) Zero inflation   *(b)* Constant inflation   *(c)* Rising inflation

Figure 8.3. Money Demand and Prices (assuming no real GDP growth)

When expected inflation is constant, real money demand is constant and nominal money demand just moves with the price level. This is true for both panels (*a*) and (*b*). In panel (*a*) there is a one-shot unexpected price increase. In panel (*c*) prices rise at an increasing rate. As inflation increases, real money demand declines, which means that the nominal money demand grows less quickly than prices.

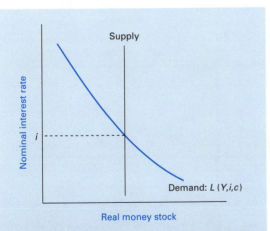

Figure 8.4. Equilibrium in the Money Market

Given the level of economic activity and the cost of converting funds, the negative slope of the money demand curve reflects the effect of the opportunity cost of holding money. When the central bank sets the money supply (the vertical supply schedule), the interest rate adjusts to clear the money market.

supply which, for a given price level, renders the real money supply exogenous, hence the vertical line in Figure 8.4. Money market equilibrium is described by the intersection of both schedules. This simple apparatus can be used to explain the short-run relationship between money and interest rates. It is only a short-run view because it takes as exogenous the real GDP, the price level, and the inflation rate: over the short run (say, a quarter) these variables normally change very little. With a constant inflation rate, the results that follow apply to both the nominal and real interest rates.

8.6.1. Money Supply Effects

Figure 8.5 shows the effect on interest rates of an increase in the real money supply, represented by a rightward shift in the vertical schedule. The demand curve does not shift, since its other determinants (real GDP and transactions costs) are assumed to remain unaffected.[13] As the equilibrium moves from *A* to *A'*, the

[13] Ch. 10 directly addresses the effects of money supply on GNP.

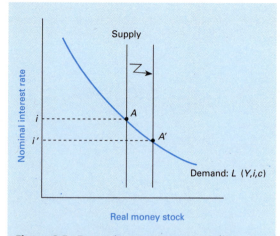

Figure 8.5. Expansionary Monetary Policy

An increase in the real money supply lowers the nominal interest rate. A decline in interest rates induces a higher demand so as to match the higher supply.

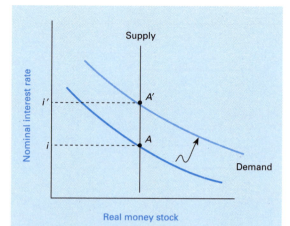

Figure 8.6. An Increase in Real Economic Activity

An increase in real economic activity increases the demand for money and the schedule shifts to the right. Starting at point A, the new equilibrium occurs at point A' and the nominal interest rate increases from i to i'. With supply unchanged, demand cannot increase in equilibrium. The interest rate must rise until its negative effect on demand exactly offsets the positive effect of the increase in GDP.

interest rate declines. This illustrates the power of the central bank to influence interest rates. A restrictive or 'tight' monetary policy occurs when the central bank contracts the real money supply, which would be represented by a leftward shift of the vertical supply schedule. In that case nominal and real interest rates rise.

8.6.2. Cyclical Fluctuations

An increase in real GDP increases money demand, and the demand schedule shifts to the right as shown in Figure 8.6. If the real money supply remains unchanged, the interest rate must rise until the increased demand induced by the higher GDP is entirely offset by the higher opportunity cost of holding money. This is one reason why interest rates are procyclical, rising in booms and declining in recessions.

8.6.3. Transaction Costs

If the nominal cost of converting wealth between interest-bearing assets and money decreases, more wealth is held in the form of interest-bearing assets and less in the form of money. The money demand curve shifts to the left, as in Figure 8.7, and interest

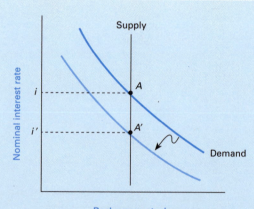

Figure 8.7. A Decline in Transaction Costs

A decline in the cost of converting assets from money to interest-bearing forms reduces the demand for money and shifts the demand schedule to the left. Since the supply does not change, the interest rate must fall to reduce the opportunity cost of holding money until demand is restored to its initial level.

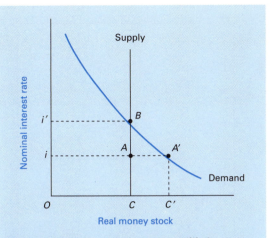

Figure 8.8. Money Market Disequilibrium

Point *A* to the left of the demand curve describes a situation of excess demand for money. At the relatively low interest rate *i*, agents want to hold more real money balances (at point *A'* on the demand curve). They attempt to sell other assets or borrow money, but with unchanged supply the interest rate rises until equilibrium is restored at point *B* at interest *i'*.

rates fall to the point where the opportunity cost is low enough to persuade agents to hold the existing money supply. An example of a decrease in transaction costs is the development and introduction of automatic teller machines. On the other hand, trans-

action costs might increase if banks decided to charge more for transfers, or if an increase in wages made individuals' leisure time more valuable.

8.6.4. The Equilibrating Role of the Interest Rate and Asset Prices

How is equilibrium achieved in the short run? Point *A* in Figure 8.8 is to the left of the demand curve: it depicts the case of an excess demand for money. At interest rate *i*, agents would like to hold real balances (point *A'*) in excess of the available supply (point *A*). To obtain additional liquidity, they attempt to sell other assets such as bonds or to borrow funds from each other. With a fixed money supply *OC*, however, these efforts cannot be successful in the aggregate. The interest rate increases as the result of competition for more money, and bond prices fall as more bonds are offered for sale.[14] Equilibrium is restored at point *B* at interest rate *i'*.

Financial markets react extremely quickly to disequilibria. This is because large losses can be incurred by holding bonds when their prices are falling. Similarly, very large capital gains are available to those who buy bonds before their prices increase. Any disequilibrium in the money market is eliminated by swift interest rate and bond price changes, and the economy promptly returns to its money demand schedule.

8.7. Equilibrium in the Money Market: the Long Run

The money market equilibrium condition also settles the long-run link between money, prices and inflation, and the exchange rate. Two very simple and powerful results emerge. First, in the long run, inflation is determined by the rate of money growth. Second, in the long run, the rate of exchange rate depreciation is determined by the rate of inflation. Figure 8.9(*a*) presents long-run averages of money growth and inflation rates for all the OECD countries. Panel (*b*) does the same for exchange rates and inflation (relatively to the dollar and US inflation). While not perfect, the

positive relationship between all three variables is unmistakable.

8.7.1. Long-Run Inflation

As the economy grows, more money is needed to facilitate more transactions. In Figure 8.10, this means that the demand schedule continuously shifts to the

[14] The link between interest rates and bond prices is presented in Box 3.2.

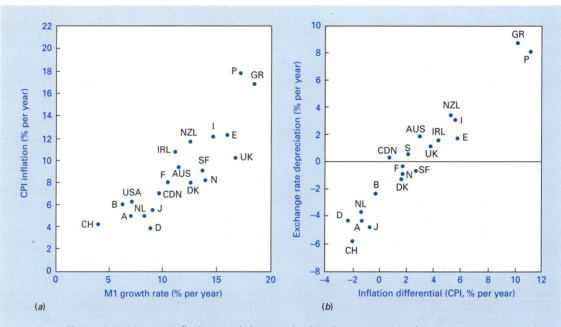

Figure 8.9. Money, Inflation, and the Nominal Exchange Rate in the Long Run: OECD Countries, 1970–1990

Averaging over many years eliminates short-run effects. Panel (*a*) shows that countries that have experienced high inflation rates are those where nominal money has grown faster. Panel (*b*) shows that the rate of change of the dollar exchange rate is about equal to the inflation differential exchange *vis-à-vis* the USA, as suggested by purchasing power parity.

Source: IMF

right. If the real money stock were held constant, the interest rate would grow from point *A* to point *A'* and then continuously further up as the demand schedule moves rightward. But we know that nominal interest rates do not grow without bounds over the long run. The two examples in Figure 8.11 show that the British and Dutch nominal interest rate rose at times of sustained inflation (after the Second World War and then in the 1970s; cf. Figure 1.5).[15] But they seem to have returned to lower levels, rather than continuing to rise. What must happen in Figure 8.10 is that the supply schedule eventually moves rightward until it passes through a point like *B*, as the real money supply matches the long-run growth in its demand. How can that be?

In the long run, the central bank controls only the *nominal* money stock. It can affect neither prices, nor

inflation, nor the real money supply. The only possibility of reconciling any discrepancy between real money demand (*M/P*) and nominal supply (*M*) growth is for prices and inflation to play the balancing act as endogenous variables. Inflation is the channel through which, in the long run, money market equilibrium is ultimately achieved. (See Box 8.4 for details.)

Consider the case shown in Table 8.5, where economic growth implies a 3% average annual increase in real money demand. If the central bank allows the nominal money stock to grow at the same 3% per year, demand and supply will coincide when the average inflation rate is 0%. Were the nominal money stock to grow at an average annual rate of 8%, inflation would have to be 5%: only then would the real money stock grow at the same 3% rate (8% nominal less 5% of inflation) as real money demand. This is why in the long run inflation is a monetary phenomenon. It is due to money growth in excess of what is strictly demanded by the public. Figure 8.9 confirms the strength of this conclusion.

[15] As explained in Ch. 20, this is related to worldwide inflation as the international monetary system built in Bretton Woods in 1944 collapsed.

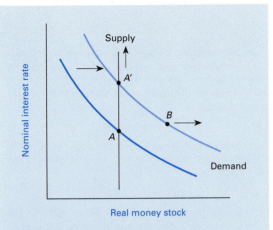

Figure 8.10. Money and Long-Run Growth

As real GDP increases, so does the demand for real money. The demand schedule shifts to the right. If the real money supply did not respond, the interest rate would rise, as shown by the move from point A to point A'. Continuous growth would result in an ever shifting demand schedule and an ever rising interest rate. The absence of long-run trend in the nominal interest rate means that, somehow, the supply curve must shift over time to move from A to B, and further to the right.

8.7.2. Inflation and the Fisher Principle

Section 8.5.1. considered the role of the price level in the demand for money. The rate of inflation, i.e. the rate of increase in the price level, has an independent effect on money demand. The distinction is subtle and is illustrated in Figure 8.3 above. A once-and-for-all increase in the price level raises nominal money demand proportionately. In contrast, continuous price increases—inflation—erode the purchasing power of money. For example, with a 10% annual inflation rate, a given stock of money in real terms is worth 10% less a year later.

The effect can be understood by the distinction between nominal and real interest rates. By definition, the real interest rate (r) is the difference between the nominal interest rate (i) and the expected rate of inflation (π^e):

$$(8.6) \qquad r = i - \pi^e.$$

For real decisions such as consumption and investment, we have seen that the real interest rate is the one that matters. In principle, no one would lend money at a nominal interest rate lower than expected inflation because the interest payment does not compensate for the loss of purchasing power. Implicitly, at

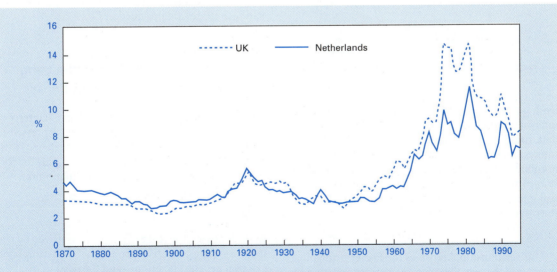

Figure 8.11. Nominal Interest Rates, UK and the Netherlands, 1870–1990

Over very long periods the nominal interest rate is trendless, despite shorter-run fluctuations and possible 'staircase behaviour' reflecting the higher inflation rate of the 1970s and 1980s.

Sources: Homer (1963); IMF

BOX 8.4. THE ALGEBRA OF LONG-RUN INFLATION

The money demand function $L(Y, i, c)$ identifies three determinants of the real money stock. As long as the transaction cost c is constant in real terms, it can safely be ignored. Similarly, when the interest rate does not exhibit any long-term trend, despite considerable variability, it does not affect real money in the long run. This just leaves the real GDP. If η is the elasticity of the demand for money with respect to GDP, an annual GDP growth rate of g translates into an annual growth rate ηg in money demand. Noting that the growth rate of the real money stock is the difference between the growth rates of the nominal money stock and the price level, we have the equilibrium condition:

$$(8.3) \qquad \frac{\Delta(M/P)}{(M/P)} = \mu - \pi = \eta g,$$

where $\mu = \Delta M/M$ and $\pi = \Delta P/P$. Given the real growth rate g, this expression shows that the long-run inflation rate is the difference between the nominal money growth rate and the rate of growth of real GNP, up to the elasticity factor η:

$$(8.4) \qquad \pi = \mu - \eta g.$$

The relationship (8.4) can be combined with relative PPP in equation (8.9) to yield the long-run rate of exchange rate depreciation:

$$(8.5) \qquad \varepsilon = (\mu - \mu^*) - (\eta g - \eta^* g^*).$$

Faster money growth at home (η) than abroad (η^*) leads in the long run to a depreciation. Faster output growth at home (g) than abroad (g^*) leads to an appreciation if the faster demand for money is not accommodated by a faster growth in the money supply.

Table 8.5. Inflation and Money Growth in the Long Run: a Rule of Thumb (assuming that real money demand grows at 3% p.a.)

Nominal money supply (%)	Inflation rate (%)
0	−3
3	0
8	5
50	47
103	100

least, borrowers and lenders agree that a positive real interest rate should remunerate the lender. Indeed, the data presented in Figure 5.7 indicated that the real interest rate shows little trend over long periods. The nominal rate can therefore be seen as the sum of the reward to the lender, or the cost of borrowing (the real interest rate), and expected inflation. This is (8.6) rewritten as

$$(8.7) \qquad i = r + \pi^e.$$

This relationship, known as the **Fisher principle**,[16] shows that the negative effect of expected inflation on real money demand is already captured by the nominal interest rate. The nominal rate includes both the forgone real opportunity cost (r) and the expected

[16] After Irving Fisher, the Yale economist referred to in Ch. 3.

capital loss on the nominal value of the loan (π^e). The store-of-value and standard-of-deferred-payment properties of money are eroded when its value in terms of the goods it can buy is deteriorating, that is when prices increase. Figure 8.12 shows a few examples of **hyperinflation**—when inflation reaches rates in excess of 50% per month. As expected, domestic money holdings fall dramatically and shattered confidence is not easily restored afterwards. More details on these fascinating episodes are provided in Box 8.5.

8.7.3. The Exchange Rate in the Long Run: Purchasing Power Parity

The real exchange rate (λ) is defined in Chapter 7 as the ratio of foreign to domestic prices, expressed in same currency ($\lambda = EP^*/P$). Its rate of change is the sum of the rate of nominal depreciation plus the foreign inflation rate less the domestic inflation rate:

$$(8.8) \qquad \frac{\Delta\lambda}{\lambda} = \frac{\Delta E}{E} + \frac{\Delta P^*}{P^*} - \frac{\Delta P}{P}.$$

In the long run, the real exchange rate is driven by real factors—tastes, relative productivity, accumulated external net asset position—and the need to meet the nation's budget constraint. When these real factors remain unchanged, the equilibrium real exchange rate is constant. The real exchange rate is constant when the nominal exchange rate depreciates at a rate ($\varepsilon = \Delta E/E$) equal to the difference between the domestic

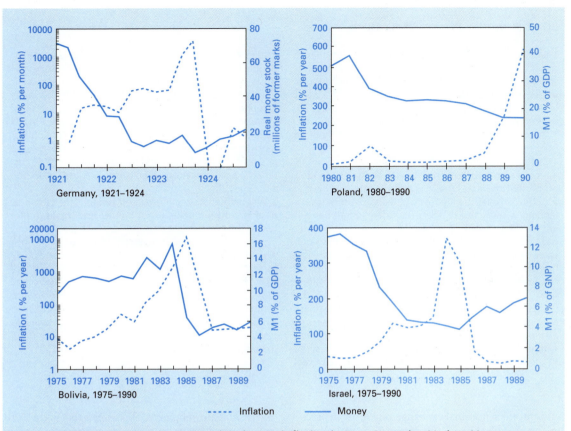

Figure 8.12. Money Demand and Hyperinflation in Four Countries, Various Years

The ratio of money to GDP or GNP declines when the expected rate of inflation rises. When hyperinflation is credibly eliminated, the ratio should go back up to normal levels. The three recent cases illustrate setbacks: a temporary decline in inflation, usually arising from administrative price controls, fails to persuade the public; confidence is not restored and the public continues shunning money, sometimes long after inflation has come down. The German hyperinflation episode in 1922–3 is the best known case. By early 1923 inflation stood at about 40% per *month* and the demand for money (the ratio of M1 to the consumer price index) had already fallen dramatically. Monthly inflation went on to an annual rate of 32,400% in October 1923.

Sources: IMF; for Germany, Sargent (1982)

$(\pi = \Delta P/P)$ and foreign $(\pi^* = \Delta P^*/P^*)$ inflation rates, the **inflation differential**:

(8.9) $\varepsilon = \pi - \pi^*$.

When the real exchange rate is constant, a country with a higher rate of inflation than the rest of the world must have a depreciating currency, whereas a low-inflation-rate country will have an appreciating currency. This principle is called **relative purchasing power parity** (PPP). Figure 8.9 provides strong support for PPP.

Exactly as in (8.9), for each country the link between the depreciation of its currency *vis-à-vis* the dollar and the inflation differential *vis-à-vis* the USA is quite tight.

Bringing together PPP and the explanation of long-run inflation, we see that the long-run rate of exchange rate depreciation depends on the difference between the rate of money growth at home and abroad. This reasoning is formalized in Box 8.4. Countries with fast money growth have more inflation than those with slow money growth. If the real exchange rate is

BOX 8.5. MONEY IN HYPERINFLATIONS

There is no clear border between high inflation and hyperinflation. Conventionally, hyperinflation corresponds to price increases in excess of 50% per month. Under such circumstances, inflation seems to assume a life of its own and to continue rising inexorably. In Central Europe a wave of hyperinflations occurred in the early 1920s. Rates of 10% per *hour* were actually observed for brief periods.

In countries with chronically high inflation, nominal interest rates are often indexed: loan contracts include a clause that stipulates that the interest rate be adjusted for inflation over the lifetime of the loan. Alternatively, lending is restricted to short maturity, sometimes not longer than a week. Because these loans are then renewed at the prevailing interest rate, it is roughly equivalent to indexation. Consequently, as inflation rises borrowers and lenders attempt to keep the real interest rate unchanged, and the nominal interest rate rises along with inflation. This explains why, in Figure 8.12, the money stock (as a percentage of nominal GDP) dramatically declines when inflation picks up speed. The real demand for money (M/P) becomes very small compared with the volume of transactions and real GDP (Y), so M/PY declines. Fearing ever-increasing losses on the real

value of money and with nominal interest rates rising, people hold increasingly smaller amounts of cash, sometimes just enough for the day's shopping. The velocity of money increases. People convert their wealth into assets immune to inflation. They hold durable goods of all sorts, including precious metals as well as less standard assets such as TVs, refrigerators, or even cigarettes. Foreign currency begins to circulate openly, with goods prices quoted and traded in both local and foreign (mostly dollar) currencies, a phenomenon called *currency substitution* (see also Box 8.2).

When inflation is finally beaten, nominal interest rates decline, and the demand for money rises again in real terms. This effect is called *reliquification*. It is a signal that people believe the inflationary episode to be over. Since we cannot observe expectations of inflation, a good proxy for them is money demand relative to real output (M/PY). The examples displayed in Figure 8.12 show that successes against inflation are not always convincing. Temporary successes are followed by relapses, and even long after hyperinflation is vanquished, real cash balances remain low, suggesting that once-burned agents continue to be sceptical for a while.

constant, their nominal exchange rate must depreciate. On the other hand, the demand for real money rises rapidly in fast-growing economies. Given the rate of growth of the nominal money supply, the nominal exchange rate tends to appreciate.

A much stronger version of this idea is **absolute**

purchasing power parity. This asserts that price levels are equalized across countries once they are converted in the same currency: not only is λ assumed to be constant, but it is assumed to be equal to unity, and therefore $P = EP^*$. Box 8.6 provides some details on the failure of absolute PPP to hold.

BOX 8.6. THE LAW OF ONE PRICE AND ABSOLUTE PURCHASING POWER PARITY

A key ingredient in the logic behind absolute PPP is the law of one price. This 'law' asserts that the same good should trade everywhere at the same price, when prices are expressed in the same currency. If prices were to differ significantly, it is asserted, enterprising traders would buy the goods where they are cheapest and sell them where they fetch a higher price. This process of arbitrage would push prices towards each other until the incentive for profit is removed. The law of one price is known to be grossly violated. Table 8.6 provides some telling examples. More examples and some of the reasons behind the results were presented in Chapter 7. Yet in the long run, if countries have access to similar technologies and converge to similar wealth levels, absolute purchasing parity becomes a much more reasonable proposition—not good

by good, but across broad baskets of goods. This might characterize price-level convergence in Europe.

Table 8.6. Prices in the USA and in France (in FF at $1 = FF5.0615)

	Levi's Jeans	Computer Mac SE	Walkman Sony WM55	Big Mac
France	430	18,500	405	18.10
USA	192	9,110	349	11.10

Source: International Herald Tribune, 19 October 1990

8.8. Summary

1. Money is an asset that is generally accepted as a means of payment. This definition leaves some room for interpretation, especially as payment technologies change over time.

2. Money has four attributes: it is a medium of exchange, a unit of account, a store of value, and a standard for deferred payment. Bearing no or low interest, it is dominated by other assets. Its desirability stems from its unique ability to resolve the problems of the double coincidence of wants and of information asymmetry.

3. Money is a public good. The fact that it is easily recognized and generally accepted generates benefits for the community. This is why there is a role for the government in issuing and guaranteeing money.

4. Money is simultaneously an asset of the private nonbanking sector and a liability of the banking system. Currency is a liability of the monetary authority (central bank), while sight deposits are a liability of commercial banks.

5. The demand for money is a demand for real money. Agents are interested in the purchasing power of money, not in its nominal or face value.

6. The demand for real money increases with the volume of transactions, approximated by the real GDP. It decreases, with the nominal interest rate, the opportunity cost of holding money. The demand for money increases with transaction costs because agents have an incentive to limit the number of transactions between money and other assets.

7. An unexpected and once-for-all increase in the price level does not affect the real demand for money. It affects the nominal demand for money, which increases in proportion with the price level.

8. Inflation reduces the purchasing power of money. An expected increase in inflation leads agents to reduce their real demand for money. This effect is captured by the nominal interest rate, the sum of the real interest rate, and the expected rate of inflation.

9. In the short run, money market equilibrium occurs rapidly through changes in the interest rate and bond prices. In the long run, money market equilibrium is achieved through changes in the price level and/or the rate of inflation.

10. In the long run, relative purchasing power parity holds in the absence of real disturbances. Then the rate of nominal exchange rate depreciation is equal to the inflation differential.

Key Concepts

- commodity monies
- monetary aggregates (M1, M2, etc.)
- medium of exchange
- double coincidence of wants
- unit of account
- store of value
- standard of deferred payment
- dominated asset
- information asymmetry
- parallel currency
- fiat money
- public good
- balance sheet

- net worth
- neutrality of money
- transactions costs
- nominal interest rate
- opportunity cost
- money demand function
- velocity of money
- Fisher principle
- inflation, hyperinflation
- inflation differential
- purchasing power parity (PPP), absolute and relative
- dichotomy

Exercises: Theory

1. Each central bank publishes the definition of its own monetary aggregates. Find the definitions for money aggregates in your own country.

2. Using Figure 8.1, consolidate the balance sheets of the central bank and of the banking sector. What is the definition of money corresponding to the liability side (excluding net worth) of the consolidated banking sector?

3. Banks routinely exchange domestic currency against foreign currencies for their customers. Imagine that a customer brings in a large amount of foreign currency and asks that her checking account be credited by the corresponding amount in domestic currency. In the balance sheet of the commercial banking (Figure 8.1), show what happens:

   (*a*) when the commercial bank keeps the foreign currency in its vaults.
   (*b*) when the bank turns over the foreign currency to the central bank and receives domestic currency in return.

4. In the consolidated balance sheet of the government and nonbank private sector, suppose we know the following:

(*a*) Deposits of the government and the private sector amount to 2000.

(*b*) Total net worth is 400.

(*c*) The net public debt of the government is 800 and its gross debt 1000, the difference being in bank deposits. (The government has no real assets.)

(*d*) The gross private debt is 1600.

(*e*) Private real assets total 600.

What is the value of bank notes and currency in circulation? What is M1?

5. Credit cards offer their holders the ability to obtain immediate credit up to a given ceiling. What are arguments for

(*a*) including the total amount of ceilings in the definition M1?

(*b*) using only the amounts actually used up?

(*c*) not including it at all?

6. Give a reason why the ratio of money to nominal GDP might increase when standards of living are rising. (*Hint*: think about leisure.)

7. If inflation is positive, simply maintaining the nominal money supply at some constant level amounts to a contractionary monetary policy. True or false?

8. What is the effect on the velocity of money of an unexpected increase in the rate of inflation that is:

(*a*) temporary?

(*b*) permanent?

9. In Figure 8.1, show the effect of an increase in the government's borrowing from

(*a*) the nonbank private sector.

(*b*) commercial banks.

(*c*) the central bank.

What do you conclude about the link between public debt and money?

10. The real interest rate rises from 2% to 4% while the nominal interest rate remains unchanged at 9%. All other determinants of money demand are assumed to be constant.

(*a*) How can you explain this?

(*b*) What is the effect on the demand for real money?

11. As inflation increases and the nominal interest rate rises, the demand for money declines. What does this imply for the relative growth rates of money and prices?

Exercises: Applications

1. The percentage effect on real money demand of an increase of one percentage point of the interest rate (say, from 5% to 6%) is sometimes called the interest rate semi-elasticity of the demand for money. Suppose it takes the value −0.1. The income elasticity of money demand (the percentage effect of an increase of 1% of real GDP on real money demand) is 0.8. Find the increase in the interest rate required to maintain money market equilibrium, at unchanged real money supply, when output increases by 1%, 2%, and 5%.

2. With an interest rate semi-elasticity of the demand for money equal to −0.2, what happens to the real money demand when the interest rate rises from 5% per annum to

   (a) 10% per annum?
   (b) 10% per month?

3. Explain the reliquification problem using question 2 above by considering what happens when a rate of inflation of 10% per month is eliminated.

4. In the early phases of inflationary periods, it is not uncommon to observe that nominal interest rates remain below the inflation rate. How can this be explained?

5. Consider the French data in Figure 8.2. Suggest reasons why the ratio of M1 to nominal GNP declined in France from the mid-1960s to the early 1980s while the ratio of M2 to nominal GNP was rising.

6. Many countries have introduced deregulation measures in the banking sector, with the intention of increasing bank competition.

   (a) How will this affect (i) interest rates? (ii) money demand?
   (b) What can central banks do if they want to keep the real money stock unchanged?

7. When the Polish government cut subsidies to state-owned corporations in 1990, Polish firms began extending commercial credit to each other by deferring payments on their respective purchases.

   (a) How is this similar to the creation of a parallel currency?
   (b) How is it different?

8. Iceland consistently had an inflation rate of between 20% and 30% per annum in the 1980s.

   (a) How do you explain this?
   (b) At what level do you suppose nominal interest rates were?

Suggested Further Reading

The classic formal articles on the inventory theory of money demand are:

Baumol, William (1952), 'The Transactions Demand for Cash: an Inventory Theoretic Approach', *Quarterly Journal of Economics*, 56: 545–56.

Tobin, James (1956), 'The Interest Rate Elasticity of the Transactions Demand for Cash', *Review of Economics and Statistics*, 38: 241–7.

A survey of the large number of empirical studies of the demand for money is:

Goldfeld, S. and Sichel, M. (1989), in B. M. Friedman and F. Hahn (eds.), *Handbook of Monetary Economics*, North-Holland, Amsterdam.

Appendix: An Inventory Model of the Demand for Money

This appendix presents a simple inventory model of money demand by individual households. It is due to Baumol (1952) and Nobel Prize laureate James Tobin (1956). (A more elaborate and difficult model for the firm's optimal holding of money can be found in Miller and Orr (1966).)

We imagine an agent who receives a nominal income of PY in each period and consumes at a constant rate over the period. There is no savings carried over from one period to the next. She receives her income in the form of a cheque at the beginning of the period, say, the month. At a minimum, she must visit the bank once, in order to deposit all her salary in her bank account, so that it is available for spending. In general, she will probably choose to keep some wealth in the form of an interest-bearing savings account as well as in her current account. Each visit to the bank or transaction has a nominal cost c. (c should be thought of as the opportunity cost of time spent queueing, 'shoe leather' used up while running to the bank, and or bank fees for such transactions.) If n is the number of visits to the bank during the month, the monthly cost will be nc. To reduce such costs, she might want to hold more sight deposits, but then she faces an opportunity cost. If i is the monthly interest rate served on the savings account, holding an average nominal balance M over the month implies an opportunity cost iM.

Figure 8.13 shows the amount of money that the agent has in her checking account for various numbers of monthly trips to the bank. The height of each triangle represents the amount withdrawn from the savings account and deposited in the checking account. It is PY/n. As trips to the bank, which are evenly spaced, occur every $(1/n)$th day of the month, the area of each triangle represents her average money held between two trips:

Average money held between two trips

$$= \frac{1}{2} \times \frac{PY}{n} \times \frac{1}{n} = \frac{PY}{2n^2}.$$

Her opportunity cost is the interest forgone on this average money holding:

Opportunity cost = $\underset{\text{interest rate}}{i} \times \underset{\substack{\text{no. of trips}}}{n} \times \underset{\substack{\text{av. holding in} \\ \text{between two trips}}}{(PY/2n)^2}.$

Total costs TC (trips plus opportunity costs of holding M1) are therefore

(A8.1) $$TC = i\frac{PY}{2n} + cn.$$

Table 8.7 presents the breakdown of total costs when PY = ECU 2000 per month, with a cost of transferring money of c = ECU 1 and a nominal interest rate of 12% (about 1% per month). Total costs are minimized for three trips to the bank over the month.

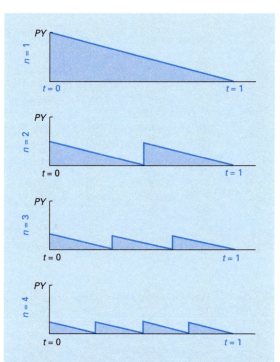

Figure 8.13. Trips to the Bank and Average Money Holdings

For one trip per month to the bank ($n = 1$), the average balance is simply $PY/2$. For two trips ($n = 2$), there are two triangles, each with area $(PY/2) \times (1/2) \times (1/2)$, so the average monthly balance is $PY/4$. For n trips per month, the average holding between trips is $PY/2n^2$ and the average monthly balance is $PY/2n$.

Table 8.7. Costs of Cash Inventory (in ECUs)

No. of trips	Interest cost $(PY/2n)i$	Trip's cost (cn)	Total cost
1	10.00	1.00	11.00
2	5.00	2.00	7.00
3	3.33	3.00	6.33
4	2.50	4.00	6.50
5	2.00	5.00	7.00
6	1.67	6.00	7.67

The more general mathematical formulation of the problem is:

(A8.2)
$$\min_{n} TC = i\frac{PY}{2n} + cn.$$

Ignoring the fact that n must be a whole number, the optimum is obtained by setting the marginal cost equal to zero:[17]

(A8.3)
$$\frac{\partial TC}{\partial n} = -\frac{iPY}{2n^2} + c = 0.$$

The optimal n is:

(A8.4)
$$n^* = \sqrt{\frac{iPY}{2c}},$$

which leads to the 'square root' formula describing the optimal holding money stock:

(A8.5)
$$M^* = \frac{PY}{2n^*} = \sqrt{\frac{PYc}{2i}}.$$

As the demand-for-money function (8.1), this expression states that the optimal average money holding is:

- a positive function of real economic activity Y
- a positive function of the price level P
- a positive function of transactions costs c
- a negative function of the nominal interest rate i

If we further define the *real* cost of transactions c^R as $c^R \equiv c/P$, the square root formula can be expressed in terms of real money demand:

(A8.6)
$$\frac{M^*}{P} = \sqrt{\frac{Yc^R}{2i}}.$$

We can further rewrite (A8.6) as

(A8.7)
$$\left(\frac{M}{P}\right)^* = Y\sqrt{\frac{c^R/Y}{2i}}.$$

If the transaction cost is a fixed proportion of income, c^R/Y is constant and the demand for money is proportional to the real GDP. The income elasticity of money demand is unity, and the elasticities with respect to (c^R/Y) and i are both 0.5:

$$\frac{\partial(M/P)^*/\partial(c^R/Y)}{(c^R/Y)/(M/P)} = \frac{1}{2}$$

and

$$\frac{\partial(M/P)^*/\partial(i/Y)}{(i/Y)/(M/P)} = -\frac{1}{2}.$$

---

[17] This is a local minimum because the second-order condition is satisfied.

9

The Supply of Money and Monetary Policy

By playing upon the reserves of the bank, the note-issuing authority can induce an expansion or a contraction of credit at will. But in order to do so, it must have at its disposal some machinery for issuing and withdrawing notes easily and promptly. A Government which can only withdraw notes by raising the necessary funds from the public by taxes or loans does not fulfil this condition. The best instrument for the regulation of the supply of paper money is a State Bank or else a Central Bank which, while not itself a part of the Executive Government, is willing regularly to co-operate with it.

R. G. Hawtrey

9.1. Overview

Chapter 8 presented the demand for money and money market equilibrium under the assumption that the central bank controls the nominal money supply. Indeed, in all countries the control of the money supply is formally attributed to the central bank. Yet, the sole component of money directly controlled by the monetary authorities is currency, which represents a small part of any definition of money—M1, M2, or wider aggregates. To influence the supply of bank deposits, the central bank must resort to indirect methods. This chapter describes the complex process of monetary control and the relationship between the central bank and the commercial banks, a curious mixture of regulation and partnership in the money creation process. Most advanced countries rely on an active money market where the authorities face the public at large—those who demand money—through the mediation of banks and other financial institutions. This is where the scarcity or abundance of money is revealed and priced and where the economy-wide interest rate is determined. At the heart of this process are the bank reserves, the sum of commercial banks' vault cash and funds deposited in accounts at the central bank.

Money markets across the world are tightly linked. Domestic monetary conditions directly affect the exchange rate, and international capital movements impinge on the process of monetary control. Not infrequently, conflicts arise between the domestic and foreign monetary policy objectives of the central bank. These conflicts originate in the linkages between the money supply process and foreign exchange market intervention by the monetary authorities.

While the principles guiding the process of monetary control are fundamentally the same across countries, institutions and procedures can differ significantly. In what follows, the *differences* between central banks, which may matter at times, are intentionally downplayed. Wherever possible we highlight similarities, and attempt to describe a monetary system that is a common denominator of various arrangements observed in developed economies.[1]

---

[1] Ch. 16 draws some important implications of the choice of particular institutions for the effectiveness of monetary control. Ch. 21 considers the steps necessary for the establishment of a monetary union in Europe.

9.2. The Money Supply Process

9.2.1. Money Creation: the Rules of Central and Commercial Banks

9.2.1.1. The central bank and the monetary base

The **central bank** is a public or quasi-public agency with an explicit legal mandate.[2] It is often called the 'bankers' bank', through which banks can settle claims against each other, and it may also serve as a clearing house of cheques written by depositors. With a few exceptions, it does not take deposits from the private sector, but often functions as the government's bank. It may also gather, process, and analyse information about the financial and real economy. Most importantly, the central bank establishes the standard of payment. It does so by issuing currency, one of the components of M1. It also creates **bank reserves**, which are claims on the central bank and are owned by commercial banks. The sum of currency in circulation and commercial bank reserves is known as the **monetary base**, sometimes called M0.[3] The monetary base is represented by the shaded area in Figure 9.1 and is depicted in Table 9.1 as the first two liability entries in the balance sheet of the German central bank, the *Bundesbank*.

9.2.1.2. The role of commercial banks in money creation

As **financial intermediaries**, commercial banks collect funds from depositors and lend them to borrowers, channelling resources from savers to investors. They also play a payment-clearing role in settling accounts among their customers and with those of other banks. Much more important, however, is their role in the money supply process. Were it not for banks, the only circulating medium of exchange would be currency. In fact, the bulk of the money supply used in modern economies is bank deposits actually created by the commercial banking system. The money-creating function of banks is what distinguishes them from other financial intermediaries such as savings banks, brokers, and stock markets. All of those collect, lend, and invest funds, but none of them has the right to create money because none of them may legally lend more than they have received in deposits.

By lending money that they do not possess, commercial banks are in effect issuing money. How do they do it? We will learn below that, by granting a loan to a

---

[2] The Bank of England was a private institution from its founding in 1694 until its nationalization in 1946, much like the Banque de France, founded in 1800 and nationalized in 1945. The Bundesbank was established in 1949 as a successor to the Deutsche Reichsbank founded in 1876. The oldest central bank is the Swedish Riksbank, founded in 1668, while other dates of foundation are: Bank of Japan, 1882; Banca d'Italia, 1893; Austrian National Bank, 1816; Swiss National Bank, 1905. The Federal Reserve of the USA was founded in 1913 and is owned by the member banks, although profits above a statutory maximum are remitted, as in most countries, to the government (Goodhart 1988).

[3] Other expressions used are 'high-powered' or 'central bank money'.

Table 9.1. The Balance Sheet of the Deutsche Bundesbank, November 1995 (DM bn)

Assets		Liabilities	
Gold and foreign reserve assets	126.1	Reserves held by commercial banks	46.8
Claims on banks	202.5	Currency outside commercial banks	238.2
Claims on government	8.7	Government deposits	0.2
Other assets	9.9	Other deposits and liabilities	36.9
		Net worth	25.1
Total	347.2	Total	347.2

Source: Deutsche Bundesbank *Monthly Report*

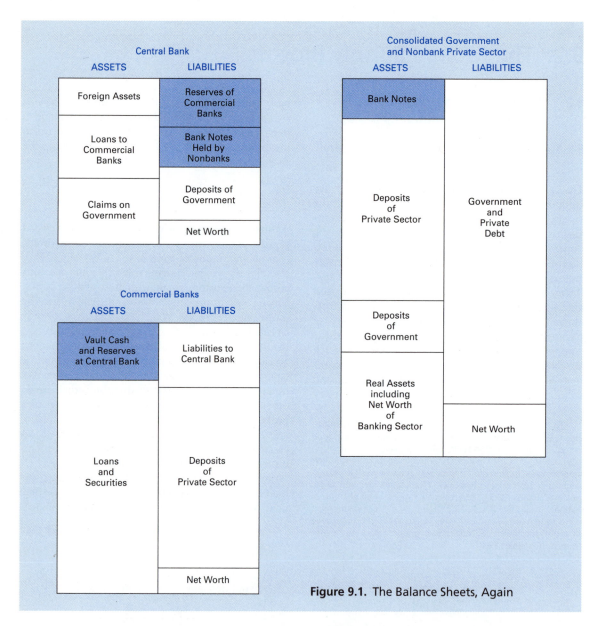

Figure 9.1. The Balance Sheets, Again

customer, a bank increases the volume of its assets, as shown in Figure 9.1. The increase is matched on the liability side by the amount of the loan credited to the customer's bank account. That is new money created by a bank. However, this is only the beginning of the story.

9.2.1.3. Prudential and legal reserves requirements

Bank reserves constitute the money that banks use to conduct transactions themselves. They generally yield little or no income to the bank that owns them. Vault cash merely gathers dust in the bank's safe, while reserves deposited at the central bank may, but usually do not, pay interest. When they do, commercial banks will strive to hold as little vault cash as possible, given the transaction costs of converting deposits into currency.

Commercial banks therefore face an opportunity cost similar to that of firms and households holding money: the return (interest) forgone on other assets such as loans and securities (see Figure 9.1). Nevertheless, commercial banks hold reserves for both

Table 9.2. Reserve Requirements on Demand Deposits, 1995

Country	Reserve requirement (%)
Italy	15.0
Spain	2.0
Portugal	2.0
Switzerland	none
Belgium	none
Netherlands	1.4–4.4
UK	0.35
France	
Sight deposits < 9 days' maturity	1.0
Time deposits up to 1 year's maturity	0.5
Savings deposits up to 2 years' maturity	1.0
Savings deposits more than 2 years' maturity	0.0
Germany	
Sight deposits	2.0
Time deposits	2.0
Savings deposits	1.5
Japan	
(a) Domestically based banks	
Time yen deposits	0.05–1.2
Other yen deposits	0.1–1.3
Time foreign currency deposits	0.2
Other foreign currency deposits	0.25
(b) Foreign-based banks	
All deposits	0.15
USA	
Net transactions account of	
0–$4.2 million	0.0
$4.2–$54 million	3.0
above $54 million	10.0

Sources: National central banks

prudential and legal reasons. First, banks must have enough currency at hand to meet withdrawals by customers. For that purpose, they use vault cash or draw on their deposits at the central bank. Further, banks need a means of settling payments among themselves and on behalf of their customers. Settlements between banks are usually made by transfers from the central bank account of one bank to another. For example, suppose that a customer of Natwest receives in payment a cheque drawn on Barclay's Bank. He proceeds to deposit the cheque in his Natwest account. Natwest would simultaneously credit its customer's account and deposit the cheque with the Bank of England. The Bank of England then debits Barclay's reserves account and credits Natwest's account. For such transactions, a positive balance is necessary with the Bank of England. During a given period, any commercial bank may receive large amounts in deposits and face large withdrawals. If the two about balance, which is normally the case, they actually need very limited amounts of reserves; but occasionally withdrawals may exceed deposits by a large amount. This is why commercial banks always find it *prudent* to hold some fraction of their assets in the form of either vault cash or deposits at the central bank.

A second reason for banks to hold reserves is a legal one. In many countries, deposit-taking banks are *required* by law to hold a fraction of outstanding deposits in the form of bank reserves. These so-called **reserves ratios**, a part of the many obligations imposed on banks, are normally set as a proportion of deposits. Some examples of reserves ratios are displayed in Table 9.2. They vary considerably from one country to another, although the trend has been to reduce them. Reserve requirements are not always binding; banks may hold reserves in excess of the legal amount. On the other hand, they usually refrain from going too far in this direction because of the associated opportunity cost.

9.2.2. The Mechanics of the Money Multiplier

The link between deposits at banks and bank reserves, whether compulsory or purely prudential, allows central banks to control the money supply. Whenever banks lend, they create new deposits, and need to obtain correspondingly more reserves at the central bank. The central bank acts on the availability, quantity, and price of reserves to steer the money supply. The link between reserves and deposits implies a relationship, known as the **money multiplier**, between the monetary base and the targeted monetary aggregate. The multiplier process is both simple and striking. It is presented in two different ways. The first stresses the end result, while the second tracks the relatively involved way in which the money is actually created.

9.2.2.1. Reserve ratios and reserve multipliers

A bank's balance sheet (Figure 9.1) includes four main items in addition to net worth. Two of them correspond to costly activities. Banks pay interest when they borrow from the central bank, and deposit-taking and administration require setting up and maintaining a network of branches with personnel, equipment, and office rental. In addition, they often pay some interest on deposits when allowed. The third item, reserves, yields little income. How then do banks earn money? Obviously, by lending to their customers and possibly holding interest-yielding assets, the fourth item on the balance sheet. Good banking practice therefore calls for lending as much as is prudently possible. This is easily done: it is enough to credit the customer's account. As long as the interest on the loan exceeds the cost of managing the deposit, it is profitable to do so.

If this is the case, why don't banks simply increase both sides of their balance sheets without bounds? The brake is the reserves ratio, whether it is regulatory (imposed by the authorities) or prudential (self-imposed). As illustrated in Figure 9.2, the reserves may not be less than the reserves ratio (rr) times the volume of deposits:

(9.1)   Reserves $\geq rr \times$ deposits.

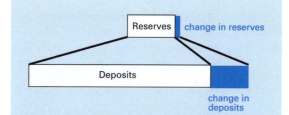

Figure 9.2. The Reserves–Money Stock Link

When reserves are a constant proportion (rr) of deposits ($R = rrD$), deposits cannot grow without an increase in reserves. Conversely, a change in reserves ΔR allows banks to increase their deposits—by granting loans—in much larger amounts. The money multiplier is the inverse of the reserve ratio.

The figure may be read in a different but equivalent way: the volume of deposits cannot exceed a multiple of existing reserves. The tinted area in Figure 9.2 shows that an increase in reserves can be multiplied up into a larger volume of deposits. The logic is simple enough: because the reserves are a fraction of deposits, deposits are a multiple of reserves. Formally, rearranging (9.1) gives

(9.2)   Deposits $\leq (1/rr) \times$ reserves.

The factor $(1/rr)$ is often called the *reserve multiplier*. Equation (9.2) means that commercial banks cannot expand their money creation beyond a multiple of reserves. Monetary control becomes a question of reserves management by the central bank.

9.2.2.2. The monetary base multiplier

While the central bank can control M0, the sum of currency and bank reserves, it cannot control its components directly. The public decides how much of M0 will be in the form of currency. The remainder can serve as reserves for deposits. Figure 9.2 did not distinguish between currency and bank deposits at the central bank. Figure 9.3 corrects that omission. Since the central bank is interested in controlling the aggregate money stock (M1, M2, or broader aggregates), rather than reserves *per se*, more attention is paid to the *monetary base multiplier*, which relates the monetary base to a monetary aggregate, for example M1:

(9.3)   Monetary base multiplier = M1/M0.

Henceforth we shall simply use the term **money multiplier**.

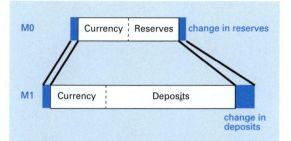

Figure 9.3. The Reserves–Money Stock Link with Currency

The public holds currency as well as bank accounts. As reserves are a constant proportion of deposits, any increase in reserves allows an increase in deposits, with a multiplier equal to the inverse of the reserve ratio. The central bank, however, controls the monetary base M0, not the breakdown between its components, currency and reserves. If the money multiplier is defined as the effect of an increase in the monetary base on the money supply M1, it is smaller because part of the money created by the commercial banks will be converted in currency, leaking out of the banking system.

Table 9.3 presents actual ratios of the money supply (M1) to the monetary base (M0) for several countries. A comparison with the reserves ratio in Table 9.2 reveals that the multipliers are much smaller than the inverse of the reserves ratio as predicted by formula (9.1). Why is that so? In the absence of currency, all monetary base would be held by commercial banks, and all M1 would take the form of bank deposits. When the public chooses to hold part of their money in the form of currency, however, the banking system loses some of its reserves, which limits its loan-making activity. The larger is the share of currency in M0, the less reserves are available to the banking system and the smaller is the multiplier. Box 9.1 shows formally that the monetary multiplier is much lower than the inverse of the reserves ratio. The monetary base multiplier declines when the reserves ratio increases and when the public holds more currency. Table 9.3 shows that countries with a predilection for currency tend to have low multipliers.

9.2.2.3. Leakages

The multiplier is lower when conversions of bank deposits into currency act as a drain on commercial banks' reserves. A number of other leakages produce the same effect and help explain the relatively low money multipliers reported in Table 9.3. Leakages occur when money is deposited in nonbank financial institutions, which cannot create money or which operate with a 100% reserve requirement. Money can also leak abroad, in the form of currency, and this reduces the amount of reserves available for the banking system. Box 9.2 shows that, in the case of the USA and Germany, this leakage can be sizeable.

9.2.2.4. A variable multiplier

It has been assumed so far that commercial banks use any reserve in excess of the minimum level to extend loans and that they have no difficulty finding customers. Neither of these assumptions need *always* be correct. Banks manage their assets and liabilities very carefully with an eye to the future. If they expect economic conditions to worsen, they may consider that some loans are too risky and may actually refrain from lending the maximum amount possible, given their reserves. Instead, they may simply buy securities that

Table 9.3. M0, M1, Money Market Multipliers, and Currency in Five Countries, 1994

	M0 (% of GNP)	M1 (% of GNP)	Multiplier M1/M0	Currency (% of M1)
France	3.61	21.24	5.88	15.06
Germany	10.34	24.58	2.38	30.86
Japan	10.54	32.32	3.07	23.54
UK	3.97	37.73	9.51	7.43
USA	6.45	18.28	2.83	28.78

Sources: IFS; central banks' bulletins

BOX 9.1. THE MONEY MULTIPLIER WITH CURRENCY

Assuming that the public wishes to hold a proportion cc of M1 in the form of currency (CU), and that the banks keep a fraction rr of deposits (D) in bank reserves (R) (for simplicity, ignore vault cash), the two aggregates M0 and M1 can be written as

$$(9.4) \qquad M0 = CU + R = ccM1 + rrD$$

$$(9.5) \qquad M1 = CU + D = ccM1 + D.$$

Then (9.5) implies $D = (1 - cc)M1$. Inserting this value of D in (9.4) gives

$$(9.6) \qquad M0 = [cc + rr(1 - cc)]M1,$$

so

$$(9.7) \qquad \text{Money multiplier} = M1/M0$$

$$= \frac{1}{cc + rr(1 - cc)}.$$

The money market multiplier is $1/rr$ if the public holds no currency (if $cc = 0$). It is equal to 1 if all M1 is cash ($cc = 1$).

Table 9.4 shows how the multiplier varies with different values of the currency-to-M1 ratio cc and the reserves ratio rr.

Table 9.4. Theoretical Values of the Money Multiplier (M1/M0)

Currency/M1	Reserve ratio		
	5%	10%	20%
0%	20.0	10.0	5.0
5%	10.3	6.9	4.0
10%	6.9	5.3	3.6
20%	4.2	3.6	2.8
30%	3.0	2.7	2.3

already exist.[4] They may also withhold lending if they expect interest rates to increase in the future, which would improve the profitability of their loans. It appears that the response of banks to reserve changes is much less automatic than implied by the money multiplier formulae. As conditions change, or are expected to change, the actual multiplier may fluctuate in value.

Similarly, when banks want to expand their lending activity, they need to find customers. They may attempt to lure them by reducing the interest rate that they charge. The private sector's reaction is by no means guaranteed. Again, fears of worsening economic conditions, or the expectation of declining interest rates, may well limit the amount of new credit that the public wants to borrow. The money multiplier then appears to be low.

9.2.2.5. Required or self-imposed reserves ratios?

Some countries have zero or symbolic reserve requirements. In the UK, for example, the ratio of 0.45% is officially justified to offset operating costs of the Bank of England,[5] yet for all practical purposes is nil. British banks do not by any means take excessive risks. In fact, such countries as Switzerland, Belgium, the Netherlands, and Luxembourg, which do not have reserve requirements, are considered perfectly safe places to hold banking accounts.

Reserve requirements serve several purposes. Initially, they were imposed to reduce the riskiness of banking systems. Next, they guaranteed a role for the central bank in the business of money creation. Finally, they became the means for central banks to control the money supply. All that is needed is a legal or voluntary reserves ratio; as long as $rr > 0$, deposits are linked to central-bank-controlled reserves. Self-imposed reserves ratios can fulfil this need as well as required ratios of the same magnitude. At the same time, because reserves receive little or no interest, high reserve requirements represent a form of taxation on the banking system. Since banks typically hold much less reserves in the absence of a legal minimum, required reserves ratios subject the domestic banking sector to a competitive disadvantage relative to other countries with low or non-existent reserve requirements. The process of European financial integration is sharpening this handicap and has led to a steady decline in reserve requirements over time.

---

[4] Of course, if all banks buy securities at the same time, their price will rise and their yield will fall. This yield is the opportunity cost against which banks will assess lending to customers. Lending will therefore tend to increase.

[5] The argument that interest forgone on required reserves covers the cost of clearing and other central bank services is often used by the Bundesbank.

9.2.3. The Multiplier Process

This section presents a two-step illustration of the process of money creation by banks, which can be skipped by readers satisfied with the previous exposition. The first step tracks down the process, bank after bank. The second step consolidates the banking sector.

9.2.3.1. Step-by-step money creation

Imagine that a customer of Dresdner Bank finds DM 10,000 in her garden. This used to be money, but since it stopped circulating a long while ago, it has been written off.[6] When the customer deposits the cash into her checking account, she effectively re-creates currency. Panel (*a*) in Figure 9.4. shows that Dresdner Bank has now increased its liabilities (the new deposit of the customer) and its assets (the cash deposited, now part of the reserves) by DM 10,000.[7] What will the manager of Dresdner Bank do? If the required reserves ratio in Germany is 10%, he may decide to keep DM 1000 in reserves (cash in the vault). The remaining DM 9000 can be lent as shown in panel (*b*). The bank hands over the cash to its customer, which decreases the reserves by DM 9000. (More realistically, the bank may credit the customer's bank account.) As soon as the money is spent, Dresdner 'loses' the DM 9000 in currency exactly as if the loan had been paid out in cash.

Next, the customer uses her loan to buy a car, and the car dealer takes the sale proceeds to his own bank, Commerzbank. Commerzbank finds itself in the same position as Dresdner did before, i.e. with a new deposit and new loanable funds. This is depicted in panel

(*c*). Like Dresdner, Commerzbank holds 10% of the DM 9000 as reserves and lends out the remaining DM 8100. The same process occurs again: the DM 8100 of banknotes that are loaned are deposited with the Deutsche Bank and so on.

In Figure 9.4, M1 increases by DM 10,000 in panels (*a*) and (*b*) (the new deposit at Dresdner), then by DM 9000 in panel (*c*) (a new deposit at Commerzbank), and by DM 8100 in panel (*d*) (a new deposit at Deutsche). So far, the total increase in M1 is DM 27,100. Letting the process continue *ad infinitum* in the same fashion, the total increase in M1 turns to be DM 100,000.[8] The commercial banks have 'multiplied' the initial deposit tenfold. As (9.2) established, with a 10% required reserves ratio, the reserves multiplier is 10. In the absence of currency holdings, the money multiplier is also 10.

9.2.3.2. A one-step interpretation

The process can be summarized in just one step if all German banks are consolidated into a single entity, German Bank AG. The manager of German Bank AG who receives the initial DM 10,000 will reason differently from the previous example. The bank manager can simply keep the cash in a vault or deposit it at the central bank. As Figure 9.5 shows, either way German Bank AG now has DM 10,000 additional reserves which could potentially 'support' DM 100,000 of additional deposits. Given the initial DM 10,000 deposited, it can extend more loans and can credit the corresponding amounts to customers' accounts up to DM 90,000. The initial DM 10,000 increase in reserves

---

[6] How does the Bundesbank know? It does not know for sure, of course, but central banks try to account for what they consider depreciation or loss of previously issued currency.

[7] The original money creation—the unearthing of DM 10,000—increased M1 first in the form of currency, then in the form of bank deposits. As long as the cash is in the bank's vault, it is not circulating in public hands and therefore is not counted as money.

[8] This follows from the formula for a geometric series: for any x such that $-1 < x < 1$, we have $1 + x + x^2 + x^3 + \ldots = \ldots \Sigma_{i=0}^{\infty} x^i = 1/(1-x)$. Here, with a reserve ratio $r = 0.1$, an initial deposit D gives rise to a first loan of $D(1-r)$, and a second loan of $D(1-r)^2$; etc. The total increase is: $D[1 + (1-r) + (1-r)^2 + (1-r)^3 + \ldots] = D/[1-(1-r)] = D/r$.

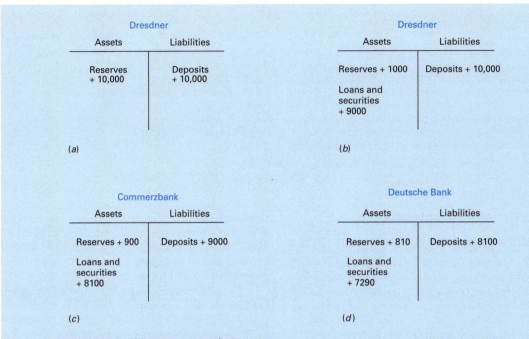

Figure 9.4. The Money Supply Process

In panel (*a*) the Dresdner Bank receives a currency deposit of 10,000. Its assets (reserves) and liabilities (deposits) increase by 10,000. With a reserve requirement of 10%, the bank lends 9,000 in cash to another customer in panel (*b*). The loan customer spends the 9,000, which is next deposited at Commerzbank (panel (*c*)). Commerzbank in turn lends out 9/10 of the new deposit, also in cash, and holds 1/10 in reserves at the central bank; and the process repeats itself, this time at the Deutsche Bank (panel (*d*)). The total increase in money will be the sum of all such increments. While the number of potential increments is infinite, the sum of them is finite.

(the cash reintroduced) again triggers a total increase in money ten times larger. By keeping the reserves, German Bank AG has captured all the money-creating potential of the initial reintroduction of DM 10,000. As the only bank in town, it cannot lose reserves to other banks: the German Bank AG reproduces the successive actions of the whole banking sector in a single step.

9.3. The Conduct of Monetary Policy: Controlling the Money Supply

9.3.1. The Logic of Monetary Policy

There are several ways for the central bank to control commercial banks' reserves, and different countries use different procedures. The principle underlying them, however, is the same and is best illustrated by imagining a country that experiences economic growth. Its demand for nominal money increases as predicted by the demand-for-money function of Chapter 8:

(9.8) $$L(Y, i, c).$$

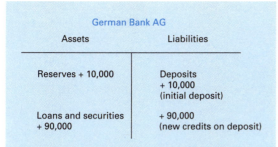

Figure 9.5. The Money Supply Process in One Step

If there is a single commercial bank—which in fact represents the whole banking system—it does not lose reserves to other banks. The bank creates a loan and credits the account of its customer. When the customer pays for her expenditures by writing cheques, these cheques are all deposited in the bank and none of the newly created money leaks out of the bank. Knowing this, the single bank keeps in the form of reserves all the 10,000 received as cash, and grants loans ten times that amount. The final outcome is the same as in Figure 9.4, but it is reached in just one step.

According to equation (9.8), households and firms react to an increase in income (Y) by increasing their demand for real balances. Where do households and firms find the money that they need to carry out an ever-increasing volume of transactions? The first natural reaction is for them to borrow from their banks. As the banks respond by granting loans, their need for reserves increases. Although individual banks may be able to obtain reserves from each other, viewed as a whole, the total supply of reserves cannot exceed that created in the past by the central bank. As the sole producer of reserves, the central bank exercises the dominant influence on their availability and cost. Day-to-day monetary policy is based on the process by which the central bank provides commercial banks with the reserves necessary for increased lending activities.

In order to enter into transactions with commercial banks, central banks typically own a portfolio of government debt, foreign exchange, and other obligations.[9] Box 9.3 provides details of these transactions. Typically, the central bank might purchase securities from a commercial bank and credit the reserve account of that bank. The result is the creation of central bank money. Figure 9.6 depicts the change in the balance sheet of a single bank representing the banking sector as a whole (as in the previous section). Panel (*a*) shows the first step, the purchase of DM 100,000 worth of securities by the central bank from a commercial bank. It takes the form of a swap on the asset side of the balance sheet: the selling bank now owns 100,000 less of securities and 100,000 more of reserves. With more reserves on its books, the bank can make new loans to its customers. If the reserves ratio is 10%, it can lend up to 1,000,000. This second step—the money multiplier mechanism once more—is shown in panel (*b*). The central bank can also perform the opposite operation: it can sell securities to commercial banks. A sale of securities reduces banks' reserves and bank deposits, and thereby reduces the money supply.

---

[9] Some banks are prohibited by law from holding certain forms of government debt. It is possible that the future European Central Bank will also be restricted in this way.

BOX 9.3. TRANSACTIONS BETWEEN CENTRAL AND COMMERCIAL BANKS

Only a limited range of assets are accepted in transactions between a central bank and commercial banks. Central banks do not normally take commercial risks, so they deal only in Treasury bills and/or securities of the most financially secure firms. If the central bank buys government debt, it indirectly grants credit to the government. It transforms a liability to the public that has to be serviced with interest and eventually repaid (the public debt) with a liability that bears no interest and is not expected to be repaid (M0). If the central bank purchases a private firm's securities, it is the firm that is indirectly financed by the central bank: although the firm still must honour its debt, it helps to have less of it floating on the market.

Although the central bank may buy securities outright, the usual practice is to buy securities with a promise by the seller to buy them back after some specified period. This transaction is called a **repurchase agreement** ('repo' for short). A repurchase agreement can be thought of as a loan by the central bank collateralized by securities. The price at which the security is bought by the central bank is less than the price at which it is sold back. The loss borne by the commercial bank is equivalent to the interest paid for a loan from the central bank. All transactions generally are for very short maturities, from just overnight to a few months.

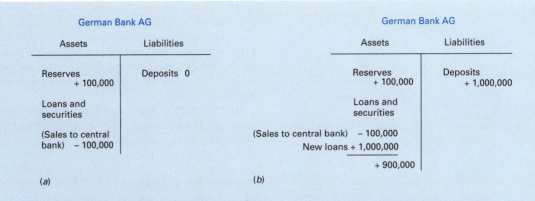

Figure 9.6. Creation of Reserves and Money

Money creation proceeds in two steps. In panel (a) the central bank provides reserves to the commercial bank by purchasing DM 100,000 worth of securities and crediting its account by that amount. Its reserves have increased, not its deposits. In the second step, the single bank uses this opportunity and grants DM 1,000,000 in new loans. Its reserves are now again 10% of its deposits.

9.3.2. Open Market Operations

In the last section we saw how the central bank can influence the supply of money by controlling the availability of bank reserves. The procedure that entails the purchasing or selling of securities is called an **open market operation**. The open market can be thought of as a network of financial intermediaries (mostly commercial banks, but also insurance companies and sometimes very large corporations) which deal in securities that the central bank accepts to sell or buy. In some countries, this function is fulfilled by the **interbank market**, which brings together commercial banks.

On any normal business day, some commercial banks hold reserves in excess of what is required, while others fall short. The interbank market allows participants to trade these reserves, borrowing and lending at very short maturities (overnight, one day, one week, one month). The interest rate at which these transactions occur is continuously set to equilibrate demand and supply. The interbank market is the best gauge of monetary conditions because, as a wholesale market for money, it determines how much banks charge their own customers. This rate is called the money market rate, with special names in some countries, the best known being the Federal Funds Rate in the USA.

The central bank is not merely an active player on the interbank market. Since it is the ultimate net supplier of bank reserves—the 'commodity' being traded —it can orient or even control the market on a minute-by-minute basis. Most often, the central bank deals with the market at a distance via dealers or brokers. It intervenes anonymously to keep the other market participants guessing, as a way of increasing its influence in the market. Through its net interventions, the central bank can determine directly the size of its liability, the monetary base. The multiplier then takes over.

9.3.3. Monetary Policy Instruments: Money and the Interest Rate

Central banks are not merely interested in controlling the quantity of money, but may feel responsible for the level of interest rates as well. These objectives may be difficult to reconcile. Panel (a) of Figure 9.7 illustrates money targeting. The central bank decides on the supply of base money M0. Demand for M0 originates with the banks (as they need to adjust reserves to their lending activity) and from the public. Given the central bank's money target, the interest rate fluctuates in response to demand conditions. Panel (b) illustrates the other extreme case, in which the central bank decides on the interest rate. For the open market to be in equilibrium, the central bank must then be ready to let the supply of base money respond to demand fluctuations.

Central banks adopt various practices in setting the interest rates, and these practices also evolve over time. The oldest procedure is **discount lending** or

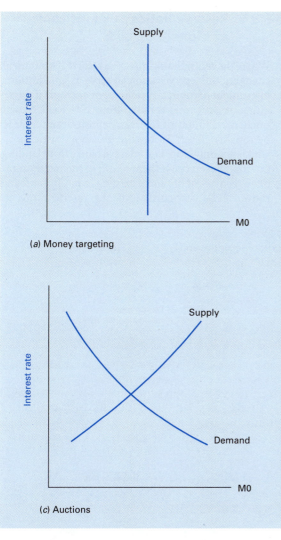

(a) Money targeting

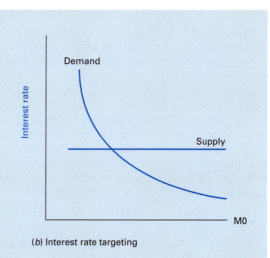

(b) Interest rate targeting

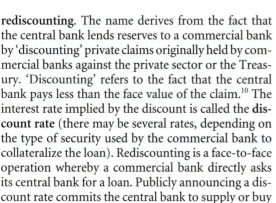

(c) Auctions

Figure 9.7. Monetary Policy Procedures

The central bank may adopt various procedures. Panel (a) represents the case where the central bank aims at the money supply, leaving it to the market to determine the interest rate. Conversely the central bank may decide to aim at a particular interest rate; in that case, corresponding to panel (b), it must provide the market with whatever volume of base money is demanded. Finally, as illustrated in panel (c), the central bank may supply additional reserves only at higher market interest rates.

rediscounting. The name derives from the fact that the central bank lends reserves to a commercial bank by 'discounting' private claims originally held by commercial banks against the private sector or the Treasury. 'Discounting' refers to the fact that the central bank pays less than the face value of the claim.[10] The interest rate implied by the discount is called the **discount rate** (there may be several rates, depending on the type of security used by the commercial bank to collateralize the loan). Rediscounting is a face-to-face operation whereby a commercial bank directly asks its central bank for a loan. Publicly announcing a discount rate commits the central bank to supply or buy

any quantity of base money; this is represented as a horizontal supply line in panel (b). In practice, however, most central banks avoid open-ended commitments to supply monetary base; in general, access to the discount window is limited, with commercial banks facing either an explicit quota (e.g. in Germany) or implicit restrictions (e.g. in the USA).

Another procedure is to organize auctions. Two types of auction are possible. In a 'rate tender' the central bank invites commercial banks to submit tenders or bids for fixed amounts of the money base: the interest rate is the one at which all demands at this rate or below are satisfied. A quantity tender sets a fixed (administered) interest rate and allocates money to the banks that are willing to pay that rate according to the size of their bids. By combining these methods,

---

[10] Discounting, as well as the inverse relationship between security prices and yield, is explained in Ch. 3.

the central bank can achieve the upward-sloping supply schedule shown in panel (*c*). Under the auction system the central bank can flexibly trade off increases in the interest rate against increases in the money supply.

While different countries adopt different procedures, the tendency is to combine all three procedures. In that case central banks typically encourage a particular channel by setting the corresponding interest rate lower than for the others. Box 9.4 presents the procedures adopted by the Bundesbank, which tend to be adopted by other European central banks in anticipation of the adoption of a single currency.

9.3.4. Reserve Ratios as an Instrument of Monetary Policy

Where the central bank imposes a reserve requirement, changing the reserve ratio can serve as an additional instrument of monetary policy. For example if the required reserve ratio is raised from 10% to 12%, with unchanged supply of reserves, deposits must contract by roughly 20%.[12] To be sure, this is a drastic move, which not only stops commercial banks from lending, but might even cause them to *call in* (demand immediate repayment of) some existing loans. Because this move can be very costly to banks, reserve ratios are

---

BOX 9.4. THE BUNDESBANK'S INSTRUMENTS

Figure 9.8 presents the key interest rates used by the German Bundesbank (nicknamed Buba) to steer the money market. The discount rate is the lowest. At that rate the Buba is willing to buy back from commercial banks high-grade bills of trade. (Bills of trade are the unpaid obligations—bills—owed by commercial enterprises.) The Buba uses this rate to set a floor to the cost of money, so it holds the discount rate fairly steady. Since it is the lowest rate, it is the one most attractive to the banks. To limit money creation through this channel, each bank is given a quota—based on its size—of discount borrowing at the lower rate.

The upper limit is determined by the Lombard rate. Banks borrow at this rate only in emergencies. It is usually considerably higher than the interbank market rate. The repo rate corresponds to frequently held auctions and is the main channel used by the Buba. Repo stands for 'repurchase agreements', as explained in Box 9.3.[11] The figure shows how the central bank uses the discount and Lombard rates to signal its intentions: during 1993, as it wanted to see the interest rates go down, it reduced in a quick succession both ceiling and floor rates. Note how the repo rate moves within the tunnel set by the discount and Lombard. This shows how the Buba uses both the tunnel and the repo to signal its intentions to the banking and financial community. Indeed, the repo is closely followed by the money market rate, the true (opportunity) cost of money to banks. Table 9.5 shows that the use of repos by the Buba has increased steadily over the past decade.

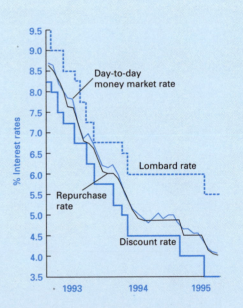

Figure 9.8. Key Interest Rates in Germany

The discount and Lombard rates, respectively, determine a floor and a ceiling for the interbank rate. These two 'signalling' rates are set rather infrequently, and are used by the Bundesbank to signal important shifts in its policy. The repurchase rate—'repo'—is set at frequently held auctions and is meant to be a more precise indicator of the Buba's intentions. As such, it is usually 'shadowed' by the interbank rate.

Source: Monthly Report, Bundesbank, December 1995

---

[11] One reason for this complex procedure is that the Bundesbank is not allowed to buy public debt. A repo can be technically described as a loan to a commercial bank collateralized by Treasury bills. Another reason, which makes repos popular among other central banks, is that the loan can be called back before maturity. This gives central banks significant power over commercial banks.

[12] When banks hold no excess reserves and currency holdings are nil, equation (9.2) implies that, if reserves are constant deposits change in the same proportion but in the opposite direction, like the reserve ratio. In the example, $\Delta rr/rr = +0.2$ implies that $\Delta D/D = -0.2$.

Table 9.5. Structure of Commercial Bank Refinancing by the Bundesbank, 1980–1993

	Discount credit under rediscount and refinancing quotas plus special quotas	Security-based repurchase agreements (repos)	Lombard or special Lombard loans
1980	83.5	6.0	10.5
1981	86.6	6.9	6.5
1982	79.9	14.8	5.3
1983	83.9	8.0	8.1
1984	76.5	15.9	7.6
1985	64.0	34.7	1.3
1986	66.2	33.2	0.6
1987	66.7	33.0	0.3
1988	51.6	47.7	0.7
1989	39.0	59.9	1.1
1990	42.2	56.3	1.5
1991	37.9	61.1	1.0
1992	34.0	65.4	0.6
1993	27.7	71.8	0.5

Note: Excludes open market transactions in trade bills under repo, foreign exchange swaps, shifts of federal funds under section 17 of the Bundesbank Law, and 'quick tenders'.

Source: Issing (1994)

normally changed only in small increments, and then only in emergency situations.

9.3.5. Direct Credit to the Government

Finally, the central bank may lend directly to the government. The central bank credits the government account (see Figure 9.1) with a newly created monetary base. As soon as these balances are used by the government to purchase goods or services, the monetary base enters the commercial banking system as recipients of government payments deposit these funds in their bank accounts. An open market purchase of Treasury bills or rediscounting achieves the same result indirectly. This modern version of the printing press is called the **monetization** of the public debt.

9.3.6. Monetary Policy Targets

So far we have looked at the monetary policy *instruments* used by central banks. But what do they try to achieve? As the following chapters will show, mon-etary policy is one of the tools used by the authorities to try to improve economic conditions. As they carry out their responsibilities, central banks often define their goal by specifying some *targets*. Because macroeconomic policy often aims at conflicting objectives—no inflation, fast growth, full employment—the choice of a target is not easy, and the debate about which are the proper targets for a central bank highlights the existence of serious policy dilemmas.

We have seen above that central banks already face a problem in deciding whether to set the money supply or the interest rate as an instrument. The same issue resurfaces under the debate on what are the proper targets. As discussed in Chapter 8, a main incentive for setting monetary aggregates lies in the long-term control of inflation. In the shorter run, however, monetary policy affects the interest rate and economic conditions.[13] Accordingly, central banks often feel torn between their long-run commitment to control money growth and inflation and the pressures to improve the short-run macroeconomic situation. As was made clear by Figure 9.7, in general the central bank cannot

[13] This link may be unclear at this stage. It is the object of the next five chapters.

at the same time restrict the money supply *and* bring the interest rate down.

Emerging from the 1970s with high interest rates, most central banks in the OECD area opted to target the rate of money growth explicitly. The procedure, still in use in Germany, is to announce ahead of time, usually a year in advance, the rate of money growth for a chosen aggregate. Figure 9.9 shows how this determines a maximum and a minimum growth rate. However, once inflation was brought down a decade later, political attention focused again on interest rates. Two further considerations have contributed to disenchantment with money targets. First, the link between money growth and inflation has become less predictable over the policy planning horizon (two to three years). Second, the link between money base and wider monetary aggregates became clouded in the mid-1980s. Both developments are related to instability in the demand for money following widespread financial deregulation in the mid-1980s. (See Box 9.5 for the case of the UK, which was followed by similar changes in Scandinavia.)

As it has become less essential to control M0, most of the central banks, which used to target monetary aggregates during the 1980s, have moved to target interest rates at the beginning of the 1990s. Some central banks (in the UK, New Zealand, Canada, and Spain, among others) have also decided to target inflation directly.

Figure 9.9. The Bundesbank Money Growth Targets

Annually, the Bundesbank announces its targets for M3 between the fourth quarter of the current year and next. It announces a minimum and a maximum growth rate, thereby defining a funnel. If it were fully prepared to ignore the interest rate or other economic variables, the Buba could achieve its target. The fact that it does not shows that its approach to monetary targeting is quite flexible.

Source: *Monthly Report*, Bundesbank, December 1995

9.4. Monetary Policy in an Open Economy

9.4.1. Exchange Market Interventions

Monetary policy is also influenced by foreign exchange markets. As can be seen in Figure 9.1, the central bank holds foreign assets. These are usually interest-bearing deposits with foreign central banks denominated in foreign currencies. What happens when this item of its balance sheet changes, and why would the central bank modify its holdings of foreign assets? Central banks frequently use their foreign assets to *intervene* on the foreign exchange market to influence the exchange rate. To prevent a nominal depreciation, i.e. a loss in its external value, a central bank might buy back its own currency on the foreign exchange markets, using some of its foreign assets. Conversely, to prevent an appreciation, the central bank sells its own currency and acquires foreign assets. For example, as

a member of the European Exchange Rate Mechanism, the Banque de France is committed (since 1995) to selling francs and buying Deutschmarks (DM) when the exchange rate falls below FF 2.888/DM, or to buying francs and selling Deutschmarks if the exchange rate rises above FF 3.895/DM. When the Banque de France pays for French francs with Deutschmarks, two things happen, as reported in panel (*a*) of Figure 9.10. On the asset side, the stock of foreign assets declines; on the liability side, the monetary base is reduced since some domestic currency is withdrawn from circulation. By the working of the money multiplier, M1 in France is consequently reduced.

There is strong similarity between exchange market and open market interventions. Both affect the monetary base and the asset side of the central bank's balance sheet. In both cases, the money multiplier then

BOX 9.5. WHILE THE BANK OF ENGLAND SLEPT, 1986–1988

In the mid-1980s things went wrong with British money demand and monetary policy. Shortly after Nigel Lawson was appointed Chancellor of the Exchequer in 1983, the UK economy began to recover from a very deep recession. As the economy grew, the demand for money expanded and was met by a rapid rate of increase in the money supply. The deregulation of financial markets, including the abolition of exchange controls and a liberalization of rules governing 'building societies' (a type of savings institution) in 1983, led to much greater competition in the supply of mortgage finance. Despite a rise in both nominal and real interest rates in 1985 and 1986, mortgage lending expanded rapidly, and was used to finance both house purchase and other forms of consumption. Easy access to credit, combined with a reduction in income taxes, resulted in a remarkable boom in consumption and a very fast GDP growth rate, documented in Table 9.7. Demand for money soared, not only because of increased activity, but because of easier access to credit.

The Bank of England understood that money conditions were changing radically, but it could not quantify the change with any precision. Facing a whole new world, the Bank—under tight control by Mr Lawson—had to make a decision: either prevent the interest rate from rising, accommodate demand, and let the money supply grow—as in panel (b) of Figure 9.9—or tighten the money supply at the possible cost of very high interest rates—as in panel (a). The Chancellor elected to err on the side of excessive money growth rather than excessive tightness. Over the period 1986–9, the nominal interest rate remained roughly unchanged and the real interest rate actually declined. To achieve the goal of interest rate stability, money was allowed to grow at an average annual rate of about 20% for three full years. This is regarded as the main cause of rapid inflation in 1989–90.

Table 9.6. Economic Indicators in the UK, 1984–1990 (%)

	1984	1985	1986	1987	1988	1989	1990
Real GDP growth	2.1	3.5	3.9	4.8	4.3	2.3	0.8
Real consumption growth	1.6	3.4	6.2	5.2	7.4	3.5	1.0
Inflation	5.0	6.1	3.4	4.1	4.9	7.8	9.5
M1 (nominal) growth	14.0	16.5	22.4	26.5	13.7	10.8	11.4
M1 (real) growth	9.0	10.4	19.0	22.4	8.8	3.0	1.9
Nominal interest rates (% p.a.)	9.9	12.2	10.9	9.7	10.3	13.9	14.8
Real interest rates (% p.a.)	4.9	6.1	7.5	5.6	5.4	6.1	5.3

Sources: OECD, *Economic Outlook*; IMF

amplifies the initial effect of the intervention. The difference concerns the matching items on the asset side: domestic assets (e.g. Treasury bills) for a money market intervention, foreign exchange reserves for an exchange market intervention. This similarity highlights the possibility of a conflict between monetary control and exchange rate control. Later chapters explore this issue in detail. The next section outlines a procedure often used in an attempt to avoid this conflict.

9.4.2. Sterilization

The similarity between money and foreign exchange market intervention suggests a 'quick fix' for the tension between monetary and exchange rate control. In the previous example, the Banque de France could offset, or *sterilize*, the impact of its foreign exchange intervention on the money supply with a money market purchase of securities which creates the same amount of the monetary base as was destroyed during the foreign exchange market intervention. Figure 9.10 (*b*) shows that the end effect of **sterilization** is a reshuffling of the asset side of the central bank's balance sheet—an increase in domestic asset holdings matched by a reduction of foreign exchange—leaving the liability side, in particular the monetary base, unchanged. Later, we shall see that this latter aspect creates problems for the 'quick fix'.

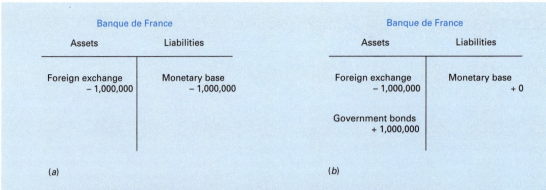

Figure 9.10. Foreign Exchange Market Intervention and Sterilization

In panel (*a*) the Banque de France intervenes in the exchange market to support the franc. It sells some of its foreign exchange reserves and buys back its own currency. With some currency withdrawn from circulation, the monetary base is reduced, and the money supply will decline further through the multiplier effect. In panel (*b*) the central bank counters the money-reducing effect by sterilizing its exchange market intervention. It buys an equivalent amount of securities from commercial banks. This replaces the monetary base previously destroyed.

Table 9.7. Seigniorage Finance (% of GDP)

	Monetary base in 1987	Seigniorage in 1987	Seigniorage av., 1979–81
Belgium	8.0	0.6	1.3
Denmark	5.2	0.4	0.7
France	6.9	0.6	0.9
Germany	10.0	0.6	0.9
Ireland	10.3	0.8	1.2
Italy	15.3	0.9	2.1
Netherlands	8.2	0.5	0.7
Spain	22.5	1.4	1.8
UK	4.3	0.3	0.8

Sources: IMF; Gros (1991)

9.5. Links between Monetary and Fiscal Policy

9.5.1. Seigniorage as a Means of Financing the Deficit

Either directly (in some countries) or indirectly via money market interventions, the central bank finances government deficits. Direct financing means that the Treasury borrows from the central bank, which in-creases the monetary base. The result is no different from debt monetization, when the central bank buys Treasury bills, as explained in Section 9.3.5. Both procedures are called **seigniorage**, a reminder of the Middle Ages when financially strapped local lords—who had the right of coinage on their lands—discreetly shaved gold coins. Table 9.7 shows that seigniorage

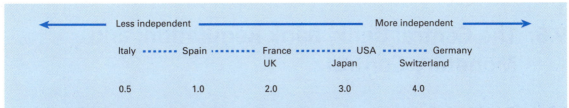

Figure 9.11. The Independence of Central Banks

This is a ranking on a scale from 0 (not independent) to 5 (completely independent) of how independent some central banks are from their respective governments. The ranking is based on criteria such as the rules of appointment and reappointment and the length of the mandate of the governor, the composition of the board, who controls the interest and exchange rates, and the ease of access by the Treasury to central bank financing of budget deficits.

Source: Alesina (1988 *b*)

was a substantial source of revenue during the high-inflation period of the 1970s; in more recent years, it has become almost negligible.[14]

The financing of government deficits by money creation should not be confused with the **inflation tax**. Seigniorage is a tax because the authorities (the government and the central bank together) obtain goods and services from the public (the work of civil servants, cars, weapons, buildings) by handing out something which it can produce at no cost: money. The inflation tax works by eroding the real value of the government debt owned by the public (individuals, corporations, banks). Nominal assets are not protected from inflation; in contrast, the value and yields of real assets are adjusted for inflation.[15] Money and non-indexed bonds are examples of nominal assets; real assets include property, artwork, rugs, jewels, and explicitly indexed financial instruments. The government benefits from the inflation tax because the public debt is rarely indexed, so that an unanticipated increase in inflation reduces its real value. When it is unanticipated, the inflation tax also redistributes income within the private sector, hurting holders of nominal assets and benefiting borrowers. In the aggregate, the private sector is normally a net holder of publicly issued nominal debt and stands to lose from unanticipated inflation. Only if inflation is correctly anticipated

is the private sector protected, for then the nominal interest rate increases one-for-one with inflation (the Fisher principle): the capital loss on the principal is exactly compensated by the higher nominal yield (Chapter 8), owing to the erosion of its purchasing power. Inflation tax falls only on money balances since the interest on money is zero and cannot be adjusted.

9.5.2. Independence of the Central Bank

The temptation for governments to engage in inflationary finance is strong. Since central banks are responsible for controlling inflation, their instinct is to refuse to finance government budget deficits. It is no surprise, then, that governments have a perpetual desire to control the central bank. In some countries central banks enjoy a high degree of independence from the government. An evaluation of the degree of central bank independence, as of 1988, is presented in Figure 9.11.[16] The famed strength of the German mark and the Swiss franc is often credited to the independence of their central banks. Conversely, much has been said about the rather limited independence that their counterparts enjoy in the UK, France, or Italy, to name a few examples.[17]

[14] Seigniorage is discussed in more detail in Ch. 15.
[15] Formally, seigniorage is the real value of the monetary base created: $\Delta M0/P = (\Delta M0/M0)M0/P$. In contrast, the inflation tax on the monetary base is the inflation rate π times the real stock of the base, or π (M0/P). They will be equal only if $\Delta M0/M0 = \pi$, which is generally not the case because long-run inflation is normally less than long-run money growth (see Ch. 8).

[16] Since then, a number of countries have granted their central banks independence. This is the case in Europe (France, Spain), where central bank independence is mandated by the Treaty of Maastricht. This issue is taken up in Ch. 21.
[17] Ch. 16 treats the issue of central bank independence in detail.

9.6. The Central Bank, Bank Regulation, and Monetary Control

9.6.1. Central Bank Oversight

The privilege of creating money conferred to commercial banks does not come without risks and restrictions. Banks are officially registered by the central bank or related agencies and often must satisfy strict operating requirements. Most of them are a consequence of the risks involved in creating money. These risks reflect the information asymmetry problem: commercial banks have less information about their customers' creditworthiness than the customers themselves. A customer who seeks a loan from a bank has an incentive to misrepresent her situation if it is likely to lead to a refusal of credit. For this reason, bank lending is riskier than intended. As stressed in Chapter 8, in a modern banking system most of the money supply is created by commercial banks, so confidence and acceptability of money is not self-evident. Confidence in money issued by the central bank is established in part by the legal-tender requirement for currency, and in part by the quality of the central bank. For money created by the commercial banks to be accepted as a virtual substitute for currency, users must be assured that bank-created money is always freely and immediately convertible into currency. Banks must always have enough cash to meet withdrawals. The history of commercial banking is full of bank failures, which often turned into bank panics as worried depositors attempted to withdraw as much cash as possible, not only from the failing bank but from all financial institutions.

The reason for such chain reactions is **systemic risk**. Systemic risk arises when banks (and, more generally, financial institutions) hold large amounts of each other's assets. Then, should one bank go bankrupt, its liabilities, held as assets by some other banks, become worthless. These losses may lead in turn to more bankruptcies. Even if that does not happen, the public often becomes suspicious and attempts to withdraw what it perceives to be endangered funds. In some cases the result is a generalized collapse of the banking system.

To reduce these risks, all countries have instituted bank regulations. Regulations include the supervision of bank accounts and operations, limits on competition perceived dangerous to the stability of banks, and restriction on asset ownership and banking activities. The purpose is to restrict the amount of risk-taking by banks, to give monetary authorities advance warning in case of failure, and to guarantee the supply of good banking services, including the public good described in Chapter 8. An example of protection is compulsory bank insurance. If a bank fails, its customer can be indemnified against loss. Table 9.8 provides a few examples of existing insurance systems.

9.6.2. Lender of the Last Resort

Another example of public protection of bank customers is the function of **lender of last resort**. Under the principle of lender of last resort, the central bank

Table 9.8. Bank Insurance

Country	Coverage of deposits
Belgium	Fully up to ceiling (ECU 11,820)
France	Fully up to ceiling (ECU 57,310)
Germany	Up to 30% of bank equity
Italy	Fully up to ECU 130,290, 75% of next ECU 521,170
Netherlands	Fully up to ceiling (ECU 18,600)
UK	75% of first ECU 28,570
Switzerland	none

Sources: Chiappori *et al.* (1991); Baltensperger and Dermine (1987) for Netherlands and Switzerland

BOX 9.6. LENDER OF LAST RESORT: A DOUBLE-EDGED SWORD

When the value of commercial bank money becomes suspicious, depositors attempt to withdraw their funds by converting them into cash. In such *bank runs* it is impossible for all deposits to be paid out, because banks hold only part of their assets in cash. Suspicion is contagious and in this case fatal to the banking system. This is why the monetary authorities may intervene as lender of last resort. As they stand ready to create whatever money is required to honour withdrawals, it is in their power to placate depositors' anxieties and put an end to bank runs.

Central banks often deny in public that they are ready for this lender-of-last-resort function. First, such interventions may require them to create a vast amount of monetary base, which runs against their objective of keeping money creation under control. Second, lender-of-last-resort protection may encourage banks to take excessive risks. This is why monetary authorities generally maintain a large degree of uncertainty as to what they would do in case of bank failure. As a matter of principle, the lender-of-last-resort function is not extended automatically, so that depositors are expected to keep an eye on their banks. Often, the central bank initially injects cash into a bank and then lets it go bankrupt. This way depositors are at least partly protected while shareholders are not, providing them with the incentive to exercise their control over management.

provides failing banks with sufficient monetary base to avoid immediate bankruptcy. Under some conditions, depositors may be reassured that they can always exchange bank deposits for currency. This guarantee is normally exercised when a commercial bank is unable to meet deposit withdrawals with cash. Bank crises occurred on a large scale in the USA during the Great Depression of the 1930s. The failure of the Federal Reserve Board (the US central bank) to act as lender of last resort is widely blamed for deepening the recession and led to the Banking Act, which strengthened its powers to deal with failing banks. In the wake of the first oil shock in 1974, many central banks conducted a 'lifeboat' operation to keep afloat a number of financial institutions; drawing the consequences of the risk of contagion, several central banks created the Basle Committee, described in the next section.

9.6.3. Capital Adequacy Ratios

Historically, regulation of the financial system has differed considerably across countries. In the 1970s, and at an increasing rate in the 1980s, financial integration among the advanced economies has brought their financial and banking systems into close contact with each other. This increasing integration has had two consequences. First, systemic risk is not limited to one country but may spread internationally at great speed. Even with relatively slow communication, the 1929 collapse of Wall Street quickly affected financial centres throughout the world; with the current technology, bank regulators have become convinced that instability has increased and requires new or strengthened measures. Second, banks compete directly with each other across borders. This calls for a level playing field to ensure fair competition. In 1989, an international agreement among most advanced economies was reached to establish minimum levels of **capital adequacy**. Banks are required to have minimum net worth as a fraction of total risky assets (see Figure 9.1). Net worth is sometimes called owners' capital or equity; it represents the owners' stake in the bank, after the value of liabilities is subtracted from total assets. Capital adequacy regulations ensure that more capital (the property of the banks' owners) can act as a 'shock absorber' for the bank's balance sheet and protect depositors against bad contingencies. Details are provided in Box 9.7.

9.6.4. Technological Innovation in Banking and Monetary Control

Banks are constantly inventing new ways of satisfying the financial needs of their customers. Many of these developments are also prompted by the banks' attempts to escape monetary policy and regulation. The central banks' objective of reining in money growth generally runs counter to individual banks' attempts to increase their profitability. Similarly, banking regulation aims at protecting customers by limiting the range of banking activities, including risk-taking. Pressed by competition and helped by continuous technological innovations—in computer power and in financial instruments—banks often innovate by exploiting loopholes in existing legislation. As a result, monetary control is weakened and banks may become more fragile. This fragility is confirmed by continuing

BOX 9.7. CAPITAL ADEQUACY RATIOS

Capital adequacy regulations are designed to protect the integrity of the banking system from individual bank risk, by requiring that capital (on the right-hand side) be a constant fraction of total risky assets (on the left-hand side) in their balance sheets. While a good case can be made for bank capital regulations, they sometimes put banks at a competitive disadvantage in international markets. Countries with little or no regulations may operate with lower levels of capital for a given stock of earning assets, and may earn better rates of return. In response to this problem, the Committee on Banking Regulation and Supervision (also know as the Basle Committee) has agreed on standard measures of bank capital adequacy.[18] The G-10 (the ten largest industrial countries) and the EC agreed to enforce these capital adequacy standards by end-1992 (by March 1993 in the case of Japan).

The principle is to link the amount of risky assets that banks hold with owners' equity, i.e. resources committed by the shareholders of the bank. Figure 9.12 shows the symmetry with the reserves ratios. The capital adequacy ratios cover the weak part of a bank's assets with the captive part of its liabilities, while reserves ratios cover the weak part of the liabilities with safe assets. One capital adequacy rule requires that primary or 'core' capital, consisting of paid-in equity and retained earnings, not fall below 4% of total risk assets. Secondary capital should equal at least an additional 4% of risk assets. Secondary

capital is defined as hidden reserves, general loan-loss provisions, asset revaluation, and certain 'near equity' such as convertible bonds, subordinated debt, and perpetual floating rate notes. The volume of risk assets is defined by a weighting scheme that increases with the riskiness of the asset involved.

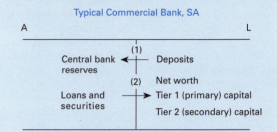

Typical Commercial Bank, SA

Figure 9.12. Reserve and Capital Adequacy Ratios

Primary or 'core' capital consists of the stakes of the owners in the bank. Secondary capital includes resources close to equity, such as hidden reserves, general loan-loss provisions, asset revaluation, convertible bonds, subordinated debt. Reserve ratios (1) link safe assets to potentially volatile deposits. Capital adequacy ratios (2) link safe liabilities to risky assets.

---

[18] The Basle Committee (established 1975) is a permanent forum for the discussion of international aspects of bank regulation, consisting of representatives of the G-10 central banks and bank supervisory bodies. Its name comes from the fact that it is housed by the Bank for International Settlements (BIS) situated in Basle. The BIS was founded after the first World War to provide settlement, research, and other services to the world's central banks.

bank failures in the USA (including a large part of the savings bank system) and in Europe (the collapse of BCCI, a bank that exploited loopholes in national regulations), and bank crises in the Nordic countries and Japan, as well as the collapse of one of the world's oldest and most prestigious banks, Barings of Britain.

9.7. Summary

1. Since most of the money stock is created by commercial banks, control of the money supply by the central bank can be only indirect. The key instrument is the reserve ratio, whether imposed by regulation or self-imposed by banks. This ratio establishes a link between bank reserves of the monetary base—a liability of the central bank—and bank deposits, a component of the money stock.

2. Because bank reserves represent a fraction of deposits, an increase in the monetary base and bank reserves translates into a much larger increase in deposits. This multiplicative factor is called the money multiplier.

3. The money multiplier is inversely related to the reserve ratio. Other factors that determine the multiplier are related to leakages out of the commercial banking system—into currency held by domestic residents or foreigners.

4. Individual commercial bank behaviour also limits the size of the money multiplier. One particular bank will see a large fraction of the money it creates leak away into deposits at other banks. As long as the newly created money remains in the banking system, the money multiplication process goes on in successive steps by commercial banks, but with a finite limit.

5. Central banks ensure monetary control through different means in different countries. By controlling liquidity in the market, the central bank directly affects the money supply and interest rates. A similar effect results from central bank rediscounting of securities; the difference is that the discount rate is pre-announced, at which the central bank stands ready to lend the monetary base.

6. An additional instrument available to the central bank is the required reserve ratio, when it exists.

7. Part of the monetary base creation is related to the financing of budget deficits. This can be done directly when the central bank lends money to the Treasury. In some countries such practices are forbidden; yet, buying government debt from banks on the money market amounts to the same thing.

8. When the exchange rate is fixed, the central bank is committed to intervene on the exchange markets. This ultimately means that the central bank cannot independently control the money supply. The same conflict arises when the central bank pursues interest rate and money supply targets which are inconsistent with each other.

9. The monetary financing of budget deficits, called monetization, should be distinguished from the effect of inflation on the value of outstanding non-indexed government debt, the inflation tax. Both effects imply that treasuries have a strong incentive to influence monetary policy. This is why central bank independence is often viewed as desirable.

10. Foreign exchange interventions can be offset by sterilization operations. Sterilization means that the central bank intervenes simultaneously on the foreign exchange and money markets, offsetting with one operation the effect on the monetary base of the other.

11. In addition to establishing the standard of payment, the central bank ultimately guarantees the value of money. This is done by a variety of regulations and the lender-of-last-resort function. Bank deposits are guaranteed—sometimes up to a certain level—through a combination of insurance schemes and implicit understanding that the central bank will create sufficient monetary base in case of bank failure. In return, the central banks may impose constraints on banks, designed to reduce their vulnerability.

12. The process of money control takes the form of an endless game between the commercial banks, which innovate and invent new unregulated forms of money, and the central bank, which adapts its operating procedures to remain in control. This is why definitions of money are both arbitrary and short-lived.

Key Concepts

- central bank
- monetary base
- bank reserves
- financial intermediaries
- reserves ratio
- money multiplier
- parallel currency
- repurchase agreement
- open market operations
- interbank market

- discount lending or rediscounting
- discount rate
- monetization
- sterilization
- seigniorage
- inflation tax
- systemic risk
- lender of last resort
- capital adequacy

Exercises: Theory

1. The central bank can control the sum of its liabilities, the monetary base, but not its breakdown between currency and banks' reserves. Explain why, and who does decide.

2. Consider the case of a country where banks are not forced to hold reserves but do so voluntarily. How might the behaviour of commercial banks frustrate the efforts of the central bank to control the money supply?

3. The central bank buys ECU 50 million worth of Treasury bills from commercial banks. It pays for it partly in foreign currency—the equivalent of ECU 10 million—and partly in local currency.

   (a) Show the effects in the balance sheets of the central bank and of the commercial banking system.
   (b) Show what commercial banks will do if the required reserves ratio is 25%.

4. Compute the multiplier when the required reserves ratio is 1% and the public chooses to hold 25% of its money (M1) in cash. What should the central bank do to increase M1 by ECU 10 million?

5. ECU 200 million worth of foreign currency was purchased by the central bank just as the central bank had decided to increase in M0 of ECU 50 million. Using the balance sheets in Figure 9.1, show what the central bank will do to keep to its original plan.

6. Imagine that the Bank of Denmark intervenes on the foreign exchange market to prevent an appreciation of the krone.

   (*a*) Describe the effect on the Danish money stock.
   (*b*) Does it make a difference if the foreign currency bought by the central bank on the foreign exchange markets was owned by foreigners?
   (*c*) Does it make a difference whether the kroner sold by the Bank of Denmark are deposited in Danish banks or in banks abroad (e.g. in London)?

7. Explain why large required reserves ratios allow governments to extract more seigniorage. Since seigniorage is a form of taxation, who bears the costs?

8. The inflation tax works only when inflation is unexpected. Explain. Do commercial banks benefit or lose from the inflation tax?

9. It is sometimes asserted that strict capital adequacy ratios reduce the money multiplier. Explain why or why not. (*Hint*: what is binding—the reserves ratio or the capital adequacy ratio?)

10. Commercial banks may want to hold reserves in excess of the minimum required because it is more convenient. Yet it is costly when reserves bear no interest. Assuming that the banks' demand for reserves resembles the public's demand for money, what is the effect of an increase in the interest rate on the money multiplier? Draw a schedule representing the supply of deposits by commercial banks as a function of the nominal interest rate.

11. Why are central banks generally reluctant to commit themselves to the lender-of-last-resort function?

12. In the text the money market multiplier was computed as $1/[cc + rr(1 - cc)]$ when the public maintains a constant fraction, cc, of the total money stock in currency form. If instead the private sector holds a constant fraction α of its deposits in the form of currency, show that the money multiplier is $(1 + \alpha)/(rr + \alpha)$, where rr is the reserves ratio.

Exercises: Applications

1. Under the gold standard (which ended in 1914), central banks were obliged to exchange paper money for gold on demand. Furthermore, banks stood ready to buy gold at some fixed price. What does this imply for the conduct of monetary policy by central banks?

2. It is a fact that in some countries the minting of coins is the activity of the Treasury rather than the central bank. Explain why national treasuries are usually in favour of increasing the maximum denomination of coins. Why would the central bank resist such a proposal?

3. When the French franc was weak in the early 1980s, the Banque de France imposed lower required reserves ratios on bank deposits by non-residents than on deposits by residents. Conversely, in the mid-1970s, the Bank of Switzerland imposed taxes on non-residents' deposits when the Swiss franc was appreciating. What could have been the logic behind these actions?

4. A number of countries (Italy, France, and the UK, for example) have used credit controls in the past. Credit controls can be thought of as an administrative limit on the volume of bank lending. Assume that the money supply is upward-sloping and money demand downward-sloping, when drawn with money on the horizontal axis and the nominal interest rate on the vertical axis.

   (*a*) Represent graphically how credit controls operate. What is the implication for the interest rate?
   (*b*) Can you think of any likely problems with operating such a policy?

5. Sterilized foreign exchange market interventions are designed to retain both an exchange rate target and monetary independence.

   (*a*) Why is this only temporarily feasible?
   (*b*) Which central banks are likely to give up first: those that prevent a depreciation or those that prevent an appreciation?

6. In the future we might cease using currency altogether. Realizing Wicksell's dream, all payments might be done electronically. What would this imply for reserves and monetary control by the central bank?

7. Some countries prefer to use open market operations as the primary tool for monetary policy, while others prefer to manipulate the discount rate. What are some possible factors that might affect this choice?

8. For several years now, Argentina has operated a currency board arrangement: the liabilities of the central bank must be equal to its foreign exchange reserves.

   (*a*) Show the balance sheet of the central bank by amending Figure 9.1.
   (*b*) What do you expect would be the effect on the interest rate of a capital outflow? Can the central bank prevent that by sterilizing operations?
   (*c*) In early 1995, capital outflows became massive (following a crisis on the Mexican peso). What would you expect the effect on commercial banks to be?
   (*d*) To alleviate pressure on commercial banks, the central bank reduced the required reserve ratio. Explain the logic of this action.

9. (*Hard*) In 1990, before monetary union occurred between East and West Germany, it was suggested that the Bundesbank should purchase East German marks (*Ostmarks*) on the open market to increase their market price. Why do you think the Bundesbank resisted this idea vigorously? (*Harder*) How would you explain their resistance to a similar proposal allowing them to sterilize the Ostmark purchases by selling foreign exchange or other securities?

Suggested Further Reading

Two useful references (the first historical and descriptive, the second analytical) on central banking are:

Goodhart, Charles A. E. (1988), *The Evolution of Central Banks*, MIT Press, Cambridge, Mass.

Tobin, James (1963), 'Commercial Banks as Creators of "Money" ', in D. Carson (ed.), *Banking and Monetary Studies*, Richard D. Irwin, Homewood, Ill., pp. 408–19.

On banks and banking deregulation in Europe, see:

Baltensperger, Ernst, and Dermine, Jean (1987), 'Banking Deregulation in Europe', *Economic Policy*, 4: 63–110.

Chiappori, Pierre-Andre, Mayer, Colin, Neven, Damien, and Vives, Xavier (1991), 'The Microeconomics of Monetary Union', in *Monitoring European Integration*, Centre for Economic Policy Research, London.

Pagano, Marco, and Roell, Ailsa (1990), 'Trading Systems in European Exchanges', *Economic Policy*, 10: 63–115.

On the debate on what the central bank should target, see:

Fischer, Stanley (1995), 'The Unending Search for Monetary Salvation', *NBER Macroeconomic Annual* 1995: 275–86.

Issing, Otmar (1994), 'Experience Gained with Monetary Policy Instruments in Germany', *Bankhistorisches Archiv*, Beiheft 27, Fritz Knapp Verlag, Frankfurt.

Walsh, Carl (1995), 'Recent Central Bank Reforms and the Role of Price Stability as the Sole Objective of Monetary Policy', *NBER Macroeconomic Annual* 1995: 237–52.

PART IV

Macroeconomic Equilibrium

This part integrates the real macroeconomy of Part II, where money played no role, with the monetary sector of Part III. It proposes a coherent framework which looks at the macroeconomy across its three key markets: the goods market, the money market, and the labour market. This framework is then used to analyse what it takes to achieve simultaneous equilibrium in all three markets. The result is macroeconomic equilibrium: the simultaneous determination of output, employment, the price level, and the interest rate.

This framework is first used in Chapter 10 to clarify the respective roles of output and prices in achieving equilibrium. Two competing hypotheses are presented and characterized: the neoclassical view, according to which it is price adjustments that bring demand and supply in line; and the Keynesian view, which considers that prices are too slow to move, leaving the burden of adjustment to be borne by output and employment. Chapter 11 then takes the Keynesian view as relevant for the short run and proceeds to explain cyclical fluctuations in the level of activity and interest rates. It shows the crucial role of exchange rates in shaping these fluctuations and the possible policy responses.

10

Output, Employment, and Prices

At the core of the Keynesian polemics . . . is the relationship between price flexibility and full employment. The fundamental argument of Keynes is directed against the belief that price flexibility can be depended upon to generate full employment automatically. The defenders of the classical tradition, on the other hand, still insist upon this automaticity as a basic tenet.

Don Patinkin

10.1. Overview

This chapter integrates the real macroeconomy of Part II, where money played no role, with the monetary sector of Part III. It proposes a coherent framework which looks at the macroeconomy across its three key markets: the goods market, the labour market, and the money market. This framework is then used to analyse the conditions under which simultaneous equilibrium is achieved in all three markets. Yet, there are two different ways of thinking about market equilibrium. The first—sometimes called the **neoclassical approach** to macroeconomics—assumes that prices perform the task of bringing the economy to equilibrium. By 'prices' we mean here not only the price level of goods in terms of money, but also the interest rate and real wages. Under these conditions, the real and monetary sectors do not affect each other.

A second approach takes a different tack. It assumes that some prices are sticky, at least for a while. Equilibrium in this case is achieved by adjusting the quantities traded: the volume of goods and services (i.e. GDP) and the quantity of labour employed. This second viewpoint is called Keynesian, in reference to J. M. Keynes, who criticized the neoclassical approach.

Despite the fact that both approaches arrive at radically different conclusions, both are derived from the same common framework. This framework is synthesized in two powerful graphical instruments: the *IS–LM* model, which highlights the interactions between the goods market and the money market; and the demand-and-supply model, which brings in the labour market and the behaviour of firms that produce goods and services and sell them in the goods market. Both tools are used extensively in the rest of the text; they are the bread and butter of macroeconomics.

Chapter 10 stresses the concept of equilibrium in both approaches. An economic model is said to be in equilibrium when it is at rest and there are no net forces moving it away from that resting point. Chapter 10 can be thus seen as an intermediate step towards the analysis of Chapter 11, which considers the effect of changes in exogenous variables on the equilibrium of the economy. A second point is that Chapter 10 first considers the case of the **closed economy**, which does not trade with, borrow from, or lend to other countries. A closed economy can be regarded as a metaphor for the world economy; this chapter will therefore be most suitable for dealing with global issues of macroeconomic equilibrium. Chapter 11 considers the case of a small open economy, which trades goods, services, and assets with the rest of the world.

10.2. The Goods Market and the *IS* Curve

10.2.1. Equilibrium in the Goods Market

We first consider the goods market, which is broadly defined to include services. The point of departure is the behaviour of households and firms, which demand

consumption and investment goods. In this chapter the focus is on the short run, taking the long run as given. The analysis can therefore be seen as the first of the two periods used in Chapters 3 and 4.

In a closed economy, the GDP as final expenditures

can be broken down into private consumption, investment, and government purchases. In the 'first period', this means

(10.1) $$Y_1 = C_1 + I_1 + G_1.$$

The components of private demand were analysed in Chapter 4. Today, in period 1 the consumption and investment functions are:

(10.2) $\quad C_1 = C(\underset{+}{\Omega}, \underset{+}{Y_1^d})\quad$ (consumption function)

(10.3) $\quad I_1 = I(\underset{-}{r_1}),\quad\quad$ (investment function)

to which is added the assumption that government spending and taxing is set exogenously by the government:

(10.4) $\quad G_1 = \overline{G}\quad\quad$ (government purchases)

$\quad\quad T_1 = \overline{T}.\quad\quad$ (net taxes)

Consumption (C) depends positively on private wealth Ω, and disposable income $Y^d = Y - T$. Because the direct effect of the real interest rate on consumption is ambiguous, only an indirect effect will be considered here: a rise in interest rates reduces household wealth and thereby consumption. For simplicity, investment is a function of the interest rate only: an increase in the real interest rate reduces the attractiveness of investment by increasing the opportunity cost of capital.[1]

The crucial step taken in this chapter is that (10.1) is no longer considered merely an accounting identity. Rather, it is now a condition for equilibrium in the goods market. The left-hand side represents the *supply* of output, while the right-hand side depicts the *demand* for it. The supply of output is determined by an economy's productive capacity, meaning its capital stock, its labourers and their skill endowments, and the state of technology.[2]

How is equilibrium, the equality between demand and supply, achieved? There are two approaches to this question. The first, which assumes that it is the chore of prices, is the object of Section 10.5, and is most often considered by economists as representing the long run, or the second period in the two-period world. It could also apply to the first period, however. Another approach is to assume that supply adjusts to demand while prices are sticky. The implications of this alternative **assumption** are studied in Section 10.6.

To start, a choice between the two competing approaches is deferred. We first ask not how equilibrium is achieved, but what it looks like when it is achieved. More precisely, we seek values of the interest rate and output for which the goods market is in equilibrium, or for which (10.1) holds. For the moment, the price level in the first period is taken as given, and equal to the price level in the second period. Inflation is zero, so the nominal interest rate i_1 is equal to the real interest rate r_1.

10.2.2. Desired Demand and Equilibrium Output

The demand for goods depends on current income through two channels: wealth and disposable income. This is seen by formulating the **desired demand function**, which combines the behavioural relationships (10.2)–(10.4):

(10.5) $\quad DD_1 \quad = C(\Omega, Y_1 - \overline{T}_1) + I(i_1) + \overline{G}_1$

$\quad$ desired demand = sum of demands for goods given i and Y

The schedule relates total planned spending or *desired* demand to income (GDP). The link is shown diagramatically in Figure 10.1. It is upward-sloping because when GDP rises, so does consumption. Aggregate demand must therefore also rise. If the GDP increase is temporary, consumption smoothing implies

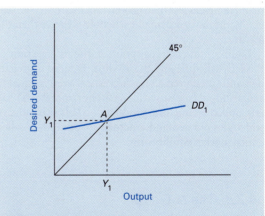

Figure 10.1. The 45° Diagram

Total desired demand responds positively but less than proportionately to a temporary increase in real GDP; hence the slope of the upward-sloping demand schedule is less than 45°. Equilibrium output is the GDP level Y_1 at which demand equals supply along the 45° line.

---

[1] Put in terms of Ch. 4, a rise in interest rates reduces Tobin's q and the attractiveness of investment.

[2] The determinants of long-run output were discussed in detail in Ch. 5.

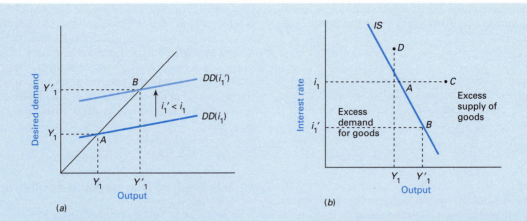

Figure 10.2. Deriving the *IS* Curve

The *IS* curve traces out combinations of the nominal interest rate (*i*) and output (*Y*) for which the goods market is in equilibrium, for given values of the exogenous variables. A reduction in interest rates from i_1 to i_1' leads to an increase in real investment. In panel (*a*) the *DD* demand curve shifts up, leading to a new equilibrium output Y_1', corresponding to moving along the curve from point *A* to point *B*. The results are shown in panel (*b*).

a smaller increase in consumption.[3] If the GDP increase is permanent, consumption should be expected to rise by a comparable amount. Since tomorrow's situation is assumed to be exogenous, changes in today's income are always considered temporary, so demand increases less than proportionately to GDP. This is why the desired demand schedule is flatter than the 45° line.

Equilibrium occurs at point *A*, the intersection of the DD_1 schedule and the 45° line. Desired aggregate demand (measured along the vertical axis) is equal to actual output (measured along the horizontal axis) and is supplied by ongoing production. This situation, in which desired demand is actually produced, is called **goods market equilibrium**.

10.2.3. The *IS* Curve

In Figure 10.1 the DD_1 schedule shows the dependence of demand on output for a given interest rate. What happens if the interest rate changes? The first panel of Figure 10.2 gives the answer, using the 45°

line diagram. The starting point *A* is on the desired demand schedule drawn for an interest rate (nominal and real) i_1. A decline in the interest rate, from i_1 to i_1', has two effects. First, wealth increases, since a given stream of future expected returns is discounted at a lower rate. This leads to an increase in consumption. Second, assuming all other things equal, investment increases because the cost of capital declines and also future profits are now discounted at a lower rate.[4] As a result, both consumption and investment spending increase—as implied by the consumption and investment functions (10.2) and (10.3). To the higher desired spending level there corresponds a higher desired demand schedule. The move from point *A* to point *B* means that equilibrium output increases from Y_1 to Y_1'.

The second panel of Figure 10.2 summarizes this discussion. Points *A* and *B* correspond respectively to the initial (interest rate i_1 and GDP Y_1) and final (i_1' and Y_1') outcomes. The same reasoning can be repeated for any a number of interest rates, producing more points like *A* and *B*. All of them confirm a negative relationship between the interest rate and equilibrium output depicted by the downward-sloping

[3] Consumption smoothing was discussed in Ch. 4.

[4] In terms of Ch. 4, Tobin's *q* rises.

schedule known as the *IS* curve.[5] *For given values of exogenous variables, the IS curve represents the combinations of nominal interest rate i and real GDP that are consistent with the goods market equilibrium.* Formally, the *IS* curve is the set of Y_1 and i_1 such that output Y_1 is equal to desired demand DD_1:

(10.6) $Y_1 = C(\Omega, Y_1 - \overline{T}_1) + I(i_1) + \overline{G}_1$.

It is downward-sloping because a higher (real) interest rate reduces private spending. For equilibrium to be maintained, output Y_1 must be lower.

The fact that the *IS* curve represents points of equilibrium means that all points *off* the *IS* curve must imply goods market **disequilibrium**. Disequilibrium occurs when, at given output or interest rate levels, desired demand is not equal to output. What happens if, starting from point A, the interest rate remains constant while today's output increases so that we move to point C? A higher income implies a higher level of demand, but, because of consumption smoothing of temporary fluctuations, demand will rise by less than output/income. At point C, therefore, there is not enough demand to absorb all of the new output: this is a situation of **excess supply** on the goods market. Similarly, moving vertically up from point A to, say, D corresponds to an increase in the interest rate with unchanged output. This would also lead to excess supply in the goods market as aggregate demand declines. Thus, the region above and to the right of the *IS* curve represents a situation of disequilibrium: excess supply on the goods market. Similarly, the region below and to the left of the *IS* curve corresponds to a situation of **excess demand** for goods and services. The *IS* curve divides panel (*b*) into those pairs of interest rates and output levels that imply excess supply, and those that imply excess demand. The *IS* curve, the border of the two regions, represents only the combinations where GDP and the interest rates are compatible with goods market equilibrium.

10.3. The Money Market and the *LM* Curve

The next step is to apply the same logic to the money market. As in Section 10.2, we ask which real GDP and interest rate levels are compatible with equilibrium in the money market, given the price level. Panel (*a*) of Figure 10.3 reproduces the equilibrium condition established in Chapter 8. The nominal money supply is controlled by the central bank and is assumed exogenous and equal to $\overline{M}$. Because the price level is taken as given, the real money supply is equal to $\overline{M}/P$, hence the vertical supply schedule. Money demand corresponds to a particular GDP level Y_1 and to an exogenous level of transaction costs. **Money market equilibrium** occurs at point A where demand and supply are equal, $\overline{M}/P = L(Y_1, i_1, c)$.

An increase in the GDP from Y_1 to Y_1' raises the demand for money. The money demand schedule shifts out and the new equilibrium occurs at point B: the interest rate has risen from i_1 to i_1'. This result is reported in panel (*b*), with corresponding points A (Y_1 and i_1) and B (Y_1' and i_1'). The money market equilibrium condition imposes a positive relationship between GDP and the interest rate. This is the **LM curve**.[6] *The LM curve is the combination of income and interest rates for which the money market is in equilibrium, given the price level and the exogenous variables.* Formally, the *LM* curve is the set of Y and i such that (10.7) holds.[7]

All points *off* the *LM* curve correspond to disequilibrium in the money market. Suppose, for example, an increase in real GDP from Y_1 to Y_1' at an unchanged interest rate takes us from an equilibrium point A to point C. What is the consequence when exogenous variables do not change? A higher GDP raises the demand for real money balances. At an unchanged real supply (given exogenous variables and given the price level), an excess demand for money

---

[5] The name of this curve comes from the identity (2.6): $I - S = T - G + CA$, and was first derived by Nobel Prize laureate Sir John Hicks. For simplicity, he assumed the budget to be in equilibrium and no foreign trade, so the identity reduced to $I = S$. We draw the *IS* curve as a line because we do not really know, nor do we need to know, its exact shape. For an derivation of the *IS* curve using calculus, see the Appendix.

[6] '*LM*' originates from the fact that along the curve, the demand for liquidity (L) equals the money supply (M) in (10.8).

[7] For an explicit derivation of the slope of the *LM* curve using calculus, see the Appendix.

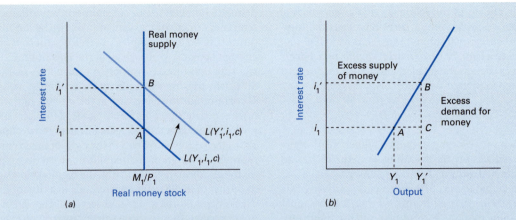

Figure 10.3. Deriving the *LM* Curve

The *LM* curve traces out the combinations of interest rates and output consistent with money market equilibrium. Panel (*a*) depicts the money market equilibrium. The demand curve going through point *A* corresponds to output Y_1. For a higher output level Y_1', demand for money is higher, and the interest rate rises from i_1 to i_1'. Points *A* and *B* in panel (*b*) correspond to the same points in panel (*a*).

arises. To restore equilibrium under these conditions, a higher interest rate is necessary, until point *B* is reached. At that point equilibrium is re-established: a higher interest rate increases the cost of holding money and therefore brings demand back into line with real money supply.

The region below and to the right of the *LM* curve thus represents disequilibrium situations of excess demand on the money market. Restoration of equi-librium requires either a rise in the interest rate, or a reduction in income and output levels. Similarly, the region above and to the left of the *LM* curve corresponds to an excess supply of money: equilibrium can be restored with a decrease in the interest rate or an increase in income and output. The border between these two regions, the *LM* curve, is where the money market is in equilibrium, i.e. in a state of neither ex-cess supply nor excess demand.[8]

10.4. General Equilibrium

10.4.1. Goods and Money Markets Together

The two previous sections have established equilib-rium conditions for the interest rate and GDP in goods and money markets, given the price level and exogenous variables. A natural next step is to look at both markets together. In Figure 10.4, the intersec-tion of the *IS* and *LM* curves yields the condition for both markets to be in equilibrium simultaneously.

Given the price level, there is now only one interest rate and one level of GDP compatible with equilib-rium in both markets. This GDP level can be thought of as representing **aggregate demand**, for it is the

---

[8] The result is more powerful than it appears. The *LM* curve also describes equilibrium in the market for interest-bearing assets. The reason is that the demand for money represents the choice of keep-ing wealth in non-interest-yielding form. Implicit in this choice is the decision of how much wealth is held in the form of interest-yielding assets such as bonds or stocks.

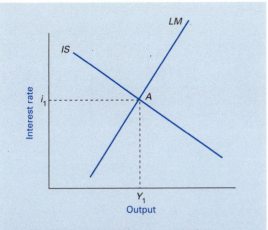

Figure 10.4. Goods and Money Market Equilibrium

The *IS* curve describes the output and interest rate levels compatible with equilibrium in the goods market. Similarly, along the *LM* curve, the money market is in equilibrium. At point *A* both markets are simultaneously in equilibrium: there is just one such point, and just one combination of output and the interest rate.

amount of income which, given the interest rate, wealth, public spending, and taxes, gives rise to an equal amount of *desired* spending. The *IS–LM* diagram is an example of a more general approach followed to find **general equilibrium** in economic systems. First, each market is examined separately and independ-

ently, and equilibrium conditions are established for each. Then these conditions are brought together, and the intersection of these conditions gives the general equilibrium.

Nevertheless, the *IS–LM* diagram does not alone suffice to establish a general equilibrium in the economy, for two reasons. First, the price level also must be determined, or at least accounted for; the thought experiments above take the price level as given. Second, until now we have not mentioned the labour market, an important element of the economic system which is intimately connected with the *production* of GDP. In the following sections this omission is redressed.

10.4.2. Output and the Labour Market with Flexible Real Wages

Figure 10.5 summarizes a number of results established in Chapters 5 and 6. Since it is clear that reference is made to the first period, from now on subscripts indicating the first period will be suppressed. The top panel represents the labour market. The focus remains on period 1, so the capital stock is given by accumulated past net investment and is exogenous. As a result, the marginal productivity of labour is declining, hence the downward-sloping labour demand schedule. The supply curve represents collective wage-setting. It is upward-sloping as workers or their representatives trade off employment and higher real wages. If real wages

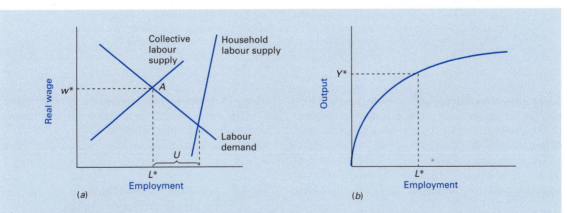

Figure 10.5. Output and Employment

When wages are fully flexible, wages adjust to clear the labour market at point *A* (panel (*a*)). This determines the amount of labour used by firms. Given the stock of capital, output is fully determined by employment by the production function (panel (*b*)).

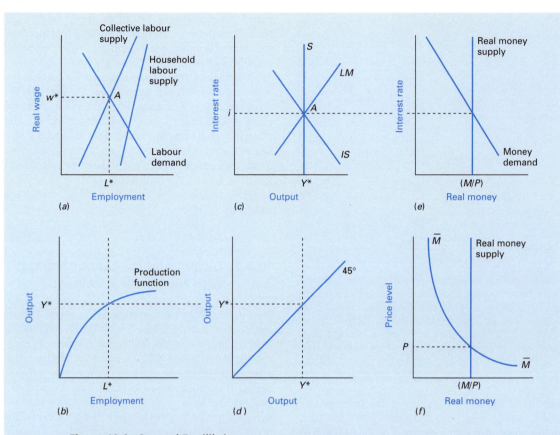

Figure 10.6. General Equilibrium

When real wages are fully flexible, they adjust to clear the labour market at point *A* (panel (*a*)). This determines the amount of labour used by firms. Given the stock of capital, the level of output is fully determined by employment as shown in panel (*b*). Using the 45° degree line in panel (*d*), the level of output that firms intend to supply is shown as the economy's vertical supply schedule *S* in panel (*c*). Panels (*e*) and (*f*) show the money market and the corresponding price level. At point *A* in panel (*c*), all three markets (labour, goods, money) are simultaneously in equilibrium. This is called the general equilibrium of the economy.

adjust instantaneously to equilibrate demand and supply, the market settles at point *A*. If there is involuntary unemployment (U), it is only from the perspective of households.[9]

The lower panel of Figure 10.5 represents the production function, given the stock of capital. At the real wage determined in the labour market, the firms hire

a level *L** of employment (man-hours) and produce *Y**. Thus, equilibrium in the labour market can be used to determine the output level.

10.4.3. General Equilibrium Determination of Output, Interest Rates, and Prices

Figure 10.6 brings together results from this and other chapters together in a single diagram. This graphical apparatus is important and powerful. It shows how to

---

[9] The difference between collective and household labour supply was discussed extensively in Ch. 6. The real wage/employment outcome is associated with involuntary unemployment from the household perspective. None of the main conclusions of the present chapter hinges on real wage flexibility, however. An exercise asks you to check this.

BOX 10.1. THE INTEREST RATE IN GENERAL EQUILIBRIUM

In Chapter 5, the interest rate was taken as given by the rest of the world. In this chapter, it is *determined* by the world's preferences and resources. The interest rate will be that which equilibrates the supply of savings—excess of output over private and government consumption—with the demand for investment.

Figure 10.7 shows the properties of this equilibrium. The economy starts with a private endowment at point A, which represents the consumption possibilities available if no investment is undertaken, and given government purchases G_1. By forgoing consumption in amount I, the economy can increase the present value of its wealth as described in Chapter 3 (Figure 3.7). The amount of consumption it is ready to give up for additional consumption tomorrow depends on its tastes, summarized by its indifference curves. By moving from A to A', the economy reaches a higher indifference curve. The real interest rate which clears the world's supply of savings and its demand for investment will be equal to the marginal rate of substitution between goods tomorrow for goods today.[10]

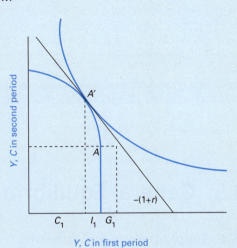

Figure 10.7. Interest rate in General Equilibrium

The interest rate is determined endogenously as the price that allocates output Y_1 among various types of demand. It will depend on tastes for consumption today versus consumption tomorrow, which are given by indifference curves, and productive possibilities, which are given by the slope of the production function. Starting from a private endowment at A, savings and investment allow the economy to reach point A'.

find the general equilibrium of the economy, i.e. when all three markets—goods, money, and labour—are in equilibrium at the same time.

Panels (a) and (b) in the left part of the figure reproduce Figure 10.5. They depict the supply side of the economy: how equilibrium in the labour market determines today's output Y. This is the level of output that is what firms will voluntarily supply. The top centre panel (c) shows the IS and LM schedules of Figure 10.4. The intersection of these two curves determines the aggregate demand of the economy: how much households, firms, and the government want to spend on today's output Y given prevailing interest rates.[11] As Box 10.1 shows, the interest rate so determined is also compatible with consumers' desires to

allocate their consumption over time, as derived in Chapter 4. The supply of goods is represented in panel (c) by a vertical line S. It is found by 'reflecting' the output level found in the lower left panel (b) using the 45° line of panel (d).

The top right panel (e) recalls the money market equilibrium condition shown in Figure 10.3(a). The link between the price and the real money stock is represented in the lower right panel (f).[12] It is assumed that the nominal money supply $\overline{M}$ is kept constant throughout. The $\overline{M}\overline{M}$ curve in panel (f) shows that a lower price level raises the real value of the money supply $\overline{M}/P$. Given $\overline{M}$, therefore, the real money supply depends only on the price level P. Along with private behaviour described by the demand-for-money schedule, the real money supply determines the LM curve in panel (c).

---

[10] In Ch. 4, many arguments were that consumers may be restricted in the amount they may borrow or lend. While this modification will change the results in Fig. 10.7 quantitatively, they are qualitatively the same.

[11] In Ch. 11, we include the net demand for goods and services from the rest of the world in an open economy.

[12] It is given by the simple formula $P = \overline{M}/(M/P)$. In simple terms, it tells us what price level P is necessary to make an exogenous nominal money supply $\overline{M}$ consistent with a certain level of real balances M/P.

The central question is whether output supplied as seen in panel (b) is compatible with equilibrium in the goods and money markets depicted in panel (c). As drawn, the IS and LM curves go through point A on the supply line S, so that demand and supply balance. This is the case of simultaneous equilibrium in all three markets.

That all three markets are simultaneously in equilibrium may seem like pure luck. What if instead, as drawn in Figure 10.8 (c), the IS and LM schedules intersect at point B with aggregate demand different from supply Y^* given by the labour market plus the production function? Equilibrium will hold in the goods and money markets either at point B, or in the goods and labour markets at point A off the LM curve (with excess demand on the money market), or in the money and labour markets at point C off the IS curve (excess supply of goods). The beauty of market economies is that powerful forces are at work in the economy to eliminate such disequilibria. What these forces are, and how they operate, form the subject of the rest of this chapter.

10.5. General Equilibrium with Flexible Prices

10.5.1. Supply-Determined Output

In the classical view, prices play the equilibrating role. This section shows that, with full price flexibility, all three markets are always jointly in equilibrium. This is shown in Figure 10.8. At point B, the output (desired demand) level compatible with both goods and money equilibrium Y is insufficient to absorb the output Y^* supplied by firms given labour market equilibrium. A decrease in the price level can, however, restore equilibrium. The process is as follows.

First, note that in panel (e) the demand-for-money schedule is defined for the supply level Y^* and will not shift. Combined with the money supply schedule, it yields the LM curve which goes through point C where output is Y^*. A reduction in the price level will increase the real money supply (panel (f)). This translates into a rightward shift of the real money supply line in panel (e) and a corresponding move from LM to LM' in panel (c). There will be a price level low enough for LM' to go through point A, where general equilibrium is achieved. In the figure, the equilibrating price level is P', which in panel (e) corresponds to the real money supply schedule $(M/P)'$.

This example shows that there is a price level that establishes general equilibrium when the interest rate and the real wage adjust to clear the money and labour markets. Put differently, full flexibility of all relevant prices (the price of goods, the interest rate, i.e. the price of money, and the real wage, i.e. the price of labour) results in general equilibrium.[13] The adjustment does not affect the supply side, which is shown in panels (a) and (b). These panels correspond to the labour market and the firms' decision to hire labour and to supply a given output level. Two important conclusions can be drawn.

First, when the price level adjusts freely, the economy's general equilibrium is always found at the intersection of the IS and the goods supply schedule S in the top centre panel. The IS schedule can be interpreted as the economy's demand schedule. The output level is **supply-determined**.

Second, price adjustments restore equilibrium through the real value of money. They shift the LM curve until it goes through the intersection of the supply and IS schedules. In the case of point B, i.e. a situation where demand is weak relative to what firms are prepared to supply, a fall in the price level is needed to raise the real value of money. This in turn leads to a lower interest rate, and a higher level of aggregate demand.

A similar story can be told where aggregate demand exceeds aggregate supply. If the IS and LM curves were to intersect at point D, this would be the case. An increase in the price level would be required to reduce real money balances, raising the interest rate and reducing desired consumption and investment spending.

10.5.2. Dichotomy and Money Neutrality

When prices are perfectly flexible so that the economy is always in a situation of general equilibrium, a very

---

[13] We have only established the existence of general equilibrium. That the relevant prices always move in the right direction to achieve general equilibrium (the issue of stability) is beyond the scope of this book. The question of price adjustment is developed more fully in Chs. 12–14.

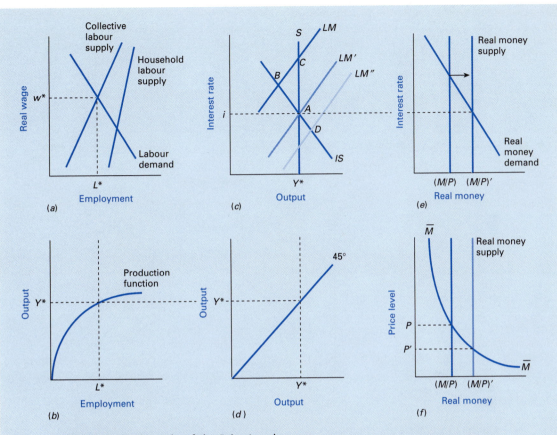

Figure 10.8. The Role of the Price Level

When the three schedules do not go through the same point as shown in panel (c), price changes change the real value ($\overline{M}/P$) of a given stock of nominal money supply $\overline{M}$. The result is a shift in the LM curve until it goes through the point where the supply and IS schedules intersect. At point B demand falls short of supply, so a reduction of the price level is needed to shift the LM curve to the right. Conversely, at point D supply falls short of demand, which is curtailed when the real money supply decreases following an increase in the price level. At point A equilibrium obtains in goods, money, and labour markets.

important property holds: nominal and real variables do not affect each other. More precisely:

1. real variables (real GNP, equilibrium unemployment, relative prices, including the real exchange rate) are unaffected by the level of the money supply;
2. money affects one for one all nominal variables (i.e. those denominated in terms of the domestic currency).[14]

---

[14] This is linked to the proposition in Ch. 8 that the rate of inflation is proportional to the rate of money growth.

Why this is so can be seen by returning to Figure 10.8. The general equilibrium is found at the intersection of the S and IS schedules, which describe the real side of the economy (goods and labour markets). The LM curve, which describes the nominal side of the economy (money and other financial markets), plays no role in determining the general equilibrium. It simply shifts to pass through the intersection of the two 'real curves'. When the price level adjusts immediately and the economy is always in general equilibrium, the principle of **classical dichotomy** holds: nominal variables do not affect real variables. Only technology and tastes affect the real side of economic activity (growth,

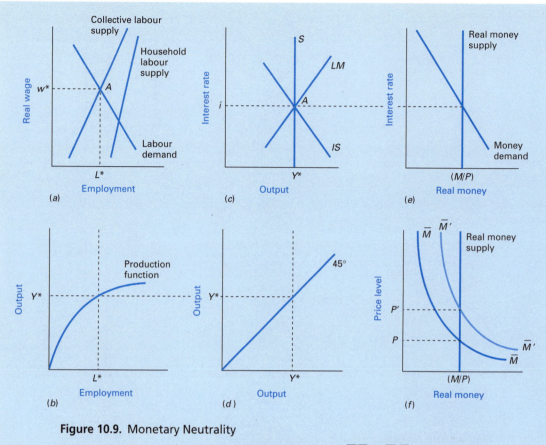

Figure 10.9. Monetary Neutrality

An increase in the nominal money supply causes a shift from $\overline{M}\overline{M}$ to $\overline{M}'\overline{M}'$ which leads to a proportional increase in the price level. All real variables are unchanged.

unemployment, real consumption, etc.). In particular, output is determined entirely by aggregate supply conditions. Monetary factors, such as the money supply and nominal interest rates, play no role.

The effects of a change in nominal money are shown in Figure 10.9. An increase in the supply of nominal money shifts the $\overline{M}\overline{M}$ curve out to $\overline{M}'\overline{M}'$ in panel (f). At a given price level, this would increase the supply of real balances and shift down the LM schedule. This is not consistent with general equilibrium, since aggregate demand exceeds aggregate supply in panel (c). To restore equilibrium, a price-level adjustment is necessary to return the LM curve to its original position. For that to occur, nominal money changes must be offset by proportional changes in the price level,

leaving the real money supply unchanged, as is shown in panel (f).[15] This result is sometimes referred to as the principle of **monetary neutrality**. Monetary neutrality means that money does not affect the real side of the economy: neither the labour market conditions (panels (a) and (c)), which determine the supply of goods (the S line in panel (b)), nor spending decisions (the IS curve) are influenced by changes in the money supply (the LM curve).

A related conclusion has already been reached in Chapter 8, where it is shown that inflation and the rate of exchange rate depreciation are driven entirely by

[15] When M and P change in the same proportion, M/P remains constant.

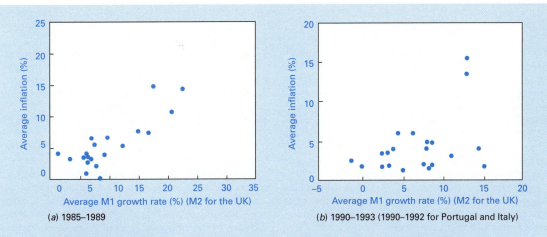

Figure 10.10. Money and Prices in the Short Run, 21 Countries, 1985–1993

Over short five-year intervals, the linkage between monetary growth and inflation is less obvious than in Figure 8.9.

The 21 countries are: USA, Japan, Germany, France, Italy, UK, Canada, Australia, Austria, Belgium, Denmark, Finland, Greece, Iceland, Ireland, Netherlands, New Zealand, Portugal, Spain, Sweden, Switzerland.

Sources: IMF, OECD

the rate of growth of the nominal money supply over longer time intervals. The view that prices adjust even in the short run, so that the economy is always dichotomized, is the **(neo)classical assumption**.[16] Its validity for the real world remains controversial. The evidence presented in Figure 8.9 suggests that monetary variables do not affect the real economy in the long run. To a first approximation, the principles of

dichotomy and money neutrality provide a good benchmark for the long-run behaviour of the macroeconomy. At the same time, evidence such as that in Figure 10.10 suggests that strict monetary neutrality does not obtain from year to year; and that changes in nominal money do not lead to instantaneous price changes. The next section takes up the implications of price rigidity for macroeconomic equilibrium.

10.6. General Equilibrium with Sticky Prices

10.6.1. Demand-Determined Output

A radically different approach to thinking about the macroeconomy assumes that the price level is no longer

perfectly flexible, but instead is *constant*. This step is often called the **Keynesian assumption**. Is this assumption realistic? Chapter 1 (Table 1.4) offers evidence that prices are considerably less volatile than output. Box 10.2 presents some good reasons why firms, which actually set prices, may change them only occasionally. This section shows that, under the Keynesian assumption, output is **demand-determined**. This means that suppliers produce whatever is demanded at the given

---

[16] It is the rival to the Keynesian view that prices are sticky. The term '*classical*' comes from Keynes's initial attack. '*Neoclassical*' refers to the revival of pre-Keynesian ideas, first in the 1960s around Milton Friedman in Chicago, and since then the mid-1970s.

BOX 10.2. THE KEYNESIAN ASSUMPTION

The assumption that the price level is insensitive to aggregate demand in the short run follows a tradition that began with John Maynard Keynes (1883–1946) in a book written after the Great Depression. His purpose was to explain how the level of activity could fall dramatically. (Industrial production declined by 10%–20% between 1929 and 1931.) Today the Keynesian assumption is a practical step towards constructing a macroeconomic framework; but Keynesians would go beyond that, claiming its validity as a good 'working assumption'. Dennis Carleton from the University of Chicago has studied how often firms change their prices. He has found that price changes are rare, often no more than every 18 months, even during periods of moderate inflation.

Critics of the Keynesian assumption prefer to think that prices move fast enough to clear the markets. They often ask: Why should price-setters not adjust to changing economic conditions? What kind of behaviour could rationalize price rigidity? The Keynesians have three responses. First, **menu costs** might be significant. These are administrative costs associated with changing prices, relabelling packages, and advertising these changes. Yet it is puzzling that catalogue prices, which are easy to change, are not changed very often either. Similarly, modern supermarkets which use bar coding pricing should not find it too costly to change entries in the central computer. This suggests that there must be other important reasons for price rigidity.

A second explanation emphasizes *customer relationships*. To maintain a good reputation *vis-à-vis* its customers, a firm may keep its price lists unchanged in the face of considerable fluctuations in demand. For example, in August 1995 VAT tax was raised by 2% in France. Many stores announced that they would not change their prices *inclusive of the tax*. Thus, to keep prices constant, they were willing to absorb—for a time at least—the 2% tax hike and to pay for advertisements to make this known to their customers. A third explanation notes the role of *contracts*. Firms may be locked into implicit or even explicit contracts to deliver goods at a specified price for some period of time.

price level. In this sense, the Keynesian case can be thought of as the polar opposite of the classical case, in which output is set by supply conditions alone.

Figure 10.11 reproduces Figure 10.8 to illustrate the difference between the flexible and sticky price equilibria. The starting point is the same: the three schedules in panel (*c*) do not go through the same point. The demand-for-money schedule in panel (*e*) corresponds to output level *Y* since the corresponding *LM* curve in panel (*c*) goes through point *B*. Now the price level *P* does not change. With a fixed money supply $\overline{M}$ and a fixed price level, the real money supply in panel (*e*) is exogenous, and the position of the *LM* curve is given in panel (*c*). The *IS* curve, which gives conditions for equilibrium in the goods markets, has no reason to move either. As a result, the only resting point for the economy is at point *B*, where the *IS* and *LM* curves intersect. Point *B* is an equilibrium.

The equilibrium cannot be completely described without looking at the labour market. Here too there is a divergence from market-clearing. Employment is determined by aggregate demand *Y*. Aggregate demand differs from the supply-determined level *Y** corresponding to point *A* in panels (*a*) and (*c*). If firms produce less, they need less labour; panel (*b*) shows that employment is *L*, below the level *L** corresponding to equilibrium in the labour market. When prices

are sticky and demand- and supply-determined outputs differ, there cannot be full general equilibrium. Rather, aggregate demand will determine employment as the labour required to produce the demanded output level. In panel (*a*), it is assumed that the real wage was rigid at level $\overline{w}$, which corresponds to the marginal productivity of labour at the previous equilibrium. In that case there is unemployment, as labour supply exceeds demand by the distance *AB*. This is, however, one of many possibilities.[17]

The main difference between the flexible and sticky price cases can now be summarized in a convenient way. With flexible prices, the direction of causality in Figure 10.6 is counter-clockwise, moving from panel (*a*) to panels (*b*), (*c*) and (*d*): labour market equilibrium determines output. Panels (*e*) and (*f*) then show what price level is consistent with general equilibrium. With sticky prices, the right-hand panels (*e*) and (*f*) are no longer informative. The logic now is to 'move clockwise', from panel (*c*) to panels (*d*), (*b*) and (*a*):

---

[17] It is important to note that, because aggregate demand determines output, firms generally will not be on their labour demand curves. In fact, any position between *B* and *C* is possible: not being on the labour demand curve means that firms make extra profits as they pay less for labour than its marginal productivity. Lower real wages in turn will reduce involuntary unemployment.

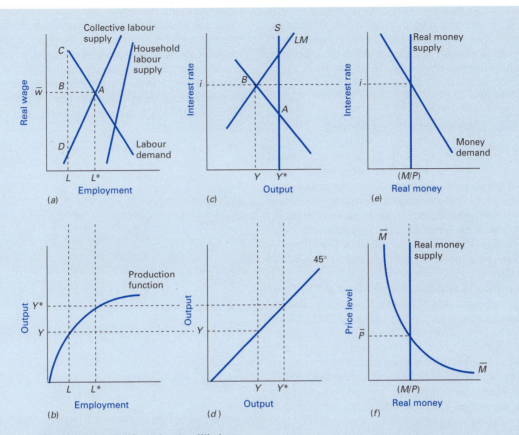

Figure 10.11. Sticky Price Equilibrium

Starting from a situation where all three schedules do not go through the same point in panel (b), with sticky prices and a given nominal money supply $\overline{M}$, the real money stock ($\overline{M}/P$), and therefore the LM curve, cannot change. It is the structure of demand, and therefore the IS schedule, that determines the sticky price equilibrium at point A. Reflecting the demand-determined output level via panel (d), we find in panel (b) the level of employment L needed to produce Y. The labour market need not be in equilibrium however, and in general will be characterized by unemployment. In panel (a) it is assumed that firms pay real wage $\overline{w}$ compatible with employment L*, so that there is involuntary unemployment corresponding to AB.

labour market no longer determines the goods market, *but rather is determined by it*. The difference between the labour demanded and labour supplied at some non-clearing real wage $\overline{w}$ is unemployment. The case considered here, where demand falls short of supply, is the archetypal sticky-price Keynesian case. It is possible to consider the opposite case, where demand exceeds supply.[18] This case, sometimes called 're-

pressed inflation', is however rarely observed in market economies.[19]

With sticky prices, true general equilibrium does not occur as in Figure 10.6, except by pure chance. The goods and money markets are in equilibrium, but the labour market is not. At an intuitive level this might seem realistic. We do not observe firms producing

---

[18] See theoretical exercise 7.

[19] It was, however, often observed in centrally planned economies, when prices were sometimes set low relative to demand for political reasons. Apparently it was more important to be paid than to have something to buy with your pay!

unwanted goods for very long when demand is weak, nor do we see persistent shortages when demand exceeds supply. As was noted in Chapter 8, money markets are notoriously fast to adjust. On the other side, unemployment is obviously a feature of life.[20]

10.6.2. Non-neutrality of Money

A key implication of sticky prices is that the classical dichotomy no longer holds. This can be seen in Figure 10.12 using a single diagram. Output determines employment, so all the variables involving the real side of the economy (GDP, employment, consumption, investment, real interest rates, etc.) are subject to influences originating in the money market. Since the price level does not move, changes in nominal money have real effects.

A corollary of the failure of the classical dichotomy is the non-neutrality of money. Graphically, changes in the nominal money supply in Figure 10.11 shift the LM curve, and thereby affect output, employment, and all other real variables. Monetary neutrality held in the classical case beause the price level moved to equate real money supply $\overline{M}/P$ with real money demand $L(Y, i, c)$, where this real money demand was consistent with the output level and interest rate delivered by

equilibrium in the goods and labour markets. In effect, the price level moved enough to bring the LM curve through the intersection of the goods supply and IS schedules. When the price level is fixed, it is money demand that adjusts to money supply. This, in turn, requires changes in the interest rate and output. These changes remain compatible with goods market equilibrium: graphically, the economy moves along the IS curve from A to A'.

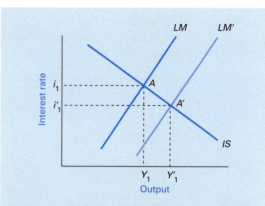

Figure 10.12. Monetary Neutrality Fails when the Price Level is Fixed

An increase in the money supply leads to excess supply of money on points along the old LM curve. The new LM curve lies below and to the right of the old one. Equilibrium in goods and money markets implies a lower interest rate and higher real GDP than at A.

---

[20]   Such 'sticky price general equilibria' are sometimes called non-Walrasian, after Leon Walras (1834–1910), a French mathematical economist who first conceptualized the idea of general equilibrium. Walras emigrated to Lausanne in Switzerland when his theories were rejected by his French peers, who ultimately drove him to exile.

10.7. Summary

1. The IS curve is the set of real GDP levels and interest rates compatible with goods market equilibrium, given the price level. This schedule is downward-sloping because an increase in the interest rate depresses consumption and investment spending; equilibrium requires that output be lower.

2. The money market equilibrium condition is represented by the LM curve, a positive relationship between real GDP and the interest rate, given the real money supply. The slope of the LM curve is positive because an increase in the interest rate, which reduces the demand for money, must be offset by an increase in GDP, which increases demand.

3. On the labour market, there exists a real wage and a level of employment which deliver equilibrium with no involuntary unemployment, at least from the perspective of the collective bargaining parties.

4. When all three markets (goods, money, labour) clear simultaneously, the economy's general equilibrium is achieved. Whether, and how, it is reached depends very much on price-level adjustments.

5. Price-level adjustments affect the real money supply and drive the *LM* curve to pass through the intersection of the supply-determined output schedule and the *IS* curve, which represents demand conditions.

6. With flexible prices the economy is dichotomized: real and nominal variables do not affect each other. Monetary neutrality is the absence of real effects of nominal money changes. Money affects only prices and other nominal variables.

7. The assumption that prices are flexible is a useful way of thinking about the long run of the economy. However, while it is borne out in the long run, the short run is less likely to be characterized by full price flexibility.

8. When prices are sticky, output is determined by demand conditions. The equilibrium occurs at the intersection of the *IS* and *LM* curves. In general, the corresponding output differs from intended supply. This discrepancy leads to disequilibrium on the labour market, often resulting in involuntary unemployment.

9. With sticky prices, the classical dichotomy and monetary neutrality principles do not apply. Money matters for the real side of the economy.

10. The Keynesian assumption, that the price level is constant and that output adjusts to achieve goods market equilibrium, is a convenient short cut for analysing the short-run determination of GDP and interest rates.

11. The flexible and sticky price cases can be analysed with the same graphical apparatus. With flexible prices, GDP is supply-determined and prices adjust; with sticky prices, GDP is demand-determined and the output of firms adjusts.

Key Concepts

- neoclassical approach
- closed economy
- desired demand function
- goods market equilibrium
- *IS* curve
- disequilibrium
- money market equilibrium
- *LM* curve

- aggregate demand
- general equilibrium
- supply- and demand-determined output
- classical dichotomy
- monetary neutrality
- neoclassical assumption
- Keynesian assumption
- menu costs

Exercises: Theory

1. Desired demand is represented by the following simplified function:
   $1500 + 0.8\,(Y - T) + G - 80i$. T is constant and equal to 3000.

   (a) Find GDP compatible with equilibrium when $G = 3000$ and $i = 5\%$, assuming that the price level remains constant.

   (b) To trace out the *IS* curve, compute GDP compatible with equilibrium keeping $G = 3000$ for $i = 2\%$ and $i = 8\%$.

   (c) Same question as (b) when $G = 4000$ for $i = 5\%$, then for $i = 2\%$ and $i = 8\%$.

2. The *IS* and *LM* curves define four quadrants in Figure 10.4. Any position off a curve corresponds to market disequilibrium, which can be characterized as excess demand or supply in either goods or money markets, or both. Define each quadrant accordingly, e.g. excess demand in the goods market and excess supply in the money market; etc.

3. Suppose the money demand curve is represented by the following linear function:
   $L(Y, i) = 0.5Y - 300i$. Suppose $M/P = 2000$. Plot the *LM* curve in the i, Y space.

4. Explain with the graphical apparatus of Figure 10.6 the following rule of thumb: when demand-determined output exceeds supply-determined output prices tend to rise; in the opposite case they tend to decline.

5. Using the diagram in Figure 10.6, show the effect of productivity gains (an outward shift of the production function) on employment, output, prices, real wages, and interest rates when prices are flexible. How does your answer change when they are sticky?

6. Consider the case where real wages are sticky and such that, in Figure 10.6(a), there is some involuntary unemployment. Show that, if prices are flexible, equilibrium is still possible in other markets and that output remains supply-determined. Show that the economy is dichotomized and that money is neutral. (This exercise establishes that the flexible price results apply in the presence of real wage rigidity.)

7. Consider the Keynesian case as in Figure 10.11. Now, however, let the *IS* and *LM* curves intersect on the right of the supply schedule in panel (c). Show the new situation in panels (a) and (c).

   (a) In panel (a), assume that the market is driven by the demand for labour: firms set the real wage low enough to hire all the necessary labour to produce the level of demand-determined output. Does this outcome seem possible to you? Explain how measures such as longer work hours, delayed retirement, and immigration may, or may not, make this situation possible.

   (b) In panel (a), assume that employees are powerful enough to impose a real wage corresponding to the amount of labour demanded. What does it mean for firms' profitability? How likely is this outcome?

(c) Discuss the view that prices may behave asymmetrically: flexible in the case of this exercise and sticky in the case depicted in Figure 10.11.

8. Two concepts of price and wage stickiness have been used in this chapter: nominal price stickiness and real-wage stickiness. Explore the general equilibrium outcomes with all the possible combinations, e.g. sticky prices and flexible real wages, or flexible prices and sticky real wages. What lesson can you draw?

9. Using the desired demand function from exercise 1, assume that output is produced using the production function $Y = \sqrt{(KL)}$. Further, assume that $K = 20{,}000$ and $L = 5000$ $\overline{T} = 3000$ and $\overline{G} = 3300$.

(a) What is the equilibrium level for output, real wages, and interest rates?
(b) Using the money demand function $L(Y, i) = 2Y - 800i$, solve for the price level in this economy for $\overline{M} = 16{,}000$.

10. Now assume the Keynesian case with $\overline{P} = 1$ for simplicity. Solve for the effect of an increase in M from 9000 to 10,000 on Y and i. What happens to L? What key assumptions have you made in solving this problem?

Exercises: Applications

1. What is the effect of increased labour militancy, as captured by an upward shift of the collective labour supply schedule in Figure 10.6(a)? Consider separately the cases of fixed and flexible prices.

2. Using the graphical apparatus, show the effects on GDP, employment, the price level, and the interest rate of an increase in the transaction costs c which affect money demand. You should consider the cases of both fixed and flexible prices.

3. After the end of the Cold War, defence expenditures could have been slashed. Consider the effect this would have on GDP, employment, and interest rates in a closed economy. As a neoclassical economist (believing that prices are flexible), what would be your view about such spending cuts? What if you believe prices are sticky?

4. Assume that we start with full equilibrium as in panel (c) of Figure 10.6, but with some involuntary unemployment as in panel (a) of Figure 10.9. Now, to reduce unemployment, workers accept a reduction in real wages such that the labour market clears with no involuntary unemployment as in panel (a) of Figure 10.6. What is the resulting situation in panel (c): (i) with flexible prices? (ii) with sticky prices? What is your conclusion about the desirability of wage cuts in the presence of involuntary unemployment?

5. The authorities control public spending G and the nominal money supply M. Explain how they can change the interest rate (a) when prices are flexible; (b) when prices are flexible.

6. Formerly planned economies emerged with an antiquated capital stock. This means that new investment will quickly raise productivity. Assuming that they start from general equilibrium as in Figure 10.6,

   (a) Show the effect of investment in panels (a) and (b).
   (b) Interpret the resulting situation in panel (c).
   (c) In the case of flexible prices, what is expected to happen to GDP, the interest rate, and prices?
   (d) Now answer the same question as (c) in the case of sticky prices.
   (e) Can the outcome of question (c) be reached with sticky prices if the central bank changes the nominal money supply in a judicious manner?

7. After the fall of communism, it was recognized that the countries of Central and Eastern Europe were suffering from a deficit of productive capital when compared with Western Europe. Suppose this implies a shift in investment demand, with no strong tendency for consumers to save. What does the classical model predict as a consequence for output and interest rates of these countries joining the world's market economies? What does the Keynesian model predict?

8. Suppose there were a drastic plague which wiped out half of the labour force in an economy. What does the general equilibrium apparatus with flexible prices predict for current output, interest rates, and prices? You may assume that the nominal money supply is kept constant.

9. (*Harder*) Drawing on your knowledge from Chapter 5, what would be the consequence of the plague—meaning the loss of a large portion of the labour force—for the marginal product of capital? Although it is not included in the investment function (10.4), what would this imply for investment? How would you modify the model to incorporate this effect?

Suggested Further Reading

The classics are:

Keynes, John Maynard (1936), *The General Theory of Employment, Interest, and Money*, Macmillan, London/Harcourt Brace, New York.

The paper that founded macroeconomics and 'summarized' the *IS–LM* framework is:

Hicks, John (1937), 'Mr Keynes and the Classics', *Econometrica*, 5: 147–59.

The seminal characterization of flexible and sticky price equilibria is:

Patinkin, Don (1948), 'Price Flexibility and Full Employment', *American Economic Review*, 38: 543–64.

An advanced treatment is:

Sargent, Thomas, J. (1987), *Macroeconomic Theory*, Academic Press, New York.

Appendix: A Mathematical Treatment of the Macroeconomic Equilibrium with Flexible and Fixed Prices

This appendix derives formally some of the results presented in the text.

Macroeconomic Equilibrium under Flexible Prices (the Classical Model)

The Labour Market

Aggregate labour supply is assumed to be given by

(A10.1) $$L^S = L^S(w, \overline{N}),$$

where w is the real wage and $\overline{N}$ is the exogenous number of individuals of working age. Assumptions are $L_w^S > 0$, $L_{\overline{N}}^S > 0$. The supply of labour could be viewed more generally as the role of collective bargaining or union behaviour instead of households.

Aggregate labour demand was derived in (A6.8) as

(A10.2) $$L^D = L^D(w, \overline{K}),$$

with $L_W^D < 0$, $L_K^D > 0$. Equilibrium is given by

(A10.3) $$L^D(w, \overline{K}) = L^S(w, \overline{N}) = L,$$

which determines two unknowns, employment L and the real wage w.

The Goods Market

Goods supply is given by the output of firms that produce goods using labour which they have hired according to (A10.2). Capital is fixed in the first period, so we can write the production function simply as $Y = F(\overline{K}, L)$. Since employment is determined in the labour market as the solution to (A10.3), we can define $\overline{L}$ and $\overline{w}$ as the corresponding equilibrium employment and wage, so

(A10.4) $$Y^S = F(\overline{K}, \overline{L}).$$

To derive goods demand, set inflation expectations $\pi = 0$, so the real interest rate r is the same as the nominal interest rate i. Following Chapter 4, final expenditure of households, firms, and government can be written for this closed economy as

(A10.5) $$Y = C(\Omega, Y^d) + I(i) + \overline{G},$$

where Y is GDP, C is consumption, I is investment expenditures, and $\overline{G}$ is government purchases, denominated in real terms. Government purchases $\overline{G}$ are exogenous, as is the lump-sum (net) tax $\overline{T}$. Disposable income Y^d is given therefore by $Y - \overline{T}$. In principle, $\overline{T}$ need not be positive; if negative it could be an exogenous transfer or a tax exemption. Wealth Ω is taken as exogenous.

Equation (A10.5) is the IS curve drawn in Figure 10.2, which is an equation in Y, i, and (trivially) the price level P. Total differentiation of (A10.5) results in

(A10.6) $$dY = C_\Omega d\Omega + C_{Y^d} dY - C_{Y^d} d\overline{T} + I_i di + d\overline{G}.$$

The slope of the IS curve in (i, Y) space is given when all exogenous variables are constant in (A10.6), when we set $d\Omega = d\overline{G} = d\overline{T} = 0$:[21]

$$dY = C_{Y^d} dY + I_i di$$

or

(A10.7) $$\frac{dY}{di} = \frac{I_r}{1 - C_{Y^d}} < 0$$

for any value of the price level P. Goods market equilibrium obtains when supply and demand of goods are equal, or

(A10.8) $$F(\overline{K}, \overline{L}) = Y = C(\Omega, Y^d) + I(i) + \overline{G}.$$

Money Market

The supply of nominal money is determined by the central bank at $\overline{M}$. Demand for real balances was derived in Chapter 8 as

(A10.9) $$\mathcal{L}(Y, i)$$

with $\mathcal{L}_Y > 0$, $\mathcal{L}_i < 0$. Equilibrium in the money market is given by

(A10.10) $$\overline{M}/P = \mathcal{L}(Y, i),$$

which is the LM curve. Total differentiation of (A10.10) results in

(A10.11) $$\frac{d\overline{M}}{P} - \frac{\overline{M}}{P^2} dP = \mathcal{L}_{Y^d} Y + \mathcal{L}_i di.$$

For P, given $dP = 0$, the slope of the LM curve can be found when $dM = 0$ in (A10.11), or

(A10.12) $$\frac{di}{dY} = -\frac{\mathcal{L}_Y}{\mathcal{L}_i} > 0.$$

Note that the 'last market', the market for interest-bearing assets, can be assumed to clear if the money market clears. This is said to be an application of Walras's Law, discussed in any good microeconomics textbook.

---

[21] The assumption that wealth is constant could be modified, as will be done in the next chapter's appendix. It reflects the view that transitory (current) movements in interest rates and output should not affect household wealth, which is based on a longer-term horizon.

General Equilibrium with Flexible Prices

Thus, we have:

S curve: $Y = F(\overline{K}, \overline{L})$
IS curve: $Y = C(\Omega, Y - T) + I(i) + \overline{G}$
LM curve: $\overline{M}/P = \mathscr{L}(Y, i)$,

a system of three equations for Y, i, and p. They are represented by the three curves in panel (c) of Figure 10.6. Since output supply is given, the equilibrium interest rates solves

$$\overline{Y} = C(\Omega, Y^d) + I(i) + \overline{G},$$

and the price level adjusts to obey (the MM curve)

$$P = \frac{\overline{M}}{\mathscr{L}(\overline{Y}, i)}.$$

Macroeconomic Equilibrium under Fixed Prices

We now assume that, for whatever reason, P is exogenously given at level $\overline{P}$. Generally, not all markets will clear; in particular, it is assumed that the labour market remains out of equilibrium, and that $L = L^D < L^S \neq \overline{L}$. For simplicity, we also assume that the nominal wage is fixed at $W = \overline{W}$ so that the real wage is also fixed at $\overline{W}$.[22] Labour demand is demand-determined; that is, employment is simply labour demanded to produce output Y. Under these conditions, we can consider equilibrium only in the goods and money markets. Equilibrium in the bond market will obtain if the money market clears, as before.

---

[22] This assumption is not necessary. For example, Keynes (1936) assumed that only nominal wages were rigid, while prices could adjust fully. Alternatively, one could assume rigid prices plus flexible nominal *wages*, assuming that individuals are on their labour supply curve, or rigid prices plus flexible nominal wages but with the latter determined along a *collective* rather than the household labour supply schedule.

Goods Market

Demand for goods is given by (A10.5). The supply of goods is perfectly elastic at price $\overline{P}$; firms are willing to supply more output at that price. The goods market equilibrium is given by

$$Y = C(\Omega, Y^d) + I(i) + \overline{G}.$$

Because changes in Y are considered short-run, Y is assumed not to affect wealth, or $\Omega_Y = 0$. The slope of the IS curve remains as given in (A10.7).

Money Market

The money market equilibrium condition is unchanged except for the exogeneity of prices:

(A10.10)′ $\overline{M}/\overline{P} = \mathscr{L}(Y, i)$.

The LM curve has slope given by (A10.12). The MM curve is given by

$$P = \frac{\overline{M}}{M/P} = \frac{\overline{M}}{\mathscr{L}(Y, i)}.$$

General Equilibrium with Fixed Price Level

IS curve: $Y = C(\Omega, Y - T) + I(i) + \overline{G}$.
LM curve: $\overline{M}/\overline{P} = \mathscr{L}(Y, i)$.

These two relationships are shown in panel (c) in Figure 10.9. The S curve depicts the output that would have obtained under flexible wages and prices, but is shown only for reference purposes. Note that equilibrium output and interest rates will not generally coincide with those under flexible prices.

Unemployment

Unemployment is given by $L^S(\overline{w}, \overline{N}) - L$, where L satisfies $\overline{Y} = F(\overline{K}, L)$.

11

Aggregate Demand and Output

11.1. Introduction

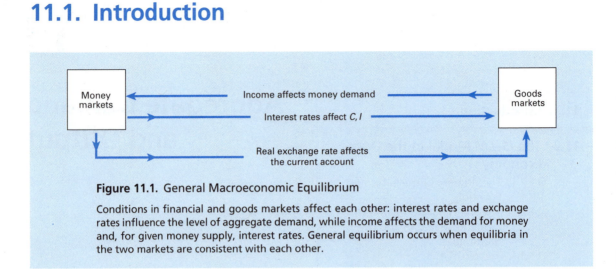

Figure 11.1. General Macroeconomic Equilibrium

Conditions in financial and goods markets affect each other: interest rates and exchange rates influence the level of aggregate demand, while income affects the demand for money and, for given money supply, interest rates. General equilibrium occurs when equilibria in the two markets are consistent with each other.

This chapter takes up where Chapter 10 leaves off. There, we saw that when prices are sticky money is not neutral in the short run, and the economy deviates from its flexible price equilibrium. This chapter continues to maintain the Keynesian assumption that prices are constant. This is a valid point of departure for the short run. Later chapters will study how output and prices move together. As a result of the Keynesian assumption, output is determined by demand. Equilibrium in the goods market is achieved through changes in production, which passively adjusts to aggregate demand with no change in prices and wages. The money market described in Chapters 8 and 9 influences the real economy through the interest rate. At the same time, the level of real economic activity affects the demand for money and thereby the interest rate. Figure 11.1 summarizes the conceptual framework of what has been called the **Keynesian model**.

The result is an interpretation of cyclical fluctuations, phases when the economy grows faster (a boom or an expansion) or slower (a recession) than its trend growth rate. Figure 11.2 illustrates these departures of the real GDP from its long-run trend. Demand, prone to spontaneous fluctuations, drives the economy. In that case, governments can use their instruments, monetary and fiscal policies, to moderate the amplitude of macroeconomic swings, even maybe to eliminate them altogether.

For many decades the Keynesian model was considered the alpha and omega of macroeconomics. Many policy-makers adopted this framework in the

1960s, paying detailed attention to the demand side of the economy and ignoring how the supply side sets prices, and forgetting that prices are not constant. The result was inflation in the 1970s and unemployment in the 1980s. Even though the shortcomings of the sticky price view are now well recognized, the analysis presented here remains a most useful 'rule of thumb' for thinking about the short run. Most macroeconomists and policy-makers have this framework in mind when they assess short-run macroeconomic conditions or make policy decisions.

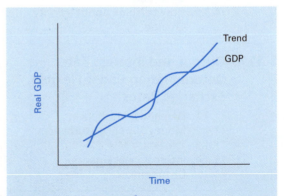

Figure 11.2. Cyclical Fluctuations

The Keynesian assumption is designed to study short-run fluctuations of real GDP around its long-run growth trend.

An important step taken in this chapter is to draw attention to the crucial role of external, or foreign, factors through trade in goods and assets. As Figure 11.1 shows, the exchange rate will be an important link between goods and asset markets. The primary current account, which was studied in Chapter 7, summarizes trade in goods and (non-interest-bearing) services and drives a wedge between domestic spending and domestic income. This will lead to an important modification of the *IS* curve. Second, cross-border movements of financial assets and other forms of wealth requires that we analyse a new market. In par-

ticular, transactions on the capital account can lead to pressures for the exchange rate to appreciate or depreciate. The consequences depend crucially on the **exchange rate regime**. The exchange rate may be fixed, so that the central bank maintains the value of the domestic money in terms of another currency or group of currencies. Alternatively, the central bank may let the exchange rate float freely. This distinction turns out to be crucial to the behaviour of the economy. For this reason, we study separately the two regimes of fixed and flexible exchange rates.

11.2. The *IS–LM* Model in the Open Economy

It will be useful to keep in mind which variables are exogenous and which ones are endogenous, and therefore are to be explained. The exogenous variables are: the price level $\bar{P}$ (the Keynesian assumption), the policy instruments, both fiscal (government purchases $\bar{G}$ and taxes $\bar{T}$[1]) and monetary (the nominal money stock M), and foreign variables such as GDP Y^* and the price level P^*. Since both domestic and foreign prices P and P^* are assumed constant, the real exchange rate ($\lambda = EP^*/\bar{P}$) is exogenous when the nominal exchange rate (E) is fixed. It is endogenous when the exchange rate is flexible. Since prices are constant, inflation is zero and nominal and real interest rates are equal ($i = r$).

11.2.1. The Primary Current Account Function

When an economy is open, the primary current account is not necessarily zero, so the basic accounting identity includes trade in goods and (non-factor) services with the rest of the world:

(11.1) $Y = C + I + G + PCA.$

This decomposition can also be seen as the condition for equilibrium in the goods market. As in Chapter 10, we use simplified versions of the consumption and investment functions established in Chapter 4. Con-

sumption depends on wealth Ω and disposable income Y^d:

(11.2) $C = C(\Omega, Y^d),$ (consumption function)
$\qquad\qquad\quad + \quad +$

while investment is described as

(11.3) $I = I(q, r),$ (investment function)
$\qquad\qquad\quad + \quad -$

and public spending is:

(11.4) $G = \bar{G}.$ (government purchases)

In comparison with Chapter 10, the investment function now includes not only the negative effect of interest rates, but also the positive effect of Tobin's q. This touch of realism will allow us to consider changes in 'animal spirits'—the outlook of businessmen with respect to the rate of return on capital investment. Exogenous increases in animal spirits will raise q, all other things equal; an exogenous increase in pessimism concerning prospective future returns will depress q.

What remains to be specified is the behaviour of the primary current account (PCA). Chapter 7 linked the PCA to the real exchange rate λ, the relative price of traded goods produced abroad in terms of those produced primarily at home. A real depreciation—an increase in λ—makes foreign goods more expensive, and therefore discourages imports. Conversely, a real appreciation—a decline in λ—boosts imports which are now cheaper.

At the same time, we know from Chapter 2 that the primary current account surplus is the difference

---

[1] Net taxes $\bar{T}$ are exogenous; in the appendix net taxes are allowed to depend positively on income Y.

between exports (X) and imports (Z) of goods and services:

$$(11.5) \qquad PCA = X - Z.$$

Imports represent a part of domestic spending, or absorption, $A = C + I + G$, and therefore will follow its fluctuations. The greater is overall absorption A, the greater will be imports. This discussion can be summarized as the **import function**:

$$(11.6) \qquad Z = Z(A, \lambda).$$
$$\qquad\qquad\qquad\quad + \quad -$$

Since our exports are the imports of the rest of the world, exactly the same arguments apply, but seen from the foreign perspective—that is, relating our exports to foreign absorption A^*, and its determinants, foreign wealth Ω^*, disposable income Y^{d*}, Tobin's q^*, etc. The result is the **export function**:

$$(11.7) \qquad X = X(A^*, \lambda).$$
$$\qquad\qquad\qquad\quad + \quad +$$

The signs underneath are the same as for the import function with the exception of the real exchange rate. A real depreciation makes our goods cheaper and therefore boosts exports, hence the + sign.

The primary current account is given by the difference between exports and imports in (11.7) and (11.6):

$$(11.8) \qquad PCA = X(A^*, \lambda) - Z(A, \lambda)$$
$$\qquad\qquad\qquad\quad + \quad + \qquad\quad + \quad -$$
$$\qquad\qquad = PCA(A, A^*, \lambda)$$
$$\qquad\qquad\qquad\qquad\quad - \quad + \quad +$$

The signs underneath are easily understandable: anything that boosts domestic absorption (increases in wealth, disposable income, Tobin's q, real growth, or a decline in the interest rate) will increase imports and worsen the primary current account; on the contrary, anything that boosts foreign spending (increases in foreign wealth, disposable income, Tobin's q, real growth, or a decline in the interest rate) will increase exports and lead to an improvement of the primary current account. Finally, a real exchange rate depreciation (an increase in λ) improves the primary account as exports rise and imports fall.

Finally, (11.1) shows that $A = Y - PCA$; absorption is simply the difference between GDP and the PCA. It follows by substitution and a little thought that the dependence of the PCA on absorption is fundamentally a dependence on GDP. This observation leads us to rewrite (11.8) as

$$(11.9) \quad PCA = PCA(Y, Y^*, \lambda). \qquad \text{(current account}$$
$$\qquad\qquad\qquad\quad - \quad + \quad + \qquad\qquad \text{function)}$$

The PCA is negatively related to domestic real income, and positively related to foreign income and the real exchange rate.

11.2.2. The 45° Diagram Revisited

In Chapter 10, we derived the IS curve using the 45° diagram and ignoring the PCA. What is changed when we introduce the PCA function? As it turns out, qualitatively, nothing at all. To see this, we briefly review the steps followed in the previous chapter. The desired demand function, which represents the demand for domestic goods, including exports and eliminating imports, is now written as

$$(11.10) \quad DD_1 = C(\Omega, Y_1 - \overline{T}_1) + I(r_1, q_1) + \overline{G}_1$$
$$\qquad\qquad\qquad + PCA(Y_1, Y_1^*, \lambda_1).$$

The desired demand schedule was shown to be an increasing function of GDP (Y). Now GDP exerts a negative effect on demand via the PCA function. Thus the presence of the PCA function simply reduces the size the effect of determinants of absorption (Ω, Y^d, r), but it does not change the direction of their effects. The desired demand schedule shown in Figure 11.3, is upward-sloping as in Figure 10.1, but it is flatter to account for the fact that the primary current account worsens as income increases, drawing in more imports from abroad, and reducing the net effect on aggregate demand.

11.2.3. Demand Leakages and the Multiplier

Under the Keynesian assumption that prices are sticky, the 45° diagram is interpreted as showing how output adjusts to match desired demand. The output level corresponding to point A at the intersection of the desired demand schedule and the 45° line is equal to demand. Fluctuations in output are interpreted as being caused by exogenous changes in demand. Figure 11.4 provides an illustration, the case when one component of demand, government spending, increases by $\Delta\overline{G}$, from $\overline{G}$ to $\overline{G}'$.

The economy starts at point A with real GDP level

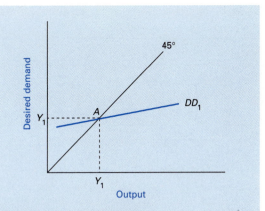

Figure 11.3. The 45° Diagram

Total desired demand responds positively but less than proportionately to increases in real GDP, hence the slope of the upward-sloping demand schedule. Equilibrium output is the GDP level Y at which demand equals supply along the 45° line.

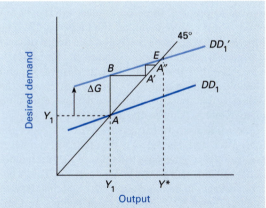

Figure 11.4. The Multiplier

An exogenous increase in government spending shifts up the demand schedule vertically by $\Delta \overline{G}$. Supply equals demand, and the economy's equilibrium output increases to point Y^*. The multiplier effect—that Y^*-Y exceeds the initial impulse $\Delta \overline{G}$—can be understood by following the staircase up from point A. The direct effect, an increase in demand and output, raises GDP to point A'. This point however is still not an equilibrium, because DD lies above the 45° line. Thus, desired demand and output increases again, to point A'', and so on.

Y_1. The change $\Delta \overline{G}$ increases aggregate demand at any level of output. The desired demand schedule shifts upward by that amount. If output remains unchanged at Y_1, the new situation is described by point B, with desired demand exceeding output. What happens when desired demand and output differ? Normally, if demand exceeds supply, producers make up the difference by sales from inventories of finished goods; we say that inventories are decumulated. Producers then adjust output to match demand until equilibrium output is reached. Thus, unexpected drawdowns of inventory are likely to be followed by production increases. (Conversely, when production exceeds demand, inventories are involuntarily accumulated and this will lead to a production slowdown.) As output expands to meet demand, the economy moves to point A' on the 45° line.

The process does not stop at A'. The increase in production and income leads to higher consumption, further increasing aggregate demand and, by the 45° line, output. Demand and output both rise again until equilibrium is reached at point A''. The process continues until, step by step, the economy reaches E, which is on the new desired demand schedule and the 45° line. What is important to notice is that, in the end, GDP increases by a *multiple* of the initial demand increase $\Delta \overline{G}$, an effect called the (Keynesian) **demand multiplier**.[2] No matter where they originate, positive or negative disturbances are transmitted to the whole economy as aggregate demand responds to income changes in a process that may take several months to complete.

This is the simplest interpretation of cyclical fluctuations: the GDP responds to fluctuations in aggregate demand. The multiplier effect corresponds to the fundamental insight provided by the circular flow diagram in Chapter 2: each individual's spending is someone else's income. An exogenous increase in demand induces further increases in spending by other households. As long as output responds passively to demand, this will lead to additional income; and so on. GDP growth will not continue *ad infinitum*, however. The multiplier is finite, because at each stage of spending

---

[2] The demand multiplier discussed here should not be confused with the money multipliers of Ch. 9, which linked central bank money and the money supply used by the public. They do have the following formal aspect in common. Consider an equilibrium condition which takes the form: $x = a(x) + b$. A multiplier effect occurs when a change in b delivers an effect on x given by $\Delta x/\Delta b = 1/[1 - a'(x)]$. If $0 < a'(x) < 1$, the multiplier is $1/[1 - a'(x)] > 1$. In the present case, x corresponds to output, $a(x)$ to the endogenous components of aggregate demand, and b to the exogenous components.

Table 11.1. Demand Multipliers

	Year 1	Year 2	Year 3	Year 4	Year 5
Germany	1.26	1.13	0.63	0.55	0.43
France	1.39	1.98	1.81	1.20	0.43
UK	1.04	1.11	0.68	0.37	0.28
USA	1.81	1.63	0.37	0.09	—

Source: EC Commission

some positive fraction of income leaks from the circular flow of income, into either taxes or savings or imports.[3] For example, adding the PCA, as we have done in this chapter, flattens the desired demand schedule; it is easily verified that the flatter the schedule, the smaller is the multiplier effect.

Table 11.1 presents some values of the demand multiplier for the largest economies as estimated by the EC Commission's model QUEST. Such models include a large number of relationships like (11.1)–(11.9), but with considerably more detail, and they are routinely used by policy-makers to predict the effects of potential decisions or to produce forecasts. These models usually fail to distinguish between temporary and permanent disturbances, so these numbers should be regarded with caution. Nevertheless, they are useful for two reasons. First, they give an idea of the size of the multiplier. Second, they show that the multiplier takes time to work out its effects: four years later, at least according to QUEST, residual effects still persist.

11.2.4. The *IS* curve

11.2.4.1. Slope of the *IS* curve

The open-economy *IS* curve is derived just as in Chapter 10: by examining the effect of changes in the interest rate on output in the 45° line diagram. Starting from *A* in Figure 11.5, what happens if the central bank lowers the interest rate from *i* to *i*′? First, wealth increases, since a given stream of future expected returns is discounted at a lower rate. This increases desired consumption. Second, assuming no change in business expectations, Tobin's *q* increases because future profits

[3] Only if at each stage all additionally generated income were completely spent on domestic goods would the multiplier be infinite, an implausible outcome.

are now discounted at a lower rate. This increases investment spending, as does the interest rate directly. In the end, the desired spending schedule shifts up in Figure 11.5(*a*) and the goods market is brought back to equilibrium when point *B* is reached, output having risen from Y_1 to Y_1'.

The move from point *A* to point *B* can be decomposed in Figure 11.5(*b*) into two steps. The drop in the interest rate, keeping GDP constant, takes the economy from point *A* to point *C*, off the *IS* curve: this is a situation of excess demand in the goods market. Equilibrium requires an increase in output, from point *C* to point *B*, to accommodate the rise in demand. The *IS* curve is flatter, the longer is *CB*. The slope is flatter (1) the greater the sensitivity of consumption and investment to changes in interest rates, as measured by the vertical shift of the desired demand schedule (*AA*′) in panel (*a*), and (2) the larger the multiplier that translates the initial demand effect into the total effect, as measured along *A*′*B*.

The multiplier, in turn, is larger, the steeper the desired demand schedule. Yet the multiplier can never be infinitely large because the slope of the desired demand schedule will always be less than 45°. This is because **leakages** in demand occur in the circular flow of income. Figure 2.2 shows that taxes, savings, and imports can be seen as subtractions from GDP. To be sure, these items can be used to support spending, but demand is already accounted for. (Remember that we are now following how exogenous demand-generated income changes further affect demand.) These three leakages represent domestic income not *automatically* re-spent on domestic goods and services. The size of the leakages, and therefore of the multiplier, depends on saving behaviour, on the tax system, and on how much additional income is spent on imports, a measure called the *marginal propensity to import*. Table 11.2, for example, presents some estimates of degrees of openness. The large economic blocs (the EC, the USA,

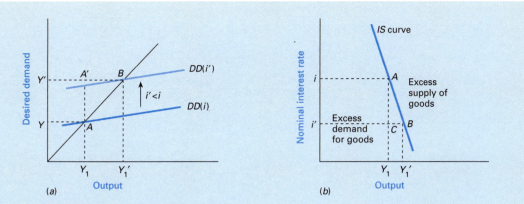

Figure 11.5. Slope of the *IS* curve

A reduction in the interest rate from *i* to *i'* leads to an increase in consumption and invest-ment, which is met by an increase in output. The *IS* curve is flatter the larger is the required output increase, as measured by the distance *CB* in panel (*b*). The length of *CB* in turn de-pends on: (1) the responsiveness of demand to interest changes, represented by the size of the vertical shift of *DD*, or *AA'*, in panel (*a*); (2) the multiplier effect, measured by distance *A'B*. The multiplier is larger the steeper is the desired demand schedule, i.e. the more sens-itive is demand to changes in output.

Japan) are fairly closed and able to lock inside the ef-fects of demand disturbances. Individual smaller coun-tries, in contrast, are quite open.

11.2.4.2. A key distinction: movements along or shifts of the *IS* curve

In order not to confuse *shifts* of the *IS* curve with move-ments *along* it, one must maintain a clear distinction between exogenous and endogenous variables. The *IS* curve is the goods market equilibrium condition imposed on two endogenous variables, GDP (*Y*) and interest rates (*i*), *everything else remaining unchanged.*

The position of the *IS* curve is determined by the exogenous variables. As long as these remain un-changed, the economy is restricted to the same *IS* curve. Whenever any of the exogenous variables changes, the *IS* curve shifts. Figure 11.6 shows that the *IS* curve shifts up and to the right when the exogenous change is expansionary. The *IS* curve shifts leftwards in the opposite case of exogenous declines in aggre-gate demand.

What are the most frequent reasons why the *IS* curve shifts? One is fiscal policy actions, when the govern-ment significantly changes its purchases of goods (e.g. military procurement or road construction) or services

Table 11.2. Measures of Openness: Marginal Propensities to Import in 1985 (%)

Belgium	53.0	Italy	22.7	EC10	13.4
Denmark	23.8	Netherlands	30.0	USA	10.1
Germany	23.8	Portugal	30.6	Japan	11.4
Spain	18.8	UK	22.4		
France	18.6	Greece	31.2		
Ireland	48.0				

Note: For the three blocks (EC, USA, and Japan), openness is measured by the share of imports in GNP.

Source: Drèze *et al.* (1987)

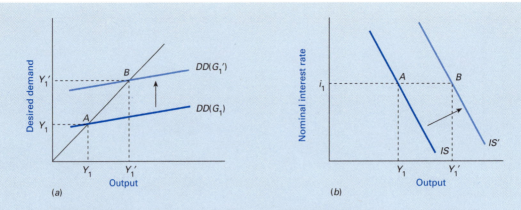

Figure 11.6. An Exogenous Increase in Aggregate Demand

At unchanged interest rate i_1, an increase in any of the exogenous components of demand is represented in panel (a) by an upward shift of the aggregate demand schedule. Equilibrium occurs at point B and the new equilibrium output Y_1' is higher than the initial level Y_1. Panel (b) shows that the IS curve shifts to the right for the given interest rate.

(e.g. the wages or number of civil servants). Another important reason is changes in domestic wealth, which can result from fluctuations in asset prices, such as stocks (which would also affect Tobin's q), bonds, housing, etc. Thus, the Great Depression of the 1930s is associated with the worldwide collapse of stock prices following the crash of Wall Street. Similarly, sharply falling housing prices preceded the recession of the early 1990s in the UK, Sweden, Japan, and many other countries.

The preceding examples all describe home-made fluctuations. A third important reason for shifts in the IS curve is related to the international transmission of disturbances. The current account is not only a source of leakage, but a source of foreign disturbances. Export-led expansions or recessions occur when a country's increase or decline in demand leaks abroad where it affects exports, as represented in equation (11.8) by the term A^*. All other things equal, an increase in A^* will increase the PCA and cause the IS curve to shift outwards.

11.2.5. International Capital Flows, Interest Parity, and the *LM* Curve

11.2.5.1. Capital Flows and Interest Parity

The primary current account function captures the link with the rest of the world operating through the

goods market, i.e. trade in goods and services. The second link is financial: it operates through international capital movements. Under the **small country assumption**, financial conditions abroad are not affected by what is happening domestically. The 'foreign' rate of return i^*—denoted as the return on one Euro invested abroad—is exogenous. For simplicity, it is further assumed to be constant. This return includes the possible expectation of a depreciation or appreciation of the exchange rate. For example, if the domestic currency depreciates, the value of foreign assets expressed in the domestic currency declines, and domestic holders suffer a capital loss; conversely, they enjoy a capital gain when the exchange rate depreciates. The overall return on foreign assets is therefore made up of two parts: the interest rate and capital gains/losses.

When capital is freely mobile, it is impossible for returns on similar assets to differ systematically across countries. Similarity is defined by the risk category (e.g. Treasury bills and bonds are usually considered safe, as are those issued by large corporations) and by the structure of the asset, mainly its maturity. Arbitrage among asset yields is practised on a minute-by-minute basis by financial institutions which have access to considerable amounts of funds and face negligible transaction costs. As they restlessly scan the world, they promptly eliminate any difference in returns. They sell assets or borrow where the rate of return is low and buy assets or lend where the return is high. No matter how successful they are individually, their activity means that worldwide returns for assets of similar characteristics are equalized across countries. The result is the **interest rate parity** condition:[4]

(11.11) $$i = i^*.$$

This condition is depicted as the horizontal **financial integration line** in Figure 11.7. When capital movements are restricted, as they were occasionally until the late 1980s in many European countries, the interest rate parity condition does not hold and the domestic interest rate is (relatively) free to move away from the line.

11.2.5.2. Slope of the *LM* curve

The *LM* curve, which describes the money market, and more generally the financial markets, is not directly affected by the interest parity condition. The *LM* curve describes the equilibrium condition on the *domestic* money market. The financial integration line represents the equilibrium condition on the *international* financial market. In general equilibrium, both conditions must be satisfied.

The slope of the *LM* curve is understood by returning to its construction, as in Chapter 10. Consider

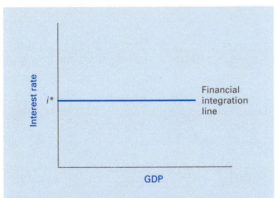

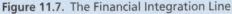

Figure 11.7. The Financial Integration Line

When capital can move freely across borders, and when financial markets are efficient, assets of similar quality (in terms of maturity and risk) should yield the same return. Otherwise, there would be unexploited profit opportunities (borrowing where interest is low and lending where it is high); this is incompatible with the assumptions of free mobility and market efficiency. Note that i^* denotes the return on foreign assets, which includes possible capital gains or losses arising from changes in the exchange rate.

point *C* in Figure 11.8(*b*). Being off the *LM* curve, this point corresponds to a situation of disequilibrium in the money market. The move from *A* to *C* corresponds to an increase in GDP. Holding the interest rate constant, money demand rises. To eliminate the excess demand for money—the money supply is exogenous and assumed unchanged—the interest rate must rise until we reach point *B*. This is what is needed to induce economic households and firms to reduce their demand. The *LM* curve is steeper, the longer is the segment *BC*. First and foremost, the length of *BC* depends on the sensitivity of money demand with respect to real economic activity. A high elasticity implies a large increase in money demand and requires a large compensating interest rate increase, hence a steep *LM* curve. Second, the length of *BC* depends on the sensitivity—called the elasticity—of money demand with respect to the interest rate: if the interest elasticity is small, the interest rate must move a lot to re-establish equilibrium for a given increase in GDP, hence again a steep *LM* curve.[5] To summarize, the *LM* curve is steeper the more sensitive is money demand to output and the less sensitive it is to the interest rate.

11.2.5.3. Moving along or shifting the *LM* curve

To avoid confusion between shifts of the *LM* curve and movements along it, the same rule applies as for the *IS* curve. A particular *LM* curve is drawn for given (fixed) values of the exogenous variables: the real money supply (M/P) and transaction costs (c). As long as these exogenous variables remain unchanged, the economy remains on the same *LM* curve. Whenever any of the exogenous variables changes, the *LM* curve shifts. It is intuitive, and easy to check, that the *LM* curve shifts rightward when the real money supply increases (the nominal supply increases or the price level falls) and if money market transactions become more expensive.

For example, Figure 11.9 shows how changes in the nominal money supply shift the *LM* curve out. The *LM* curve shifts whenever the real money supply (M/P) and demand $L(Y, i, c)$ do not change at the same time by the same amount. In practice, money demand is relatively stable, so that sudden shifts of the *LM* curve are related to the behaviour of the money supply. If the real supply outpaces demand, the *LM* curve moves to the right; when supply is held down below demand, the *LM* shifts to the left.

[4] Ch. 18 describes the financial markets and arbitraging activity. Ch. 19 pursues the analysis of the interest rate parity condition and considers the role of the exchange rate explicitly.

[5] For an explicit derivation of the slope of the *LM* curve using calculus, see the Appendix.

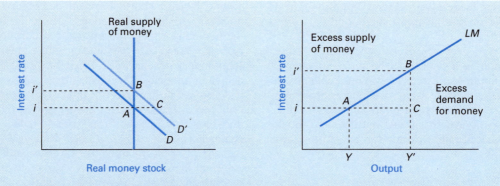

Figure 11.8. Slope of the *LM* curve

An exogenous increase in GDP raises the demand for money at any interest rate, hence the shift from *D* to *D'* in panel (*a*). At the initial interest rate *i*, we now have excess demand, as represented by point *C* in both panels. The size of the this excess demand (measured by the length *AC*) is proportional to the responsiveness of money demand to output. The return to money equilibrium is achieved through an increase in the interest rate which reduces demand. The required increase from *i* to *i'* (measured by *AB* in panel (*a*) and by *BC* in panel (*b*)) is inversely proportional to the responsiveness of money demand to the interest rate. If money demand is very interest-sensitive, a small increase in the interest rate is sufficient to eliminate the excess demand.

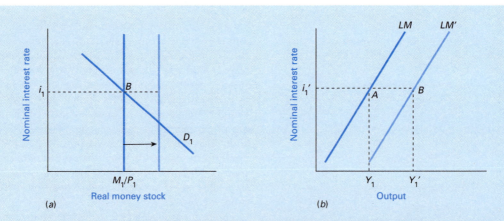

Figure 11.9. An Increase in the Money Supply Shifts the *LM* Curve Outward

An increase in the money supply at a given level of interest rates creates a situation of excess money supply. This means that all points on the original *LM* curve now represent (*i*, *Y*) combinations of excess supply of money. To restore equilibrium, the demand for money must be higher. To achieve this, either the interest rate must be lower or income must be higher. Thus, the new *LM* curve lies below and to the right of the old one.

Changes in the real money supply, in turn, may be the outcome of changes in the nominal supply, given prices, or of prices, given the money supply. In a word, where inflation is never really zero but positive, prices are constantly rising, even if very slowly, every day or month. The rule then is that the *LM* curve shifts, say, to the right when the rate of growth of the real money supply—the difference between the growth rate of the nominal supply and the rate of inflation[6]—is higher than the rate of growth of demand.

11.2.6. Macroeconomic Equilibrium and the Exchange Rate Regime

We now summarize this section and contrast it with Chapter 10. There, we dealt with three markets—the goods market equilibrium (*IS*), the money market (*LM*), and the labour market—which, along with the existing capital stock, determine the supply side of the economy. In the present chapter, the assumption that prices and wages are sticky implies that the supply side becomes irrelevant. Supply passively adjusts to demand and employees provide whatever amount of labour is needed to produce the required output.

In addition, this chapter recognizes links with the rest of the world. Trade in goods and services enriches, but does not fundamentally alter, the analysis of the goods market. It is simply incorporated in the *IS* curve. Trade in assets introduces the international financial market. Under conditions of full capital mobility, this market's equilibrium condition is represented by the financial integration line. The economy is in general, fixed-price or Keynesian equilibrium when, as in Figure 11.10, the three market equilibrium schedules all pass through point *E*.

The rest of this chapter uses this framework to explain how the GDP and interest rates respond to various exogenous disturbances in the economy. We require that the three schedules go through the same point because none of the three markets can be out of equilibrium for long. Inventory adjustment and output changes restore equilibrium in the goods market. Disequilibrium in the goods market would manifest itself by persistent queues in front of empty stores in the case of excess demand, or by unsold goods in the case of excess supply. It is a distinguishing feature of market economies that these situations do not occur on any significant scale. As for the money and inter-

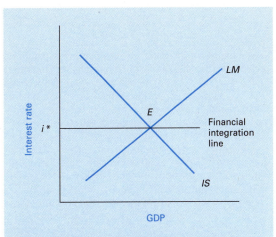

Figure 11.10. General Equilibrium

When both goods and money markets are in equilibrium and full arbitrage occurs, the real GDP and the interest rate are determined by the intersection of three schedules: the *IS* and *LM* curves and the arbitrage (financial integration) line.

national financial markets, they are known for the rapidity at which they clear.

The analysis proceeds by asking what is the effect of a change in an exogenous variable. The approach is always the same. The first step is to determine which of the three schedules shifts in response to the exogenous disturbance. The second step is to find out what must happen for the three schedules to go through a single point. The last step is to interpret the result: how and why has the economy moved from the initial to the new general equilibrium?

The approach embodied in Figure 11.10 is often referred to as the **Mundell–Fleming model**.[7] The implications of openness to trade and particularly to capital movements are dramatic, as a comparison with Chapter 10 will make clear. In particular, the exchange rate regime profoundly affects the results. Section 11.3 describes the case of a country committed to a fixed exchange rate regime. This is the case in many European countries, either because they are explicitly part of the European Monetary System, or because they peg their currency, formally or informally, to another currency of their choice. Section 11.4 considers the polar opposite case, in which the exchange rate is freely floating. This corresponds to the situation of the USA and Japan, or the EMS member-countries jointly

---

[6] It can be shown that $\Delta(M/P)/(M/P) = \Delta M/M - \Delta P/P$.

[7] It is named after the Canadian Robert Mundell from Columbia University and the Briton Marcus Fleming, who worked at the IMF.

BOX 11.1. EXCHANGE RATE REGIMES IN EUROPE, 1996

At the beginning of 1996, European countries could be grouped in five categories. A first category, the members of the European Monetary System (EMS), jointly fixed their exchange rates within agreed-upon margins of fluctuations.[8] A second group includes countries, mostly from Eastern Europe, that have adopted a basket of foreign currencies to which they peg their own. Some of them—Hungary for example—have an explicit programme of frequent depreciation, the so-called crawling-peg. Countries in the third group do not declare any official parity but actively limit exchange rate fluctuations. Countries in the fourth group in principle have freedom of action. The two Baltic countries that make up the fifth and final group have adopted currency boards: they peg

to the Deutschmark and allow the money base to change only when their foreign exchange reserves change. (By law, in M0 = $R + D$, D is not allowed to change.)

1. *EMS members*: Austria, Belgium–Luxembourg (currency union), Denmark, France, Germany, Ireland, Netherlands, Portugal, Spain
2. *Basket-peggers* (pegged to the US dollar): Croatia, Czech Republic, Hungary, Iceland, Norway, Poland, Russia
3. *Managed floaters*: Albania, Bulgaria, Finland, Latvia, Turkey, Slovak Republic, Slovenia, Sweden, Switzerland
4. *Free floaters*: Italy, UK, Greece
5. *Currency board*: Estonia, Lithuania

vis-à-vis the rest of the world. In between these two extremes are various degrees of managed floating, where the authorities do not commit themselves to a

particular rate but nevertheless attempt to prevent large fluctuations. Box 11.1 summarizes the choice of European countries in early 1996.[9]

11.3. Output and Interest Rate Determination under Fixed Exchange Rates

11.3.1. Money Supply Disturbances

To study the role of monetary policy, suppose the central bank raises the money supply from M to M'. In Figure 11.11 the LM curve shifts down and to the right from LM to LM'. Starting from initial general equilibrium at point A, there are now two candidates for the new equilibrium: point B at the intersection of LM' and IS, and point C at the intersection of LM' and the financial integration line.

Which one to pick? At point B the domestic interest rate is lower than the yields available on foreign assets. This prompts arbitrageurs to sell domestic assets, and to purchase foreign assets. As a result, the exchange rate comes under pressure to depreciate; this forces the monetary authorities to step in and buy the domestic currency on foreign exchange markets, using its foreign exchange reserves. This intervention reduces

the money supply, and the LM curve shifts leftwards.[10] The process must go on as long as the return on domestic assets (i) is less than the return on foreign assets ($i*$), that is until the LM curve has returned to its initial position. We asked whether the new equilibrium occurs at point B or point C. The answer is that neither of these points can be a general equilibrium, because neither lies on all three schedules describing the three equilibrium conditions. The economy returns to the original point A.

Monetary policy is ineffective under fixed exchange rates. This conclusion should not be too surprising. Chapter 9 already established that monetary policy independence is lost under a fixed exchange rate regime. The balance sheet of the central bank, simplified to the monetary base on the liability side and to foreign exchange (F) and domestic credit or securities (DC) on the asset side, implies that

---

[8] More precisely, they belong to the Exchange Rate Mechanism of the EMS. The margins, which used to be ±2.25%, were expanded to ±15% in 1993. Ch. 21 presents details.

[9] More detail is provided in Ch. 19. The situation can, and will, change over time.

[10] S. 9.4 explains the links between foreign exchange rate market interventions and the money supply.

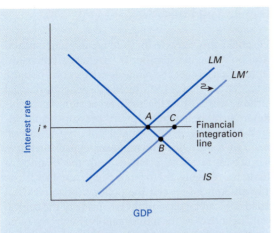

Figure 11.11. Money Supply Disturbance under Fixed Exchange Rates

A money supply increase implies a rightward shift of the LM curve from *LM* to *LM'*. At point *B*, with *i < i**, capital outflows force the central bank to intervene and the money supply contracts until the economy returns to point *A*. Monetary policy is ineffective.

$$(11.10) \qquad M0 = F + DC.$$

Initially, in order to raise the money supply, the central bank creates additional monetary base (M0) by purchasing domestic securities (*DC*). During the ensuing foreign exchange market interventions, however, the central bank spends foreign exchange rate reserves (*F*), negating its initial action.

In principle, the central bank could sterilize its sale of foreign exchange reserves in order to maintain the initial increase in the money supply, raising *DC* one

for one as *F* declines. This cannot go on for ever, though, because the stock of foreign exchange reserves is depleted along the way. The financial integration line in Figure 11.11 simply says that the central bank of a 'small' open economy must accept that the domestic interest rate cannot be altered. In order to forestall this outcome and to break the link between *i* and *i**, some countries have been tempted to use **capital controls** or restrictions on the international movement of capital. Box 11.2 explains how these capital controls operate.

11.3.2. Demand Disturbances

Figure 11.12 illustrates the effect of an increase in any of the exogenous components of demand, such as improving business expectations, a fiscal policy expansion (an increase in public spending or tax reductions), or rising exports (following a foreign expansion). As in Figure 11.6, the positive demand disturbance is represented as a rightward shift of the *IS* curve, from *IS* to *IS'*. As in the previous section, two points are candidates for the new equilibrium: point *B* at the intersection of *IS'* and *LM*, and point *C* at the intersection of *IS'* and the financial integration line.

Moving from *A* to *B* along *LM*, output increases to meet a higher demand, and money demand rises to finance more transactions. Since the money supply (nominal and real) is by assumption constant, the interest rate must rise to maintain equilibrium in the money market. The higher interest rate, in turn, adversely affects stock prices (Tobin's *q*) and investment spending. This last effect is often referred to as **crowd-**

BOX 11.2. CAPITAL CONTROLS AND MONETARY INDEPENDENCE[11]

Capital controls refer to a variety of administrative measures which prevent the residents of one country from freely moving assets across borders. Some measures are designed to repel capital inflows, others to forestall outflows. If the controls are effective, arbitrageurs cannot equalize returns on domestic and foreign assets. The domestic interest rate is then decoupled from foreign returns—or at least, the link is less tight. In the case of a monetary expansion as represented in Figure 11.11, it becomes possible to aim at point *B*. In principle, the monetary authorities recover some independence as the

financial integration line is 'suspended'. In practice, however, the profits from dodging the controls—exploiting the difference between asset returns—is so high that many agents develop great skills and invest large amount of resources in the fine art of evasion. Given time—sometimes a few months, more often a few days—monetary policy independence is eroded again. A similar result holds for the case of aggregate demand disturbances studied in the next section: in Figure 11.11, point *B* becomes possible under fixed exchange rates, at least for some time.

---

[11] This box is a brief introduction to the question of capital controls, which are studied in Ch. 19.

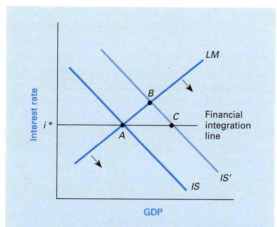

Figure 11.12. Demand Disturbance under Fixed Exchange Rates

The demand expansion is shown as shifting the IS curve from *IS′* to *IS′*. At point *B*, the goods and money markets are in equilibrium but the interest rate exceeds the world level. The combination of capital inflows and exchange market interventions raises the money supply, shifting the LM curve down and to the right. This proceeds until the LM curve passes through point *C*.

11.3.3. The Policy Mix

The **policy mix** refers to the joint use of monetary and fiscal policies. An expansionary monetary policy under fixed exchange rates alone does not work, because its tendency to lower the interest rate generates capital outflows which offset the initial expansion. An expansionary fiscal policy puts upward pressure on the interest rate and generates capital inflows. When well balanced, a joint fiscal and monetary expansion leaves the interest rate unaffected, as both the IS and LM curves move rightward to point B in Figure 11.13. The only difference between the policy mix and a fiscal expansion can be seen on the asset side of the central bank. In both cases the money supply rises by the same amount. With a policy mix, however, it rises because the central bank provides additional monetary base by buying securities from banks; with pure fiscal expansion, the central bank provides the additional base by increasing its foreign exchange reserves.

11.3.4. International Financial Disturbances

When returns on foreign assets rise from *i** to *i*′*, the horizontal financial integration line shifts upwards in Figure 11.14. The *IS* and *LM* schedules remain initially unchanged, but at point *A*, where both goods and money markets are in equilibrium, the interest rate is too low. Capital outflows prompt foreign interventions by the central bank, the money supply contracts, and the *LM* curve shifts leftwards until it goes through point *B*. The domestic economy cannot be shielded from international financial disturbances. If interest rates rise worldwide, they must rise at home, which provokes a recession (*Y* declines). This example illustrates the phenomenon of *monetary interdependence*. Under fixed exchange rates, foreign interest rate changes are transmitted directly to domestic interest rates.

ing out, the fact that an exogenous increase in demand may induce a reduction in investment brought about by higher interest rates.

Point *B* cannot represent complete equilibrium since the domestic interest rate exceeds the foreign rate of return, *i**, and the arbitrage condition is not satisfied. The higher domestic return immediately triggers a capital inflow. As foreign currency is converted into domestic currency, the exchange rate comes under pressure and an appreciation will occur unless the monetary authorities intervene. Committed to a fixed exchange rate, the central bank sells its own currency and acquires foreign exchange reserves. The logic of equation (11.10) is that the money stock must rise and the *LM* curve will shift rightward. How far? When it goes through point *C*, general equilibrium occurs at the intersection of the three equilibrium schedules.

Once again, it is essential to remember that monetary independence is lost under fixed exchange rates. The *LM* curve must pass through the point defined by the *IS* and arbitrage schedules. The money supply —and the *LM* curve—is endogenous, beyond the control of the monetary authorities. One way of attempting to reassert control is to restrict capital movements, as explained in Box 11.2. Box 11.3 provides an illustration of the pressure on money and exchange rates from a sharp demand expansion.

11.3.5. How to Think about a Parity Change

That monetary policy is ineffective under fixed exchange rates does not mean that monetary policy cannot be used. If exchange rate changes are possible, as is usually the case with all fixed exchange rate regimes, a weaker form of monetary policy independence can be

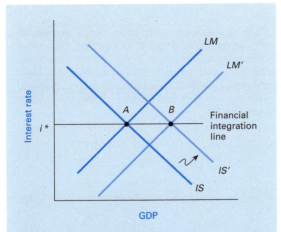

Figure 11.13. Policy Mix

When both monetary and fiscal policies are combined in an expansionary fashion, the economy moves from point *A* to point *B*. While the outcome is the same as with just a fiscal policy expansion (Figure 10.11), in the present case the increase in the monetary supply is achieved through securities purchases by the central bank.

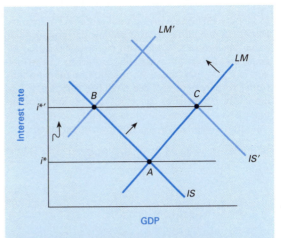

Figure 11.14. A Financial Disturbance

The increase in the rate of return on foreign assets induces a capital outflow. Under a fixed exchange rate, the central bank intervenes to prevent a depreciation. The money supply contracts and the LM curve shifts to *LM′*. The new general equilibrium is at point *B*. Under flexible exchange rates, the exchange rate depreciates. The gain in competitiveness increases the demand for domestic goods. The IS curve shifts to *IS₂* and equilibrium occurs at point *C*.

restored. In **a revaluation** or **devaluation**, the monetary authority unilaterally changes the parity rate at which it buys and sells foreign exchange. For given price levels at home and abroad, a nominal devaluation, for example, implies a depreciation of the real exchange rate, and shifts the *IS* curve outwards in Figure 11.16. In order to enforce the new parity, the central bank must sell its own currency and purchase foreign exchange. Alternatively, market participants

may take advantage of the higher price of foreign currency now on offer and sell their holdings to the central bank. In either case, the supply of high-powered money and thus of the money supply itself expands and the *LM* curve shifts out to the right in Figure 11.16.[12] A devaluation thus is tantamount to a monetary expansion, whereas a revaluation corresponds to a monetary contraction. In brief, monetary and exchange rate policies are just two sides of the same coin.

11.4. Output and Interest Rate Determination under Flexible Exchange Rates

11.4.1. Demand Disturbances

An exogenous increase in aggregate demand is shown as the rightward shift of the *IS* curve from *IS* to *IS′* in Figure 11.17. Again, the question is whether the economy will settle at point *B* or point *C*, or indeed anywhere else. The key rule is that, when the exchange rate is freely floating, the central bank does not inter-

vene in the money market and therefore control the money supply. In that case the position of the *LM* curve

[12] Another possibility is that the devaluation has already been anticipated by the market. In this case, the financial integration curve shifts upwards because financial markets require a higher return in the home currency. Capital outflow ensues, and the rest can be understood in the context of the preceding section. This is why interest rates often rise sharply before a devaluation actually occurs.

BOX 11.3. WHEN SPAIN JOINED THE COMMON MARKET

In January 1986 Spain joined the European Community. Over the previous years, its economic performance had been unimpressive. Along with membership in the EC, Spain achieved political stability and access to the markets of its new partners. Both Spanish firms and multinational corporations realized that the combination of moderate labour costs, good skills, and open borders made Spain an attractive place to build up productive capacities. Table 11.3 reveals that investment quickly triggered a home-made demand expansion. Figure 11.15 shows the increase in capacity utilization, a clear sign of supply responding to demand. As expected, the current account turned into a large deficit. At the same time, capital inflows were significant and, as the central bank intervened repeatedly on a large scale to (successfully) prevent the peseta from appreciating, the money stock increased rapidly.

Table 11.3. Spain, 1980–1989

	1980–5	1986	1987	1988	1989
Real Growth in:					
Investment[a]	−2.9	14.2	21.0	14.1	15.6
Consumption	0.4	4.1	5.8	4.7	5.5
GDP	1.4	3.8	5.6	5.2	4.8
Growth in M1	11.1	15.3	14.4	21.3	16.9
Effective nominal exchange rate[b]	100.0[c]	102.1	103.3	100.2	95.9

[a] Non-residential investment.
[b] The effective exchange rate is defined in Ch. 7. It is given in European terms as an index: 1985 = 100.
[c] 1985.

Sources: OECD, *Economic Outlook*; IMF

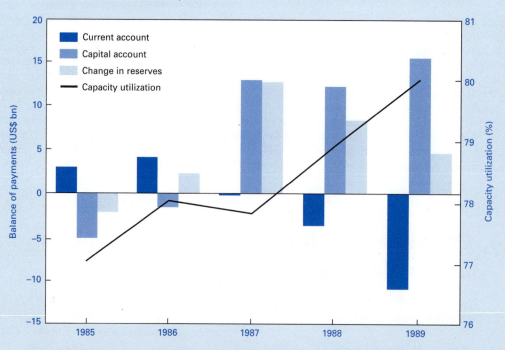

Figure 11.15. The Spanish Boom after 1986

The rate of capacity utilization is a measure of the cyclical position of the economy. It rises after Spain's entry into the EC on 1 January 1986. The current account worsens and capital flows in. The Bank of Spain intervenes heavily on the exchange market, acquiring foreign exchange reserves and supplying pesetas.

Sources: IMF; OECD

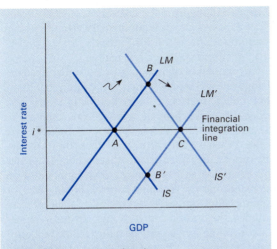

Figure 11.16. A Devaluation

A devaluation shifts the IS curve out to IS'. At the same time, the money supply rises as central banks purchase foreign exchange, and the LM curve shifts downwards.

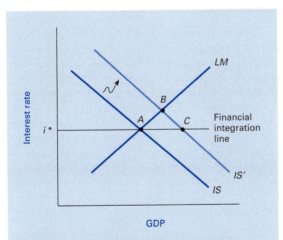

Figure 11.17. Demand Disturbance under Flexible Exchange Rates

As real demand increases, the IS curve shifts rightwards. At point B, capital flows in and the exchange rate appreciates. This loss of external competitiveness leads to a fall in net foreign demand for domestic goods until the IS curve returns to its initial position. The demand disturbance is 'crowded out'.

is exogenous. At point B the domestic interest rate exceeds the return available on foreign assets. Capital flows in, but now, in the absence of central bank intervention, the exchange rate appreciates. With domestic prices assumed constant, the real exchange rate also

appreciates, which hurts competitiveness and leads to a deterioration of the primary current account. Total demand for domestic output declines, and the IS curve shifts leftward. This process goes on as long as the domestic interest rate is above the financial integration line: the exchange rate appreciates until the loss in competitiveness has brought the IS curve back to point A.

In sharp contrast with the fixed exchange rate case, aggregate demand disturbances leave output and the interest rate unaffected when the exchange rate is freely floating. Increases in domestic demand entirely leak abroad as a result of the loss of competitiveness. The link between a home-made demand expansion and a worsening of the current account is now one for one. The return to point A is not instantaneous. In contrast to the exchange rate, which responds immediately to capital inflows, the effect on trade and the current account will take time to complete.

The result applies to any of the exogenous components in (11.10). In particular, an expansionary fiscal policy—raising public spending or reducing taxes—merely leads to an exchange rate appreciation and to a worsening of the current account. Similarly, a surge in business optimism and the resulting investment boom has no demand effect: it simply crowds out net demand in the foreign sector. Under flexible exchange rates an economy cannot lift itself up via demand, nor can it be lifted up by world demand. As foreign customers attempt to purchase more of our exports, they end up bidding up the exchange rate, which discourages their initial move. In the end, under floating exchange rates, *domestic demand impulses are neutralized by exchange rate changes and the economy is insulated from foreign demand disturbances.*

11.4.2. Money Supply Disturbances

A monetary expansion is represented by the shift of the LM curve from LM to LM' in Figure 11.18. At point B, the low interest rate prompts capital outflows and therefore an exchange rate depreciation. The attendant gain in external competitiveness increases foreign demand for domestic goods, and the current account improves. Graphically, the additional net foreign demand—more exports and fewer imports—shifts the IS curve to the right until it passes through point C.

In contrast to the fixed exchange rate case, monetary policy is effective under flexible rates. As described, monetary policy works entirely through its effect on the exchange rate and the current account, rather than through the interest rate, which remains

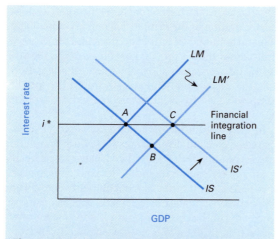

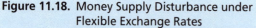

Figure 11.18. Money Supply Disturbance under Flexible Exchange Rates

An increase in the money supply shifts the LM curve to *LM′* from *LM*. At point *B*, with low domestic interest rates, the exchange rate depreciates which leads to a current account surplus. This shifts the IS curve rightwards until local interest rates are equal to the foreign rate of return *i** at point *C*.

governed by foreign returns. Monetary policy is sometimes considered a **beggar-thy-neighbour** policy: it diverts world demand away from foreign goods and towards domestic goods. Beggar-thy-neighbour policies raise opposition from trade partners if the exchange rate depreciation is perceived as being unjustified, merely an attempt to achieve an 'artificial' trade advantage. Box 11.4 describes recent tensions in

Europe resulting from the EMS crises of 1992–3. The legacy of bruising trade fights in the 1930s is often cited as an important reason for Europe's marked preference for a fixed exchange rate regime.

The impotence of monetary policy under fixed exchange rates is directly related to the result that monetary policy is effective under flexible rates precisely because it works through exchange rate changes. In the end, monetary policy is the same as exchange rate policy. When the authorities wish to use the monetary instrument, they must decide what exchange rate they will be aiming at if they want to have any effect on the real economy. If capital controls are in place, or if financial integration is less complete than hitherto assumed, the domestic interest rate can depart somewhat from the foreign rate of return. (Box 11.2 elaborates on this case.) In particular, part of the effect of monetary policy may come through a decline in interest rates.

11.4.3. The Policy Mix

Fiscal policy is ineffective under flexible exchange rates because it exerts an upward pressure on interest rates and the resulting capital inflows provoke a currency appreciation. The authorities may prevent this exchange rate movement by changing the money supply. A monetary expansion appropriately coupled with a fiscal expansion prevents the exchange rate from appreciating. This case is shown in Figure 11.14 as the move from point *A* to point *B*. With no reduction in foreign demand, the additional spending generated by

---

BOX 11.4. BEGGAR-THY-NEIGHBOUR POLICIES IN EUROPE?

In the summer of 1992 two large EMS member-countries, Italy and the UK, gave up their fixed exchange rates in the face of violent speculative crises.[13] In both cases, the exchange rate immediately depreciated by nearly 20% and the interest rates fell, a sign of monetary relaxation. The British Chancellor of the Exchequer, Norman Lamont, celebrated the recovery of policy independence by stating that from then on 'British monetary policy [would] work for Britain'. Within a few months, the Spanish peseta, the Portuguese escudo, and the Irish punt, while remaining pegged within the EMS, were also devalued by sizeable amounts (between 10% and 20%). Given price

stickiness, the real exchange rates depreciated in similar proportions. Put differently, those currencies that did not devalue suffered serious competitiveness losses. Figure 11.19 shows that Lamont was right: both Italy and the UK enjoyed a pick-up in growth following the depreciation of their currencies. In the aftermath, a number of firms in 'strong' currency countries complained loudly about unfair trade practices. The French authorities even proposed introducing 'compensatory amounts', a system of taxes and subsidies close in effects to tariffs, which would violate the spirit of the Common Market.

---

[13] The events that led to this outcome, and their analysis, are presented in Ch. 21.

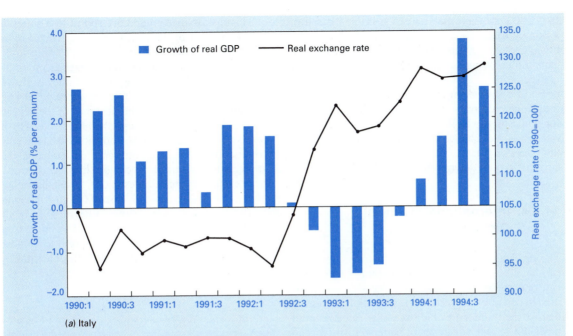

(a) Italy

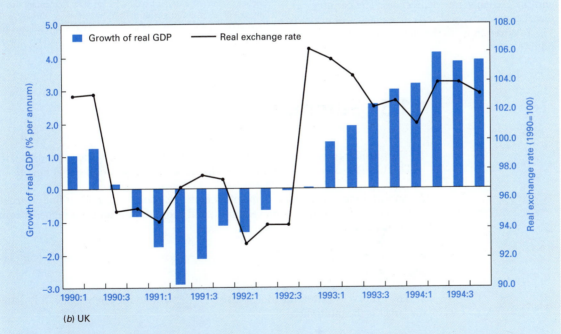

(b) UK

Figure 11.19. Growth After EMS

Italy and the UK were in a recession when the 1992 exchange crisis erupted. Forced out of the exchange rate mechanism of the EMS, the lira and the pound depreciated by about 20%, boosting growth. Some of their trading partners felt that they had been made victims of a competitive depreciation.

Sources: IMF; OECD

the fiscal expansion materializes at home instead of leaking abroad. What is the difference between a combined fiscal and monetary policy mix and just monetary policy? When an expansionary monetary policy is used alone, the exchange rate depreciates: world demand is shifted towards domestic goods, and it is the primary account improvement that boosts demand for domestic goods. With a policy mix, the exchange rate remains unchanged. In this case, the expansionary effect originates in domestic demand while the current account deteriorates.

11.4.4. International Financial Disturbances

The effect of an increase in returns from foreign assets (i^*) has already been described in Figure 11.15 in the case of fixed exchange rates. The same diagram can be used to describe the effects of an international financial disturbance under flexible exchange rates. Capital flows out to take advantage of better returns abroad and the exchange rate depreciates. The country's external competitiveness and current account improve. The *IS* curve shifts to the right until it goes through point *C*.

This disturbance could correspond to a situation where the 'rest of the world' adopts a stricter monetary policy. (This can be thought of as a shift in the *LM* curve of the rest of the world, upwards and to the left, resulting in higher foreign interest rates and lower foreign GDP.) While GDP declines abroad, it rises at home. This is just another instance of the beggar-thy-neighbour effect, except that it now works in reverse: the monetary contraction abroad has an anti-contractionary effect at home as 'their' exchange rate appreciation is 'our' depreciation. In contrast, under fixed exchange rates, domestic GDP also falls following a monetary contraction abroad (point *B* in Figure 11.15).[14] 'Foreign' monetary policy has the same qualitative effect on foreign and domestic GDPs under fixed exchange rates—the transmission is said to be positive—and the opposite effect under flexible rates—a negative transmission.

---

[14] That monetary policy abroad reduces foreign GDP under fixed exchange rates might appear to contradict the result that monetary policy is ineffective under fixed exchange rates. Remember that we make the 'small country assumption' and consider 'abroad' as the rest of the world. The rest of the world cannot be a 'small country'. One way to think about it is that 'abroad' represents a larger hegemonic economic power.

11.5. Summary

1. The primary current account improves when the rest of the world expands and the real exchange depreciates, and worsens when GDP and absorption rise at home.

2. An autonomous increase in demand for domestic goods triggers a multiplier mechanism: more demand means more output, and more output means a higher income and hence a new round of demand increases.

3. The multiplier process is dampened by leakages in the income–demand chain: savings, taxes, and imports.

4. The *IS* curve is flatter, the more sensitive is demand to the interest rate. It is flatter, the larger is the multiplier.

5. When a country's financial markets are well integrated in world markets, the domestic interest rate is tied to worldwide financial conditions. Under conditions of complete capital mobility, the domestic interest rate is equal to the (home currency) rate of return on foreign assets. This provides a third equilibrium condition which must be fulfilled to achieve complete general equilibrium.

6. The *LM* curve is steeper the more sensitive money demand is to output and the less sensitive it is to the interest rate.

7. When the exchange rate is fixed, demand disturbances affect domestic GDP. Monetary disturbances have no effect on real GDP. Monetary policy is ineffective because the central bank's commitment to uphold the declared parity of its currency renders the money supply endogenous. Under a fixed exchange rate regime, foreign financial disturbances affect domestic interest rates and GDP.

8. When the exchange rate is freely floating, the economy is shielded from demand disturbances. Discrepancies between the domestic and foreign interest rates trigger capital flows, which lead to an exchange rate change and affect the current account. Monetary policy is effective because it works through the exchange rate and the current account. Foreign financial disturbances also affect the domestic GDP via the exchange rate: an increase in foreign interest rates leads to an increase in the GDP because the exchange rate depreciates in the wake of capital outflows. Fiscal policy is ineffective because the real exchange rate effect on the primary current account entirely offsets the policy effect on domestic demand.

9. Table 11.4 summarizes the results of the impact of disturbances under fixed and flexible exchange rates.

Table 11.4. The Mundell–Fleming Model: A Summary

Exogenous change	Effect on real GDP	
	Fixed exchange rates	Flexible exchange rates
Expansionary demand disturbance	Increase	No effect
Expansionary monetary policy	No effect	Increase
Increase in foreign interest rates	Decrease	Increase

Key Concepts

- Keynesian model
- exchange rate regime
- import, export, and PCA functions
- (Keynesian) demand multiplier
- leakages
- small-country assumption
- arbitrage
- interest rate parity
- financial integration line
- general equilibrium
- Mundell–Fleming model
- crowding out
- capital controls
- policy mix
- monetary interdependence
- revaluation/devaluation
- beggar-thy-neighbour policies

Exercises: Theory

1. Desired demand is represented by the following simplified function:

$$1500 + 0.8(Y - T) + G - 80i + 300E.$$

The price level is assumed constant throughout. Initially $G = T = 3000$, and $i = 5\%$ throughout. E is the nominal exchange rate, and foreign and domestic prices are constant and are set equal to 1.

   (a) Compute the effect on GDP of an increase in T from 3000 to 3500. Show your result graphically. What is the value of the lump-sum tax multiplier?
   (b) Compute the effect on GDP of an increase in G from 3000 to 3500. Show your result graphically. What is the value of the government spending multiplier?
   (c) Compute the net effect on GDP when both G and T increase by the same amount, from 3000 to 3500. Show your result graphically. What is the value of the balanced budget multiplier?
   (d) Compare your results and interpret the balanced budget multiplier.

2. What are the three sources of leakage that prevent the Keynesian multiplier from being infinite? What do you think is most important for your country?

3. The IS, LM, and financial integration curves define six regions in Figure 11.10. Any position off a curve corresponds to market disequilibrium which can be characterized as excess demand or supply in either goods or money markets or short capital inflow or outflow. Define each region accordingly, e.g. excess demand in the goods market and excess supply in the money market.

4. Show the effects on GDP and the interest rate of an increase in the transaction costs c which affect money demand. You should consider cases of both fixed and flexible exchange rate regimes.

5. Suppose the money demand has the form $L(Y, i, c) = 0.5Y - 300i + 50c$. Let $M/P = 2500$ and $c = 10$. Plot the LM curve in the i, Y diagram.

6. Using the IS and LM curves from questions 1 and 5, find the equilibrium interest rate and real GDP. Holding $E = 1$ (fixed exchange rate regime) and $i^* = 10$, what is the effect of an increase in government expenditure from 3000 to 3500?

7. In problem 6, what happens to the money supply? Explain in words how the central bank allows this to occur.

8. Reconsider the desired demand schedule from problem 1:

$$1500 + 0.8(Y - T) + G - 80i + 300E,$$

where E is the fixed nominal exchange rate (domestic and foreign nominal prices are set equal to one). Solve for the effect of an increase in E from, say, 0.5 to 0.75. Plot the IS curve in the i, Y diagram. What would equilibrium output be if $M/P = 2000$?

9. Assuming the same *IS* and *LM* curves from questions 1 and 5, and assuming a *flexible* exchange rate system with $\overline{M/P} = 2500$, $i^* = 10$, $c = 10$, what is the effect of an increase in *taxes* from 3000 to 3500, when *G* (government purchases) remains at 3000?

10. Suppose the exchange rate in the previous question is fixed at 0.5, and the economy is at equilibrium $(i = i^* = 10)$. Assess the effect of an increase in the foreign exchange rate i^* to 15 on equilibrium output and interest rates. If the exchange rate is allowed to float and *M/P* is exogenous, how will your answer change?

Exercises: Applications

1. *France, 1981–3.* In 1981 a Socialist government took power in France and attempted to reflate the economy while the rest of the world was falling deeper into recession. The expansionary policy consisted of increased government spending with no tax increases and an accommodative to expansionary monetary policy. (One-third of the deficit was money-financed.) Despite this, growth was only 1.8% in 1982 and 0.7% in 1983.

   (a) Using the *IS–LM* diagram, map out the Mitterrand policy in 1981–2. France fixed its exchange rate in the European Monetary System. What must have happened to the current account?

   (b) Within a few months of the programme's outset, capital outflows were significant. What does this indicate? (*Hint*: think about the current account.) What was the gain (at least, the perceived gain) of instituting capital controls in France?

   (c) Why was the demand policy of Mitterrand doomed to failure before it even began?

2. *Norway, 1986.* Norway faced a precipitous drop in the real value of oil exports in 1986. This occurred both because the dollar price of oil declined and because the dollar depreciated. Describe the impact using the *IS–LM* diagram. What options were available to Norway? Norway fixes its exchange rate to a basket of currencies.

3. *Belgium–Luxembourg, 1990.* The Belgium–Luxembourg monetary union operated until 1990 under a two-tier exchange market, separating out current account transactions (the commercial Belgian franc, which was fixed) from capital account transactions (the financial Belgian franc, which was freely floating). What would be the effect of a monetary expansion on the interest rate and GDP?

4. *Sweden, 1982.* By early 1982, Sweden was facing a growing budget deficit, rising unemployment, and a deepening imbalance on the current account. The krona was devalued by 16% while public spending was sharply cut. By 1986 the current account was back in balance, the budget deficit was much improved, unemployment was declining after peaking in 1983, and investment was up by 40%. Interpret this episode graphically, using the *IS–LM* diagram.

5. *Finland, 1991, I.* The collapse of the Soviet Union in 1991 meant a decline of at least 25% of exports for Finland. Explain the consequences of this export decline for GDP and interest rates in Finland. It may help to know that Finland pegged the markka to a basket of currencies.

6. *Finland, 1991, II.* On 15 November 1991 the Finnish markka was devalued by 12.3%. Explain the impact of such a move, using the *IS–LM* diagram.

7. *Sweden, 1991.* On Thursday, 5 December, Sweden announced a 600-basis-point (6%) rise in the discount rate to banks from 11.5% to 17.5%. The increase was said to be necessary after a sudden capital outflow of SKr26 billion in the course of two-and-a-half weeks. (Some blamed this on the Finns' devaluation mentioned in the preceding question.) Analyse this situation using the *IS–LM* diagram. It will help to know that Sweden pegged its exchange rate to a basket of currencies.

8. *German reunification and the EMS, 1990.* One result of German economic and monetary union in 1990 was the huge requirements of the former German Democratic Republic for needed infrastructure and transfers. These have been assumed by West Germany.

   (*a*) What is the effect of increased public spending on the *IS* curve in Germany? Recall that Germany fixes its exchange rate in the European Monetary System.
   (*b*) Suppose the German central bank decides instead not to increase the money supply. Is such a decision consistent with a fixed exchange rate regime?
   (*c*) Other countries have perceived higher German interest rates as an upward movement of the financial integration line. How might this help explain the prolonged recession observed in Germany's EC neighbours in 1991?

9. *Italy, 1992, I.* Before September 1992 Italy pegged its exchange rate to the ECU, a basket of European exchange rates. Show the effects of

   (*a*) an increase in world interest rates resulting from restrictive monetary policy in Germany;
   (*b*) a tightening of the budget (increasing taxes, cutting government spending).

10. *Italy, 1992, II.* After September 1992 the Banca d'Italia (central bank) let the lira float. As a result, the exchange rate depreciated from roughly L850/DM to L1275/DM in March 1995. What would you expect to be the effect of this devaluation? How would your answer to question 9 change if the lira is floating?

Suggested Further Reading

The Mundell–Fleming model refers to:

Fleming, J. M. (1962), 'Domestic Financial Policies under Fixed and Floating Exchange Rates', *IMF Staff Papers*, 9: 369–79.

Mundell, R. A. (1962), 'Capital Mobility and Stabilization Policy under Fixed and Flexible Exchange Rates', *Canadian Journal of Economic and Political Science*, 29: 475–85.

A more advanced treatment can be found in:

Gärtner, Manfred (1993), *Macroeconomics under Flexible Exchange Rates*, Harvester Wheatsheaf, Brighton.

Appendix: A Mathematical Treatment of Policy Multiplier in the *IS–LM* System

This appendix derives formally some of the results presented in the text for the *IS–LM* model of an open economy, under fixed and flexible exchange rates. Both foreign and domestic price levels are exogenous throughout, so changes in the nominal exchange rate are equivalent to changes in the real rate; if E is the nominal and λ is the real exchange rate, then $dE = d\lambda$.

The Model

The *IS* curve is given by

(A10.1) $Y = C(\Omega, Y^d) + I(q, i) + G + PCA(Y, Y^*, \lambda),$

where Y is GDP, C consumption, I investment expenditures, $\overline{G}$ government purchases, and PCA the current account, all denominated in real terms (at constant prices). The functions are largely as in the main text. Government purchases are exogenous, as is the tax rate and the lump-sum (net) tax. Disposable income Y^d is given therefore by $Y(1 - \tau) - \overline{T}$. In principle, $\overline{T}$ need not be positive; if negative, it might be regarded as an exogenous transfer or a tax exemption. Investment is a positive function of q and the interest rate. q is assumed to be a positive function of expected future marginal products of capital (exogenous) and a negative function of the interest rate (endogenous). Note also that the primary current account is only a function of domestic GDP, foreign GDP, and the real exchange rate.

Total differentiation of (A10.1) yields the following local characterization of the *IS* curve:

(A10.2) $dY = C_Y(1 - \tau)dY - C_Y Y d\tau - C_Y d\overline{T}$
$$+ C_\Omega(\Omega_i di + \Omega_E dE) + I_q q_i di + I_i di$$
$$+ d\overline{G} + PCA_\lambda d\lambda + PCA_Y dY,$$

where subscripts here refer to partial derivatives of the underlying functions; i.e., $C_Y \equiv \partial C/\partial Y^d$. By assumption, $1 > C_Y > 0$, $C_\Omega > 0$, $\Omega_i < 0$, $\Omega_E \lessgtr 0$ (depending on whether the net foreign asset position is positive or negative), $I_q > 0$, $q_i < 0$, $I_i < 0$, $PCA_Y > 0$, and $PCA_\lambda < 0$. The slope of the *IS* curve is given when $d\tau = d\overline{T} = dE = d\overline{G} = d\lambda$

$$\frac{di}{dY} = \frac{1 - C_Y(1 - \tau) - I_Y - PCA_Y}{C_\Omega \Omega i + I_q q_i + I_i} < 0.$$

The *LM* curve is given by equilibrium in the money market, i.e. by

(A10.3) $M/\overline{P} = \mathcal{L}(Y, i),$

so total differentiation results in

(A10.4) $dM/\overline{P} = \mathcal{L}_Y dY + \mathcal{L}_i di,$

with $\mathcal{L}_Y > 0$ and $\mathcal{L}_i < 0$, for reasons given in Chapter 8. The slope of the *LM* curve is $di/dY = -\mathcal{L}_Y/\mathcal{L}_i > 0$.

Fixed Exchange Rates

The nominal exchange rate (units of domestic currency per unit of foreign currency) is pegged at $\overline{E}$, and the domestic interest rate i is continuously equal to the exogenous foreign required rate of return i^*. Thus, $d\overline{E} = di = 0$. The money supply is endogenous. The *IS* curve reduces to

(A10.5) $dY = C_Y(1 - \tau)dY - C_Y Y d\tau + C_Y d\overline{T} + d\overline{G}$
$$+ PCA_Y dY,$$

and the *LM* curve is

(A10.6) $dM/P = \mathcal{L}_Y dY.$

The money supply is endogenous, and we will ignore the *LM* curve for the rest of the fixed exchange rate analysis. It is sufficient to manipulate (A10.5). To derive the fiscal multipliers, we seek the change in the endogenous variable Y for changes in the policy instruments: $\overline{G}$, τ, and $\overline{T}$. Thus, the government spending multiplier obtains from (A10.5) when $d\overline{G} \neq 0$ but $d\tau = d\overline{T} = 0$:

$$\frac{dY}{d\overline{G}} = \frac{1}{1 - C_Y(1 - \tau) - PCA_Y} > 0.$$

Similarly, the lump-sum tax multiplier obtains when $d\overline{T} \neq 0$ and $d\tau = d\overline{G} = 0$:

$$\frac{dY}{d\overline{T}} = \frac{-C_Y}{1 - C_Y(1 - \tau) - PCA_Y} < 0.$$

Note that $dY/d\overline{G} > -dY/d\overline{T}$, so one might think of a balanced budget multiplier which applies when changes in government purchases are matched by tax increases or transfer reductions ($d\overline{G} = d\overline{T} \neq 0$, $d\tau = 0$):

$$\frac{dY}{d\overline{G}}\bigg|_{d\overline{G} = d\overline{T}} = \frac{1 - C_Y}{1 - C_Y(1 - \tau) - PCA_Y} > 0.$$

The tax rate multiplier ($d\overline{G} = d\overline{T} = O$, $d\tau \neq 0$) is given by

$$\frac{dY}{d\tau} = \frac{-YC_Y}{1 - C_Y(1 - \tau) - PCA_Y} < 0.$$

Floating Exchange Rates

Under a floating exchange rate regime, the money supply is exogenous, so $M = \overline{M}$. As before, i^* is given as well. Consequently, the domestic interest rate clears the domestic money market, and the exchange rate moves to clear the demand and supply of foreign exchange, assumed to be determined by relative rates of return. The financial integration condition is simply[15]

$$(A10.7) \qquad dE = \theta(i - i^*) \qquad \text{with } \theta < 0.$$

Equation (A10.7) simply states that, when nominal interest rates exceed the required rate of return abroad, the exchange rate tends to appreciate. The *IS* curve is given by (A10.2), the *LM* by (A10.4). It is possible to solve (A10.2), (10.4), and (A10.7) to obtain the analogous multipliers under floating exchange rates:[16]

It is revealing to compare these multipliers with those of the previous section. For two reasons, the fiscal multipliers are smaller than they are under fixed exchange rate regimes. First, there is a crowding out of interest-sensitive expenditure as interest rates rise. Second, higher domestic interest rates are associated with an appreciated exchange rate (E lower), which crowds out exports and encourages imports. The extent of this crowding out depends on the slope of the *LM* curve ($\mathcal{L}_Y/\mathcal{L}_i$); as the *LM* curve becomes flatter, we move closer to the fixed exchange rate regime case. Note also that, as capital becomes perfectly mobile ($\theta \to \infty$), the fiscal multipliers tend to zero, and the monetary policy multiplier tends to $1/(\overline{P}\mathcal{L}_Y)$.

$$\frac{dY}{d\overline{G}} = \frac{1}{1 - C_Y(1 - \tau) - PCA_Y + (\mathcal{L}_Y/\mathcal{L}_i)\left[C_\Omega\Omega_i + I_q q_i + I_i + \theta(PCA_\lambda + C_\Omega\Omega_E)\right]} > 0,$$

$$\frac{dY}{d\overline{T}} = \frac{-C_Y}{1 - C_Y(1 - \tau) - PCA_Y + (\mathcal{L}_Y/\mathcal{L}_i)\left[C_\Omega\Omega_i + I_q q_i + I_i + \theta(PCA_\lambda + C_\Omega\Omega_E)\right]} < 0,$$

$$\frac{dY}{d\tau} = \frac{-YC_Y}{1 - C_Y(1 - \tau) - PCA_Y + (\mathcal{L}_Y/\mathcal{L}_i)\left[C_\Omega\Omega_i + I_q q_i + I_i + \theta(PCA_\lambda + C_\Omega\Omega_E)\right]} < 0.$$

It is also possible to derive the monetary policy multiplier as

$$\frac{dY}{d\overline{M}} = \frac{\left[C_\Omega\Omega_i + I_q q_i + \theta(PCA_\lambda + C_\Omega\Omega_E)\right]/\overline{P}\mathcal{L}_i}{1 - C_Y(1 - \tau) - PCA_Y + (\mathcal{L}_Y/\mathcal{L}_i)\left[C_\Omega\Omega_i + I_q q_i + I_i + \theta(PCA_\lambda + C_\Omega\Omega_E)\right]} < 0.$$

---

[15] In Ch. 9 we will explore this relationship in detail.

[16] These three equations are a system in three unknowns dY, di, and dE. These unknowns can be solved for in terms of the exogenous variables in a variety of ways. One is brute force. Another is to write the system in matrix form $Ax = b$, where x is the vector of endogenous variables, A is a conformable matrix of the coefficients, and b is the set of exogenous terms; if A is invertible, the solution is $x = A^{-1}b$.

PART V

Inflation and Business Cycles

Finally, the synthesis of modern macroeconomics is reached. All previous chapters are brought together in a coherent framework which distinguishes between factors that affect aggregate supply from those that affect aggregate demand. Chapter 12 focuses on aggregate supply, stressing the role of labour markets, and using concepts developed in Part II. Chapter 13 introduces inflation in the *IS–LM* analysis and derives the aggregate demand schedule. Bringing together the aggregate demand (*AD*) and aggregate supply (*AS*) schedules provides a powerful tool which is used to explain both inflation and business cycles. Chapter 14 then focuses on business cycles. It proposes some stylized facts and studies how far they can be explained by the *AD–AS* framework, and by its competitor the Real Business Cycle view.

12

Aggregate Supply and Inflation

When the demand for a commodity or service is high relative to the supply of it we expect the price to rise, the rate of rise being greater the greater the excess demand. Conversely when the demand is low relatively to the supply we expect the price to fall, the rate of fall being greater the greater the deficiency of demand. It seems plausible that this principle should operate as one of the factors determining the rate of change of money wage rates, which are the price of labour services.

A. W. Phillips

12.1. Overview

Two issues are discussed explicitly for the first time in this chapter: inflation, and the **supply side**. The supply side, the mobilization of productive resources for the delivery of goods and services, has already been mentioned in previous chapters—Chapters 5 and 7 described the evolution of the economy's trend growth path; Chapter 6 examined how the labour market settles on an equilibrium unemployment rate. This chapter looks at the exact same issues but from a different viewpoint: it considers why and how GDP and unemployment fluctuate about their equilibrium levels, an issue already raised in Chapter 11. Assuming that prices are fixed, the familiar GDP decomposition has been interpreted as a causal relationship running from demand (the right-hand side) to output (the left-hand side):

(12.1) $$Y = C + I + G + PCA.$$

In the present chapter, the question is: does the supply side really respond passively to the demand side? What are the incentives for producers to behave in this fashion? or for workers to adjust by changing the numbers of hours worked? This chapter develops the idea that demand increases are actually met by a combination of output expansion *and* price increases. The mix varies over time, however. In the short run, prices are sticky and most of the response is in output. In the long run prices rise and the economy returns to its trend growth path. The short run is Keynesian; the long run is characterized by the neutrality principle.

The chapter begins with two 'stylized facts': Okun's law, which links output and unemployment, and the Phillips curve, which links unemployment and inflation. Despite their name, 'stylized facts' are not facts at all, but regularities in the data. As such, they will help us begin to analyse the supply side of the economy and the process through which wages affect prices and prices affect wages.

These issues are highly controversial. This is where Keynesians and Monetarists part company. The chapter takes a pragmatic approach, initially proposing a simple accounting of the inflation process and leaving the controversies for later on.[1]

12.2. Okun's Law

In the long run, output increases as a result of a combination of additional capital, labour, and technical progress. Over the short run, when demand fluctuates and firms respond by adjusting their output, the only significant margin of flexibility is labour input. Capital accumulation and technical progress make at best a small contribution to supplying additional output when demand rises.[2] When demand declines temporarily, firms implement short-time work schedules, freeze hirings, or in the worst cases dismiss workers.

To change labour input, firms may vary the number of hours per worker or the number of employed workers, or both. The temporary deviations of GDP from its trend, which appear in Figure 12.1, constitute the **output gap**. The figure relates the output gap of

[1] Ch. 16 presents the debate between Keynesians and Monetarists.
[2] Capital usage may be increased through overtime work, using the same equipment more hours per day, and possibly operating more days per week.

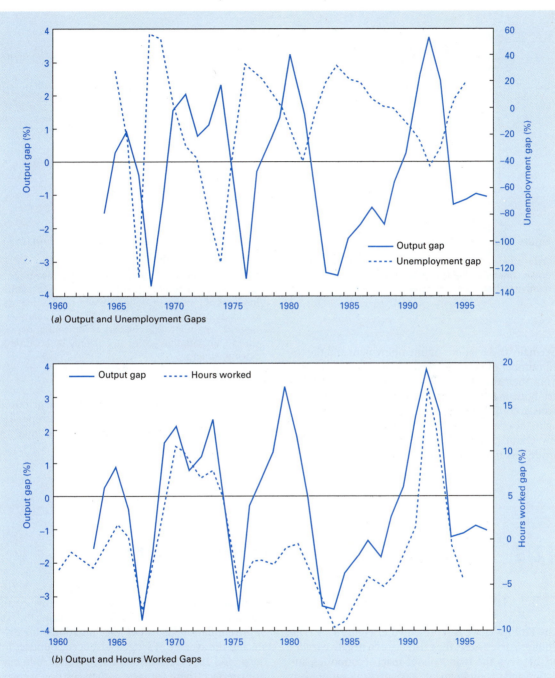

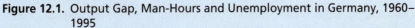

(a) Output and Unemployment Gaps

(b) Output and Hours Worked Gaps

Figure 12.1. Output Gap, Man-Hours and Unemployment in Germany, 1960–1995

The output gap (deviations of real GDP from its trend) is presented alongside deviations from the trends of the rate of unemployment and of total hours worked per month. When business conditions vary, firms adjust the supply of goods and services and their demand for labour. For example, when the economy goes into a recession, firms reduce man-hours, partly by using fewer workers partly by reducing the number of hours worked.

Notes: Trend real GDP and unemployment are estimated (by second-order polynomial functions of time).

Sources: OECD, *Economic Outlook*, June 1995, and *Main Economic Indicators*

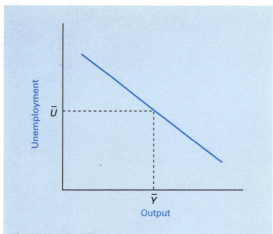

Figure 12.2. Okun's Law

Okun's law implies that, when the economy slows down, unemployment increases; when output rises relative to trend, unemployment declines.

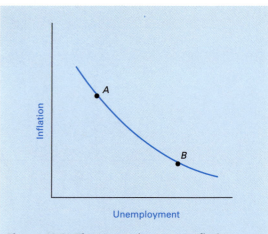

Figure 12.3. The Unemployment–Inflation Trade-off

The Phillips curve was once seen as a negative trade-off between unemployment and inflation, representing a set of possible options from which governments could choose. For example, it could keep unemployment down (point *A*) at the cost of some inflation, or could limit inflation (point *B*) but only by accepting unemployment.

Germany to deviations of unemployment and the total number of hours worked per week or per month from their own trends. The figure shows that firms use both margins of adjustment in varying proportions according to circumstances. Although not airtight, the effect on unemployment is known as **Okun's law**. Okun's law associates fluctuations of real GDP Y around its trend growth path $\overline{Y}$, with fluctuations in

the opposite direction of the unemployment rate U around its equilibrium rate $\overline{U}$. The relationship is displayed in Figure 12.2 and summarized as follows:

$$(12.2) \qquad U - \overline{U} = -g(Y - \overline{Y}).$$

12.3. The Phillips Curve: a Stylized Fact?

12.3.1. The Early Phillips Curve

The **Phillips curve** is represented in Figure 12.3. The Phillips curve asserts the existence of a negative *trade-off* between the twin evils of macroeconomics, inflation and unemployment. A country can suffer from high inflation but have low unemployment (point *A*), or from high unemployment but with low inflation (point *B*). This relationship is named after A. W. Phillips of the London School of Economics. At the end of the 1950s he plotted the annual rate of growth of nominal wages, or **wage inflation**, in Britain during the period 1861–1957 against the rate of unemploy-

ment and found a remarkably robust negative correlation. Figure 12.4 plots Phillips curves—using the rate of price inflation instead of wage inflation—for Britain and the average of sixteen advanced countries for the period 1921–73 (excluding war years).[3] While far from perfect (there are a few outliers, no doubt corresponding to exceptional events), the Phillips curve is suggestive of an important systematic relationship.

[3] Unweighted average of observations for Australia, Austria, Belgium, Canada, Denmark, Finland, France, Germany, Italy, Japan, Netherlands, Norway, Sweden, Switzerland, the UK, and the USA. For some years some countries are missing.

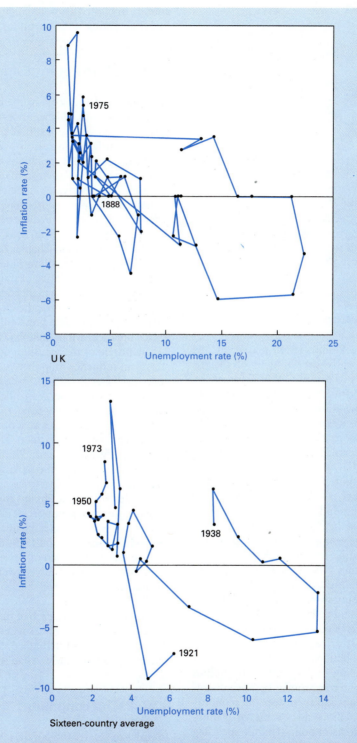

UK

Sixteen-country average

Figure 12.4. Phillips Curves: the UK (1888–1975) and a Sixteen-Country Average
(1921–1973, excluding 1939–1949)

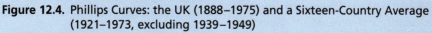

Sources: Maddison (1991); Mitchell (1978)

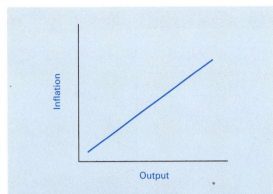

Figure 12.5. Aggregate Supply

Combining the Phillips curve and Okun's law delivers a supply curve. The supply curve states that inflation must rise to induce suppliers to produce more output.

12.3.2. A Supply Curve Interpretation

The discovery of the Phillips curve played an important role in the early development of macroeconomics and its everyday use by policy-makers. Economists had been frustrated by the 'missing link' between output and inflation: they knew full well that the assumption that prices are fixed, which is used to derive the IS and LM curves, cannot literally be true. The IS–LM system explained output fluctuations given prices; Okun's law explained how unemployment varies with output. Then, to have a complete macroeconomic theory, all that was needed was to explain how prices respond to unemployment. This was the status accorded the Phillips curve and also represented as an **aggregate supply curve**, as displayed in Figure 12.5: when output increases relative to trend, unemployment declines (Okun's law) and inflation rises (the Phillips curve). It is called a supply curve because it answers the question raised earlier: how and why does output respond to demand? The interpretation was that suppliers of goods and services increase output if they can raise prices and profits.

The message of the Phillips curve to policy-makers was simple and appealing: pick a point on the Phillips curve, i.e. choose a good compromise between unemployment and inflation, and then steer the economy to the designed point. This could be achieved by moving the IS curve using fiscal policy (public spending and taxes) or the LM curve using monetary policy, or a mix of both. A country that favoured low unemployment would choose a point like A in Figure 12.3; a

country interested in low inflation would aim at a point like B, accepting some unemployment.

12.3.3. More Recent Evidence

Not long after its discovery, the interpretation of the Phillips curve—that higher prices elicit more output—was perceived as tenuous. If all prices and wages rise simultaneously, relative prices—real interest rates, real wages, and real exchange rates—are unchanged. Only if workers and firms suffer from **money illusion**—that is, if they act on increases in their own prices or wages without taking contemporaneous increases in all other prices into account—will there be an incentive to raise output. (This follows from the discussions of labour supply and demand in Chapter 6.) The Phillips curve rested on weak foundations indeed. Figure 12.6 presents some representative examples of the relationship between unemployment and inflation during the period 1965–96: at times, the Phillips curve seems to have disappeared. The link, still present in the late 1960s, breaks down in the following decade.

The puzzle of the vanishing Phillips curve had as strong an influence on policy-making as the Phillips curve itself (see Box 12.1). Over nearly a century, the inverse relationship between inflation and unemployment seemed relatively robust. Yet the breakdown occurred in all countries at about the same time and in a similar systematic fashion. The challenge is to explain both the existence of a Phillips curve and its disappearance, as well as the striking similarity between different countries' experiences.

In order to solve the Phillips curve mystery, we need to make use of some important clues. First, the timing of the sharpest increases in inflation—first around 1973–4, and then around 1979–80—seems related to the two oil shocks, when oil prices increased fourfold in 1973–4 and then doubled over again in 1979–80.[4] Second, in between the oil shocks, and after the second oil shock, it is possible to observe the re-emergence of Phillips curves. Third, each of these curves lies to the right of the previous one, suggesting that the unemployment rate was fluctuating about an equilibrium unemployment rate which had increased over time.

12.3.4. The Long Run

In order to resolve the puzzle, it will prove helpful to start with the long run. In particular, the principle of

[4] The evolution of oil prices is displayed in Fig. 4.6.

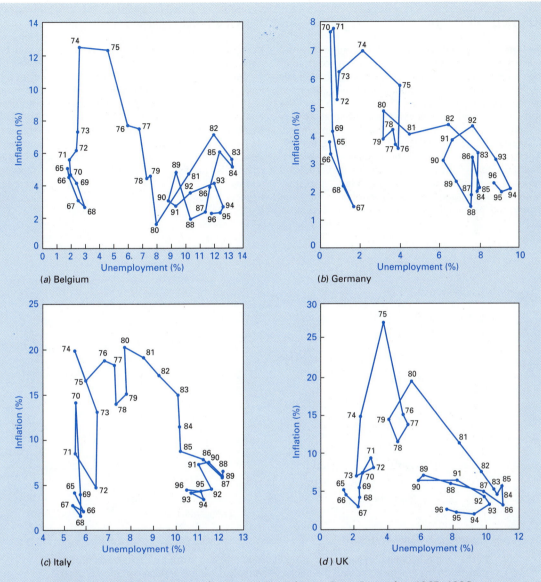

Figure 12.6. Philips Curves: the Recent Experience, Four Countries, 1965–1996

The Phillips curve broke down at the end of the 1960s. In almost all countries, the sharpest departures occur during the years 1973–5 and 1979–81.

Sources: IMF; OECD

neutrality asserts that the economy is dichotomized in the long run: real and nominal sectors of an economy cease to influence each other. In particular, the output level is on its trend growth path $\bar{Y}$ and unemployment is at its equilibrium rate $\bar{U}$, *no matter what the rate of inflation is*. The rate of inflation is determined by the

rate of money growth.[5] Graphically, if in the long run unemployment returns to its equilibrium level, the **long-run aggregate supply** and Phillips 'curves' are simply vertical lines, as displayed in Figure 12.7.

[5] This principle is established in S. 8.7 of Ch. 8.

BOX 12.1. THE PHILLIPS CURVE AND ECONOMIC POLICY DOCTRINES

The history of the Phillips curve has profoundly influenced policy-making. Because the curve had been accepted as their own by the Keynesians, its vanishing in the early 1970s presented them with a major difficulty. The main lesson from the Phillips curve was believed to lie in the trade-off between unemployment and inflation; a simultaneous increase in both inflation and unemployment, or **stagflation**, was ruled out. Milton Friedman, the Chicago economist and Nobel Prize laureate, often considered the leader of the Monetarist school, had predicted the end of the Phillips curve as early as 1967. When stagflation occurred, the Monetarists were able to claim victory and to benefit from the attendant decline in Keynesian influence on policy-making. (It should be noted, however, that a Keynesian, Edmund Phelps of Columbia University, had also predicted instability of the Phillips curve in 1967!) Ever since, the Keynesians have been on the defensive, hard pressed to explain why prices and wages should ever be fixed or simply sticky. The Monetarists were at the forefront of the successful battle against inflation during the 1980s. While controversies persist today, the interpretation developed in this chapter is broadly accepted by both schools of thought and indeed is closer to the Monetarist than to the earlier Keynesian view.

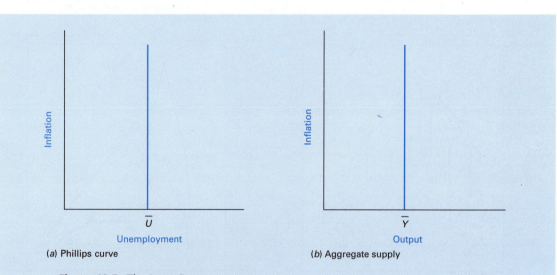

(a) Phillips curve   (b) Aggregate supply

Figure 12.7. The Long Run

In the long run, unemployment is at its equilibrium rate and output is on its trend growth path. Both the Phillips curve and the aggregate supply curve are vertical. Inflation is determined by money growth, independently of output or unemployment.

12.4. Accounting for Inflation

If in the short run prices are thought of as sticky and in the long run the Phillips curve is vertical, then the Phillips curve puzzle must be related to the behaviour of inflation over the medium run. This section proposes an inflation accounting exercise. It starts with the observation that firms set prices. They do so with one eye on the market and the other on production costs. Focusing next on production costs, the emphasis is put on wages, labour productivity, and wage bargaining. Consolidating price-setting and wage-setting provides an explanation of why a Phillips curve existed, and why it has sometimes disappeared.

BOX 12.2. THE GEOMETRY OF A MONOPOLIST

A firm with market power is described in Figure 12.8. It faces a downward-sloping demand schedule. The demand schedule also represents average revenue, i.e. the price of one unit sold. The marginal revenue from selling one more unit to the marginal customer is the sales price *less* the loss from lowering the price charged to all other consumers. This is why the marginal revenue schedule (MR) lies below the demand schedule.[6] The figure also shows the marginal cost curve (MC): it measures how much it costs to produce one more unit, all things given. The marginal cost curve is rising: since the stock of productive capital is fixed in the short run, the marginal productivity of other factors decreases when production is expanded. Microeconomic principles, formally reproduced in the Appendix, establish that the firm maximizes its profit when its marginal cost equals its marginal revenue, i.e. at point *B* where the two schedules intersect. The reason is quite intuitive. Point *B* corresponds to production level *Q*.

To sell this quantity, the firm must choose point *A* on the market demand schedule by setting the price at *P*. To see why this is the best that it can do, consider point *A'*. Starting from the price and quantity corresponding to point *A'*, the firm considers selling one more unit. Its profit increases because its marginal revenue (point) exceeds its marginal cost (point *C'*). The firm will surely produce more until marginal revenue exactly equals marginal cost, that is at point *A*. The same reasoning can be applied to any point to the right of *A* on the demand schedule: profits rise by selling and producing less.

For our purposes, the key result is that the selling price will be set equal to (marginal) cost—corresponding to distance *BQ*—plus a profit margin or mark-up—corresponding to the distance *AB*. The mark-up depends on the sensitivity of the market to price changes, measured by the price elasticity of demand. When demand is highly elastic—the demand curve is flat—the mark-up is small because the firm has little market power; even a small price increase would reduce demand dramatically. This is the case of perfect competition. Conversely, with a less elastic demand, the firm has an incentive to take advantage of the market's insensitivity to price increases and to charge a high mark-up. If the elasticity is constant— a reasonable approximation—the mark-up will also be constant.

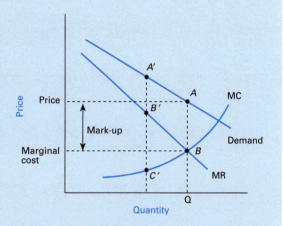

Figure 12.8. Mark-up Pricing

Given the demand curve for its product, the firm chooses point *A* because that is where it maximizes its profits. The optimum occurs when the marginal revenue from an additional unit of output and the marginal cost of producing it are equal. The corresponding point *B* determines how much to produce, and point *A* shows how to price the product accordingly.

12.4.1. Output and Prices Given Costs

If perfect competition reigned in all markets, firms would not have any latitude in setting prices. In order to be able to think of effective price-setting, we need to imagine firms that have some market power, so that they can use prices as a strategic tool. Producers of non-differentiated products such as milk or copper have little or no market power. Most firms, however, can make their products sufficiently different, in one

---

[6] Formally, the demand curve is the function $P(Q)$ linking the price P and the quantity sold Q. Total revenue is $TR = P(Q)Q$. Average revenue is $TR/Q = P(Q)$, the demand curve. Marginal revenue is $MR = \partial TR/\partial Q = P(Q) + Q(\partial P/\partial Q)$. Since $\partial P/\partial Q$ is negative (it is the slope of the demand curve), we have $MR < AR$.

way or another, to establish some market power. (For example, car manufacturers use all sorts of gimmicks as well as advertisement to make each model look different.) The reward from product differentiation is higher (monopolistic) profits. The difference between perfect competition and monopolistic pricing is explained in Box 12.2. The main result is **mark-up pricing**: a firm with market power sets the price (P) of its products above the marginal production cost (MC). Mark-up pricing is summarized as follows:

$$(12.3) \quad P = \theta MC \quad \text{where } \theta > 1 \text{ is the mark-up.}$$

To keep things simple, we consider (rather realistically) that the mark-up is constant. Then, the rate of

Table 12.1. Wage Share of Value Added by Country and Selected Industries, 1993 (%)

	Total economy	Manufacturing	Chemicals	Basic metal industries	Wholesale/ retail trade
Belgium[a]	52.9	59.1	42.9	54.9	50.1
Denmark	54.3	67.1	59.6	78.0	58.8
France[a]	51.8	58.7	42.8	56.1	50.7
Germany[c]	54.3	69.6	57.0	74.3	65.6
Italy	44.0	56.0	62.9	63.8	26.9
Netherlands	53.7	61.0	43.7	72.4	59.5
Norway[b]	51.9	68.7	55.2	72.1	68.5
Sweden	59.5	68.7	45.8	73.4	81.2
USA[b]	60.5	66.7	49.9	73.8	60.4
Japan	57.3	55.1	29.0	44.9	70.7

[a] 1990
[b] 1991
[c] 1992

Source: OECD National Acounts, 1995

inflation is simply the rate of growth of nominal marginal costs:[7]

$$(12.4) \qquad \pi = \Delta P/P = \Delta MC/MC.$$

If the firm has no market power whatsoever, there is no possibility of setting a mark-up over costs: $\theta = 1$, and the price is equal to the marginal cost ($P = MC$). As the mark-up is constant, (12.4) remains valid.

Accounting for inflation therefore requires accounting for marginal costs. Marginal costs, however, are difficult to measure. We approximate them by **average** or **unit costs**—total costs per unit produced.[8] It is convenient to break down production costs into two main categories: labour costs, and non-labour costs. For the economy as a whole, labour costs are the single largest component of production costs. Their share of value added ranges from 50% to 60% in developed countries, being usually much higher in labour-intensive services than in capital-intensive industries (Table 12.1).[9] If non-labour costs represent a fraction

α of all production costs, the rate of growth of average nominal costs is:[10]

$$(12.5) \qquad \frac{\Delta(\text{average costs})}{\text{average costs}}$$

$$= (1 - \alpha)\frac{\Delta(\text{average labour costs})}{\text{average labour costs}}$$

$$+ \alpha\frac{\Delta(\text{average non-labour costs})}{\text{average non-labour costs}}.$$

12.4.2. Labour Costs Given Prices

The change in average nominal labour costs can be decomposed into two parts. The first is the growth in wages (w), which includes costs such as direct labour taxes, social security contributions, and other benefits paid by employers. The second component is growth in the amount of labour services, measured in

---

[7] Here we apply the rule (called rule of logarithmic differentiation) that, if $z = xy$, then $\Delta z/z = \Delta x/x + \Delta y/y$. Since we assume that the mark-up is constant, $\Delta\theta/\theta = 0$.

[8] The Appendix provides a justification of this assumption.

[9] In interpreting these numbers, it is important to remember the difference between value added and turnover or total sales. As a percentage of total sales, wage shares are much lower because turnover includes the costs of intermediate goods.

[10] Formally, if total unit costs are $TC = LC + NLC$, where LC are labour costs and NLC non-labour costs, we have:

$$\Delta TC = \Delta LC + \Delta NLC;$$

i.e. $\dfrac{\Delta TC}{TC} = \dfrac{\Delta LC}{TC} + \dfrac{\Delta NLC}{TC} = \dfrac{\Delta LC}{LC}\dfrac{LC}{TC} + \dfrac{\Delta NLC}{NLC}\dfrac{NLC}{TC}$,

where $1 - \alpha = LC/TC$ and $\alpha = NLC/TC$.

man-hours, needed to produce one unit of output. This is the same thing as the inverse of average labour productivity (LP), the amount of output produced by one hour of work. Average labour costs therefore grow as the difference between hourly wage growth and productivity growth:[11]

$$(12.6) \quad \frac{\Delta(\text{average labour costs})}{\text{average labour costs}} = \frac{\Delta W}{W} - \frac{\Delta LP}{LP}.$$

Just as **real wage rigidities** prevent equilibrium unemployment from achieving full employment in the long run, **nominal wage rigidities** prevent the actual unemployment rate from reaching its equilibrium level in the short run. The next question to ask is: who sets wages? In all democratic countries the answer is that wages are negotiated, between employers and either workers or their unions. The following sections will show that three main factors influence wage negotiations and drive the rate of growth of nominal wages: core inflation, productivity growth $\Delta LP/LP$, and the state of demand in the labour market:

$$(12.7) \quad \frac{\Delta W}{W} = \overline{\pi} + \frac{\Delta LP}{LP} - f(U - \overline{U}),$$

where the last term says that, when actual unemployment U is above its equilibrium rate $\overline{U}$, wages tend to slow down, and conversely.[12]

12.4.2.1. Core inflation

Both sides of the table during wage negotiations—employees and employers—care about *real* labour costs and *real* wages. Yet bargaining can only be about *nominal* wages.[13] Naturally, employees want to protect wages against inflation. Employers normally agree to incorporate inflation in wage settlements but worry about overestimating inflation. Other things equal, both sides wish to maintain the real wage W/P 'on target'. For this reason, the rate of inflation to be fully incorporated into wage settlements is usually a central part of wage negotiations.

But which rate of inflation should wage negotiators take into account? Often wages seem to reflect past inflation. This is the backward-looking part of wage negotiations, which sometimes takes the form of explicit or implicit **indexation** clauses which commit nominal wages to rise in line with past price increases. Yet at the same time, nominal wages are often set for a period during which the inflation rate may be expected to change. This is the forward-looking part of wage negotiations. Because it is not clear exactly how this is done, we refer loosely to the rate of inflation taken into account during wage bargaining as the **core (or underlying) rate of inflation**, and it appears in (12.7) as $\overline{\pi}$.

The core rate of inflation is a central part of the analysis, but, it must be admitted, its precise behaviour remains highly controversial, as Chapter 13 will make abundantly clear. At this stage it is important to grasp the logic of the concept, rather than its operational definition. Core inflation could be measured by asking wage negotiators directly what rate they factored in. Typically, this rate includes a correction of the past. During the previous negotiations, they may have underestimated subsequent inflation, penalizing the employees, or overestimated it, thus pushing up wages too fast. Thus, core inflation has a backward-looking component. At the same time, wages are set for a given period of time (one or two years, sometimes more), so the negotiators must also guess the future course of inflation in setting wages, possibly including a pre-arranged increase after a year. Thus, core inflation also includes a forward-looking component. During periods of high inflation, wages are set for shorter period because forward-looking guesses are too difficult and errors lead to very significant distortions; indexation then can become automatic. In low-inflation periods, there is little difference between the backward and forward-looking components, and between core and actual inflation.

12.4.2.2. Productivity gains

Productivity gains accrue little by little and are not a feature of the short run. All things equal, they improve firms' profitability. Negotiators typically argue about the financial health of firms. Unions demand, usually successfully, that wages rise with improvements in labour productivity. This is why labour productivity gains contribute one for one to raise wages in (12.7).[14]

12.4.2.3. Cyclical effects

Figure 12.9(*a*) depicts the changing balance of power during wage negotiations. When employment

---

[11] Nominal average labour costs are $LC = (WL/Y)$, where W is nominal hourly wages, L hours worked, and Y real GDP. Average labour productivity is $LP = Y/L$. With $LC = W/LP$, $\Delta LC/LC = \Delta W/W - \Delta LP/LP$.

[12] Formally, $f(U - \overline{U})$ is increasing and $f(0) = 0$.

[13] First, everyone consumes a different bundle of goods so it would be difficult to decide 'whose' bundle should be used. Second, the price level, even when measured by the rate of change in the CPI, is measured only with a lag. Third, the future is unknown!

[14] This is consistent with the implication, derived in Ch. 6, that it is optimal for firms to equate real wages to the marginal productivity of labour.

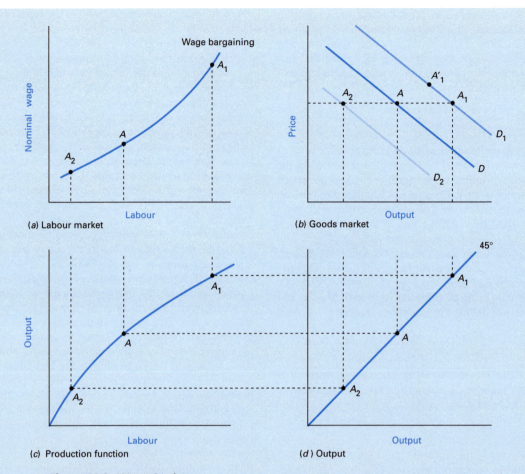

Figure 12.9. Wage-Setting

The long-run equilibrium is represented by point A. The goods demand schedules D_1 and D_2 in panel (b) correspond to fluctuations in aggregate demand. When prices are sticky, firms respond by producing at A_1 or A_2. Via panel (d), the changes in output in panel (c) are translated into changes in the use of labour. Panel (a) shows how wage bargaining is affected by the level of employment. Given the price level, wages increase during an expansion (point A_1) and decline during a recession (point A_2).

increases, the unions' bargaining position improves and they extract higher wage settlements. Conversely, with employment falling, unions may be weaker and concerned more with unemployment than wages.[15] Panel (b), which reproduces Figure 12.8, describes the pricing and output decisions of a firm with market power. Panel (c) represents the short-run production function: with a fixed capital stock, firms change output by varying the amount of labour that they use.

Panel (d) links panels (b) and (c). Point A represents a situation of long-run equilibrium: output is on its trend growth path. While not depicted, unemployment is at its equilibrium rate ($\overline{U}$).

Cyclical fluctuations in the demand for goods are represented by temporary shifts of the demand schedule in panel (b): to D_1 for an expansion, to D_2 in a recession. Prices are a fixed mark-up over costs, and costs have not changed yet, so the price level remains temporarily unchanged—this is the Keynesian assumption. The supply response of firms to demand fluctuations is shown as shifts to points A_1 or A_2. As a result, the quantity of labour in use changes as depicted

[15] This is the short-run equivalent of the collective labour supply curve of Ch. 6, where unions trade off higher real wages against more employment.

in panel (*c*). Panel (*a*) shows that, when the economy is booming and firms are eager to hire more labour, the union's bargaining position is enhanced and the negotiators ask for higher wages (point A_1). Conversely, in a cyclical downturn, unions are concerned with unemployment and agree to lower wage settlements (point A_2). As costs rise, prices will have to adjust according to the mark-up principle. This process is picked up in Box 12.3.

Unemployment would remain unaffected by fluctuations in the goods market if the wage bargaining schedule were vertical. This would require full nominal wage flexibility, i.e. a readiness by workers and their unions to accept any nominal wage level consistent with equilibrium unemployment. Nominal wage rigidity is the reason why short-run fluctuations in unemployment occur during business cycles. That wages respond to pressure from the goods market transmitted to the labour market is captured by the cyclical—or bargaining power—factor $f(U - \bar{U})$ in (12.7).

12.4.3. Non-Labour Costs[16]

The remaining 'non-labour' production costs correspond to the other factors of production—capital,

land—and to intermediate inputs—unfinished goods, materials, and energy. The costs for a firm of intermediate inputs are the sales prices charged by other firms. When aggregating at the country level, one firm's cost is another's selling price, tracked down by the overall inflation rate. Imported intermediate goods and raw materials are therefore left out of this aggregation process. Their prices rise with the exchange rate; as long as PPP remains approximately true, in the end they too simply reflect domestic inflation. Similarly, the cost of capital includes dividend payments to shareholders and interest payments on bonds or bank loans. These costs also broadly track the inflation rate.

The variety of taxes borne by the firms relate directly to production and affect the final selling price—value added or excise taxes, profit taxes, establishment and property taxes, and so on. Other costs imposed by governments are implicit, but may have a significant impact (environment protection or consumer protection legislation, for example). All of these government-induced costs affect only the *price level*; to have an effect on the rate of inflation—the *rate of change* in the price level—they would have to increase continuously, which seems less likely.

All in all, it is safe to think of non-labour costs as following core inflation $\bar{\pi}$ plus an additional component—denoted *s*—which is meant to capture **supply shocks** such as the oil shocks, or other exogenous increases in non-labour production costs such as tax hikes or additional regulation:

---

[16] This section is slightly more difficult than the rest of the text. Students may jump to the last paragraph without loss of continuity.

Table 12.2. Variability of Inflation, Unemployment, and Imported Commodity Prices in Britain, 1888–1990[a]

	1982–90	1969–82	1888–1965
Inflation	0.36	0.44	2.29
Unemployment	0.20	0.49	0.92
Real commodity prices	0.09	0.20	0.17

[a] Variability is measured as the coefficient of variation, the ratio of the standard deviation to the mean. Commodity prices are deflated by the consumer price index.

Sources: Mitchell (1978; 1988); Maddison (1991)

$$(12.8) \quad \frac{\Delta(\text{average non-labour costs})}{\text{average non-labour cost}} = \bar{\pi} + s.$$

The supply shock term can be positive or negative. It is a catch-all for exogenous disturbances affecting production costs, hence its label. As long as non-labour costs simply follow the core rate of inflation, the supply shock term is zero. The way to think about it is that it is close to zero most of the time or on average, with occasional significant positive or negative deviations.

12.4.4. Putting It All Together

Having seen how firms set prices given costs, and then how costs are set given prices, all that remains is to consolidate the accounts. First, labour costs increase if nominal wages grow faster than labour productivity (see (12.6)). Nominal wage growth, in turn, exceeds labour productivity gains by the core rate of inflation and the cyclical factor (see (12.7)). So productivity effects cancel out and labour costs simply follow trend inflation *plus* the cyclical or bargaining power effects. Adding (12.6) and (12.7) gives

$$(12.9) \quad \frac{\Delta(\text{average labour costs})}{\text{average labour cost}} = \bar{\pi} - f(U - \bar{U}).$$

Having accounted for both labour and non-labour costs, it is now a short step to arrive at the final description of price setting:[17]

---

[17] This is obtained by inserting (12.9) and (12.8) into (12.5), and combining the result with (12.4), plus the assumption that the rate of change of marginal and average costs is equal:

$$\pi = \Delta MC/MC = \Delta AC/AC$$
$$= (1 - \alpha)[\bar{\pi} - f(U - \bar{U})] + \alpha(\bar{\pi} + s)$$
$$= \bar{\pi} - (1 - \alpha)f(U - \bar{U}) + \alpha s$$

$$(12.10) \quad \underset{\substack{\text{actual} \\ \text{inflation}}}{\pi} = \underset{\substack{\text{core} \\ \text{inflation}}}{\bar{\pi}} - (1 - \alpha)\underset{\substack{\text{cyclical} \\ \text{demand} \\ \text{pressure}}}{f(U - \bar{U})} + \underset{\substack{\text{supply} \\ \text{shock}}}{\alpha s.}$$

The step-by-step accounting of price- and wage-setting decisions points to three main sources of changes in the inflation rate: (1) core or underlying inflation, as perceived by wage negotiators and also affecting the pricing of non-labour costs; (2) cyclical demand pressure, transmitted from labour markets to goods markets; and (3) occasional positive or negative supply shocks.

12.4.5. Solving the Puzzle: the Augmented Phillips Curve

Does this accounting explain the Phillips curve puzzle—both its existence over decades and its apparent instability over particular periods of time? The Phillips curve claims that inflation depends only on the level of unemployment. The inflation account (12.10) shows that cyclical labour market conditions do indeed matter, but along with core inflation and occasional supply shocks. For a Phillips curve to be visible, core inflation and non-labour production costs must be stable.

Table 12.2 presents the year-to-year average variability in the rate of inflation, the rate of unemployment, and commodity prices over selected sub-periods in Britain. It turns out that, over the period surveyed by Phillips, commodity prices were quite stable. Furthermore, the general level of prices was largely trendless; inflation therefore was negligible, and core inflation was probably near zero, at least rather stable. During this period, focusing on unemployment as the Phillips curve view of inflation makes sense.

During the 1970s, however, price and commodity

shocks were a major source of instability. As inflation rose, core inflation rose as well, and became more variable, reflecting changing expectations of the future. The Phillips curve's demise reflects the emergence of two other explanatory factors of inflation. Modern Phillips curves are therefore **augmented**, meaning that they incorporate core inflation, and allow for supply shocks.

12.5. Inflation and Unemployment

12.5.1. The Phillips Curve Reconstructed

The inflation account (12.10) shows that, when supply shocks are zero and when actual unemployment equals its equilibrium rate, actual inflation equals its core rate:

(12.11) With $s = 0$, $\pi = \bar{\pi} - (1 - \alpha)f(U - \bar{U})$;

so: $\pi = \bar{\pi}$ when $U = \bar{U}$.

This situation corresponds to point A in Figure 12.10. At point B unemployment is below equilibrium so the demand pressure pushes inflation above its core rate. Conversely, point C corresponds to the case where inflation is below its core rate because the unemployment rate is above equilibrium. While this resembles the Phillips curve, there is a crucial difference: its position is determined by point A, that is, by the core inflation rate $\bar{\pi}$ and the equilibrium rate of unemployment $\bar{U}$.[18]

There is no presumption whatsoever that either core inflation or the equilibrium rate of unemployment is constant over time. If either changes, point A moves, and so does the Phillips curve. Potentially, there exists an infinity of Phillips curves, corresponding to the infinity of values that the core inflation rate or the equilibrium rate of unemployment can take. It just so happened that, over the hundred years surveyed by Phillips, the core rate of inflation and the equilibrium rate of unemployment did not change much, so there seems to have been just one Phillips curve.

12.5.2. Core Inflation and the Long Run

The notion of core inflation was introduced as a way of capturing the rate of inflation agreed upon during wage negotiations. It has both a backward-looking (catching up with past inflation) and a forward-looking component (what inflation is expected to be in the future). Somehow, it must be related to the actual rate of inflation. How this is so in the short run is considered in the next chapter. Here we deal with the long run.

As negotiators consider the amount of inflation to be factored in wage settlements, they strive to guess it accurately. Of course, employees have an incentive to overstate the core rate of inflation, but employers have the opposite incentive. If there were no uncertainty and both sides always knew *ex ante* what inflation would be over the lifetime of the wage contract, core and actual inflation would just be equal. Uncertainty

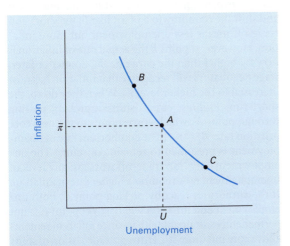

Figure 12.10. The Augmented Phillips Curve

By definition, point A represents the case where actually observed inflation π is at its core rate $\bar{\pi}$ and where unemployment is at its equilibrium rate. When unemployment is low, actual inflation is above core inflation rate (point B). When unemployment is high, actual inflation is below core inflation (point C).

[18] This is why the equilibrium rate of unemployment is sometimes called the NAIRU: the non-accelerating inflation rate of unemployment. At point B inflation accelerates above its core rate; at point C it decelerates. Only at A does it stabilize.

means that core inflation must be guessed. More often than not, the guesses are wrong. Yet, the principle of rational expectations implies that wage negotiators do not make systematic forecast errors. On average, although forecasts are almost always incorrect, the errors are largely unsystematic and average to zero.

This observation has two important implications. One is that there must be a link between actual inflation π and core inflation $\bar{\pi}$. Somehow core inflation must track, albeit imperfectly, actual inflation. The backward-looking component implies that core inflation *lags* behind actual inflation, but the forward-looking component implies that core inflation *leads* actual inflation. It is the presence of both components that makes the link rather clouded.

The second implication concerns the long run. If actual and core inflation rates are equal on average, (12.11) establishes that, in the absence of supply shocks, on average unemployment is at its equilibrium level. This is why the long-run Phillips curve is vertical as in Figure 12.7. The long run corresponds to the time it takes for core and actual inflation to catch up with each other. Views vary about how quickly this happens, and herein lie the deepest controversies in macroeconomics. These are studied in Chapter 16.

The vertical Phillips curve describes the long run if we believe that core inflation is slow to catch up with actual inflation. Alternatively, we can look at it as a representation of the 'average' when we consider that core inflation simply moves about actual inflation. In any case, there cannot be a long-lasting trade-off between unemployment and inflation. Demand policies cannot move the actual unemployment rate permanently away from its equilibrium level. This is why one of the lessons to be learned from Figure 12.6 is that actual unemployment rates move about equilibrium levels that have shifted over time, as reported in Table 6.8. These successive changes in equilibrium unemployment imply rightwards shifts of short-run Phillips curves.

12.5.3. From the Short to the Long Run

Figure 12.11 displays a short-run and a long-run Phillips curve. Point A, which is on both curves, represents the long-run equilibrium, when actual and core inflation are equal $(\bar{\pi}_1)$ and actual unemployment is at

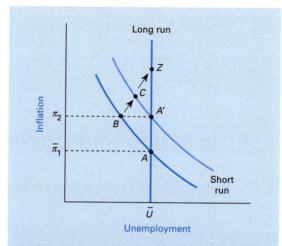

Figure 12.11. From the Short to the Long Run

For a given core rate inflation, the economy can sustain lower unemployment at the cost of higher inflation. This trade-off is not permanent, however. When core inflation rises to be consistent with higher actual inflation, the short-run Phillips curve shifts up. In the long run (point Z) there is no trade-off.

its equilibrium level. By construction, the particular short-run Phillips curve that goes through point A corresponds to core inflation rate $\bar{\pi}_1$. Now imagine a demand expansion designed to reduce unemployment and shift the economy to a point like B: the short-run trade-off means less unemployment but more inflation. However, at point B the actual rate of inflation is now π_2, higher than the core rate $\bar{\pi}_1$. Sooner or later, wage negotiators will recognize that inflation has now increased to the higher level π_2. When they do so, the short-run Phillips curve shifts upward, passing through point A', which corresponds to the new core inflation rate $\bar{\pi}_2 = \pi_2$. (The equilibrium rate of unemployment is presumed to remain constant.) The unemployment-inflation trade-off worsens: any level of unemployment now requires a higher rate of inflation. If the authorities react by picking point C, both unemployment and inflation will rise. Yet point C is not permanently sustainable either, since inflation remains above core inflation $\bar{\pi}_2$. Through a succession of shifts in the short-run Phillips curve and associated—increasingly desperate—policy reactions, eventually unemployment must return to the equilibrium rate.

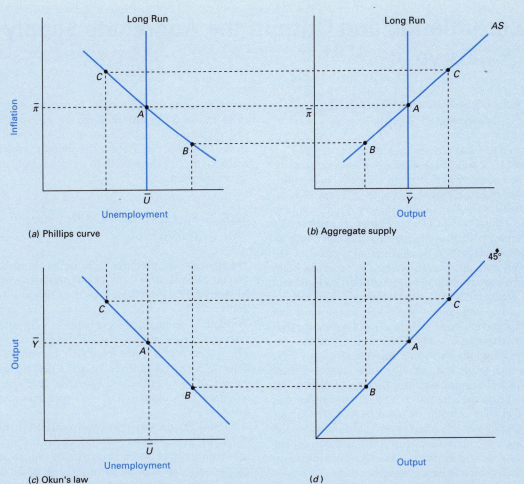

Figure 12.12. The Aggregate Supply Curve

Point *A* represents the long-run equilibrium: inflation is determined by money growth, unemployment is at its equilibrium rate, and output is on its trend growth path. Point *B* represents higher than equilibrium unemployment. Panel (*a*) shows that actual inflation is below
core inflation, and this is reported in panel (*b*). Panel (*c*) shows that the higher unemployment occurs when output is below its trend growth level. The lower output level is reflected
via panel (*d*) to panel (*b*) to determine the corresponding point *B*. The same procedure finds
point *C* in panel (*b*) which corresponds to point *C* in panel (*a*). The aggregate supply curve is
upward-sloping: for a given rate of core inflation, inducing suppliers to produce more requires more inflation. The position of the aggregate supply curve is determined by core
inflation $\bar{\pi}$ and trend output $\bar{Y}$.

12.6. Inflation and Output: the Aggregate Supply Curve

12.6.1. Long-Run and Short-Run Aggregate Supply

Section 12.3 has already indicated that the Phillips curve can be seen as a description of aggregate supply. This section derives the aggregate supply curve, which is used extensively in later chapters. Figure 12.12(a) reproduces the short- and long-run Phillips curves. Panel (c) uses Okun's law to convert fluctuations in unemployment into fluctuations in GDP about its trend growth path $\bar{Y}$. Using panel (d) to recover GDP delivers both inflation and output in panel (b). Point A is the long-run equilibrium: output is on trend and actual inflation is equal to core inflation. This fact can be used to determine the position of the short-run Phillips curve. To equilibrium unemployment in panel (a) corresponds trend GDP in panel (b) and the corresponding long-run vertical aggregate supply (AS) schedule. Point B in panel (a) describes a cyclical downturn: unemployment is high and inflation has fallen below the core rate $\bar{\pi}$. Okun's law implies that the real GDP is below its trend level $\bar{Y}$. The corresponding point B in panel (b) is below and to the left of long-run equilibrium point A. Similarly, an expansion is described by point C. The result is a short-run upward-sloping aggregate supply curve.

An alternative way of obtaining the aggregate supply curve is to substitute Okun's law (12.2) into the inflation account (12.10) to obtain:[19]

$$(12.12) \qquad \pi = \bar{\pi} + (1 - \alpha)h(Y - \bar{Y}) + \alpha s.$$

When there is no supply shock ($s = 0$), this relationship implies that when GDP is at trend ($Y = \bar{Y}$) actual and core inflation are equal ($\pi = \bar{\pi}$), hence at point A in Figure 12.12(b). When GDP is above trend ($Y > \bar{Y}$), the demand pressure from the labour market pushes actual inflation above the core inflation rate ($\pi > \bar{\pi}$), hence to point C. Conversely, point B corresponds to GDP below trend ($Y < \bar{Y}$).

The aggregate supply curves convey two messages. In the short run, it is possible for GDP to fluctuate about its trend growth path, and such fluctuations are accompanied by movements of inflation about the core rate, in the same direction. In the long run, GDP must return to its growth path, regardless of what the inflation rate is: the economy is dichotomized. In the long run, real forces determine the growth of real activity and the growth of money supply determines inflation.

12.6.2. Factors that Shift the Supply Curve

The aggregate supply curve shifts for the same reasons that the Phillips curve shifts. Its position is determined by point A, that is by trend growth GDP and core inflation. This gives two reasons for the curve to shift. The first is a change in the core or underlying inflation rate: an increase in core inflation shifts the curve up. The second reason is that trend GDP rises as the outcome of long-run growth. To avoid dealing with a curve that always moves to the right, later chapters will draw the output gap ($Y - \bar{Y}$) on the horizontal axis.

A third reason why the supply curve may shift is the occurrence of real supply shocks. An s % increase in real non-labour production costs—owing to an exchange rate depreciation or to a rise in commodity prices—raises inflation and the curve by αs %. If the increase is temporary, the curve will return to its initial position.

Are commodity prices an important source of disturbances affecting the aggregate supply curve? Figure 12.13 recalls the oil shock and also illustrates the role of exchange rates. A currency appreciation makes foreign goods cheaper when expressed in domestic prices, including imported materials and primary commodities. Exchange rate changes and commodity price changes may reinforce or offset each other. For example, the well-timed appreciation of the German currency in the 1970s had the effect of cushioning the blow of the first oil shock on Germany, since it made the price of oil increase by less in Deutschmarks than in dollars.[20]

---

[19] The function $h(Y - \bar{Y})$ is increasing in $Y - \bar{Y}$ and $h(0) = 0$. It is defined as $h(Y - \bar{Y}) = f[g(Y - \bar{Y})]$.

[20] Formally, let P^* be the price of oil in \$, P the price in DM, and E the exchange rate (DM per \$). Then $P = EP^*$: when E declines (the DM appreciates) P increases by less than P^*. Formally: $\Delta P/P = \Delta P^*/P^* - \Delta E/E$.

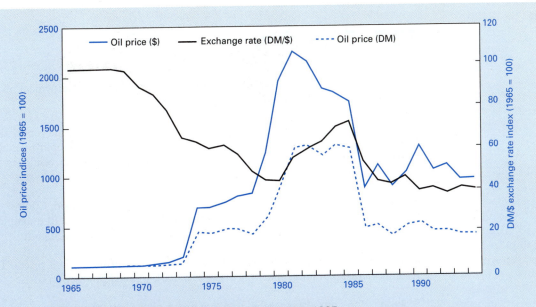

Figure 12.13. The Oil Shocks and the DM, 1965–1995

The Deutschmark (DM) propitiously appreciated in the early 1970s (shown as a decline in the index, calculated in European terms) when oil prices, set in US dollars, quadrupled. Valued in DM, oil prices rose much more modestly. At the time of the second oil shock in 1979–80, in contrast, the DM depreciated *vis-à-vis* the dollar, which worsened the supply-side effect in Germany. In 1986 the counter-oil shock was accompanied by another appreciation of the DM, and therefore an even stronger positive supply shock for Germany.

Source: IMF

BOX 12.4. WHICH PRICE: THE CPI OR THE GDP DEFLATOR

Which price measure should be used when thinking about the Phillips curve or aggregate supply? Wage-earners care about their purchasing power and therefore use the consumer price index (CPI) in wage negotiations. Domestic producers set prices looking at their value added, and the GDP deflator is based on value added. The CPI includes imported goods used for consumption and, indirectly, imported materials incorporated into locally produced and consumed goods; the GDP deflator ex-cludes both. As an example, consider a supply shock, say an increase in commodity prices. This does not affect the GDP deflator but feeds through production costs to the CPI as in equation (12.10). On the other hand, wages are tied to the CPI. As they increase firms face increased pro-duction costs and, through mark-up pricing, a rising GDP deflator. In the end, the answer is: to a first approxima-tion, it does not matter too much which price measure is used.

12.7. Summary

1. Price or wage rigidities explain fluctuations of output and unemployment about their long-run or equilibrium levels.

2. The Phillips curve was once considered a sufficient description of the supply side. Its message was that there existed a permanent trade-off between unemployment and inflation. Thus, output could rise to meet an increase in demand but would, in the process, generate a higher rate of inflation.

3. Since the late 1960s, apparently stable Phillips curves have vanished. Contrary to the notion of an inflation–unemployment trade-off, both inflation and unemployment rose in the mid-1970s and early 1980s, a phenomenon called stagflation.

4. Accounting for inflation starts with the study of how firms set their prices. The result is mark-up pricing, or setting prices as a mark-up over production costs.

5. Production costs are separated into two broad categories: labour and non-labour costs. Labour costs rise when wages—and related costs—increase faster than labour productivity.

6. Wages are set through negotiations that acknowledge three main factors: core inflation, productivity gains, and the relative bargaining strength of employees and employers.

7. Wage contracts attempt both to catch up on past inflation and to protect wages from future inflation. Core inflation captures both these backward- and forward-looking aspects.

8. The consolidation of inflation accounts describes the actual rate of inflation as responding to: core inflation, demand pressure transmitted from the labour markets to goods markets, and occasional supply shocks.

9. The inflation accounts explain both why a Phillips curve may have existed for a century, and why it disappeared as the result of mounting inflation and the two oil shocks of 1973–4 and 1979–80.

10. In the long run, unemployment returns to its equilibrium rate. Equivalently, the real GDP cannot permanently stray away from its growth trend. In the long run the Phillips curve and aggregate supply schedules are vertical. The economy is dichotomized, growth and real rigidities determine the GDP and unemployment, money growth determines inflation, and there is no trade-off between inflation and unemployment.

11. The Phillips curve describes the supply side and can be transformed into an aggregate supply curve using Okun's law. The supply curve says that, for increased output to be supplied, inflation increases because production—mainly labour—costs are higher.

12. The core rate of inflation and the equilibrium unemployment rate determine the position of the short-run Phillips curve. The position of the aggregate supply curve is

determined by the core rate of inflation and trend GDP. Any change in one of these variables leads to shifts in the short-run schedules.

Key Concepts

- supply and demand sides
- output gap
- Okun's law
- Phillips curve
- wage inflation
- aggregate supply curve
- money illusion
- stagflation
- long-run aggregate supply

- mark-up pricing
- average or unit costs
- real wage rigidity
- nominal wage rigidity
- indexation
- core or underlying inflation rate
- menu costs
- supply shocks
- augmented Phillips curve

Exercises: Theory

1. A government that underestimates the equilibrium rate of unemployment may attempt to reduce the unemployment rate below the equilibrium rate by stimulating aggregate demand. Show the likely outcome of such a policy using the short- and long-run Phillips curves.

2. Show the effect on the short- and long-run Phillips curves of an oil shock, i.e. a once-and-for-all increase in the price of imported energy, assuming that core inflation remains unchanged.

3. Explain how inflation accounting might be modified if wages are fully indexed to the rate of inflation. What difference could it make whether indexation applies on a yearly rather than a monthly basis?

4. What could be the effect on inflation of an increase in value added taxes (VAT) raised to finance government expenditures? Of an increase in corporate profit taxes? Of an increase in personal income taxes? State your assumptions carefully.

5. Incomes policies are designed to prevent wages from rising with inflation. They work by imposing a ceiling on nominal wage increases. How can such policies be interpreted in the Phillips curve framework?

6. Give reasons why contractionary monetary policy under flexible exchange rates reduces inflation.

7. 'Only inflation surprises can affect the rate of unemployment.' Discuss.

8. Give at least three interpretations to the concept of 'imported inflation'.

9. How might an expansionary fiscal policy be a source of reduced inflation in an open economy with flexible exchange rates? Why might an expansionary monetary policy under flexible exchange rates increase inflation?

10. 'The Phillips curve exists as long as governments can refrain from exploiting it.' Comment.

11. Give examples of why the core rate of inflation might be (*a*) partly backward-looking; (*b*) partly forward-looking.

12. A Phillips curve is represented by the following relationship:

$$\pi - \bar{\pi} = -10(U - \bar{U}) + s, \qquad \text{where } s \text{ is a supply shock term.}$$

(*a*) Draw the curve when $\bar{\pi} = 4\%$ and $\bar{U} = 7\%$; when core inflation rises to 6%.
(*b*) A reform reduces equilibrium unemployment to 5%. Explain the effect on inflation and unemployment in the short term, and then in the long term.
(*c*) Okun's law is given by: $U - \bar{U} = -(Y - \bar{Y})/10{,}000$. Write down and draw the *AS* curve for the same values as (*a*); for $\bar{Y} = 10{,}000$.

Exercises: Applications

1. It is often asserted that some central banks (e.g. the German Bundesbank or the Swiss National Bank) have anti-inflation 'credibility': they have a reputation for keeping inflation low. How does this affect the core inflation rate? In particular, how might it influence the reaction of core inflation to commodity price shocks?

2. When an oil shock occurs, does it matter for the Phillips curve whether the country is an oil-importer or is self-sufficient like the UK?

3. Three types of consumer price index are being used in the UK: the retail price index (RPI), RPIX, which excludes the interest charge on mortgage loans, and RPIY, which also excludes indirect taxes (VAT, duties, local taxes, etc.). These distinctions have been introduced because, using the CPI, a restrictive monetary or fiscal policy might be *inflationary* in the short run. Explain why.

4. In both Western and Eastern Europe, many basic goods such as bread, milk, meat, etc., are directly or indirectly subsidized. One argument in favour of maintaining subsidies is that their removal would be inflationary. Evaluate this argument, being careful to distinguish between a process of *ongoing* inflation and a one-shot price increase.

5. Monetary authorities often try to influence inflation by 'talking', i.e. making pronouncements carefully designed to influence various markets. This can take the

form of being conspicuously optimistic or overly pessimistic, soothing or threatening. Describe the channels by which 'central bank talk' might affect the inflation rate in an economy.

6. Find data to build a Phillips curve for your own country. Try to interpret the evolution from one year to another, using any supplementary information at your disposal.

7. How could a depreciation be a supply shock?

8. Why are wage and price controls usually ineffective? That is, why is it that as soon as they are lifted inflation usually rises rapidly again?

9. Imagine yourself in the 1960s, when the Phillips curve was believed to be stable. How do you imagine political parties were arguing over the most desirable position on the curve?

10. Some Central and Eastern European countries battling inflation in the early 1990s imposed a tax on 'excess wages': the government would set a 'normal' wage level and firms would pay a high tax (sometimes more than 100%) for all wages above that level. How could this affect inflation? Can you think of problems that might be caused by the measure? (Think of the microeconomics of labour markets.)

Suggested Further Reading

The three classics on the Phillips curve are:

Friedman, Milton (1968), 'The Role of Monetary Policy', *American Economic Review*, 58: 1–17.

Phelps, Edmund S. (1968), 'Money-Wage Dynamics and Labor Market Equilibrium', *Journal of Political Economy*, 76: 687–712.

Phillips, A. W. (1958), 'The Relationship between Unemployment and the Rate of Change of Money Wage Rates in the United Kingdom, 1861–1957', *Economica*, 100: 283–99.

For critical views, see:

Gordon, Robert J. (1990), 'What is New Keynesian Economics?' *Journal of Economic Literature*, 28: 1115–71.

Tobin, James (1972), 'Inflation and Unemployment', *American Economic Review*, 62: 1–18.

More recent explanations of the inflation–output trade-off and approaches to contain inflation can be found in:

Ball, Lawrence, Mankiw, N. Greg, and Romer, David (1988), 'The New Keynesian Economics and the Output–Inflation Trade-off', *Brookings Papers on Economic Activity*, 1: 1–65.

Leiderman, Leonard and Svensson, Lars O. (eds.) (1995), *Inflation Targets*, CEPR, London.

For an article that defines and quantifies the concept of core inflation, see:

Quah, Danny and Vahey, S. P. (1995), 'Measuring Core Inflation', *Economic Journal*, 432: 1130–44.

Many central banks (in the UK, Spain, Sweden) now regularly publish an *Inflation Report* which contains detailed analyses and data about current inflationary developments.

Appendix: A Formal Presentation of Mark-up Pricing

The demand for output Q declines with the price of the good. It is represented by the demand function $Q(P)$, where $Q'(P) < 0$. The elasticity of demand η is (minus, to be positive) the logarithmic derivative:

$$(A12.1) \qquad \eta = -\frac{\partial \ln(Q)}{\partial \ln(P)} = -\frac{\partial Q/\partial P}{Q/P}.$$

Let total costs $C(Q)$ be the sum of fixed costs f and variable costs $c(Q)$, with $c'(Q) > 0$, and $c(0) = 0$. The firm's total profit is:

$$(A12.2) \quad \text{Profit} = \underset{\substack{\text{total} \\ \text{revenue}}}{R(Q)} - \underset{\substack{\text{total} \\ \text{costs}}}{C(Q)}$$

$$= \underset{\substack{\text{total} \\ \text{revenue}}}{QP(Q)} - \underset{\substack{\text{fixed} \\ \text{costs}}}{f} - \underset{\substack{\text{variable} \\ \text{costs}}}{c(Q)}.$$

To maximize profit, the firm sets its derivative with respect to output equal to zero. This implies that marginal revenue equals marginal cost:

$$(A12.3) \quad R'(Q) = C'(Q) \qquad \text{or} \qquad MR = MC.$$

It can choose either the quantity produced and sold or the price level, given demand $Q(P)$. If it chooses quantity, then the first-order condition for maximization of profit (A12.2) is:[21]

---

[21] We assume that the second-order condition is satisfied.

$$(A12.4) \qquad P + Q\frac{\partial P}{\partial Q} - C'Q = 0,$$

where $C'(Q)$ is the marginal cost MC. Note that

$$(A12.5) \qquad Q\frac{\partial P}{\partial Q} = \frac{P(\partial P/\partial Q)}{P/Q} = -\frac{P}{\eta}.$$

Then we find that the profit is highest when

$$(A12.6) \qquad P = \frac{C'(Q)}{1 - 1/\eta}.$$

This says that the price level is set as a mark-up θ over marginal cost:

$$(A12.7) \quad P = \theta MC \qquad \text{where } \theta = \frac{1}{1 - 1/\eta} > 1.$$

The mark-up is larger than unity. If the elasticity of demand is constant, so is the mark-up. (In the limiting case where competition is perfect, the elasticity of demand is infinite, the mark-up is equal to one, and firms set marginal costs equal to the (exogenously) given price level.) Note also that, when average costs are constant, average and marginal costs are equal. Average costs are $AC(Q) = C(Q)/Q$ are constant when $\partial AC/\partial Q = (QC' - C)/Q^2 = 0$. This implies that $QC' = C$, or that C' (marginal costs) $= C/Q$ (arerage costs).

13

Aggregate Demand and Aggregate Supply

> Money influences only monetary variables and not real variables in the long run. The problem is 'how long is long?' The 'Keynesian' answer embodied in the concept of the Phillips curve was 'too long to matter!': the 'monetarist' rejoinder was 'shorter than the Keynesians think!'; extreme rationalism provides the answer 'too short for anything else to matter!'—answers that no one concerned with either the history or the practice of stabilization policy is likely to accept.
>
> Harry G. Johnson

13.1. Overview

This chapter presents a unified framework for thinking about output and inflation. This framework integrates and unifies many results of previous chapters, and, together with the *IS–LM* diagram, represents the 'workhorse' of macroeconomists. Its main analytical strength lies in the distinction between aggregate demand and aggregate supply. Aggregate demand has been analysed within the *IS–LM* framework under the assumption that prices are constant. The first task is to amend this framework to account for variable prices (inflation). The result is the downward-sloping curve labelled *AD* in Figure 13.1: a higher inflation rate, all other things equal, reduces aggregate demand. The upward-sloping aggregate supply curve is already familiar from the previous chapter. In a market economy demand equals supply, so the position of the economy is described by the intersection of the *AD* and *AS* curves. Separating the two blades of the scissors is often the best way to approach any economic issue.

The *IS–LM* analysis of Chapter 11 showed that the exchange rate regime (fixed or freely floating) is of crucial importance in understanding an economy's reaction to real and financial disturbances. This observation remains valid in the presence of inflation, so this chapter continues to distinguish between the two regimes.

The aggregate supply curve stresses the difference between the short run, when a trade-off is possible between unemployment and inflation, and the long run, when the supply curve is vertical. This distinction is fundamental. In the long run, demand and monetary factors have no effect on real economic conditions. Nominal variables such as inflation and the nominal exchange rate depend only on the money supply. Real variables—for example real GDP, unemployment, or the real exchange rate—are independent of money. In stark contrast, monetary and real factors interact with each other in the short run. Linking the economy's short run to the long run is a key function of the aggregate demand and supply framework. The chapter concludes with a number of examples of the framework's usefulness.

13.2. Aggregate Demand and Supply under Fixed Exchange Rates

13.2.1. Aggregate Demand

13.2.1.1. A long-run restriction

The first channel by which changes in the price level can affect aggregate demand is via the real exchange rate. When the nominal exchange rate (E) is fixed, the real exchange rate (λ) depends on the evolution of prices at home (P) and abroad (P^*). The real exchange rate is:[1]

$$(13.1) \qquad \lambda = \frac{EP^*}{P}.$$

---

[1] Various definitions of the real exchange rate are presented in Ch. 7.

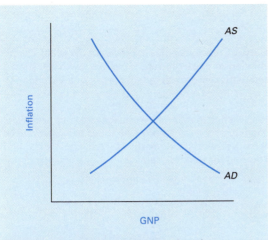

Figure 13.1. Aggregate Demand and Aggregate Supply

The macroeconomy can be fully described by the intersection of the aggregate demand and supply curves. Movements of these curves help to interpret fluctuations in output and inflation.

If domestic inflation (π) exceeds the foreign inflation rate (π^*), the real exchange rate appreciates, external competitiveness worsens, the primary current account deteriorates, and demand for domestic goods decreases. Conversely, if inflation is lower at home than abroad, competitiveness is enhanced, the primary current account improves, and demand for domestic goods rises. The link between the real exchange rate (λ) and the inflation differential under a fixed exchange rate is

(13.2) $$\frac{\Delta\lambda}{\lambda} = \pi^* - \pi.$$

The principle of **purchasing power parity (PPP)**, as we accept it here,[2] implies that the real exchange rate is constant in the long run. If the nominal exchange rate is fixed, PPP rules out a *permanent* difference between domestic and foreign inflation. If domestic and foreign inflation rates diverge, the real exchange rate will appreciate or depreciate without end. Barring continuous exchange rate revaluations or devaluations —studied in Section 13.2.4—deviations between domestic and foreign inflation can only be temporary. Formally,

---

[2] PPP is studied in Ch. 8. To recall, PPP is based on the idea that prices at home, prices abroad, and the nominal exchange rate move to keep the real exchange rate constant.

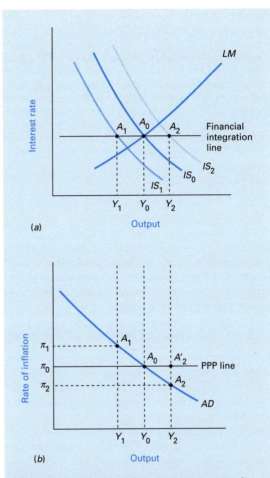

(a)

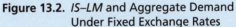

(b)

Figure 13.2. *IS–LM* and Aggregate Demand Under Fixed Exchange Rates

Starting from inflation π_0 at point A_0, an increase (respectively reduction) in the rate of inflation to π_1 (resp. π_2) reduces (resp. improves) the country's external competitiveness. The *IS* curve shifts leftward (rightward) in panel (a). The resulting decrease (resp. increase) in demand is reported in panel (b).

(13.3) $$\pi = \pi^* \qquad \text{in the long run.}$$

This restriction is represented in Figure 13.2(b) as the horizontal long-run PPP line. Since money growth determines inflation in the long run, the PPP line is in fact a restriction on monetary policy. The result that monetary policy independence is lost under a fixed exchange rate regime with fixed prices—the *IS–LM* (Mundell–Fleming) framework—is also true in the presence of inflation. As the central bank intervenes in foreign exchange markets to defend the parity, the

---

BOX 13.1. MONEY GROWTH UNDER FIXED EXCHANGE RATES

The real money supply must match the needs of a growing economy. If the economy grows at a rate g, and the elasticity of demand is η, then money demand, in real terms, grows at rate ηg. The nominal money growth rate is the sum of the real money growth rate and inflation. With inflation given by the rest of the world and the GDP growth rate given by real factors in the long run, the rate of nominal money growth consistent with a fixed exchange rate is[3]

$$(13.4) \qquad \Delta M / M = \mu = \pi^* + \eta g.$$

The same relation applies in the rest of the world, linking inflation abroad to the rate of money growth (μ^*) abroad and to the real growth rate of the rest of the world (g^*):

$$(13.5) \qquad \pi^* = \mu^* - \eta g^*.$$

Then we find that, for the exchange rate to be held fixed, domestic money must grow at about the same rate as abroad, faster if the domestic GDP growth is higher, and slower in the opposite case:

$$(13.6) \qquad \mu = \mu^* + \eta(g - g^*).$$

---

domestic money supply is endogenous and money growth must be consistent with the requirement imposed by PPP on the domestic inflation rate. Box 13.1 formally derives the endogenous rate of growth of money under fixed exchange rates.

13.2.1.2. The effect of inflation on demand

In the shorter run, what happens to aggregate demand when the inflation rate increases—or decreases—while nothing else changes? The question can be answered using the IS–LM system, keeping all other factors affecting the position of the IS and LM curves constant. Besides a change in the domestic price level, which affects the IS curve through the real exchange rate, the other exogenous factors are: the 'animal spirits' of businessmen; private wealth and expectations of future conditions; public spending and taxation; and foreign demand, which influences the current account. The position of the LM curve is determined by transaction costs, which are assumed constant, and the real money supply. Under fixed exchange rates with full financial integration, the nominal money supply is endogenous and the LM curve moves to meet the IS curve and the financial integration line.

In Figure 13.2(a) the initial situation at point A_0 is one where the rate of inflation (π_0) is the same as abroad ($\pi_0 = \pi^*$) and where the real money supply is constant because the nominal money supply grows at the same rate as the price level ($\mu_0 = \pi_0$). The IS curve IS_0 corresponds to this inflation rate π_0. What happens when the rate of inflation rises from π_0 to π_1? The real exchange rate appreciates and competitiveness is eroded. The primary current account worsens and demand for domestic output declines. After, say, a

year, the IS curve has shifted to IS_1. Along the LM curve, the interest rate declines, triggering capital outflows and sales of the domestic currency on the exchange markets. To maintain the same parity, the central bank intervenes and buys back its own currency. The money supply declines, and the LM curve moves to the left until it passes through point A_1 at the intersection of the new IS curve and the financial integration line. The effect of a higher inflation rate, after one year, is to reduce aggregate demand. Conversely, if inflation falls below the foreign rate, competitiveness improves, the IS curve shifts to the right, and the higher demand after one year is described by a point like A_2 in panel (a).

In panel (b) the inflation rates and output levels corresponding to points A_0, A_1, and A_2 trace out the short-run **aggregate demand curve**. The curve is downward-sloping because a rising inflation rate weakens the country's external competitiveness which reduces the demand for domestic goods by both domestic and foreign customers. Along the aggregate demand curve, both goods and money markets are in equilibrium. This is because the AD schedule is derived by tracking intersections of IS and LM schedules: being on the IS schedule captures goods market equilibrium, while being on LM corresponds to the money market equilibrium. It is a short-run curve because, as long as domestic inflation differs from foreign inflation, demand continues to change (so that a year later, say, output would have moved further away from Y_0 in Figure 13.2, flattening the demand curve).

13.2.1.3. What Moves the Aggregate Demand Schedule

Under fixed exchange rates, any change that shifts the IS curve, say, rightward also shifts the aggregate demand schedule to the right. For example, at the initial

---

[3] The link between money growth, inflation, and real GDP growth is established in Ch. 8, Box 8.5.

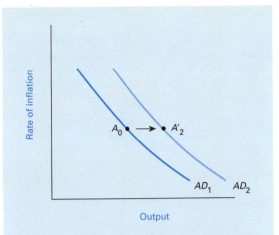

Figure 13.3. Shifts in the Aggregate Demand Curve

Exogenous changes in demand which shift the *IS* curve also shift the short-run aggregate demand curve in the same direction. Point A_2' corresponds to the same point in Figure 13.2, showing a demand increase at the initial inflation rate π_0.

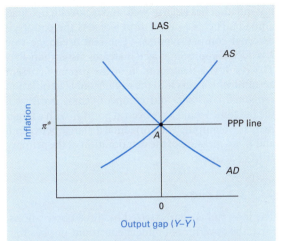

Figure 13.4. Aggregate Demand and Supply under Fixed Exchange Rates

In the long run output is at its trend growth level (a zero output gap) and inflation must be equal to the foreign inflation rate. The short run is determined by the *AD* and *AS* curves. The figure depicts a situation of long-run equilibrium where all four curves intersect.

inflation rate π_0, an increase in government spending is represented in Figure 13.2(*a*) by a shift from IS_0 to IS_2. In panel (*b*) the corresponding point is A_2'. The new demand schedule which passes through A_2' must lie to the right of the initial schedule as shown in Figure 13.3. An exogenous decline in demand shifts the *AD* curve leftwards.

13.2.2. The Complete System

Demand and supply are brought together in Figure 13.4. The demand side comes in two parts: the downward-sloping short-run aggregate demand schedule *AD*, and the horizontal long-run PPP line, which reminds us of the endogeneity of money in fixed exchange rate regimes. The supply side is brought from Chapter 12 and also comes in two parts: the upward-sloping short-run supply curve *AS*, and the vertical long-run schedule *LAS*. In the long run, on the supply side, actual and core inflation are equal ($\pi = \underline{\pi}$). On the demand side, the domestic inflation rate is equal to the foreign rate ($\pi = \pi^*$). The two long-run schedules intersect at point *A* where actual GDP is on its trend growth path. The corresponding zero output gap ($Y - \overline{Y} = 0$) reflects the principle of long-run

dichotomy.[4] The situation depicted in Figure 13.4 corresponds to a long-run equilibrium because the two short-run schedules also go through the long-run equilibrium point *A*. The following sections examine several cases of short-run equilibria distinct from the long-run position and explain how to go from the short to the long run.

13.2.3. Fiscal Policy

13.2.3.1. Short run

An example of fiscal expansion—an increase in public expenditures or a tax reduction—is shown as the rightward shift of the *AD* curve in Figure 13.5. Initially, at point *A*, the economy is long-term equilibrium. (Output *Y* is at its trend level $\overline{Y}$ and actual and core inflation are both equal to the world inflation rate π^*.) The new *AD'* curve shows the short-run effect of fiscal policy, say after one year. At point *B* output has increased—as with the Mundell–Fleming framework—

---

[4] For convenience, the horizontal axis has been redrawn to measure deviations around trend output, or the output gap. This rescaling allows us to focus on the business cycle and to ignore trend output $\overline{Y}$, which is growing continuously over time.

but inflation has risen as well, and is now higher than abroad.[5] The rise in inflation worsens the country's external competitiveness. (The real exchange rate $\lambda = EP^*/P$ appreciates as P increases faster than P^*.) The result is a deterioration of the primary current account which cuts into the expansion. Had inflation remained constant, and competitiveness preserved, the outcome would have been at point B' with a larger increase in output. The horizontal distance between B and B' is a measure of the deterioration of the primary current account.

13.2.3.2. Long run

The long run is characterized by three observations. First, the government budget constraint implies that there can be no permanent fiscal expansion: eventually the expansion move must be reversed and the aggregate demand curve must return approximately to its initial position AD.[6] Second, output must return to the long-run aggregate supply line, so there can be no permanent real effect of a fiscal expansion. Third, and most importantly, inflation cannot deviate for very long from the foreign inflation rate if the exchange rate is to remain fixed. Thus, the inflation rate must return to its long-run PPP line. The conclusion is that in the long run the economy must return to point A.

13.2.3.3. Transition

The actual path taken by the economy from the immediate short run at point B to the long run at point A can be broadly reconstituted using a couple of observations. First, the budget constraint of the government implies that an expansion today must be matched by a contraction later on to pay for debt. That means that the AD curve must eventually shift back, and even remain for some time *below* its initial position. Figure 13.5 is drawn on the assumption that the policy reversal occurs soon after point B has been reached. Another reason for the demand curve to shift back towards its initial position is that, under fixed exchange rates, *only the foreign rate of inflation π^* can ultimately sustain a higher demand curve, i.e. a permanently higher*

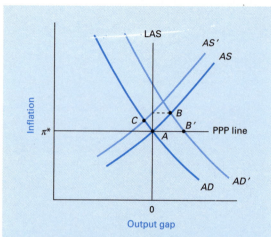

Figure 13.5. Fiscal Policy under Fixed Exchange Rates

Starting at point A, a fiscal policy expansion shifts the AD curve rightwards to AD'. In the short run the economy moves to point B. Thereafter, the fiscal policy expansion must be rescinded to meet the budget constraint, so the AD curve shifts back to its initial position. In the long run the economy will return to its initial position, because inflation must equal foreign inflation: it cannot change if the exchange rate is to remain fixed. In the short run, as trend inflation trails actual inflation, the AS curve shifts upward and the economy moves to point C. As trend inflation returns to its long-run level, the economy ultimately returns to point A.

inflation rate at zero output gap. This is once again the logic of the PPP line.

Second, the backward-looking component of core inflation will begin to react to actual inflation conditions, 'catching up' with (or perhaps even anticipating) current inflation. As a result, the short-run AS curve will shift upward. This leads to a position like point C or even further down along AS'; since AD is temporarily below its initial and long-run position, GDP will be below trend level and the inflation rate will be declining. GDP is below trend because there is no further expansionary impulse coming from fiscal policy, while a higher inflation rate worsens the primary current account. From now on, with output below trend, core inflation exceeds actual inflation.[7] With

---

[5] This shows that the Mundell–Fleming framework can be seen as a special case when the AS curve is flat. Indeed, with prices constant and supply meeting all demand fluctuations, the AS curve is horizontal at the $\pi = 0$ level.

[6] In the meantime, the public debt has risen and must be paid for by a permanent primary budget surplus, which requires that the AD curve shifts back beyond AD. Overlooking this effect is acceptable if the initial expansion does not last long enough to seriously increase the debt–GDP ratio. Ch. 15 returns to this issue at length.

[7] This is a key result of the analysis of the supply curve in Ch. 12: whenever we are to the left of the long-run AS curve, by construction, actual inflation is below core inflation.

BOX 13.2. MITTERRAND'S ECONOMIC POLICIES: FROM SOCIALISM TO FRANC FORT[8]

When François Mitterrand was elected President of France in May 1981, he promised to carry out a Socialist programme of classic vintage. His government implemented a sharp increase in the minimum wage, a new tax on wealth, extensive nationalization of key industries, a work-week reduction at unchanged monthly wages, and new laws further limiting the right of firms to lay off workers. The AS curve shot up and to the left, since these measures had strong adverse supply-side implications: higher labour costs increased inflation in the short run and led to slower growth and more unemployment in the long run as the equilibrium rate of unemployment rose (or, equivalently, the trend GDP decreased). At the same time, the government embarked on expansionary monetary and fiscal policies with the intent of pulling France out of the post-oil shock recession which afflicted all of Europe. Roughly a third of the increase in government spending was financed by borrowing from the central bank, i.e. creating money. This had the effect of moving the AD curve up and to the right. The result was higher inflation and, since the demand boost exceeded the supply shock in the short run, more output. Indeed, France was one of very few advanced countries that did not experience negative growth in the early 1980s. Table 13.1 compares France and its main EMS partner, Germany.

France's expansionary monetary policy was inconsistent with its fixing of the exchange rate in the European Monetary System. The current account deteriorated, and France devalued its currency no less than three times between October 1981 and March 1983. In the end, the Mitterrand government was forced to reverse its earlier policies. On the demand side, fiscal austerity was implemented to undo the earlier easing: public spending was frozen and taxes were raised—there was a surcharge on social security and a compulsory subscription to public borrowing. Monetary policy turned restrictive. By the mid-1980s France had embarked on the 'Franc fort' policy, effectively harnessing monetary policy to the German model: interest rates closely followed Germany's (the horizontal financial integration line of the IS–LM framework) and money growth was officially dedicated to the goal of making the franc as good as the DM (the horizontal PPP line in the AS–AD framework). On the supply side, wage moderation has been pursued relentlessly as an official goal. Promises to reduce the working week still further were quietly shelved. Taxes on corporate profits were reduced.

By 1990 the French inflation rate had fallen below Germany's. Officially, the franc has not been devalued vis-à-vis the DM since 1987. Yet the radical programme of the early 1980s has left severe scars on the supply side of the French economy. Among these is one of the highest indirect tax levels on labour income in the industrialized world. Unemployment has also remained high, despite a return to normal, if not high, rates of GDP growth.

Table 13.1. French and German Economic Performance, 1980–1995

	Money growth (%)		Inflation (%)		GDP growth (%)		Unemployment (%)		Current account (% GDP)	
	France	Germany[a]	France	Germany[b]	France	Germany[b]	France	Germany[a]	France	Germany[b]
1980	9.6	6.2	11.4	5.0	1.6	1.0	6.2	2.7	−0.6	−1.7
1981	11.1	5.0	11.4	4.2	1.2	0.1	7.3	3.9	−0.8	−0.6
1982	12.4	7.1	11.7	4.4	2.5	−0.9	8.0	5.6	−2.1	0.8
1983	13.1	5.3	9.7	3.2	0.7	1.8	8.2	6.9	−0.8	0.9
1984	11.0	4.7	7.5	2.1	1.3	2.8	9.7	7.1	0.0	1.4
1985	7.4	7.6	5.8	2.1	1.9	2.0	10.1	7.1	0.1	2.4
1986	6.6	6.6	5.2	3.2	2.5	2.3	10.3	6.5	0.5	4.3
1987	9.7	5.9	3.0	1.9	2.3	1.5	10.4	6.3	−0.2	4.1
1988	8.4	6.9	2.8	1.5	4.5	3.7	9.9	6.3	−0.3	4.3
1989	9.4	5.5	3.0	2.4	4.3	3.6	9.4	5.6	−0.5	4.8
1990	8.9	4.2	3.1	3.2	2.5	5.7	9.0	4.8	−1.0	3.5
1991	2.5	6.3	3.1	3.9	0.8	5.0	9.5	4.2	−0.5	−1.1
1992	5.3	7.6	2.3	5.5	1.2	2.2	10.0	4.5	0.1	−1.2
1993	−1.4	10.9	2.3	3.9	−1.0	−1.1	10.8	5.6	1.0	−1.4
1994	−1.7	8.1	1.6	2.8	2.2	2.5	11.3	6.3	0.6	−1.4
1995			2.1	2.2	3.2	3.0	11.0	6.2	0.6	−1.1

[a] West Germany only.
[b] West Germany 1980–91, unified Germany 1992–5.
Note: Money is M3; inflation is measured by GDP deflator.

Source: European Economy (59), Dec. 1994

core inflation declining, the *AS* curve continues to shift down. The economy moves down along the *AD* curve which eventually settles back at its long-run position as a period of low inflation re-establishes external competitiveness. The trajectory is roughly from point *C* to point *A*.[9]

To summarize, a fiscal expansion is necessarily temporary. Initially it achieves its aim, although at the cost of an increase in the inflation rate and a deterioration in the external position. Over time the GDP returns to its trend path while inflation winds down, tracing out a broad spiral from *A* to *B*, to *C*, and then towards *A* from below. The experience of France in the early 1980s, described in Box 13.2, illustrates the role of a fixed exchange rate regime in shaping economic policies.

13.2.4. Monetary Policy and Realignments

In fixed exchange rate regimes, monetary policy is beyond the control of the central bank. The bank's task is to keep its interest rate close to the rate prevailing in the country to which it pegs its exchange rate, and therefore to supply money as demanded by the public at that interest rate. The loss of monetary independence is illustrated in Box 13.3 for the case of the Netherlands, which has successfully tied the guilder to the Deutschmark.

The only possibility of retaining some degree of

---

[9] Actually, the economy will need to move below point *A*, because a period of lower inflation than abroad is required to bring the real exchange rate back to its initial level.

monetary independence under fixed exchange rates is to introduce capital controls and to change the parity from time to time. Figure 13.7 illustrates the case of a country that undertakes a monetary expansion. When capital controls work, they prevent arbitrageurs from linking domestic interest rates with the foreign rate of return. Consequently, the financial integration line ceases to be binding in panel (*a*) and the monetary authorities can shift the *LM* curve to *LM'*, raising the rate of growth of money and reducing the interest rate. In panel (*b*), the monetary expansion is represented by a rightward shift in the aggregate demand schedule to *AD'*. Point *B* in both panels shows that the desired expansionary effect is achieved at the cost of some inflation. However, the effect is temporary, for two reasons.

First, at point *B* actual inflation exceeds core inflation. Over time, core inflation catches up and the *AS* curve shifts upward until it passes through point *C*. There, the rate of inflation has increased by the same amount as the rate of money growth ($\Delta \pi = \Delta \mu$); the real money supply is constant—more precisely, it is growing along with the economy's real growth—and monetary policy has run its course and ceases to have any expansionary impact. Yet—and this is the second reason—point *C* is not sustainable in the long run either, because it is above the PPP line. Inflation is higher at home than abroad, the real exchange rate keeps appreciating, and competitiveness deteriorates. As demand weakens, the *IS* curve shifts to the left and the *AD* curve moves back from *AD'* to *AD*.

There are two ways of restoring external competitiveness eroded by inflation. The first is to reduce inflation below the foreign rate for some period of time. This is rarely done because it implies a long period of low output and high unemployment. One celebrated

---

BOX 13.3. MONETARY POLICY IN THE NETHERLANDS: THE DM STANDARD

Since the creation of the European Monetary System in 1979, the Bank of Netherlands has undertaken to maintain a fixed parity *vis-à-vis* the Deutschmark. Only in two instances, in 1979 and 1982, was the guilder depreciated *vis-à-vis* the mark, each time by a mere 2%. Figure 13.2 illustrates the functioning of a truly fixed exchange rate regime and the loss of monetary independence. The increasing closeness of Dutch and German interest rates seen in panel (*a*) vividly captures the meaning of the financial integration line in the Mundell–Fleming framework. Panel (*b*) shows that the obligation of the Bank of

Netherlands to accommodate domestic money demand at the German interest rate leads to an erratic money growth pattern from year to year. The contrast with the smooth pattern of money growth in Germany is striking. Third, starting in 1990, the Bundesbank has had to tighten its monetary policy because of inflationary pressure from reunification. The Netherlands, of course, had no such reason to adopt a restrictive monetary policy, but nevertheless followed the German lead and let interest rates rise steeply.

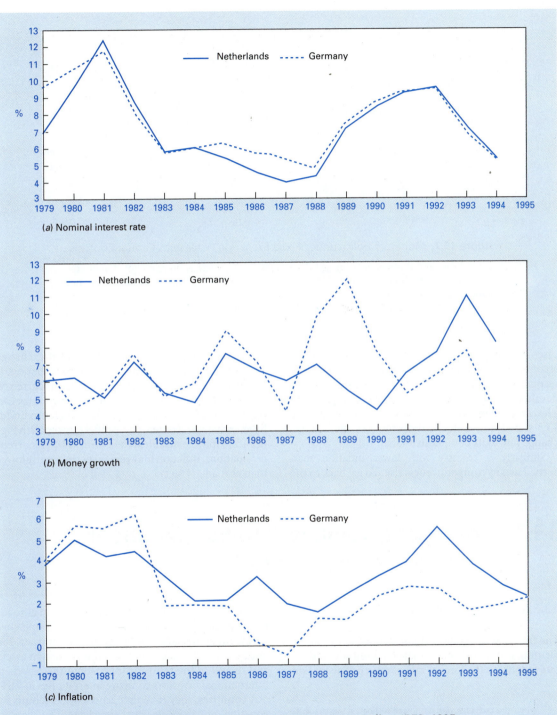

Figure 13.6. Netherlands and Germany: One Monetary Policy, 1979–1995

The near-perfect financial integration of the two countries combined with a fixed exchange rate regime implies that at least one central bank will lose its autonomy. The erratic growth of the Dutch money supply as well as the leading nature of German interest rates suggest that the Netherlands has given up having an independent monetary policy, with the reward of an inflation record even better than its neighbour's.

Source: European Economy

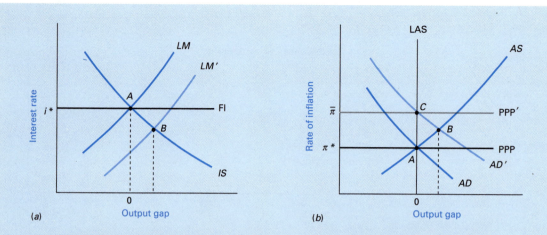

Figure 13.7. Monetary Policy under Fixed Exchange Rates with Capital Controls

Capital controls, if effective, suppress the interest rate constraint in panel (*a*). A monetary expansion succeeds in shifting the *LM* curve to *LM'* and the *AD* curve to *AD'*. At the new equilibrium (point *B* in both panels) domestic inflation exceeds the foreign rate. Periodic devaluations of this sort shift up the PPP line and make point *C* possible.

case—that of Britain after the First World War—is recounted in Box 13.4. Most countries choose the second option, changing the exchange rate parity. A **devaluation** resets an overvalued real exchange rate to a level that restores external competitiveness.[10] Figure 13.8 shows how a devaluation restores the real exchange rate to its competitive value.

Similarly, a country with lower inflation than abroad sees its competitiveness rise. To get back to the initial situation with unchanged nominal exchange rate, it needs to endure a period of higher inflation. It may instead choose periodically to **revalue** its currency. Provided capital controls are effective, a country can regain limited monetary policy independence under fixed exchange rates; temporary effects (point *B* in Figure 13.7) may be sustained for a while. With recurrent revaluations, inflation may remain permanently lower than abroad.

13.3. Aggregate Demand and Supply under Flexible Exchange Rates

13.3.1. Interest Rate Parity Revisited

The financial integration condition of the Mundell–Fleming framework states that the domestic interest rate is equal to the foreign rate of return. The foreign rate of return is not simply the rate of interest abroad, because returns must be compared in the same currency. An appreciation of the domestic currency, for example, reduces the domestic value of foreign assets and therefore the return from holding them. When international investors compare interest rates in various countries, they take that aspect into account by equating returns *given expected exchange rate changes*. Denoting by ε the expected rate of nominal depreciation of the domestic currency ($\varepsilon = \Delta E/E$), the modified **interest rate parity** condition is[11]

---

[10] When the exchange rate is allowed to float, its movements occur in response to market conditions, on a continuous basis. These movements are called an **appreciation** when the currency's value increases), or a **depreciation** in the opposite case. When the exchange rate is fixed, it is the monetary authorities that decide its value. They can change the parity: they can make the currency more valuable in terms of foreign currencies, (a **revaluation**), or they can lower its value (a **devaluation**).

[11] The exact derivation of this condition as well as its modification for risk is presented in Ch. 19.

BOX 13.4. CHURCHILL VERSUS KEYNES

During the First World War the price level doubled in Britain while the fixed exchange rate of sterling against gold was suspended. It was always understood that, once the war was over, sterling would return to the pre-war parity of 85s. per ounce of fine gold. Winston Churchill, the young Chancellor of the Exchequer, was determined to carry out this task and indeed restored the gold parity in 1925. By ruling out a devaluation, Britain's competitiveness could be restored only through falling domestic prices. Table 13.2 shows that the deflation was massive and, true to the Phillips curve, was accompanied by a significant rise in unemployment. In fact, although Britain maintained the gold parity in 1931, prices never quite recovered to the pre-war level, and unemployment remained high, even before the Great Depression. John Maynard Keynes, who was critical of this policy, wrote later that 'the loss of national wealth entailed . . . was enormous. If we assume that only half the unemployment was abnormal, the loss of national output may be estimated at more than £100 million per annum—a loss that persisted over several years.'[12]

Table 13.2. Britain after the First World War: the Consumer Price Index, Inflation, and Unemployment, 1913–1931

	CPI (1913 = 100)	Inflation (%)	Unemployment (%)
1913	100	2.0	2.1
1919	219	9.5	2.4
1920	248	13.2	2.4
1921	224	−9.7	14.8
1922	181	−19.2	15.2
1923	176	−2.8	11.3
1924	176	0.0	10.9
1925	176	0.0	11.2
1926	171	−2.8	13.7
1927	167	−2.3	10.6
1928	167	0.0	11.2
1929	167	0.0	11.0
1930	157	−6.0	14.6
1931	148	−5.7	21.5

Sources: Maddison (1991); Mitchell (1978)

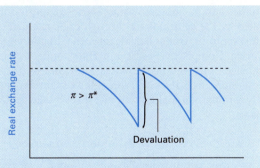

Figure 13.8. Realignments Restore the Real Exchange Rate

With a higher rate of inflation at home, the real exchange rate appreciates. A devaluation resets the real exchange rate to restore competitiveness. Repeating this procedure periodically permits the economy to sustain a higher rate of inflation than abroad.

(13.7) $i = i^* + \varepsilon.$

In this expression, i^* represents the nominal foreign interest rate. If the domestic currency is expected to depreciate by, say, 5% over the next year, the domestic interest rate must be 5% higher to compensate for the capital loss.[13] If instead an appreciation is anticipated, ε is negative and the domestic interest rate is lower than abroad.

13.3.2. Aggregate Demand and the Complete System

13.3.2.1. The effect of inflation on demand

The effect of inflation on aggregate demand is explored in Figure 13.9(*a*). Once again, we start by assuming that all the exogenous factors that affect demand (the *IS* and *LM* curves) are assumed to remain unchanged. This applies to fiscal policy instruments and private expectations affecting consumption and investment.

---

[12] J. Keynes (1930: 165).

[13] In Ch. 11 we implicitly assume that $\varepsilon = 0$. Given that prices are taken to be constant at home and abroad, PPP would indeed predict a constant exchange rate.

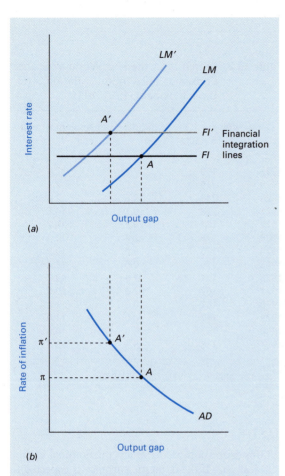

(a)

(b)

Figure 13.9. *IS–LM* and Aggregate Demand under Flexible Exchange Rates

The figure shows the effect of an increase in the rate of inflation on aggregate demand when the rate of nominal money growth remains constant (μ). Starting at point *A* with an inflation rate π, inflation rises to π'. This reduces the rate of real money growth and moves the *LM* curve to the left in panel (*a*). Demand is reduced (point *A*), hence the downward-sloping curve in panel (*b*).

An 'unchanged monetary policy' means a constant rate of nominal money growth (μ), which, under flexible exchange rates, determines the rate of inflation in the long run.[14]

Given the rate of growth of money, when the rate of inflation increases from π to π', the rate of growth of the real money supply (*M/P*)—measured as (μ − π)—decreases and the *LM* curve reaches, say, after a year

the position *LM'* in panel (*a*). If, as is likely, the higher inflation rate prompts the expectation of an exchange rate depreciation, the expected return on foreign assets increases and the financial integration line shifts up since a higher rate of interest is now required.[15] The subsequent behaviour of the *IS* curve depends on what happens to the real exchange rate. While this is interesting in its own right, it is a difficult question to answer directly.[16] The important thing to remember is that, under flexible exchange rates, the position of the *IS* curve is endogenous (see Chapter 11): the exchange rate will adjust until, through its effect on the primary current account, the *IS* curve passes through point *A'*. The *LM* curve and financial integration line fully characterize the outcome, and we can safely ignore the *IS* curve and the real exchange rate.

The overall effect of a higher rate of inflation is a decline in output. Reporting this result in panel (*b*) establishes that the short-run aggregate demand curve is downward-sloping. It is a short-run curve because, as long as the inflation rate stays high, the real money stock growth rate is declining and the *LM* curve keeps shifting to the left.

The short-run aggregate demand curve is downward-sloping under both fixed and flexible exchange rates, but for different reasons. When exchange rates are fixed, inflation affects demand through external competitiveness. Inflation does not affect the real money supply because money is endogenously supplied by the central bank through exchange market interventions. Under flexible rates, the situation is reversed. Competitiveness is under the dominating influence of the nominal exchange rate, not of prices. Inflation affects the evolution of the real money supply for any nominal growth rate μ set by the central bank.

13.3.2.2. What moves the demand curve

The strong result from Chapter 11—that over time movements in the *IS* curve are 'crowded out' by exchange rate movements—remains valid. In the end, neither fiscal policy, nor animal spirits, nor any other exogenous change in demand can shift the aggregate demand curve for very long because these impulses are offset by a change in the real exchange rate. The

---

[14] According to (8.4), the long-run inflation rate is π = μ − η*g*.

[15] This is not automatic because in the long run inflation must return to its initial level if the rate of money growth remains unchanged, and PPP predicts that the rate of depreciation is driven by the inflation differential. If the interest rate is of short maturity, it is shorter-run inflation that matters. For longer maturities the financial integration line may remain unchanged. The conclusions are not affected by this distinction.

[16] However, this is an excellent, if challenging, exercise.

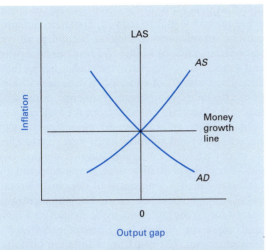

Figure 13.10. Aggregate Demand and Supply under Flexible Exchange Rates

In the long run output is at its trend growth level (a zero output gap) and the money growth rate determines the rate of inflation. The figure depicts long-run equilibrium when the short-run aggregate demand and supply curves pass through the same point as the long-run schedules.

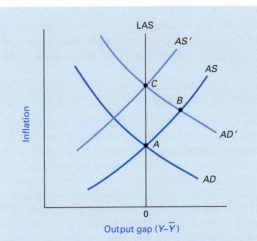

Figure 13.11. Monetary Policy under Flexible Exchange Rates

Starting at point A, a monetary policy expansion shifts the AD curve rightwards to AD'. In the long run the economy will settle at point C, with GAP equal to trend output and the increase in inflation equal to the increase in the money growth rate. Short-run equilibrium occurs at point B. Thereafter core inflation tends to its long-run level and the economy moves from point B towards point C.

aggregate demand curve shifts when the *LM* curve does, primarily when the real money supply is changing. *Under flexible exchange rates, the nominal growth rate of the money supply is the sole determinant of the position of the AD curve.*

13.3.2.3. The complete system

Figure 13.10 presents the complete system under flexible exchange rates. It includes the short- and long-run aggregate supply curves as well as the short-run aggregate demand curve. The horizontal **money growth line** is the equivalent of the PPP line under fixed rates, except that now the monetary authorities control its position. Being free to choose the rate of growth of nominal money, they can determine the long-run inflation rate. The PPP principle ensures that, in the long run, the exchange rate makes up the difference between the domestic and foreign inflation rates. The figure depicts a long-run equilibrium: actual output is equal to trend output—a zero output gap—as required by the supply side, and inflation is set by money growth as required by the demand side. If the foreign rate of inflation is below the domestic rate, the exchange rate is depreciating; in the opposite case, it is appreciating.

13.3.3. Monetary Policy

13.3.3.1. Long run

The long-run effects of an expansionary monetary policy, i.e. of an increase in the rate of growth of the nominal money supply, are straightforward. The principle of neutrality implies that inflation will increase by the same amount, and so will the rate of change of the exchange rate. The real side of the economy is left unaffected. In Figure 13.11, the economy moves from point A to point C and the vertical distance AC represents the increase in the money growth rate.

13.3.3.2. Short run

The expansionary effect of an increase in money growth is described in Figure 13.11 by the shift of the aggregate demand curve from AD to AD'. The economy moves to point B in the short run: output is raised (and unemployment declines); inflation increases, but by less than the money growth rate; and therefore the real money supply expands. If inflation were to rise immediately in the same proportion as money, the long run would be achieved instantaneously. For a (temporary) expansionary effect to occur, the wage- and price-setting process must have some inertia arising from rigidities somewhere in the economy.

13.3.3.3. Transition

The transition will take the economy in steps from point *B* to point *C*. At point *B*, where output is above its growth trend level, the actual rate of inflation exceeds the core rate. What happens during the transition—and therefore the details of the trajectory—depends on the behaviour of the core rate of inflation. To the extent that it is backward-looking, core inflation is sluggish. Initially the *AS* curve does not move and the economy reaches point *B*. As core inflation begins to track actual inflation, the short-run *AS* curve shifts upward and the economy moves from *B* towards *C*, along curve *AD′*. Along the path from *B* to *C*, actual inflation exceeds the core rate of inflation, while output declines as the real money growth rate is eroded by the rise in inflation.

Yet, core inflation has a forward-looking component which could anticipate that the long run is achieved at point *C*. If core inflation were purely forward-looking, it would immediately adjust to the long-term inflation rate. If the short-run *AS* curve shifts at once to position *AS′*, the transition bypasses point *B* and the economy jumps directly from point *A* to point *C*. In that case neutrality occurs instantaneously and

monetary policy loses its effectiveness. Two conditions are required for that to happen. First, core inflation must be entirely forward-looking. Second, price- and wage-setters must be willing and ready to raise prices and wages to the full extent of the change in core inflation. The existence of either price or wage stickiness or of a backward component in core inflation is what makes the short run different from the long run.

In summary, an expansionary monetary policy increases output and inflation. In the long run the effect is entirely on higher inflation and not at all on output—this is the neutrality result. In the short run, the backward-looking component of core inflation and price or wage stickiness create the non-neutrality needed for an output effect, while the forward-looking component tends to bring neutrality forward to the shorter run. The role of core inflation obviously requires closer scrutiny. This is the task of Chapter 15.

13.3.4. Fiscal Policy

Fiscal policy fails to move the *IS* curve, and therefore aggregate demand, because its effects are ultimately frustrated by the exchange rate reaction. A fiscal expansion leaks abroad because a real appreciation leads to a worsening of the primary current account. A fiscal contraction provokes a real depreciation which generates an increase in demand. For all practical purposes, the aggregate demand curve does not move.

13.4. How to Use the *AS–AD* Framework

This section illustrates how the complete system may be used to analyse important questions. It serves three main purposes: to develop familiarity with the framework; to bring up the role of a number of principles developed earlier; and to consider some recent economic developments of general interest.

13.4.1. Supply Shocks

Supply shocks occur when the production conditions change. Adverse supply shocks include the exogenous increase in factors of production or natural disasters

(bad crops, earthquakes). It also characterizes the shift from central planning to markets in Eastern and Central Europe. Favourable supply shocks result for example from technological advances or the discovery of natural resources. They create difficult problems for policy-makers who are typically ill-equipped to face the consequences—Box 13.5 recalls how oil shocks shattered the world economy after 1973.

13.4.1.1. Short-term policy dilemmas

Until now, the short-run aggregate supply curve has been drawn assuming away supply shocks. When, for example, commodity prices increase faster than goods prices, producers face increased production costs.

Chapter 12 shows that, when producers pass higher intermediate goods prices (s) on to their own prices, inflation is higher for any level of output and of the core rate of inflation:

$$(13.8) \qquad \pi = \bar{\pi} + (1 - \alpha)h(Y - \bar{Y}) + \alpha s.$$

In Figure 13.13 the short-run aggregate supply curve shifts upward from AS to AS'. The move from point A to point B represents **stagflation**, a combination of declining real growth and rising inflation. If the relative price increase is just a one-off event, it might seem that the AS curve will shift back to its initial position. This interpretation is optimistic, however. Facing higher prices, workers may demand higher nominal wages. The backward-looking component of core inflation $\bar{\pi}$ rises, which means that, even after the commodity price increase has been absorbed (s goes back to zero in (13.8)), the AS curve is unlikely to shift back quickly.

This poses a serious dilemma for governments. One solution is to attempt to soften the blow on output and unemployment by adopting an expansionary policy (monetary or fiscal, depending on the exchange rate regime). Aiming at point C, and shifting the AD curve to AD' in Figure 13.13, hastens the return to trend growth but at a higher rate of inflation. Another solution is to attempt to prevent inflation from ever rising so that core inflation never changes. This calls for a prompt *contractionary* policy reaction, moving down the short-run aggregate demand schedule until

it goes through point D. Once the shock has worked itself through (and $s = 0$), the aggregate supply curve moves back to AS and the restrictive demand policy may be lifted to return to point A.

13.4.1.2. The exchange rate regime

What drives the evolution of the short-run aggregate supply curve after the initial shock is core inflation. It tends to increase because of its backward-looking component. The forward-looking component depends on which long-run equilibrium is expected to be reached eventually. If the authorities are known to aim at point A in Figure 13.13, with a restrictive monetary policy, the forward-looking component is likely to act towards bringing core inflation down and the trajectory will shift roughly from A to B and back to A. If instead policy is lax, aiming at point C, core inflation will rise for a while, pushing the AS curve above AS'. The trajectory will be from A to B and beyond, higher and to the left of B along the new AD' curve. However, since we have a negative output gap, core is above actual inflation, so the AS curve will eventually start shifting back towards AS', even though the one-off supply shock is over. The economy winds up at point C.

Under flexible exchange rates, each country can choose its long-run inflation rate and therefore can determine whether point A or point C will be reached. This is not the case with a fixed exchange rate regime where the long-run position is determined by the PPP

BOX 13.5. THE OIL SHOCKS OF THE 1970S AND 1980S

The two oil shocks of 1973–4 and 1979–80 represent a turning point in postwar economic history. We can see from Figure 13.12 how the oil shocks marked the end of the rapid growth performance of most European countries and Japan, and were followed by markedly higher inflation and unemployment rates. By the end of the 1980s inflation had been rolled back, but employment and output growth remained significantly below the golden levels of the 1960s. The challenge posed by oil shocks in fact led to the development of many of the ideas presented in this chapter, just as the *IS–LM* framework was a response to the Great Depression.

Major commodity prices started to rise in the early and late 1970s. While most of these increases were quickly reversed, nominal oil prices increased sixfold in two steps, with a partial reversal in 1986. The role of policy is high-

lighted by the choice of the exchange rate regime. At the time of the first shock, the industrial countries were trying to preserve a system of fixed exchange rates, including several European countries regrouped in the 'Snake' arrangement.[17] Countries that were determined not to let inflation rise did not wish to maintain a fixed exchange rate with a more complacent rest of the world. Some countries, including Austria, Germany, Switzerland, and the Netherlands, opted for the low-inflation strategy; Japan, Italy, Spain, and the UK implicitly opted for the high-inflation approach; most other European countries adopted an intermediate stance with little or no policy reaction. Along the way, the international monetary system based on fixed exchange rates could not accommodate such policy divergences and collapsed.

---

[17] Ch. 20 describes the international monetary arrangements; Ch. 21 focuses on the European experience.

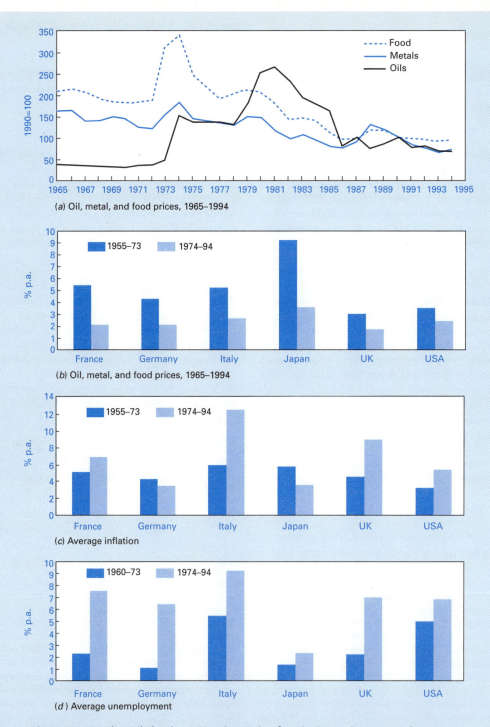

(a) Oil, metal, and food prices, 1965–1994

(b) Oil, metal, and food prices, 1965–1994

(c) Average inflation

(d) Average unemployment

Figure 13.12. The Oil Shocks: A Turning Point for Six Countries, pre and post 1973

Panel (a) shows the prices of key commodities relative to the average consumer price index in the advanced economies. Real oil prices increased from 1973 until 1981, then declined significantly at the time of the counter-oil shock in 1986. Other commodity prices increased earlier, in 1971–2, but were quickly reversed, and in fact declined over the following decade. Panels (b)–(d) confirm that, with few exceptions, since the first oil shock of 1973–4 all key macroeconomic variables (growth, inflation, unemployment) have changed for the worse in OECD countries.

Sources: IMF; OECD *Main Economic Indicators*

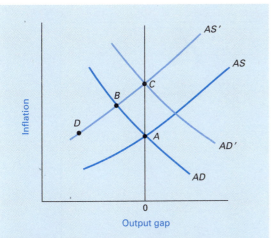

Figure 13.13. An Adverse Supply Shock

An adverse supply shock shifts the *AS* curve up to *AS'*. The economy undergoes stagflation as it moves from point *A* to point *B*. If the authorities decide to avoid a fall in output and a rise in unemployment, they can adopt expansionary demand-side policies and drive the economy back to long-run equilibrium at point *C*. If instead they decide to prevent inflation from rising, they can adopt contractionary demand-side policies and aim at point *D*.

line, i.e. the 'foreign' rest of inflation. What this means is that, in presence of a serious supply shock, a fixed exchange rate regime can be maintained only among like-minded countries, with compatible views of how they will react. Box 13.5 explains the role this issue played after the oil shocks.

13.4.1.3. Lessons from supply shocks

Three general lessons can be drawn. First, an adverse supply shock is bad news. It adversely affects growth, unemployment, and inflation, in contrast with the Phillips curve trade-off. Second, demand management instruments are not appropriate for a supply shock. When the aggregate supply curve moves up and to the left, demand management cannot deal with both inflation and output. Demand-side policies must make the difficult choice between taking the shock as an increase in inflation or as a drop in output with higher unemployment. Third, the exchange regime becomes crucial. A fixed exchange rate can be maintained only among countries that adopt the same strategy.

13.4.2. Demand Shocks

The years 1990–3 were characterized in Europe by a marked slowdown in growth and an increase in unemployment. Figure 13.14 shows the evolution of a measure of agents' expectations in France during this period, alongside the behaviour of the unemployment rate. The confidence indicator is obtained from polls of consumers and firms asked about their spending intentions. The collapse in confidence, which began with the Gulf Crisis in mid-1990, seems to have led the economic downturn. As 'animal spirits' turned skittish, spending slowed down, as did GDP in the familiar income multiplier fashion.

In Figure 13.15 an adverse demand shock is represented by a leftward exogenous shift of the short-run aggregate demand curve. The economy moves from point *A* to point *B*. In principle, the government has instruments at its disposal—monetary or fiscal policy, or both—that could restore the *AD* curve to its original position. This was the standard policy response of the 1960s. During the 1990s, however, the reaction has been remarkably subdued in European countries.

This reluctance is not difficult to explain. After a decade dedicated largely to erasing the inflation scars from the oil shocks (bringing core inflation down), most countries felt that the results had to be consolidated. This meant that monetary growth could not be allowed to rise again. Another policy achievement of the 1980s was the generally successful control over public indebtedness. Most governments felt that their intertemporal budget constraint precluded any decisive use of fiscal policy to counteract a weakening of aggregate demand.[18]

13.4.3. Disinflation

When an economy has settled on a high rate of inflation, how does it come down? Under flexible exchange rates, the answer is simple: reduce the growth rate of the nominal money supply. Under a fixed exchange rate arrangement, it means real appreciation. In both cases, it means bringing the short-run aggregate demand curve from *AD* to *AD'* in Figure 13.16, in an attempt to move from point *A* to point *B* on the long-run aggregate supply curve. The short-run effect of disinflationary policy corresponds to point *C*: inflation

---

[18] Ch. 16 provides more details on governments' reluctance to use their demand management instruments. Ch. 15 studies the public debt situation.

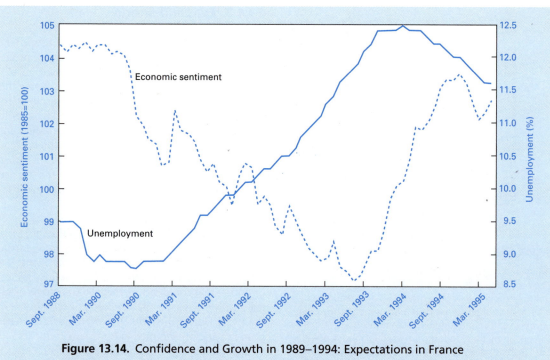

Figure 13.14. Confidence and Growth in 1989–1994: Expectations in France

Consumers' and businesses' confidence as measured by surveys turned downward in 1989 and were further shattered by the invasion of Kuwait and the war with Iraq. Gloom paved the way for a marked slowdown in economic activity and rising unemployment.

Sources: European Economy; OECD, Main Economic Indicators

declines but so does output, while unemployment rises. At point *C* actual inflation is below core inflation. Eventually, the short-run aggregate supply curve returns to *AS'* and the disinflation is complete.

The interesting question is: how long does it take to move from point *C* to point *B*, and how much output is lost along the way? One measure of the **output cost of disinflation** is the **sacrifice ratio**. It compares the cumulated increase in the rate of unemployment with the reduction in inflation achieved during that period. For example, the Phillips curves in Figure 12.6 show disinflation in Italy and the UK over the period 1980–3. In both countries the unemployment rate rose significantly; the corresponding sacrifice ratios over this period are roughly 8 percentage points of inflation for 1 point of unemployment. Clearly, this ratio is only a descriptive device, as it does not control for the credibility of disinflation policies—an important determinant of how quickly core inflation declines.

The output cost of disinflation is lower the faster the *AS* curve comes down. That, in turn, depends on the speed at which core inflation adapts to a declining

inflation rate. The backward component of core inflation is the source of sluggishness. The forward-looking component accelerates the movement. The importance of the backward-looking component is that it depends on wage- and price-setting institutions. The next section looks at the role of wage indexation, and Box 13.6 evaluates the role of the timing of wage negotiations. The forward-looking component is often referred to as the 'psychological' nature of price- and wage-setting. Wage negotiators may have opposing incentives in stating their expectations. It may be good bargaining tactics for workers to argue that prices will rise considerably, while employers invariably prefer to predict declines in the rate of inflation. Jointly, however, employers and employees have an incentive to be as close as possible to target, for errors may be costly in terms of competitiveness and profitability. This often leads to a conservative approach in assessing the future path of inflation: core inflation tends to move slowly over time. Negotiators may be influenced by outside indicators. In particular, the government may play a role by signalling its intentions and calling

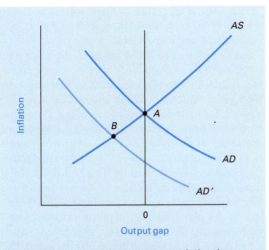

Figure 13.15. An Adverse Demand Shock

An adverse demand shock is represented by a leftward exogenous shift of the short-run aggregate demand curve. The economy moves from point *A* to point *B*. In principle, the government has instruments at its disposal—monetary or fiscal policy, or both—which could restore the *AD* curve to its original position. This was the standard policy response of the 1960s. During the 1990s, however, the reaction has been remarkably subdued in European countries.

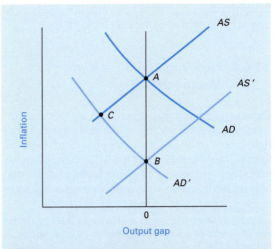

Figure 13.16. Disinflation

Disinflation aims at bringing the economy from point *A* to point *B*. Using demand-side policies implies adopting contractionary monetary or fiscal policies, pushing the aggregate demand curve from *AD* to *AD'*. The short-run equilibrium at point *C* explains why disinflation is usually painful: it requires a period of low output and high unemployment. Long-run equilibrium is achieved at point *B* when the short-run aggregate supply curve has shifted to *AS'*. The speed of this shift depends on the time taken by core inflation to catch up with lower actual inflation.

BOX 13.6. WAGE NEGOTIATIONS: THE TIME DIMENSION

In most European countries and in the USA, wage negotiations are *staggered* over a year or more. One wage negotiation takes into account the previous one, and may even anticipate the next one. Employees do not want to be bettered by other employees. Employers do not want to be underpriced and must hold their labour costs in line. In contrast, in Japan wage negotiations are *synchronized*. They take place every year at roughly the same time, the so-called 'spring offensive' (*shunto*). Each industry opens up bargaining, but closely monitors the state of play elsewhere. When one bargain is struck, it sets the trend and all the others follow quickly. In northern Europe, wage negotiations were for a time centralized and therefore highly synchronized. Elsewhere they are stag-

gered, but some negotiations are *trend-setting*: they result in similar agreements later on and sometimes even trigger readjustments to previously reached agreement, thus injecting a dose of synchronization. With wage staggering, aggregate nominal wages (the average of all nominal wages) move slowly, which retards the return to equilibrium unemployment. The *AS* curve will appear flatter. With full synchronization, average nominal wages are stable between negotiations, and then jump. This implies a steeper *AS* curve. The implications for the economy are profound: either a quick return to the equilibrium unemployment rate if the real wages are set right, or a prolonged departure if they are set incorrectly.

for moderation.[19] In some countries the government may actually even sit at the negotiating table.

13.4.4. Nominal Rigidities and Wage Indexation

Departures from trend growth and equilibrium unemployment occur because of **nominal wage and price rigidities**. Why do those who set prices and wages fail to bring them to a level that would keep the economy on its long-run trend with unemployment at its equilibrium level? Even if wages could be reset every day or

[19] One of these signals might be the rate of wage increase in the public sector, which may be part of government spending (G) but also acts to set a lower bound on expected $\Delta w/w$. More on this can be found in Chs. 15 and 16.

every month, it takes time to know with some degree of accuracy the evolution of the price level. Errors, even if short-lived, are unavoidable.

One solution is to index wages to the price level, matching price increases with wage increases, one for one. Partial indexation compensates for only some fraction of inflation. **Wage indexation** has been adopted, formally or informally, in many countries in an attempt to reduce the risks involved in setting wages when there is much inflation uncertainty. However, indexation institutionalizes the backward-looking component of core inflation. This is a drawback at times of disinflation: Section 13.4.3 has shown that disinflation is faster and less painful the weaker is the backward-looking component of core inflation. This is one reason why the practice has been reduced or abandoned in the 1980s, as is further explained in Box 13.7.

BOX 13.7. PROBLEMS WITH WAGE INDEXATION

Some countries used to have mandatory or mutually agreed indexation schemes for wages. Brazil was particularly advanced, indexing virtually *all* nominal prices, including house rents, corporate balance sheets, taxes, and public utilities rates. Although wage indexation removes some of the costs of high inflation to households and firms, it has serious adverse side-effects. First, indexation generally perpetuates any real wage gain achieved. This gives an incentive to any group of wage-earners to be the first to bid for higher wages. The result is that all groups rush, as much to protect themselves as to achieve a head-start. Second, indexation reduces both public and government support for anti-inflation policies. This is why Germany, ever since its famous hyperinflation in the 1920s, has made indexation illegal. The third drawback is

that indexation makes disinflation costlier in terms of unemployment. When inflation is on the way up, nominal wages trail behind prices: real wages are reduced and labour demand is robust. When inflation is on the way down, wages indexed on past inflation trail actual inflation: real wages rise, firms' profits are squeezed, and unemployment rises. This is why most European countries with legal or simply widespread indexation clauses eliminated them in the 1980s (Belgium, France, the UK, and possibly Italy), much against the will of trade unions. Fourth, indexation eliminates downward real wage flexibility as real wages are at least constant unless there is a sharp burst in inflation. The lack of flexibility is a source of unemployment when an adverse supply shock occurs.

13.5. Summary

1. The macroeconomy is analysed as the interplay of aggregate demand and aggregate supply. This framework emphasizes the distinction between the short run and the long run, when output returns to its trend growth path.

2. The short-run aggregate demand curve is downward-sloping. Under fixed exchange rates, an increase in inflation above the foreign rate erodes external competitiveness and reduces total demand for domestic goods. Under flexible exchange rates, for a given growth rate of the nominal money supply, an increase in the inflation rate lowers the rate of growth of the real money stock, and hence has a contractionary effect on aggregate demand.

3. In the long run, inflation is restricted to be equal to foreign inflation under fixed exchange rates. Under flexible rates, the inflation rate is determined by the rate of growth of the nominal money supply.

4. Only under flexible rates can the monetary authorities set the money growth rate. Some independence can be achieved under fixed exchange rates by the use of capital controls. The possibility of devaluing or revaluing the currency further allows a country under otherwise fixed exchange rates to choose its long-run rate of inflation.

5. Under fixed exchange rates, fiscal policy can affect aggregate demand and output. The effects of a fiscal policy action are, however, temporary for two reasons. First, in the long run output must be back on trend and inflation is determined by the foreign rate of inflation. Second, the fiscal policy action itself is temporary because of the government's budget constraint.

6. A fiscal expansion initially raises the output level at the cost of a higher rate of inflation. Over time, as core inflation rises and the unavoidable retrenchment of fiscal policy occurs, demand returns to trend output.

7. Under fixed exchange rates monetary policy is ineffective. This is also the case for fiscal policy under flexible exchange rates.

8. Under flexible exchange rates, a monetary expansion initially raises output and inflation. Over time, inflation continues to increase, eroding the real money supply and bringing output back to its trend growth path.

9. A supply shock simultaneously lowers output and raises inflation. Demand management policies are ill equipped to deal with a supply shock. They may cushion the fall in income at the cost of more inflation, or reduce the inflationary impact at the cost of a deeper fall in output and more employment.

10. Disinflation requires reducing the rate of monetary growth. It can be costly in terms of lost output and above-equilibrium unemployment.

11. The faster core inflation adjusts, the lower the costs of disinflation. Wage indexation and the staggering of wage negotiations are among the institutional factors that reinforce the backward-looking component of core inflation.

Key Concepts

- PPP line
- aggregate demand curve
- appreciation, depreciation
- revaluation, devaluation
- interest rate parity
- money growth line
- stagflation
- output costs of disinflation
- sacrifice ratio
- nominal wage and price rigidity
- indexation

Exercises: Theory

1. Using the diagrams of Figure 13.2, show the effect of a higher inflation rate on demand, under fixed exchange rates, (*a*) after one year; (*b*) after two years; (*c*) after three years.

2. Using the *IS–LM* and *AS–AD* diagrams, show the effects of a tight fiscal policy action combined with an expansionary monetary policy (tight fiscal–easy money mix):

   (*a*) under flexible exchange rates;
   (*b*) under fixed exchange rates.

3. Referring back to question 2, show the effect on demand of a combination of an expansionary fiscal policy and a tight monetary policy (easy fiscal–tight money mix) under both fixed and flexible exchange rates.

4. A government wants to use monetary policy under a flexible exchange rate to keep actual GDP above its trend growth rate for ever. In the *AS–AD* diagram, show graphically the consequences of such a policy.

5. During wage negotiations, the future rate of inflation must be guessed. What are the effects on firms' competitiveness and profitability of overestimating future inflation? Of underestimating it?

6. Assume that core inflation is entirely forward-looking and that expectations are rational. What are the effects of fiscal policy (under fixed exchange rates) and monetary policy (under flexible exchange rates) on output and inflation? Consider both cases of expansionary or restrictive policies, at your discretion.

7. Assume that core inflation is entirely forward-looking and that expectations are rational. Under flexible exchange rates, what is the difference between a bond-financed and a money-financed fiscal expansion? (Bond-financed means that the increase in the budget deficit is covered by public borrowing; money-financed means that it is paid for by money creation.)

8. Consider a small open economy under flexible exchange rates.

   (*a*) What is the effect of a large exchange rate depreciation on inflation? on the short-run aggregate supply curve? on the aggregate demand curve?
   (*b*) If core inflation is entirely forward-looking, what is the effect on output and inflation of a large expected depreciation?
   (*c*) What does this suggest for the impact effect on output of an expansionary monetary policy?

9. Stickiness in core inflation implies that disinflation requires some loss of output. Comment.

10. Trace out the effects, from the short to the long run, of an adverse supply shock when the authorities refrain from any fiscal or monetary policy response whatsoever.

11. It is said in the text that, under fixed exchange rates, the PPP line is determined by the foreign rate of inflation. Does that apply to the case of a country that adopts permanently an expansionary monetary policy which leads to recurrent devaluation?

Exercises: Applications

1. Consider two countries linked by a fixed-but-adjustable exchange rate agreement. Hermania fears inflation, Mediterranea uses money to finance budget deficits. How can you foresee the operation of their exchange rate arrangement? In your answer, describe the evolution of inflation, the real exchange rate, the current account, output and unemployment, and the interest rate in both countries.

2. Is it possible, in principle, to fight inflation by fixing the exchange rate to the currency of a country known for its commitment to a low rate of inflation? In your answer, explain what happens to the real exchange rate and the money supply.

3. In the early 1980s, Italy made it mandatory in wage indexation to use a new price index which excludes energy costs. What could be the rationale for such a rule?

4. Over the 1970s, many governments imposed mandatory ceilings on the rates of increase of individual prices and wages. Show in the *AS–AD* framework what the effects of such a policy could be. Why has such an approach been abandoned?

5. Immediate postwar periods are usually accompanied by very high rates of inflation. Can you explain why?

6. Most Eastern and Central European countries have initially undergone a burst of very high inflation (monthly rates of 20%–50% or more were the rule rather than the exception) while output collapsed. Using the *AS–AD* framework, can you imagine why?

7. It has been proposed that central banks should target the nominal GDP, e.g. that they should set the nominal money growth equal to the desired rate of nominal GDP growth. Evaluate the rationale, advantages, and disadvantages of such a proposal.

8. At the time of the German monetary unification in July 1990, the Bundesbank issued large amounts of DM for the former Eastern Germany. Do you think this represented a permanent source of inflation? A temporary one? None at all?

9. The Netherlands is on a rigidly fixed exchange rate with Germany. What is the effect on output and inflation of (*a*) a temporary and (*b*) a permanent increase in German inflation? (*Hint*: use the *AS–AD* diagram.) Discuss the possible policy actions.

10. Looking at the long-run restrictions on demand, compare the relative disciplinary effect on inflation of fixed and flexible exchange rates. Does it matter if realignments are ruled out or considered as a possibly desirable course of action?

Suggested Further Reading

The aggregate demand and supply framework is fully set up and used to analyse the oil shock and its aftermath in:

Bruno, Michael, and Sachs, Jeffrey (1985), *The Economics of Worldwide Stagflation*, Harvard University Press, Cambridge, Mass.

Episodes of inflation and its eradication in Western Europe are described in the following articles:

Bean, Charles, and Symons, James (1989), 'Ten Years of Mrs. T', NBER *Macroeconomics Annual*, MIT Press, Cambridge, Mass.
Blanchard, Olivier J. (1987), 'Reaganomics', *Economic Policy*, 5.
Dornbusch, Rudiger, and Fischer, Stanley (1986), 'Stopping Hyperinflations Past and Present', *Weltwirtschaftliches Archiv*, 122: 1–47.
Giavazzi, Francesco, and Spaventa, Luigi (1989), 'Italy: the Real Effects of Inflation and Disinflation', *Economic Policy*, 8: 133–72.
Hellwig, Martin, and Neumann, Manfred (1987), 'Economic Policy in Germany: Was There a Turnaround?' *Economic Policy*, 5: 103–46.
Sachs, Jeffrey D., and Wyplosz, Charles (1986), 'The Economic Consequences of President Mitterrand', *Economic Policy*, 2: 261–322.

Episodes of very high inflation in Eastern Europe and history can be found in:

Balcerowicz, Leszek (1994), 'Poland: the Economic Outcomes', *Economic Policy*, 19S: 71–87.
Havrylyshyn, Oleh, Miller, Marcus, and Perraudin, William (1994), 'Deficits, Inflation and the Political Economy of Ukraine', *Economic Policy*, 19: 353–401.
Sargent, Thomas (1982), 'The End of Four Big Inflations', in R. E. Hall (ed.), *Inflation*, University of Chicago Press.

Appendix: The *AS–AD* Model

Derivation of *AS* and *AD* curves

This appendix provides a formal presentation of the model underlying the *AD–AS* framework. The aggregate supply curve is described by the following equation:

(A13.1) $$\pi = \bar{\pi} + (1 - \alpha)h(Y - \bar{Y}) + \alpha s.$$

The supply shock term *s* is assumed to remain equal to zero.

Aggregate demand is derived from the *IS* and *LM* curves. For simplicity, we assume that there is no GDP growth trend ($g = 0$). The price level *P* moves as follows:

(A13.2) $$P_t = P_{t-1}(1 + \pi_t).$$

This implies that the real exchange rate is

(A13.3) $$\lambda_t = \frac{E_t P_t^*}{P_t} = \lambda_{t-1} \frac{(1 + \varepsilon_t)(1 + \pi_t^*)}{1 + \pi},$$

where ε is the (expected and actual) rate of change of the exchange rate and π^* is the foreign rate of inflation assumed to be constant.

If μ is the growth rate of the nominal money stock, we have, between period $t - 1$ and t,

(A13.4) $$(M/P)_t = (M/P)_{t-1}(1 + \mu_t - \pi_t).$$

The *IS* curve, linearized around the long-run equilibrium (a bar above a variable denotes its long-run value),[20] is written as

(A13.5) $$Y_t - \bar{Y} = \beta FP_t + \gamma(\lambda_t - \bar{\lambda}) - \phi(r_t - \bar{r}),$$

where β, γ, and ϕ are fixed parameters, *r* is the real interest rate, and *FP* is an indicator of fiscal policy (a catch-all formulation which includes both public spending and tax effects) which is equal to zero in the long run. The real exchange rate captures the effect on demand via the current account. The real interest rate is:

(A13.6) $$r_t = i_t - \pi_t.$$

Without loss of generality, we assume that $\bar{r} = 0$; i.e. the long-run equilibrium value of the real interest rate is zero.

The *LM* curve describes equilibrium in the money market. It is expressed, again in a linearized first-difference form, as

(A13.7) $$(M/P)_t - (M/P)_{t-1} = (M/P)_{t-1}(\mu_t - \pi_t)$$
$$= a(Y_t - Y_{t-1}) - b(i_t - i_{t-1}).$$

Long-Run Equilibrium

It is useful first to characterize the long-run equilibrium to which the economy will converge. The no-growth assump-

tion implies that the economy is stationary and settles to its long-run equilibrium when all real variables are constant. By (A13.3), the real exchange rate is constant when the rate of exchange rate change is equal to the inflation differential, the PPP relationship:[21]

$$\lambda_t = \lambda_{t-1} = \bar{\lambda} \qquad \text{where} \qquad \frac{(1 + \bar{\varepsilon})(1 + \pi^*)}{1 + \bar{\pi}} = 1,$$

is approximated as $\qquad \bar{\varepsilon} = \bar{\pi} - \bar{\pi}^*$

Similarly, the real money stock is constant when the rate of inflation is equal to the rate of money growth. Indeed, (A13.6) and (A13.7) imply that the nominal interest rate equals the rate of inflation, and

$$(M/P)_t = (M/P)_{t-1} \qquad \text{when } \mu = \bar{i} = \bar{\pi}.$$

We obtain the super-neutrality property: all real variables are unaffected by the rate of growth of nominal money, and all nominal variables grow at the rate μ, except the nominal exchange rate which follows PPP.

Fixed Exchange Rate Regime

Aggregate demand

Under a fixed exchange rate regime, $\varepsilon_t = 0$, $E_t = \bar{E}$, and the interest rate is tied to the foreign interest rate, which is assumed to be constant:

(A13.8) $$i_t = \bar{i} = i^*.$$

The money supply is endogenous, and therefore (A13.7) simply determines its growth rate given inflation, real GDP, and the previous period real money stock:

(A13.9) $$\mu_t = \pi_t + \frac{a(Y_t - Y_{t-1})}{M/P_{t-1}}.$$

There is no independent monetary policy, exactly as with the Mundell–Fleming model. Aggregate demand is therefore entirely determined by the *IS* curve:

(A13.10) $$Y_t - \bar{Y} = \beta FP_t + \gamma(\lambda_t - \bar{\lambda}) - \phi(\bar{i} - \bar{\pi}_t).$$

Note that inflaton must be equal to the foreign inflation rate to preclude realignments:

(A13.11) $$\pi_t = \pi^*.$$

The aggregate demand curve is found by substituting (A13.4), (A13.8), and (A13.11) in (A13.10) and noting that the real interest rate abroad is equal to zero, as is the long-run rate at home:

---

[20] The only exception is trend inflation, noted $\bar{\pi}_t$ out of equilibrium and $\bar{\pi}$ in equilibrium.

[21] Taking logs, we have $\ln(1 + \bar{\varepsilon}) + \ln(1 + \bar{\pi}^*) - \ln(1 + \bar{\pi}) = 0$. Then we use the approximation $\ln(1 + x) = x$.

$$\text{(A13.12)} \quad Y_t - \bar{Y} = \beta FP_t + \gamma\left(\lambda_{t-1}\frac{1+\pi^*}{1+\pi_t} - \bar{\lambda}\right).$$

Demand depends on: (1) fiscal policy, as in Chapter 11; (2) domestic inflation. An increase in the rate of inflation leads to a real appreciation as domestic goods become more expensive, an effect not offset by a change in the exchange rate. This is the reason why the AD curve is downward-sloping.

Fiscal policy

Consider a one-period fiscal expansion, captured by a one-off increase in FP from $FP_0 = 0$ to FP_1.[22] We assume that at time $t = 0$ the economy was in its long-run equilibrium position. In period $t = 1$ demand and supply are given by, respectively,

$$\text{(A13.13)} \quad Y_t - \bar{Y} = \beta FP_1 + \gamma\bar{\lambda}\left(\frac{\pi^* - \pi_1}{1+\pi_1}\right)$$

$$\text{(A13.14)} \quad \pi_1 = \pi^* + (1-\alpha)h(Y_1 - \bar{Y}).$$

Linearizing the supply equation (i.e., h is taken to be a fixed parameter) and using the approximation $1 + \pi_1 \approx 1$, (A13.13) and (A13.14) are solved to yield

$$\text{(A13.15)} \quad \pi_1 = \pi^* + \frac{(1-\alpha)\beta h FP_1}{1+(1-\alpha)\gamma h\bar{\lambda}}$$

$$\text{(A13.16)} \quad Y_1 = \bar{Y} + \frac{\beta FP_1}{1+(1-\alpha)\gamma h\bar{\lambda}}$$

$$\text{(A13.17)} \quad \frac{\lambda_1 - \bar{\lambda}}{\bar{\lambda}} = -(\pi_1 - \pi^*) = -\left(\frac{(1-\alpha)\beta h FP_1}{1+(1-\alpha)\gamma h\bar{\lambda}}\right).$$

The first-period effect of the fiscal expansion is an increase in both inflation and output, and a real appreciation arising from higher inflation at a constant real exchange rate.

Moving to period $t = 2$, FP returns to its initial value FP_0. We have demand and supply given respectively by

$$\text{(A13.18)} \quad Y_2 - \bar{Y} = \beta FP_0 + \gamma\left(\lambda_1\frac{1+\pi^*}{1+\pi_2} - \bar{\lambda}\right)$$

$$= \gamma\left(\lambda_1\frac{1+\pi^*}{1+\pi_2} - \bar{\lambda}\right)$$

The solution is:

$$\text{(A13.19)} \quad \pi_2 = \bar{\pi} + (1-\alpha)h(Y_2 - \bar{Y}).$$

(A13.20)

$$\pi_2 - \pi_1 = -\left(\frac{(1-\alpha)\beta h FP_1 + (1-\alpha)\gamma h\bar{\lambda}\frac{1+\pi^*}{1+\pi_1}(\pi_1 - \pi^*)}{1+(1-\alpha)\gamma h\bar{\lambda}\frac{1+\pi^*}{1+\pi_1}}\right)$$

[22] The government budget constraint implies that there cannot be a permanent expansion. It also requires that an expansion be matched by an eventual contraction. We disregard the latter for simplicity. Eager students will explore this case on their own.

$$\text{(A13.21)} \quad Y_2 - Y_1 = -\left(\frac{\beta FP_1 + \gamma\bar{\lambda}\frac{1+\pi^*}{1+\pi_1}(\pi_1 - \pi^*)}{1+(1-\alpha)\gamma h\bar{\lambda}\frac{1+\pi^*}{1+\pi_1}}\right).$$

In period $t = 2$, the inflation rate declines and output falls. This is the result of two effects which work towards contracting demand: fiscal policy is withdrawn, and the overvalued exchange rate hurts the current account. The process will continue until the initial equilibrium is re-established, including inflation returning to the foreign rate. Note that this will require a transition period during which inflation will fall below the foreign rate to bring the real exchange rate back to its equilibrium level after an initial period of appreciation.

Flexible Exchange Rate Regime

Aggregate demand

With the exchange rate no longer expected to remain constant, the domestic interest rate follows the parity condition:

$$\text{(A13.22)} \quad i_t = i^* + \varepsilon_t,$$

where ε is the expected rate of change of the nominal exchange rate. PPP implies that it is equal to the expected inflation differential:

$$\text{(A13.23)} \quad \varepsilon_t = \bar{\pi}_t - \pi^*.$$

Together, (A13.21) and (A13.22) show that the domestic and foreign real interest rates are equal (and both nil by assumption):

$$\text{(A13.24)} \quad i_t = i^* + \bar{\pi}_t - \pi^*$$
$$\Rightarrow r_t = i_t - \bar{\pi}_t = i^* - \pi^* = r^* = 0.$$

The real exchange rate is now determined endogenously by the goods market equilibrium condition (IS) and is derived from (A13.5) given (A13.23):

$$\text{(A13.25)} \quad \lambda_t - \bar{\lambda} = \frac{(Y_t - \bar{Y}) - \beta FP_t}{\gamma}.$$

This equation says that an increase in output requires a depreciation to pull in foreign demand for the domestic goods. An increase in demand, via fiscal policy, requires a real appreciation to crowd out foreign demand.

Domestic demand is determined by the money market equilibrium condition (LM), i.e. (A13.7) with (A13.21) and (A13.22):

$$\text{(A13.26)} \quad Y_t - Y_{t-1} = \frac{(M/P)_{t-1}(\mu_t - \pi_t) - b(\bar{\pi}_t - \bar{\pi}_{t-1})}{a}.$$

For given inflation and a given rate of nominal money growth, an increase in actual inflation leads to a reduction in demand by reducing real cash balances. This is the reason why the AD curve is downward-sloping.

Fiscal policy

Fiscal policy is ineffective under flexible exchange rates by the same reasoning as in Chapter 11: (A13.26) shows that demand cannot change unless the real money supply is changed, and (A13.25) shows that any change in fiscal policy is entirely absorbed by the real exchange rate—an expansionary fiscal policy leads to a real appreciation. When the fiscal policy impulse is reversed, the exchange rate returns to its original position.

Monetary policy with backward-looking core inflation

We begin by considering the polar case in which core inflation is purely backward-looking, as would be the case with full wage and price indexation:

$$(A13.27) \qquad \pi_t = \pi_{t-1}.$$

Nominal money is exogenous, and we can consider first an exogenous increase in its growth rate from μ_0 to μ_1, again assuming that the economy was in equilibrium value $\bar{Y}$, so both actual and core inflation, the nominal interest rate, and the rate of change of the exchange rate all increase in the long run by the same proportion as the increase in money growth:

$$(A13.28) \qquad \bar{\pi} - \pi_0 = \bar{\varepsilon} - \varepsilon_0 = \bar{i} - i_0 = \mu_1 - \mu_0.$$

This raises a small difficulty with the monetary equilibrium condition $M/P = L(Y, i)$. The increase in core inflation $\bar{\pi}$ implies an equal increase in the nominal interest rate and a permanent reduction in the real money stock. This requires that, for some period of the adjustment process, inflation overshoots its long-run level $\bar{\pi}_1$. In period 1, aggregate demand and supply are given respectively as

$$(A13.29) \qquad Y_1 - Y_0 = \frac{(M/P)_0(\mu_1 - \pi_1) + b(i_1 - i_0)}{a},$$

$$(A13.30) \qquad \pi_1 = \bar{\pi}_0 + (1-\alpha)h(Y_1 - \bar{Y}_0).$$

Since inflation in period 1 is unaffected, it follows that $i_1 = i_0$. The solution of (A13.29) and (A13.30) is

$$(A13.31) \qquad \pi_1 - \pi_0 = \frac{[(1-\alpha)h/a](M/P)_0}{1 + [(1-\alpha)h/a](M/P)_0}(\mu_1 - \mu_0),$$

$$(A13.32) \qquad Y_1 - Y_0 = (1/a)(M/P)_0(\mu_1 - \mu_0).$$

The monetary expansion leads to an increase in inflation which is less than the increase in money growth, unless we have extreme cases ($a = 0$, $h = \infty$). Since long-run inflation will ultimately reach the rate of money growth (by (A13.28)), we find that the acceleration is gradual. Output rises as well. Detailed treatment of the path of exchange rates is deferred to Chapter 19.

In subsequent periods inflation continues to rise as core inflation tracks actual inflation with a lag, which raises nominal interest rates and decreases the demand for money. Inflation will eventually overshoot its long-run level in order to reduce real money balances to the starting (equilibrium) value.

Monetary policy with forward-looking core inflation

The other polar case is when core inflation is forward-looking, meaning that agents recognize that inflation will increase by exactly the amount of the increase in money growth. Core inflation is thus set at its new long-run rate:

$$(A13.33) \qquad \bar{\pi}_t = \bar{\pi} = \mu_1 \qquad \forall t = 1, 2 \ldots$$

Monetary policy has no effect on the real economy. Nominal variables jump immediately to their new long-run equilibrium (which is the same as in the previous case). This can be seen by noting that (A13.22) implies that the exchange rate in period $t = 1$ immediately adjusts to its new long-run rate of depreciation:

$$(A13.34) \qquad \varepsilon_1 = \varepsilon_0 + (\mu_1 - \mu_0).$$

From (A13.23), we see that the real exchange rate in period $t = 1$ is given by

$$\frac{\lambda_1}{\lambda_0} = \frac{(1 + \varepsilon_1)(1 + \pi^*)}{1 + \pi_1} = \frac{(1 + \pi^* + \mu_1)(1 + \pi^*)}{1 + \pi_1} \approx 1,$$

so the real exchange rate remains constant at its equilibrium level. The IS curve implies that, with no changes in fiscal policy, real output too remains unaffected. The price level must jump discretely immediately after the event to bring down the real money stock as demand has been reduced by the increase in the nominal interest rate.

14

Business Cycles

Almost all of the phenomena of economic life, like many other processes, social, meteorological, and others, occur in sequences of rising and falling movements, like waves.

Eugen E. Slutsky

14.1. Overview

Economies tend to grow over time, but in an uneven fashion. They tend to *fluctuate* around their long-term trends, as shown in Figure 14.1. Chapter 5 studied trend growth, overlooking shorter-run fluctuations; this chapter is dedicated to fluctuations around trend. For centuries, the tendency for an economy to fluctuate has been considered for centuries a key puzzle of economic life, going as far back as the Bible's observation that seven years of feast are followed by seven years of famine. It has long been observed that these patterns of expansion and contraction in activity, or **business cycles**, occur with some regularity. A recession does not necessarily mean negative growth, however. For fast growing countries like South Korea and China, a year when the economy grows by 'merely' 4%–5% is considered a slump!

Many questions come to mind when thinking about cycles. Is there such a thing as a 'typical' cycle? What is its frequency? Are cycles a result of purely predictable factors—we say *deterministic*—or are they random in

nature? Does each period of expansion sow the seeds of an unavoidable recession? Conversely, is it the case that **recessions** are invariably followed by **booms**, if one is willing to wait long enough? Which aspects of economic life are subject to cyclical movements and which ones seem unaffected by boom and bust?

This chapter begins by establishing some stylized facts about the business cycle. Business cycle watchers, economic forecasters, and policy planners study the economic scene intently to detect signals of future macroeconomic developments. They are especially concerned with **turning points**, those times when the economic cycle reaches a **peak** or a **trough** in the cycle of economic activity. To that end, they watch a number of variables that tend to move systematically with, or even anticipate, the business cycle. Why do they care about turning points? Because entering into a period of expansion means that firms will have to hire more workers and invest in additional capacities if they do not want to run out of goods to sell. In a recession, on the contrary, capital accumulation and new hiring slows down. Thus, the whole economic (and political) climate radically changes.

This chapter's goal is to explain business cycles. Previous chapters have already laid the key building blocks. The *IS–LM* and *AS–AD* analyses are precisely designed to explain deviations of GDP from trend, but more is needed. Two things, really. First, we want to draw all the implications from the previous analyses and track down explicitly the behaviour of other variables than GDP—unemployment, prices, wages, firms' profitability, interest rates, etc. Second, we have used the *IS–LM* and *AS–AD* frameworks by assuming some exogenous changes (e.g. in the money supply, or in entrepreneurial spirits), but is there something more systematic in these changes? Can they be explained—and become endogenous?

Two general viewpoints exist. The first is that business cycles are largely predictable self-perpetuating movements, much like the mythical perpetual motion

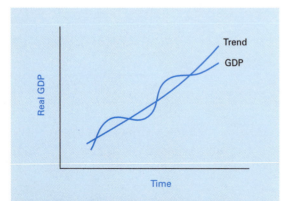

Figure 14.1. The Business Cycle

Economies tend to fluctuate around their trend growth path in a cyclical but irregular fashion.

machine. Section 14.3 describes what would be needed for that to happen and concludes that it is highly unlikely. An alternative, more fruitful, insight conceives of the economic system as a 'black box', receiving stimuli at one end and transforming them into business cycles at the other end. This view of an 'impulse-propagation' mechanism is the subject of the rest of the chapter.

What are the stimuli, and how exactly do they get transmitted? Here two main answers exist, which correspond to the distinction introduced in Chapter 10 between price stickiness and flexibility. Section 14.4 presents the sticky price view, which can be seen as an extension of ideas introduced in Chapters 11–13. Section 14.5 explains the alternative case of flexible prices, which is often called the theory of **real business cycles**. The last section summarizes the current state of thinking on the two competing paradigms.

14.2. Stylized Facts about Business Cycles

As with growth in Chapter 5, a useful first step is to identify 'stylized facts', i.e. features that tend to be common to all business cycles over time and across countries. Business cycles are usually studied using quarterly data, in order to reveal enough details within the time period—usually just a few years—that a typical cycle takes to unfold.

14.2.1. The Duration and Magnitude of Cycles

Panel (*a*) of Figure 14.2 presents the evolution of GDP in the UK since 1970. It displays an estimated trend which 'smooths out' the uneven movements of real GDP. These fluctuations are even more evident in panel (*b*), which presents the deviations of actual from trend GDP, or **detrended** GDP, magnifying the deviations revealed in the upper panel. Cycles seem to be recurrent, with two to three years above trend, two to three years below. When the economy turns down from its peak, the recession phase starts. As it runs up from a trough, this is the time of recovery, leading to an expansion.

> Stylized Fact 1: In advanced economies, real GDP growth fluctuates in a recurrent but irregular fashion, with an average cycle length of five to eight years.

Although business cycle episodes tend to be similar, Figure 14.2 shows that they are far from identical. For example, the 1976 recovery was short-lived, leading to a 'double-dip' in 1977 following the 1975 recession. Conversely, the recovery that followed the early 1980s recession was long-lived. This irregularity makes it a

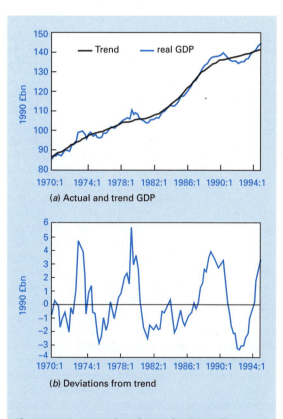

Figure 14.2. Actual and Trend GDP and Detrended GDP, UK, 1970:1– 1994:2 (GDP by expenditure)

Panel (*a*) shows the evolution over time of actual and trend real quarterly GDP in the UK. Panel (*b*) displays the series after it has been detrended, or separated from its trend.

Source: OECD, *National Accounts*

Table 14.1. Descriptive Statistics of Business Cycles, 1970–1994

	No. of completed cycles	Av. cycle length (quarters)	Max. cycle length (quarters)	Min. cycle length (quarters)	Av. deviation from midpoint (%)
UK	2	31.5	42	21	2.5
France	2	35	48	22	2.1
Germany	2	36	48	24	2.9
Italy	3	24	41	11	3.4
Japan	2	36.5	44	29	2.7
USA	3	22	35	6	3.0

Source: IMF, authors' calculations

delicate exercise to pinpoint peaks and troughs in the business cycle. In the USA, the task has long been held by the National Bureau of Economic Research (NBER), which appoints a business cycle committee of independent economists. They declare as a peak the quarter that immediately precedes two consecutive quarters of decline in GDP. Similarly, a trough immediately precedes two consecutive quarters of positive growth. In Europe, business cycle dating is just as widely practised, although not on such a formal basis. For comparison, Table 14.1 identifies peaks as immediately preceding declines in output below trend for a period of four or more quarters. Troughs are defined in a similar fashion. In the case of the UK between 1970 and 1994 (see Figure 14.2), this rule identifies three troughs and three peaks. From peak to peak, the first cycle lasted just over 5 years while the second one spans more than 10 years. Table 14.1 presents a few descriptive statistics for business cycles in several countries.[1] The average peak-to-peak cycle length is about 30 quarters or 7.5 years, with large differences in minimum and maximum length. While these are the cycles most widely monitored and referred to as business cycles, a number of cyclical fluctuations in economic activity have long fascinated researchers. Box 14.1 describes some of these cycles.

Popular discussions of economic conditions emphasize the short-run fluctuations associated with business cycles, to the point that cycles can have significant political repercussions, including bringing

governments down. Yet the last column of Table 14.1 shows that these fluctuations represent only 2%–5% of average GDP from peak to trough. Movements of GDP around its trend are clearly dwarfed by the evolution of the trend itself, as Figure 14.2 amply illustrates. Thus, the second stylized fact:

Stylized Fact 2: Measured relative to average GDP and relative to the growth process, the amplitude of business cycle fluctuations is small.

To detect common aspects of business cycles, we will use **Burns–Mitchell diagrams**. This important tool summarizes visually the behaviour of variables over cyclical periods.[2] The diagrams show the behaviour of macroeconomic variables over the typical business cycle, as a deviation from the value taken at the peak. Figure 14.3 displays these 'reference cycles' for real GDP for several OECD countries. Note that the data are not detrended to keep them free of manipulation. Consistent with stylized fact 2, the figures reveal the importance of the growth trend, even at the short horizon of business cycles. Business cycles do appear to be similar across countries; for example, the average

---

[1] The table presents data on *completed* cycles, from peak to peak. Looking at Fig. 14.2, it might seem that we observe three cycles but the last one is not yet complete; i.e. the peak had not been reached in the interval observed.

[2] Named after US economists Arthur Burns and Wesley Mitchell, two of the most influential empirical researchers on the 'trade cycle' in their time. They developed this technique at the NBER in the 1940s and 1950s. Their work was severely criticized in 1947 by Dutch-born Chicago economic theorist and econometrician Tjalling Koopmans as 'measurement without theory'. His attack turned several generations of economists away from the descriptive approach developed by Burns and Mitchell. While Koopmans was correct in his reasoning, he was probably responsible for the demise of the data-driven Burns–Mitchell approach since the 1950s. Almost a half-century later, Burns and Mitchell are making a comeback of sorts.

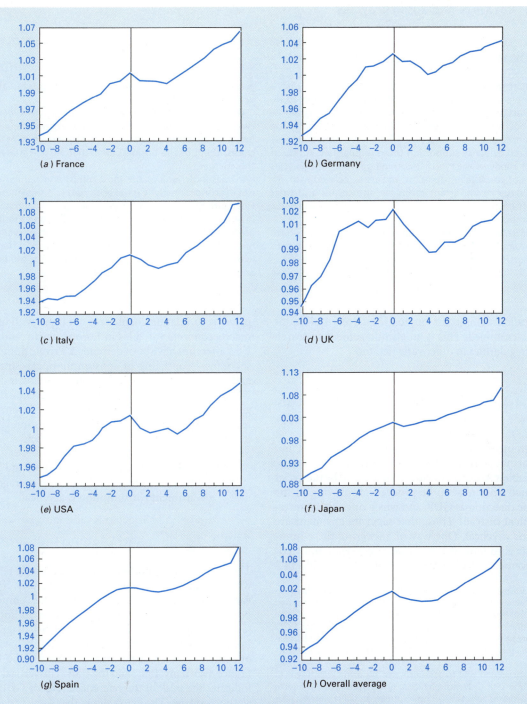

Figure 14.3. Burns–Mitchell Diagrams for Real GDP, 1970–1994

The Burns–Mitchell procedure can be described as follows. First, for each country, cyclical peaks over the period are identified. Second, within a standard 'business cycle window' of 22 quarters (10 before the peak, 12 afterwards), GDP is normalized relative to its cyclical peak. Third, real GDP is averaged across all identified business cycle periods. The figure displays this average for each country and, in the last graph, for the average of all seven countries. Note that the scale differs across countries; for example, it is larger in Japan than in the UK, reflecting higher trend growth rates.

Source: OECD, *Quarterly National Accounts*

BOX 14.1. FAMOUS CYCLES

Older generations of students were presented with a whole array of typical cycles which were thought to interact with each other and produce the data we observe. Modern statistical methods, designed to extract cyclical components from time series data, have turned up only mixed evidence supporting those regularities. A few of the survivors are worth mentioning.[3] *Kondratieff cycles* are of 40–60 years' duration, and are associated with discoveries or important technical innovations and their diffusion (electricity, the steam engine, railroads, computers).

Kuznets cycles, which are associated with long-term accumulation of factors of production (investment, construction, and migration) have periods of 15–23 years.

At higher frequencies, *Kitchin cycles* (duration: 2–4 years) are associated with inventory movements but also with bank clearings and wholesale prices.

Of all cyclical patterns studied, those known as *Juglar cycles*—which involve fluctuations of investment spending, GNP, inflation, and unemployment—are perhaps the closest thing to the business cycle that we will study in this chapter.

Interestingly, one of the most robust and regular cycles in economic activity is the *seasonal cycle*, which coincides with the seasons of the year. Movements of output in agriculture, manufacturing, construction, and tourism have obvious seasonal components which often swamp business cycle fluctuations in magnitude, as do patterns in overall output associated with bank holidays, summer and winter weather, and harvests.

---

recession seems to last four to five quarters in all countries examined. This is an encouragement to search for regularities in other variables, too.

14.2.2. Correlation with Output over the Cycle

Movements in GDP are used to identify cycles, but what happens to other important macroeconomic variables? Are they systematically affected by the cycle? Which ones tend to be **procyclical**, moving in the same direction as GDP, and which ones are **countercyclical** instead? Those that seem independent are called **acyclical**. One way of answering these questions is to look at the degree of covariation, or co-movement, of each variable with GDP.[4] Table 14.2

[3] Business cycles, like comets, bear the names of their discoverers. Simon Kuznets was a Russian-born US economist who received a Nobel Prize for his work on growth. Russian economist Nikolai Kondratieff developed his theory of long-wave cycles in the 1920s before he was arrested and disappeared; the official *Soviet Encyclopaedia* then wrote about his work: 'this theory is wrong and reactionary'. It was also in the 1920s that Joseph Kitchin, a South African statistician and gold trader, uncovered his own cycles. Clement Juglar, a 19th C. French physician, first studied cycles in human births, deaths, and marriages before turning his skills to interest rates and credit conditions (information taken from the *New Palgrave's Dictionary*).

[4] The concept of correlation is introduced informally in Ch. 1. Two variables are statistically correlated when they exhibit a tendency to move together, and this tendency is summarized by the correlation coefficient. Procyclical variables would have positive values of the correlation coefficient near +1; countercyclical variables would have negative correlation coefficients with output near −1; acyclical variables would have correlation coefficients near 0.

presents correlation coefficients of output with other macroeconomic variables in Europe, Japan, and the USA after they have been detrended. Private domestic spending—consisting of consumption, investment, and imports—is procyclical. Public spending is quite smooth and acyclical: it would be countercyclical if the government were systematically offsetting movements in private spending, procyclical if it were stimulating it. This is robust enough to be a stylized fact:

> **Stylized Fact 3: The components of private expenditures are procyclical, while on average government consumption is acyclical.**

14.2.3. Leading and Lagging Indicators

The correlations reported in Table 14.2 only tell us which variables move together simultaneously. If one variable systematically leads or lags another, contemporaneous correlation may be nil and yet an important link may still exist. The Burns–Mitchell diagrams in Figure 14.4 display the average cyclical behaviour of some key macroeconomic variables for the UK, France, Germany, Italy, and the USA. The vertical line indicates the peak of the reference cycle for GDP for all the countries. The figure shows that some variables tend systematically to peak ahead of, and others systematically to trail behind, real output. For example, the degree of capacity utilization, investment in inventory, real share prices, and real money balances are examples of **leading indicators**. They tend to predict the emergence of recessions and expansions. Other variables, such as unemployment and inflation, tend

Table 14.2. Business Cycle Correlations of Macroeconomic Variables with Output[a]

	Consumption	Investment	Gov. spending	Exports	Imports	Prices	Inflation
EU	0.84	0.89	0.11	0.79	0.92	−0.76	0.09
Japan	0.49	0.81	−0.19	−0.10	0.16	−0.27	0.17
USA	0.85	0.90	0.09	0.18	0.56	−0.59	0.19

[a] The 'European Union' is computed as the unweighted average of the UK, France, Germany, and Italy. Correlations are taken over quarterly time intervals ranging from 1957–89 to 1965–89.

Sources: Danthine and Donaldson (1993: Table 3); inflation rate correlations are taken from Chadha and Prasad (1994). Except for inflation, variables are seasonally adjusted and detrended using the Hodrick–Prescott filter

to be **lagging indicators**. Interest rates are an example of a **coincident** indicator.

Stylized Fact 4: Some variables systematically lead GDP over the cycle (inventories, capacity utilization, stock prices, real money balances), while others (inflation, unemployment) systematically lag behind. Still others (interest rates) are coincident.

14.2.4. Relative Variability

Another feature of business cycles is how much key economic variables move over the cycle relative to each other. Table 14.3 indicates several regularities across countries. Prices are less variable than output, which is consistent with the 'Keynesian assumption' that was introduced in Chapter 10. Consumption is smoother than output, output is smoother than investment expenditures, and trade (exports and imports) represents the most unstable component of GDP. A broader view of the relative variability of spending components is given by Figure 14.5. With the exception of government purchases, all variables peak together with GDP. Clearly, the most volatile are investment spending, inventory investment (Figure 14.4), and the current account; in comparison, private consumption and government purchases of goods and services are relatively smooth.

Stylized Fact 5: Investment—especially inventory investment—is more volatile and consumption less volatile than GDP. Exports and imports are highly variable, while government purchases are relatively acyclical.

Our knowledge of the macroeconomy can explain these regularities. Evidence on capacity utilization from Figure 14.4 shows that firms begin reducing production about two to three quarters before a cyclical peak, i.e. before the GDP, which measures spending and income, turns around and starts slowing down. How can aggregate spending and output differ from each other? When spending exceeds production, inventories of finished goods are sold to make up the difference. When output exceeds spending, inventories are accumulated.[5] Thus, moving towards a cyclical peak, firms act to satisfy part of demand by selling from inventories. The opposite occurs near the trough: firms begin to restock inventories in anticipation of a recovery. A similar logic applies to total investment spending, another leading indicator. As the cyclical peak approaches, forward-looking firms decelerate their spending on new productive equipment, which is not needed in a recession; conversely, anticipating rising demand, they begin expanding capacity in advance of cyclical peaks. This also explains why real share prices—one measure of Tobin's q shown in Figure 14.4—are a leading indicator: financial markets also anticipate the next phase of the cycle and, for example, expect poorer profitability during the downturn phase.

That consumption is less volatile than GDP is consistent with the consumption smoothing principle established in Chapter 4; the volatility of investment is a consequence of its forward-looking nature, as captured by Tobin's q. Two main factors account for the

---

[5] Inventories are goods produced but not yet sold as well as goods in process and intermediate goods used in production. In the National Income Accounts (see Chapter 2), inventory changes are counted as part of investment, so additions to inventories represent positive investment.

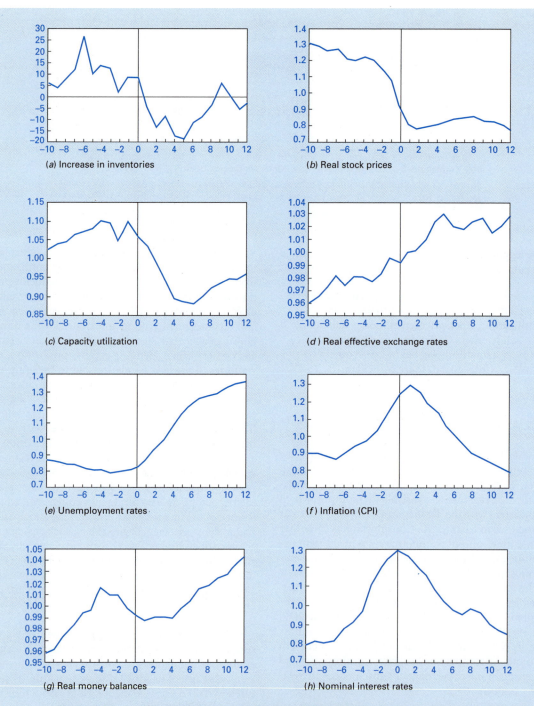

Figure 14.4. Leading and Lagging Indicators, 1970–1994

These Burns–Mitchell diagrams show the evolution of key economic variables averaged over five countries (France, Germany, Italy, the UK, and the USA) and over each country's business cycles. The vertical line corresponds to the cyclical peak (of output).

Sources: OECD, *Quarterly National Accounts, Main Economic Indicators*; IMF, *International Financial Statistics*

Table 14.3. Variability of Key Macro Variables over the Cycle[a]

	Output	Consumption	Investment	Gov. spending	Exports	Imports	Prices (GDP deflator)
	(%)	standard deviation relative to standard deviation of output					
EU	1.12	0.87	2.23	0.47	2.35	3.26	1.00
Japan	1.66	0.73	2.80	3.76	6.99	11.67	1.98
USA	1.73	0.71	3.01	1.18	6.82	5.17	0.90

[a] Variability is measured as the standard deviation of seasonally adjusted and detrended values using the Hodrick–Prescott filter; see Appendix for details.

Source: Danthine and Donaldson (1993: Table 3)

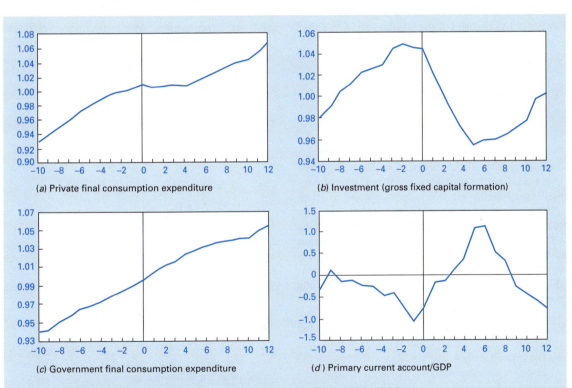

(*a*) Private final consumption expenditure

(*b*) Investment (gross fixed capital formation)

(*c*) Government final consumption expenditure

(*d*) Primary current account/GDP

Figure 14.5. Components of Aggregate Spending, 1970–1994

These Burns–Mitchell diagrams show the evolution of the components of aggregate spending averaged over five countries (France, Germany, Italy, the UK, and the USA) and over each country's business cycles. The vertical line corresponds to the cyclical peak.

Source: OECD, *Quarterly National Accounts*

acyclical nature of government purchases. First, as a policy variable, government purchases are likely to be employed countercyclically, rising to reduce a recession and declining during expansions. Second, a large component of government consumption is the wages of civil servants, which also tend to be smooth over time.

14.3. Deterministic and Stochastic Interpretations of the Business Cycle

Why should economic fluctuations occur in a seemingly endless and systematic way? The long-held belief that cycles occur with perfect regularity has been disproved by closer scrutiny. Yet the list of stylized facts shows that cycles do not unfold in a completely random fashion, either. They exhibit important regularities and seem to follow an internal logic. This tension lies behind all theories of the business cycle. We shall now look at two interpretations of the cycle.

14.3.1. Deterministic Cycles: the Example of the Multiplier-Accelerator

Might it be possible that cycles go on reproducing themselves, just like the rising and falling of the tides? This would be the case if the economic system constantly generated forces that successively speeded it up and then slowed it down. It turns out that it is quite possible to imagine how this can come about. One necessary condition, which applies to any explanation of business cycles, is some systematic delay in economic responses to changing conditions. For example, the consumption function links current spending to current income and wealth. This may just hold for consumers' *intentions*, but they may take time in transforming that into effective *action*. This is the so-called **Robertson lag**. It is equally plausible that output does not rise immediately to meet increases in demand: the behaviour of inventories shows that firms initially supply additional demand by running down inventories, the so-called **Lundberg lag**.[6]

In the end, we expect GDP to depend on its own past—in fact, in a fairly rich and complex way. Appendix II shows how the *AS–AD* model indeed displays this pattern. To illustrate this using a simpler example, we introduce the so-called multiplier-accelerator

model, which has played an important role in the development of ideas about business cycles. The framework itself is presented in Box 14.2. The main element is the accelerator principle presented in Chapter 4, which relates the level of investment positively to changes in GDP. If GDP was unusually high last period, it is likely to be smaller this period. As GDP declines, investment slows down. Since investment is itself a component of GDP, declining investment spending will reduce current GDP. Graphically, this example can be summarized in Figure 14.6 as the

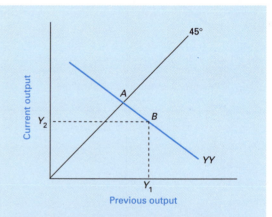

Figure 14.6. Current GDP as a Declining Function of its Past Level

The downward-sloping *YY* schedule represents the case when current GDP—represented along the vertical axis—tends to be lower the higher was GDP in the previous period—represented along the horizontal schedule. This occurs, for example, when a component of demand such as investment depends on the change in GDP between the current and previous period. Stationarity (GDP stops fluctuating) occurs at point *A* where current and past GDP are equal. Point *B* correspond to a non-stationary situation: with past GDP at Y_1, current GDP is at Y_2.

---

[6] Named respectively after the British economist D.H. Robertson and the Swedish economist Erik Lundberg.

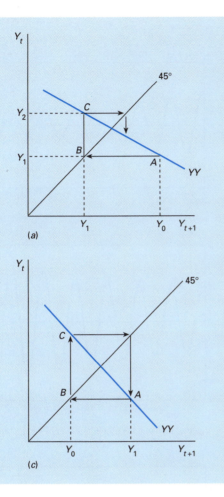

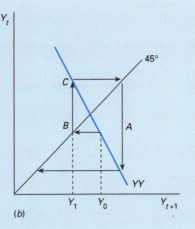

Figure 14.7. The Possibility of Deterministic Cycles

These diagrams show that the cycle depends on the slope of the demand schedule relating today's to last period's output. In panel (a), in which the YY schedule is relatively flat, the cycle converges. When the YY schedule is steep (panel (b)), there is divergence. When the slope of YY is exactly equal to – 1 as in panel (c), the cycle goes on for ever.

downward-sloping *YY* schedule which states that an unusually high GDP yesterday leads to an unusually low GDP today, and conversely.

When studying business cycle fluctuations, a useful reference point is the stationary GDP level, i.e. the level at which GDP is no longer fluctuating or is constant. In our example, this occurs when $Y_t = Y_{t-1}$; graphically, this corresponds to the 45° line. Given the natural evolution of GDP represented by the *YY* schedule, stationarity occurs at point *A* where the *YY* schedule crosses the 45° line.

For other positions than point *A*, the economy will fluctuate. Three possible outcomes are displayed in the three panels of Figure 14.7. In panel (*a*) we start in period 1 at point *A*, with GDP in the previous period

equal to Y_0. The *YY* schedule shows that next period's GDP will be Y_1, which is lower than Y_0. If nothing else changes, GDP in period 2 can be determined using the 45° line, which permits us to move one period ahead: at point *B*, Y_1 becomes last period's GDP, which corresponds to point *C*, the new current GDP Y_2. In the first case, in panel (*a*), each of these steps takes the economy closer to the stationary equilibrium, the intersection of the *YY* schedule with 45° line. In this case, the economy exhibits cycles that die out over time, or are **damped**.

Panel (*b*) shows an **explosive cycle:** when the *YY* schedule is steep (consumption and investment react strongly to changes in GDP), each step takes the economy further away from its equilibrium.

BOX 14.2. THE MULTIPLIER–ACCELERATOR MODEL[7]

Consider an economy in which consumption and investment are simple linear functions of GDP or its change, omitting all forward-looking variables, such as wealth in the consumption function and real interest rates or Tobin's q:

(14.1) $C_t = a_0 + a_1 Y_t$,   with $0 < a_1 < 1$
$I_t = b_0 + b_1(Y_t - Y_{t-1})$,   with $b_1 > 0$.

Since GDP is $Y_t = C_t + I_t + G + PCA$ (we take G and PCA as given),

(14.2) $Y_t = a_0 + a_1 Y_t + b_0 + b_1(Y_t - Y_{t-1}) + c_0$,

where $c_0 = \overline{G} + PCA$ constant, which can be rewritten as

(14.3) $Y_t = \dfrac{a_0 + b_0 + c_0 - b_1 Y_{t-1}}{1 - a_1 - b_1}$,

where it is assumed that $a_1 + b_1 < 1$. This 'reduced form' of the model is a difference equation describing the evolution of Y over time. The long-run stationary state corresponds to $\overline{Y} = Y_t = Y_{t-1}$, which in (14.3) gives $\overline{Y} = (a_0 + b_0 + c_0)/(1 - a_1)$.

The dynamics of the difference equation depend on the values taken by the parameters a_1 and b_1. When $b_1/(1 - a_1 - b_1) < 1$ (i.e. when $a_1 + 2b_1 < 1$), damped oscillations results (panel (a) of Figure 14.7). This is the case when the responsiveness of consumption and investment to GDP is not too strong (a_1 and b_1 not too large). Explosive oscillations occur in the opposite case. Perpetual cycles occur when $a_1 + 2b_1 = 1$.

The saw-toothed pattern shown by Y_t is due to the simplicity of the lag structure. More plausible dynamics results from more complex lag structures. For example, suppose that both consumption and investment react with a one-period (Robertson) lag to output and output changes, respectively:

$C_t = a_0 + a_1 Y_{t-1}$ and $I_t = b_0 + b_1(Y_{t-1} - Y_{t-2})$.

Then the model becomes

(14.4) $Y_t = a_0 + b_0 + c_0 + (a_1 + b_1)Y_{t-1} - b_1 Y_{t-2}$.

The steady-state level of output in this case is once again $\overline{Y} = (a_0 + b_0 + c_0)/(1 - a_1)$.

Difference equations like (14.4) have a solution (as a function of time t only) of the form $Y_t = k_1 \lambda_1^t + k_2 \lambda_2^t$, where λ_1, λ_2, k_1, and k_2 are constants, and depend on a_0, b_0, c_0, a_1, b_1, and the initial values of Y. To obtain λ_1 and λ_2, one must solve the quadratic equation,

---

[7] This model was developed by Paul Samuelson of MIT and the late Sir John Hicks from Oxford, both Nobel Prize laureates. We present a version close to that developed by the late Chicago economist Lloyd Metzler.

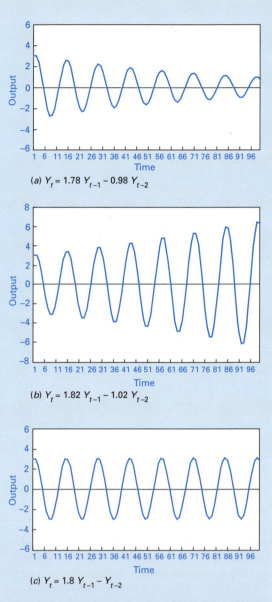

(a) $Y_t = 1.78\, Y_{t-1} - 0.98\, Y_{t-2}$

(b) $Y_t = 1.82\, Y_{t-1} - 1.02\, Y_{t-2}$

(c) $Y_t = 1.8\, Y_{t-1} - Y_{t-2}$

Figure 14.8. Deterministic Cycles: What Do They Look Like?

These diagrams correspond to the variant of the multiplier-accelerator model presented in Box 14.2. Panel (a) depicts 100 observations of a variable generated by the formula $Y_t = 1.78 Y_{t-1} - 0.98 Y_{t-2}$, starting from values of $Y_0 = 3$, $Y_{-1} = Y_{-2} = 0$. In panel (b), the formula $Y_t = 1.82 Y_{t-1} - 1.02 Y_{t-2}$ was used instead. The data in panel (c) were generated by the equation $Y_t = 1.8 Y_{t-1} - Y_{t-2}$.

$$\lambda^2 - (a_1 + b_1)\lambda + b_1 = 0.$$

It can be shown that the solution to (14.4) will be oscillatory if $(a_1 + b_1)^2 < 4b_1$, and is dampened or explosive, depending on whether λ_1 and λ_2 are smaller or larger than unity in absolute value. In the oscillatory case, this is the same as whether b_1 is greater or less than one. Three cases of dynamics generated by this example are shown in Figure 14.8.

The last and most interesting is panel (c), where the schedule YY has a slope of exactly −1 and is perpendicular to 45° line: now the economy oscillates for ever around equilibrium, but never reaches it. This is the case of undamped oscillations. Under these conditions, business cycles can recur in a systematic, never-ending fashion, like self-perpetuating cycles. This example illustrates the deterministic view of the business cycle.

More general patterns can be generated by taking into account more complete descriptions of the behaviour of aggregate demand and aggregate supply. What matters at this stage is not the details of the cycles but the possibility of explaining actual business cycles with this approach. Could it be, indeed, that what we observe is the consequence of a pendulum-like motion started some time far back in the past and self-perpetuating ever since? The answer is no, for at least two reasons. First, cycles produced by deterministic models are regular, a clear contradiction of stylized fact 1. Second, oscillations in such models can be damped, explosive, or permanent. Damped oscillations eventually die down, in contradiction with the endless recurrence of business cycles. Explosive cycles do not seem to correspond to reality either. The only case that delivers recurrent cycles is the last one, which requires a very special combination of characteristics of the economy. Most economists believe that the probability that this combination arises is so low as to make it an unlikely candidate to explain business cycles. This opens the way for an alternative approach.

trepreneurial animal spirits or the consumer mood, which can alternatively turn optimistic or pessimistic; policy actions) as well as supply (e.g. exceptionally bad or good crops and natural disasters; important inventions or discoveries like the steel furnace, railroads, electricity, or computers, as well as minor ones; social unrest). For example, a favourable shock will raise current GDP and shift the economy to point A in Figure 14.7.

The list of potential shocks is endless. Imagine events, small or large, favourable or unfavourable, which occur regularly if not predictably. Like drops of rain generating ripples on a lake, these shocks shake the economy off its existing position and trigger a chain reaction. Figure 14.9 describes this vision. These shocks, often referred to as **impulses**, change the demand or supply conditions in the economy. Once randomly disturbed, the economy embarks on the kind of deterministic adjustment described in the previous section, until the occurrence of the next shock. The propagation mechanism transforms impulses into oscillations. It does not crucially matter any more whether the oscillations are damped or explosive: they are continuously replaced by new ones corresponding to new shocks. In contrast to the previous section, it is unnecessary to search for the unlikely existence of a self-perpetuating cycle. It is sufficient to accept the view than an economy is regularly buffeted by endless series of shocks, and never really settles down to its stationary state. The rest of this chapter follows on this

14.3.2. Stochastic Cycles: the Impulse-Propagation Mechanism

A more plausible explanation starts by asking a question. In the previous section, the economy oscillates because it starts away from its stationary-state equilibrium; but what displaced it out of the stationary state in the first place? It is illuminating to imagine that an economy is subject to random, but recurrent disturbances, or shocks. These can affect demand (e.g. en-

Figure 14.9. The Impulse-Propagation Mechanism

Random shocks hit the economic system which reacts by generating business cycles. The cycles result from the averaging or cumulation of these random disturbances over time.

BOX 14.3. COMPUTERS, SCIENTISTS, AND BUSINESS CYCLES

The discovery that purely random events can be responsible for cycles was made independently by Slutsky and Frisch in the 1930s. Evidence that such events can generate cycle-like behaviour typical of actual economies was not forthcoming until the late 1950s with the first computers. Frank Adelman, a nuclear physicist, and his wife Irma, an economist, studied an economic model developed by Lawrence Klein, Nobel Prize laureate from the University of Pennsylvania, and Arthur Goldberger, now at the University of Wisconsin. (This model consisted of 25 equations summarizing the most important variables in the US economy.) First, the Adelmans found that the Klein–Goldberger model could not generate a cycle on its own (a deterministic cycle), because the fluctuations were dying down as in Figure 14.7(a). Yet, when perturbed by random shocks, it produced data that had the same statistical properties as *actual* US business cycles. They concluded that:

Ever since the pathbreaking article of Frisch on the propagation of business cycles, the possibility that the cyclical movements observed in a capitalistic society are actually due to random shocks has been seriously considered by business cycle theories. The results we have found in this study tend to support this possibility . . . The agreement between the data obtained by imposing uncorrelated perturbation upon a model which is otherwise non-oscillatory in character is certainly consistent with the hypothesis that the economic fluctuations experienced in modern, highly developed societies are indeed due to random impulses. (Adelman and Adelman 1959: 620)

The Adelmans simulated, or solved, their model 100 years into the future on an IBM 650 and were proud that 'computations for one year could be made during an operating time of about one minute'. Now that simulations take seconds or less on a laptop, this approach has become routine. Much effort has gone into improving and enlarging the models and the algorithms used for simulations. More recently, Robert E. Lucas of the University of Chicago, and the 1995 Nobel Prize laureate in economic sciences, made this research strategy explicit:

Our task as I see it . . . is to write a FORTRAN [a programming language] program that will accept specific economic policy rules as 'input' and will generate as 'output' statistics describing the operating characteristics of time series we care about, which are predicted to result from these policies.

lead, which is the cornerstone of modern business cycle theory.[8]

How likely is it that purely random impulses working their way through the economy actually generate the kind of behaviour corresponding to our earlier stylized facts? Can it be that shocks which continuously move the economy away from the intersection of the YY schedule and the 45° line and are followed by the cyclical response shown in Figure 14.7 actually explain business cycles? Box 14.3 recalls how this question received an affirmative answer at the dawn of the computer era.

This possibility is more precisely illustrated in Figure 14.10. Panel (a) displays 200 purely random shocks.[9] Such observations could represent a succession of unforeseeable events, big or small. They are the impulses. Panel (b) shows the evolution of GDP when these shocks are 'filtered' through a propagation mechanism; in this case we use the example of the multiplier-accelerator model described in Box 14.2. The result is a succession of artificial business cycles which resemble the UK data presented in Figure 14.2(b). Although the impulses are not cyclical, the transformed variable exhibits irregular, periodic movements similar to business cycles.

This impulse-propagation mechanism is the dominant way of thinking about business cycles, because it accords well with the stylized facts. Since they are random, the shocks will typically generate cycles of different sizes and magnitudes, as in stylized fact 1. If many of these impulses are related to technological innovations, not only will they trigger cycles, but in the long run they will also cumulate into a process of unending growth. This is consistent with stylized fact 2: in the long run, the growth process (the accumulation of positive shocks) dwarfs business cycles (the reaction to individual productivity and other shocks).[10]

Some important questions remain, however. First, what is the exact nature of these impulses? Second,

---

[8] The discovery that cycles can be generated from purely random factors was made in the late 1920s and early 1930s by the Russian Eugen Slutsky and the Norwegian Ragnar Frisch, who was awarded the first Nobel Prize. Slutsky was a researcher at the Conjuncture Institute in Moscow during Stalin's dictatorship and was unable to publish this discovery until eight years later when his work was finally translated into English.

[9] Such a random variable which is identically and independently distributed is often called *white noise*. White noise has the property that current and past values contain no information helpful in forecasting future values.

[10] We need to assume that the impulse-propagation mechanism is of the 'damped' variety, which corresponds to the empirical evidence.

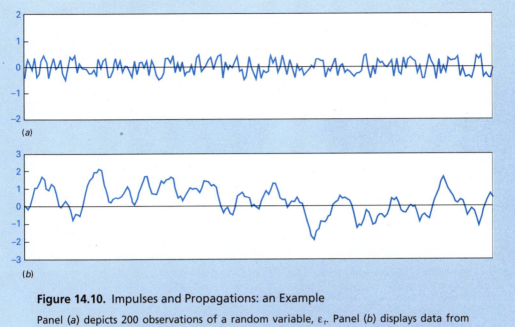

Figure 14.10. Impulses and Propagations: an Example

Panel (a) depicts 200 observations of a random variable, ε_t. Panel (b) displays data from panel (a) after they were transformed, or 'filtered', by the formula $Y_t = 1.3Y_{t-1} - 0.4Y_{t-2} + \varepsilon_t$, starting from a given Y_0 and Y_{-1}. This 'filter' has the ability to mimic a true data series.

what is the impulse-propagation mechanism? We have used a simple example to show that such a mechanism is plausible. Yet this is not good enough: the objective is to show that the 'shocks' correspond to well-known disturbances. A 'good' business cycle theory is one that can also replicate the key stylized facts discussed at the beginning of this chapter.

Two competing approaches to thinking about the impulse-propagation mechanism have been developed. The first follows the Keynesian tradition of sticky prices and takes the *AS–AD* framework as its point of departure; it is presented in the next section. The second asks whether cycles may exist when all prices are perfectly flexible; it is studied in Section 14.5.

14.4. Sticky Price Business Cycles

14.4.1. Impulses and Propagation in the *AS–AD* Framework

Chapter 13 showed how to use the *AS–AD* model to understand the determinants of output and inflation in the short and long run. It can also be used to study business cycles. The point of departure is to identify the shocks as factors that shift either the *AS* or *AD* curves. Those that shift the *AD* schedule are called **demand shocks**, while **supply shocks** are those that

affect the *AS* curve. Both demand and supply shocks can be positive or negative. Positive shocks, for example, move the relevant schedule rightwards.

The multiplier-accelerator model demonstrated that lags in economic relationships are the central source of dynamics. This is also true in the *AS–AD* framework. Lags exist for various reasons: slow responses of demand to income and of supply to demand imply that the *AD* schedule reacts gradually to demand disturbances; the supply side may also be a

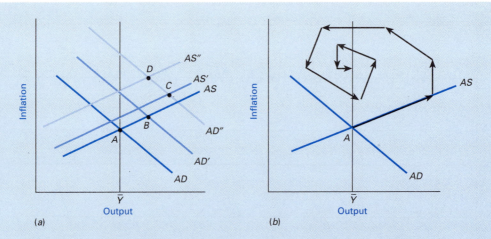

Figure 14.11. The *AS–AD* Framework as an Example of the Propagating Mechanism

The initial impulse is an increase in the rate of money growth. In panel (*a*), from its initial stationary equilibrium at point *A* the economy first moves to point *B*, as the *AD* curve begins to respond to the monetary impulse. Gradually, core inflation catches up with actual inflation, and the *AS* curve—whose position depends on core inflation—slides to *AS'*: when the *AD* curve reaches position *AD'* the economy is at point *B*. Further lagged responses of demand to money growth, and of core inflation to actual inflation, result in gradual shifts of the *AD* curve towards *AD''* and of the *AS* schedule towards *AS''*, bringing the economy to point *D*. Because output has begun to decline, the *AD* curve begins a descent. As inflation declines, core inflation follows and the *AS* curve also moves downwards. Tracking down this evolution, the economy will follow a loop of the kind exhibited in panel (*b*).

source of **persistence**, if core inflation only gradually catches up with past inflation.

As an example, consider a permanent increase in money growth in a system of flexible exchange rates. Core inflation is simply equal to last period's inflation. The cycle triggered by this disturbance is tracked down in Figure 14.11. (Appendix II provides a formal analysis.) For simplicity, we start with an economy in stationary state at point *A*.[11] The monetary expansion growth takes the economy to point *B* in panel (*a*), with an increase in both output and inflation. Owing to demand lags, the initial shift of the *AD* curve to *AD'* represents only an initial, partial, response. For a time, the *AD* schedule will continue to move rightwards towards *AD''*. Indeed, the lagged response of output means that the longer-run shift of the *AD* curve always exceeds that of the short run and that, as output rises, the *AD* keeps moving to the right.

At the same time, the *AS* curve shifts upward as core inflation gradually catches up with the actual inflation rate. Over time, the economy moves towards point *C*. With actual output in excess of its trend level, inflation catches up and eventually overtakes money growth.[12] This implies that the real money stock starts declining and with it output. Declining output means that the *AD* curve begins to move leftwards. Actual inflation then starts to decline, followed by core inflation and a downward shift of the *AS* schedule (not shown). Pursuing this reasoning, it appears that the adjustment will be characterized by the 'loops' shown in panel (*b*), with alternating periods of output above and below equilibrium level—i.e. business cycles.

---

[11] This is simpler because there is no cycle under way that would interfere with the new one under study.

[12] How do we know? We know that, as long as money growth exceeds inflation, the real money stock M/P rises. In the long run, the economy returns to trend GDP and the demand for money roughly returns to its initial value (since $M/P = L(Y, i)$ and both Y and i approximately return to their initial levels). For M/P to return to its initial level, inflation *must* exceed money growth at some point.

14.4.2. Identifying Demand and Supply Shocks and their Propagation

The example of the previous section shows how the *AS–AD* framework can be used to explain business cycles. The next step is to identify the characteristics of cycles, as predicted by the *AS–AD* framework. This naturally points to a distinction between demand and supply shocks. The case studied in the previous section—an increase in money growth—is an example of a demand shock. Is the theory's prediction, that demand shocks lead to loops of the type depicted in Figure 14.11, borne out by the facts?

The case of German unification, seen from the perspective of West Germany, provides an easily identified demand shock.[13] While output in the east was collapsing, consumption, investment, and government spending by East German residents was rising rapidly. Consumers who had been repressed for several decades and anticipated an increase in their future incomes met West German banks eager to attract new customers, especially as none of them was indebted. Most of this spending went to West German firms, which were poised to produce this extra demand.

Figure 14.12 shows that the outcome was indeed a counterclockwise loop. The initial demand was met without inflation pressure. After two years of expansion, the tell-tale signs of overheating emerged: increasing nominal wage demands by unions, high capacity utilization rates, etc. In the end, the Bundesbank refused to allow any further money growth. By allowing market interest rates to rise, and by raising the discount and Lombard rates several times, the German central bank effected a prompt return to non-inflationary conditions.

The second example traces an economy's reaction to a supply shock, the first oil price increase in 1973–4. Panel (*a*) of Figure 14.13 shows the theory. The *AS* curve shifts up to *AS'* because the cost of a major input, energy, abruptly rises. Without any policy reaction, the impact has the effect of moving the economy from point *A* to point *B*. Thereafter, once the initial burst of cost increases is absorbed, the *AS* curve moves back to its initial position—but only gradually so, since core inflation is on the rise, trailing actual inflation. Similarly, with a reduced GDP, the *AD* curve also moves down, so that the return is shown as the curved trajectory from *B* to *A*. If instead the authorities decide to fight the inflationary implication of the oil shock and tighten up demand, the *AD* curve shifts left-

[13] For East Germany, it was more likely a mixture of negative demand and supply shocks.

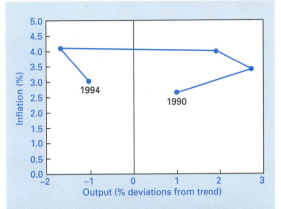

Figure 14.12. An Example of a Demand Shock: the Effect of German Unification on West Germany, 1990–1994

German economic and monetary unification occurred in 1990. Spending by former East German households, firms, and governmental authorities increased dramatically, and most of this demand fell on West German producers. The figure traces out the effect on West German GDP—measured as a deviation from its trend—and rate of inflation.

Sources: OECD National Accounts; *Main Economic Indicators*

wards to *AD'* and the economy moves from *B* to *C* and will return to point *A* via point *D*, for example.

Panels (*b*) and (*c*) give two examples of reactions to the oil shock. Panel (*b*) shows that the Swiss National Bank adopted the low inflation solution. After the shock, in 1974 inflation increased and output continued to grow as it completed the expansion phase started a few years before. But then, restrictive policies provoked a sharp recession followed by a gradual decline in inflation—the overall cycle matching trajectory *ABCD* in panel (*a*). In contrast, British authorities did not act to curb inflation: panel (*b*) depicts a loop similar to the *ABA* trajectory in panel (*a*).

14.4.3. The Contribution of Demand and Supply Shocks

With plausible lags on both the demand and supply side, the *AS–AD* framework can broadly explain patterns observed in actual business cycles. The results of this analysis are consistent with an impulse-

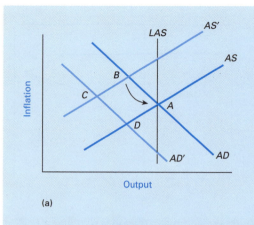

(a)

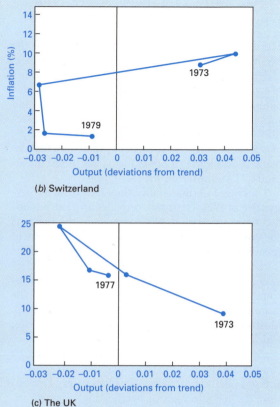

(b) Switzerland

Figure 14.13. An Example of a Supply Shock:
the Oil Price Shock of 1973–1974

An adverse supply shock is captured by an upward jump
of the AS schedule to AS'. Once oil prices stabilize, the
AS curve gradually comes back down. A country intent
on fighting inflation, like Switzerland shown in panel
(b), also curbs demand, bringing the AD schedule down
to AD'. The UK, shown in panel (c), does not exhibit
the same aversion to inflation, so its cycle is more like
the trajectory from point A to point B and back to A in
panel (a).

Source: OECD, *Main Economic Indicators*

(c) The UK

propagation interpretation of business cycles, operating through the sticky price framework developed in
Chapter 13. The next section considers an alternative
interpretation.

As an important by-product of this interpretation,
attention is drawn to the distinction between demand
and supply shocks. To think about cycles—and how
to deal with them—it helps to know which types of
shock are more frequent. Table 14.4 presents estimates
for five of the G7 countries. In this study, two kinds of
demand shock are identified: (1) monetary shocks,
which are related to exogenous changes in monetary
policy, and (2) real demand shocks, reflecting public
action (fiscal policy), private spending behaviour, or
foreign demand via the current account.[14] According

to this study, monetary shocks are less important while
demand and supply shocks are predominant. At the
same time, there are significant differences from country to country.

Table 14.4. Decomposition of the variance of
GDP, 1979:1–1993:4 (%, 1 year after
shock)

Country	Demand	Supply	Money	Total
Canada	54	34	12	100
France	19	80	1	100
Germany	66	31	3	100
Italy	40	51	10	100
Japan	11	87	2	100
UK	32	64	4	100
USA	20	71	8	100

Source: Gerlach and Smets (1995)

[14] How this is done is somewhat technical. The authors identify
the shocks by *defining* them in terms of their effects on real GDP:
demand shocks do not have permanent effects (they do not affect
the LAS schedule); supply shocks have both temporary and permanent effects (both the AS and LAS schedules shift); monetary shocks
have neither instantaneous nor permanent effects. (It takes time for
money to affect output and it leaves the LAS schedule unchanged.)

14.5. Real Business Cycles

14.5.1. Productivity Shocks as Impulses

The *AS–AD* framework implies that business cycles are propagated because prices are sticky. Does this mean that business cycles are impossible when prices are perfectly flexible? This is the challenge undertaken by the real business cycle (RBC) theory, which argues that business cycles can be viewed as a market-clearing, equilibrium phenomenon. The challenge is demanding. As Chapter 10 shows, an economy with fully flexible prices is perfectly dichotomized, even in the short run, and departures from the long-run AS (LAS) schedule are impossible. In that case, the only shocks that affect the real economy are supply shocks, which shift the LAS schedule. To the extent that monetary and fiscal policies do not affect the LAS line, they are irrelevant. At the same time, if the economy is always on its long-run supply schedule, the propagation mechanism of the *AS–AD* model is shut down: real GDP simply moves randomly in response to random supply shocks. So it would seem that such an economy would be free from cyclical tendencies.

The hallmark of RBC theory is the development of other propagation mechanisms besides those related to price stickiness. It starts by focusing on supply shocks related to the production technology: the main source of impulses are new discoveries, inventions, product innovations, or process improvements. Propagation occurs because these shocks alter the productivity of factors of production, change the environment of economic agents, and cause them to change their behaviour. Figure 14.14 shows movements in total factor productivity—as measured by the Solow residual—in the case of Germany.[15] In the RBC framework, these are the exogenous impulses that hit the economy.[16]

The propagation mechanism assumed in the RBC theory is directly related to the paradigm of Robinson Crusoe presented in Chapters 3 and 4. In fact, the RBC

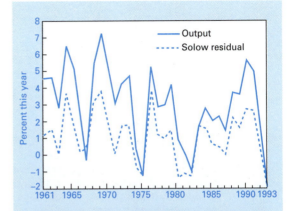

Figure 14.14. The Solow Residual and GDP, Germany, 1961–1993

The figure shows that growth in total factor productivity, as measured by the Solow residual, is strongly correlated with output. To some extent, the innovations themselves appear random.

Sources: OECD; *Statistiches Bundesamt*; authors' calculations.

approach can be seen as a variant of the growth theory exposed in Chapter 5.

The effect of a productivity shock is illustrated in Figure 14.15:[17] it raises the marginal productivity of both capital and labour. In the short run, given the stock of capital, the rate of return on capital rises.[18] For the time being, labour supply is assumed inelastic—the labour supply schedule is vertical—so the real wage rises. Output goes up since the same amounts of capital and labour are now more productive. On the demand side, wealth rises because both wage and earnings profits are higher, so consumption also increases. This is the short-run effect of a favourable supply shock. What about propagation? The RBC identifies two main channels.

[15] The Solow residual was introduced in Ch. 5. It is the percentage change in output minus a weighted average of growth in labour and capital inputs, where the weights are the respective factor shares of labour and capital respectively. The weights can be justified if both labour and capital are paid their marginal products and the aggregate production function exhibits constant returns to scale.

[16] In the sticky price interpretation, fluctuations of the Solow residual—which is highly correlated with real GDP—are endogenous and constitute one of several manifestations of a normal business cycle.

[17] This figure is the same as Fig. 5.5.

[18] If the same shock affects the whole world, the world real interest rate is likely to rise. If it affects only one country, the real interest rate can still rise temporarily even if the nominal interest rate cannot change when the exchange rate is fixed: expected inflation absorbs the difference.

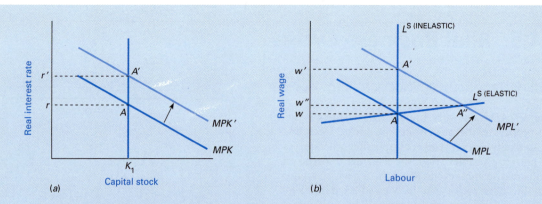

Figure 14.15. A Productivity Shock

A productivity shock raises the marginal productivity of capital and labour. In the short run, the stock of capital is unchanged and the real interest rises. In the inelastic aggregate labour supply ($L^{S(INELASTIC)}$) case, the labour supply curve is assumed to be vertical so the effect on productivity gain is to raise the real wage rate without any change in employment. When aggregate labour supply is elastic ($L^{S(ELASTIC)}$), the response is little change in wages and a larger fluctuation in employment.

14.5.2. Two Propagation Channels: Capital Accumulation and Intertemporal Substitution of Labour

The first propagation channel involves physical capital. The increase in marginal productivity of capital provides an incentive to accumulate more. Given the real interest rate, we now have $MPK > r$. (Alternatively, Tobin's q increases.) The build-up of capital results in a higher output level. If the technology shock is temporary, its passing will mark a decline in the productivity of capital, triggering a process of decumulation and a fall in productive capacity back to the initial level. The result is a flexible-price business cycle.

The second propagation channel is related to the other factor of production, labour. One feature of the previous story is unappealing: if labour supply is inelastic, there is no change in employment over the cycle. This contradicts evidence that employment and unemployment fluctuate a lot, suggesting that aggregate labour supply is elastic. In that case, productivity shocks will be accompanied by changes in the supply of labour, and the overall response of output will be reinforced. For this channel to work, we need a good reason for the aggregate elasticity of labour supply to be so high.

The primary determinant of the slope of labour sup-

ply, as Chapter 6 showed, is the contemporary leisure–consumption choice: each period a worker decides whether to work, earn money, and consume—or to enjoy leisure. Our conclusion, backed by empirical evidence, was that the labour supply is quite inelastic at the household level. Thus, a flat aggregate labour supply curve would only result from the aggregation of different households (see Box 6.1 and Figure 6.6).[19] In addition, the RBC approach emphasizes another channel: the *intertemporal* choice between leisure today and leisure tomorrow.

This choice is represented in Figure 14.16 and resembles Robinson Crusoe's choice of consumption over time analysed in Chapter 3. Preferences are represented by indifference curves, and express the trade-off that workers perceive between leisure today, ℓ_1, and leisure tomorrow, ℓ_2. Ignoring profits and other financial wealth, Robinson's 'budget constraint' is determined by wealth Ω, which in turn is determined by wage income, i.e. today's wage plus the discounted value of tomorrow's wage:

$$(14.5) \qquad \Omega = w_1(\overline{L}_1 - \ell_1) + \frac{w_2}{1 + r}(\overline{L}_2 - \ell_2).$$

[19] In principle, a flat collective bargaining curve would achieve the same result, but the RBC approach has generally avoided considering these forms of market imperfections.

The slope of this constraint is $-w_1(1 + r)/w_2$, that is, the ratio of today's wage w_1 to the present value of tomorrow's wage $w_2/(1 + r)$. As usual, the optimum choice is where the utility curve is tangent to the budget line.

A productivity shock that is temporary will raise today's wage w_1 and the real interest rate. This in turn will have two effects. A higher wage and a higher real interest rate mean a steeper budget line; work effort is worth more today relative to tomorrow. (Put differently, leisure today is more expensive than leisure tomorrow.) The substitution effect means that Crusoe works harder today. The income effect, in contrast, implies that Robinson Crusoe works less in both periods, since with the same work effort he can afford more leisure in both periods. If the substitution effect dominates the income effect, the labour supply schedule in Figure 14.16 is elastic and more labour is supplied.

This is the second propagation mechanism of the RBC theory. A favourable productivity shock leads workers to supply more labour today, and GDP rises over and above the direct productivity effect. In the following period, workers 'cash in' and work less; as labour supply is reduced, GDP decreases. All of that occurs without invoking any wage or price rigidity.

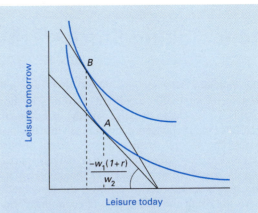

Figure 14.16. Intertemporal Substitution of Leisure

Robinson Crusoe decides on his work effort by comparing, in present value terms, the wage today w_1 and tomorrow $w_2/(1 + r)$: the slope of his 'budget line' is the ratio of these wages. The combination of an increase in both today's wage w_1 and the real interest rate triggers substitution (work more today, less tomorrow) and income (work less today and less tomorrow) effects. In this particular case, Robinson reacts to a temporary wage increase by enjoying less leisure and working harder today, and taking more leisure tomorrow.

14.5.3. Optimality Properties of the Cycle

RBC theory offers an alternative view of business cycles. Technology and other factors shift the production function out and raise the productivity of capital and labour. This causes firms to increase the stock of capital and workers to supply more labour. These reactions of the factors of production during the upswing phase of the cycle amplify the direct effect of the productivity impulse. More interesting, in a second stage, GDP declines as capital is decumulated and workers enjoy leisure or households incurring high costs of going to work stay home. These cyclical responses are optimal for all concerned. It is the best that agents can do, and there is no (involuntary) unemployment and no lost opportunities. This inter-

pretation stands in sharp contrast to the sticky price interpretation, which stresses unemployment and inefficient utilization of resources in recessions.

Thus, one important conclusion of the RBC approach—and one that is disturbing for many economists and therefore highly controversial—is that it is impossible to use demand management policies to attempt to improve matters. Indeed, a striking implication of the RBC theory is that it is not even desirable to even out business cycles, since both households and firms are by definition doing the best they can given changing constraints, so there is nothing to lament about. Deep recessions, for example, are seen as the economy's best response to severe adverse productivity shocks. In Chapter 15 we shall return to this important issue in more detail.

14.6. Taking Stock of the Two Theories

The previous two sections introduced two self-contained, internally consistent accounts of how impulses—shocks to demand, supply, or both—are translated via a propagation mechanism into business cycles. The *AS–AD*, or sticky price, account of business cycles relies on disequilibrium in markets—prices that do not adjust immediately to changing demand and supply conditions. In contrast, the RBC theory views the rising and falling tides of economic conditions as an equilibrium response to productivity shocks. It studiously avoids the terms 'demand' and 'supply', since in the RBC framework shocks to technology affect both simultaneously, and economic agents are fully aware of this. Given the current state of affairs, there is no reason for agents to behave differently and there is nothing to worry about.

Where do we stand? How do the theories match up with the facts? The following sections assess some of the evidence.[20]

14.6.1. Productivity, Real Wages, and Employment

Additional stylized facts about the labour market over the business cycle can be used to sharpen the debate. Figure 14.17 shows the cyclical behaviour of labour productivity, employment, the real wage, and the wage share for several OECD countries. Labour productivity—the ratio of output to employment—is procyclical and a coincident indicator. Employment is also procyclical. These facts are good news for the RBC view and a potential weakness of the *AS–AD* framework. With diminishing returns, given that the stock of capital cannot change much during a cycle, the marginal product of labour (and thereby the average product for all workers) should decline when production and employment increase. The RBC theory provides a plausible interpretation. If business cycles are driven by productivity shocks, then upswings necessarily coincide with periods of high productivity. High productivity plus intertemporal substitution of leisure or a flat aggregate supply curve then explain why labour demand and supply both rise during the upswing.

However, the extreme volatility of total factor productivity, as shown in Figure 14.15, is suspect. Neither labour nor capital is always fully employed by firms. Because dismissal costs are positive and human capital is often firm-specific, firms avoid firing employees immediately in downturns, even though production is reduced; workers are often asked to perform tasks less related to the direct production process, such as maintenance, building improvements, painting, and cleaning. During the expansion phase, there is a reserve of workers' effort which can be tapped. The same argument applies to the stock of capital; indeed, capacity utilization is not constant over the cycle (see Figure 14.4). The stylized fact of procyclical total factor productivity might therefore be due to a faulty measure of inputs: in recessions labour is employed but not in directly productive activities—we say labour is *hoarded*—and it is gradually put back to more directly productive use in the upturn that follows.

Another feature of Figure 14.17 is that real wages are acyclical.[21] Since the wage share is the ratio of real wages to labour productivity, it follows that the wage share—the proportion of total value added paid out in labour costs—is countercyclical.[22] Figure 14.6 confirms that the wage share promptly rises once the peak of the cycle has passed. Given its emphasis on intertemporal substitution of labour, the RBC approach now fares poorly: the procyclicality of employment is predicated on *procyclical* wages. Even if real wages were mildly procyclical, a very high elasticity of intertemporal substitution or labour supply would be required to explain the observed employment response. Almost all available data on individual behaviour point to inelastic labour supply, at least for heads of households. To the contrary, the small responsiveness of real wages to labour market conditions favours the sticky price view, and also lends evidence to the view that real wage rigidity is the source of involuntary unemployment.[23]

---

[20] To save space, we do not use our graphical apparatus (*IS–LM*, *AS–AD*, demand and supply as in Fig. 14.15) to explain every point. Careful readers will find it useful—indeed, an excellent exercise—to check their understanding by drawing their own graphs and reproducing the arguments.

[21] Inspection of the individual countries reveals no distinguishing patterns; in some cases there is weak evidence of procyclicality, in other cases, weak countercyclicality.

[22] The wage share is $WL/PY = (W/P)/(Y/L)$.

[23] RBC theorists counter that the reason is that job contracts do not usually provide for flexibility in the number of hours worked: they are rather of the all-or-nothing variety, i.e. work the normal work-week or don't work at all. (Recall Fig. 6.5.) If individual labour supply responses are 'discontinuous', with individuals shifting from zero hours to a fixed normal work-week and back, this might explain the high aggregate elasticity of employment observed.

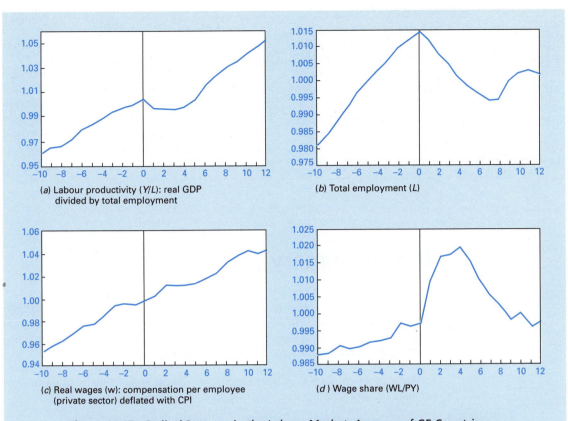

(a) Labour productivity (*Y/L*): real GDP divided by total employment

(b) Total employment (*L*)

(c) Real wages (w): compensation per employee (private sector) deflated with CPI

(d) Wage share (WL/PY)

Figure 14.17. Cyclical Patterns in the Labour Market, Average of G5 Countries, 1970–1994

Labour productivity and employment are procyclical and coincident. Wages are acyclical, while the wage share is anticyclical and lagging. The five countries are France, Germany, Italy, the UK, and the USA.

Source: OECD *National Accounts*; Business Sector Data Base

14.6.2. Money, Credit, and the Cycle

As noted above, the RBC admits no role for money in causing the business cycle.[24] This is because the *AS* curve is always vertical, and money is neutral in the short run. We saw however, in the stylized facts of Figure 14.4, that the real money stock is procyclical and in particular a leading indicator. In the sticky price business cycle (*AS–AD*) model, this is consistent with money growth leading and causing booms. It is not, however, consistent with the fact that nominal (and real as well) interest rates are procyclical and coincident. Indeed, in the *IS–LM* framework, a money supply impulse is expected to work on output via *declining* interest rates. Procyclical money and interest rates can be reconciled in the sticky price world if the primary impulses to the cycle come from the real demand side (spending, fiscal policy, the current account). In that case, an increase in demand-led GDP is accompanied—or led—by an increase in demand for money that is passively supplied by the central bank. Indeed,

[24] This has been an issue for a long time. It is interesting that, while the real business cycle idea has gained momentum only since the early 1980s, the difficulty of associating business cycles with money and credit was not lost on another keen observer, Karl Marx, who wrote:

Among other things, the superficiality of political economy becomes apparent when it assigns a causative role to the expansion and contraction of credit, which is really only a symptom of boom and bust of the industrial cycle. Just as heavenly bodies constantly repeat their revolutions once set in motion, so it is with production as soon as it is hurled into its pattern of expansion and contraction. Effects become for their part causes, and alternating conditions of the process, which constantly reproduce themselves, take on a periodic form. (Marx 1867: i, ch. 23)

private spending—investment and inventory accumulation in particular—is both procyclical and leading (stylized fact 4). In addition, forward-looking variables are likely to react more forcefully to expectations (the stock market and sentiment indicators). This explains why investment and spending on durable goods are volatile.

Does such evidence seal the debate in favour of the sticky price view? Certainly not! The RBC view is that credit and money demand are passive, expanding with the economy but without any notable influence on real variables. This is also consistent with the coincident and procyclical behaviour of interest rates in Figure 14.4, which the AS–AD framework can explain only if shifts to the underlying IS curve predominate, while monetary policy works with a lag.

In the end, the central issue remains the flexibility of prices. Evidence from Section 14.2 indicates that prices—measured as aggregate indices—do appear to be rigid. It is this element of realism that is lacking in the RBC theory of macroeconomic fluctuations and prevents its acceptance by a wide spectrum of the economics profession, despite its intellectual rigour.

14.7. Summary

1. Real output in economies tends to grow, but in a fluctuating, unsteady manner. Cyclical fluctuations of 5–10 years' duration are known as business cycles. They seldom deviate by more than 2%–5% of output from average, and yet are assigned considerable significance in modern industrial societies.

2. Fluctuations in output are accompanied by fluctuations in many other macroeconomic variables. Some lead, some lag, and most are coincident.

3. Components of GDP exhibit differing degrees of volatility, which confirms that the economic forces behind them are different. Private consumption is smoother than investment, and exports and imports are perhaps the most volatile of all for small open economies.

4. Two theoretical approaches have been used to study business cycles: deterministic cycles, and stochastic cycles. The more modern and widely accepted view is that cycles represent the transformation of random shocks over time.

5. The impulse-propagation mechanism transforms purely random shocks into more regular fluctuations. Crucial to the mechanism is the existence of lags in responses of some key variables to their determinants.

6. The AS–AD framework—which rests on the assumption that prices are sticky in the short run—is one example of an impulse-propagation framework. It rests on lags in the response of demand to GDP and of core to actual inflation. This view emphasizes the distinction between demand and supply shocks.

7. The real business cycle theory offers an alternative to the sticky price interpretation of business cycles. Random, exogenous productivity shocks are the underlying impulses that are propagated through two main channels: capital accumulation, and the intertemporal substitution of leisure.

8. Both interpretations of the business cycle have strengths and weaknesses. The AS–AD framework has difficulties explaining procyclical productivity and procyclical

interest rates. Yet it can account for the high variance of employment and the apparent short-run rigidity of nominal prices and real wages.

9. The RBC theory is ill-equipped to account for high fluctuations in employment given the acyclical behaviour of real wages. Most objectionable for RBC theory is its assumption that prices are perfectly flexible and that fluctuations represent society's best response to a changing environment which cannot be improved upon.

Key Concepts

- business cycles
- boom, recession
- turning points
- peak, trough
- detrending
- Burns–Mitchell diagram
- procyclical, countercyclical, acyclical
- leading and lagging indicator
- coincident indicator
- multiplier–accelerator model

- Robertson and Lundberg lags
- stationary GDP
- damped, explosive and oscillating cycles
- impulse-propagation mechanism
- sticky price business cycle theory
- demand shock
- supply shocks
- persistence
- real business cycle theory

Exercises: Theory

1. We saw that in the long-run stationary state of the multiplier-accelerator model $Y_t = Y_{t-1}$, which implies $\overline{Y} = (a_0 + b_0 + c_0)/(1 - a_1)$. In what sense can $1/(1 - a_1)$ be thought of as a multiplier?

2. What is the *economic* intuition for the fact that $\overline{Y}$ defined in the previous problem becomes infinite when $a_1 = 1$? (*Hint*: think about Figure 14.6.)

3. Figure 14.11 shows the *AS–AD* response to a money shock. In the background, the *IS–LM* apparatus is operating. Show how the same cycle unfolds in the *IS–LM* diagram.

4. Using the *AS–AD* diagram, trace graphically the dynamic reaction of an economy under fixed rates to a permanent decline in the foreign rate of inflation.

5. Box 14.2 presents two versions of the multiplier-accelerator model. Both have the same steady-state solution. Why? Do they have the same short-run multiplier?

6. Trace the effect of a positive technological shock on the *AS–AD* model with constant monetary and fiscal policy.

7. Suppose supply shocks predominated in an economy. What would the *AS–AD* model predict the sign of the correlation to be between output and inflation? What if demand shocks predominated instead?

8. In Figure 14.3, it is evident that PCA is on average a leading indicator and is countercyclical, meaning that the primary current account tends to deteriorate before the peak is reached. Given the evidence from Figures 14.4 and 14.5, which components of aggregate demand can best explain this fact?

9. Consider the real business cycle model as described in the text. Describe the effect of a temporary positive productivity shock on the optimal behaviour of the representative household. What should be the effect on household wealth? How will it react? Does it matter if households face borrowing constraints?

Exercises: Applications

1. Flip a coin 50 times, recording the outcomes in the order they occur (e.g. heads, tails, tails, heads, tails, etc.). Starting with $t = 1$ (the first flip), assign the value $+1$ to heads, -1 to tails. Now construct a data series according to the formula

$$x_t = 1.3x_{t-1} - 0.5x_{t-2} + \varepsilon_t,$$

where ε_t is the outcome of the flip. (Assign the value 0 to the initial conditions x_0 and x_{-1}.) How many cycles do you observe?

2. How does your answer to question 1 change if you use instead the formula

$$x_t = 1.3x_{t-1} - 0.9x_{t-2} + \varepsilon_t?$$

Can you explain the difference?

3. Now compute the coin-flipping exercise using

$$x_t = 1.3x_{t-1} - 0.3x_{t-2} + \varepsilon_t.$$

What do you notice about the behaviour of x over time? Can you explain what is going on?

4. In Table 14.2, the cyclical behaviour of exports differs considerably in Europe, Japan, and the USA. Can you offer an explanation for these differences?

5. Given that the PCA is the difference between exports and imports, explain why its cyclical behaviour may well depend on whether cycles are synchronized or not at home and abroad (i.e. whether we reach our peak at the same time as do our main trading partners, or when they reach their trough).

6. How can the *AS–AD* account for the strongly procyclical behaviour of real and nominal interest rates in the data? (*Hint*: go back to the *IS–LM* diagram.) What does this tell you about the relative importance of real versus monetary shocks in the data? (*Hint*: look at Table 14.3.)

7. In the Burns–Mitchell diagram below, (West) German net exports exhibit a clear divergence from the 'average' pattern displayed in Figure 14.5; i.e., net exports *lead* the cycle, and do so in a procyclical fashion.

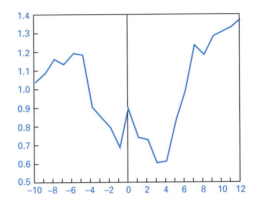

   (*a*) How might the sticky price view of the business cycle explain this fact?
   (*b*) Can you think of a real business cycle interpretation of procyclical net exports? Does it make sense to think of Germany as being 'different' from the other countries considered in the averages of Figure 14.5?

8. If you were to construct a Burns–Mitchell diagram for spending on consumer *durable* goods, what would you expect to find and why?

9. In Sweden in the early 1990s, a drastic collapse in house and share prices significantly reduced net wealth of Swedish households. For the first time in many years, households' net savings turned positive. Trace through the effects of such an event on Swedish output. (You should know that Sweden was fixing its exchange rate during the period.) What would you have expected had Sweden been pursuing a floating exchange rate regime?

10. After Britain left the ERM in 1992, it was in a deep recession; that is, *Y* was below $\bar{Y}$, and inflation was declining. The Bank of England reacted by pursuing an openly expansionary monetary policy. What would you expect to observe regarding *C*, *I*, *PCA*, interest rates, inflation, unemployment, and total output? How would you explain the fact that inflation in fact took a while to begin to creep upwards again?

Suggested Further Reading

The classics:

Burns, Arthur, and Mitchell, Wesley (1946), *Measuring Business Cycles*, NBER, New York.

Friedman, Milton, and Schwartz, Anna (1963), *A Monetary History of the United States*, Princeton University Press.

On historical episodes:

Bruno, Michael, and Sachs, Jeffrey (1985), *Economics of Worldwide Stagflation*, Basil Blackwell, Oxford.

Kindleberger, Charles (1986), *The World in Depression*, University of California Press, Berkeley, Calif.

Romer, Christina, and Romer, David (1989), 'Does Monetary Policy Matter? A Test in the Spirit of Friedman and Schwartz', *NBER Macroeconomic Annual*: 121–84.

Temin, Peter (1989), *The Cause of the Great Depression*, MIT Press, Cambridge, Mass.

On the modern debate:

Plosser, Charles I. (1989), 'Understanding Real Business Cycles', *Journal of Economic Perspectives*, 3, 51–77.

Mankiw, N. Gregory (1989), 'Real Business Cycles: A New Keynesian View', *Journal of Economic Perspectives*, 3, 79–90.

Stadler, George W. (1994), 'Real Business Cycles', *Journal of Economic Literature*, 32:1750–83.

Summers, Lawrence (1986), 'Some Skeptical Observations on Real Business Cycles', *Federal Bank of Minneapolis Review*, 10(4):23–7.

Appendix I: Trends in Macroeconomic Data and Detrending Procedures

Most macroeconomic data are trended: real variables like real GDP, consumption, exports, etc., have a tendency to grow secularly. Nominal variables also increase because inflation is positive on average. These trends dwarf fluctuations that are more relevant for the study of business cycles or the dynamics of inflation. To see these fluctuations around trend, we need to detrend the original variable.

Many techniques are available for removing trends. Some of them are shown in Figure A14.1, using the real GDP of Italy. Panel (a) illustrates the simplest procedure, a *linear trend*. A linear trend is simply a linear function of time: $y_t = a + bt$. Because GDP tends to grow exponentially, this is an undesirable procedure. Panel (b) displays a *linear logarithmic trend*, which looks like a linear trend once the real GDP is plotted on a logarithmic scale. The corresponding formula is $\log(y_t) = a + bt$. While this trend performs better, it fails to capture an apparent long-lasting slowdown in growth which occurred in the late 1970s. One way to cope with this difficulty is to used *split* log-linear trends, as in panel (c): we look for two different trends, one for the period 1970:1–1980:4 and one for the period 1981:1–1994:4. Yet another alternative is to model the trend as a nonlinear function of time. We often use, as in Figure 12.1, a fourth-degree polynomial (of the form $y_t = a_0 + a_1 t + a_2 t^2 + a_3 t^3 + a_4 t^4$).

In panel (d) a more elaborate technique, the *Hodrick–Prescott filter* is employed, producing a smoothly variable trend. This procedure minimizes the distance between actual GDP and the estimated trend, while allowing the user to choose how smooth the trend should be.[25] The corresponding cyclical component shown in panel (e) is simply the difference between actual GDP and its estimated trend, and thereby magnifies the fluctuations.

These methods all assume that the trend is *deterministic*: the trend is estimated as a smooth continuous function of time and is not allowed to jump over time. In that case, all the randomness of the original GDP series is absorbed by the difference between the actual variable and its trend as in Figure 14.2. Another approach assumes that the trend itself evolves randomly. For example, one might think that the evolution of technology—or total factor productivity, as measured by the Solow residual in Chapter 5—is simply the cumulation of random shocks, representing important discoveries and innovations that occur by chance. One way to allow for a random trend is *first-differencing*, simply subtracting the previous value from the current one and considering that this is the cyclical component.[26] The result, shown in panel (f), is not very different from the detrended series obtained in panel (e).

---

[25] Known to engineers as the Whittaker type B, this trend $\bar{y}_t$ is formally the solution to the problem: choose the sequence $\{\bar{y}_t\}$ for $t = 1, T$

$$\min \sum (y_t - \bar{y}_t)^2 + \lambda \sum [(y_t - \bar{y}_t) - (y_{t-1} - \bar{y}_{t-1})]^2,$$

where T is the length of the sample, and λ can be chosen at will. The higher is λ, the smoother is the series.

[26] Decompose GDP y_t into a trend T_t and a cyclical component C_t. The trend includes a determinist part $(a + bt)$ and a random component ε_t. Taking the first difference gives $y_t - y_{t-1} = (T_t - T_{t-1}) + (C_t - C_{t-1}) = b + (\varepsilon_t - \varepsilon_{t-1}) + (C_t - C_{t-1})$. The fluctuations in the first difference of real GDP reflect fluctuations in the cyclical component $(C_t - C_{t-1})$ *plus* fluctuations in the random component of the trend $(\varepsilon_t - \varepsilon_{t-1})$.

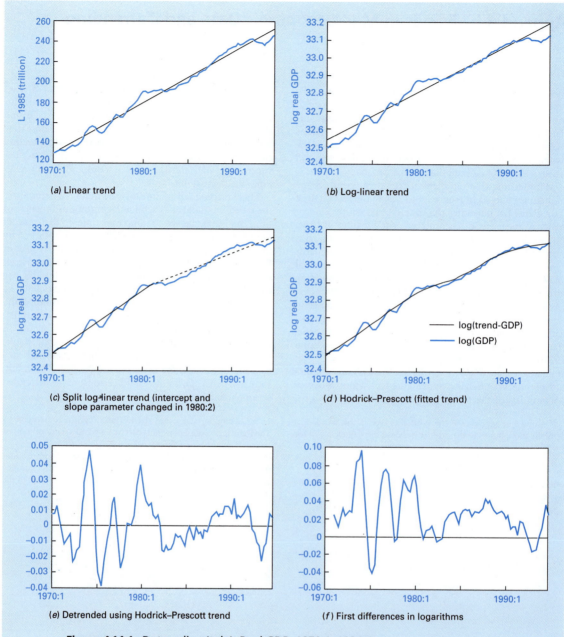

(a) Linear trend

(b) Log-linear trend

(c) Split log-linear trend (intercept and slope parameter changed in 1980:2)

(d) Hodrick–Prescott (fitted trend)

(e) Detrended using Hodrick–Prescott trend

(f) First differences in logarithms

Figure A14.1. Detrending Italy's Real GDP, 1970:1–1994:4

Source: OECD, *National Accounts*

Appendix II: A Dynamic *AS–AD* Model of the Business Cycle[27]

This appendix presents an example of a formal dynamic *AS–AD* model and solves it. The model takes the form of a system of linear difference equations. For simplicity, most absolute constants are set to zero. Aggregate demand is given by

$$(A14.1) \qquad Y_t = a_1 Y_{t-1} + a_2(\mu_t - \pi_t) + d_t,$$

where

Y_t = real output in t
μ_t = nominal rate of money growth in t
π_t = inflation rate in t
d_t = one-off non-monetary demand shocks (fiscal policy)

It is assumed that $a_1 > 0$, $a_2 > 0$, and that d_t is a random variable with expected value zero; that is, it averages to 0 over time.

Aggregate supply is given by

$$(A14.2) \qquad \pi_t = \overline{\pi}_t + b_1(Y_t - \overline{Y}_t) + s_t,$$

where

$\overline{\pi}_t$ = core inflation rate in t
$\overline{Y}_t$ = trend (equilibrium) level of output
s_t = one-off supply shocks (e.g. oil price increases, indirect tax increases)

It is assumed that $b_1 > 0$, and that s_t also has expected value 0.

Finally, core inflation is determined by

$$(A14.3) \qquad \overline{\pi}_t = \lambda \pi_t + (1 - \lambda)\pi_{t-1},$$

where $\overline{\pi}_t$ = core inflation rate in t. The constant λ is restricted so that $0 < \lambda < 1$.

The model can be solved in the following fashion:[28] Substitute core inflation from (A14.3) into (A14.2) and solve for π_t to obtain

---

[27] We are very grateful to Francis X. Hof (Technische Universität Wien) for numerous constructive suggestions concerning this appendix.
[28] The model can also be written and solved in matrix form. The system $[Y_t \, \pi_t]'$ then can be written

$$\begin{bmatrix} Y_t \\ \pi_t \end{bmatrix} = \left(\frac{1 + a_2 b_1}{1 - \lambda}\right)^{-1} \left\{ \begin{bmatrix} a_1 & -a_2 \\ \dfrac{a_1 b_1}{1 - \lambda} & 1 \end{bmatrix} \begin{bmatrix} Y_{t-1} \\ \pi_{t-1} \end{bmatrix} \right.$$

$$\left. + \begin{bmatrix} a_2 \mu_t + d_t + \dfrac{a_2}{1 - \lambda}(b_1 \overline{Y}_t - s_t) \\ \dfrac{b_1(a_2 \mu_t + d_t) - (b_1 \overline{Y}_t - s_t)}{1 - \lambda} \end{bmatrix} \right\}.$$

Obtaining this form requires writing (A14.1) and (A14.3) as a vector equation with the vector $[Y_t \, \pi_t]'$ as a function of itself, $[Y_{t-1} \, \pi_{t-1}]'$ and a vector of constants. This equation is then solved to eliminate $[Y_t \, \pi_t]'$ on the right-hand side, yielding the above equation.

$$(A14.4) \qquad \pi_t = \pi_{t-1} + \frac{b_1}{1 - \lambda}(Y_t - \overline{Y}_t) + \frac{s_t}{1 - \lambda}.$$

Next, subtract from equation (A14.1) the same equation holding in period $t - 1$:

$$(A14.5) \quad Y_t - Y_{t-1} = a_1(Y_{t-1} - Y_{t-2}) + a_2[(\mu_t - \mu_{t-1})$$
$$- (\pi_t - \pi_{t-1})] + d_t - d_{t-1}.$$

From (A14.4),

$$\pi_t - \pi_{t-1} = \frac{b_1}{1 - \lambda}(Y_t - \overline{Y}_t) + \frac{s_t}{1 - \lambda},$$

so (A14.5) can be rewritten as

$$(A14.6) \quad Y_t = \alpha_1 Y_{t-1} + \alpha_2 Y_{t-2} + \alpha_3 \Delta\mu_t + \alpha_4 \Delta d_t$$
$$+ \alpha_5 \overline{Y}_t + \alpha_6 s_t,$$

where

$$\alpha_1 = \frac{(1 + a_1)(1 - \lambda)}{1 - \lambda + a_2 b_1}$$

$$\alpha_2 = \frac{-a_1(1 - \lambda)}{1 - \lambda + a_2 b_1}$$

$$\alpha_3 = \frac{a_2(1 - \lambda)}{1 - \lambda + a_2 b_1}$$

$$\alpha_4 = \frac{1 - \lambda}{1 - \lambda + a_2 b_1}$$

$$\alpha_5 = \frac{a_2 b_1}{1 - \lambda + a_2 b_1}$$

$$\alpha_6 = \frac{-a_2}{1 - \lambda + a_2 b_1},$$

and where Δ signifies first difference, e.g. $\Delta\mu_t = \mu_t - \mu_{t-1}$, etc. Equation (A14.6) will be stable (non-explosive) as long as $a_1 < 1$.[29] The model will exhibit cyclical or oscillating deterministic behaviour in response to a single shock if and only if output is sufficiently sluggish (a_1 close to 1) and/or expectations are sufficiently forward-looking (λ close to 1).[30] Naturally, if the model is hit by many random shocks,

---

[29] Technically, stability for a second-order difference equation requires that the characteristic roots must lie inside the unit circle (i.e. have modulus less than unity). The roots of (A14.6) are

$$\left\{ \left[\alpha_1 - \sqrt{(\alpha_1^2 + 4\alpha_2)}\right]/2, \left[\alpha_1 + \sqrt{(\alpha_1^2 + 4\alpha_2)}\right]/2 \right\}.$$

Given the other assumptions on the parameters, the equation is stable as long as $a_1 < 1$.
[30] Cyclical behaviour in the deterministic version of the model (that is, when d, s, and μ are identically zero) arises when the characteristic roots are conjugate complex. From the previous footnote, this occurs when $\alpha_1^2 + 4\alpha_2 < 0$, or when $(1 - a_1)^2(1 - \lambda) < 4a_1 a_2 b_1$.

oscillatory behaviour can arise all the same, just as Slutsky predicted.

It is useful to observe that, as the backward-looking element of core inflation becomes dominant ($\lambda \to 0$), equation (A14.6) becomes

$$(A14.6') \quad Y_t = \frac{1+a_1}{1+a_2 b_1} Y_{t-1} - \frac{a_1}{1+a_2 b_1} Y_{t-2} + \frac{a_2}{1+a_2 b_1} \Delta \mu_t$$

$$+ \frac{1}{1+a_2 b_1} \Delta d_t + \frac{a_2 b_1}{1+a_2 b_1} \overline{Y}_t - \frac{a_2}{1+a_2 b_1} s_t,$$

whereas, as the forward-looking element of core inflation becomes dominant ($\lambda \to 1$), equation (A14.6) becomes

$$(A14.6'') \quad Y_t = \overline{Y}_t - (1/b_1)s_t.$$

Thus the effects of demand shocks decline as core inflation becomes forward-looking. The case $\lambda = 1$ corresponds to full price flexibility: output only responds to supply shocks as in the RBC model. Inflation can be solved as a second-order difference equation in a way similar to (A14.6):

$$(A14.7) \quad \pi_t = \alpha_1 \pi_{t-1} + \alpha_2 \pi_{t-2} + \frac{a_2 b_1}{1-\lambda + a_2 b_1} \mu_t$$

$$+ \frac{b_1}{1-\lambda + a_2 b_1} d_t - \frac{b_1}{1-\lambda + a_2 b_1} \overline{Y}_t$$

$$+ \frac{a_1 b_1}{1-\lambda + a_2 b_1} \overline{Y}_{t-1} + \frac{1}{1-\lambda + a_2 b_1} s_t$$

$$- \frac{a_1}{1-\lambda + a_2 b_1} s_{t-1}.$$

As the backward-looking element of core inflation becomes dominant ($\lambda \to 0$), equation (A14.7) becomes

$$(A14.7') \quad \pi_t = \frac{1+a_1}{1+a_2 b_1} \pi_{t-1} - \frac{a_1}{1+a_2 b_1} \pi_{t-2} + \frac{a_2 b_1}{1+a_2 b_1} \mu_t$$

$$+ \frac{b_1}{1+a_2 b_1} d_t - \frac{b_1}{1+a_2 b_1} \overline{Y}_t + \frac{a_1 b_1}{1+a_2 b_1} \overline{Y}_{t-1}$$

$$+ \frac{1}{1+a_2 b_1} s_t - \frac{a_1}{1+a_2 b_1} s_{t-1}.$$

As the forward-looking element of core inflation becomes dominant ($\lambda \to 1$), equation (A14.7) becomes

$$(A14.7'') \quad \pi_t = \mu_t + \frac{1}{a_2} d_t - \frac{1}{a_2} \overline{Y}_t + \frac{a_1}{a_2} \overline{Y}_{t-1}$$

$$+ \frac{1}{a_2 b_1} s_t - \frac{a_1}{a_2 b_1} s_{t-1}.$$

PART VI

Macroeconomic Policy

Macroeconomics originated as a field largely because of its proximity to policy-making. Part V has shown how, in theory, macroeconomic policies can prevent recessions, unnecessarily high unemployment, and inflation. Part VI explores the limits of demand management—ranging from the government's budget constraint to the interactions of private expectations with policy effectiveness—and the role of politics in policy-making. It also develops the principles of supply-side policies, the possibility of altering incentives to work, save, and produce, and how this affects the long-run capacity of the economy.

15

Fiscal Policy, Debt, and Seigniorage

Chancellor:	In my old age I have been freed from pain.
	Listen and look at this portentous bill
	Which has made welfare out of all our ill:
	'Be it known to all men who may so require;
	This note is worth a thousand crowns entire.
	Which has its guarantee and counterfoil
	In untold wealth beneath imperial soil.
	And this is hereby a substitute approved
	Until such time as the treasure can be moved.'
Emperor:	And do my people think it negotiable?
	Do army and court take it for pay in full?
	Strange though I think it, I must ratify it.
Steward:	To collect those fluttering notes, one couldn't try it;
	once issued, they are scattered in a flash.
	The Exchanges stand wide open for the queue
	Where every bill is honoured and changed for cash—Silver and gold—
	at a discount it is true.
	And then to butcher, baker, pub it goes,
	Half the world only seems to think of stuffing;
	While the other half in brand new clothes goes puffing.
	The clothier cuts the cloth, the tailor sews.
	Long live the Emperor! Makes the cellars gush
	In a cooking, roasting, platter-clattering crush.

Goethe, *Faust*, trans. L. MacNeice

15.1. Overview

Governments are big, and have been growing bigger for most of the postwar period. Table 15.1 shows that governments in the European Union spend and tax close to half of GDP. A large part of this spending represents redistribution of income among citizens—about a third of GDP on average. Yet, governments are also big consumers. They spend close to one-fourth of what all households do on goods and services. Nor are governments known to be particularly strict in managing their budgets. Deficits are frequent, and most governments are heavily indebted to the private sector and foreigners. On average, public debt in Europe represents about three-fourths of a year's GDP, and in some countries, such as Belgium, Italy, or Ireland, the stock of public debt far exceeds a full year of domestic product.

This chapter looks at the economic functions of governments and how they fulfil their tasks. Why do governments have an economic role to play at all? This question has been debated since time immemorial between right, left, and centre, between partisans of

laissez-faire economics and interventionists. In this chapter we focus on two roles of government in the national economy: microeconomic (the provision of

Table 15.1. General Government Spending and Finances: EU, USA, and Japan, 1995

	EU[a]	USA	Japan
Total spending (% of GDP)	50.1	33.4	37.4
Public consumption			
% of GDP	16.5	17.0	10.1
% of private consumption	26.6	25.0	15.1
Budget surplus (% of GDP)	−4.7	−1.8	−4.1
Gross debt (% of GDP)	72.6	63.0	88.9

[a] EU includes unified Germany, except for gross debt (only West Germany).

Sources: European Economy; OECD Economic Outlook

public goods and services, income redistribution) and macroeconomic (stabilization of aggregate activity). The stabilization function is performed both through active policies designed to negate the effects of business cycle fluctuations—perhaps originating in the private sector—and through the working of automatic stabilizers embedded in the public budget.

In this process, governments often find themselves running budget deficits: they pay out more than they take in. To meet their intertemporal budget constraints, they must either close the deficit or borrow and accumulate public debt. This process is inherently

explosive, since existing debt must be serviced. (At least, the interest must be paid.) An alternative for the government is to pay its bills simply by printing some money (Mephistopheles' solution in Faust), effectively exploiting its monopoly right to create legal tender. **Seigniorage**, as this is called, relieves the government of the need to borrow, but it has potential implications for money supply and inflation. Still another, less frequently used, option is partial or total default, whereby the government solves its budget constraint by a confiscation of wealth from its creditors.

15.2. Fiscal Policy and Economic Welfare

15.2.1. Provision of Public Goods and Services

Governments 'produce' goods and services, mostly for collective consumption. Why are they involved in that activity? The general response is that without the state these goods would not be provided at all, or would be provided in insufficient quantity. First, these goods are often collective goods. Second, they are produced under increasing returns.

The particularity of public goods is that they cannot be appropriated for individual consumption. This applies, for example, to law and order, defence, public gardens, or foreign affairs. Another characteristic of public goods is that their use by one person benefits another person. This is called an **externality**.[1] A good example is education. All of society benefits from mass literacy; workers can interact more effectively, which raises their productivity. Indeed, Chapter 5 has shown that there is a direct link between the education level of a population—its human capital—and a country's growth performance and well-being. The generic feature of collective goods is that, without the government, they would not be produced at all privately, or would be produced in socially insufficient quantities, because individuals would not be willing to pay for the externality that benefits society as a whole.

Another reason for the undersupply of some categories of goods and services is the presence of increasing returns in production. One example is the usage

of streets: the cost of building and operating a street is roughly the same whether there are few or many users. Streets could be private and their use charged to users, and this would undoubtedly relieve traffic congestion in cities.[2] On the other hand, there is a risk that individually each of us reacts to street tolls by cutting down our use of such streets to the point where the cost per remaining user could be so large to be dissuasive, resulting in no streets in some areas.

While there is a strong justification for *some* government consumption—in reality, the provision of collective goods—there is no clear-cut border between goods and services that can be provided only publicly and those that can in principle be provided privately. This relates to such differing cases as education (private schools and universities exist alongside public education), social security (health and retirement insurance are increasingly often privately provided), and utilities (highways are built and run by private companies; electricity and telephone networks are privately owned and operated). Consider, for example, police protection. This service could be privately organized, but it benefits all concerned whether they pay for it or not; in practice, only better-off, homogeneous neighbourhoods could afford to set it up. Furthermore, the state has an incentive to combat lawlessness on a wider scale than do individuals interested only in protecting their own safety.

The absence of unequivocal criteria for deciding what should be publicly provided explains why there

[1] The concept of externality is presented in Ch. 5.

[2] Much as public goods are undersupplied by the market, free goods are overconsumed.

Table 15.2. Government Transfers, Various Countries, 1960 and 1995

	Transfers as % of GDP		Transfers as % of government outlays	
	1960	1995	1960	1995
Austria	14.8	25.0	51.8	51.9
Belgium	12.7	27.7	44.8	53.4
Denmark	7.6	26.6	35.1	45.9
Finland	9.0	31.1	41.6	52.3
France	16.3	27.6	53.5	54.3
Germany	14.1	22.4	50.2	49.3
Greece	5.3	16.6	30.6	37.3
Ireland	9.6	17.1	38.7	44.8
Italy	11.2	22.4	45.4	44.6
Japan[a]	4.5	13.5	34.5	50.3
Netherlands	8.6	29.8	na	60.1
Portugal	3.7	16.4	24.5	41.8
Spain	2.9	21.0	23.1	49.1
Sweden	8.6	32.1	32.2	48.4
Switzerland[a]	5.9	20.5	34.2	55.7
UK	9.0	15.4	30.7	38.4
USA[a]	6.0	14.1	24.4	39.3

[a] 1993; *source*: IFS.

Source: OECD, *European Economy*

is much soul-searching on the issue. Recent privatizations throughout Europe reflect a trend towards reduced public ownership, a reversal of a long trend in the other direction. Whatever the ultimate evolution of thought on this matter, however, some government spending will always be considered desirable.

15.2.2. Redistributive Goals: Equity versus Efficiency

Productive efficiency—meaning the optimal use of available productive resources—is achieved when each factor of production is paid its marginal productivity. This may result in a very unequal distribution of income and wealth. The reality of economic life is the coexistence of much individual wealth alongside grinding poverty. While this outcome may be efficient from a productive point of view, an altogether different logic emphasizes that human beings all have similar needs and should be able to meet them. **Equity** or fairness is often seen as a requirement for society to be cohesive and stable. Yet equity and efficiency often

work against each other; there is a fundamental **equity–efficiency trade-off**.

Governments can reduce inequalities. Progressive income taxes reduce the differences in post-tax incomes. Taxes levied on the better-off pay for transfers to the worse-off. In fact, a significant part of public spending is dedicated to income redistribution. Table 15.2 shows the size of transfers, both as a share of GDP and as a proportion of total government outlays. In some countries, this is the single largest item in the government budget. Not surprisingly, different countries deal differently with the equity–efficiency trade-off. Sweden and the Netherlands seem to place more weight on equity than Japan or the USA, for example.

The trade-off, however, implies that income redistribution for the sake of equity has disincentive effects. Highly paid—and presumably highly productive—people may reduce their work effort in response to heavy taxation, or may even move abroad. On the other hand, those who receive transfers from the state may find it pointless to work hard for little net reward.[3]

---

[3] The topics of incentives and taxation are treated in Ch. 17.

15.3. Macroeconomic Stabilization

Providing public services and redistributing income does not imply that government spending differs from revenues. The government could perform its functions without running budget imbalances. As Table 15.3 shows, however, significant surpluses and deficits are the rule rather than the exception. This section looks at a second function of government budgets: stabilizing aggregate income and spending as well as unemployment. To achieve these goals, governments shift resources intertemporally, dissaving during recessions and saving at times of expansions. That there exist valid reasons for public imbalances does not mean that imbalances are always justified, of course.

15.3.1. Long-Run Consumption and Tax Smoothing

The flow of (usually freely provided) public goods and services constitutes an integral part of each indivi-

Table 15.3. Primary Budget Balances, Various Countries, 1972–1995
% of GDP

	1972	1975	1980	1985	1990	1995
Austria	3.0	−1.2	0.0	0.4	1.0	−1.0
Belgium	−1.3	−1.8	−4.0	0.9	4.3	4.3
Denmark	2.7	−2.4	−2.8	4.1	1.8	1.3
Finland	3.3	1.9	1.9	2.1	3.6	−3.9
France	1.1	−1.7	0.8	−0.8	0.8	−1.6
Germany	−0.8	−5.6	−1.6	1.1	−0.1	1.2
Greece	0.6	−2.1	−0.3	−6.7	−3.8	2.9
Ireland	−1.4	−8.5	−8.5	−4.3	4.0	1.4
Italy	−7.4	−8.1	−3.9	−5.2	−1.8	3.3
Japan	−0.4	−2.8	−3.4	0.9	3.5	−3.5
Netherlands	1.2	−1.2	−1.5	0.8	−0.6	1.3
Norway	4.6	3.9	5.9	8.7	0.9	1.3
Spain	0.3	0.1	−1.9	−4.2	−0.8	−1.1
Sweden	2.5	0.6	−4.4	−0.8	4.3	−5.6
UK	1.2	−1.2	−0.3	0.5	1.2	−1.7
USA	0.7	−2.9	−0.1	−1.0	−0.4	0.4

[a] + indicates a surplus, − indicates a deficit

Source: OECD *Economic Outlook*

dual's consumption. In general, individual agents prefer a smooth pattern of consumption over time, and that applies to collective as well as private consumption. It is the social responsibility of governments—and a factor of their electoral success—to provide a steady flow of public goods and services.

To purchase these goods and services, the government must levy taxes. Taxes, however, reduce individuals' incomes and, therefore, their means to consume. For this reason, it is inefficient to lighten the tax burden for a while and then raise it sharply to satisfy the government intertemporal budget constraint.[4] A well-run government wants to finance a steady flow of spending by a steady rate of taxation. **Tax smoothing** is the normal companion to **consumption smoothing**.

This principle has a central implication for the conduct of fiscal policy. If a series of bad years reduces the country's income and the ability to pay taxes, the government's best course of action is not to cut spending and maintain the budget in balance. Rather, it should endeavour to maintain a steady flow of public goods and services, and finance the tax revenue shortfall by borrowing. (Public sector borrowing can be done domestically or abroad. Globally, a country with a temporary fall in income must borrow. As a first approximation, it does not matter whether it is the private or the public sector that borrows abroad.[5]) Conversely, a few particularly good years during which taxable income rises sharply should be used not to raise government consumption temporarily, but to increase savings. Acting on behalf of the public at large, a government must behave like any economic agent, meeting temporary income disturbances by saving or borrowing, of course within the limits of its budget constraint. Similarly, if the need for public spending rises or declines temporarily, the appropriate response is to borrow or save while keeping tax pressure steady. Box 15.1 applies the principle of tax smoothing to the controversial case of Germany's unification.

Budget deficits met by public borrowing increase the public debt. Figure 15.1 shows how public debts (as a percentage of GDP) have evolved over the past century. It is fairly clear that debts rise, sometimes spectacularly, during wars and decline afterwards. Wars

---

[4] This is especially true if households have imperfect access to credit markets, and thus cannot offset the government's actions. Consumption smoothing is studied in Ch. 4.

[5] S. 15.5.4 returns to this issue.

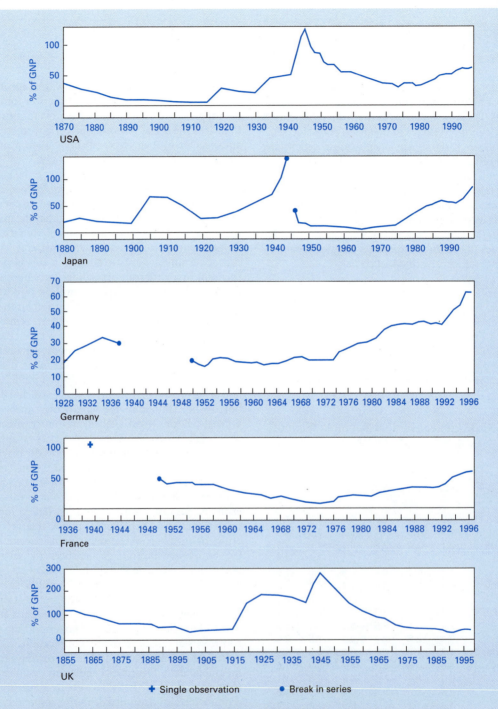

Figure 15.1. Historical Evolution of Public Debts, Five Countries

The UK had a debt to GDP ratio of over 100% in 1855, a legacy of the Napoleonic wars. During the First World War the British debt rose to about 200%, and during the Second World War to 300%. The war efforts are also visible for the USA (including the Civil War) and Japan.

Source: OECD

BOX 15.1. TAX SMOOTHING AFTER GERMAN REUNIFICATION

When he endorsed swift reunification early in 1990, Chancellor Helmut Kohl promised that there would be no new taxes for West Germans. Yet, the former East Germany entered the Federal Republic with precious little dowry, a hugely inefficient productive sector, a large external debt (mostly to West Germany), poor infrastructure, and considerable environmental liabilities. In the eastern provinces, output fell by about 50%, unemployment—official and unofficial—rose to about 30%, and state-owned enterprises needed cash to stay afloat until they could be sold. From a budgetary viewpoint, the eastern provinces required massive public spending but could not contribute much to the financing. The pressure on the federal budget is apparent in Table 15.4. Yet, this evolution is best regarded as temporary. Within a decade or two the eastern provinces will have very good prospects of catching up with the West. Facing a temporary shock, tax smoothing calls for accumulating public debt and limiting tax increases, as well as for current account deficits (i.e. foreign borrowing). Yet, considerable anguish has mounted as the full costs of reunification were tallied. The Chancellor has come under public pressure to stem the rise of the national debt and close the external deficit, even if there are good economic reasons to put up with it.

Table 15.4. Fiscal Implications of German Reunification (% of GDP)

	1988	1989	1990	1991	1992	1993	1994	1995	1996
Goverment expenditures	46.3	44.8	45.1	47.9	48.6	49.4	49.0	49.1	48.6
Budget surplus	−2.2	0.1	−2.1	−3.3	−2.9	−3.3	−2.5	−2.3	−2.2
Gross public debt	44.4	43.2	43.4	42.7	47.3	51.8	54.6	62.5	62.5
Current account	4.2	4.8	3.3	−1.1	−1.1	−0.8	−1.1	−0.7	−1.2

Source: OECD *Economic Outlook*, June 1995

are periods of unusually high public expenditure, yet they are rarely expected to last very long. The tax-smoothing principle seems to have been applied here (even if some countries eventually defaulted on part of their debts). Similarly, the oil shocks of the 1970s were met in many countries by debt accumulation.

15.3.2. Short-Run Stabilization

The principle of public spending and tax smoothing applies to shorter-run cyclical fluctuations as well. A cyclical downturn means that personal incomes decline temporarily. The *laissez-faire* view is that, facing a temporary income fluctuation, individuals should borrow and/or save to smooth their consumption pattern, with government playing no particular role. This prescription would be correct if all individuals could indeed borrow their way out of a recession. Credit rationing, however, changes the situation.[6] Individuals who cannot borrow, or cannot borrow as much as needed, are unable to smooth out their consumption.

Not only are they hurt, but their declining demand deepens the slowdown through the demand multiplier effect. In Figure 15.2, starting from long-run equilibrium at point *A*, the aggregate demand curve shifts from *AD* to *AD'*. Under fixed exchange rates, the government can stop this process of spiralling demand decline. To keep the curve in its *AD* position and prevent the move from point *A* to point *B*, it either increases its own spending or provides tax relief. In effect, the government borrows on behalf of its credit-constrained citizens. Conversely, a demand boom provides the government with the opportunity to run a budget surplus and pay back the debt accumulated during previous downturns.[7]

When demand exogenously falls, the economy moves from point *A* to point *B*. In the absence of stabilization policy, it will eventually move to point *C*. Fiscal policy can be used to speed up a return to trend output at point *A*, or even to prevent the *AD* schedule from shifting.

The fact that unemployment rises during recessions provides another rationale for countercyclical fiscal

---

[6] Ch. 4 explains the mechanism and importance of credit rationing.

[7] The principle does not apply in case of permanent disturbances when complete adjustment is necessary.

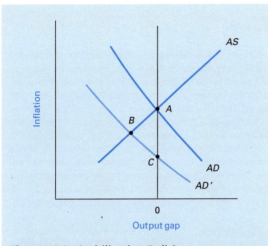

Figure 15.2. Stabilization Policies

When demand exogenously falls, the economy moves from point A to point B. In the absence of stabilization policy, the economy will eventually move to point C. Fiscal policy can be used to speed up a return to trend output at point A, or even to prevent the AD schedule from shifting.

policies. The mere increase in unemployment is not a justification for active fiscal policies. If unemployment rises because its equilibrium level has permanently increased, the economy will eventually settle along its long-run aggregate supply schedule and demand management is bound to fail. Attempts to keep unemployment below equilibrium through fiscal expansions will only lead to more public debt. However, short-run fluctuations in unemployment around its equilibrium rate occur because price and wage rigidities prevent an optimal utilization of available resources. **Countercyclical fiscal policy** may be a corrective device to keep unemployment at its equilibrium level, and output near its trend growth path. Sustaining aggregate demand with public spending when private demand weakens, or directly boosting private demand with tax relief, could eliminate business cycles altogether.

15.3.3. Automatic Stabilizers

Public budgets tend to go into surplus during upturns and into deficits during recessions. While government consumption is largely unaffected by cyclical

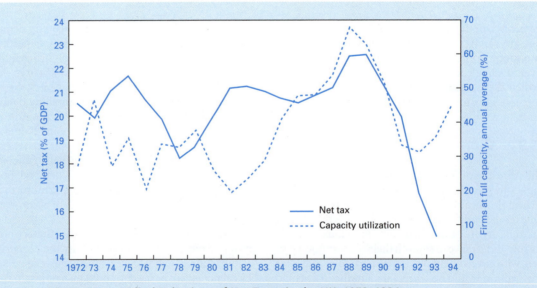

Figure 15.3. Cyclical Behaviour of Net Taxes in the UK, 1972–1994

When the economy enters into a slowdown (the rate of capacity utilization declines), usually with a lag of a year or two, tax receipts fall and transfers rise. Taxes net of transfers are procyclical.

Source: OECD

BOX 15.2. THE BUDGETARY PROCESS

All democracies follow roughly the same budgetary process. Once a year, the government presents a budget to its parliament, which then debates on—and sometimes amends—each item before voting on it. One part of the budget concerns spending by the various ministries or departments; the other part concerns tax revenue. The parliament approves tax rates, literally hundreds of them, from VAT to income, from petrol to corporate profits or property. While spending authorizations are set in amounts, tax receipts are uncertain, depending upon how much is to be taxed at the set rates. This is why parliament cannot decide exactly what the deficit or surplus will be. Instead, it is presented with a forecast of GDP which underlies a forecast of tax receipts and the associated deficit or surplus. It is well understood that economic conditions will settle the matter as the fiscal year goes on. Table 15.5 shows the amount of 'error' involved, first in the case of France. The higher-than-expected GDP growth of 1988 delivered a slightly lower deficit than planned, with the opposite effect in 1992. Naturally, most governments have a tendency to forecast high growth, large tax receipts, and small deficits, since such forecasts are not binding. It takes an unusually good year to have a better budgetary outcome then announced, while a moderate slowdown easily results in massive slippages.

Table 15.5 also shows the particular situation of Russia in 1995. The budget passed by the Russian parliament was based on an unrealistically low inflation target. The higher outcome led to higher tax receipts but not to higher spending, since spending had been voted upon in nominal terms. This was the ploy used by the government to get a spending-oriented parliament to adopt a rigorous budget.

Table 15.5. Expected and Realized Budgets, France, 1988–1992, and Russia, 1995

	France					Russia			
	Budget deficit (FF bn)		Real GDP growth (%)				Budget deficit (% of GDP)		Inflation (%)
	Target	Actual	Target	Actual			Target	Actual	Target	Actual
1988	115.0	114.7	2.2	4.5	1995	7.9	3.1	30	131
1992	89.9	226.3	2.1	1.3				

Sources: France: Les Notes Bleues, IMF; Russia: RECEP

fluctuations, net taxes, i.e. taxes less transfers from the government to the private sector, are strongly procyclical, as shown in Figure 15.3.[8] The reason is that nearly all taxes are set as *rates* applied to incomes or spending. When incomes and spending rise, tax collection automatically rises, and conversely. Public transfers, on the other hand, and unemployment benefits in particular, rise during recessions and decline during booms. Only if the government takes explicit steps to alter its budget can the cyclicality of public budgets be avoided. Given the nature of the budgetary process described in Box 15.2, this seems unlikely.

When an economy slows down, if the budget is not amended—which would require a new law voted by the legislature—its planned budget deficit will increase, or its planned surplus will shrink (or shift into deficit). This automatic lowering of taxes amounts to an implicit fiscal expansion. Conversely, a better-than-expected economic performance reduces the budget deficit or increases the surplus because of enhanced tax income for the government. This can be looked upon as a contractionary fiscal policy. In the end, we see that exogenous shifts in private demand are automatically cushioned—if not completely offset—by shifts in public demand: these are the so-called **automatic stabilizers**. They work in the absence of any policy action: simply by enacting the budget as approved by the parliament, the government finds itself conducting a countercyclical fiscal policy, dampening both recessions and expansions.

---

[8] Remember that the budget deficit is the difference between government purchases and net taxes or, equivalently, is consumption plus transfers less tax revenues.

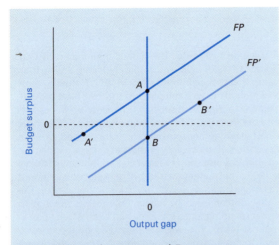

Figure 15.4. Endogenous and Exogenous Components of Budgets

The line *FP* describes how the actual budget responds to cyclical fluctuations of output about its trend for a given fiscal policy stance. The move from line *FP* to line *FP'* describes a more expansionary policy stance. The cyclically adjusted budget is measured assuming a zero output gap. For fiscal policy stance *FP* it is given by point *A*, and for *FP'* by point *B*.

15.3.4. How to Interpret Budget Figures

The mechanism of the automatic stabilizers implies that the budget is partly endogenous. Policy choices determine a planned surplus or deficit; economic conditions determine the outcome. This is why budget figures do not always fully reveal the government's intentions. Table 15.3 shows that most countries underwent budget deficits in 1975 and 1980. Did this reflect a collective enthusiasm for expansionary policies? In fact, these years coincided with the post-oil-shock recessions (the exception being Norway, an oil-exporting country).

The endogeneity of budgets means that it is not straightforward to determine the stance of fiscal policy as tight or easy. To do so requires separating out exogenous policy decisions from endogenous responses to cyclical fluctuations. To eliminate the cyclical component, we ask what would have happened to the budget balance if real GDP had been on its trend path. In Figure 15.4 a given upward-sloping schedule represents a budget as approved by parliament. The positive slope of each schedule represents the automatic stabilizer: given tax and spending rules, an increase in the GDP improves the budget balance. The budget corresponding to schedule *FP* is tighter—less

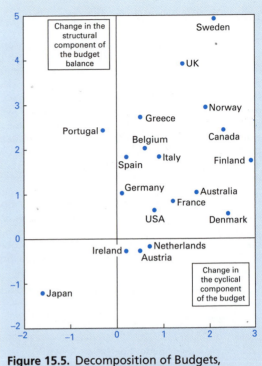

Figure 15.5. Decomposition of Budgets, 1993–1996: Estimates by OECD (% of GDP)

Forecasted budget deficit changes between 1993 and 1996 are decomposed into two parts: on the vertical axis are shown changes in the cyclically adjusted budget (i.e. exogenous changes in the stance), sometimes called the structural component; the horizontal axis measures the remaining cyclical part (computed as the total change less the cyclically adjusted change). Towards the south-east, for example, are the countries where fiscal policy is expanding but where the budget tends to improve because of a cyclical upturn (like the move from point *A* to point *B* in Figure 15.4). Between 1993 and 1996 most countries emerged from the recession of the early 1990s, which improves the budget balance. At the same time, they have pursued restrictive fiscal polices. Japan stands out: it has plunged into a recession, hence a worsening of the cyclical component of the deficit, and is conducting expansionary fiscal policies, hence a worsening in the cyclically adjusted component.

Source: OECD, *Economic Outlook*, June 1995

expansionary—than the budget represented by *FP'*: for any given GDP level, the surplus is larger because of either less spending, or more taxes, or a combination of both.

The figure reveals why it is difficult to interpret

budget figures. If, for example, the economy moves out of a recession at the same time as tax rates are reduced, it goes from point A' to point B'. As drawn, the budget improves, from a deficit to a surplus. The reason for the improvement is purely cyclical, however; in fact, the authorities have relaxed the budget by cutting taxes. The actual improvement in the budget can easily be misconstrued as a sign that fiscal policy has been tightened.

In order to better interpret the fiscal stance of the authorities, we would like to have a measure free of cyclical effects. The usual procedure is to compute the **cyclically adjusted budget**. This is the budget surplus or deficit that would occur if the economy were on its trend growth path, when the output gap is nil. In the figure, cyclically adjusted budgets are represented by

points A and B. For FP, the cyclically adjusted budget is in surplus, even though a recession could lead to an actual deficit at point A'. The fiscal relaxation from FP to FP' is confirmed by the move from point A to point B where the cyclically adjusted budget is in deficit. Yet, the exogenous relaxation is more than offset by the endogenous effect of the cyclical expansion, so that the actual budget is in surplus at point B'. Figure 15.5 applies the distinction between actual and cyclically adjusted deficits. Countries where the cyclically adjusted budget has improved (above the horizontal axis) are countries where fiscal policy has been exogenously tightened up. The diagram makes clear that many countries have used the recent period of cyclical improvement in the budget as an opportunity to correct structural imbalances.

15.4. Deficit Financing: Public Debt and Seigniorage

Whether budget imbalances are justified by tax smoothing and consumption smoothing considerations, by active stabilization policies, or by the spontaneous operation of the automatic stabilizers, the intertemporal budget constraint prevents the permanent accumulation of public debt. Yet, in many industrialized countries public debts are very large, as seen in Table 15.6.[9] What is troublesome in the more recent period is that the largest European debts have grown in peacetime, mostly during the 1970s. This section, which extends the two-period reasoning of Chapter 3 to many periods, shows that the debt process is explosive and requires careful management. For this reason, **debt stabilization** has emerged as a central concern of fiscal policy (which is confirmed by Figure 15.5).

15.4.1. The Public Debt with No Growth and No Inflation

The government budget deficit is the sum of the primary deficit—the excess of purchases G over net tax

receipts T—and of debt service—the real rate of interest r times the existing debt stock B. To finance the deficit, in the absence of monetary financing, the government must borrow and issue new debt ΔB:

Table 15.6. Gross Public Debt, Various Countries, 1970–1996 (% of GDP)

	1970	1980	1990	1996
Austria	19.4	37.2	56.2	61.4
Belgium	67.6	81.1	130.7	136.4
Denmark	11.3	33.5	59.7	68.4
Finland	12.1	11.9	14.8	73.4
France	na	30.9	40.1	60.9
Germany	18.4	32.8	43.4	62.5
Greece	17.8	23.1	77.7	120.2
Ireland	na	71.3	96.0	79.1
Italy	41.7	59.0	100.5	120.5
Japan	12.1	52.0	69.8	96.2
Netherlands	51.3	45.1	76.5	79.5
Norway	47.0	52.2	39.2	46.5
Spain	na	18.3	48.7	68.7
Sweden	30.5	44.3	44.4	86.3
UK	81.8	54.1	35.0	52.8
USA	45.4	37.7	55.6	63.7

Source: OECD *Economic Outlook*

[9] The table presents gross debts. In contrast, net debt takes into account the state's assets. Net debt figures exist but are considered unreliable because of the difficulty in determining the value of state assets.

Table 15.7. Net Debts and Primary Budget Balances, 1996[a]
% of GDP

	Net debt in 1996	Primary budget balance surplus in 1996	Required primary surplus:[b]	
			to stabilize debt	to stabilize debt–GDP ratio
Belgium	124.2	4.5	8.5	3.1
Germany	45.8	1.3	3.5	1.1
Ireland	79.1	1.2	3.6	2.0
Italy	119.0	3.9	10.8	3.0
Netherlands	60.8	1.9	4.7	1.5

[a] These are forecasts produced in 1995 by the OECD.
[b] The required surplus assumes a 5% real interest rate and a 2.5% real GDP growth rate.

Source: OECD, *Economic Outlook*, June 1995

$$(15.1) \qquad \Delta B = \underbrace{G - T}_{\substack{\text{primary budget} \\ \text{deficit}}} + \underset{\substack{\text{debt} \\ \text{service}}}{rB.}$$

$$\underbrace{}_{\substack{\text{total budget} \\ \text{deficit}}}$$

the ΔB term is labelled "debt build-up".

If the budget is in surplus, the government retires some of its existing debt or accumulates assets ($\Delta B < 0$). In the rare few instances when it is a net asset holder ($B < 0$), it can accumulate wealth.

Expression (15.1) shows that debts tend to feed on themselves. The explosive nature of the debt comes from the fact that, even when the primary budget is balanced ($G - T = 0$), the debt continues to grow. The government is borrowing to pay interest on the existing debt, which accumulates at the rate r. This feature of indebtedness is general and applies to any debt, be it public or private, domestic (i.e. held by domestic residents) or external.[10]

How can debt accumulation be arrested at some given level? The government must for ever run a primary surplus large enough to cover the existing debt service. Expression (15.1) shows that the primary surplus required to stabilize a debt that has reached the level B is

$$(15.2) \qquad \underset{\substack{\text{primary} \\ \text{budget surplus}}}{T - G} = \underset{\text{debt service}}{rB.}$$

Enforcing (15.2) can be a formidable task. The longer the government waits to do so, the larger the

debt becomes, and the larger is the surplus ultimately required to stabilize it. Table 15.7 presents debt levels and primary budget balances. The third column gives the primary surplus needed to stabilize the debt level as in (15.2), assuming a real interest rate of 5%. None of the countries shown was stabilizing its debts in 1996, and in some cases—Belgium and Italy—doing so would have required a considerable turnaround in public finances. Fortunately, the following sections show that this debt stabilization criterion is excessively stringent because it ignores both growth in GDP (the tax base) and the possibility of monetary finance.

15.4.2. The Public Debt with Growth and No Inflation

No one would seriously compare the size of the US Treasury indebtedness with that of the French or Swedish governments. The ability to service, or pay for, the debt is obviously related to the size of the country. This is precisely why all the data presented so far have been in terms of ratios to GDP, and why the appropriate objective is to stabilize the ratio of debt to GDP ratio rather than the debt level.

This distinction assumes greater importance when one recognizes that GDPs grow secularly over time. Box 15.3 shows how the debt level accounts in (15.1) and (15.2) change when we look at ratios to GDP. We see that the debt to GDP *ratio* can remain constant even if the public debt *level* keeps increasing for ever. By the same reasoning, were the stock of the debt to

---

[10] The tendency to grow is seen by looking at (15.1) when the primary budget is balanced: then, $\Delta B = rB$ or $\Delta B/B = r$. The same logic applies to a country's external debt.

BOX 15.3. DEBT-DEFICIT ARITHMETIC

Growth, no Inflation. The annual budget account (15.1), when divided by real GDP, can be transformed into a relationship which shows that the debt–GDP ratio increases with the budget deficit (as a share of GDP) and debt service on the debt–GDP ratio adjusted for GDP growth rate (g):[11]

$$(15.3) \qquad \Delta \frac{B}{Y} = \frac{G-T}{Y} + (r-g)\frac{B}{Y}.$$

As long as the real interest rate exceeds the growth rate, the debt process is explosive. For a given primary deficit as a fraction of GDP, more debt means more deficit and the need to borrow more. The primary budget surplus $(T-G)$ required to stabilize the debt–GDP ratio is

$$(15.4) \qquad \Delta \left(\frac{B}{Y}\right) = 0 \quad \text{when} \quad \frac{T-G}{Y} = (r-g)\frac{B}{Y}.$$

If the rate of interest is below the growth rate, the debt–GDP ratio can be stabilized while running a budget defi-

cit: the economy outgrows its public debt. Of course, as long as $r > g$, a surplus is still needed to stabilize the debt–GDP ratio.

Growth and Inflation. In the presence of inflation, money has to be accounted for. The Appendix shows that the budgetary accounts are simply modified to recognize that the deficit can be financed by new debt issues or by the creation of additional monetary base M0:

$$(15.5) \qquad \Delta \left(\frac{B}{Y}\right) + \frac{\Delta M0}{PY} = \frac{G-T}{Y} + (r-g)\frac{B}{Y}.$$

Stabilizing the debt–GDP ratio now requires an even smaller primary budget surplus, or can even be achieved with a primary deficit if enough monetary base is created:

$$(15.6) \qquad \Delta \left(\frac{B}{Y}\right) = 0 \quad \text{when} \quad \frac{T-G}{Y} = (r-g)\frac{B}{Y} - \frac{\Delta M0}{PY}.$$

remain stable in a growing economy, the debt-to-GDP ratio would vanish over time. Implicitly, there is a 'race' between the GDP and the public debt, or, more precisely, between the economy's trend growth rate ($g = \Delta Y/Y$) and the real interest rate (r) which determines the rate at which the debt cumulates. When the GDP growth rate exceeds the real interest rate, a balanced primary budget is sufficient for the debt–GDP ratio to shrink. When the real interest rate exceeds the economy's growth rate, the debt process is explosive; yet, the primary surplus required to stabilize the *ratio* of the debt to GDP is significantly smaller than that required to stabilize the *level* of the debt. This is illustrated by the last column in Table 15.7. Assuming a 5% real interest rate and a 2.5% real GDP growth rate, most countries had stabilized their debt–GDP ratio in 1996.

But why have debts increased so much in peacetime? The evolution of real interest rates and growth rates after 1975 provides part of the explanation. Table 15.8 shows that, over the 1960s and early 1970s, real GDP growth exceeded the real interest rate in most countries. Under such conditions, budget deficits did not necessarily result in growing debt–GDP ratios. The debt accumulation process was not explosive, at least relative to GDP, a fact that probably encouraged complacency about deficits and debts. Then real interest rates rose sharply while GDP growth declined. The

debt process became explosive and required prompt and vigorous action, but some countries failed to adjust quickly enough.

15.4.3. The Public Debt with Growth and Inflation

Inflation is a way of further relaxing the budgetary stringency required for debt stabilization. Monetary financing of the deficit occurs when the central bank purchases part of the public debt, either directly from the Treasury or indirectly on the money market. To pay for it, the central bank simply issues additional monetary base M0, a process sometimes called **seigniorage**.[12] Naturally, greater use of seigniorage results in faster money growth (via the money multiplier effect) and, eventually, higher inflation. Seigniorage is just another way of financing a deficit, as is seen by modification of the budget account (15.1) to recognize that any increase in the nominal monetary base

[11] See the Appendix for a formal derivation.

[12] This expression recalls the medieval practice of local lords, who had the power to mint coins and used it to reduce—debase—their gold content. In a similar fashion, governments exploit the monopoly power of the central bank in creating the medium of exchange to acquire valuable resources from the private sector. Modern seigniorage too is just another form of taxation, because the authorities exchange money, which is costless to produce, against goods and services: it is as if these goods and services were just taken away.

Table 15.8. Real Interest Rate and GDP Growth, Various Countries, 1961–1995 (%)

	1961–70		1971–75		1976–80		1981–85		1986–90		1990–95	
	r	g	r	g	r	g	r	g	r	g	r	g
Austria	3.7	4.5	1.2	4.0	3.3	3.4	4.0	1.3	5.2	3.0	4.1	2.1
Belgium	3.5	4.9	−0.6	3.5	3.2	3.1	5.3	0.8	6.3	3.0	5.5	1.5
Denmark	2.1	4.4	2.6	2.0	4.5	2.5	7.9	2.7	6.3	1.4	6.5	2.3
France	1.7	5.6	−0.2	3.5	−0.4	3.1	4.1	1.5	6.1	3.2	5.6	1.3
Germany	4.3	4.4	2.7	2.1	3.1	3.4	4.5	1.2	5.4	3.4	3.7	2.0
Ireland	2.5	4.3	−1.0	4.5	−0.1	4.6	2.7	2.8	6.9	5.7	6.0	4.7
Italy	3.0	5.7	−2.6	2.8	−2.3	4.8	3.4	1.4	4.9	3.0	7.1	1.2
Netherlands	1.6	5.7	−0.5	3.2	2.7	2.6	5.0	1.0	6.3	3.3	4.7	2.0
Sweden	1.9	4.7	−0.3	2.6	−0.3	1.3	3.8	1.8	5.3	2.3	5.0	−0.2
UK	3.1	2.8	−1.6	2.1	−1.1	1.8	4.7	2.0	3.9	3.3	5.3	1.4

Sources: IMF; OECD *Economic Outlook*

ΔM0 provides real resources to the government valued as ΔM0/P:

$$(15.7) \qquad \underset{\text{new debt}}{\Delta B} + \underset{\text{seigniorage}}{\Delta\text{M0}/P} = \underset{\substack{\text{primary} \\ \text{deficit}}}{G - T} + \underset{\substack{\text{interest} \\ \text{payments}}}{rB}.$$

Seigniorage is a cheap source of financing because little or no interest is paid on the monetary base.[13] More importantly, the absence of debt service on the monetary base severs the link that makes the debt process explosive. Can generous money growth allow the deficit to be financed without borrowing? Possibly in the short run, but the explosiveness is simply transferred elsewhere—into inflation. All high or hyperinflationary episodes can be linked to a government's attempt to break away from its budget constraint. Hyperinflations end when governments close their deficits, or when central banks stop financing them.

15.5. Three Ways to Stabilize the Public Debt

What are the options open to a government that wants first to stabilize, and then to reduce a high and exploding debt–GDP ratio? There are three, and only three, known ways of achieving that objective: (1) cutting the deficit, possibly going to a surplus, either by reducing public spending or by raising taxes; (2) financing by money creation (monetization); (3) defaulting on some or all of the existing debt. All three amount to forms of taxation: standard taxation in the first case, taxing those who happen to hold nominal assets (money, and nominal bonds) in the second case, and taxing those who own Treasury debt in the last case.

15.5.1. Cutting the Deficit

Deficit reduction is the hard and virtuous road to debt stabilization. Politically, though, it is also the hardest to implement. Public spending gives rise to interest groups that resist cuts, for example government employees who will fight for their jobs. Raising taxes is notoriously unpopular. And yet, deficit reduction has been the solution chosen and achieved in several European countries. As can be seen from Figure 3.10 and Table 15.3, countries with some of the most serious debt problems—Belgium, Denmark, and Ireland—have turned their primary budgets around, and Italy has made some progress. Still, debt stabilization remains precarious, especially given the ominous demographic trends described in Box 15.4.

---

[13] Ch. 9 described monetization of government deficits in more detail.

BOX 15.4. DEBT AND DEMOGRAPHY

The official debt figures reported in Table 15.6 correspond to explicit claims on the state, such as Treasury bills or bonds. Governments, however, also incur *implicit* liabilities, which are difficult or impossible to measure. Examples include unemployment benefits to be paid in the future—which depends on the evolution of the economy—or potential environmental rehabilitation likely to be imposed by future voters—which corresponds to legislation not even in place. One of the most important implicit liabilities originates in the pension system. At the time of the baby boom of the late 1940s and early 1950s, many countries adopted the 'pay-as-you-go' approach: economically active people paid taxes which were redistributed to re-

tired people. This was easy and cheap with a young and growing population. Over time, however, birth rates have dropped and life expectancy has risen. In addition, people now go to school longer and retire earlier. In the meantime, the baby boom has subsided; for example in the UK the **dependency ratio** (the ratio of people aged 65 years and older to the number of people aged from 15–64) was 24.2% in 1991, compared with 20.7% in 1970. For Europe as a whole, the OECD expects this ratio to rise from 21.5% in 1990 to 25.9% by 2005. Current legally binding arrangements to pay pensions to retirees imply huge unaccounted liabilities for European states when the baby boomers will reach retirement age early next century.

15.5.2. Seigniorage and the Inflation Tax

Inflationary finance reduces the debt burden in two ways.[14] The first is seigniorage. Table 15.9 shows how governments raise money. While not trivial, seignior-

---

[14] Both are explained in S. 9.5.1 of Ch. 9.

age income is too limited to be a major factor in large-debt stabilization. It has traditionally been highest in those countries, like Spain and Italy, that impose relatively high reserve ratios on their banks, thus generating an artificially large demand for the monetary base. (In Portugal, which has moved in the opposite direction and reduced reserve requirements, seigniorage in 1995 was negative.) The second effect is the **inflation**

Table 15.9. Government Receipts as a Percentage of GDP, Various Countries, 1995

	Taxes linked to imports and production	Income tax	Social security	Other current receipts	Total current receipts	Of which: Seigniorage[a]
Austria	16.0	13.1	15.9	3.1	48.1	0.4
Belgium	12.8	18.0	17.3	1.8	50.0	n.a.
Denmark	18.3	27.4	6.2	5.5	57.4	0.0
Finland	14.3	15.7	15.2	7.0	52.2	3.8
France	15.1	9.5	20.9	3.8	49.3	0.0
Germany	13.1	11.9	19.1	2.8	47.0	−0.2
Greece	15.5	5.3	13.1	2.6	36.4	5.3
Ireland	15.7	14.7	5.0	1.7	37.0	0.0
Italy	12.1	15.0	14.8	3.8	45.6	0.1
Luxemburg	14.4	14.2	11.7	3.5	43.9	n.a.
Netherlands	13.0	13.5	19.4	3.7	49.6	0.6
Portugal	14.0	8.8	10.9	3.8	37.5	−11.9
Spain	11.4	11.5	13.7	4.1	40.7	1.2
Sweden	14.4	22.0	14.7	9.2	60.3	2.4
UK	16.1	13.2	6.2	2.2	37.7	0.2

[a] Seigniorage is calculated as the annual increase in the monetary base, divided by nominal GDP over the year.

Sources: European Economy; IMF

tax on nominal assets. Most government debts take the form of nominal non-indexed assets. When prices rise, the value of that debt is eroded and debt-holders suffer a capital loss. The inflation tax is just the mirror image of this loss: the reduction of the real value of the debt.

Seigniorage and the inflation tax go hand in hand. Seigniorage leads to money growth and therefore to inflation and debt relief via the inflation tax. Naturally, the inflation tax applies only to debt issued in local currencies. In addition, the tax works only if inflation is unexpected. The reason is that, when debt-holders anticipate inflation, they demand a nominal interest rate which compensates them for the expected erosion of the principal. The nominal interest rate rises in line with expected inflation, leaving the real interest rate unchanged.[15] In that case, there is no gain from inflation for the government and no cost to bond-holders.

In the budget accounts ((15.1) for example) it is the real interest rate that appears. For the inflation tax to work, the real interest rate must fall. When inflation rises unexpectedly and quickly enough, nominal interest rates on existing assets cannot be changed; *ex post* real interest rates fall. Figure 15.6 documents how this happened during the period when inflation unexpectedly surged in the wake of the two oil shocks of 1973–4 and 1979–80. For long-maturity assets, the nominal interest rate cannot be modified as it is contractually set. This explains why *ex post* real interest rates are just the mirror image of inflation. Negative interest rates mean that bondholders actually pay for the right of lending money! This is a measure of the inflation tax.

Ex ante real interest rates are always positive, so to raise tax permanently governments must repeatedly produce inflation surprises. This is exactly how hyperinflations get under way. Indeed, hyperinflations do succeed in wiping out nominal assets. However, stopping a hyperinflation is so costly that it is an option used only in extreme political situations, for example in the Eastern European countries at the time of the collapse of the communist regimes.

It should be clear by now that monetary financing of the deficit is just another form of taxation. Instead of taxing incomes or consumption or petrol, monetary financing operates by reducing the value of the money base (the central bank's liability) and of the public debt (the Treasury's liability). Inflationary finance is a tax on money and bond-holders.[16]

15.5.3. Default

The most brutal way of stabilizing the debt is simply to repudiate it. Except for postwar or post-revolution periods (when the blame can be put on exceptional circumstances or previous regimes), only governments under very severe stress resort to default. This can be outright default, which is perceived as breach of confidence and leaves long-lasting scars on the reputation of governments; Box 15.5 describes the Italian experience in the Fascist era. On the other hand, it can be seen as a form of taxation, one that affects bond-holders, much as inflation. Indeed, partial default is exactly equivalent to a tax on bond income. If, for example, a government reduces the value of its debt by half, this is the same as imposing a 50% tax on interest and repayment of the principal.

15.5.4. Foreign Indebtedness

So far, it has been implicitly assumed that the public debt was held by residents. In that case, debt accumulation or stabilization amounts to a redistribution of income across generations, between those who are taxed now and those who will be taxed in the future. When debt is owned by foreigners, the situation is different. As Chapter 3 showed, honouring external debt implies transferring resources to the rest of the world. This will require running a current account surplus, i.e. spending less than is earned. In the case of domestically held debt, the government can always correct the income distribution effects through adequately counteracting taxes and transfers. This option is not available for the foreign-held public debt, and this is one reason why it is more painful.

---

[15] This is the Fisher pinciple studied in Ch. 8.

[16] More generally, inflation redistributes wealth from borrowers to lenders when the assets are nominal, i.e. set in money terms and not indexed to a price level.

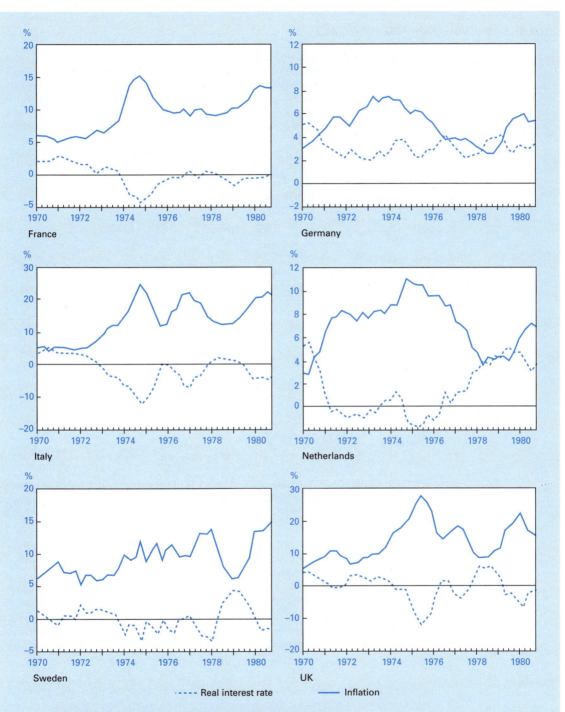

Figure 15.6. Negative Real Interest Rates, 1970–1983

Ex-post real interest rates turn negative when the nominal rate fails to match increases in the inflation rate. The figure shows that sharp jumps in inflation are usually unexpected and therefore not incorporated in the nominal interest rate.

Source: IMF

BOX 15.5. MUSSOLINI AND THE PUBLIC DEBT[17]

Italy emerged from the First World War with a large debt and a considerable budget deficit. Between 1923 and 1926, having eliminated all political opposition, Mussolini re-established near budget balance and brought the debt–GDP ratio down by reducing spending and raising taxes (Table 15.10). Yet, concerned that the debt was too short in maturity, and therefore vulnerable to market conditions, the government in November 1926 imposed a mandatory conversion of debt of less than seven-year maturity into fixed-rate (5%) longer-term bonds. In 1934, these bonds were again forcibly converted into 25-year loans bearing a 3.5% interest. The first conversion is estimated to have resulted in a partial default of 20%, the second one in a loss of 30%. After these moves, the government found it very hard to undertake new borrowing. It was forced to cease issuing short-term debt in 1927 and paid a premium estimated at 2%–3% on borrowing from banks.

Table 15.10. Public Finances in Italy, 1918–1928

	1918	1922	1924	1926	1928
Tax revenues as % of public spending	23	46	90	100	90
Debt–GNP (%)	70.3	74.8	65.1	49.7	53.8

Source: Alesina (1988a)

[17] This box draws on Alesina (1988a).

15.6. Summary

1. A first fundamental purpose of fiscal policy is to provide public goods and services. The border between what has to be produced publicly and what can be produced privately is not clear-cut.

2. A second function ascribed to fiscal policy is the redistribution of income and the alleviation of inequities that may be generated by the market mechanism. Doing so, however, may lead to inefficiencies.

3. A third function is to use the budget to offset temporary or cyclical fluctuations. This is done by running deficits in bad years—financed by borrowing—and surpluses in good years—to repay the borrowing. Countercyclical fiscal policy has three main benefits. One is tax smoothing—or the avoidance of temporary changes in tax rates; others are private consumption smoothing and private income maintenance.

4. The fact that in bad years some citizens cannot borrow on their own provides a justification for fiscal policy to step in and support private consumption smoothing.

5. If prices and wages are not fully flexible, fiscal policy can be used to stabilize demand, either directly through government spending, or indirectly through taxation by reducing fluctuations in private sector incomes. This prevents or attenuates the underutilization of productive resources during recession.

6. When they vote on the budgets, parliaments set public spending levels and tax rates. During a recession (respectively, expansion) tax receipts decline (resp. increase), leading to a deficit (resp. surplus). As a result, the budget acts as an automatic stabilizer.

7. Indebtedness is an inherently explosive process. When the primary budget is balanced and the debt is positive, it is necessary to keep on borrowing merely to service existing debt. The real debt accumulates at a rate given by the real interest rate.

8. To stabilize the level of the real debt, in the absence of money financing and real growth, the government must run a primary budget surplus equal to the interest charge. The longer it waits, the larger will be the debt and the interest burden that it faces, and the larger the required primary budget surplus.

9. In a growing economy, stabilizing the ratio of debt to GDP is a less stringent condition than stabilizing the absolute debt level. The required primary surplus is proportional to the difference between the real interest rate and the real GDP growth rate. Not only is this smaller than the real interest rate, it may well be negative, thus allowing permanent primary deficits.

10. Monetary financing reduces the debt burden for two reasons. Seigniorage provides resources directly to the government, virtually free of charge. As money growth eventually leads to inflation, the real value of nominal debt declines.

11. The inflation tax can be collected, however, only if inflation is unexpected. Otherwise the nominal interest rate rises, which protects lenders.

12. In addition to lowering the deficit—through spending cuts or tax increases—or resorting to money finance, debt can be stabilized by defaulting. This drastic form of taxation considerably hurts a government's reputation.

13. As long as the public debt is held by residents, debt stabilization or reduction implies income redistribution within the country. When part of the public debt is held by non-residents, stabilization requires a net transfer by residents to the rest of the world.

Key Concepts

- seigniorage
- public goods
- externalities
- productive efficiency
- equity–efficiency trade-off
- distortionary taxation
- consumption smoothing

- tax smoothing
- stabilization policies
- countercyclical fiscal policy
- automatic stabilizers
- cyclically adjusted budgets
- debt stabilization
- inflation tax

Exercises: Theory

1. Income taxes are typically progressive, meaning that they increase more than proportionately with income. What might be the purpose of progressivity?

2. Suppose that progressive income taxes are reduced and replaced by VAT so as to keep tax receipts unchanged. What is the effect on the automatic stabilizer?

3. A country has a large portion of its public debt issued in foreign currency. What effect does this have on the government's incentive to engage in inflationary finance? What does a devaluation do to the debt burden?

4. 'The national debt is a great scam, because it will never be repaid.' Discuss.

5. What are the differences in terms of government revenue between an anticipated and a non-anticipated increase in the rate of inflation?

6. The Tanzi effect refers to the loss of real revenues that governments face during hyperinflations when they cannot collect revenues sufficiently quickly. Explain why such an effect makes it difficult for governments to eliminate hyperinflations. What are some possible solutions?

7. By increasing the rate of money growth, the government unexpectedly increases the inflation rate to a higher, stable level. Draw a picture showing the evolution of seigniorage revenue over time.

8. The velocity of money is $V = PY/M$, where P is the GDP deflator, Y the real GDP and M a monetary aggregate (e.g. M1 or M2). How does an increase in velocity affect the monetary financing of the deficit?

9. Figure 15.3 shows a lag between capacity utilization and net tax receipts. Can you explain why we should expect such a lag and why the lag is variable?

10. Are bank notes and coins part of the public debt?

11. (*Formal*). Write down the definitions of *ex ante* and *ex post* real interest rates. Use these relationships to explain the difference between the two rates.

12. The balanced budget multiplier (*formal and difficult*). A government simultaneously reduces government spending and tax receipts by the same amount. What is the net effect on aggregate demand? (*Hint*: define c as the response to consumption to changes in GDP, the so-called the marginal propensity to consume $\partial C/\partial Y$). Use your answer to explain why it is hard to reduce the size of government, i.e. the ratios G/Y and T/Y.

Exercises: Applications

1. A country growing at a rate of 3.5% has a debt–GDP ratio of 40%. What is the primary budget surplus that keeps this ratio constant when the real interest rate is 2%? When it is 6%?

2. Suppose the debt–GDP ratio is 100%, growth is 3% per annum, and the real interest rate is 5%.

   (*a*) What is the primary government budget surplus (as a percentage of GDP) that can stabilize the debt–GDP ratio?

   (*b*) How does you answer change if interest rates fall to 2%? If growth falls to 1%?

3. The demand for (real) central bank money, the source of seigniorage, declines with the rate of inflation. Suppose, as an example, that this demand (in billions of ECUs) is:

Inflation rate							
0%	1%	2%	5%	10%	20%	25%	50%
H/P							
1000	905	819	607	368	135	82	7

   Seigniorage is a tax applied to this demand, whose rate is just the rate of inflation. Compute seigniorage as a function of the inflation rate. (*Hint*: an inflation rate of 5% corresponds to a tax rate equal to 0.05.) Which inflation rate maximizes seigniorage?

4. (*Formal version of above exercise*)   The demand for central bank money H is described by the function $H/P = A \exp(-\alpha\pi)$.[18] In long-run equilibrium the inflation rate is stable ($\partial\pi/\partial t = 0$). Seigniorage is $(\partial H/\partial t)/P$. Compute seigniorage in the long run and find the inflation rate for which the revenue is maximum. (In the previous exercise, we use $A = 1000$ and $\alpha = 10$: check your result.)

5. Public bondholders protect themselves from surprise inflation in many ways. Short-term debt is one form of indexation. Another option is to accept only debt denominated in foreign currencies: there is nothing that a government can do about them, short of default. Can you explain the patterns in the data below? (You may use data from Table 15.6.)

---

[18] This is the so-called Cagan function, named after Chicago economist Phillip Cagan, who used it in a seminal analysis of German inflation in the 1920s.

Average Maturity and Foreign Currency Components of EC National Debts, year-end 1989

	Average maturity (yrs)	Fixed-coupon, foreign currency long-term bonds (% of marketable debt)[a]
Belgium	3.4	55
Denmark	4.0	45
France	4.0[b]	na
Germany	5.0	24
Greece	0.6[c]	9
Ireland	5.9	44
Italy	2.5	20
Netherlands	5.9[b]	61
Spain	1.2	30
UK	9.4	6

[a] Initial maturity.
[b] 1987.
[c] Estimate, which excludes domestic debt indexed to foreign currencies.

Source: Missale (1991)

6. Governments face unmeasurable liabilities: Box 15.4 has dealt with one such case. Can you think of other implicit liabilities? Assets?

7. An ageing population creates difficult budgetary problems (health, retirement). What about migration? Can you think through the (politically sensitive) links between immigration policies and public debt?

Suggested Further Reading

For a careful analysis of public accounts, see:

Buiter, Willem (1985), 'A Guide to Public Sector Debt and Deficits', *Economic Policy*, 1: 13–80.

For a technical exposition of the link between budget deficits, the intertemporal budget constraint, seigniorage, and inflation, see:

Sargent, Thomas J., and Wallace, Neil (1981), 'Some Unpleasant Monetarist Arithmetic', *Federal Reserve Bank of Minneapolis Quarterly Review*, 5(3): 1–17.

Studies that deal with the public debt problem in Europe and elsewhere include:

Alesina, Alberto, and Perotti, Roberto (1996), 'Fiscal Adjustments: Fiscal Expansions and Adjustments in OECD Countries', *Economic Policy*, 21: 205–48.

Bartolini, Leonardo, Symansky, Steven, and Razin, Assaf (1995), 'G7 Fiscal Restructuring in the 1990s: Macroeconomic Effects', *Economic Policy*, 20: 109–46.

Appendix: The Algebra of Budget Deficits

Real GNP Growth

We start from the budget account (15.1) and divide both sides by real GDP, Y:

$$\text{(A15.1)} \qquad \frac{\Delta B}{Y} = \frac{G}{Y} - \frac{T}{Y} + \frac{rB}{Y}.$$

Note next that an approximation of $\Delta(B/Y)$ is:

$$\text{(A15.2)} \qquad \Delta\left(\frac{B}{Y}\right) = \frac{\Delta B}{Y} - \frac{\Delta Y}{Y}\frac{B}{Y}.$$

Then, if real growth $\Delta Y/Y$ is denoted by g, we find (15.3) in the text:

$$\text{(A15.3)} \qquad \Delta\left(\frac{B}{Y}\right) = \frac{G - T}{Y} + (r - g)\frac{B}{Y}.$$

Growth, Seigniorage, and Inflation

With seignorage and inflation, it is convenient to start from the annual budget account expressed in nominal terms, where P is the price level. (So PG is nominal public spending, PB nominal public debt, etc. Recall that M0 is the nominal stock of central bank money.)

$$\text{(A15.4)} \qquad \Delta(PB) + \Delta M0 = PG - PT + i(PB).$$

The nominal interest rate i is used for computing debt service consistently. Dividing both sides by the nominal GNP (PY), we have:

$$\text{(A15.5)} \qquad \frac{\Delta(PB)}{PY} + \frac{\Delta M0}{PY} = \frac{PG}{PY} - \frac{PT}{PY} + i\frac{PB}{PY}.$$

Using the approximation

$$\Delta\left(\frac{PB}{PY}\right) = \frac{\Delta(PB)}{PY} - \frac{PB}{PY}\frac{P\Delta Y + Y\Delta P}{PY}$$

$$= \frac{\Delta(PB)}{PY} - \frac{PB}{PY}(g + \pi),$$

and substituting into (A15.5), we obtain (15.5) in the text:

$$\text{(A15.6)} \qquad \Delta\left(\frac{B}{Y}\right) + \frac{\Delta M0}{PY} = \frac{PG}{PY} - \frac{PT}{PY} + (i - \pi - g)\frac{B}{Y}$$

$$= \frac{G - T}{Y} + (r - g)\frac{B}{Y},$$

since the real interest rate is $r = i - \pi$. Note that a surprise inflation occurs when actual inflation exceeds expected inflation $\bar{\pi}$. The *ex ante* real interest rate is $\bar{r} = i - \bar{\pi}$, while the *ex post* real interest rate is $r = i - \pi$. The difference is $r - \bar{r} = -(\pi - \bar{\pi})$. With a positive inflation surprise, $\pi > \bar{\pi}$ and $r < \bar{r}$.

16

The Limits of Demand Management

> . . . the ideas of economists and political philosophers, both when they are right and when they are wrong, are more powerful than is commonly understood. Indeed the world is fuelled by little else. Practical men, who believe themselves to be quite exempt from any intellectual influences, are usually the slaves of some defunct economist.
>
> J. M. Keynes

> As an advice-giving profession we are way over our heads.
>
> R. E. Lucas Jr

16.1. Overview

This chapter will remove a coat of gloss from the concept of demand management developed in previous chapters. Its relatively sceptical tone reflects the dramatic reappraisal of what macroeconomic policy can actually achieve. The rise in inflation, unemployment, and public indebtedness over the late 1970s, and the medicine applied in the early 1980s, left a bitter taste and little stomach for experimenting again with policy activism. At the same time, macroeconomic theory has raised a number of doubts about the efficacy of demand management; there is much less confidence that governments can systematically use fiscal and monetary policy to smooth out aggregate fluctuations.

The age-old controversy between Monetarists and Keynesians centres on relatively slim disagreements which can have sweeping implications. The first bone of contention is the speed at which goods and labour markets clear, the degree of nominal wage and price rigidity in an economy. If markets adjust rapidly, the economy is better left alone. If markets are slow to adjust, we are back in a world of trade-offs—if still only temporary—between inflation and real economic performance. In such a world, there is a place for active **demand management** policies.

The debate is also about expectations. How do expectations of inflation, which largely influence core inflation, relate to government policy or exogenous events? Shifts in policies affect expectations and, through expectations, many aspects of agents' behaviour. The implications are troubling. For example, the past may cease to be a reliable guide for the future, as 'facts' based on past experience become irrelevant.

Expectations look to the future, but the future is unbounded. When a government announces its intentions for the next year or two, or for the next legislature, we still need to ask: And what happens afterwards? What are the government's next intentions, or the next government's intentions? The absence of long-term commitments has deleterious effects; merely the freedom to carry out policy actions can have costs. The common response has been the setting up of rules, institutions, and practices dedicated to establishing credibility and reputation. A new trade-off emerges between rules, which anchor the future but limit freedom of action, and discretion, which permits policies to deal with unforeseen events but creates its own uncertainties.

These ideas inevitably lead us into the realm of politics, as we require an understanding of how present and future governments act and react each other. If voters care about economic policies, politicians will need to address this concern to stay in power, or to get into power. Economic policies are no longer exogenous. Similarly, political events, in particular electoral outcomes, may become endogenous too. One implication is that political institutions are important for economic performance, if only to create the proper backdrop for economic activity.

16.2. Monetarists and Keynesians: the Debate Made Simple

Monetarists and Keynesians have never stopped disagreeing about the proper role of government. Heirs of the *laissez-faire* school of thought, Monetarists focus on the dysfunctions of government interventions and attempts to stabilize the economy; they ask whether it is possible to stabilize. Keynesians worry about unemployment and slow growth. Because they believe that market outcomes can be improved upon, they contrive ways of correcting them by **activist policies**.

The debate is illustrated in Figure 16.1. Starting from point *A*, an expansionary policy (monetary policy under flexible exchange rates, fiscal policy under fixed exchange rates) takes the economy first to point *B*, and then to point *C*, where the effect is entirely absorbed by a permanently higher rate of inflation, ratified by a proportional exchange rate depreciation. The move from *B* to *C* depends on the speed at which the short-run *AS* curve shifts. This in turn depends on how core inflation reacts to actual inflation. Quick adjustment means a fast move to *C*: policy only creates inflation,

at best with a fleeting boost to GDP. A superior solution, then, is to aim at point *D*, where inflation is low, which in this view can be achieved at little or no output cost. That is the Monetarist perspective.

The Keynesian case starts from point *A* in Figure 16.2, where, for one reason or another, output is below its trend level, and unemployment is above its equilibrium level. Then actual inflation is below its expected level; over time, core inflation will decline and the short-run *AS* curve will shift downward until point *C* is reached. This, however may take a very long time, during which unemployment is high and some output is forgone. This means frustration among the unemployed and inefficiency as productive resources remain underutilized. The preferred solution for Keynesians is to pursue an expansionary policy, bringing the *AD* curve up and, by the same token, bringing the economy swiftly to point *B* where things would settle.

The disagreement boils down to a simple question: can the economy stay away from the long-run *AS* schedule for a long time? Put differently, is the short-run *AS* curve really distinct from the vertical *LAS*? This,

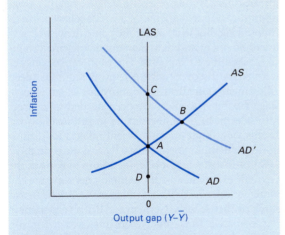

Figure 16.1. The Monetarist Case

A monetary expansion moves the economy from point *A* to point *B* in the short run and to point *C* in the long run. If deviations from trend $\bar{Y}$ are short-lived, the move is actually from point *A* to point *C*, which is not really helpful. It is more desirable to aim at point *D*, where inflation is low.

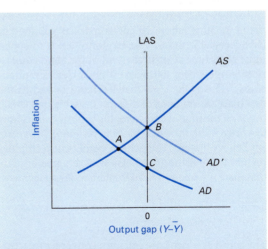

Figure 16.2. The Keynesian Case

When the economy is below trend at point *A*, waiting for prices to adjust to reach point *C* may take a long time. A monetary policy boost takes the economy promptly back to full employment at point *B*.

in turn, raises two issues. The first one is the slope of the short-run *AS* curve. If it is relatively steep, there can be no lasting departure of GDP from its trend, unemployment cannot differ much from its equilibrium level, and there is no unemployment–inflation trade-off. The second issue is the time it takes for the short-run curve to give way to its long-run version. Even if it is flat but moves quickly to its long-run position, departures from trend output are short-lived.

Monetarists argue that GDP is never far from its growth trend; Keynesians disagree. It is remarkable that so sharp a divergence about the desirability of policy actions arises from an apparently narrow disagreement concerning a point of detail. After all, one may agree on almost everything, including the whole analysis of demand and supply, and yet disagree on every aspect of economic policy simply because there is doubt about the slope of the *AS* curve or about the speed at which it shifts.

16.2.1. Market-Clearing and Rational Expectations

16.2.1.1. The slope of the aggregate supply curve

What then determines the slope of the *AS* curve and the speed at which it shifts? The slope depends on the process of **market-clearing**. Economies in which prices and wages react strongly to conditions of excess demand in either labour or goods markets will tend to have steep *AS* curves. The economy tends to spend most of its time at or near trend output and equilibrium employment: all markets must clear simultaneously. This is the view that Keynes attacked in the first place. As millions of disturbances, big and small, occur all the time everywhere, the central issue is how fast prices—and wages—move in response. Monetarists believe that markets achieve equilibrium employment roughly all the time; Keynesians disagree, arguing that there is scope and need for demand management.

16.2.1.2. The speed of *AS* curve shifts and core inflation

The speed at which core inflation converges to actual inflation is what determines the shifts of the *AS* curve. When core inflation is mostly driven by its forward-looking element and expectations are rational, the *AS* curve always shifts so that the economy remains on its long-run aggregate supply curve. This is the Monetarist view.

Keynesians think that it would be misleading to think of core inflation only as expected inflation. Even if all agents perfectly anticipate the future, they may engage in nominal contracts that lock them into prices and nominal wages that are based on rationally expected inflation, but at some earlier period in time. Thus, when inflation deviates from these older expectations, there will be some interval of time when agents can do little or nothing about their errors. During that interval, the economy is away from trend output.

16.2.1.3. An example: the debate over unemployment

If the Keynesians are right, there should be long periods of underutilization of resources. But how do we know that, for example, employment is not at its equilibrium level? Figure 16.3 shows that the British unemployment rate has fluctuated very widely over a century. Are these joint fluctuations in the actual and equilibrium unemployment rates? The latest bout of increase, after 1979, has been the object of an intense controversy. Keynesians blamed the Thatcher government for engineering a massive rise in unemployment through restrictive monetary and fiscal policies aimed at taming both inflation and the trade unions. Monetarist supporters of Mrs Thatcher countered that there was an increase in equilibrium unemployment because of the monopolistic behaviour of trade unions and distortionary labour market practices, ranging from minimum wages to unemployment benefits to closed-shop hiring. But what about the coincidence of rising unemployment and tight demand management policies, asked the Keynesians? The Monetarists' answer was that the discovery of North Sea oil[1] required a deep adjustment of the British economy, for which relative wage flexibility would have been needed to redirect resources from declining sectors to promising ones. In this view, high unemployment reflects high equilibrium unemployment caused by real wage rigidity.

Some insights might be gained from looking at the German experience with unemployment during the same period, also depicted in Figure 16.3. The broad similarity between the German and British experiences is informative. In Germany, too, unemployment rose in the early 1980s, albeit without any discovery of natural resources. Both countries, on the other hand, embarked on anti-inflation monetary policies at about the same time, and both countries tightened up their fiscal policies to reduce the public debt. This provides some evidence supporting the Keynesian view that

---

[1] The 'Dutch disease' syndrome is discussed in Ch. 7.

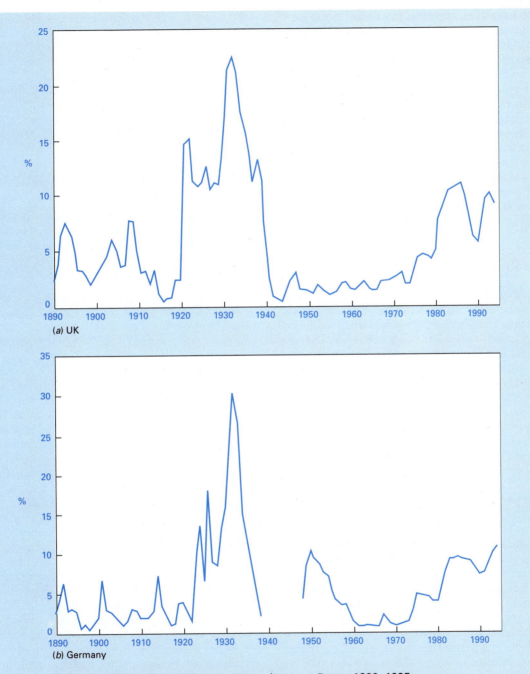

Figure 16.3. British and German Unemployment Rates, 1890–1995

Unemployment rates display considerable variability. The peaks in both countries correspond to difficult postwar conditions, the Great Depression (1929–31), and the post-oil-shock period.

Sources: Mitchell (1978); OECD *Main Economic Indicators*

tight demand management has a hand in the story. Furthermore, the sharp world-wide increase in unemployment in the 1930s, a symptom of the Great Depression and of the attendant collapse in demand, cannot easily be dismissed as mere coincidence. Yet the very fact that in both Germany and the UK unemployment has oscillated in the 1980s around a higher level than in the 1960s suggests that equilibrium unemployment has indeed risen, as the Monetarists claim. Keynesians counter that the increase in equilibrium unemployment remains short of what is needed to explain away all of the observed increase in actual unemployment, and especially the persistence of the observed fluctuations.[2]

16.2.2. Uncertainty and Policy Lags

Even if markets do not function perfectly well, a case has to be made that governments can improve the situation. The other battlefront concerns the ability of governments to conduct policy effectively. To make the case that markets fail to adjust, Keynesians argue that many prices are set in advance because of an imperfect knowledge of future conditions, and that governments may be able to offset the effects of nominal rigidities. This argument is not airtight, however. The same uncertainty or incomplete information that prevents prices from delivering full employment of available resources may also plague government actions. Why should policy-makers have a superior ability to improve market outcomes? Wrong pricing lasts only as long as it takes for private agents to discover what is going on and take remedial action.

On these grounds, Monetarists assert, the best policy is to do nothing at all. If uncertainty is the main problem, governments can help simply by not making matters worse. If the government has no information advantage over the private sector, it might even do more harm than good by trying to stabilize the economy.

This critique of macroeconomic policy goes beyond the issue of government's informational advantage. Milton Friedman has argued that, in addition to the **recognition lag** (the lag in discovering that policy intervention is called for), governments need time to formulate policy, leading to **decision lags**. Depending on the government structure, this can be coupled with

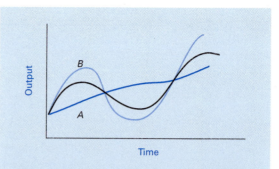

Figure 16.4. Lags and Demand Management Policy

The dark line shows the business cycle arising from fluctuations in aggregate demand in the private sector. A demand management policy correctly implemented would smooth out the fluctuations (curve *A*). If there are significant effectiveness lags, the government may need to enact these measures well in advance of the turning points in the cycle. If instead the government reacts passively, it may simply reinforce the cycle (curve *B*).

implementation lags, as ministries must originate and parliaments must pass legislation. Even if implemented quickly, policies take time to produce their effects. This is especially true of monetary policy. It takes several months before the easing of money market conditions and depreciating exchange rates have an impact on real activity. To make matters even worse, this **effectiveness lag** contains a large amount of uncertainty about it; economists cannot always get it right.

Figure 16.4 illustrates the debate. The dark line represents the path of output subjected to business cycle fluctuations of an economy left to itself. A perfectly thought-out and implemented policy would begin to stimulate the economy just when it is nearing a peak so that, given the various lags described above, its effects come into play just at the time it is needed. Similarly, it would turn restrictive just when the trough is passed, so as to moderate the strength of the upturn. Ideally, the outcome would be curve *A*. Now add uncertainty about the recognition, decision, implementation, and effectiveness lags. In the worst case, we face the risk of achieving curve *B*: the stimulus planned for the downturn affects the economy exactly when it is coming out of the recession while restraint comes into play just when the economy has peaked. Here, policy worsens matters!

In order to avoid this outcome, governments in practice use early indicators of business conditions.

---

[2] Chs. 6 and 17 study reasons behind the increase in European equilibrium unemployment.

BOX 16.1. ECONOMIC INDICATORS

Because aggregate data are produced only slowly, current conditions are known only with delay. This is why other readily available data are used as leading, coincident, or even lagging indicators. In practice, several indicators are used jointly. Chapter 14 discussed a number of empirical regularities about business cycles. These regularities can be used to anticipate business conditions. Through trial and error, analysts have developed a battery of indicators such as those listed in Table 16.1.

Table 16.1. Frequently Used Indicators

Real money supply	Leading
Orders	Leading
Inventories	Leading
Delivery lags	Leading
Credit growth	Leading
Stock prices	Leading
New business permits	Leading
Commodity prices	Leading
Long-short term interest rate spread	Leading
Employment	Coincident
Industrial production	Coincident
Unit labour costs	Lagging
Duration of unemployment	Lagging
Interest rates	Lagging
Consumer credit	Lagging

Box 16.1 describes some of their tools, some of which have already been mentioned in Chapter 14. The very fact that they need these tools, which are highly imperfect, indicates that the issue is a serious one. On the other side, it may not be as severe as supporters of *laissez-faire* would like us to think.

16.2.3. The Costs of Inflation

The by-product of the Keynesian approach to demand management is higher inflation, as depicted in Figure 16.2. Unless contractionary policy is pursued with the same vigour as expansionary policy, there will be an upward bias or drift in the rate of inflation. This raises in turn the rather important question of priorities. Couldn't lower joblessness and higher output outweigh the inconvenience of permanently higher inflation? The cost of inflation is another source of disagreement between Keynesians and Monetarists. Inflation is undesirable, yet it is surprisingly difficult to explain why.

16.2.3.1. Income distribution

One commonly held fear is that inflation has important redistributive effects. First, it redistributes income by distorting relative prices. When prices rise rapidly, unless they all move at the same speed, even small differences in rates of increase can change relative prices

quite rapidly. Typically, real wages stay ahead, which hurts firms' profitability, eventually deterring investment and harming growth. Those on fixed incomes and limited political clout, such as pensioners or dole recipients, generally lose out. Real exchange rates differ from one experience to another, yet they tend to vary enormously. Income shifts between local and foreign producers, and between the local producers of traded and nontraded goods.

Second, inflation redistributes wealth. In contrast to real assets (real estate, durable goods, foreign exchange, precious metals), the value of nominal nonindexed assets is eroded if inflation comes as a surprise: wealth shifts from lenders to borrowers when real interest rates plunge to negative levels.[3] Hyperinflations, in particular, can leave a legacy that survives many generations: 75 years on, Germans still consider inflation as an absolute evil.

16.2.3.2. The value of money

The answer to income and wealth redistribution is indexation. If all nominal values are indexed, the losers are simply those who hold money, which, by definition, is not indexed. As nominal interest rates rise, agents reduce their holdings of money balances. The losses suffered when the value of money declines steadily—more frequent trips to the bank—may seem trivial. Yet examples of hyperinflation in history show

---

[3] See Ch. 15.

BOX 16.2. OPTIMAL INFLATION

Milton Friedman has argued that the optimal rate of inflation is negative, equal to minus the real interest rate, i.e. minus the marginal productivity of capital.[4] Then the nominal interest rate is zero. The argument rests on the usual principle that a good should be supplied up to the point where its marginal cost of production equals its price, itself equal to the marginal benefit to the consumer. For the public, the price of money—the opportunity cost of holding it—is the nominal interest rate. The cost of producing money is virtually nil for the government. The government would make its citizens better off by providing them at zero cost with a public good (money) which costs nothing to produce.

The problem with this principle is that Friedman neglects the need of every government to raise taxes. Because taxes are distortionary, the overall distortion imposed by taxation is reduced when taxes are widely spread on all goods, including money. It is likely that the optimal inflation rate under this criterion is still quite small.

On the other hand, welfare is seriously undermined when inflation becomes so high that the demand for money all but vanishes. (Figure 8.12 illustrated this effect.) The costs come in several ways, mainly because valuable resources are utilized in a thoroughly unproductive activity. People spend an inordinate amount of time and energy trying to avoid the inflation tax, ranging from foreign exchange speculation to simply spending the pay cheque as quickly as possible.

that the consequences can be extremely disruptive. Box 16.2 explains these costs and the concept of an ideal or 'optimal' rate of inflation.

16.2.3.3. Uncertainty and the value of price signals

Prices are essential signals in market economies: they tell producers what and how to produce, consumers what and how to consume, whether to save, etc. In all cases, what matters is not absolute but relative prices, what a given good costs in terms of other goods. A correct interpretation of (relative) price signals is crucial to the efficiency of a market economy. High inflation is often associated with more variable inflation. The more variable inflation is, the less confidence firms

and households have that observed changes in specific prices represent relative price changes—which may require action—rather than just inflation. This can lead to distortions as firms and households take inappropriate decisions, confusing movements in the price level with changes in relative price. Figure 16.5(a) documents the link between inflation level and variability. Panels (b) and (c) show that a more uncertain inflation is associated with more variable real wages and unemployment, an indication that nominal fluctuations may have real effects. When the efficient functioning of the price mechanism is attenuated, overall productivity declines, resulting eventually in lower growth and higher unemployment. Indexation may worsen the situation because it tends to freeze the hierarchy of all relative prices and to lock in real rigidities.

16.3. Expectations of Policy

The importance of expectations on present decisions is stressed in Part II. No important economic choice can ignore the impact of the future. Consumption and saving, investment, price- and wage-setting, and of course the choice among assets are all sensitive to agents' perceptions of the future. Among the many

forces shaping the future are policy actions. Assessing the role and effectiveness of economic policies cannot, therefore, be conducted only by linking today's policies to today's outcomes. In fact, tomorrow's policies may be more important for today's outcome. This opens up a fascinating range of issues, including the puzzling recognition that current policy actions themselves may respond to agents' expectations of future policy actions.

---

[4] The argument that the real interest rate should be equal to the marginal productivity of capital is presented in Ch. 4.

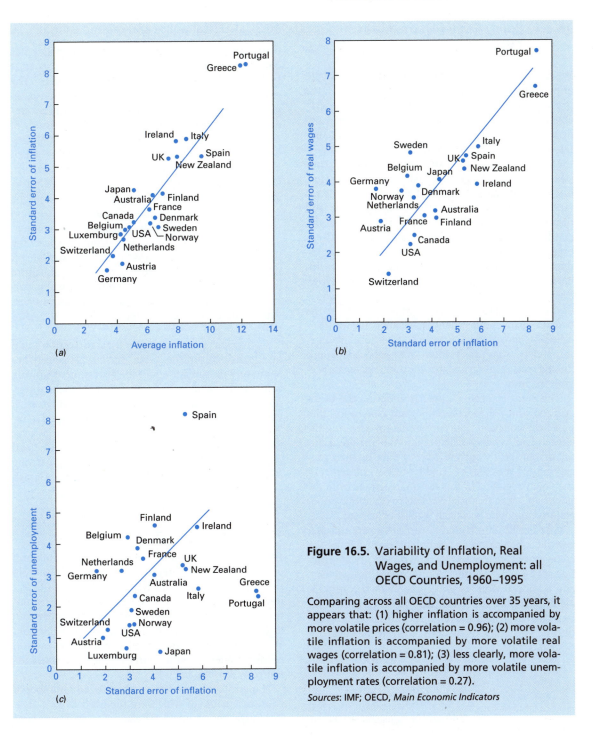

Figure 16.5. Variability of Inflation, Real Wages, and Unemployment: all OECD Countries, 1960–1995

Comparing across all OECD countries over 35 years, it appears that: (1) higher inflation is accompanied by more volatile prices (correlation = 0.96); (2) more volatile inflation is accompanied by more volatile real wages (correlation = 0.81); (3) less clearly, more volatile inflation is accompanied by more volatile unemployment rates (correlation = 0.27).

Sources: IMF; OECD, *Main Economic Indicators*

16.3.1. Policy Regimes: the Lucas Critique

We know that current consumption is driven by wealth and current disposable income. Wealth, in turn, is the present value of future net incomes. It is not observable because it depends on private expectations and because many of its components—chiefly human capital—do not have a market value. What is observable is the link between consumption and disposable income (shown in Figure 4.11). This link takes wealth as given, but what if wealth changes? Then the previously established pattern linking current consumption and disposable income ceases to hold. Since wealth depends on agents' expectations, it can change rapidly as expectations shift. For example, a temporary tax reduction affects current disposable income, but wealth hardly at all, with little effect on consumption. However, if perceived as permanent, the same tax reduction affects wealth and boosts consumption. In the end, important policy changes that affect the future—called changes in the policy regime, because they correspond to lasting policy shifts—may break the pattern linking consumption and income observed over a previous regime.

The point is a general one. It underlies the **Lucas critique** which draws the important conclusion that past behaviour can be a poor guide for assessing the effects of policy actions.[5] Expectations of private agents are driven less by current actions than by their perceptions of the rules of conduct of governments, or the **policy regime**. For this reason, reactions from the public and from financial markets to economic policy actions cannot be predicted by past behaviour.

One implication is that governments are on safer grounds when planning small steps. Important policy changes may trigger largely unexpected private reactions. This is yet another argument against activism, and a good reason for governments to be cautious. Another implication is that policy-making must combine current actions and binding commitments for the future.[6] The following sections illustrate the Lucas critique in action.

16.3.1.1. Fiscal policy and regime change

Could it be that an expansionary fiscal policy has contractionary effects and conversely? In theory at least, it is possible to have 'negative multipliers'. The case may arise if, for example, a permanent increase in government purchases is perceived as a significant reduction in private wealth. The budget constraint of the government requires that higher public spending be matched, in present value, by higher taxes which cut into private wealth.[7] Lower private wealth, in turn, leads to less private spending. If the reduction in private spending more than offsets the increase in public spending, it becomes possible that a fiscal expansion will be met by a negative effect on aggregate demand.[8] This may happen if the private sector interprets the increase in public spending as a first step towards fiscal relaxation which will, in the end, require severe future tax increases. The fall in perceived wealth, and in private spending, may be considerable, and can overwhelm the current expansionary effect of the fiscal policy change.

Conversely, a contractionary fiscal correction could be expansionary if the public, having previously become very pessimistic about the government's future ability to deal with its budget deficit and indebtedness, now reassesses the situation and sees a big increase in wealth. This intriguing idea has been developed in response to experience with stabilization policies over the 1980s. In Germany, Denmark, and Ireland, fiscal contractions have been met with a surprisingly strong economic performance. Box 16.3 presents the Danish case. A related example of France in the 1920s is presented below in Box 16.6.

16.3.1.2. Hyperinflations

Hyperinflations—when the *monthly* rate of inflation exceeds 50%—are interesting because they sharply reveal some mechanisms that are less easy to detect under normal conditions. A key aspect of hyperinflations is that core inflation becomes entirely forward-looking with an increasingly shorter time horizon. When prices rise at a rate of 50% or more per month, money-holders need to worry about price levels tomorrow, if not today.

Hyperinflations have been observed in a number of countries, some of which are reported in Box 16.4. Recently it has occurred in Poland, Serbia, Russia, and

---

[5] This principle was first established in 1976 by Robert Lucas Jr, a leader of the Chicago school and Nobel Prize laureate. The Lucas critique has radically changed the way macroeconomists think about policy and its effects on the economy.

[6] For this reason, UK authorities introduced in the mid-1980s the concept of medium-term financial strategy (MTFS): each year, the government announces its intentions for the following three years. Of course, it can renege, but at the cost of losing face or having publicly to explain departures from the announced plan.

[7] This discussion is related to the Ricardian equivalence principle presented in Ch. 3.

[8] Graphically, the *IS* and *AD* curves shift to the left, not to the right.

BOX 16.3. DENMARK IN THE MID-1980S[9]

Over the period 1979–82, the Danish debt–GDP ratio rose at an unsustainable rate of 10% per year. In late 1982 the government adopted a tight debt stabilization package, cutting public spending and raising taxes. Table 16.2 shows how the deterioration of public finances was halted and reversed. Surprisingly, however, private consumption rose just when disposable income declined because of the tax increases. Part of the explanation for this is that expected future tax liabilities fell—while current taxes were raised—because the reduction in public spending was perceived as a serious policy regime change. Government spending reductions, if believed to be per-

manent, imply an increase in private wealth which may outweigh the current increase in taxes.

Another interpretation, which does not exclude the previous one, is that the government simultaneously changed its monetary policy regime: from a policy of moderate inflation matched by exchange rate devaluations within the EMS, the central bank undertook to tie the Danish krone to the Deutschmark. This meant that monetary policy would become endogenous and would be determined by the German stance. As a result interest rates fell. Wealth, which is discounted at the going interest rate, rose, as witnessed by a stock market boom during the period. As a result, consumption increased.

Table 16.2. Fiscal Stabilization in Denmark, 1979–1986

	1979–82	1983–6
Government		
Av. growth rate of public consumption (%)	4.0	0.9
Av. change (% of GDP) in cyclically adjusted:		
Net taxes	−0.3	1.3
Budget deficit	1.8	−1.8
Private sector		
Av. growth rate (%) of		
Disposable income	2.6	−0.3
Consumption	−0.8	3.7
Business investment	−2.9	12.7
Exports	6.0	3.2
GDP	1.3	3.6
Tangible Wealth	−4.2	7.7

Source: Giavazzi and Pagano (1990)

the Ukraine following the end of central planning. One of the best-known cases is that of Germany in 1922–3. Table 16.3 shows the price index and associated rate of inflation in Germany as well as the money stock during that period. During the month of October 1923 alone, the price index rose by 29,720%. This makes for a *daily* average increase of about 19%, and it could well have been double or triple that amount on some days. Failing to adjust wages or prices for just one day would have been unacceptable. Under such conditions, nominal rigidities—which arise because it is costly to change prices too often—disappear entirely. Table 16.3 shows that money, prices, and the exchange

rate moved tightly together, indicating that neutrality held on a monthly basis.

To defeat a hyperinflation, a reduction of money growth is required. There is no getting around this. The problem is that, if governments have gone down the route of hyperinflation, it is probably for serious reasons. First and foremost, stopping a hyperinflation requires closing the budget deficit.[10] Several examples which all confirm this conclusion are given in Box 16.4. Closing the budget deficit and bringing down the rate of money growth represent a dramatically sharp combination of restrictive policies. The result is guaranteed, eventually, as long as this policy is rigorously pursued.

---

[9] This box draws on the study by Giavazzi and Pagano (1990).

[10] Ch. 15 describes the link between budget deficits, public debts, and money growth, which is at the root of all hyperinflations.

Table 16.3. German Hyperinflation: Money, Prices, and Inflation, January 1922–October 1923

	Currency (Jan. 1922 = 1)	Prices (Jan. 1922 = 1)	Inflation (% per month)
January 1922	1	1	1
January 1923	16	75	189
March 1923	45	132	−12
May 1923	70	221	157
July 1923	354	2,021	386
August 1923	5,394	25,515	1,262
September 1923	227,777	645,946	2,532
October 1923	20,201,256	191,891,890	29,720

Source: adapted from Holtferich (1980)

BOX 16.4. ENDING HYPERINFLATIONS

Key features of policies that have ended hyperinflations include the following.

Germany (1921–3): Monetary reform (the Rentenmark) introduced: 1 new Rentenmark = 10^{12} old paper marks; new central bank (Rentenbank) established with binding limits on the volume of banknotes and lending to government; government budget balanced; 25% of government employees dismissed; 10% of civil servants discharged. There was a rise in unemployment in 1924 but not by much compared with surrounding years.

Austria (1921–3): Establishment of an independent central bank bound not to finance deficits with advances of banknotes; banknote issue, backing (in terms of proportions of) gold, foreign earning assets, and commercial bills; currency reform, austerity budget, and new taxes. There was a substantial increase in measured unemployment from September 1922 to March 1923.

Hungary (1922–4): New central bank, established, prohibited from lending to government except on security of gold or foreign bills; gold reserves imposed; budget balanced by late 1924. There was a less substantial increase in unemployment this time than in other episodes.

Poland (1922–3): New central bank; 30% reserve backing of notes (gold and foreign assets) beyond which backing of silver and bills of trade required; quick government moves to balance the budget; currency reform undertaken, imposing fixed gold content. There was a rise in unemployment by 50% but stabilization thereafter; there was also a loss of discipline by the central bank, contributing to a later deterioration of the foreign exchange rate and price level.

Bolivia (1985–6): Exchange rate set by government using reserve loan from the IMF; wage freeze introduced; budget balanced; new valorized (inflation-proof) taxes introduced. Unemployment skyrocketed; output plummeted by 30%; real interest rates remained at double-digit levels for several years thereafter.

Israel (1985): Sharp cut in the budget deficit from 17% to 8% of GDP; US dollar exchange rate stabilized. There followed a rise in unemployment, new independence for the central bank, and a dramatic reduction in growth.

Poland (1990): Subsidies cut by government on 1 January 1990; currency devalued and pegged to the US dollar; loans from central bank to government severely limited. Output fell by some 10%, unemployment increased from 0 to about 10%, and real wages contracted sharply.

Sources: Sargent (1982); Dornbusch and Fischer (1986); Berg and Sachs (1992).

BOX 16.5. HETERODOX DISINFLATION POLICIES

Because in the long run money growth determines inflation, 'orthodox' disinflation policies simply cut down the rate of money growth. The risk is a protracted recession if expectations are slow to recognize the policy shift. Credibility is therefore essential to limit the costs of disinflation. This has led to the 'heterodox' strategy of announcing so-called nominal anchors. Initially experimented with in Bolivia and Israel in 1985, nominal anchors have been applied in many other countries, for example Poland in 1990.

The idea behind nominal anchors is simultaneously to announce the new money growth targets and to fix some key nominal variables, like the exchange rate or wages. Those who depend on these prices naturally stand to lose. To assuage them, heterodox policies sometimes start by raising these prices, so as to provide an 'advance compensation', and then freezing them, or slowing them down by administrative rules. In Poland wages had increased by 30% before the programme was in place. They were then allowed to grow at only a fraction of the inflation rate (30% in January 1990, 20% from February to April, and 60% for the rest of the year except for a safety valve of 100% in July). The control mechanism was a tax of 200%–500% imposed on firms on wage growth in excess of the ceilings. The exchange rate was devalued by 31.6% on 1 January 1990 and held unchanged until May 1991. The path of inflation is shown in Figure 16.6. Real wages, which initially improved, went on declining, cumulating to an average loss of 31%. The initial undervaluation of the exchange rate allowed for a boost in exports, but then became progressively overvalued as inflation picked up. Nominal anchors are designed to buttress the credibility of the plan: by administratively controlling these anchors, the government makes the continuation of inflation painful and inconsistent with its own objectives. Sticking to the anchors is a signal of a government's determination.

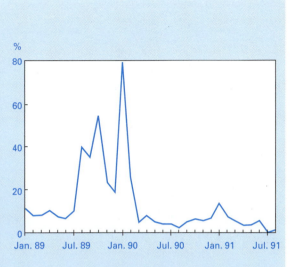

Figure 16.6. Inflation in Poland, 1989–1991: Monthly Growth Rate of the Consumer Price Index

Inflation appeared towards the end of the Communist regime, peaked in January 1990 when prices were freed and subsidies cut, and then declined sharply.

Source: Berg and Sachs (1992)

The true challenge in the short run is to limit the output costs of the disinflation, and to make it politically acceptable and sustainable. The key to success is to affect expectations in the private sector. If the policy shift is convincing enough to shake the forward-looking component of core inflation, the costs can be contained. The necessary condition is that the monetary authorities be committed as clearly and unambiguously as possible to a new policy regime of non-monetary finance of budget deficits. Merely issuing a new currency—as in Argentina and Brazil in the 1980s—without any change in the policy regime is not enough. A better example is the end of the Weimar Republic hyperinflation. In January 1924, Germany instituted a new central bank which was strongly independent and was forbidden to lend to the Treasury. These features survive in modern Germany. In fact, inflation stopped in November 1923, when the new constitution of the bank was promulgated, even before it came into existence. Quite often, the authorities attempt to supplement the bare minimum—tight money—with a set of 'anchors' designed to signal their determination and affect core inflation. Box 16.5 describes these so-called heterodox policies.

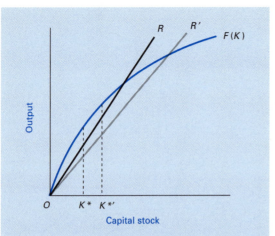

Figure 16.7. The Effect of a Reduction in Corporate Taxes

A reduction of corporate profit taxation reduces the required pre-tax rate of profit. As the ray *OR* shifts to *OR'*, the optimal capital stock rises from *K** to *K*'*, with a corresponding increase in output.

16.3.2. Reputation and Credibility

16.3.2.1. The temptation of governments to cheat

If expectations of future policy actions affect private behaviour, governments may wish to 'manipulate' expectations. This phenomenon is most apparent in the case of the Phillips curve: a promise of less inflation in the future, if believed, lowers both core and actual inflation now. Once this is achieved and inflation is low, will not the government be tempted to create an inflation surprise, for example to reduce the real value of its debt? Such attempts at manipulation may seem of little importance, because when the private sector discovers that promises are not upheld, it will simply revise its expectations.

In fact, the problem is more serious. How can a government really intent on keeping inflation low convince the public of its intentions? If it reneges on its commitments, then the public will always want to be prepared for broken promises, so will conservatively assume a higher rate of inflation than the government intends to adopt. Core, and therefore actual, inflation will not decline. Reducing core inflation requires a period of recession (as at point *A* in Figure 16.2).

Another example is the case of reduction of the tax on corporate profits. Figure 16.7 reproduces the firm's investment decision.[11] A tax reduction shifts the ray describing the cost of capital from *OR* to *OR'*. This provides incentives for firms to accumulate more capital, from *K** to *K*'*. But firms must ask themselves how the government will meet its intertemporal budget constraint once it has reduced corporate profit taxes. Could it be that the government will change its mind later on, when pressed to close the budget deficit, and tax already-installed capital? If firms suspect such a policy, they will simply ignore the initial incentive. It is essential therefore for the government to promise that future taxes will not affect installed capital. This promise is not credible, however, for when the capital is in place the government's best course of action is to renege.

These are just two examples of a wider phenomenon. A broad range of policies are **time-inconsistent**: policies that appear optimal today (low inflation, reduced taxes on corporate profits, and no taxation on installed capital) are not optimal later on, especially after agents have adjusted their behaviour accordingly.[12] If a course of action is time-inconsistent, it is not credible, because the private sector will not consider it likely to be implemented. What is left is always less desirable: a higher rate of inflation than the government wishes, and less capital accumulation.

16.3.3. Rules versus Discretion

The phenomenon of time consistency is so conspicuous that societies have designed many ways of coping with it. The most obvious is the establishment of legal rules. For example, it is against the German constitution for the Bundesbank to lend money to the government. The second strategy is for the government to build up a **reputation**, i.e. the perception that it would never pursue such policies. To do so, it may impose rules upon itself to convince the public of its will to refrain from certain actions (like printing money), even if at some point such actions prove highly desirable.

Rules have the merit of preventing time-inconsistent actions. A vivid description of rules often refers to 'binding the hands' of the policy-maker. Rules,

[11] Ch. 4 develops the principle of an optimal stock of capital.
[12] Time inconsistency is a very general phenomenon, which goes beyond economics. A son will promise to drive carefully if lent his parents' car; a person in prison always pledges not to engage in unlawful activity if released early; politicians promise the moon if elected. All of these promises are time-inconsistent. The risk is that only time-consistent solutions, which are less desirable for all involved, are adopted: no son is lent a car, no inmate is released early, and politicians are never trusted.

BOX 16.6. HIGH DEBT IN FRANCE[15]

France emerged from the First World War with a public debt of about 150% of GDP. Figure 16.8 shows the budget deficit, the wholesale price index, and an index representing the exchange rate (rising as the French franc depreciates). For a while, the French government financed huge deficits by borrowing against expected war reparations imposed upon Germany. When it became clear that Germany would not pay, sharp political disagreements made it impossible to close the deficit.[16] The alternatives under consideration were a tax on wealth ('the rich can pay' was a favourite slogan), inflation, or default. Inflation closely tracks debt stabilization attempts. The first surge in inflation (1919–20) corresponds to an early attempt at seigniorage. The second one (1923–4) followed the French occupation of the Ruhr in a last-ditch effort to extract war reparations. Inflation stopped in March

1924, when the parliament adopted an across-the-board 20% tax increase. Soon afterwards, a left-wing coalition came to power. To improve its credibility, it adopted a rule establishing ceilings on central bank advances to the Treasury, but then secretly violated them. When the truth surfaced (April 1925), inflation shot up again. Each bout of nervousness was accompanied by massive capital flight and pressure on the exchange rate.

In July 1926 Raymond Poincaré, a conservative and highly respected politician, became prime minister. He promptly raised indirect and income taxes—but not taxes on wealth—and appointed as governor of the Bank of France a staunchly independent personality, Emile Moreau. The credibility of the Poincaré–Moreau team had a visibly powerful effect: from the brink of hyperinflation, prices stopped immediately and the franc even appreciated.

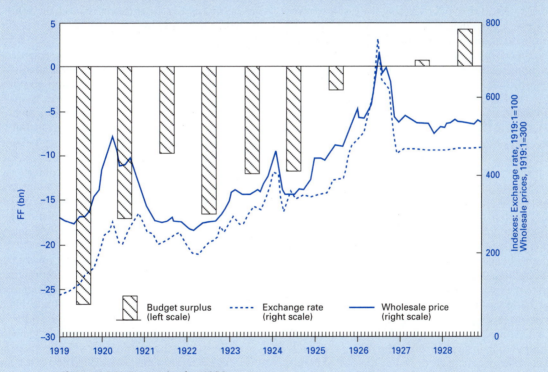

Figure 16.8. France in the 1920s

Several partial attempts at solving the postwar debt and deficit problem brought temporary price and exchange rate relief. The mere appointment of a credible prime minister and a credible governor of the Banque de France brought price and exchange rate stability.

Source: Alesina (1988a)

---

[15] This box draws on the study by Alesina (1988a).

[16] The newborn Communist Party was rising, as were far-rightist movements.

Table 16.4. Budget Deficit Rules in the USA (number of states (out of 50) with the following rules)

Governor has to submit a balanced budget (1)	Legislature has to pass a balanced budget (2)	Deficit may be carried over, but must then be corrected (3)	Deficit may not be carried over (4)
12	8	9	36

Source: Eichengreen (1990)

however, may also prevent governments from taking actions that are desirable. For example, it is often suggested that governments be forbidden from running budget deficits to avoid triggering the explosive debt process. A no-deficit rule, however, would block the automatic stabilizer mechanism. In the midst of a recession, when net taxes decline, such a rule imposes spending cuts or tax increases, i.e. contractionary policies which deepen the recession.

In the USA, budget rules exist in forty-nine of the fifty states (the exception being Vermont). They are described in Table 16.4. (Similar, although less restrictive, rules exist for the German *Länder*.) No-deficit rules exist in thirty-six states (column (4)). A solution that allows the automatic stabilizer to operate is to request balanced budgets on average, allowing deficits in bad years to be repaid in better times. This procedure exists in nine states (column (3)). Finally, more discretion is allowed in the remaining twenty states, where either the government or the legislature must adopt a budget balanced *ex ante*, not *ex post*. There is no binding rule at the federal level in the USA, nor has any sovereign state felt it necessary so far to adopt binding budgetary rules. Fiscal policy discretion is perceived as too important to be given up, or else it is felt that the time inconsistency problem can be dealt with by reputation instead of rules. The role of credibility in episodes of debt is illustrated by the case of France in the 1920s in Box 16.6.

16.3.4. Central Bank Independence

Central banks face some of the most serious time inconsistency problems. The value of money rests on the assumption that central banks will not create too

much of it, despite strong incentives to do so. One incentive is the revenue from seigniorage. History shows that this temptation is often difficult to resist. Furthermore, surprise inflation reduces the value of the public debt, and highly indebted treasuries often ask their central banks to help out.

Solutions to this problem are usually based on rules, or reputation, or both. *Rules* take several forms. The central bank may forfeit its power to impose reserve requirements (e.g. the UK and Switzerland); this reduces the demand for the monetary base which is the source of seigniorage. Another rule is to forbid the central bank from lending directly to the Treasury, and/or to limit its holdings of public debts (e.g. Germany). In general, central banks actively cultivate their reputations. One approach is publicly to adopt some explicit targets—money growth, inflation, a fixed exchange rate. Under conditions of high inflation, governments sometimes pre-announce a schedule of devaluations.[13]

In the end, however, the best way for a government to enhance its reputation is to grant its central bank independence from government influence and interference. Figure 16.9 relates the economic performance of the OECD countries to a measure of the degree of economic independence of central banks.[14] Panel (*a*) shows that where the central bank is more independent inflation tends to be lower. What about the output–inflation trade-off? From panel (*b*) it can be seen that there is no link between economic growth and the degree of central bank independence. The two panels together have a clear implication: by granting

---

[13] This strategy has been pursued in numerous Latin American countries, in Israel, and in Eastern and Central European countries.
[14] Ch. 9 presents an alternative measure of central bank independence.

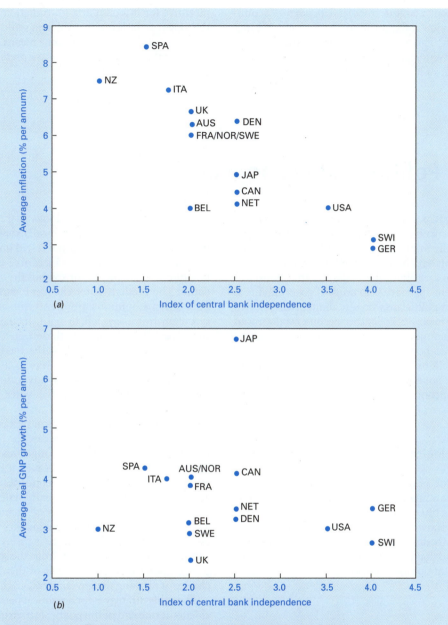

Figure 16.9. Inflation, Growth, and Central Bank Independence

Both charts link an index of central bank independence to the inflation and GDP growth performance of OECD countries over the period 1955–88. Panel (*a*) exhibits a clear relationship: inflation is lower the more independent is the central bank. Panel (*b*) fails to reveal any link between independence and GDP growth: independence delivers low inflation at no cost.

Source: Alesina and Summers (1993)

its central bank a large degree of independence, a country achieves low inflation at no cost in terms of long-run growth. This result is consistent with a vertical long-run *AS* curve. In the end, an independent central bank's main asset is its credibility. This provides a clear incentive for it to aim at a low inflation rate, and in the long run the economy will then settle in the lower portion of its LAS schedule. Some means of establishing central bank independence are presented in Box 16.7.

16.4. Politics and Economics

Reputation is meaningful only when a long-term relationship is involved. When it comes to government, this naturally implicates the political system. So far, governments have been described as well-meaning entities which care about the welfare of the country. A very different approach is to think of governments as being run by politicians who care about getting elected and staying in power. Policy then becomes endogenous to both economic and political circumstances, and, reciprocally, economic circumstances are partly shaped by policy actions. The loop is closed and provides interesting, if not always encouraging, insights into the role and function of demand management polices.

16.4.1. Electoral Business Cycles

It is risky for a government to approach an election with deteriorating economic conditions. The timing of elections often generate **political business cycles**. Table 16.6 shows that, indeed, during election years the budget tends to deteriorate relatively to the previous year and that growth is often higher, although the evidence is not particularly strong.[17]

16.4.2. Partisan Business Cycles

The partisan business cycle view claims that changes of governments lead to new policies which generate business cycles. This section looks at the macroeconomic implications of the (cynical?) view that, when in power, a political party is interested only in pursuing policies that increase its chances of re-election. The first question is how to think about the election outcome. The **median voter theorem** asserts that the population's opinions are evenly spread along the spectrum from, say, left to right. In that case there would be 50% of the votes to the left, 50% to the right, and the voter-in-the-middle—the median voter—casts the swinging vote. If that were so, a party would maximize its election chances by advocating the policy mix most palatable to the median voter. Two strategies are possible.

In the first strategy, all political parties aim at the lucky median voter, and in this case the political parties are indistinguishable. Although this description does not accord too well with reality, it explains two important facts. First, in many countries the political arena is characterized by a two-party system with parties that offer very similar choices. Second, elections are often won by a very narrow margin. In that case elections do not generate business cycles because the winner does not differ much from the loser and the public knows *ex ante* that each of them has a 50% chance of forming the government.

The other strategy is for a political party to aim decidedly at one end of the political spectrum but try to extend its appeal *up to* the median voter, thus catching just 50% of the electorate, plus one. This would describe fairly polarized political systems and would also explain the narrow margins of election outcomes. In this case, elections generate **partisan business cycles**, because policies change fairly sharply when a new party is elected.

It is customary to describe left-leaning governments as being Keynesian and right-leaning governments as being Monetarist. Then, if a left-leaning government replaces a right-leaning government, we should expect

---

[17] The fact that unemployment seems to worsen in election years in some countries is puzzling. One possibility is that exogenously bad economic outcomes lead to the downfall of governments and premature elections. Another possibility is that in Europe policy-generated expansions have not been sufficient to stop the unrelenting increase in equilibrium unemployment during most of the period studied. See Ch. 6.

BOX 16.7. THE NUTS AND BOLTS OF CENTRAL BANK INDEPENDENCE[18]

The autonomy of a central bank depends on its political independence and its economic freedom of manoeuvre. As a central bank is vested with important authority and serves the public interest, it must be subject to some measure of democratic control. The line between democratic control and political interference is a thin one, though. **Political independence** depends upon such aspects as the way in which central bank governors and boards are appointed. Long terms of appointment, with no possibility of early dismissal, offer more independence than terms with no set limit so that dismissal can occur at any time. Non-renewability of the term in office removes the incentive to please politicians. Current arrangements are described in Table 16.5. For example, the governor of the Bundesbank is appointed for a single eight-year term, whereas the governors of the Bank of Denmark, France, and Italy are appointed for an indefinite term and can be dismissed at any time. While governments often insist on being represented on the board, their formal approval for policy action may not be required. When conflicts arise, precise procedures contribute to greater autonomy. In Denmark, France, and the UK, there are no legal av-enues for resolving disagreements between the central bank and the government, which effectively means that the government can impose its will.

Economic independence depends on the practical aspects of daily operations. For example, the central bank may be able to restrict its lending to the Treasury. Yet, as open market operations can be the back-door for financing budget deficits, in some countries (e.g. Austria, France, Germany, the Netherlands) the central bank is not allowed to participate in auctions for Treasury bills. Of course, who sets the rate at which the Treasury borrows from its central bank also matters. Another important aspect is who decides on exchange rate policy, since money supply, interest, and exchange rates cannot be set independently. In Germany the exchange rate is decided by the finance minister; this is one of the rare limits on the Bundesbank's independence, one that explains its traditional coolness towards formal exchange rate linkages.[19] Bringing together these various features, it is possible to compute a synthetic index of economic and political independence.

Table 16.5. Terms of Central Bank Governors and Boards

Canada
    Governor appointed by finance minister for 3-year term, renewable
    Board appointed by government for 3-year term, renewable
Germany
    President appointed by federal president for 8-year term, non-renewable
    Council members appointed by federal president for 8-year term, renewable
Netherlands
    President appointed by government for 7-year term, renewable
    Governing board appointed by government for 7-year term, renewable
UK
    Governor appointed by government for 5-year term, renewable
Switzerland
    Directorate of 3, appointed by council for 8-year term, renewable
USA
    President appointed by senate for 4-year term, renewable
    All board members (including president) appointed for 14-year term
European System of Central Banks (Maastricht Treaty)
    President appointed by EC Council for 8-year term, non-renewable
    Executive board members (up to 5 in addition to president) appointed by EC Council for
        8-year term, non-renewable
    Council includes board members and governors of National Central Banks, each with
        terms of at least 5 years, renewable

Source: Roll *et al.* (1993)

---

[18] This box owes much to the work of Grilli *et al.* (1991).

[19] The Bundesbank is known to have been unhappy with the creation of the European Monetary System. Early in 1990 it argued against a swift monetary unification with East Germany, then against the one-Deutschmark-for-one-Ostmark conversion rate. In the end, it bowed to the government's wishes. Thus, even the considerable freedom enjoyed by such institutions can be modified if public demand for such a change is sufficiently high.

Table 16.6. Budgetary and Economic Conditions in Election Years, OECD Countries, 1972–1984

	Does the budget deteriorate in election years?		Is output growth higher in election years?		Is unemployment lower in election years?	
	Yes	No	Yes	No	Yes	No
Austria	1	2	1	2	0	3
Belgium	4	0	3	1	0	3
Denmark	3	1	2	2	1	3
Finland	3	0	2	1	0	3
France	2	1	0	3	0	3
Germany	0	4	2	2	2	1
Netherlands	2	1	2	1	0	3
Norway	1	2	0	3	2	1
Sweden	2	2	3	1	3	1
UK	2	1	3	0	2	1
USA	2	2	3	1	3	1
Total	22	16	21	17	13	23

Note: Changes are measured as differences between election year and previous year (moved ahead one year if election is in Jan.–June). For unemployment, two cases are not classified because the rate did not change significantly.

Sources: Alesina (1989) and own calculations from OECD *National Accounts*

to see GDP growth increase and unemployment decrease, possibly at the expense of rising inflation. Based on twenty years of observation, Table 16.7 confirms this presumption. The table can equally be read as indicating the effect of a shift to the right by merely changing the signs. In all cases, GDP growth picks up, and in all but two cases (the Netherlands and Norway[20]) unemployment declines.

[20] The estimated effects in these two cases are not statistically significant; i.e. they are not really different from zero.

Table 16.7. Effects on Real GNP Growth and Unemployment of a Change to the Left, OECD Countries, 1966–1986

	Growth	Unemployment		Growth	Unemployment
Australia	0.87	−0.29	Germany	0.39	−0.50
Austria	1.04	−0.24	Netherlands	0.67	0.36
Belgium	0.21	−0.53	Norway	1.04	0.01
Denmark	0.67	−0.42	Sweden	1.44	−0.16
Finland	2.32	−1.00	UK	1.51	−0.42
France	0.31	−0.67	USA	2.51	−0.66

Note: each country's growth and unemployment are measured relatively to the average of the other countries listed in the table.

Source: Alesina (1989)

16.5. Summary

1. While demand management policies can in principle smooth business cycle fluctuations, recent experience and economic principles suggest caution.

2. Monetarists and Keynesians mostly disagree on the *degree* to which actual prices and markets achieve efficient allocation of resources and optimal satisfaction of individual needs. Monetarists contend that market-clearing is a good first-order approximation, and that markets are closer to perfection than governments. Keynesians consider that markets suffer from a host of imperfections and that economies can suffer from persistent underutilization of resources.

3. Uncertainty plays an important role in the debate. For Keynesians, it means that private decisions are taken with imperfect knowledge of future conditions. This results in wrong pricing and resource allocation decisions. For Monetarists, uncertainty means that policy mistakes are as likely to make matters worse as they are to improve them. Keynesians want discretion in policy-making, whereas Monetarists favour rules.

4. Because expectations crucially shape private behaviour, limited policy changes may not affect private behaviour patterns, while regime policy changes may change them abruptly. The Lucas critique implies that policies that look good given previous policies may turn out to deliver very different outcomes from those desired.

5. Time inconsistency arises when the policy plans that are best today become less desirable at a later stage, possibly after the private sector has reacted. This represents a powerful incentive for governments to renege on promises once the private sector has acted in the belief that the promises will be carried out. Time-inconsistent policies are not credible.

6. There are two ways of making time-inconsistent policies credible: legally binding rules, and reputation. Rules invariably restrict policy discretion and activism. Reputation requires that governments refrain from actions even if they are, at the time, desirable.

7. Monetary policy is a fragile instrument because of severe time consistency problems. This has led central banks to seek rules (independence) and reputation. Independent central banks tend to be associated with lower inflation rates.

8. In reality, citizens have different interests and opinions. Real-life governments are not necessarily well-meaning, but instead care mainly about being re-elected. This may lead some governments to use economic policy in a politically opportunistic way.

9. Political business cycles may take the form of expansionary policies being introduced just before elections, to be followed by corrective contractionary policies after elections. Partisan business cycles may result from the alternation of governments that defend the interests of their constituencies.

Key Concepts

- Monetarism
- Keynesianism
- activist policies
- market-clearing
- recognition, decision, implementation, and effectiveness lags
- Lucas critique
- policy regime

- nominal anchors
- time inconsistency
- credibility
- reputation
- rules *v.* discretion
- median voter theorem
- political business cycles
- partisan business cycles

Exercises: Theory

1. It has been suggested that real interest rates on public debts are related to the size of the budget deficit, not to the size of the debt. Can you provide an explanation? (*Hint*: think about the long-term implications for the budget constraint.)

2. Imagine a sudden and unexpected wave of high wage settlements. What would be the likely solutions proposed (*a*) by a Monetarist? (*b*) by a Keynesian? Argue their cases.

3. Why are quickly rising debts sometimes accompanied by increasing inflation, even if money growth is held tight?

4. What are the costs of inflation? Are there any advantages of inflation? If so, what are they?

5. Monetary policy works through either the interest rate or the exchange rate. Do you think that the effectiveness lag differs according to the exchange rate regime? If so, explain why and how.

6. Why do large budget deficits often result in exchange rate depreciations? Identify at least two channels.

7. 'By reducing the costs of inflation, indexation raises an economy's steady state inflation rate.' Comment.

8. Using the *AS–AD* framework, illustrate how influencing inflationary expectations could be an important policy instrument.

9. Describe the lags that affect economic policy-making and their consequences for the effectiveness of: (*a*) fiscal policy; (*b*) monetary policy.

10. Discuss arguments for and against a zero budget deficit rule.

Exercises: Applications

1. Over the period 1955–86, New Zealand experienced an annual money growth of 6.4% and CPI inflation of 8.0%, translating into reduction of real balances at roughly 1.6% per annum over a period of three decades. Yet, at the same time, the economy grew at a respectable 3.0% per annum. How might this be explained?

2. The following numbers have been taken from the International Monetary Fund's *International Financial Statistics* for the Republic of Bolivia:

	1984	1985	1986	1987
$\mu(\Delta M/M)$	18,900	58,800	83.3	38.3
$\pi(\Delta P/P)$	13,800	12,100	376	10.6

A stringent disinflation programme was undertaken in 1986, successfully bringing inflation down to 10%. How can one explain the rapid increase in real money balances in 1987 (high money growth in 1987 despite the low inflation)? What additional evidence would you require to determine whether the Bolivian programme has collapsed or succeeded?

3. In Germany, *Länder* (states) are in principle allowed to borrow only an amount equal to or less than the public investments that they undertake. What is the economic rationale for this so-called 'golden rule of public finance'?

4. The Italian public debt is considerably higher than 100% of GDP. Why is most of it short-term and denominated in Italian lira? The Treasury has started to issue debt in ECUs: how can that improve its credibility?

5. Belgium has one of the largest public debts in Europe. In 1990 its central bank announced a determination to keep for ever the parity of the franc *vis à vis* the Deutschmark. What might affect the credibility of this proposal?

6. The Swedish government has often tried to slow down inflation by asking trade unions and employers to agree on moderate wage settlements, offering tax reductions in return. Why is such an attempt at a 'social contract' unlikely to be credible?

7. 'Italy will never solve its public debt problem unless its electoral system is thoroughly modified.' Comment.

8. For more than two decades, European governments have severely regulated the ability of employers to dismiss workers for economic (business-cycle-related) reasons. In recent years some governments have announced that these regulations would be relaxed, with the hope of reducing the equilibrium unemployment rate. How might the time inconsistency argument be used to explain why employers have not created as many jobs as one might have hoped?

Suggested Further Reading

On the debate between Keynesians and Monetarists, see the special issue of *Economic Policy*, 5 (1987) as well as the symposium on 'Keynesian Economics Today' in the *Journal of Economic Perspectives*, 7 (Winter 1993); also:

De Long, J. Bradford, and Summers, Lawrence H. (1988), 'How Does Macroeconomic Policy After Output?' *Brookings Papers on Economic Activity*, 2: 433–94.

Friedman, Milton (1953), 'The Effect of Full Employment Policy on Economic Stability: a Formal Analysis', in his *Essays in Positive Economics*, University of Chicago Press.

Lucas, R. E. Jr (1978), 'Unemployment Policy', *American Economic Review Papers and Proceedings*, 68: 353–7.

Recollections by leading economists involved in policy-making are presented in:

Tobin, James, and Weidenbaum, Murray (eds.) (1988), *Two Revolutions in Economic Policy: the First Economic Reports of Presidents Kennedy and Reagan*, MIT Press, Cambridge, Mass.

The original (and technical) exposition of the Lucas critique can be found in:

Lucas, R. E. Jr (1976), 'Economic Policy Evaluation: a Critique', in K. Brunner and A. Meltzer (eds.), *The Phillips Curve and Labor Markets*, Carnegie–Rochester Conference Series, North-Holland, Amsterdam.

On credibility, see:

Barro, Robert, and Gordon, Robert D. (1983), 'Rules, Discretion, and Reputation in a Model of Monetary Policy', *Journal of Monetary Economics*, 12: 101–22.

Cukierman, Alex (1992), *Central Bank Strategy, Credibility and Independence*, MIT Press, Cambridge, Mass.

Goodhart, Charles (1994), 'Game Theory for Central Bankers', *Journal of Economic Literature*, 32(1): 101–14.

On the cost of inflation, see:

Fischer, Stanley (1986), *Indexing, Inflation, and Economic Policy*, MIT Press, Cambridge, Mass.

On the link between politics and economics, see:

Alesina, Alberto (1988), 'Macroeconomics and Politics', *NBER Macroeconomics Annual*, 3: 13–62.
Alesina, Alberto (1989), 'Politics and Business Cycles in Industrial Democracies', *Economic Policy*, 8: 55–98.

Figure 16.9, showing the effect of central bank independence on inflation, is from:

Alesina, Alberto, and Summers, Lawrence (1993), 'Central Bank Independence and Macroeconomic Performance: Some Comparative Evidence', *Journal of Money, Credit, and Banking*, 25: 151–62.

This and other results on central bank independence can be found in:

Grilli, Vittorio, Masciandaro, Donato, and Tabellini, Guido (1991), 'Political and Monetary Institutions and Public Financial Policies in the Industrial Countries', *Economic Policy*, 13: 341–92.
Roll, Eric *et al.* (1993), *Independent and Accountable: a New Mandate for the Bank of England*, CEPR, London.

17

Supply-Side and Unemployment Policies

For almost twenty years now, European unemployment has been a major social problem and the sign of underutilized resources at a time of unfilled needs . . . Faced with such a prospect, European economists cannot remain silent.

Jacques Drèze and Edmond Malinvaud

17.1. Overview

In contrast with demand-side policies discussed in the previous chapter, supply-side policies do not require the uncomfortable trade-off between output and inflation. Their aim is to increase permanently the potential GDP ($\overline{Y}$). The attractiveness of such policies can be seen in Figure 17.1, which plots GDP itself rather than its deviation from $\overline{Y}$ on the horizontal axis. Successful supply-side policies raise potential GDP from $\overline{Y}$ to $\overline{Y}'$ faster than if were it left to the normal process of economic growth. In the short run, more output and lower inflation are possible as the economy moves from A to A'.[1] Bad supply-side policies reduce $\overline{Y}$, causing higher inflation in the short run and higher unemployment in the long run.

Since the late 1970s enthusiasm for demand man-agement has waned, while it has grown for supply-side policies. This chapter reports on the many types of supply-side policies that have since been tried. One lesson is that supply-side policies require time to work and do not produce immediate miracles. They are microeconomic in nature; measures that increase the production of a single good may allow an increase in the production of all goods by freeing up productive resources for alternative uses.

Two broad areas of supply-side policies can be identified. First, markets sometimes do not function correctly; this can justify government activity to correct these malfunctions. Second, the presence of governments in the marketplace may itself be disruptive. One example of this is regulation; another is taxation. Many of the principles developed in this chapter rely on analyses of previous chapters. Supply-side policies are simply the application of sound economic principles.

17.2. Improving the Efficiency of Markets

17.2.1. The Benchmark of Efficiency: Perfect Competition

One of the most important results of modern microeconomics is the proof that Adam Smith was right.[2] Under ideal conditions, market economies should achieve optimal employment of resources. For that to happen, all markets must be free to work and prices must adjust completely. In practice, this rarely happens. An example is the labour market described in Chapter 6 and especially Figure 6.10. Firms' demand for labour is given by the labour demand curve, which is simply the marginal product of labour (MPL); firms hire labour to the point at which its marginal productivity equals the real wage. Employing labour beyond this point reduces the MPL below the real wage, and thereby reduces profits. Conversely, reducing employment below the optimal point would mean a rise of the MPL above the real wage, so that it would pay to hire more labour again. In a similar way, workers competing in the marketplace decide how much labour to supply given the real wage. Where the two curves intersect, demand equals supply, but also the value of an additional hour of workers' time is equal to the value

---

[1] Note that the short-run effect of the shift is a reduction in the rate of inflation, as the new short-run and long-run AS curves shift rightward. For a given rate of monetary growth the inflation rate returns to its previous level (point A''), although complicated dynamics may characterize this adjustment process, as Ch. 14 showed.

[2] Adam Smith (1723–90), perhaps the most famous economist of all time, claimed in his book *The Wealth of Nations* that efficient resource allocation was best left to the market system. A formal proof was accomplished much later by Nobel laureates Kenneth Arrow of Stanford and Gerard Debreu of Berkeley, who in the 1950s identified the conditions under which a market economy reproduces the socially optimal allocation of resources.

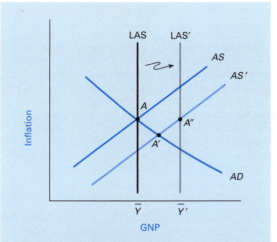

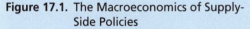

Figure 17.1. The Macroeconomics of Supply-Side Policies

Supply-side policies aim at mobilizing productive resources to increase equilibrium output. Shifting the aggregate supply curve yields both more output and less inflation in the short run (point *A'*). In the longer run, inflation returns to its previous level but output is permanently higher.

placed on it by firms in the marketplace. The market outcome maximizes the employment of resources given the desires of workers. This ideal situation occurs when, and only when, the real wage is free to reach its market-clearing level.

If instead wages were above the market-clearing level, firms would restrict employment, resulting in the underutilization of labour. Or if real wages were too low, firms would find no workers to man their equipment, which would mean underutilization of capital, and low returns on investment. This conclusion is general: for the economy to achieve its optimum, all markets must clear. Either all prices are right and full employment of all productive resources is achieved, or none of them is and underutilization and inefficiency spreads throughout the economy.

If all markets behave in this fashion, there is no economic reason for governments to interfere with their working. This is the case for *laissez-faire*. In practice, very few markets meet the high requirements set forth by Adam Smith. Such market failures open up the case for government interventions. Supply-side principles rest on two ideas. First, interventions should be limited to clearly identified market failures. Second, the interventions should be targeted directly at the market failure so as not to create additional distortions of their

own. The next sections present a number of generic distortions and the associated supply-side principles.

17.2.2. Competition Policy

Every economic agent has an interest in shielding itself from competition by developing some ability to behave as a monopolist and earn profits above the normal rate of return, or what economists sometimes call **economic rents**. For firms, sources of monopoly power are increasing returns and product differentiation. When production exhibits increasing returns to scale, smaller firms may be squeezed out by larger ones, which come to dominate the market. Second, firms may attempt to erect barriers to prevent others from entering their markets. Most means of maintaining dominance in a market are explicitly illegal, including threats against retailers and blackmail. It is standard practice, however, for producers to try to differentiate their products from others on the market. Customers are willing to pay more for a particular product or brand that they perceive as special. Firms use clever marketing as a means of obtaining and defending this monopoly power, and the amounts spent in that activity are suggestive of the profits possible through product differentiation. Product differentiation thrives on individuals' desire for variety in the marketplace.

Measures that aim at increasing competition, and thereby economic output, are called **competition policy**. Two interesting cases of EU competition policy are discussed in Box 17.1. Most countries regulate monopolies caused by increasing returns. Firms are seldom allowed to acquire excessive shares of their markets. Cartels and price-fixing schemes are illegal, although sometimes difficult to prove in court. More recently, governments have limited the ability of firms to dominate their input and output markets. In the USA, a court forced the telephone company AT&T to divest itself of its regional telephone service companies. Similarly, the UK government has separated electricity generation from electricity distribution and the EU Commission envisages moving in this direction at the Community level. More generally, as European integration progresses, anti-monopoly powers are being transferred to Brussels, which now examines market shares at the EU level.

Labour markets are also characterized by non-competitive behaviour. Wages are often set through bilateral negotiations and trade unions can be seen as monopolists striving for high real wages.[3] With high

---

[3] The analysis of trade unions is developed in Ch. 6.

BOX 17.1. CASSIS DE DIJON AND THE REINHEITSGEBOT

While Germany is well known for its antitrust office, it has been seen as less inclined to reduce the monopoly power of German firms under attacks from EC competitors. Twice Germany has been taken to the European Court of Justice, which has the final word in matters of competition policy. The first case concerned Cassis de Dijon, a French alcoholic beverage made from blackcurrants used to make *kir* (when mixed with white wine). Germany claimed that its alcohol content did not satisfy German standards and that the cassis could not be imported.

As for beer, Germany has long honoured the so-called beer purity law dating back to 1516, which limited the content of beer to four ingredients (water, yeast, barley, and malt). This law was used to exclude 'impure' foreign beer which did not meet the exacting standards of the *Reinheitsgebot*. In both cases, the European Court of Justice felt otherwise. Still, most German beer drinkers prefer to buy German beer. These two cases set a precedent which relates to *grani duro* Italian pasta and all other idiosyncratic national preferences.

real wages, labour demand is low and equilibrium unemployment high. If the majority of their members are ready for the trade-off, trade unions press for an outcome that is not optimal from a social point of view. A similar situation arises on the other side of the bargaining table. In response to unionization, management has organized itself into employers' associations. These associations often take decisions that may be binding also on non-members (usually smaller firms). For example, if they set wages in collective bargaining without considering the interest of non-members, the level of competition is reduced.

While trade unions may have adverse economic effects, they fulfil important social purposes. Historically, they have protected workers from abuses and they continue to play an important role in this regard. Reducing their market power requires reducing their overall role in the workplace. It is also true that an overwhelming majority (90%–95%) of workers are employed, so that their domination over the unemployed might even be regarded as democratic, and is mitigated by unemployment benefits in any case. Often social and economic objectives clash, leaving con-

flicts to be settled by politics. This is why reducing the market power of trade unions may be dangerous. In general, governments find it difficult to reform labour market institutions because their interventions are often regarded as interference in the collective bargaining process. One rare example of a major reform is the case of Britain under Mrs Thatcher, presented in Box 17.2.

17.2.3. Search and Information Externalities

While prices themselves reveal much information, many markets require even more to operate efficiently. For example, buyers are often unable to determine the quality of products, especially those that have a high technical content. Buyers and sellers may have difficulty locating each other, for example in real estate or antiques. Organized physical markets overcome this difficulty but cannot be set up for all goods. (The marketplace itself has aspects of a public good.) The

BOX 17.2. MRS THATCHER, UNION BUSTING, AND THE EQUILIBRIUM UNEMPLOYMENT RATE

One of the legacies of Prime Minister Margaret Thatcher was a radical overhaul of the UK collective bargaining system. In a series of legislative actions, she restricted the wide immunity enjoyed by unions from civil torts to those directly involving industrial action, and forced unions to elect their officials in secret balloting. In a series of open confrontations, she limited trade unions' ability to disrupt the workings of the economy. In the decade 1980–9, union membership in the UK declined by 21% and union density declined from 50.7% to 41.5%. Over the same period unemployment declined considerably, as

seen in Figure 17.2. Because the Conservative government often 'redefined' unemployment, we also display OECD standardized unemployment which adjusts for such changes in definition. Both show a dramatic decline. The Phillips curve shown in Figure 12.7 suggests that a significant part of the decline in actual unemployment also represents a fall in equilibrium unemployment. This illustrates the key difference between temporary successes to be had from demand management policies and permanent gains from supply-side policies.

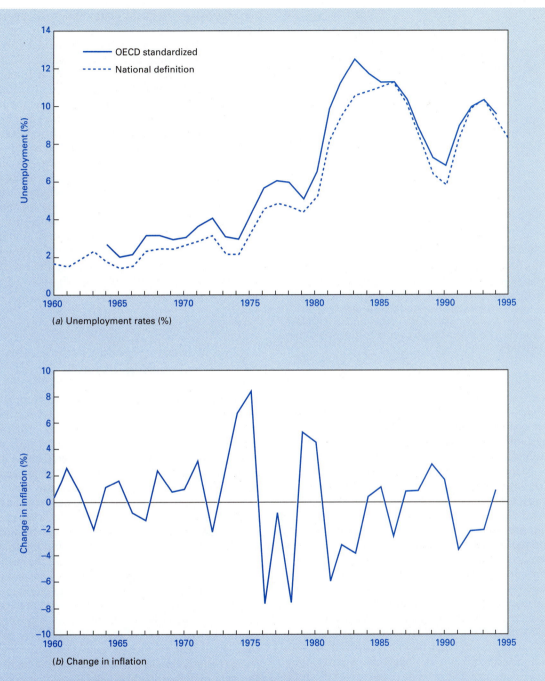

(a) Unemployment rates (%)

(b) Change in inflation

Figure 17.2. British Unemployment, 1960–1995

Has equilibrium unemployment declined in the 1980s? The UK is one of the rare European countries where actual unemployment declined significantly. Up until about 1987, the combination of declining unemployment and declining inflation suggests a fall in equilibrium unemployment as well.

Sources: OECD; IMF

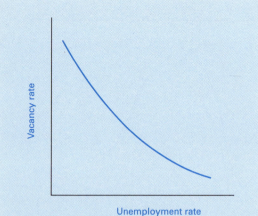

Vacancy rate

Unemployment rate

Figure 17.3. The Beveridge Curve

The Beveridge curve is the empirical inverse relationship between vacancies and unemployment. In a recession vacancies tend to decline and unemployment increases. The more efficient is the job matching process—the way unemployment workers and unfilled job vacancies are matched—the closer to the origin the Beveridge curve is.

government can help enhance—or at least try not to hinder—markets in need of additional information. For example, it can set standards and provide a stable legal infrastructure, laws governing the behaviour of business, the enforceability of contracts, and so forth.

An important case where the lack of information may have a significant effect is the labour market, which matches job offers by firms—sometimes called 'vacancies'—and unemployed workers. This is a complex process because jobs and workers are often very specific. The efficiency of the **job-matching** process is revealed by the **Beveridge curve** shown in Figure 17.3. This curve, named after the British economist William Beveridge who first described it in the 1940s, relates the unemployment rate on the horizontal axis to the vacancy rate on the vertical axis. During a recession, firms offer fewer jobs and unemployment is higher; as the vacancy rate declines, the unemployment rate rises, and the economy moves along a downward-sloping Beveridge curve. The position of the curve reflects the efficiency of the job-matching process. Efficient matching means that vacancies are quickly filled so that the curve is close to the origin. Indeed, the coincidence of a large number of vacancies with high unemployment—a Beveridge curve far away from the origin—suggests that workers are either badly informed, or unable to take up the offers for lack of

mobility or adequate skills, or unwilling to change and adapt.

Figure 17.4 displays examples of Beveridge curves. In Belgium, France, the UK, and Germany, the Beveridge curve seems to have shifted away from the origin since the mid-1970s, suggesting increasingly inefficient labour markets—in fact, a rise in the equilibrium rate of unemployment. In the USA and Sweden, on the other side, the curve seems relatively stable. Shifting the Beveridge curve towards the origin—to reduce the equilibrium unemployment rate—requires improving the job-matching process. One approach is to improve information on job openings, hence the multiplication of job agencies in many countries. Second, the adaptability of workers' skills may be enhanced via job retraining programmes. Another possibility is to increase workers' and firms' geographical mobility, for example by making the housing market more efficient or providing subsidies to firms in search of new locations.

17.2.4. Managing Market Failures and the Provision of Public Goods

A number of important goods and services simply do not have a price and are not sold in the market. This is the case of public goods and externalities.[4] The consumption of public goods by one person does not diminish their consumption by another. Externalities occur when one agent's action affects other agents. Some externalities are **pecuniary** because they are *actually transmitted* by the price mechanism. As an example of a negative pecuniary externality, a large firm which increases the size of its staff drives up the wages paid by all firms in the industry. The most important externalities are **non-pecuniary**, because the market has no natural way of mediating their effects. An example is environmental pollution: if no one is made to pay, the problem remains unsolved. Often it is enough for the government to establish property rights.[5] In the case of pollution, if citizens are given the right to clean air, then the public authorities must charge polluters for the costs they inflict. Alternatively, the right to pollute might be sold to polluter, for example by auctioning licences. If the right to pollute were instead given to companies, the public would have to organize and bribe the firms to stop polluting.

---

[4] Public goods and externalities were discussed in Chs. 5 and 15.
[5] This general principle was first established in 1960 by Nobel laureate Ronald Coase.

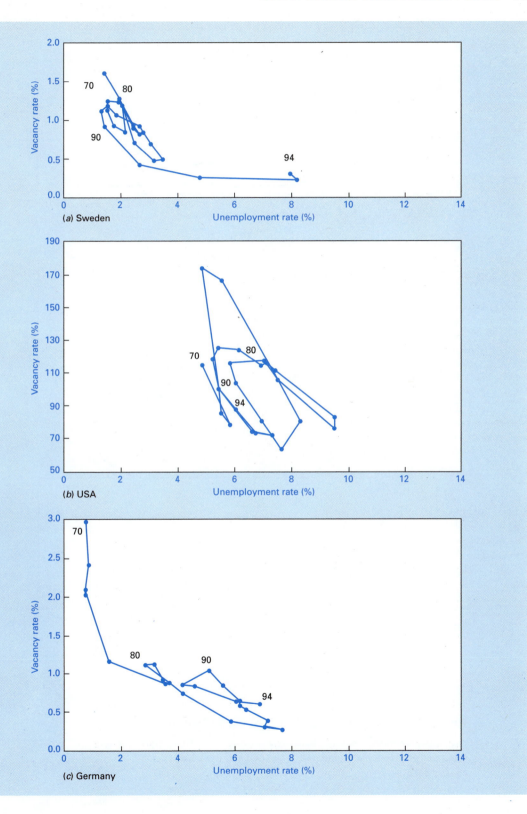

(a) Sweden

(b) USA

(c) Germany

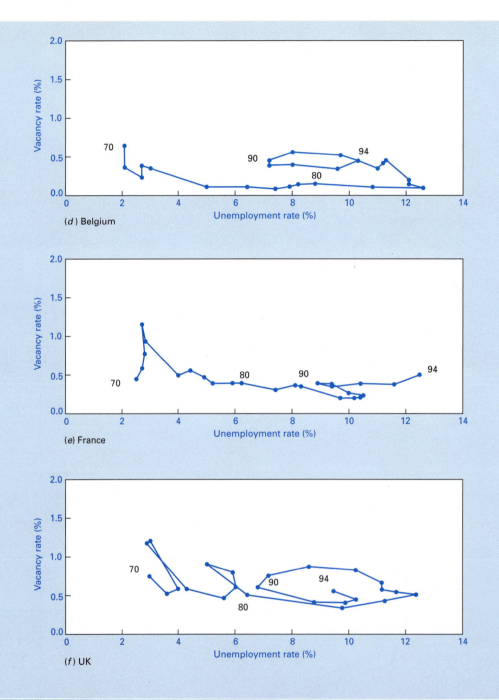

Figure 17.4. Beveridge Curves, Six Countries, 1970–1994

Over the past thirty years, the Beveridge curve seems to have shifted outward in several European economies, although not in Sweden and the USA.

Sources: OECD; IMF

In all cases of non-pecuniary externalities, public intervention is generally needed. Box 17.3 gives another example of a market failure which public policy can help to solve and which can have significant positive supply-side effects: the market for education and for **human capital**.[6]

17.3. Reducing the Adverse Effects of Government Intervention

17.3.1. Price Controls and Regulations

Beyond unspecified 'excesses of markets', two main reasons are usually invoked by governments when they impose controls on prices and regulate the conditions under which certain goods can be sold. The first is the need to provide social protection for the poor; this translates into price restrictions on goods identified as necessities—bread, potatoes, and so on. The other justification is the fight against inflation and the desire to avoid restrictive and unpopular demand policies.

Except for very short periods of time, price controls are usually inefficient. The poor are better helped by direct transfers, rather than through interference with the price mechanism. Price controls are also notoriously inefficient in the face of inflation, and they affect the supply side adversely. When prices are unrealistically low goods are not produced, and when they are they appear not on the shelves of shops but on the black market. Former centrally planned economies in Eastern Europe are a case in point. Within a month of price liberalization in January 1991, Polish shelves, which had been bare for decades, suddenly filled up. Even though most ordinary citizens could not afford what they saw initially, many new firms rushed in to make profits, increasing supply and lowering prices in the end. Since the 1970s, West European countries have gradually abandoned the use of price controls. Yet, decades of habits die slowly, especially in the presence of pressure groups which benefit from price controls at the expense of society (see Box 17.4).

The conclusion concerning price controls extends beyond product markets: labour markets (e.g. minimum wages) and financial markets (usury laws and other interest ceilings) normally do not benefit from government interference. Recall the familiar case of minimum wages.[7] Under free market conditions, an adverse disturbance (for example an oil shock) works itself out through a combination of lower real wages and reduced employment. If real wages do not decline, employment generally will. In particular, minimum wages result in a decline in the employment of the less qualified—often young—workers whose productivity no longer matches their costs to firms. The same applies to any category of labour whose real wages are not free to respond to market conditions.

Regulations are justified in principle when markets are not well-behaved. One example is to be found in financial markets. Banks and financial intermediaries collect savings to finance investment by firms and public deficits. This process is essential for economic growth, and yet few countries have well-developed financial markets. In fact, financial markets are often considered with suspicion, partly because of markets' tendencies to undergo violent crises. In response, financial markets have been regulated, mostly by limiting the range of operations that can be performed by particular intermediaries. The result has been to prevent some services from coming into existence—limiting the variety of assets available to savers or the borrowing arrangements offered to firms—and to limit competition, a feature sometimes encouraged by the financial industry itself to obtain state-sponsored cartellization.

Where should the line be drawn on regulation? For many decades after the Second World War many countries adopted capital controls, restrictions on the movement of assets to and from the rest of the world. Over-regulation may have created inefficiencies, but national financial systems also enjoyed protection from international competition. Greater integration of financial markets in the 1980s has forced authorities to reconsider their options, for fear that their financial industries will be found non-competitive *vis-à-vis* those established in countries with leaner regulation. The wave of stock market deregulation described in Box 17.5 is a telling example of this process. In 1974

---

[6] Human capital is discussed in Ch. 5.
[7] Minimum wages are discussed in Ch. 6.

BOX 17.3. MARKET FAILURES IN THE HUMAN CAPITAL MARKET

The parable of Robinson Crusoe neglected the obvious fact that workers are not identical. One dimension in which they differ is human capital—their education, training, and work experience. Individuals accumulate human capital just as firms accumulate physical capital.[8] By investing in education and training, they acquire skills which they then 'rent' to their employers. Human capital accumulation is crucial to growth and improvement in standards of living, and is therefore an economic activity of major social importance. Yet it takes place in the midst of numerous market failures. Two aspects of human capital result in socially insufficient investment: it is intangible, and it produces positive externalities.

First, individuals are ready to borrow in order to pay for their own education, just as firms borrow to accumulate physical capital. In contrast to firms, individuals often cannot put up collateral for their loans. Employers might invest in their employees with the hope of recouping their outlays in the future, but there is a risk that workers, once trained, will quit to work for the competition.[9] Because many individuals cannot secure the necessary financing, insufficient investment in human capital

is actually undertaken. Second, human capital produces positive externalities. Better trained people share their knowledge with co-workers and their own children. If they are not fully compensated for this externality, individuals will not accumulate as much human capital as is socially desirable.

For these reasons, encouraging the accumulation of human capital can represent good macroeconomic supply-side policy. The existence of state schools and training, scholarships, subsidized loans and loan guarantees, and state support for industry-wide training programmes can be justified by this argument. The impact of these policies can be seen in Table 17.1: the number of years of formal education in most countries has doubled between 1913 and 1989, while time spent in higher education has increased by roughly tenfold. At the same time, public education is susceptible to the same failures as state-owned enterprises (see Section 17.3.4 below): performance criteria are unclear, and deficits are covered automatically; subsidies are paid out to what have become large bureaucracies.

Table 17.1. Human Capital Accumulation

Average number of years of formal education

	Total		Primary		Secondary		Higher	
	1913	1989	1913	1989	1913	1989	1913	1989
France	6.2	11.6	4.3	5.0	1.8	5.3	0.1	1.3
Germany	6.9	9.6	3.5	4.0	3.4	5.2	0.1	0.4
Japan	5.1	11.7	4.5	6.0	0.6	5.0	0.0	0.7
Netherlands	6.1	10.5	5.3	6.0	0.6	3.8	0.1	0.7
UK	7.3	11.3	5.3	6.0	1.9	4.8	0.1	0.5
USA	6.9	13.4	4.9	6.0	1.8	5.7	0.2	1.7

Source: Maddison (1991)

the USA underwent a fundamental deregulation of its financial markets on 'May Day'; in 1986 the London Stock Market underwent its 'Big Bang', triggering a process of banking and financial deregulation which has spread throughout the European Union. The question is whether competition among financial systems in Europe will lead to a competition towards less regulation and eventually under-regulation.

17.3.2. Taxation

17.3.2.1. The effects of taxation

Chapter 15 put forward arguments in favour of government provision of some goods and services. Once some level of government activity has been chosen,

[8] Ch. 5 provides more details on the role of human capital and knowledge in growth.

[9] This might be an economic argument in favour of slavery. There is no evidence, however, that slaves were better educated than poor freemen. A lost opportunity?

BOX 17.4. RENT CONTROLS AND HOUSING SHORTAGES

In many countries—e.g. France, Italy, and some parts of the USA—rents are still controlled. As a result, housing is not as lucrative as other forms of investment and not enough of it is produced. Shortages that plague most large cities is testimony to the failure of this policy. Ironically, rent controls were adopted to protect the 'little people'. Over the years, a decline in housing production has resulted in a dramatic excess demand for dwellings while unregulated office space is plentiful. As a consequence, the 'little people' have been driven out of inner cities and spend considerable time commuting daily to centrally located offices. Furthermore, when they lose jobs and need to relocate, the shortages limit their mobility. It is sometimes argued that unemployment rates could be significantly reduced by removing rent controls.

BOX 17.5. BIG-BANG IN EUROPE[10]

The October 1986 'Big Bang' in London was launched by the British Department of Trade and Industry to enhance competition in Europe's largest financial market. It turned out be one of the most significant deregulations in British history. Old cosy arrangements restricting stock market membership and prescribing non-negotiable commissions were scrapped, and computerized trading systems began replacing the old-fashioned yelling and screaming that symbolized finance to many ordinary citizens. The result was a lowering of the cost of doing business in London. As Table 17.2 shows, part of this was due to a reduction in the stamp duty on securities transactions. The rest has come from lower profits earned by security firms in the form of commissions and the difference between the selling and buying price called the 'touch'. As costs fell, the London City boomed and rapidly asserted itself as the financial powerhouse of Europe. In 1988 the Paris Bourse, alarmed by a growing loss of customers to London, initiated a series of similar reforms, including its own computerized system and the suppression of negotiated commissions and the monopoly held by the now-extinct *agents de change*. Amsterdam reacted similarly in 1987, followed by Madrid and Milan in 1989. Importantly, in most cases dealerships have been opened to foreigners.

Table 17.2. Cost of Buying and Selling in London Before and After the 'Big Bang' (% cost of a £500,000 round trip transaction)

	Before	After
Stamp duty	1.00	0.50
Average commission	0.31	0.25
Average touch	1.56	1.24
Total	2.87	1.99

Source: Pagano and Roëll (1990)

resources need to be raised in order to pay for it. This is done through taxation of goods and services, either on an *ad valorem* (at some percentage rate), per-unit, or lump-sum basis. Taxation generally distorts markets by driving a wedge between the cost of producing goods and the price paid by the consumers. This effect is shown in Figure 17.5 for an *ad valorem* tax. Demand and supply for a given good or service depend on its price. Under perfect competition, the demand curve describes the marginal utility of a representative consumer for the good, and the supply curve describes the marginal cost of producing it. At point *E*, where the two curves intersect, the consumer at the margin is willing to pay exactly what the producer requires; perfect competition achieves the social best. Taxes alter the situation: the price paid by the buyer must differ from the after-tax price received by the seller. The new supply curve *S'* shows that the producer receives only a fraction of the market (relative) price. At the new market equilibrium point *D* the price is higher and the amount consumed and produced is lower. Both consumers and producers are worse off. Box 17.6 provides more details on who lose and why.

Non-distortionary taxes do not affect economic behaviour. An example would be lump-sum taxes levied on individuals without any reference to incomes, wealth, or spending, or taxes levied unexpectedly on past incomes and wealth so that it is too late to react.

[10] This box draws on Pagano and Roell (1990).

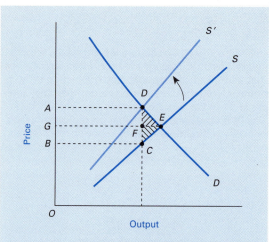

Figure 17.5. The Effect of Taxation

Taxes introduce a wedge between the price faced by the buyer and the price charged by the seller. Here a sales tax (e.g. VAT) shifts the supply curve upward. The new equilibrium occurs at point *D*, with less output, a higher buying price, (distance *OA*), and a lower selling price (*OB*) than at the tax-free equilibrium point *E*. Tax revenue for the government is measured by area *ABCD*, the quantity sold times the tax rate (the difference between the two prices). Consumers, who could buy quantity *GE* at price *OG*, suffer a 'welfare loss' measured by the area *ADEG*. Similarly, producers suffer a loss represented by the area *GECB*. Of these two losses—area *ADECB*—the government receives *ABCD*. What is left, the triangles *DEF* and *EFC*, represent, respectively, lost consumer and producer surpluses—deadweight losses—arising from the tax.

For this reason, non-distortionary taxes are appealing to governments. In practice, however, retroactive taxation is considered illegal precisely because it takes people by surprise. Lump-sum taxes are also unpopular, as Mrs Thatcher's fateful experience with the poll tax in 1990 showed. As a result, nearly all taxes are distortionary.

17.3.2.2. Tax efficiency and the size of government

An alternative means of reducing tax distortions is simply to reduce the size of the government. This must be balanced against the needs of society for a welfare state, providing collective services and insurance against ill health, accidents, and old age. The size of public spending has considerably expanded since 1913 but it still varies from one country to another. In the 1980s, views have been shifting against 'big government'. Many political leaders promised to reduce the size of the government even if, in the short run, reducing government spending decreases output through its (Keynesian) demand effect—the IS curve shifts back. In principle, however, there is no long-run effect. Indeed, in Figure 17.6 for a cross-section of OECD countries there is little discernable correlation between growth in real output and growth in public spending.

17.3.2.3. The Laffer curve

Because distortionary taxes move the economy away from its first-best equilibrium, it is entirely conceivable that higher tax rates actually result in lower tax yields. This effect is sometimes called the **Laffer curve**

BOX 17.6. THE DEADWEIGHT LOSS FROM TAXATION

What are the losses to an economy from **distortionary taxation**? Figure 17.5 gives us the answer. The loss to consumers of not enjoying the price *OG* is given by *ADEG*. This can be thought of as consumers' willingness to pay above the market-clearing price, or **consumer surplus**. At the same time, the lower price (net of tax) to producing firms means that firms will lose profits on goods they would have sold at cost lower than the no-tax price. The existence of these profits is due to the fact that the supply curve is upward-sloping. This second area *BCEG* is known as **producer surplus**.

This consumer and producer surplus are not lost entirely. Despite the price rise, purchases of *AD* will still occur. The

tax income from an *ad valorem* tax is given by the rectangle *ABCD*. This leaves the two triangles, *DEF* and *CFE*, which represent lost consumer and producer surplus, or deadweight loss to society.

In raising a given amount of money, an objective of government should be to minimize the 'deadweight loss' arising from taxation, represented by the triangles of producer and consumer surplus in Figure 17.5. This can be achieved by taxing most heavily those goods with the most inelastic (i.e. steepest) demands and supplies. This is known as the **Ramsey principle of public finance**.

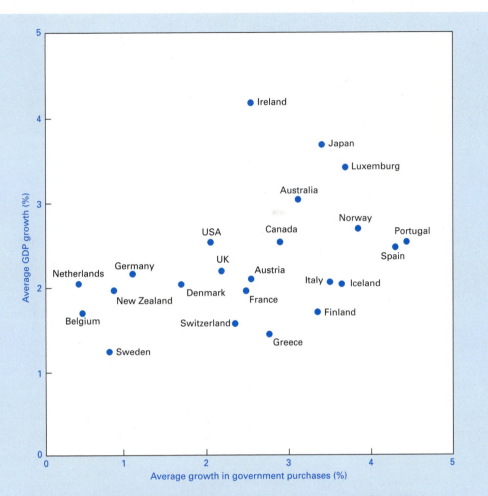

Figure 17.6. Growth in Real GDP and Government Purchases in the OECD Countries, 1981–1994

There is little clear correlation in the long run between real growth and growth in government purchases in the OECD countries. This contrasts with the short-run effect of changes in government purchases and GNP.

Note: Italy, Luxemburg, and Portugal: 1981–92; Japan, Greece, Ireland, and New Zealand: 1981–93

Source: IMF

and is depicted in Figure 17.7.[11] This curve aims at describing a theoretical relationship between *total* government tax revenues on the vertical axis and the *average* tax rate (the ratio of tax receipts to GDP) on the horizontal axis. The tax rate ranges from 0 to 100%; at a 0% rate, tax revenue is nil (point *A*); when the tax

rate reaches 100%, no one is likely to work or produce at all so tax receipts are also nil (point *B*). At intermediate tax rates, tax receipts are positive, as at point *C*. The hump-shape of the curve indicates that the tax rate so distorts the economy that beyond a point taxable incomes decline faster than tax rates increase. The threshold point *D* corresponds to the average tax rate for which tax receipts are maximum. Any rate of taxation to the right of point *D* is inefficient because the same tax income can be raised with a lower tax rate,

[11] Economist Arthur Laffer, then from Chicago, is reported to have been quite influential in persuading President Reagan to cut taxes in the early 1980s.

Table 17.3. Government Spending: the 1970s and 1980s (% of GDP)

	1971	1975	1980	1985	1989	1992
Government expenditure						
Belgium	37.8	44.4	51.0	55.4	49.3	51.1
Italy	20.4	26.7	30.5	40.5	39.5	40.9[a]
Sweden	26.4	29.4	39.5	44.8	39.3	46.0
UK	31.6	38.9	38.2	39.5	34.0	43.2
USA	19.8	21.5	22.0	24.2	22.8	23.9
Public final consumption						
Belgium	14.4	16.8	17.8	17.1	14.6	14.8
Italy	14.8	14.4	15.0	16.7	16.9	17.7
Sweden	22.1	23.5	29.1	27.6	25.7	26.7
UK	18.3	22.3	21.6	21.1	19.7	22.3
USA	17.7	17.2	16.0	16.8	16.5	16.2
Current disbursements						
Belgium	34.4	41.2	48.3	53.0	48.8	50.1
Italy	32.5	36.4	37.9	45.3	46.9	51.2
Sweden	39.8	45.3	58.1	62.1	57.7	65.1
UK	32.8	39.3	40.1	41.7	35.5	40.3
USA	31.4	34.5	32.9	33.8	32.8	35.4

[a] 1991

Sources: IMF; OECD, *Economic Outlook*

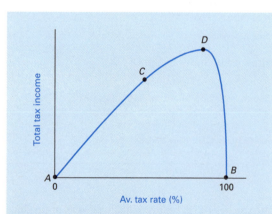

Figure 17.7. The Laffer Curve

When the average tax rate is 0% there is no tax income (point *A*). When it is 100%, tax income is also likely to be zero (point *B*). At intermediate tax rates, there is some tax income, e.g. at point *C*. By continuity, the Laffer curve assumes a hump-shaped relationship between tax income and average tax rates. The maximum tax intake occurs at point *D*.

i.e. less distortion. The Laffer curve is not taken too seriously for policy purposes, since its most important detail is unknown: the location of point *D*. In the early 1980s, Laffer claimed that the USA had passed this point; the USA did cut tax rates, but tax revenue actually declined.[12]

17.3.3. Minimizing Adverse Effects on Incentives

Efficiency in labour markets is enhanced when workers give up jobs in which relative wages have fallen behind and move to better paid positions. For individuals, this represents a number of difficult steps: abandoning skills, retraining, possibly moving, and developing new social networks. Quite naturally,

[12] It is true that richer people in the USA ended up paying more taxes, since it made less sense to hire expensive lawyers to devise complicated tax breaks. Another important effect is that the underground economy tends to come out into the open when tax rates are lower.

Table 17.4.	Subsidies to Firms, Various Countries, 1975 and 1989 (% of GDP)	
	1975	1989
Belgium	4.1[a]	4.9[b]
France	4.0	5.3
Germany	4.2	4.8
Italy	5.3	3.7[b]
Netherlands	3.1	3.6
Spain	0.4	3.6[b]
Sweden	4.6	6.6
USA	0.2	0.2

[a] 1977   [b] 1988

Source: OECD National Accounts

workers resist such changes, especially if there is some chance that their old jobs will return. In the meantime unemployment is likely to rise. Supply-side policies include training and manpower programmes which provide workers with incentives to undergo the adjustment process as well as reducing existing disincentives. Generous unemployment benefits fulfil the important objective of cushioning the blow of becoming unemployed, but they also have the side-effect of offering an alternative to painful adjustment.

17.3.4. Subsidies, State-Owned Enterprises, and Industrial Policy

For a variety of non-economic reasons, many countries operate elaborate systems of subsidies designed to shield certain firms from the discipline of the market. Table 17.4 displays the evidence for some OECD countries. Subsidized firms can sustain losses and refrain from adjusting to changing economic conditions. In doing so, they keep resources (e.g. labour) employed, but inefficiently. They do not face the full cost of their operations (part of the costs are charged to taxpayers), or else the factors of production are paid more than their true marginal productivity.[13] In fact,

[13] For example, after the oil shocks, a reduced world demand for tankers and the emergence of competitors in Asia (Japan, Korea) combined to create major difficulties for European shipyards. The UK, Germany, France, and many other countries reacted by subsidizing their shipbuilding companies. In the end, the costs became too large and the situation too hopeless for the subsidies to be maintained. While the subsidies did save jobs for a few years, they did so in a very inefficient way.

they may even keep factor prices artificially high and hurt productive activities that are not subsidized.

Public ownership is another form of subsidization. Unlike private firms, state-owned enterprises (SOEs) rarely face demanding shareholders and are almost never shut down. When they lose money, they generally receive public resources. This may come either as an explicit subsidy from the government to cover the loss, or as a loan to the company at interest rates usually unavailable to other firms. SOEs operate in virtually every major industry in Western Europe. While there may be valid reasons to have SOEs, supply-side considerations have led a number of governments to privatize their companies. **Privatization** means selling part or all of SOEs to the private sector. Especially in the UK, but also in France, Sweden, Spain, and Portugal, major privatization programmes started in the 1980s.

The lesson to be drawn from this experience is mixed. While the rigours of the market place improved the performance of many SOEs, the privatization of monopolies may be counterproductive. State-owned monopolies are usually prevented from abusing their dominant position, while profits are remitted to the government anyway. Once privatized, monopoly profits are captured by the new owners. This is why privatization is a complex operation. often requiring more than just selling companies.[14]

Most countries regard certain economic activities as indispensable for strategic or political reasons. These include defence-related industries such as steel, energy, high technology, aircraft, and shipbuilding. As many of these activities exhibit increasing returns to scale, governments often try to guarantee that the firms are large enough. This is often the underlying logic behind **industrial policies**. Industrial policies amount to official backing of national corporations or whole industries. It takes the form of subsidies, public orders, and trade policies. **Trade policies** include tariffs on foreign goods, quotas on imports, export credits financed at concessionary rates, and procurement policies whereby domestically produced goods are chosen over cheaper foreign ones, not to mention 'buy domestic goods' campaigns.

The ultimate effect of these policies is to raise prices above competitive levels. Consumers or taxpayers make up the difference. Once again, the optimality principle, that prices reflect efficient production costs, is violated. Supply-side considerations have led to a

[14] An extreme case was ex-communist Eastern Europe, where all firms were state-owned. These firms were known to operate under soft-budget constraints: profits, if any, were returned to the government, and losses were automatically covered by the public budget.

reassessment of strategic requirements. The European Single Act (1992) bans most of the trade policies mentioned above for intra-European trade. Yet industrial and trade policies survive, and are now being conducted at the European rather than the national level, with such celebrated examples as Airbus and Ariane.

17.4. An Example: Structural Unemployment as a Supply-Side Problem

Unemployment is generally regarded as a curse of modern market economies. In Europe, unemployment levels have risen to dramatic proportions. Figure 6.16 showed that, while European unemployment has risen steadily over successive business cycles, the USA has maintained a relatively steady equilibrium unemployment rate. To the extent that unemployment is involuntary and does not reflect the preferences of the unemployed, it represents a supply-side problem. As the leading quote at the beginning of this chapter indicated, an important challenge for the nations of Europe is to address this issue, perhaps using the ideas and concepts developed in this chapter.

Yet it is for this reason that unemployment should be interpreted carefully. To the extent that the jobless are really 'unemployed resources', they represent a lost opportunity and a reason that trend GDP is lower than it could be. A number of reasons were presented in Chapter 6 why unemployment might emerge, and why workers ready to work at current wages are unable to do so. On the other hand, 'full employment' remains a slippery and probably unusable concept.[15] To some extent, unemployment is an efficient response to changing economic conditions. Information is incomplete and workers do not know the full range of offer when they begin to search. As Chapter 6 showed, some frictional unemployment is to be expected. In addition, preservation of workers' skills, education, and productive characteristics—the **human capital** discussed in Box 17.3—might be inconsistent with 'full employment' at all times. Job losers may possess a large amount of industry- or firm-specific human capital which would be lost or unutilized (unemployed) were the worker forced to accept the first new job that came

along. A policy-maker must carefully evaluate the unemployment problem before choosing the appropriate set of supply-side reforms.

17.4.1. Labour Taxes

The logic of Figure 17.5 can be fruitfully applied to the labour market: labour taxes lead to higher pre-tax real wages and lower employment in the sector that pays the tax.[16] There exist three main labour taxes: income taxes, social insurance charges paid by employers, and social security contributions by the employees. All three can be added up, as they either reduce the workers' net receipts and thus affect the supply of labour, or increase the cost of labour and reduce demand. (Box 17.6 provides a formal treatment.) Indeed, labour is one of the most highly taxed 'commodities'. Despite high unemployment, little effort has been made so far to alleviate the tax burden placed on the labour market.

Table 17.5 in Box 17.7 shows the rate of taxation on labour in various countries in its various guises. What is not known is how distortionary labour taxes really are and therefore what is to be expected from a reduction of these taxes. If collective labour supply is relatively inelastic—perhaps reflecting the inelastic labour supply of households—workers will pay the tax, and employment will be little affected. In Europe, however, wages are set in collective bargaining, possibly leading to a flatter collective labour supply curve. Under these conditions, high labour taxes might reduce employment significantly, and be associated with a large loss of consumer and producer surplus.[17]

[15] A truly fully employed economy—with zero unemployment—is rarely observed. It is probably only achievable for any long period of time in slave economies or totalitarian communist regimes. Furthermore, if one restricts attention to 'fully employing' those who seek work, one runs the risk of ignoring those who have left the labour force—the so-called discouraged workers.

[16] This qualification is important. If some type of labour is untaxed, demand, employment, and wages may rise when labour taxes rise elsewhere. The obvious example is the underground economy, which always thrives when labour taxes are high.

[17] Ch. 6 provides more details on the collective labour supply curve; producer and consumer surplus are defined and discussed in S. 17.3.2.

BOX 17.7. TAXES AND THE LABOUR MARKET IN EUROPE

Labour taxes are considerable, especially in Europe. Perhaps this is because they are the most expedient to implement politically—it is usually a faceless ministry (rather than the prime minister or president) that announces the increase. Employees rarely see these taxes on their labour, since they are paid on their behalf by their employers. In France firms now report the *charges patronales* in order to show their employees exactly what they cost the company. (Many are incredulous when they find out!) Some of these charges cover unemployment benefits, national health insurance, retirement and pension benefits, disability insurance, 'solidarity funds' with various causes including low-cost housing and special retraining programmes, etc. All these charges increase the cost of labour to the firm, unless workers are willing to reduce their after-tax wage.

Formally, let τ_F be the employer's wage tax rate, let W be the wage of the employee before his own income taxes and employee social security contributions, let τ_W be the rate of contribution of the employee, and let τ_P be the personal (average) tax rate. The after-tax wage for the worker will be

$$W_{\text{take home}} = (1 - \tau_W)(1 - \tau_P)W,$$

while labour costs to the firm is given by

$$W_{\text{labour costs}} = (1 + \tau_F)W = \frac{1 + \tau_F}{(1 - \tau_W)(1 - \tau_P)}W_{\text{take home}}.$$

The multiplicative factor

$$\frac{1 + \tau_F}{(1 - \tau_W)(1 - \tau_P)}$$

is often called the **labour tax wedge**. Holding $W_{\text{take home}}$ constant, increases in the tax wedge tend to reduce the demand for labour. Unless after-tax wages fall, the outcome is therefore an increase in the equilibrium unemployment rate.

In addition to all this, workers also pay income tax on their take-home salary. In Europe, the income tax rises rapidly at the margin: it is **progressive**. Table 17.5 documents the various tax rates as well as the maximal marginal tax rate in European countries. At such high marginal tax rates, it makes economic sense to work in the underground economy, or to take overtime pay in the form of a holiday (leisure), as is often done in Scandinavia. It is likely that such high taxes make hiring labour unattractive, and that a reduction of such taxes would be associated with more employment. The problem for governments is how to replace the revenue that would be lost.

Table 17.5. Taxes on Labour, Various Countries, 1988 (%)

	Av. employer labour tax rate (τ_F)[a]		Income tax rate (τ_P)	Av. employee tax rate (τ_W)	Overall marginal tax[b]
	Required	Total			
Austria	na	22.8	5.9	27.9	na
Belgium	23.3	33.0	15.4	36.9	66.3
Canada	5.8	11.0	3.7	27.1	55.1
Finland	na	23.2	2.4	35.6	66.1
France	31.8	39.3	20.9	16.5	63.4
Germany	17.8	24.3	19.9	23.7	63.8
Italy	26.4	37.3	11.2	33.8	62.0
Japan	9.4	16.2	8.8	15.3	22.2
Netherlands	22.2	29.4	27.9	26.2	70.8
Norway	17.7	na	11.2	29.4	62.9
Sweden	31.1	37.4	1.2	50.8	62.6
Switzerland	6.2	15.0	12.6	24.2	na
UK	7.5	14.1	6.8	21.2	50.4
USA	7.5	19.9	7.3	20.8	38.5

[a] Required employer tax is the minimum compulsory rate. Total employer tax includes voluntary contributions to insurance and retirement schemes, etc.

[b] 1978–92.

Sources: OECD National Accounts; Hagemann *et al.* (1988); *OECD Job Study* (1994).

Table 17.6. Job Security and Managers' Attitudes towards Notice Requirements and Severance Pay

Country	Overall job security ranking	% of firms judging a positive employment impact from a reduction in:		
		Notice periods and legal procedures for redundancies	Redundancy payments	Av. unemployment rate, 1988–93
	(1)	(2)	(3)	(4)
Italy	1	88	78	10.5
Belgium	2	74	63	8.2
France	3	48	22	10.0
Sweden	4	—	—	3.4
Germany	5	63	46	5.2
Japan	6	—	—	2.3
UK	7	28	23	8.7
Netherlands	8	47	12	7.8
Denmark	9	—	—	10.2
USA	10	—	—	6.1
EC average	—	58	42	9.2

Sources: column (1): Bertola (1990); cols. (2) and (3): Emerson (1988); OECD standardized unemployment rates except Denmark; column (4): OECD

17.4.2. Regulations in Labour Markets

Perhaps because of their social and political aspects, labour markets are often heavily regulated, more so in Europe than in the USA. Regulations cover a wide range of aspects: paid holidays, the length of working days and weeks, safety standards, works councils, union representation, and other facets of the employment relationship. One important form of regulation governs dismissals. Prior notice to workers or to the labour ministry may be required by law, and 'social plans' may be mandated for large-scale redundancies. Severance payments are often required for workers dismissed for economic reasons.

While such regulations make it difficult for firms to reduce employment in the short run, they also increase the effective cost of labour to firms. Mandatory severance payments and red tape make firms more reluctant to hire in good times, because they worry about consequences in bad times. Table 17.6 reports a ranking of the degree of 'job security' provisions provided in a number of industrial countries, as well as the results of a survey of European businessmen by the EC Commission. The table shows that managers do consider hiring and firing regulations, as well as severance payments, to be an obstacle to job creation. It is note-

worthy that the two countries whose youth unemployment rates are highest in the survey—Italy and Belgium—are perceived as having the most restrictive dismissal laws.

How should a country reform such laws? Several problems arise with simply 'deregulating'. First, many companies that had wanted to reduce employment under the old regime will take advantage of deregulation, so layoffs may actually increase in the short run. In most European countries, the political consequences of such a move are severe enough to make reform unthinkable. Second, an issue of *time consistency* arises.[18] Suppose a firm that would like to hire more employees expands its employment in response to deregulation. At this point, a government seeking approval with job-security-conscious voters may reimpose the dismissal regulations, 'trapping' such firms at higher employment levels. Naturally, firms will anticipate this, with the sad result that no new workers will be hired, despite deregulation! Governments will need to precommit themselves to a 'no-re-regulate' regime before employers are convinced.

One noteworthy approach is that followed by Spain, which has a serious structural unemployment

---

[18] Time consistency is discussed in Ch. 16.

Table 17.7. The Degree of Centralization in Collective Bargaining

1 = most centralized; 17 = least centralized	
1. Austria	10. Australia
2. Norway	11. France
3. Sweden	12. UK
4. Denmark	13. Italy
5. Finland	14. Japan
6. Germany	15. Switzerland
7. Netherlands	16. USA
8. Belgium	17. Canada
9. New Zealand	

Source: Calmfors and Driffill (1988)

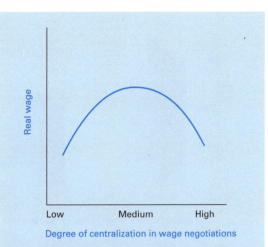

Figure 17.8. The Hump Shape

When wage negotiations are very centralized or very decentralized, trade unions have an incentive to show restraint. This tends to lead to lower real wages and less unemployment than in intermediate cases of industry-level or craft-by-craft negotiations.

problem. Since the mid-1980s, temporary contracts for workers have been permitted, with some restrictions.[19] Such contracts allow firms to hire workers without restrictions on a limited-time, contractual basis. As a result, roughly four-fifths of all new employment in Spain since the late 1980s has been under such limited-time contracts. This response suggests that firms are willing to hire more workers when job security obligations are absent. Second, young people have been the primary beneficiary of such reforms, which has helped relieve the youth unemployment problem so acute in Spain. Finally, increasing the relative number of workers who have jobs with less protection may help establish a consensus for broader reforms in the future.

17.4.3. Labour Relations

Labour relations are not all alike from one country to another. One difference is the degree of centralization of collective bargaining. Table 17.7 presents country rankings based on the late 1980s. At one end of the spectrum, one trade union and one employers' association negotiate a basic wage agreement for all workers at a national or very broad industrial level. Unions then are in a natural position to understand that the labour demand curve is downward-sloping, and that high real wages cost jobs. This in turn leads to moderate wage claims. At the other end, negotiations take

[19] For example, firms were not allowed to 'roll over' the same worker in a series of short-term contracts. Naturally, employers have devised numerous loopholes to deal with this restriction.

place at the plant level. Workers recognize that excessive wage settlement will hurt the firm, and jeopardize their own jobs, if competition in the goods market prevents firms from raising their prices to cover higher costs. Such a direct threat of bankruptcy or employment reduction makes for moderate wage claims here, too. In between, negotiations take place at the industry level, bringing together firms that would otherwise compete against each other. Since all firms in the industry are affected by wage negotiations in the same way, they accommodate higher wage demands by simply raising their prices. At least within a country, there will be little competitive pressure to fight back.

The result is the hump-shape relationship between centralization and wage moderation depicted in Figure 17.8. Very centralized and very decentralized wage negotiations deliver more moderate real wage settlements and therefore higher levels of employment. At the same time, one might expect the hump-shape curve to be less pronounced in countries facing competitive world markets for their exports.

This reasoning can be broadened to include the degree to which trade unions feel responsible for the economic health of the economy. The degree to which trade unions, management, and government work together is called **corporatism**. Corporatist trade unions—for example in Sweden or Austria—take the view that they have common interests with the

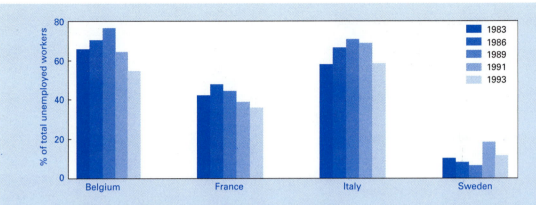

Figure 17.9. Long-Term Unemployed, Four Countries

The long-term unemployed are defined here as workers whose current spell of unemployment started more than a year ago. Staying out of employment for too long has deleterious effects on a worker's human capital and contact with the labour market. The figure dramatically illustrates the difference between the Scandinavian and EC ways of dealing with the unemployment problem.

Source: OECD, *Employment Outlook*

employers; that healthy firms provide well-paid jobs. Non-corporatist unions tend to focus more on income distribution, taking the view that firms always look after themselves; these unions always attempt to increase the labour share. Countries with corporatist unions tend to have less unemployment.

17.4.4. The Social Safety Net and Active Labour Market Policies

The social safety net refers to the system of transfers and benefits designed to help the disadvantaged and vulnerable in society. These include unemployment benefits, social welfare, old-age pensions, early retirement, health insurance, and disability benefits. Table 15.2 shows a clear difference between European countries, which transfer between 20% and 30% of their national income to individuals or firms, and the USA, Japan, and Switzerland, which transfer only 10%–15%. This might lead a casual observer to conclude that high European unemployment is a product of the 'social welfare state', which puts weight on solidarity but at the cost of productivity and economic efficiency.

It would be unfair to generalize that Europeans have erred too far in the direction of social protection, in contrast to the more spartan approach of Japan, Switzerland, and the USA. The high level of transfers observed in Europe is to a some extent a *response* to high

unemployment, which may have other underlying causes. At the same time, these transfers—in the form of unemployment benefits, welfare, and premature retirement and disability pensions—take the pressure off workers and firms to adjust to a changing world economy. The greatest danger is that the safety net becomes a trap, leading to long-term unemployment. Figure 17.9 illustrates the chronic long-term unemployment problem in Belgium, France, and Italy. Sweden stands out in this figure as an exception to the Western European rule that high unemployment rates mean high long-term unemployment rates.

The Nordic countries, which until recently had the world's lowest unemployment rates, have proved that strictly administered unemployment benefit programmes are consistent with 'European' solidarity with the unemployed. In Sweden, for example, unemployed workers may claim benefits for roughly 300 days of unemployment. Unlike most countries, however, at the end of this period benefits are not renewed. Instead, a position in a job training programme is offered. Employment offices may even require that an unemployed person move to another city. Refusal can, and often does, result in termination of benefits. As a result, the Scandinavian countries spend less on unemployment benefits and more on **active labour market policies**, i.e. programmes involving direct job creation, targeted job subsidies, retraining, relocation of families away from distressed regions, and special programmes to get young people started. In general, the unemployed are supervised more closely and kept

Table 17.8. Scandinavian Labour Market Programme Expenditure, 1994 (% of GDP)

	Denmark	Finland	Norway	Sweden[a]	West. Europe[b]
Active measures					
Training	0.5	0.5	0.3	0.8	0.3
Youth measures	0.3	0.1	0.1	0.3	0.2
Direct job creation	0.3	0.6	0.2	0.5	0.2[c]
Total active programmes	1.8	1.7	1.5	3.0	1.0
Passive measures					
Unemployment benefits	3.8	4.6	1.4	2.5	2.2
Early retirement	1.4	0.5	—	0.0	0.5[c]
Total insurance[d]	5.2	5.0	1.4	2.5	2.0
Total	7.0	6.7	2.9	5.4	3.4
Long-term unemployment rate (%)	2.7[e]	5.4[e]	1.3	1.4	5.7[e]

[a] Sweden 1994–95
[b] Unweighted average of France (1993), Germany (1993), Spain (1993) and UK (1993/4)
[c] Data for Spain and UK not available
[d] Passive measures
[e] 1993

Source: OECD *Employment Outlook; Economic Outlook*

in touch with the labour market. Table 17.8 shows that Nordic countries spend considerably more on labour market policies than other Western European countries, while maintaining much lower long-term unemployment rates. More recently, aggressive implementation of active labour market policies in the Czech Republic, a formerly centrally planned economy, has confirmed the Swedish success story in maintaining turnover among the unemployed.

At the same time, policy-makers should recognize the limitations of active labour market policies in the face of massive structural change. In recent years, the rise in overall unemployment rates in Finland and Sweden associated with the sharp recession of the early 1990s and the collapse of the Soviet Union seems to contain a 'structural' element. Put in terms of the past chapters, the equilibrium rate of unemployment does seem to have risen in these countries. This is supported by the fact that inflation in Sweden had ceased to decline by 1995. This is indeed a sign that active labour market policies alone cannot solve severe unemployment problems.

17.5. Summary

1. Supply-side policies are appealing because, in contrast to demand-side policies, they do not imply a short-run trade-off between unemployment and inflation. They increase output permanently at any given level of inflation and economic growth, and may even increase the rate of growth itself.

2. One principle underlying supply-side policies is that markets do not function perfectly. By removing market imperfections, the economy's overall output and productivity can be enhanced.

3. Markets often lack competition, either because of increasing returns—as in the case of natural monopolies—or because firms have erected barriers to entry into their

markets. Competition policies are designed to increase competition and market efficiency.

4. Markets require information. The government can play a role by enhancing the exchange of information. The process of matching workers and jobs in labour markets can be made more efficient by improving the exchange of job information or increasing worker mobility.

5. A whole range of supply-side policies deals with the fact that markets do not exist for some goods. This is the case with public goods, which governments may provide because the market cannot.

6. The government engages in many types of regulation, primarily for non-economic reasons. These can have significant economic costs and can reduce the economy's overall performance.

7. Modern governments raise money through taxation. Taxation is a source of inefficiency because it drives a wedge between the price paid by the consumer and the price received by the producer, reducing demand and supply.

8. Taxes cannot be eliminated because they are needed to finance government activities. Supply-side considerations call for limiting public spending to the production of goods and services that cannot be produced by the private sector. There is much debate on the correct size of government.

9. Governments often subsidize firms and industries. Although the objective is to protect firms, these policies remove the incentive to compete, and ultimately cost jobs. State ownership has similar effects. The supply-side response is to cut down on subsidies and to privatize.

10. High structural unemployment is a supply-side problem. It arises as a result of labour market distortions, some of which are due to private agents and others to interventions of government.

11. Eliminating structural unemployment is possible by better management of labour taxation, severance regulations, labour relations, and the social safety net. Active labour market policies can help prevent the emergence of long-term unemployment. Such reforms may be politically difficult to implement, however.

Key Concepts

- economic rents
- competition policy
- job matching
- Beveridge curve
- pecuniary and non-pecuniary externalities
- human capital
- distortionary taxation
- consumer and producer surplus
- Ramsey principle of public finance
- Laffer curve

- privatization
- industrial policies
- trade policies
- labour tax wedge

- progressive tax
- corporatism
- active labour market policies

Exercises

1. Trace through the macroeconomic effects, in the short and long run, of a policy that reduces equilibrium output $\bar{Y}$ (for example, an increase in labour taxation). Under what conditions could this lead to a permanent increase in the rate of inflation? (*Hint*: Chapter 13.)

2. 'A cut in social security contributions by firms, replaced by revenue raised by the income tax, would have significant supply-side effects.' Comment.

3. Why is there a shortage of dwellings in cities, even in cities without rent control but with a history of it? Why might a promise *never* to impose rent control help solve the problem?

4. According to the Ramsey principle of public finance (see Box 17.6), on which would you levy higher taxes, jewellery or petrol? Labour income or capital income?

5. Under what conditions will an increase in the minimum wage affect equilibrium output? Under what conditions will an increase in unions' pay settlements have the same effect?

6. Why didn't the Laffer curve work when President Reagan cut taxes in 1982? Do you think it will work for Sweden?

7. Immigration policy is often considered to be a type of supply-side policy. How might this be so?

8. In Chapter 7 we discussed the Dutch disease. This was the reaction of the real exchange rate to an increase in domestic wealth associated with a resource discovery. In the case of Britain and Norway, both countries enjoyed the benefits of the North Sea oil discoveries of the 1970s. Norway subsidized its exporting industries as a response, while Britain used the resources to help balance the budget and therefore pay for transfers and government spending. Why might a subsidy be good supply-side economics in this case?

9. Discuss proposals that can help reduce the equilibrium rate of unemployment. Which are most relevant for your country? Who might stand to lose from such proposals?

Suggested Further Reading

The classic statement of why markets achieve the social best is:

Smith, Adam (1776), *The Wealth of Nations*, London.

Modern restatements are:

Friedman, Milton, and Friedman, Rose (1979), *Free To Choose*, Harcourt Brace Jovanovich, New York (classic popular summary of the most important supply-side arguments).

Gilder, George F. (1981), *Wealth and Poverty*, Basic Books, New York.

Other useful references on supply-side effects and policies are:

Bertola, Giuseppe (1990), 'Job Security Provisions, Employment and Wages', *European Economic Review*, 34: 851–86.

——, and Ichino, Andrea (1995), 'Crossing the River: a Comparative Perspective on Italian Employment Dynamics', *Economic Policy*, 21: 359–420.

Blanchard, Olivier, and Diamond, Peter (1989), 'The Beveridge Curve', *Brookings Papers on Economic Activity*, 1: 1–60.

Giavazzi, Francesco, and Pagano, Marco (1990), 'Can Severe Fiscal Policy Contractions be Expansionary? Tales of Two Small European Countries', NBER *Macroeconomics Annual*, MIT Press, Cambridge, Mass.

Jackman, Richard, Pissarides, Christopher, and Savouri, Savvas (1990), 'Labour Market Policies and Unemployment in the OECD', *Economic Policy*, 11: 449–90.

Matthews, Kent, and Minford, Patrick (1987), 'Mrs Thatcher's Economic Policies 1979–87', *Economic Policy*, 5: 57–102.

Yarrow, George (1986), 'Privatization in Theory and Practice', *Economic Policy*, 2: 323–64.

Some concrete proposals with respect to the European situation can be found in:

Alogoskoufis, Georges, Bean, Charles, Bertola, Giuseppe, Cohen, Daniel, Dolado, Juan, and Saint-Paul, Gilles (1995), 'Unemployment: Choices for Europe', *Monitoring European Integration*, 5, CEPR, London.

Calmfors, Lars, and Richard, Layard (eds.) (1987), *The Fight against Unemployment*, MIT Press, Cambridge, Mass.

Drèze, J., and Malinvaud, E. (1994), 'Growth and Employment: the Scope of a European Initiative', *European Economic Review*, 38: 489–504.

Lindbeck A. *et al.* (1993), 'Options for Economic and Political Reform in Sweden', *Economic Policy*, 17: 219–64.

PART VII

Financial Markets and the Exchange Rate

18. Financial and Exchange Markets

19. Exchange Rates in the Short Run

20. The International Monetary System

21. Policy Co-ordination and Exchange Rate Crises: the EMS and the EMU

Financial markets play a crucial role in the allocation of resources. They are the conduit that channels the savings of households and firms into physical investment, finance of government deficits, or the purchase of foreign assets. In the process, financial markets provide a means of protection against risk.

Foreign exchange markets, one of the most important components of the world network of financial markets, shape the day-to-day behaviour of exchange rates, in a way much different from the long-run interpretation discussed in Chapter 7.

The two concluding chapters bring together the principles of macroeconomics and the analysis of exchange rates to deal with issues of international policy co-ordination. The first issue concerns the international monetary system. Chapter 20 reviews the evolution of international monetary arrangements and discusses the current mixed system of managed exchange rate blocks and free floating. Chapter 21 describes the European Monetary System and its evolution towards a monetary union.

18

Financial and Exchange Markets

18.1. Overview

The wild gyrations of exchange rates, the booms and busts of stock markets, and the legendary earnings of market participants often create the impression that financial markets are casinos with no real economic function. Far from being a sideshow, however, markets for financial assets fulfil the key economic role of putting a price tag on the future and on uncertainty. Financial markets are the meeting place for millions of households and firms who wish to shift resources intertemporally—either saving or borrowing—or intratemporally—from one form of asset or liability to another. To this end, they can act on their own behalf or indirectly through **financial intermediaries**. Financial intermediaries funnel resources from savers to borrowers and investors, helping economies avoid the same 'double coincidence' problem that arose in Chapter 8; they divorce the act of saving (deferred consumption) from the act of investment (creation of physical productive capacity).

A second function of financial markets is to help deal with risk. Because the future is unknown, uncertainty is inherent to saving and investing. When buying an asset from someone—e.g. a share in a company, a deposit at the bank, or a Treasury bond—we must trust that the borrower will be able to pay us back, according to the terms agreed upon. This, in turn, presumes that the borrower will realize the expected return on the projects financed with our money. None of these steps can be absolutely guaranteed. Just as it is possible to protect ourselves against the costs of car accidents, house fire, unemployment, and death by purchasing insurance, so we can protect ourselves against financial uncertainty. Financial markets allow savers to spread their risks by holding their wealth in many different forms. By engaging in **diversification**, savers can reduce the total risk that they bear by purchasing a mix of several different assets.[1] Diversification can also be supplied by the market in the form of new composite assets backed by a mix, or portfolio, of underlying risky assets. Again, the composite asset is less risky than its individual components. When risk must be borne financial markets offer compensation of it, called the **risk premium**: the interest rate paid on assets tends to be higher, the riskier they are. Borrowers too benefit from markets: each one taken individually is risky and would have to pay a high yield to attract wary savers. Going through intermediaries who pool these individual risks, borrowers end up paying lower interest rates.

This chapter describes how financial markets function, the instruments that are used, and the economic role they play. It prepares us for the more detailed analysis of exchange rates and monetary arrangements in the following chapters.

18.2. Financial Markets: Nuts and Bolts

18.2.1. Trades in Stocks, not Flows

One important characteristic of financial markets must be emphasized at the start: while most markets deal in *flows* (e.g. kilograms of potatoes or numbers of cars produced per month or year), financial markets deal in *stocks*. Assets traded on financial markets—shares in a company, bonds, contracts for future delivery of orange juice or pork bellies, or precious metals—have the following two common features. First, they are standardized and can be traded in large quantities with ease in well-organized markets. Second, they are durable because their storage is relatively inexpensive.

These two aspects alter the usual demand and supply analysis. On the one hand, households' supply of savings is ostensibly a flow, as is the demand for savings by borrowers who need to finance current spending. Yet, durability implies that the entire stock of accumulated savings in the form of financial assets may at any moment be sold or purchased. Because for most assets the volume of stocks dwarfs the volume of flows, asset prices move to clear the demand and supply of the former rather than the latter. Durability also means that today's asset price reflects its anticipated resale value in the future. Rapidly changing demand and supply of stocks can result in volatile market condi-

---

[1] Savers make use of a statistical result that is known as the 'law of large numbers'. The law of large numbers implies that the adding together of uncertain events delivers an 'average event' which is less risky than any individual event taken in isolation.

Table 18.1. Stock Exchange Turnovers, Various Cities, 1988 (% of GNP)

London	43.8
Frankfurt	8.6
Paris	7.1
Zurich	37.7
Milan	3.8
Amsterdam	13.0
Madrid	6.2
Brussels	7.0

Sources: Pagano and Roëll (1990); IMF

tions, depending on market assessments of the future. This description alerts us to the fact that the reasoning applies not just to strictly defined assets, but to any durable good that can be (relatively) easily stored and sold—artwork, commodities, even stocks of grains or sugar yet to be harvested. In fact, all these durable goods are traded on markets which often resemble those for financial assets.

18.2.2. Facts about Financial Markets

Most individuals do not deal in quantities sufficiently large to be traded directly on financial markets. Instead, they work through intermediaries who place orders for several customers at once, or may 'make a market' for their customers by selling from or adding to their own inventories. In this way, intermediaries themselves become asset-holders. Because of the inherent uncertainty regarding asset prices, asset-holding is risky and intermediaries constantly strive to reduce their exposure to risk.

These two concerns—seeking high returns and reducing risk—lead intermediaries to trade on their own account as well on the account of their customers. In fact, the amounts traded on financial markets are many times what the end users actually sell or buy. Because clever rearrangement of assets can reduce a portfolio's overall riskiness, the amounts traded can be large in the major financial centres, which deal in stocks of companies from all over the world. Table 18.1 reports that stock market trading volume, or turnover, is often a sizeable portion of GDP. This is undoubtedly far beyond the average citizen's individual needs and leads to a frequent misperception of financial markets as casino houses spinning their own roulette wheels. Yet it is the consequence of competition among interme-

diaries in providing fast and affordable services to their customers.

18.2.3. Professional Trading

Financial markets deal with highly standardized assets of known quality and content, and are designed primarily for wholesale business among professionals. One consequence is that traders accept and execute large orders on the basis of mutual trust; another is that they charge each other relatively small fees.

Financial markets take different forms. Best known are the stock markets, with swarms of screaming and gesturing traders wading through seas of hastily scribbled papers. In fact, most markets are now computerized, and market participants can often trade from terminal screens virtually anywhere in the world. Computerization and automation mean that markets located in different cities and continents are linked through telephone lines. We are not far from a single world market. Indeed, almost at any moment in time, twenty-four hours a day, a financial market is open somewhere in the world. Figure 18.1 shows that when Frankfurt or Paris is opening Singapore and Hong Kong are closing, while New York opens when European markets are still operating, and closes after Tokyo has opened. Because the system is so well integrated, traders generally can rest assured that they are getting the 'market' price, even for fairly large trades. This is perfect competition!

18.2.4. Euro- or Offshore Markets

Because of the sums involved and the history of market collapses, not to mention fraudulent behaviour, financial markets tend to be tightly regulated by the central bank of the country in which they are located. Naturally, regulation breeds discontent. Central banks in the 1950s and 1960s placed strict controls on markets which were still recovering from the twin disasters of the Great Depression and the Second World War. At a stroke of genius, financial intermediaries set up **offshore markets** for assets denominated in US dollars—now called Euro-dollars—outside the USA.[2] London has emerged as the premier Euro-market and

[2] The first financial institution to engage in offshore activities was probably the Soviet-owned Bank for Northern Europe, which wanted to deal in dollar-denominated assets but, for political reasons, did not want to operate from New York or hold its assets within a territory under US jurisdiction. So it arranged for holding US assets in London.

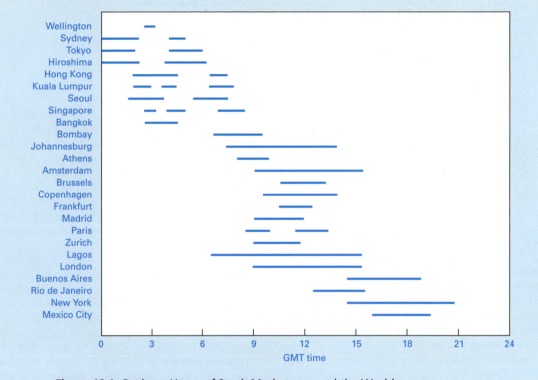

Figure 18.1. Business Hours of Stock Markets around the World

Stock markets are located around the world. As the world turns, some market somewhere is open, processing new information and pricing assets accordingly.

Source: de Caires (1988)

all sorts of assets can be traded there. Tax evasion also motivates the existence of such markets in places like Luxembourg, the Bahamas, and Singapore which offer lenient treatment of capital income.[3] A particular feature of offshore markets that attracts our attention is that the same assets, in the same currency, can be traded in both domestic and offshore markets. We return to this below.

18.3.   Arbitrage and Market Efficiency

18.3.1.   Arbitrage and the Unbridled Pursuit of Profit

A hallmark of properly functioning financial markets is that participants are engaged in a never-ending search for profit opportunities, either for their customers or for their own accounts. As a result of the amounts of money at stake and the speed at which information flows, it is unlikely that profit opportunities not involving additional risk will be left unexploited for more than a few minutes at the most. For this reason, it is convenient to assume that market efficiency imposes a **no-arbitrage condition**: i.e. opportunities for arbitrage—earning a profit by simultaneously purchasing and selling identical or equivalent assets—are absent.

[3] Despite their location, these non-European centres are still sometimes referred to as Euro-markets; more often they are simply called 'offshore'.

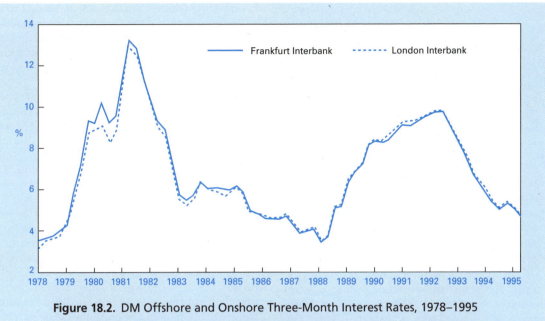

Figure 18.2. DM Offshore and Onshore Three-Month Interest Rates, 1978–1995

With a brief exception in 1979–1980, capital mobility has been complete between offshore and onshore financial centres. Spatial arbitrage has been near-perfect, equalizing interbank interest rates on DM interbank transactions in Frankfurt and London.

Source: IMF

There are many types of arbitrage. **Spatial arbitrage** occurs when investors identify a divergence of prices of identical assets in different market locations. For example, large commercial banks borrow from each other at the so-called interbank interest rate. For the major currencies, these loans take place simultaneously on several markets. Figure 18.2 compares the interbank rates on the Deutschmark in Frankfurt and London. If these rates were to diverge, enterprising banks present in both cities would immediately borrow in the cheaper market and lend in the dearer one. The figure shows that arbitrage seems to have worked pretty well, except for a brief period of time in late 1979 and early 1980 when Germany imposed a withholding tax on short-term foreign deposits.

Yield arbitrage applies to assets that are equivalent in terms of their risk characteristics. Markets do not allow yields on shares in top-rated corporations or rates of return on Treasury bills of reliable governments to differ radically. Any significant difference triggers a wave of selling and buying. Of course, since yields of risky assets are uncertain *ex ante*, it is always possible that two assets that are identical are quite different after uncertainty is cleared up.

Finally, **triangular arbitrage** occurs whenever the relative prices of three—or more—assets are not consistent with each other. For example, if US dollars are selling at FF5/$ and the DM is selling at FF3.4/DM, the DM–dollar rate must be (FF5/$)/(FF3.4/DM) = 1.470588. Otherwise profit would be possible. Suppose instead that the DM price of US dollars were 1.50: then every dollar purchased with Deutschmarks through French francs at a cost of DM1.470588 could be resold for DM1.50, or a profit of 2%. A DM price of 1.45 would call for trade in the opposite direction. (see Figure 18.3.)

18.3.2. Arbitrage versus Risk-Taking

By definition, arbitrage involves no risk.[4] As a result, it imposes equality of returns among riskless assets. When assets are risky, we no longer expect strict equality: the market will demand compensation for bearing

---

[4] In financial market jargon, this distinction is not always so clear. For example, traders who search for information on corporate takeovers in order to take a position in the stock 'in play' are sometimes called risk arbitrageurs. Technically, this is a contradiction in terms: if a takeover is called off, the 'risk arbitrageur' may be left holding a great deal of stock and may suffer a large loss.

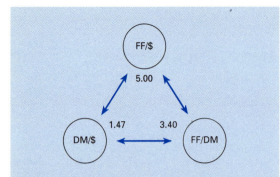

Figure 18.3. Triangular Arbitrage

When two exchange rates among three currencies are set, the exchange rate between the remaining pair of currencies is also set: triangular arbitrage eliminates any discrepancy.

ket efficiency requires two things: that markets collect all the information about the future that is available, even at cost; and that they process information correctly, i.e. based on principles that are not systematically contradicted by the facts (they have a 'correct' understanding of the economy).

If markets are efficient, the rest of us do not need to go scrambling for information: the market reveals it to us by the price it places on assets. If stock prices fall today, we do not really need to find out why: the market has received the relevant information and drawn the correct implications. At best we can agree. As a corollary, it is very unlikely that anyone will outperform the market consistently, year in and year out. The myths of traders systematically beating the markets are more likely a sign of good luck than much else. For every winner we hear about, there are just as many losers who have since disappeared from the market either because they have run out of capital or because they have been dismissed by their bosses. Using this line of argument, Milton Friedman has argued that speculation cannot be destabilizing: those traders who drive the asset price away from its 'fundamental' price—those who buy high and sell low—will exit the market. Similarly, a number of financial advisers promise unusual returns; again, if markets are efficient, these advisers must be overstating what they can do for their (gullible?) customers.

this risk. To see this, consider the following two assets. The first promises to pay 10% with no risk. A second investment yields 5% with probability 0.5 and 15% with probability 0.5; the expected value of the return is $(0.5) \times 15\% + (0.5) \times 5\%$, i.e. the same 10%. Most people will prefer the first investment, since it delivers on average the same return, but with no risk of doing worse. The fact that the 'risk' of doing better does not make up for the downside is a sign of **risk aversion**. If all investors are risk-averse, the asset corresponding to the second investment will fetch a lower market value, and the difference between the two will be the market valuation of risk. There is no arbitrage possible between the two assets, since they differ in their level of uncertainty.[5]

18.3.3. Market Efficiency

18.3.3.1. The principle of market efficiency

With so much hardware and cash floating around, it is only natural to expect financial markets to be 'efficient'. The precise definition of **market efficiency** is that prices fully reflect all available information.[6] Mar-

18.3.3.2. Existing evidence

The evidence for market efficiency is fairly convincing. Financial markets around the world continuously scan the news on teletypes and terminal screens, and react without delay to relevant information. Figure 18.4 shows the average price index on a few stock exchanges between July 1990 and January 1991. The invasion of Kuwait in early August and subsequent related news shaped the behaviour of all indices up until the rebound and upward trend following the beginning of the war. All along, markets were evaluating the implications for business profitability and for exchange rates. This illustrates what market efficiency entails: information first, but also the assessment of what it means for returns both now and in the future.

At the same time, some studies do turn up statistically measurable deviations from market efficiency. For example, if stock prices decline today, there is a good probability that they will revert somewhat in the distant future towards their previous values. This could imply that markets overreact to news, and that the markets may not be efficient. Why does no one buy these assets now when it is profitable to do so? This

---

[5] The theory of finance emphasizes that risk is rewarded with higher average returns. If there are sufficiently many investors who are indifferent to risk, they will not require higher returns and the distinction between arbitrage and speculation will break down. Similarly, diversification means that the market will ask only to be compensated for undiversifiable risk.

[6] The idea of market efficiency is related to the rational expectations hypothesis introduced in Ch. 3. Rational expectations assume that agents do not make systematic forecasting errors. Market efficiency applies this concept to markets and price-setting.

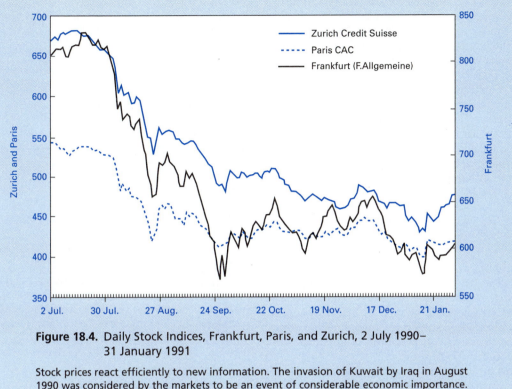

Figure 18.4. Daily Stock Indices, Frankfurt, Paris, and Zurich, 2 July 1990–31 January 1991

Stock prices react efficiently to new information. The invasion of Kuwait by Iraq in August 1990 was considered by the markets to be an event of considerable economic importance. Most markets are measured by indices averaging a number of much-traded asset prices, like the Credit Suisse index in Zurich.

Source: DRI/FACS

would restore the price to its fundamental value immediately. The answer may lie in risk aversion, the fact that too few traders are willing to take positions and hold them long enough for this to occur. But then markets are efficient: they eliminate all profit opportunity *given that the risk has its own price:* forgone profits are not sufficient to compensate for risk-taking.

18.3.3.3. Explanations for deviations from efficiency

How and why might deviations from market efficiency arise? It is always tempting to write off financial markets as irrational and prone to fads. But there are often more satisfying answers which can be illustrated with two examples. One of them is the coexistence of professional traders and inexperienced amateurs. The other is the phenomenon of rational speculative bubbles.

Not all traders need be bulwarks of rationality. In this view, only a subset of traders are informed and have access to information about the true underlying value of assets, whereas the remainder are **noise traders**. These noise traders can be either irrational or simply misinformed, and they behave accordingly. The result is that they systematically lose money to the informed traders. Noise traders arrive continuously on the scene, with new ones replacing those who lose on average and quit in disgust, so that there are always some of them around. Despite perfectly efficient and rational behaviour on the part of the professionals, stock prices may again diverge from their fundamental value for long periods of time.

The other interpretation of deviations from efficiency is the presence of **speculative bubbles**, persistent deviations of market prices from their fundamental values. To see how bubbles may arise, consider the following simple example. Investors can choose between a Treasury bill with a fixed interest rate and a company share which pays a fixed dividend for ever.

To make things as simple as possible, we assume that there is no uncertainty, so that arbitrage can take place and equalize the returns expected from both assets. The hitch is that, while the Treasury bill pays a fixed yield, the yield on the stock consists of the dividend plus capital gain or change in the market price of the asset. Capital gains and losses are taken into account by rational investors. If r denotes the interest rate on the Treasury bill, d the dividend per share per period, and q the share price, the rate of return on the private asset is the dividend yield, d/q, plus the perfectly foreseen future capital gain, $\Delta q/q$ (gain if $\Delta q > 0$, loss when $\Delta q < 0$). Arbitrage imposes

$$(18.1) \qquad r \;=\; \underbrace{\underbrace{d/q}_{\substack{\text{dividend} \\ \text{yield}}} + \underbrace{\Delta q/q}_{\substack{\text{capital} \\ \text{gain}}}}_{\text{return on shares}}$$

return on
Treasury
bills

This arbitrage condition has a puzzling interpretation. The expected future change in the share price is $\Delta q = q_{t+1} - q_t$. If we take dividends d and the return r on the Treasury bill as given, (18.1) can be seen as determining today's stock price q_t as a function of next period's price q_{t+1}.[7] Expectations of the future price drives today's stock price.

This curious—but intuitive—result that today's stock price is determined by our expectation of tomorrow's implies that there is an infinity of paths of stock prices that satisfy (18.1). To see why, ask what happens if expectations of tomorrow's price change exogenously. Let us take the case where the price is now expected to be higher. For the arbitrage condition to be satisfied, it is sufficient for today's price to rise. More generally, any expected share price any time far into the future is compatible with the arbitrage condition as long as previous prices and price expectation from today are 'right', i.e. satisfy the arbitrage condition (18.1). Stock prices rise because they are *expected* to, without violating any market efficiency condition. Figure 18.5 shows this by plotting possible evolutions of the share price over time, for given r and d.[8] Only one of them does not 'explode', and that is the one in which the share price $\bar q$ is equal to the ex-

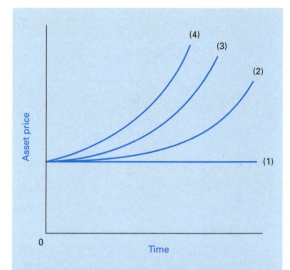

Figure 18.5. Possible Stock Price Paths

Path (1) is the no-bubble value of the asset that satisfies the arbitrage condition. The price of the stock is equal to the present value of the dividend d, which is assumed constant. Paths (2)–(4) also satisfy the arbitrage condition, but are explosive bubbles.

pected value of receiving the constant dividend d for ever:

$$(18.2) \qquad \bar q = d/r \qquad \text{and} \qquad \Delta q/q = 0.$$

This value $\bar q$ is called the stock's fundamental value. It is the present discounted value of an infinite stream of dividends d when the interest rate is r. The other paths, which are exploding without any apparent fundamental justification, are self-fulfilling price paths. The share price keeps increasing, reducing the rate of return d/q but generating compensating capital gains at the same time. The apparently inexorable growth of the share price is called a speculative bubble: a bubble because it keeps growing until it bursts, speculative because its growth is due to the expectation of growth in the future. Note that (18.1) implies that the price of a bubble is always above its fundamental since the dividend yield must be lower—and therefore the price higher, given the dividend—when there are capital gains. What is efficient or rational about that? As long as traders believe that the bubble will continue to grow, they are willing to hold the asset because its growth guarantees a 'normal' return. Such beliefs are enough to keep the bubble going. In such a bubble, the beliefs themselves are validated *ex post*.

---

[7] (18.1.) states that $r = d/q_t + (q_{t+1} - q_t)/q_t$, which can be rewritten as $q_t = (d + q_{t+1})/(1 + r)$.

[8] For the mathematically minded, the equation in the previous footnote $q_t = (d + q_{t+1})/(1 + r)$ can be iterated forward to give $q_t = \{d/(1 + r)[1 + 1/(1 + r) + 1/(1 + r)^2 + \ldots] + q_{t+n}/(1 + r)^n\} = d/r + q_{t+n}/(1 + r)^n$. This infinity of solutions corresponds to the infinity of possible non-zero values of the last term as n goes to infinity, which occurs when q_{t+n} grows at least at the rate r. (Since asset prices cannot be negative, rational economic agents will rule out a priori 'negative bubbles').

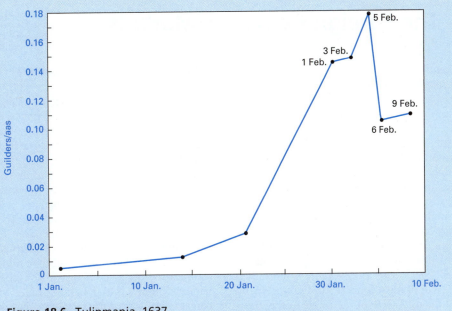

Figure 18.6. Tulipmania, 1637

History has given us several instances of price behaviour that looks like speculative bubbles. In Holland, the price of rare tulip bulbs during the seventeenth century rose by extraordinary rates within a month's time, only to collapse thereafter.

Source: Garber (1990)

The price must be believed to grow for ever. If there is a known date at which the price will stabilize, the situation will unravel. When the price stabilizes, (18.1) shows that, with $\Delta q/q = 0$, the asset price must be equal to its fundamental from that point on. In the period just before the price stabilizes, for it to be a bubble, the price must be expected to rise, and therefore to be below the fundamental value. This is a contradiction, however, with the earlier observation that the price of a bubble is always above its fundamental. So the period just before stabilization of the price cannot be *below* the fundamental, it can only be *at* the fundamental. Working backwards, it is easy to see that the same reasoning applies all the way to the present: there can be no bubble that is expected to stop growing. This logic can be extended to uncertainty, when traders believe the bubble will end with some probability.[9]

A famous historical bubble episode is Holland's 'Tulipmania' in the seventeenth century.[10] The bubble involved exotic varieties of tulip bulbs, therefore objects of fundamental value. Figure 18.6 displays the price of tulip bulbs in the first two months of 1637, when they increased by over 3000%, and then collapsed sharply. For example, the price of the Switser variety is reported to have fallen to one-twentieth of its 2 January 1637 price. More recent historical episodes that have bubble-like characteristics are the gold price in the late 1970s, the run-up of the world's stock markets before the crashes of 1929, 1987, and 1989, and the explosion of property prices in Japan, the UK, Sweden, and several other countries in the late 1980s. In each of these instances, reports by contemporaries indicate that market participants were convinced that the boom would continue.

---

[9] See Theory exercise 9 at the end of this chapter.

[10] This description is taken from Peter Garber's (1990) survey of the Tulipmania boom.

18.4. The Foreign Exchange Markets

As with other financial markets, the market of foreign exchange arose in response to commercial demands. Banks carry out transactions for their customers, i.e. firms engaged in international trade. In the process, they acquire foreign currencies and face the risks associated with exchange rate fluctuations. As they take steps to protect themselves against risk, they end up trading mainly on their own accounts. This is why the link between international trade and exchange market activity is at best tenuous, as is apparent in Table 18.2. The numbers are staggering. According to a survey of worldwide exchange markets, the average daily trading volume was estimated at more than $1.3 trillion in April 1995, compared with roughly $650 billion in April 1989.[11] This *daily* volume is more than the *annual* GDP of most countries in the world, and one-fifth of the total GDP of the whole of the European Union. This is more than four times the total *stock* of foreign exchange reserves held by EC central banks (about ECU 385 billion).

[11] Since 1986, every three years, 26 central banks conduct a survey of their local exchange markets. This worldwide survey is co-ordinated by the Bank for International Settlements.

18.4.1. Where is the Market?

Foreign exchange means foreign money. Since most money (M1) is in the form of deposits, i.e. liquid liabilities of the commercial banking system, the foreign exchange market is most accurately described as a market for demand deposits denominated in foreign currencies. The big players in these markets are the commercial banks. Interbank transactions account for roughly 90% of total trading.

The US dollar has become the *de facto* world numeraire currency. It solves the same 'double coincidence of wants' problem described in Chapter 8. Just as agents seek a common medium to minimize transaction costs, foreign exchange traders most often swap national monies into dollars. A trader who wants to convert Zimbabwe dollars into Canadian dollars would need to conduct two transactions: from Zimbabwe into US dollars, and from US into Canadian dollars.

Unlike most national stock exchanges or the markets for commodity futures, which involve the physical presence of the participants, the foreign exchange market is not found in a single location. Business is conducted either over the telephone or on computer terminal screens linking national markets. Central banks are the other big players in the foreign exchange

Table 18.2. Exchange Markets, April 1995

Total average daily market turnover (billions of US dollars)							
	London	New York	Tokyo	Singapore	Hong Kong	Zurich	Frankfurt	Paris
April 1989	184.0	115.2	110.8	55.0	48.8	56.0	55.0[a]	23.2
April 1995	464.5	244.4	161.3	105.4	90.2	86.5	76.2	58.0

Use of currencies on one side of transaction (% of total)							
	US dollar	DM	Yen	Sterling	FF	SF	ECU	Other EMS
April 1989	45	13.5	13.5	7.5	1	5	0.5	1.5
April 1995	41.5	18.5	12	5	4	3.5	1	6.5

[a] April 1992

Source: Bank for International Settlements

BOX 18.1. BUYING $10 MILLION OVER THE PHONE

The phone call might proceed like this:[12]

Barclays: Hi Jan, Andrew here. How are you?
Amro: Just fine Andrew.
Barclays: Jan, what are you doing in dollars for sterling today?
Amro: Well, Andrew, we're doing 85/75 [which means that Amro is selling sterling for US$1.985 and buying at US$1.975 per pound].
Barclays: OK, we'll buy 10 [million US dollars] at [1.9]75.
Amro: I'll do 5 [million US dollars], Andrew.

Barclays: Great. Talk to you later.

Initially Barclays trader doesn't reveal his trading intentions. He does so only after he knows the bid–ask quote of Amro. Technically, Barclays needn't have taken up Amro's offer either, simply saying 'par' or 'parity', meaning that it viewed Barclays quote as the right rate. In the process, Amro's trader has found out that there is a large transaction under way and he may expect the rate to change. This may be why he was willing to sell only half of the $10 million that Barclays wanted to buy.

---

market. They have a special role since they actually create the object that is traded (or at least one form of it): the currency. In some countries they are in the market daily, attempting to smooth out exchange rate fluctuations.

Since no physical presence is involved, there is no auctioneer, outcry, or body contact as in other exchanges. Trading takes place on a **bid–ask spread** basis. At any point in time, there are two quoted prices: the bid, at which one can sell to the market, and the ask, at which purchase is possible. The system works as follows. Suppose Barclays Bank requires, for a British customer's account, $10 million. This is quite a lot of money, and it is likely that the customer wants it fairly quickly, so the bank cannot wait several weeks for a favourable rate. Yet, it wants to find the best deal possible in a market where the situation is continuously changing, often rapidly. Information is exchanged continuously, for example by telephone as illustrated in Box 18.1. One of Barclays traders rings the Dutch bank Amrobank, which in this example is a **market maker**. A market maker stands ready to buy or sell any amount from the minimum standardized trade (say, $5 million) up to some maximum. Big banks 'make' a number of bilateral rates, and presumably Amro is one candidate market maker.

If Amro knew Barclays intentions, it would try to take advantage of the latter's urgency by charging a higher price. That of course, is the beauty of the bid–ask system: Barclay's does not divulge this information at the outset of the phone call. As a market maker, Amro commits both to buy and sell at its quoted bid–ask. In the course of the trade, Barclays forces Amro to reveal its view of the market. At the same time, Barclay's must reveal the extent of its needs. Thus, not

only do our two traders conclude a deal, but they also learn something about each other. Thousands of such exchanges comprise the trader's day and guarantee swift dissemination of all relevant information.

Transactors in foreign exchange have alternatives to a market maker. They could avail themselves of a computerized trading system (Reuters and Telerate are the leaders in this field), which transmits a continuous display of the running bid and ask postings. In such a system, traders have continuous news of the most recent bid and ask. A trader has the option of taking the bid price (selling foreign exchange to the bidder), taking the ask price (buying foreign exchange from the seller), or 'seizing' the bid–ask by posting his own. Many banks both make markets and subscribe to such services, so the two systems generally are well synchronized.

Another procedure for a trader is to seek out a broker. This is done for very large amounts. Why? Every market maker has the right to refuse very large amounts and trade only a fraction. As soon as this occurs, of course, the market learns the identity of a very large trader and the exchange rate will be bid up automatically by others eager to take advantage of the situation. A broker, on the other hand, acts as a third party and conceals the identity of the transactor. Brokers, who now represent anywhere between 30% and 50% of trading volume, often work outside the normal market channels, or serve as a mask behind which the transactor can act. They work on a commission basis.

18.4.2. The Market Instruments

Since the foreign exchange rate is the relative price of two national monies, there are always two ways of quoting an exchange rate: either by the number of

---

[12] The brackets are indicated to help the reader; the rest is understood by the participants.

foreign monetary units per domestic unit (British terms) or by the number of domestic units per foreign unit (European terms). The quotation conventions, used in the newspapers or by professional traders, are often simply the outcome of institutional factors or historical accident.[13] To maintain consistency with previous chapters, we continue to use European terms when quoting exchange rates.

18.4.2.1. Spot transactions

The best known type of transaction, the one described above, is for immediate delivery, where 'immediate' means within forty-eight hours. The rates quoted there are those that are published daily in many newspapers, an example of which—from the *Financial Times*—appears in Table 18.3. The exchange rate that is quoted applies to wholesale, interbank transactions: the minimum transaction is generally of the order of $2–$5 million. Even large corporations do not trade directly in the **spot market** unless they have large and steady requirements for foreign exchange. 'Spot' means European terms except for the UK (of course), Ireland, and the ECU. The first column reports the lowest bid and the highest ask prices quoted during the day. The second column displays the bid and ask prices when the market closed. Comparing the first two columns indicates how volatile the market has been on the reported day. The third and fourth columns report the forward premium (pm) or discount (dis) for two different maturities: as explained in Box 18.2, these are calculated in percentage points.[14]

18.4.2.2. Forward transactions

In order to provide their customers with prompt service, commercial banks must maintain an inventory of various currencies. Technically, when a bank holds a foreign currency asset or liability it is said to take a position. Yet taking positions in foreign exchange puts the bank at risk, given the tendency of exchange rates to move quickly: the domestic value of inventory holdings may vary and entail serious losses (and gains,

too).[15] This is why it is routine practice for banks to remove this exposure to risk by **hedging**. Hedging means taking an offsetting position in the market, negating the source of risk. For example, a trivial way of hedging against exposure is simply to sell the currency immediately in the spot market. Another approach is to use the **forward market**. The forward market is the market for foreign exchange delivered and paid for at some point in the future, rather than in two days, but at a price agreed upon today. Box 18.2 provides details on forward markets.

For example, a Swiss bank that just bought $10 million may not wish to hold this on its books at the end of the day. With some luck, it may have another customer asking for just this amount. It is more likely that this will not happen, however, and so the bank will simply sell the $10 million forward at some date in the future. The bank has eliminated its exposure because it knows for sure the price that it will receive for its dollars at the time of delivery; whatever happens to the exchange rate between now and then does not affect the forward rate, which remains unchanged. In the meantime, it will receive interest on the dollars it purchased by depositing them immediately in a Eurodollar account or a US subsidiary. In fact, most of the time banks simply execute the spot purchase (sale) and forward (sale) purchase at the same time. This bundling of transactions is called a **swap transaction**.

Banks are not the only users of forward contracts. A European exporter who will receive dollars in six months actually owns these dollars even if she does not yet hold them; we say that she is 'long' in dollars. She is at risk; unless she wants to speculate, it makes sense for her to sell these dollars forward to her bank at a known rate (plus a commission, of course). Similarly, an order placed by a European concern in the USA involving payment of US dollars in the future implies foreign exchange exposure, too: in this case the importer is 'short' in dollars, as she must pay them at some future date. To hedge her short position (the risk is that the dollar might rise in the next six months, implying a more expensive payment in the home currency), she would purchase forward dollars.[16] The fees and commissions paid for such transactions to the

---

[13] The origin of the designation 'British terms' does not reflect any particular Anglocentricity in the foreign exchange markets, or the considerable influence exerted by the UK in the development of world financial markets in the 19th C. Rather, it is an artefact of the nondecimal monetary system that existed in the UK until 1969, which would have made rapid quotation of rates in European terms very difficult indeed.

[14] It is a good exercise to determine which one corresponds to the bid rate and which one is the ask (or offer) rate.

[15] If the Banque Nationale de Paris were to have a daily dollar exposure of US$20 m (4–5 average trades for the day), then a movement of the exchange rate from FF 5.00 to FF 4.99 would imply a loss of roughly FF 200,000, the monthly salary of its director!

[16] Note that, if the dollar depreciates with no forward protection, the company walks away with a handsome capital gain. But since the company's main business is presumably something else, it doesn't make sense to speculate or assume this type of risk. The manager might as well go to the casino.

BOX 18.2. THE FORWARD MARKETS

Table 18.3 shows forward rates as quoted in the *Financial Times*. Currencies are generally sold forward at standardized intervals (e.g. 1, 3, or 12 months), but in the retail market banks are willing to customize forward rates to the desires of their customers—within limits and always for a price, of course. The price for such a contract is usually stated as a **forward premium or discount** with respect to the spot price. A forward premium on the Danish krone *vis-à-vis* the US dollar exists when the forward price of dollars in krone is lower than the current spot price: the dollar is cheaper on the forward market or, equivalently, the krone is more expensive.

The forward premium or discount is usually expressed as a per-annum rate. If F_{t+1} is the forward rate agreed at time t for delivery at date $t+1$ and E_t is the spot rate at date t, the forward discount is $(F_{t+1} - E_t)/E_t$; it is a discount if positive because an increase in the exchange rate means a depreciation when quoted in European terms. $(F_{t+1} - E_t)/E_t$ is similar to a rate of interest over the period of the contract. To obtain its per-annum equivalent we compound it; for example, for a three-month contract we compute $(1+r)^4$, which gives $(F_{t+1}/E_t)^4$ since $1 + (F_{t+1} - E_t)/E_t = F_{t+1}/E_t$. A discount of 2% per annum on the three-month Danish krone/US dollar forward rate means that $(F_{t+1}/E_t)^4 = 1.02$ so that $F_{t+1}/E_t = 1.00496$: F_{t+1} is 0.496% above E_t. This is the way forward rates are reported in Table 18.3. For each maturity (1, 3, and 12 months), the table reports the forward rate and then the annualized percentage deviation from the spot rate; a positive number corresponds to a premium, a negative number to a discount.

Table 18.3. Spot and Forward Exchange Rates

POUND SPOT - FORWARD AGAINST THE POUND

May 1	Day's spread	Close	One month	% p.a.	Three months	% p.a.
US	1.7785 - 1.7855	1.7845 - 1.7855	1.03-1.01cpm	6.86	2.78-2.75pm	6.20
Canada	2.1150 - 2.1225	2.1215 - 2.1225	0.70-0.66cpm	3.85	2.00-1.90pm	3.68
Netherlands	3.2900 - 3.3025	3.2925 - 3.3025	½-¼cpm	0.91	1⅛-⅞pm	1.14
Belgium	60.10 - 60.50	60.40 - 60.50	9-4cpm	1.29	14-5pm	0.63
Denmark	11.3275 - 11.3575	11.3425 - 11.3525	¾-¼orepm	0.46	1¾-¼pm	0.26
Ireland	1.0945 - 1.0995	1.0975 - 1.0985	0.01-0.04cdis	−0.27	0.01-0.08dis	−0.16
Germany	2.9275 - 2.9350	2.9275 - 2.9325	½-¼pfpm	1.28	½-¼pm	0.34
Portugal	245.50 - 247.00	246.00 - 247.00	50-75cdis	−3.04	149-197dis	−2.81
Spain	183.60 - 184.10	183.75 - 184.05	19-26cdis	−1.47	88-101dis	−2.06
Italy	2196.00 - 2205.50	2202.25 - 2203.25	1-3lliredis	−1.09	9-12dis	−1.91
Norway	11.4300 - 11.4825	11.4725 - 11.4825	⅜-⅛orepm	0.39	1⅛-parpm	0.20
France	9.8700 - 9.8875	9.8750 - 9.8850	1-½cpm	0.91	⅜-⅛pm	0.15
Sweden	10.5625 - 10.5900	10.5800 - 10.5900	⅜-1⅛oredis	−1.20	3⅛-4⅜dis	−1.42
Japan	236.25 - 237.25	236.25 - 237.25	1¼-1⅛ypm	6.02	3⅜-3¼pm	5.60
Austria	20.57 - 20.65	20.59 - 20.62	2⅜-1¼gropm	1.06	5⅜-2¼pm	0.79
Switzerland	2.6725 - 2.6950	2.6725 - 2.6825	⅝-½cpm	2.24	1¼-1pm	1.68
Ecu	1.4255 - 1.4285	1.4275 - 1.4285	0.09-0.03cpm	0.50	0.10-0.02pm	0.17

Commercial rates taken towards the end of London trading. Six-month forward dollar 5.17-5.12pm. 12 Month 8.85-8.75pm

DOLLAR SPOT - FORWARD AGAINST THE DOLLAR

May 1	Day's spread	Close	One month	% p.a.	Three months	% p.a.
UK†	1.7785 - 1.7855	1.7845 - 1.7855	1.03-1.01cpm	6.86	2.78-2.75pm	6.20
Ireland†	1.6160 - 1.6265	1.6240 - 1.6250	0.87-0.84cpm	6.32	2.51-2.44pm	6.09
Canada	1.1880 - 1.1920	1.1890 - 1.1900	0.25-0.27cdis	−2.62	0.75-0.79dis	−2.59
Netherlands	1.8450 - 1.8645	1.8470 - 1.8480	0.89-0.92cdis	−5.88	2.62-2.66dis	−5.72
Belgium	33.80 - 34.00	33.80 - 33.90	16.00-18.00cdis	−6.03	46.00-50.00dis	−5.67
Denmark	6.3525 - 6.3925	6.3550 - 6.3600	3.55-3.95oredis	−7.08	9.40-10.10dis	−6.13
Germany	1.6395 - 1.6515	1.6405 - 1.6415	0.83-0.84pfdis	−6.11	2.43-2.45dis	−5.95
Portugal	139.10 - 139.60	139.15 - 139.25	121-129cdis	−10.78	318-333dis	−9.36
Spain	102.90 - 103.60	102.90 - 103.00	73-75cdis	−8.63	215-220dis	−8.45
Italy	1232.00 - 1240.75	1233.75 - 1234.25	0.84-0.89liredis	−0.84	2.50-2.60dis	−0.83
Norway	6.4200 - 6.4450	6.4275 - 6.4325	3.40-3.80oredis	−6.72	10.00-10.60dis	−6.41
France	5.5300 - 5.5700	5.5325 - 5.5375	2.93-2.97cdis	−6.40	8.50-8.56dis	−6.16
Sweden	5.9225 - 5.9500	5.9275 - 5.9325	3.93-4.18oredis	−8.21	11.55-12.10dis	−7.98
Japan	132.50 - 133.35	132.65 - 132.75	0.08-0.09ydis	−0.77	0.20-0.22dis	−0.63
Austria	11.5650 - 11.6100	11.6050 - 11.6100	5.55-5.90grodis	−5.92	16.00-17.00dis	−5.69
Switzerland	1.4980 - 1.5175	1.4995 - 1.5005	0.65-0.66cdis	−5.24	1.83-1.85dis	−4.91
Ecu	1.2420 - 1.2510	1.2475 - 1.2485	0.68-0.65cpm	6.39	1.94-1.87pm	6.11

Commercial rates taken towards the end of London trading. † UK, Ireland and ECU are quoted in US currency. Forward premiums and discounts apply to the US dollar and not to the individual currency.

Source: *Financial Times*, 12 January 1996

bank can be thought of as a premium for insurance against foreign exchange risk caused by long or short positions.

18.4.2.3. Currency Futures

The market provides a variety of instruments to firms and banks that want to cover exchange risk. **Futures**, like forwards, are contracts for future delivery of foreign exchange. They differ from forward contracts in two main respects: they are available only for standardized amounts, and delivery is for fixed dates, typically the last day of each quarter. Forward contracts, in contrast, can cover any amount (above a minimum level) and have a given maturity instead of standardized delivery date. Both features make currency futures a retail instrument to be purchased 'off the shelf', hence they are cheaper and are targeted to the non-bank public. Table 18.4 gives some examples of futures contracts and where they are traded. Another difference from forward contracts is the fact that payment is made up front, rather than on the terminal date. Usually traders will put up only some fraction, or margin, of face value of the contract and borrow the rest of the purchase price. Standard practice requires traders to make additional payment if the market moves against them.

18.4.2.4. Currency Options

Perhaps the least expensive means of hedging against foreign exchange risk is the purchase of options. Options are a general class of **derivatives**, or securities which derive their value from the behaviour of other, underlying, securities. A **call option** is a contract that entitles the owner to purchase an underlying asset at some predetermined price, called the strike price, up until a fixed expiration date. A **put option** entitles the

Table 18.4. Examples of Widely Traded Futures Contracts in Various Currencies

Currency	Exchange	Contract size
Deutschmark	Chicago Mercantile Exchange	125,000
Japanese yen	Chicago Mercantile Exchange	12.5 million
Australian $	Chicago Mercantile Exchange	100,000
Swiss franc	International Money Market	125,000

Table 18.5. Examples of Options on Spot Currencies and Futures

Currency	Exchange	Contract size
Deutschmark	Philadelphia Exchange	62,500
Canadian $	Philadelphia Exchange	50,000
Deutschmark	Singapore Exchange	125,000
Pound sterling	London Traded Options Exchange	12,500

owner to sell the asset at some pre-agreed strike price. For example, a call option on common stock in XYZ Company allows its owner to purchase 100 shares at 10 Euros per share before 30 June. If the actual price of the stock is 15 Euros, the owner could 'exercise' the option, paying 1000 Euros for stock worth 1500. One would expect the market price of this option to be worth 500 Euros. In contrast, an option 'out of the money' would be one in which the strike price is higher than the current market price of the stock, for example if market price of XYZ shares were only 8 Euros per share. Interestingly, options can still have value under such conditions, since the market price may rise above 10 Euros before 30 June.

Options need not be 'exercised': the holder of an option may let the expiration date pass and do nothing, in contrast to forwards or futures, which require full completion of the deal. Thus, an option is exercised only if it is profitable to do so. If the option is not exercised, the holder loses the price paid for the option. This might be thought of as an insurance premium. On the other hand, the holder may make a profit, for example when the actual price of the asset rises above the strike price.[17]

Consider again the exporter due to receive a dollar payment. She could purchase a put option on dollars,

enabling her to sell a specified amount of dollars at some specified price over the coming months. Should the spot dollar fall below the strike price, exercising the option would allow her to avoid a loss on her anticipated dollar export receipts. The beauty of the option is that, if the dollar rises above the strike price, the exporter does not exercise the option and actually makes a speculative gain on her dollar receipts. Similarly, an importer who has a future invoice to pay in dollars could buy a call option and hedge against dollar appreciation. Table 18.5 provides some examples of options traded on foreign exchange markets.

18.4.3. Economic Interpretation

18.4.3.1. Pricing risk

The economic function of any financial market is to reallocate risk among agents, from those who wish to avoid risk to those who are willing to bear it for a price. At the same time, competition drives the price of risk down to the lowest possible level. Indeed, this is why those markets are dominated by financial intermediaries who pass along to one another the risk that each one started off accepting. This process of risk reduction occurs through two channels.

The first channel is the netting out of risks, as the following example illustrates. Suppose an exporter is

---

[17] Futures and options can be written on anything that has value: stocks, commodities, forthcoming crops, etc. Options are written on both spot foreign exchange and futures.

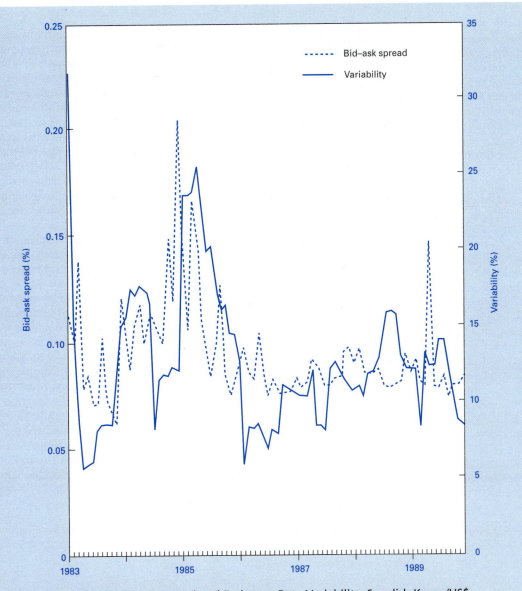

Figure 18.7. Bid–Ask Spread and Exchange Rate Variability: Swedish Krone/US$
Exchange Rate, 1983:1–1989:12

This figure plots the bid–ask spread in percentage points (which is quite small) against a
measure of the variability of the bid exchange rate. The two track each other. Variability is
measured as the standard deviation of the change in the exchange rate in the period beginning three months before and ending three months after the current month.

Source: DRI/FACS

due to receive $10 million in three months. At the same time, one or more importers must pay, possibly collectively, the same sum at the same date. If they could meet, the exporters could just agree to sell their dollars to the importers at a price agreed upon now and thus avoid all dollar exchange risk at no cost. The hitch is that they are very unlikely to meet each other. If they all deal with the same bank, the bank will do the matching, and receive a fee for it. If they bank at different institutions, the market can perform the same task, for yet another fee.

This example shows that a great deal of risk nets out. If export and import payments are exactly matched on a day-by-day basis, there is no aggregate risk whatsoever. Yet, despite market efficiency, it is unlikely that all risk can be diversified away. For example, if exports and imports are not equal, there will remain some unavoidable risk that the market as a whole must bear. This is where the risk premium is determined. In effect, the risk premium really applies only for the net-of-trade discrepancies, a tiny fraction of the total amount susceptible of seeking coverage.

The second channel of market efficiency concerns this residual risk that cannot be diversified away. Different financial intermediaries are likely to start out holding different positions in each currency. Diversification means holding a little bit of each possible position, expecting to compensate losses on some currencies by gains on others. By shifting positions around, the market allows the optimal distribution and pricing of risk; much like any well-functioning market, it distributes and prices resources according to people's endowments and tastes. From this process, a risk premium emerges as the market's 'price of risk'.

18.4.3.2. The bid–ask spread

The bid–ask spread can now be seen as the intermediary's fee for a turnaround transaction: by selling and buying the same foreign currency, she pockets the difference between the bid and the spot rate. Were things to stand still, that profit would be around 5%–7% in foreign exchange booths at banks and *bureaux de change*, about 2% for better customers, and well under 0.1% for banks for those million-dollar transactions. The fee must cover the fixed costs of putting together the transaction: the traders' salaries, the expensive equipment, the bullet-proof glass protection of the bank, etc. The bid–ask spread also includes the risk premium which compensates traders for their exposure to this risky business.

This goes quite some way towards explaining why the bid–ask spread faced by 'small players' like tourists is much greater than that faced by big banks in the interbank market. The former do not deal in large quantities, so the fixed costs are spread over a smaller volume of transactions. Second, the transactions are for cash (currency) rather than demand deposits, meaning that physical transportation of the bank notes is necessary, entailing more risk than a cheque or bank transfer. Third, inventories of the *bureaux de change* may be large with a commensurate exposure to risk. The bid–ask spread is compensation for that risk. Figure 18.7 shows how the interbank spread for the Swedish krone, the sum of operating costs and risk premia, tracks the variability of the exchange rate. Box 18.3 reports on a particularly interesting episode, the period that preceded German monetary union, between August 1989 and July 1990.

BOX 18.3. THE SHORT-LIVED MARKET FOR OSTMARKS

Even before the Berlin Wall fell on 9 November 1989, trade in the East German currency, the Ostmark (OM), was significant, and DM quotes for OM were published daily in major West German newspapers. After this historic date, volume increased by an order of magnitude as East Germans tried to convert their savings into harder currency. It remained unclear until March 1990 that monetary unification would occur, implying automatic conversion of OM currency and bank deposits into DM. The conversion rate of one DM for one OM applying to a part of East Germany's holdings and one for two for the rest—resulting in an average estimated by the Bundesbank at 1.8—was first suggested in March. It was then formal-ized as part of the state treaty of monetary and economic union between the two German states in May 1990.

Considerable uncertainty characterized this period. Furthermore, before the Berlin Wall opened, the markets were relatively thin and trade was exclusively a Western business. This is reflected in the bid–ask spread which stood at more than 30% in early 1989, as seen in Figure 18.8. As the situation became clearer, trade moved to the streets of East and West Berlin and most banks entered the game. With the decision to establish a monetary union between West and East Germany by July 1990—in effect, replacing OMs with DMs—uncertainty declined, and so did the spread.

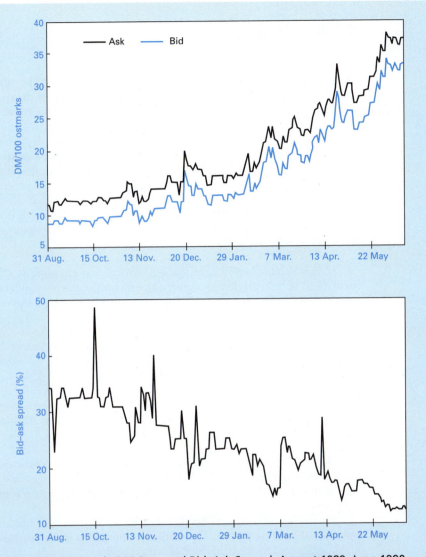

Figure 18.8. Ostmark–DM Rate and Bid–Ask Spread, August 1989–June 1990

As monetary union approached, the risk involved in holding Ostmarks, the currency of the vanishing German Democratic Republic, declined. This is reflected in the bid–ask spread, which fell significantly.

Source: Burda and Gerlach (1990)

18.5. Summary

1. Financial markets put a price tag on the future and on risk. They allow households and corporations to decide on saving and borrowing without themselves having to gather the whole array of uncertain information that affects their own future.

2. Financial assets are traded with ease in large well-organized markets, they are durable, and they are cheap to store. This is why financial markets are understood as equating the demand and supply of asset stocks, rather than the flow increments to the stocks that are created each period.

3. While financial intermediaries can be thought of as intervening on financial markets on the behalf of their customers, in fact most of the transactions correspond to trade among intermediaries.

4. Market equilibrium in asset markets involves large existing stocks. In order for these stocks to be held willingly, returns among similar assets—similar in terms of risk and maturity—must be equalized. The activity that brings about this equality without risk-taking is arbitrage.

5. Arbitrage should not be confused with risk-taking. The former implies the absence of risk, while the latter involves a conscious decision on the part of the investor to assume it. Agents are, on average, risk-averse.

6. Markets are efficient when they gather all the available information and treat it to the point where prices reflect fully what is known and the risks attached to any single asset.

7. The evidence on market efficiency is mostly favourable. Yet there exist a number of anomalies that suggest either that markets are not fully efficient or that efficiency is consistent with phenomena such as speculative bubbles or noise trading.

8. The foreign exchange market deals in national monies, the liquid liabilities of the commercial banking system. The market is dominated by commercial banks but is highly influenced by the behaviour of central banks.

9. Transactions in the foreign exchange market are made on a bid–ask basis among well-known market makers via a large informal telephone network and a computerized system. The bid–ask convention allows the potential transactor to conceal his intentions *vis-à-vis* the market maker. Brokers can also serve as a method of executing larger transactions with anonymity.

10. Forwards, futures, options, and other financial instruments allow their owners to either reduce or increase their exposure to the risk of asset price fluctuations. On the other hand, the net amount of aggregate risk is fixed and can be reallocated only within the markets.

Key Concepts

- financial intermediaries
- risk premium
- diversification
- offshore markets
- no-arbitrage condition
- spatial, yield, triangular arbitrage
- risk aversion/risk neutrality
- market efficiency
- noise traders
- speculative bubbles
- fundamentals
- bid–ask spread

- market maker
- European terms, British terms
- spot market
- hedging
- forward premium or discount
- swap transaction
- position (long or short)
- futures
- derivatives
- options (call and put)
- undiversifiable risk

Exercises: Theory

1. Explain why the bid–ask spread can be thought of as the price of risk.

2. Which type of arbitrage—spatial, yield, or triangular—do you think is most likely to be profitable? Why? How does the bid–ask spread play a role in your answer? What about technology?

3. Explain the similarities and differences between buying a put option, a call option, and a futures contract.

4. Although we usually refer to a single interest rate, usually of short duration, in fact there is a whole spectrum of maturities. Given what you know about the determination of the short-run interest rate, what kind of information do you think would affect long-term interest rates, and why? (*Hint*: see Applications question 3)

5. Insider trading occurs when some traders have superior private information which they use to 'beat' the market. In most countries insider trading is forbidden on stock markets but not in exchange markets.

   (*a*) Is it self-evident that insider trading on stocks should be banned? (*Hint*: think in terms of market efficiency.) Why do you think that insider trading is generally illegal?

   (*b*) Why do you think that insider trading is not forbidden on foreign exchange markets?

6. 'Markets are not efficient, because they place a premium on short-termism.' Comment.

7. As cars get older, their resale prices first decline and then sometimes rise. Why might this be so?

8. A market is said to be 'deep' when there are many traders at all times willing to buy and sell assets. The opposite of a deep market is a 'thin' market. How might the behaviour of prices help you distinguish a thin from a thick or deep market?

9. (*Difficult, formal*)   Consider the example of a speculative bubble in the text (Section 18.3.3.3). Now imagine that while, as before, there are two assets, investors no longer have perfect foresight. The private asset can be purchased at variable real price q_t and pays a fixed real dividend d. Now, however, there is a probability s that in the following period $q_{t+1} = 0$ (i.e. the bubble will burst), and a probability $(1 - s)$ that it will be sold at $q_{t+1} > 0$. Investors are risk-neutral and equate the rate of return on the government asset r with the expected rate of return on the private asset.

(*a*) Write down the arbitrage condition.
(*b*) Solve for the 'non-exploding' value of current q_t.

Exercises: Applications

1. Suppose that you could buy and sell US dollars in France at FF5 and Deutschmarks at FF3.4, but that at the same time the dollar–DM rate was DM1.48/$. What strategy would you pursue to take advantage of this 'money pump'? What would be the likely effect of the market's recognition of its existence?

2. The example given in the previous problem ignores the bid–ask spread. How would your answer change if the bid–ask spreads were: FF4.9925–5.00/$, FF3.395–3.405/DM, and DM1.4780–1.4790/$?

3. Suppose the interest rate for one-year Treasury rates is 5% per annum, and for two-year maturity, 7% per annum. By an arbitrage argument, at what rate should you be willing to contract to lend in one year's time over a maturity of one year?

4. Today you buy 100,000 Danish krone, selling Swiss francs at a spot rate of DKr4.48/SF, and simultaneously you sell them at a three-month forward rate of 4.54. Is this a premium or a discount? Assume that you hold the krone in cash over these next three months. What is the per-annum rate of return on this trade?

5. If the spot exchange rate on the French franc (European terms *vis-à-vis* the dollar) is 5.05 and the one-month forward premium is 4.6% (per annum), what is the one-month forward rate?

6. Suppose the three-month forward rate for sterling in Paris is FF9.9/£ and the corresponding spot rate is FF10/£. What is the forward discount on sterling? Suppose sterling interest rates are 12% while French interest rates are 10%. Do you see an arbitrage opportunity?

7. The DM–£ rate is 3. Suppose it is known that the exchange rate could move in one year with probability 1/2 to 3.1 and with probability 1/2 to 2.95. What is the value of a call option that allows the holder to buy sterling at DM 3 in one year?

Suggested Further Reading

A trader's inside view of how foreign exchange markets work can be found in the yearly publication by Swiss Bank Corporation, *Foreign Exchange and Money Market Operations*, Zurich.

An entertaining survey of the arguments in favour of market efficiency which contains a large number of references is:

Burton, Malkiel (1981), *A Random Walk Down Wall Street*, W. W. Norton, New York.

A textbook introduction to the economics of finance is:

Sharpe, William (1990), *Investments*, Prentice-Hall, Englewood Cliffs, NJ.

A lively discussion of speculative bubbles in both technical and non-technical terms can be found in the Spring 1990 issue of the *Journal of Economic Perspectives*.

19

Exchange Rates in the Short Run

> It is certain that a system of 'free exchanges' would lead to extremely undesirable results. It would incite capital flight and violent fluctuations. There are very few examples of really free exchanges in monetary history, and none that could be called a success.
>
> Gottfried Haberler

19.1. Overview

Chapter 7 explained that, in the long run, the real exchange rate is determined by real forces: the country's net asset positions and wealth, productivity in tradable goods, and world tastes. Ultimately, as a relative price of goods, the real exchange rate's role is to clear the current account and enforce the intertemporal budget constraint. This view does not, however, fit the short-run behaviour of exchange rates. Figure 19.1 presents day-to-day *nominal* exchange rate changes. The variability of nominal exchange rates is often remarkably high, with daily changes of ±1% or more per day commonplace. (A daily change of 1% corresponds to an annual compounded return of more than 3000%.) These violent fluctuations, which are often followed by movements of similar magnitude in the opposite direction, are not consistent with the behaviour of relative prices or price levels. The inescapable conclusion is that in the short run neither the nominal nor the real exchange rate can be thought of as the relative price of goods and services in different countries; rather, they should be regarded as an *asset* price— the price of national monies. This chapter first focuses on the short run—hour-by-hour or month-to-month —and then reconciles the interpretation of the exchange rate as the relative price of goods with that of the relative price of monies.

In 1979, Michael Mussa of the University of Chicago assessed the first half-decade of floating exchange rates after the end of the Bretton Woods system.[1] His observations, which remain true today, can be summarized in the following stylized facts. The goal of this chapter is to account for all seven of them:

[1] Ch. 20 presents the Bretton Woods system.

1. On a daily basis, changes in foreign exchange rates are largely unpredictable.

2. On a month-to-month basis, over 90% of exchange rate movements are unexpected, and less than 10% are predictable.

3. Countries with high inflation rates have depreciating currencies, and over the long run the rate of depreciation of the exchange rate between two countries is approximately equal to the difference in national inflation rates.

4. Countries with rapidly expanding money supplies tend to have depreciating exchange rates *vis-à-vis* countries with slowly expanding money supplies. Countries with rapidly expanding money demands tend to have appreciating exchange rates *vis-à-vis* countries with slowly expanding money demands.

5. In the longer run, the excess of domestic over foreign interest rates is roughly equal to the expected rate of appreciation of the foreign currency. On a day-to-day basis, however, the relationship is more tenuous.

6. Actual changes in the spot exchange rate will tend to overshoot any smoothly adjusting measure of the equilibrium exchange rate, the real exchange rate predicted by the analysis of Chapter 7.

7. The correlation between month-to-month changes in exchange rates and monthly trade balances is low. On the other hand, in the longer run, countries with persistent trade deficits tend to have depreciating currencies, whereas those with trade surpluses tend to have appreciating currencies.

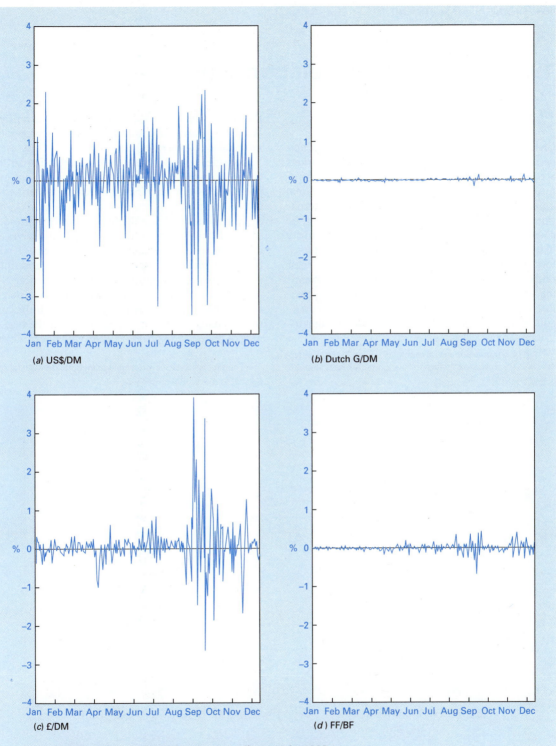

Figure 19.1. Daily Exchange Rate Changes in 1992

Day-to-day variability of the nominal exchange rate is considerable. Sharp changes in one direction are frequently undone on the following day.

Source: National central banks

19.2. Interest Parity Relationships

19.2.1. Uncovered Interest Parity

Chapter 18 showed that exchange markets' participants constantly follow events in financial markets across the globe, ready at a moment's notice to commit large resources to take advantage of even minimal differences in yields.[2] As a result, returns on international assets of similar risk characteristics should be equalized. Treasury bonds of three months' maturity in the USA, the UK, and Germany are safe and therefore roughly comparable in terms of risk. Are their returns equal? Figure 19.2 responds with a resounding 'no'. Although they seem to move broadly together, interest rates always differ, sometimes by wide margins. Thus, it is not just nominal interest rates that in

fluence the decision to shift funds across currencies. When assets are denominated in different currencies, nominal exchange rates must enter the picture.

Consider a French resident contemplating an investment in the UK, who compares investment opportunities—say, government Treasury securities—of the same maturity (one year, for concreteness) with equal riskiness and liquidity in the two countries.[3] If she holds the French asset to maturity she receives an interest income i_t; after one year, she will receive $(1 + i_t)$ francs for each franc invested, where the subscript t denotes the interest rate prevailing over period t. If instead she acquires the British asset yielding interest rate i^*, she must first buy pounds sterling. If the current exchange rate in European terms at the beginning of year t is E_t (e.g. FF8/£), then with one franc she

[2] A typical transaction may amount to 5 million Euros. A difference of 0.1% represents a return of 5000 Euros, for what amounts to a few seconds' work.

[3] Transaction costs and risk would complicate the analysis and are overlooked for the time being.

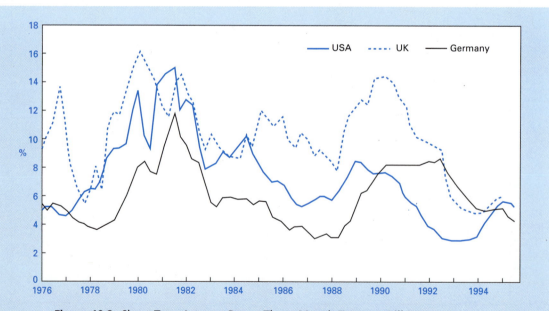

Figure 19.2. Short-Term Interest Rates: Three-Month Treasury Bill Rates, USA, UK, and Germany, 1976–1995

Despite high capital mobility between the USA, Germany, and the UK, interest rates on assets of similar quality differ even if they tend to follow similar patterns. Evidently, exchange rate fluctuations have a role to play in these differences.

Source: IMF

BOX 19.1. EXAMPLES OF INTEREST PARITY CONDITIONS

Uncovered interest parity. Imagine that sterling is expected to fall from FF10 to FF9.5 over the next year, while one-year sterling and franc assets bear interest rates of $i* = 15.00\%$ and $i = 9.00\%$ per annum, respectively. The expected yield of one franc invested in the UK, seen from the perspective of France, is:

$$(1 + i_t^*)\frac{{}_tE_{t+1}}{E_t} = (1 + 0.15)\,(9.5/10) = 1.0925,$$

or a 9.25% rate of return. Thus, it is a better investment than the available French security. If market traders were indifferent to risk, or if one well-endowed trader were, equilibrium would require that the interest differential be matched by a 5.5% expected sterling depreciation:[6]

$$\frac{E_t}{{}_tE_{t+1}} = \frac{1 + i_t^*}{1 + i_t} = 1.055 = (1 + 5.5\%).$$

How would this occur? Traders would buy sterling, raising E_t; for a given ${}_tE_{t+1}$, this would reduce the expected depreciation on sterling until yields are equalized.

Covered interest parity. With a one-year forward rate $F_t = 9.4783$, the covered return on the British investment is $(1 + 0.15)\,(9.4783/10) = 1.0900$, or exactly (to several significant decimal points) 9.00%. This is exactly the rate of return in France.

can invest $1/E_t$ pounds at the known interest i_t^*. In one year's time, she will convert the $(1 + i_t^*)/E_t$ pounds that she will receive back into francs. Suppose she expects presently, at time t, that the exchange rate in year $t + 1$ will be ${}_tE_{t+1}$.[4] Then the expected yield on the British investment, expressed in francs, is $(1 + i_t^*)\,{}_tE_{t+1}/E_t$.

The relevant yield comparison therefore is between $(1 + i_t)$ and $(1 + i_t^*)\,{}_tE_{t+1}/E_t$, which are both denominated in the same currency, and not between i_t and i_t^*, in francs and sterling, respectively. If investors are indifferent with respect to risk, they will shift funds around until the two yields are equalized. This is the uncovered interest parity condition (UIP):

(19.1) $$(1 + i_t) = (1 + i_t^*)\frac{{}_tE_{t+1}}{E_t}.$$

A frequently used approximation to (19.1) is[5]

(19.1′) $$i_t = i_t^* + \frac{{}_tE_{t+1} - E_t}{E_t}.$$

The UIP simply asserts that rates of return are equalized across countries once expected exchange rate changes are taken into account. The second term on the right-hand side of (19.1′) represents the expected rate of depreciation of the franc *vis-à-vis* the pound and can be expressed in percentage terms like interest

rates. If the UK bond offers a lower return than the French bond $(i > i*)$, the franc must be expected to depreciate *vis-à-vis* the pound. A French resident who buys British bonds suffers an interest loss, which is compensated by the expected capital gain that occurs when the pound appreciates. Box 19.1 presents a simple illustrative example.

19.2.2. Covered Interest Parity

The actual value of the exchange rate a year hence is unknown, of course, so the effective return on a sterling investment is uncertain return for the French investor. If she wishes ultimately to spend the proceeds in France, she takes a risk relative to the investment in francs. There is a way to avoid this currency—or exchange—risk by transacting in the market for forward foreign exchange. The investor may buy $(1 + i*)/E_t$ pounds' worth of francs now for delivery in a year's time—she knows precisely that this is how many pounds she will receive in one year—at a price agreed upon today. This can be routinely done on the forward foreign exchange market. Today's price of francs in terms of sterling for future delivery, the forward rate, is denoted as F_t. Her return will be $(1 + i*)F_t/E_t$ and is perfectly riskless. The foreign investment is said to be covered, or **hedged**.

Since there is no risk involved, in principle, the French investor should be indifferent between holding French bonds and holding covered British bonds. When capital is perfectly mobile and transaction costs are ignored, arbitrage ensures that the two returns are

---

[4] The first subscript refers to the period when the expectation is formed, the second one to period to which the expectation applies.

[5] Mathematically, take logarithms of both sides of (19.1) to obtain $\log(1 + i_t) = \log(1 + i_t^*) + \log[1 + ({}_tE_{t+1} - E_t)/E_t]$, and apply the approximation that $\log(1 + x) = x$ for small x.

[6] Using the approximation (19.1′) instead of the exact formula (19.1), we would find that a 6% interest differential must be matched by a 6% expected change in the exchange rate.

Table 19.1. The Performance of Free Forecasts, Various Countries (mean squared error, %)

Country	Horizon (mos.)	UIP	Forward	Lag spot
Canada	1	0.380	0.385	0.365*
	3	1.486	1.517	1.463*
	6	3.179*	3.291	3.243
UK	1	4.144	4.052	3.982*
	3	15.924	15.983	15.065*
	6	29.779*	33.783	32.039
Belgium	1	4.406	4.434	4.110*
	3	18.064	17.935	16.714*
	6	36.087	38.525	34.093*
France	1	6.277	5.881	5.460*
	3	22.803	22.280	21.493*
	6	53.252	54.189	50.555*
Germany	1	5.590*	5.636	5.687
	3	23.550*	23.737	24.501
	6	45.158*	45.415	49.972
Italy	1	2.094	2.241	2.067*
	3	8.557	8.395	7.408*
	6	12.909	13.907	12.110*
Netherlands	1	4.481*	4.554	4.545
	3	15.282*	15.385	16.135
	6	28.728*	32.717	31.768
Switzerland	1	5.448*	5.469	5.458
	3	20.864*	21.057	20.952
	6	45.881*	46.347	47.819
Japan	1	5.623*	5.671	5.704
	3	23.605*	23.788	24.500
	6	46.687	45.892*	49.947

Note: The performance criterion is the square root of the mean of squared forecast errors. Squares are used to avoid positive errors (overestimates) being compensated for by negative errors (underestimates). Entries marked * are lowest mean squared error given country and horizon.

Source: Levich (1978)

equal. This provides the **covered interest parity (CIP)** conditions:

$$(19.2) \qquad 1 + i_t = (1 + i_t^*) \frac{F_t}{E_t}.$$

In the absence of capital controls or other impediments to capital mobility, covered interest parity should hold exactly. It is approximated as

$$(19.2') \qquad i_t = i_t^* + \frac{F_t - E_t}{E_t}.$$

The second term on the right-hand side is the forward discount when positive (so that $F_t > E_t$, meaning the forward rate is depreciated *vis à vis* the spot rate), or the forward premium when negative (the currency with a higher forward in European terms is at a premium). In Table 18.3, forward discounts and premia are quoted in percentages per annum, much like the interest rates with which they are compared.

19.2.3. The Forward Rate and Prediction of the Spot Rate

When both covered and uncovered parity conditions hold, the forward rate must be equal to the spot rate that is expected to prevail at the same date. This is just an implication of (19.1) and (19.2):

$$(19.3) \qquad F_t = {}_t E_{t+1}.$$

BOX 19.2. FREE VERSUS COMMERCIAL EXCHANGE RATE FORECASTS

It is interesting to compare how free forecasts offered by the market fare *vis-à-vis* forecasting services, which cost money. These services use two main kinds of forecasting technique. Econometric models are based on economic principles, like those developed in this book, which employ statistical methods to quantify important relationships. Chartists are market analysts who track the evolution of exchange rates and 'see' regularities, which they exploit to project the trends in the future. Table 19.2 summarizes a study published by *Euromoney* in August 1983. The performance of several forecasting services is compared with that of the forward rate, the worst of the three free forecasts. It gives the number of times (in percentages) across the same nine currencies that the services do better than the forward rate. The forward rate comes out as a clear winner, although its superiority diminishes as the horizon lengthens. This is an indication that, over time, the 'exchange rate fundamentals'—to be

explained in Section 19.4.6—that are used by the econometric forecasts become more useful. It also turns out that chartists—who rely on unspecified non-fundamental information—do better than econometrics in the short run, worse in the long run.

Table 19.2. Free Forecasts versus Services, 1977–1981 (% of times when services do better than the forward rate at various horizons)

1 mo.	3 mos.	6 mos.	12 mos.
9.5	14.7.	24.2	30.5

Source: Euromoney, Aug. 1983

Thus, the market reveals its forecast of the future spot rate when it sets the corresponding forward rate. UIP also reveals what the market expects the exchange rate to be in the next period: since the current spot exchange rate (E_t) and interest rates (i_t and i_t^*) are known, (19.1) tells us that $_t E_{t+1} = E_t (1 + i_t)/(1 + i_t^*)$. If markets expectations are rational, UIP and the forward rate on average correctly predict the future spot rate, even if they are never exactly on the mark.

Is it true that markets provide free forecasts of the spot exchange rate? Table 19.1 reports how the two free forecasts—the forward rate and the rate implied by UIP—compare with each other for a number of currencies and forecasting horizons. Their performance is compared with the most naive forecast of the future spot exchange rate: the *current spot* exchange rate. The table shows that, the longer the horizon, the more inaccurate are the forecasts, which is not surprising. More surprising, the spot exchange rate generally outperforms either UIP or the forward rate. Box 19.2 further evaluates the performance of forecasting services.

19.2.4. Risk Premium

The two interest rate parity conditions differ in an important way. The covered parity is based on riskless arbitrage, while the uncovered parity condition in-

volves risk taking, or speculation. The two activities are identical only when well-endowed risk-neutral traders are ready to arbitrage away any yield difference. If, as is more likely, market participants are risk-averse, the CIP may hold while the UIP needs to be amended to allow for risk. The more volatile the exchange rate is, the more likely are investors to require compensation for sleepless nights. This compensation will take the form of a higher expected rate of return, which is increased by a **risk premium**. In the previous example, the French investor who contemplated investing in Britain will demand a risk premium. For her, sterling yields must exceed the uncovered parity condition by a premium. If we denote this risk premium by ψ_t, the approximate version of the uncovered interest parity condition is modified as follows:

$$(19.4) \qquad i_t^* = i_t - \frac{(_t E_{t+1} - E_t)}{E_t} + \psi_t.$$

At the same time, there may be British investors who hold French assets. They face exactly the same type of exchange risk, but see things the other way round: they require a premium on French assets, i.e. a relative discount on British assets and a negative ψ. In general, the sign of the risk premium will depend on the net bilateral asset position of Britain and France, but also on the positions of third parties (e.g. US or Japanese investors) in each country's assets. The size of the premium or discount will depend on the degree of risk—which varies a lot over time—and on traders' risk

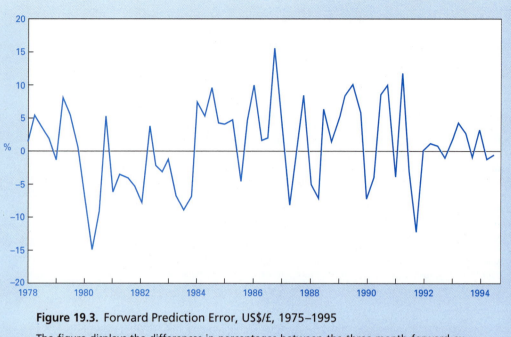

Figure 19.3. Forward Prediction Error, US$/£, 1975–1995

The figure displays the differences in percentages between the three-month forward exchange rate and the corresponding spot exchange rate. The errors are large and quite random.

Sources: DRI/FACS; Bank of England

aversion.[7] In the end, all we need is to understand that the risk premium or discount ψ_t depends upon a set of exogenous and variable factors beyond our purview. The existence of uncertainty and risk means that we should not expect the uncovered parity condition to hold exactly. It will be true right up to a—possibly volatile—risk premium. Once this is understood, we can turn things around and *define* the risk premium as the deviation from the uncovered interest parity condition:

$$(19.5) \qquad \underset{\substack{\text{risk} \\ \text{premium}}}{\psi_t} = \underset{\substack{\text{expected} \\ \text{depreciation}}}{\frac{(_t E_{t+1} - E_t)}{E_t}} - \underset{\substack{\text{interest rate} \\ \text{differential}}}{(i_t - i_t^*)}.$$

The risk premium may be decomposed further in an illuminating way. Because the CIP holds at all times in the absence of legal restrictions on capital movements, (19.2′) shows that the interest differential ($i_t - i_t^*$) is just the forward discount. The risk premium

then is the difference between the expected rate of depreciation and the forward discount. (As both of these can be negative, it is equivalent to considering the risk premium as the difference between the expected rate of appreciation and the forward premium.) This is written as

$$(19.6) \qquad \underset{\substack{\text{risk} \\ \text{premium}}}{\psi_t} = \underset{\substack{\text{expected} \\ \text{depreciation}}}{\frac{_t E_{t+1} - E_t}{E_t}} - \underset{\substack{\text{interest rate} \\ \text{differential}}}{\frac{F_t - E_t}{E_t}} = \underset{\substack{\text{forward} \\ \text{bias}}}{\frac{_t E_{t+1} - F_t}{E_t}}.$$

The risk premium is the bias separating the *expected* future spot exchange rate from the corresponding forward rate. Figure 19.3 shows a related measure, the forward forecast error, the deviation of the forward rate from the *realized* spot exchange rate E_{t+1} (which differs from the expected rate $_t E_{t+1}$):

$$(19.7) \qquad \text{Forward forecast error} = \frac{E_{t+1} - F_t}{E_t}.$$

The forward forecast error is the sum of the risk premium and the market's own error in predicting the spot exchange rate:

---

[7] The theory of finance—e.g. the capital asset pricing model—has developed formal explanations of the risk premium.

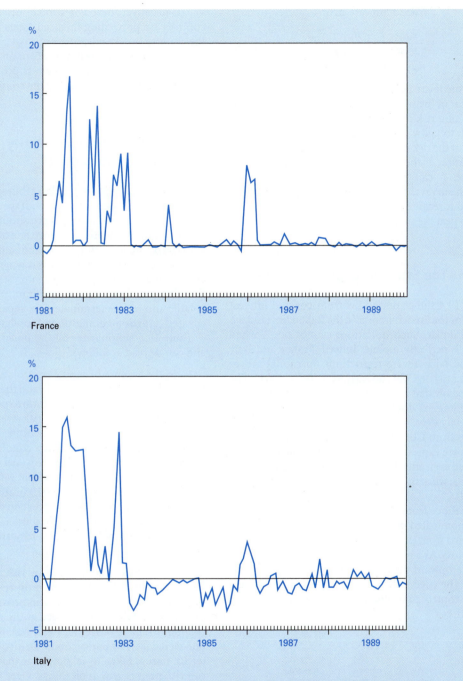

France

Italy

Figure 19.4. Deviations from Covered Interest Parity, France and Italy, 1981–1990

The deviations are measured as $i - i^* - (F_{t+1} - E_t)/E_t$. They correspond to unexploited riskless arbitrage opportunities and can be explained by capital controls.

Source: DRI/FACS

(19.8)   Forward forecast error

$$= \frac{{}_tE_{t+1} - F_t}{E_t} + \frac{E_{t+1} - {}_tE_{t+1}}{E_t}.$$

    risk premium   market forecast error

The mediocre performance of the forward rate as a predictor of the spot rate may be due either to the existence of a risk premium or to market errors.[8] It is difficult to know what determines the sign and magnitude of the risk premium because ${}_tE_{t+1}$, the market's expectation of the exchange rate, is not directly observable: it can be estimated only statistically or through surveys. The highly erratic behaviour of the forward forecast error serves to illustrate why it is so hard to beat the market.

19.2.5. The Effect of Capital Controls

Figure 19.4 shows deviations from covered interest parity for the French franc and the Italian lira vis-à-vis the US dollar. Such deviations cannot occur when capital is perfectly mobile. Indeed, France and Italy imposed fairly severe restrictions on capital movements until late 1989 and early 1990, respectively. The figures show that most of the time the restrictions are not binding, no doubt because controls can never be completely tight. It also reveals occasional sharp deviations from CIP when devaluations of the franc or the lira are expected to take place. For the franc, this occurred even after 1990, at the times of crises in 1992 and 1993, when the French authorities applied implicit controls.

Deviations from CIP occur because holders of assets denominated in currencies subject to controls are prevented from legally selling them before suffering a capital loss. As a result, domestic interest rates do not face the upward pressure generated by capital outflows.[9] The effect can be thought of as introducing a **capital control premium** ζ_p, defined as the deviation from CIP:

(19.9) $$\zeta_t = (i_t - i_t^*) - \frac{F_t - E_t}{E_t}.$$

    capital control   interest rate   forward
       premium   differential   discount

[8] Froot and Frankel (1989) find that the larger of the two is the market error.
[9] To be sure, controls are evaded but Figure 19.3 shows that evasion is imperfect: the fact that CIP does not hold in these circumstances is evidence that capital controls slow down capital movements.

When negative, there is a control discount: capital controls are preventing financial assets from leaving the country to take advantage of a covered return on foreign assets that exceeds the return on domestic assets. When the control premium is positive, restrictions are keeping money out of the country.[10]

19.2.6. When Do Which Parity Conditions Hold?

With free capital mobility, riskless arbitrage should enforce the covered parity condition. If speculators were not deterred by risk taking, there should be no risk premia. In the real world, exchange rate traders or their employers, the large international financial intermediaries, are not risk-neutral. This is why, even in fully efficient markets, the uncovered interest parity condition does not hold. A risk premium, possibly quite volatile and of indeterminate sign, separates the uncovered returns on domestic and foreign assets.

Table 19.3 summarizes all the possible situations and can be read as follows:

1. In the absence of capital controls and risk aversion, both parity conditions hold and the forward rate is an unbiased predictor of the future spot rate.

2. If market participants are risk-averse but there are no capital controls, the covered parity condition holds, while the uncovered parity condition includes a risk premium term. Then the forward rate is not an unbiased predictor of the future spot rate.

3. In the presence of capital controls, both arbitrageurs and speculators are prevented from eliminating profit opportunities. Then none of the above parity conditions hold, nor is the forward rate an unbiased predictor of the future spot rate.

If the world is characterized by risk aversion, the second line in Table 19.3 is the most relevant one in the absence of capital controls. This provides an interpretation of stylized fact 5 listed at the outset of this chapter, which is simply a careful restatement of the uncovered interest parity condition invoked in Chapter 13. Care is taken to acknowledge that in the short run risk premia may spoil things. Over the long run, however, risk premia are small and average out to zero, so the parity condition is much more likely to hold.

[10] Situations in which capital controls are instituted to prevent capital inflow, while rarer, do occur: some examples are Germany in the early 1970s, Spain and South Korea in the mid-1980s, Chile in the 1990s, and Switzerland from time to time throughout the postwar period.

Table 19.3. The Parity Conditions

	Uncovered interest parity (UIP)	Covered interest parity (CIP)
No capital controls, risk neutrality	$i_t - i_t^* = \dfrac{{}_tE_{t+1} - E_t}{E_t}$	$i_t - i_t^* = \dfrac{F_t - E_t}{E_t}$
	Risk-adjusted interest parity (RIP)	Covered interest parity (CIP)
No capital controls, risk aversion	$i_t - i_t^* = \dfrac{{}_tE_{t+1} - E_t}{E_t} - \psi_t$	$i_t - i_t^* = \dfrac{F_t - E_t}{E_t}$
	Both parity conditions fail to hold	
Capital controls, risk aversion	$i_t - i_t^* = \dfrac{{}_tE_{t+1} - E_t}{E_t} - \psi_t - \xi_t$	$i_t - i_t^* = \dfrac{F_t - E_t}{E_t} - \xi_t$

19.2.7. Real Interest Parity Conditions: the International Fisher Equation

Purchasing power parity (PPP)[11] implies a useful parity condition for real interest rates: the resulting **real interest parity** relationship is derived in Box 19.3. By definition, the difference between domestic and foreign real interest rates is equal to the corresponding nominal differential less the expected inflation differential. UIP asserts that the nominal interest rate differential is equal to expected depreciation. If private agents use PPP in forming their expectation of inflation, the expected inflation differential determines the expected rate of depreciation. The UIP condition plus PPP imply that the real interest rates are equal across countries, *ex ante*:

$$(19.14) \qquad r_t = r_t^*.$$

This relationship is called the **international Fisher equation**.[12] As it rests on PPP, it is at best a long-run proposition. Nevertheless, it is a useful benchmark to keep in mind. For example, when evaluating long-term foreign investment strategies, it implies that the real rate of interest should be largely the same in all countries and is independent of the evolution of exchange rates.

---

[11] Purchasing power parity is presented in Ch. 8. Only its relative version is used here.

[12] The name comes from the Fisher equation introduced in Ch. 8: the nominal interest rate is the sum of the real interest rate and the expected rate of inflation.

BOX 19.3. THE REAL INTEREST RATE PARITY CONDITION

Relative PPP implies that the rate of depreciation is equal to the inflation differential:

$$(19.10) \qquad \frac{E_{t+1} - E_t}{E_t} = \pi_{t+1} - \pi_{t+1}^*.$$

If agents use PPP to form their expectations of the expected rate of depreciation, they turn to the difference between expected inflation at home (${}_t\pi_{t+1}$) and abroad (${}_t\pi_{t+1}^*$):

$$(19.11) \qquad \frac{{}_tE_{t+1} - E_t}{E_t} = {}_t\pi_{t+1} - {}_t\pi_{t+1}^*.$$

Combining UIP from (19.1') and (19.11), we have

$$(19.12) \qquad i_t - i_t^* = {}_t\pi_{t+1}^* - {}_t\pi_{t+1}^*,$$

which can be rewritten as

$$(19.13) \qquad i_t - {}_t\pi_{t+1} = i_t^* - {}_t\pi_{t+1}^*.$$

Real interest rates *ex ante* are equalized as in (19.14).

19.3. Exchange Rate Determination: Forward-Looking

19.3.1. Reinterpreting the Interest Parity Conditions

The interest parity conditions build a bridge between the exchange rate and domestic financial markets (represented by the interest rate) and clarify why the exchange rate is the relative price of domestic and foreign assets. These conditions do not yet provide the theory of exchange rate determination that we are aiming at because they involve only endogenous variables. Still, they provide a number of important and fundamental insights.

Any of the interest parity conditions shown in Table 19.3 can be used to illustrate how the market thinks about today's exchange rate. For example, with no capital controls but with risk aversion,[13]

$$(19.15) \qquad \frac{_tE_{t+1}}{E_t} = \frac{1+i_t}{1+i_t^*}(1+\psi_t).$$

The UIP condition can be interpreted as a relationship linking the current exchange rate to both interest rates, to the risk premium, and to the exchange rate expected to prevail next period. This may be seen by rewriting the parity condition (19.15) as

$$(19.16) \qquad E_t = \frac{1+i_t^*}{(1+i_t)(1+\psi_t)}\,_tE_{t+1}.$$

Viewed this way, the UIP condition implies that the current spot exchange rate is determined by domestic and foreign interest rates and by the market's *expectation* of next period's exchange rate. The market cares about the future when it sets the current exchange rate. Like all financial markets, the exchange market is *forward-looking*. What happened before is irrelevant: bygones are bygones and the exchange rate is not tied to its past. It is totally free to jump to any level justified by current conditions, or by expectations of future conditions. The following newspaper report is indicative of the relevance of the future for the exchange markets:

[13] If we wanted to include capital controls we could simply redefine ψ as the sum of both risk premia ψ and ζ. If the period is annual, $_tE_{t+1}$ corresponds to next year and i_t and i_t^* have yield periods of 1 yr. If the comparison is for a period of 3 mos., the 3-mo. interest rate differential must be compared with the expected change in the exchange rate over the same period.

The foreign exchange markets yesterday focused on the possibility of a cut in US interest rates later this week, leading to continued selling pressure on the dollar. . . . This may change this week with the market anticipating a number of US economic indicators; leading indicators and the monthly national purchasing manager's survey are due today, manufacturing orders and manufacturing shipments are due on Thursday and nonfarm payroll data on Friday. The last of these figures is seen by market participants as the most significant. In recent months a sharp decrease in employment has been the trigger for an easing of monetary conditions in the US. (*Financial Times*, 1 October 1991: 42)

The interest parity condition written as (19.16) shows that an increase in the domestic relative to the foreign interest rate implies an exchange rate appreciation. It is tempting to reason as follows: the higher yield makes domestic assets more attractive and triggers capital inflows, which in turn lead to an appreciation. Yet UIP written as (19.15) says that an increase in the domestic rate is accompanied by an increase in expected depreciation—or a reduction in expected appreciation. Is this a fatal contradiction?

Not at all. The two ways of reasoning are reconciled in Figure 19.5. As the domestic interest rate rises above

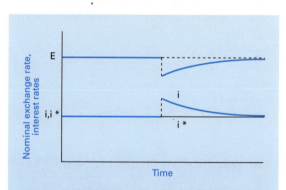

Figure 19.5. An Increase in the Domestic Interest Rate

When the domestic interest rate (*i*) rises above the world interest rate, uncovered interest rate parity requires that there be an expected exchange rate depreciation. Given an unchanged expected long-run nominal exchange rate, the exchange rate must appreciate now in order to generate that expected depreciation.

the world rate, the exchange rate temporarily appreciates: hence it is expected to depreciate back to its initial value. An expected depreciation of the domestic currency (a capital loss) offsets the interest advantage. *Given an unchanged future expected exchange rate*, the only way for the exchange rate to be expected to depreciate in the future is for it to appreciate *now*. Over time, the interest rate declines and the exchange rate will indeed depreciate back to its long-run level. Importantly, actual capital movements are not really required as long as asset returns are equalized. All that needs to happen is that markets change the pricing rather than move the assets. In highly integrated and efficient financial markets, this happens almost instantaneously.

19.3.2. Implications: Looking into the Future

Explaining today's exchange rate by that expected next period might seem trivial. Let us pursue the reasoning, all the same: next period's exchange rate will be expected to be related, like today's, to that period's interest rates and to the exchange rate expected to prevail the period after. To keep things simple we ignore uncertainty, so we can substitute E_{t+1} for $_tE_{t+1}$, E_{t+2} for $_tE_{t+2}$, etc. Applying (19.16) one period ahead yields

$$(19.17) \qquad E_{t+1} = \frac{1 + i^*_{t+1}}{(1 + i_{t+1})(1 + \psi_{t+1})} E_{t+2}.$$

Combining (19.17) with (19.16), we find that the current exchange rate depends on interest rates and risk premia in the current and next period, plus the exchange rate expected two periods ahead. Formally,

$$(19.18) \quad E_t = \frac{1 + i^*_t}{(1 + i_t)(1 + \psi_t)} \frac{1 + i^*_{t+1}}{(1 + i_{t+1})(1 + \psi_{t+1})} E_{t+2}.$$

The process can be repeated an arbitrary number of times, so that

$$(19.19) \quad E_t = \frac{1 + i^*_t}{(1 + i_t)(1 + \psi_t)} \frac{1 + i^*_{t+1}}{(1 + i_{t+1})(1 + \psi_{t+1})} \cdots$$
$$\frac{1 + i^*_{t+n}}{(1 + i_{t+n})(1 + \psi_{t+n})} E_{t+n+1}.$$

The current exchange rate is related to current and expected future interest rates at home and abroad, to the corresponding risk premia, and to the exchange rate expected to prevail at some future date. This expression shows just how important expectations of the future are for the present. Even fairly distant events can have a large impact on today's exchange rate. This is why exchange markets—and financial markets in general—are so concerned with information. Even remote future events affect the present.

19.3.3. Exchange Rates, Trends, and News

The above reasoning implies that all that is currently known about the determinants of the exchange rate, between now and the indefinite long run, is already incorporated into the current rate. What then, can make the exchange rate change? First, there are fully anticipated trends in future interest rates, at home and abroad. As we move from one period to another, the exchange rate should adjust smoothly to the evolution of interest rates, as current interest rates become part of the past, and thus no longer relevant. Box 19.4 provides details. This cannot, however, explain the volatility of exchange rate seen in Figure 19.1. To understand that characteristic, we turn to the second explanation.

Inevitably, the market will receive new information

BOX 19.4. UPDATING THE EXCHANGE RATE

As long as the expected long-run exchange rate is unchanged, the evolution of domestic and foreign interest rates over time translates into a smooth evolution of the exchange rate. It must be smooth because, from one period to the next, the change in the exchange rate results from 'dropping off' the latest period's interest rates, as is seen by comparing (19.19) and (19.20):

(19.20)

$$E_{t+1} = \frac{1 + i^*_{t+1}}{(1 + i^*_{t+1})(1 + \psi_{t+1})} \cdots \frac{1 + i^*_{t+n}}{(1 + i^*_{t+n})(1 + \psi_{t+n})} E_{t+n+1}.$$

As time passes, the successive dropping of the first terms leads to expected changes in the exchange rates. Holding E_{t+n+1} constant, it can be shown that

$$\frac{\Delta E_{t+1}}{E_t} = \frac{1 + i^*_t}{(1 + i_t)(1 + \psi_t)} - 1 \approx i^*_t - i_t - \psi_t.$$

which is the UIP condition (19.6).

between one period and the next. If this information affects any future domestic or foreign interest rate, the risk premia, or the long-run exchange rate, as earlier expectations are revised, the exchange rate changes according to (19.19). For expectations to be revised, however, something genuinely unexpected must occur: only *news* matters. To be unexpected, news cannot be systematic; information will, by definition, arrive randomly. If most of what moves the exchange rate on a daily basis is unexpected random news, changes in the exchange rate will be mostly random and nearly impossible to forecast. This is exactly the message of the first and second of Mussa's stylized facts.

When a variable changes randomly from period to period, it is said to follow a **random walk**.[14] In that case, the only change between its value today and its value tomorrow will be white noise, a random shock which can be as much positive as it can be negative, so on average it must be zero. Thus, the best next-period forecast of a variable that evolves as a random walk is simply its current value. Along with the forward rate and the UIP (see Section 19.2.3), this is another forecast available free of charge. Surprisingly, perhaps, this most naive forecast often turns out to be the best one (Table 19.1). This result lends much credit to the 'random walk' view of the exchange rate.

Indeed, exchange markets are constantly hit by news encompassing political conditions, the release of economic data, and pronouncements by government ministers, analysts, prominent businessmen, gurus, etc. After the fact, much of this 'news' will be amended, made more precise, or disavowed if not actually proved wrong. In the meantime, however, it influences crucially the evolution of the exchange rate. This provides an explanation of the short-run exchange rate behaviour shown in Figure 19.1. News—both genuine facts and rumours—can move the exchange rate up one moment, and down the next. The fact that the 'news' component is so much more important than the redating of interest rates corresponds to the second stylized fact cited at the beginning of this chapter. In practice, predictable trend changes—such as a return to PPP, a well-understood need to depart from PPP, or simply the changing profile of already expected interest rates—represent a relatively small part of short-term exchange rate movements.

19.3.4. The Long Run as an Anchor

In equation (19.19) the current nominal exchange rate is related, among other things, to the nominal exchange rate (E_{t+n+1}) expected to prevail as far into the future as we care to look. The long run serves as an anchor; given intervening interest rates and risk premia, it drives the current nominal exchange rate. We can now see the link between a short-run financial or 'assets market' view of exchange rate determination and the long-run view linking the exchange rate to trade, to competitiveness, and to the intertemporal budget constraint. Importantly, these considerations matter for the short run precisely *because* they matter for the long run. On the other hand, real (trade) considerations constitute one of many types of news that can affect the exchange rate in the short run. This helps explain stylized fact 7—which stresses the weak correlation between exchange rates and trade balances in the short run.

19.4. Exchange Rate Determination in the Short Run

Taken on its own, the UIP condition is not a complete theory of the nominal exchange rate. It is based on endogenous variables—current and future nominal interest rates—which themselves have to be explained. A complete story integrates interest rate determination (along the lines of the *IS–LM* framework and/or the Fisher equation) and the exchange rate (*via* the parity condition).

19.4.1. Money Market Equilibrium

As is often the case elsewhere in this text, it is much easier to collapse the time dimension into two periods,

---

[14] A variable x_t follows a random walk when it evolves as $x_t = x_{t-1} + u_t$ where u_t is a 'white noise', i.e. a purely random variable (with zero expectation and serially uncorrelated). At time $t - 1$, the best forecast of x_t is x_{t-1}.

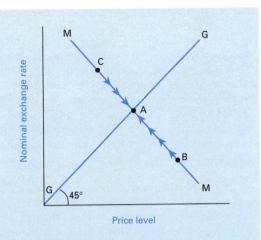

Figure 19.6. General Equilibrium

Money market equilibrium implies an inverse relation-ship between the exchange rate and the price level, the *MM* schedule. For a given nominal money stock, a price increase reduces the real money supply. Demand is equilibrated with supply by an increase in the inter-est rate which triggers an exchange rate appreciation. Goods market equilibrium is characterized by PPP. This in turn implies a positive relationship between the ex-change rate and the price level, the *GG* schedule. Equi-librium in the money market holds continuously, so positions off the *MM* schedule are not possible. In con-trast, PPP is valid only in the long run—under some conditions—so in the short run, positions off the *GG* schedule are possible. Long-run equilibrium occurs at point *A*, with equilibrium in both money and goods markets.

Given the nominal money supply, the expected future exchange rate, and the foreign interest rate, money market equilibrium imposes an inverse relationship between the current exchange rate and prices. An in-crease in the price level reduces the real money sup-ply. To restore equilibrium, demand must decline. This occurs when the opportunity cost of holding the domestic money, the nominal interest rate, rises. Since the foreign interest rate is taken as constant, UIP im-plies that the exchange rate must be expected to de-preciate. Holding the future exchange rate E_2 constant, the current exchange rate must appreciate. This is quite sensible: the excess demand for money that follows a price increase prompts domestic residents to borrow abroad; the ensuing capital inflow leads to an appre-ciation. This is represented in Figure 19.6 by the down-ward-sloping *MM* schedule.

19.4.2. Goods Market Equilibrium: the Long Run

In the long run, goods market equilibrium is charac-terized by relative PPP. If prices abroad are constant, the real exchange rate remains unchanged as long as the exchange rate and the price level remain propor-tional. This is represented by the *GG* line in Figure 19.6.[15] If the long-run equilibrium real exchange rate changes, so does the slope of the *GG* line: it rotates clockwise (case of real appreciation) or counterclock-wise (real depreciation).

19.4.3. Short- and Long-Run Equilibria

The money market is always in equilibrium: the inter-est rate and the exchange rate instantaneously jump to a level that guarantees equilibrium between money supply and demand. As a result, the economy is al-ways located on the *MM* schedule of Figure 19.6. On the other hand, PPP is expected to hold only in the long run; because of price stickiness, the economy may well be away from the PPP line in the short run. In the long run, however, PPP reasserts itself and the economy must be at point *A*.

In the short run, point *C* above the PPP line corre-sponds to an undervalued exchange rate; more pre-

today (period 1), and the indefinite future when sta-tionary equilibrium is reached (period 2). To further simplify matters, we assume that output is constant. A more general and formal presentation can be found in Box 19.5 and in the Appendix.

The familiar *LM* curve provides the money market equilibrium condition. Taking real GDP as constant, we have, in each period $t = 1$ and 2,

$$(19.21) \qquad \frac{M_t}{P_t} = L(\overline{Y}, i_t).$$

The UIP condition links the domestic money market to international financial conditions and the exchange market. Using (19.1′) in (19.20) gives, for period 1,

$$(19.22) \qquad \frac{M_1}{P_1} = L\left(\overline{Y}, i^* + \frac{E_2 - E_1}{E_1}\right).$$

---

[15] The *GG* line corresponds to $E = \lambda P/P^*$ where λ is the real ex-change rate. Here the unite for λ and P^* have been chosen so that $\lambda/P^* = 1$; it also passes through the origin.

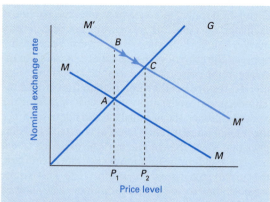

Figure 19.7. Overshooting

An increase in the money supply shifts the money market equilibrium schedule to the right, from *MM* to *M'M'*. The new long-run equilibrium obtains at point C, the intersection of the PPP (goods market equilibrium) line and *M'M'*. In the short run, with sticky prices, only the exchange rate can move. The economy jumps to point B to maintain money market equilibrium. As point B lies above the PPP line, there is excess demand for domestic goods, and prices will start to rise. Over time, rising prices reduce the real money supply, pushing up the interest rate and therefore requiring an exchange rate appreciation as we move from B to C. As point B is above point C, the exchange rate initially overshoots its long-run level. This overshooting creates an excess demand for domestic goods and puts upward pressure on prices.

cisely, either the nominal exchange rate is undervalued, or the price level is too low and there is an excess demand for domestic goods. Over time, the price level must rise or the exchange rate must appreciate. The long-run equilibrium in the goods market is restored as the economy moves down along the *MM* schedule. Conversely, at point *B* below the PPP line, the exchange rate is overvalued or prices are too high. Because they are too expensive relatively to foreign competitors, goods are in excess supply and prices tend to be falling. The return to equilibrium requires a combination of declining prices and exchange rate depreciation.

19.4.4. Exchange Rate Determination with Flexible Prices: the Monetary Approach

If prices are perfectly flexible, the goods market is always in equilibrium, and the economy is adequately

described by the intersection of the *GG* and *MM* schedules. Starting from long-run equilibrium at point *A* in Figure 19.7 (so that $E_t = E_{t+1}$ and $i = i^*$), we consider a once-for-all unexpected 5% increase in the money supply. Long-run neutrality implies that the nominal exchange rate and the price level must also increase by 5%, proportionately to the money supply. This is why the *MM* schedule shifts to the right to *M'M'*, and the long-run equilibrium is at point *C*. With fully flexible prices, neutrality occurs in the short run, and the economy immediately jumps from point *A* to point *C*.

It follows from this exercise that, when the equilibrium real exchange is stable, *all* long-run movements of the nominal exchange rate are due to changes in the nominal money supply. This is known as the **monetary approach** to exchange rate determination. If money increases by 5% more than the foreign money supply—and therefore the foreign price level—both the price level and the exchange rate increase by 5% also. This provides an interpretation of stylized fact 3, which states that countries with high inflation rates have depreciating currencies. Yet if prices are sticky in the short run, the monetary approach will fall short of being a full explanation of nominal exchange rate behaviour.

19.4.5. Exchange Rate Determination with Rigid Prices: Overshooting[16]

In the short run (period 1) it is more realistic to think of the price level as rigid, moving only slowly to eliminate goods market imbalances and deviations from the equilibrium real exchange rate. In the long run, prices recover flexibility and a 5% increase in the money supply remains described by point *C*. In period 1, however, the price level remains unchanged at P_1. At the same time, money market equilibrium requires the economy to jump instantaneously on to the new schedule *M'M'* in Figure 19.7. With prices unable to move in the very short run, the task is performed by the nominal exchange rate which takes the economy immediately to point *B*. Over time, the price level adjusts and the economy will move down along *MM* from *B* to *C*.

A key feature of short-run point *B* is that it lies *above* long-run point *C*. The nominal exchange rate **over-**

[16] The overshooting result was first established by Rudiger Dornbusch from MIT in 1976.

BOX 19.5. OVERSHOOTING AND UNDERSHOOTING IN THE *IS–LM* FRAMEWORK

The *IS–LM* framework allows us to consider the case—treated formally in the Appendix—where output varies. In Figure 19.8, we start from long-run equilibrium at point *A* (so $i = i^*$ and $E_t = {}_tE_{t+1}$). We now interpret i^* strictly as the foreign interest rate *only*. The increase in the money supply shifts the *LM* curve rightward to *LM'*. This depresses the domestic (nominal and real) interest rate and is met by a depreciation which shifts the *IS* curve to the right because of the gain in competitiveness. If spending is not too sensitive to the real interest rate (through investment) and to the exchange rate (through the current account), the *IS* curve shifts only to *IS'*. At point *B*, the domestic interest rate is below the world level and there must be a compensating expectation of exchange rate appreciation: the exchange rate overshoots. If spending is very sensitive to interest and exchange rates, the *IS* curve shifts further to *IS"* and the economy is at point *C*. The interest rate is *above* the world level; the exchange rate is expected to depreciate afterwards so it jumps less than, rather than more than, its long run change: so there is **undershooting**. In both cases, the interpretation is the same: when the money supply increases, with sticky prices money demand must rise to achieve equilibrium. (With flexible prices, the real money supply remains unchanged as the price level rises in the same proportion as the nominal money stock.) If demand does not rise enough (point *B*), the interest rate must decline on impact, and there is overshooting. If demand is very responsive, it boosts output so much that the interest rate must rise, and there is undershooting.

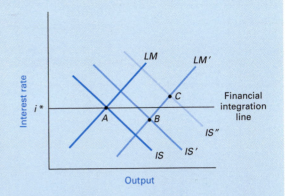

Figure 19.8. Overshooting and Undershooting in the *IS–LM* Framework

Starting from full equilibrium at point *A*, an increase in the money stock brings the *LM* curve to *LM'*. As the nominal interest rate falls, the nominal exchange rate depreciates. With sticky prices, the real exchange rate depreciates, shifting the *IS* curve to the right. With a small shift (*IS'*) at point *B*, the domestic interest rate is still lower than abroad: the exchange rate must be expected to appreciate, hence an overshooting depreciation. With a larger shift (*IS"*) at point *C*, the exchange rate undershoots: since the domestic interest rate exceeds the world level, the exchange rate is rationally expected to further depreciate and is therefore below its long-run level.

shoots its long-run level, depreciating by more than the 5% warranted by the money stock increase. From *B* to *C*, overshooting is eliminated as the exchange rate appreciates, while the price level rises to its new higher equilibrium level. That the exchange rate overshoots its equilibrium value is exactly what Mussa's stylized fact 6 asserts: actual changes in spot rates tend to overshoot any measure of the equilibrium exchange rate.

Box 19.5 provides an interpretation of overshooting using the *IS–LM* framework. Figure 19.9 shows the evolution over time of the interest and exchange rates and of the price level in the more general case when there are more than just two periods. As the money supply has increased, initially the interest rate must decline to maintain equilibrium in the money market. This raises demand for domestic goods. In response, the price level rises gradually towards its higher long-run level. The lower exchange rate must be compensated by an expected appreciation. In the

long run, the exchange rate will have moved from its initial value E_1 to E_2, which is 5% higher. In the short run, the exchange rate must jump above its long-run value: it *over*depreciates in order to appreciate thereafter. As the price level rises, the real money supply declines and the interest rate increases. A rising interest rate, in turn, coincides with an appreciating exchange rate. Figure 19.9 provides the background for stylized fact 4, which links depreciation rates in the long run to monetary growth. Money increases 'tend' to lead to depreciations, but overshooting may blur the picture as the initial depreciation is followed by a partially offsetting appreciation.

Overshooting shows that persistent deviations of real exchange rates from their equilibrium values, or **misalignments**, are possible, even with rational expectations. This would be impossible if goods prices were perfectly flexible. Box 19.6 provides some more detail on interpreting misalignments.

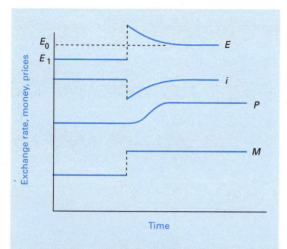

Figure 19.9. Overshooting over Time

The nominal money increase eventually leads to an equiproportionate increase in the price level and the exchange rate. Thus, we expect E to settle eventually at the level E_1, above its initial value E_0. Initially, with sticky prices, the money supply increase pushes interest rates down. This requires an expected exchange rate depreciation, hence a jump above E_1.

19.4.6. The Fundamental Determinants

The 'cumulated' interest parity condition (19.19) states that the exchange rate is determined by present and future interest rates and is anchored by its long-run value. The exchange rate **fundamentals**, therefore, are those variables that influence the current and future domestic and foreign exchange rates as well as the long-run exchange rate. Domestic and foreign economic conditions—as captured by the *IS–LM* framework—drive the domestic and foreign interest rates. The fundamentals thus include the present and future setting of monetary and fiscal policies at home and abroad. The long-run nominal exchange rate depends on two sets of factors: required competitiveness to meet the nation's intertemporal budget constraint, and the path of current and foreign prices which allow us to go from the required *real* exchange rate to the required *nominal* exchange rate. Thus, the fundamentals also include the foreign debt, the country's competitive position, and present and future inflation, both at home and abroad. The list becomes wide because of the ubiquitous role of the exchange rate as the relative price of goods and the relative price of assets. That it is so wide explains why the exchange markets react to a very broad range of indicators.

BOX 19.6. INTERPRETING REAL EXCHANGE RATE MISALIGNMENTS

The overshooting result implies that monetary disturbances can move the exchange rate away from PPP, *even in the absence of real disturbances*. This in turn affects consumption, the allocation of resources, firms' profitability, real wages, and the current account. Movements in the real exchange rate may also occur, of course, in response to real disturbances. Real disturbances, however, are relatively rare, as they are related to differences across countries in technological advances, tastes, or government policies. Figure 19.10 shows the effective nominal and real exchange rates for the three major currencies: the US dollar, the Deutschmark, and the yen. Fluctuations are sizeable (some 50% over periods of two to three years are not uncommon) but occur in the form of long swings around a fairly steady mean. Strikingly, nominal and real exchange rates move closely together, which is an indication that prices are sticky and that monetary forces play an important role in the short-run determination of the real exchange rate.

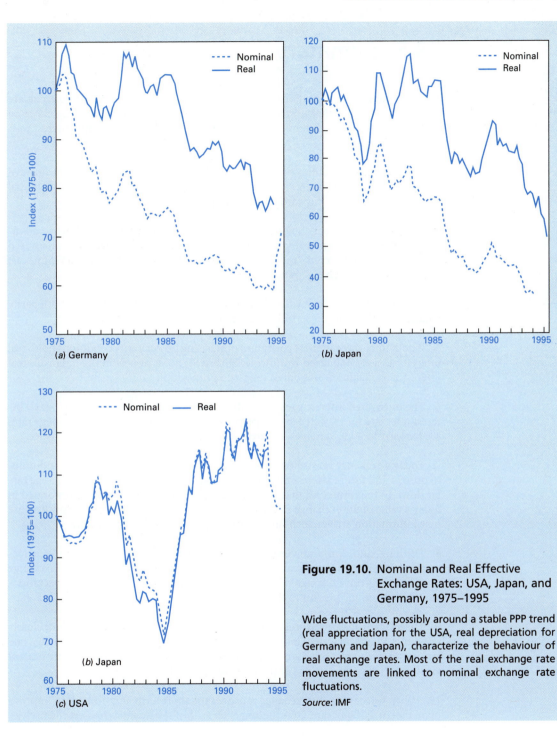

Figure 19.10. Nominal and Real Effective Exchange Rates: USA, Japan, and Germany, 1975–1995

Wide fluctuations, possibly around a stable PPP trend (real appreciation for the USA, real depreciation for Germany and Japan), characterize the behaviour of real exchange rates. Most of the real exchange rate movements are linked to nominal exchange rate fluctuations.

Source: IMF

19.5. Summary

1. When capital is internationally mobile, returns on assets of comparable risk are equalized. This is captured by the uncovered interest parity condition: an expected exchange rate depreciation must be compensated by a higher domestic interest rate, and conversely.

2. Arbitrage links the domestic interest rate, the foreign interest rate, and the forward discount. The covered interest parity condition states that the interest rate differential is matched by an equal forward discount or premium.

3. Covered interest parity holds exactly if capital movements are free. Uncovered interest parity holds up to a risk premium. In the absence of risk aversion, uncovered interest parity holds exactly and the forward exchange rate reveals the market forecast of the future spot exchange rate.

4. Capital controls, at least when they are binding, lead to a breakdown of both parity conditions. Profitable opportunities cannot be legally arbitraged away.

5. If both uncovered interest parity and purchasing power parity conditions hold, real interest rates are equalized worldwide. Since PPP holds at best in the long run, real interest rate equalization is only a long-run proposition.

6. The uncovered interest parity condition links today's exchange rate to today's interest rates and the expected exchange rate next period. Consequently, exchange rates are forward-looking variables, i.e. are free from the past and driven by the future.

7. Today's exchange rate is linked, by a chain of uncovered interest parity conditions, to present and future interest rates at home and abroad, and to the spot exchange rate far down in the future. All that is known about the future is already incorporated in today's value of the exchange rate. Changes in the exchange rate occur mostly because new information arrives, including revised expectations about the future.

8. The long- and short-run views of the exchange rate are not inconsistent. Real factors that drive the long-run real exchange rate are present in today's nominal exchange rate. The long-run exchange rate is the *anchor* that drives the stream of expectations stretching from the present to the future.

9. The forward-looking aspect of the exchange rate explains why its behaviour closely resembles a random walk. This makes it hard to see the link between the exchange rate and its fundamentals which are typically considerably less volatile. Yet, they are present via the market's expectations of their future expected values.

10. When forecasting the exchange rate over the short term, it is difficult to improve upon the current spot rate. Over the longer term, the fundamentals reassert themselves.

11. With prices sticky in the short run, an increase in the money stock leads to an exchange rate depreciation which overshoots its long-run value. All other things equal, an increase in the stock of money leads in the long run to increases of the same proportion in the exchange rate and price level.

Key Concepts

- uncovered interest parity (UIP)
- covered interest parity (CIP)
- real interest parity
- risk premium
- forward bias, forward forecast error
- capital control premium

- international Fisher equation
- random walk
- monetary approach
- undervaluation, overvaluation
- misalignment
- fundamentals

Exercises: Theory

1. In Figure 19.6 the schedules MM and GG determine four quadrants where the two markets are in disequilibrium. Characterize the market disequilibria in each quadrant, e.g. excess demand for goods and excess supply of money.

2. In Figure 19.6, moving along the MM schedule from point C to point A:

   (a) What is happening to the real stock of money?
   (b) What about the domestic interest rate? Is it approaching the foreign interest rate i^* from below (i.e. $i < i^*$) or from above (i.e. $i > i^*$)?

3. A small economy, which allows for full external capital mobility, is characterized by the following equations:

   $$M_t/P_t = 0.5\,\overline{Y} - 30{,}000[i^* + (E_{t+1} - E_t)/E_t]$$
   $$i_t = i^* + (E_{t+1} - E_t)/E_t,$$

   with $\overline{Y} = 8000$ and $i^* = 0.04$.

   (a) Draw the MM curve when $M_t = 2000$ and $E_{t+1} = 1$, limiting yourself to the cases where P_t and E_t are positive. Show what happens when M_t rises to 3000.
   (b) In the long run, purchasing power parity holds so that $\lambda = EP^*/P$, with $\lambda = 1$ and $P^* = 0.5$. Show the GG curve.
   (c) What is the long-run price and exchange rate equilibrium when $M_t = 2000$? When $M_t = 3000$?
   (d) Compute the short-term nominal exchange rate when M_t changes unexpectedly from 2000 to 3000, assuming that E was initially at its long-run equilibrium level.

4. When the money stock is increased once for all, do the nominal interest rate and inflation return to their previous levels?

5. Explore the implications of a once-for-all contraction of the money supply, tracing out the implications in the short and long run for the exchange rate, prices, and interest rates.

6. Analyse the outcome of an expected permanent increase in the growth *rate* of the money supply. It may help to start with zero money growth. Consider both the short- and long-run implications.

7. Using Figure 19.6, analyse the effect, in the short and long run, of a permanent increase in the risk premium on foreign assets, ψ. Does the long-run exchange rate appreciate or depreciate?

8. Using the apparatus of Figure 19.6, show graphically the effect on the exchange rate of a permanent exogenous increase in output. You may assume that PPP still holds. Is there an overshooting effect?

9. How does your answer to question 8 change if PPP fails to hold in the long run? Explain why a long-run real depreciation is likely to occur, so that the PPP line rotates counter-clockwise.

10. In the development of the Mundell–Fleming *IS–LM* framework in Chapter 11, the possibility of overshooting was ignored. Comment on the implications of this omission.

11. How might you interpret the forward premium or discount of exchange rates often observed between currencies in fixed exchange rate systems?

12. Using Figure 19.7, show the short- and long-run effects of a real disturbance which leads to a long-run real appreciation. Using this approach, show the short- and long-run effects of an exogenous and unexpected increase in the nation's external debt.

Exercises: Applications

1. Suppose you observe German and French three-month interbank interest rates at 8% in both countries. At the same time, the French franc is trading at a 1% discount *vis-à-vis* the Deutschmark; that is, $(F - E)/E = 1\%$ on an annualized basis. Is there a profit opportunity available? If so, how could you exploit it?

2. Suppose now that the German short-term interest rate is 8%, the French rate of the same maturity is 7%, and the forward discount of the Deutschmark is exactly 1%, annualized. Yet France and Germany fix their exchange rates to each other, so that fluctuations of the currency are infrequent. Is there a profit opportunity available? If so, how could you exploit it?

3. If you are advising a company interested in buying a business in another country, how might exchange rate volatility influence your decision?

4. Suppose we observe a long-term nominal interest rate of 8% in both the USA and Germany. Yet the measured rate of inflation is 4% in Germany and 5% in the USA. How might you reconcile this observation with real interest parity (the international Fisher equation)?

5. The same arguments we have used for interest rate parity apply to longer-run interest rates as well. Suppose you observe ten-year US bonds yielding 9% and German bonds of the same yield to maturity yielding 8%. What is the implicit depreciation of the dollar over the next ten years? How could you reconcile this with the observation that comparable five-year bonds in both countries were yielding 8%? Does the role of risk aversion affect your answer?

6. The DKK (Danish crown) interest rate for three months is 6.5% per annum; it is 7.5% for the SEK (Swedish crown). The spot exchange rate is 0.85 DKK/SEK. What is the three-month forward premium? The forward exchange rate?

7. The six-month interest rate on DM is 5.5% and 7.0% on sterling, both per annum. The expected future exchange rate six months ahead is 1.8 DM/£. What is today's spot exchange rate? What interest rate should the Bank of England choose if it wants today's spot exchange rate to be 1.82?

Suggested Further Reading

The classic description of exchange rate behaviour is:

Mussa, Michael (1979), 'Empirical Regularities in the Behavior of Exchange Rates and Theories of the Foreign Exchange Market', in K. Brunner and A. Meltzer (eds.), *Carnegie Rochester Conference Series*, 11: 9–58.

A recent survey of exchange rate behaviour is:

Froot, Kenneth, and Thaler, Jeffrey (1990), 'Anomalies: Foreign Exchange', *Journal of Economic Perspectives*, 4: 179–92.

The first derivation of the overshooting result can be found in:

Dornbusch, Rudiger (1976), 'Expectations and Exchange Rate Dynamics', *Journal of Political Economy*, 84: 1161–76.

Other useful, more technical, references include:

de Grauwe, Paul, Janssens, Marc, and Leliaert, Hilde (1989), 'Real Exchange Rate Variability from 1920–6 and 1973–82', *Princeton Studies in International Finance*, 56.
Dornbusch, Rudiger (1980), *Open Economy Macroeconomics*, New York: Basic Books.
Meese, Richard (1990), 'Currency Fluctuations in the Post-Bretton Woods Era', *Journal of Economic Perspectives*, 4: 117–34.
Rogoff, Kenneth, and Obstfeld, Maurice (1995), 'Exchange Rate Dynamics Redux', *Journal of Political Economy*, 103: 624–60.

Appendix: Models of Exchange Rate Determination

The Monetary Model: Flexible Prices

We consider two identical countries at full employment. Foreign variables are indicated by an asterisk. Except for interest rates i and i^*, it will be convenient in this appendix to use lower-case variables for the logarithms of the corresponding upper-case variables; e.g. $m = \ln(M)$.[17] When the time subscript is suppressed, contemporaneous variables are being described.

Money supplies m and m^* are set by the monetary authorities. Money demand takes the linear form

$$(A19.1) \qquad m - p = \eta y - \phi i,$$
$$m^* - p^* = \eta y - \phi i^*,$$

where m, p, and y represent the logarithms of the money stock, the price level, and real GDP; η is the elasticity of real money demand with respect to real income; and ϕ is the semielasticity of real money demand with respect to nominal interest rates.

The uncovered interest parity condition holds so that the nominal interest rates must obey

$$(A19.2) \qquad i - i^* = \Delta E_{t+1}/E_t = {}_t\Delta e_{t+1},$$

where e is the logarithm of the nominal exchange rate and ${}_t\Delta$ represent the change in the corresponding variable expected at time t; i.e. ${}_t\Delta e_{t+1} = {}_t e_{t+1} - e_t$. Substituting (A19.2 into A19.1), we have

$$(A19.3) \qquad m - p = \eta y - \phi(i^* + {}_t e_{t+1} - e_t).$$

Expression (A19.3) describes the *MM* curve in the home country.

With completely flexible prices purchasing power parity holds continuously, so $EP^* = P$ and $\lambda = EP^*/P = 1$. Taking logs,

$$(A19.4) \qquad p = p^* + e.$$

Combining (A19.1), (A19.3), and (A19.4), we see that the log exchange rate e under flexible prices must obey

$$(A19.5) \qquad e_t = m_t - m_t^* + \eta(y_t^* - y_t) - \phi({}_t e_{t+1} - e_t).$$

As in the text, the exchange rate is forward-looking: in addition to current observable variables, it depends on expectations of its own future value.

Relative liquidity between the two countries is defined as $m_t - m_t^* + \eta(y_t^* - y_t)$, and represented by the symbol l_t. Thus, if m is high relative to m^*, or y is low relative to y^*, the measure indicates a relatively higher liquidity in the home country compared with abroad. Thus we can rewrite (A19.5) as

$$(A19.6) \qquad e_t = l_t + \phi({}_t e_{t+1} - e_t) = \frac{l_t + \phi_t e_{t+1}}{1 + \phi}.$$

The current exchange rate depends on two factors: the current state of relative liquidity at home and abroad, and the *expected* future exchange rate. Note how this goes beyond the discussion in the text by actually solving for the exchange rate as a function of present and expected future exogenous variables and its own future value. The relative weight depends on the sensitivity of money demand to interest rates, ϕ. In the next period, we have

$$(A19.7) \qquad e_{t+1} = \frac{l_{t+1} + \phi_{t+1} e_{t+2}}{1 + \phi}.$$

By substituting (A19.7) into (A19.6), we obtain[18]

$$(A19.8) \qquad e_t = \frac{l_t + \dfrac{\phi}{1 + \phi}({}_t l_{t+1} + \phi e_{t+1})}{1 + \phi}.$$

This recursive operation can be repeated again *ad infinitum* to obtain

$$(A19.9) \qquad e_t = \frac{1}{1 + \phi} \sum_{i=0}^{\infty} \left(\frac{\phi}{1 + \phi}\right)^i {}_t l_{t+i}.$$

Equation (A19.9) is a closed-form solution, i.e. in terms of exogenous variables only, since the right-hand side on longer contains the exchange rate (that which was to be explained). The exchange rate appears to be the 'present value' of current and future relative liquidity. In this model, where the only market is the money market (hence its being referred to as the monetary model of exchange rate determination), the *fundamental* determinant of the exchange rate—the right-hand side of (A19.9)—simply measures the relative money supply. In the next section we consider a more general model.

The Monetary Model: Sticky Prices

When prices are not fully flexible, goods market do not clear at full-employment output. This calls for adding the *IS*-curve goods market equilibrium condition:

$$(A19.10) \qquad y_t = -\beta r_t + \gamma(e_t + p^* - p_t),$$

---

[18] This substitution makes use of a relationship ${}_t({}_{t+1}x_{t+2}) = {}_t x_{t+2}$, which is called the law of iterated projections. It says that today's expectation of what will be expected tomorrow for a latter period, is simply today's expectation for the latter period. This relationship holds when agents process information efficiently and don't 'forget'. Readers interested in a mathematical treatment of this subject might look at Sargent (1979).

[17] This is because a first difference of the logarithm of some quantity is a close approximation to the quantity's growth rate over time.

where the real interest rate r is given by Fisher's equation:

(A19.11) $\qquad r_t = i_t - (p_{t+1} - p_t)$.

The *LM* curve is given by (A19.1) as before. The fact that prices are sticky is captured by the following condition:

(A19.12) $\qquad p_t = p_{t-1} + \theta(y_t - \bar{y})$,

with $\theta > 0$. This condition says that prices move gradually to eliminate excess demand for domestic goods, since $\bar{y}$ is trend output. If θ is low, prices are very sticky. Full price flexibility corresponds to the case where θ is infinite, for then the goods market always clears for GDP at its trend level.

To keep things simple, we consider two periods, plus the initial situation of full general equilibrium ($t = 0$). In period $t = 1$, the economy is described by the previous equations and prices are sticky ($\theta < \infty$). Period 2 corresponds to a return to full equilibrium and prices have recovered full flexibility ($\theta = \infty$). With $y_2 = \bar{y}$, long-run neutrality obtains and it is easy to see that

(A19.13) $\qquad e_2 - e_0 = p_2 - p_0 = m_2 - m_2$.

Period $t = 1$ is characterized by the following:

(A19.14) $\qquad (m_1 - m_0) - (p_1 - p_0) = \eta(y_1 - y_0)$
$\qquad\qquad - \phi(i^* + e_2 - e_1)$,

(A19.15) $\quad y_1 = -\beta[i^* + (e_2 - p_2) - (e_1 - p_1)] + \gamma(e_1 - p_1)$,

(A19.16) $\qquad p_1 - p_0 = \theta(y_1 - \bar{y})$.

We now consider the case where m_t is permanently increased at time $t = 1$ from m_0 to $\bar{m}$, i.e. $m_1 = m_2 = \bar{m}$. Eliminating y_1 and p_1, we obtain

(A19.17) $\qquad \left[1 - \dfrac{(\beta + \gamma)(\eta + \theta)}{1 + \theta(\beta + \gamma)} \right] (\bar{m} - m_0)$

$$= \left[\phi + \dfrac{(\beta + \gamma)(\eta + \theta)}{1 + \theta(\beta + \gamma)} \right] (e_1 - \bar{e}).$$

In the case where

$$1 - \dfrac{(\beta + \gamma)(\eta + \theta)}{1 + \theta(\beta + \gamma)} > 0,$$

we have $e_1 > \bar{e}$: the exchange rate overshoots as it increases to a value above its new long-run level (which increases proportionately to the money stock: see (A19.13). This occurs when β and γ are not too large, so that the *IS* curve does not shift 'too much' in Figure 19.9. The case of a stronger shift corresponds to

$$1 - \dfrac{(\beta + \gamma)(\eta + \theta)}{1 + \theta(\beta + \gamma)} < 0$$

in (A19.17), and therefore $e_1 < \bar{e}$. The exchange rate undershoots, since in period 1 it has not yet increased by the full amount of its long-run depreciation.

20

The International Monetary System

> An exchange rate in its very nature is a two-ended thing, and changes in exchange rates are therefore properly matters of international concern.
>
> *Bretton Woods Conference Proceedings*, i. 867

20.1. Overview

The choice of an exchange rate regime has always been a highly controversial issue. While it is usually discussed in terms of fixed versus flexible exchange rate regimes, a whole spectrum of arrangements is possible. Arrangements as of mid-1995 are presented in Table 20.1 as classified by the **International Monetary Fund (IMF)**, a key player in the modern international monetary system. A number of the major world currencies, including the US dollar, the Japanese yen, and the British pound, are officially freely floating, and by mid-1995 they shared this status with 57 other currencies. In principle, these countries leave it to the exchange markets to determine freely the value of their exchange rates, refraining from market interventions. Another 39 currencies were considered as floating but less freely, either because they are adjusted according to particular rules or because interventions are undertaken when the authorities see fit to do so.

Moving in the direction of fixed exchange rates, we find that less than half of the world's currencies are pegged, although the relevant parity varies from country to country. Some (23) are pegged to the US dollar, some (15) to the French franc, the largest group (30) to 'baskets' of currencies, either custom-made or

Table 20.1. Exchange Rate Arrangements as of June 1995[a]

Currency pegged to					Flexibility limited in terms of a single currency or group of currencies		More flexible		
US dollar	French franc	Other currency	SDR	Other composite[b]	Single currency[c]	Co-operative arrangements[d]	Adjusted according to a set of indicators[e]	Other managed floating	Independently floating
Antigua & Barbuda	Benin	Bhutan (Indian rupee)	Libya	Bangladesh	Bahrain	Austria	Chile	Algeria	Afghanistan
Argentina	Burkina Faso	Estonia (Deutschmark)	Myanmar	Botswana	Qatar	Belgium	Ecuador	Angola	Albania
Bahamas, The	Cameroon		Seychelles	Burundi	Saudi Arabia	Denmark	Nicaragua	Belarus	Armenia
Barbados	C. African Rep.	Kiribati (Australian dollar)		Cape Verde	United Arab Emirates	France		Brazil	Australia
Belize	Chad			Cyprus		Germany		Cambodia	Azerbaijan
Djibouti	Comoros	Lesotho (South African rand)		Czech Republic		Ireland		China, P.R.	Bolivia
Dominica	Congo			Fiji		Luxemburg		Colombia	Bulgaria
Grenada	Côte d'Ivoire			Iceland		Netherlands		Croatia	Canada
Iraq	Equatorial Guinea	Namibia (South African rand)		Jordan		Portugal		Dominican Rep.	Costa Rica
Liberia	Gabon			Kuwait		Spain		Egypt	El Salvador
Lithuania	Mali	San Marino (Italian lira)		Malta				Eritrea	Ethiopia
Marshall Islands	Niger			Mauritania				Georgia	Finland
Micronesia, Fed. States of	Senegal	Swaziland (South African rand)		Morocco				Greece	Gambia, The
Nigeria	Togo			Nepal				Guinea-Bissau	Ghana
Oman				Slovak Republic				Honduras	Guatemala
				Solomon Islands				Hungary	Guinea
								Indonesia	Guyana
									Haiti

Table 20.1. (cont.)

Currency pegged to					Flexibility limited in terms of a single currency or group of currencies		More flexible		
US dollar	French franc	Other currency	SDR	Other composite[b]	Single currency[c]	Cooperative arrangements[d]	Adjusted according to a set of indicators[e]	Other managed floating	Independently floating
Panama				Thailand				Israel	India
St. Kitts & Nevis				Tonga				Korea	Iran, I. R. of
St. Lucia				Vanuatu				Lao P.D. Rep	Italy
St. Vincent and the Grenadines				Western Samoa				Latvia	Jamaica
Syrian Arab Rep.								Macedonia, FYR of	Japan
Turkmenistan								Malaysia	Kazakhstan
Venezuela								Maldives	Kenya
Yemen, Republic of								Mauritius	Kyrgyz Rep.
								Pakistan	Lebanon
								Poland	Madagascar
								Russia	Malawi
								Singapore	Mexico
								Slovenia	Moldova
								Sri Lanka	Mongolia
								Sudan	Mozambique
								Tunisia	New Zealand
								Turkey	Norway
								Uruguay	Papua New Guinea
								Vietnam	Paraguay
									Peru
									Philippines
									Romania
									Rwanda
									São Tomé and P.
									Sierra Leone
									Somalia
									South Africa
									Suriname
									Sweden
									Switzerland
									Tajikistan, Rep. of
									Tanzania
									Trinidad and Tobago
									Uganda
									Ukraine
									United Kingdom
									United States
									Uzbekistan
									Zaïre
									Zambia
									Zimbabwe

[a] Excluding the currency of Cambodia, for which no current information is available. For members with dual or multiple exchange markets, the arrangement shown is that in the major market.
[b] Comprises currencies that are pegged to various 'baskets' of currencies of the members' own choice, as distinct from the SDR basket.
[c] Exchange rates of all currencies have shown limited flexibility in terms of the US dollar.
[d] Refers to the co-operative arrangement maintained under the European Monetary System.
[e] Includes exchange arrangements under which the exchange rate is adjusted at relatively frequent intervals, on the basis of indicators determined by the respective member-countries.

Source: IMF

according to a pre-existing formula, like the IMF's special drawing right (SDR).[1] Three regional arrangements can be identified: the European Monetary System (EMS), the Gulf countries' joint management of their currencies *vis-à-vis* the US dollar, and a number of French-speaking African nations which peg to the French franc.

The present arrangements have emerged from the collapse of the postwar system, which was put in place as a reaction to the interwar experience following the abandonment of the gold and silver standards. History lays the ground for the classic debate between fixed and flexible exchange rate regimes and an analysis of some of the current proposals for international monetary reform.

20.2. History of Monetary Arrangements

20.2.1. The Gold Standard and How It Worked

For centuries, both domestic and international trade was carried out with gold and silver. Metallic monies had been in use for millennia, because, as explained in Chapter 8, they were easily recognizable and acceptable by others. Metal was scarce, and not easily subject to manipulation; it was a medium of exchange that also served well as a store of value. National currencies as we know them did not exist. The responsibility of public authorities was to guarantee the precious metal content of their money; hence the essential role of issuing agencies, which were continuously melting coins—often produced abroad—and coining their own. In fact, national authorities sometimes coined foreign money as well.

Until the late 1870s, gold and silver coexisted as the main monetary metals. Progressively over the nineteenth century, bank notes started to circulate alongside gold and silver. The invention of paper money can be seen as an economic response to the resource costs of gold- and silver-based monetary systems. Often issued by private banks, banknotes were not always fully backed by metallic reserves, however, and uncertainty about this backing led to occasional banking crises. This is one reason why central banks were created, and why they displaced private banks as issuers of paper money. Central banks were formally required to hold close to 100% gold or silver to back their issues of bank notes. These notes were convertible into gold, coins, or bullion at the holder's request, and conversion was indeed routine. With close to 100% backing, banknotes simply represented another way of holding gold or silver.

The **gold standard** lasted from 1879 to 1914, less than forty years. It emerged in the wake of the demise of bimetallism (see Box 20.1) and collapsed one month before the outbreak of the First World War. The gold standard era is sometimes nostalgically associated with the rapid industrialization of the time and is regarded as a great economic success story. This 'success' is often attributed to the gold standard's automatic adjustment mechanisms, and its resilience is seen as the outcome of the linkage that it established between domestic and international conditions. In fact, the gold standard was not without problems, nor were these adjustment mechanisms as automatic as is often believed.

20.2.1.1. Domestic operation of the gold standard

As long as gold was the sole (or main) form of money, demand was ensured by the need to carry out transactions, and supply was limited by its scarcity. Even large discoveries amounted to small disturbances, for the amounts brought out (the flows of newly coined gold) were very small in comparison to existing stocks. Monetary authorities could establish only the gold content of their own currencies. Under such an arrangement, monetary policy is well described by the Mundell–Fleming model under fixed exchange rates, described in Chapter 11. It was entirely dedicated to the defence of the exchange rate, i.e. the gold value of the currency.

20.2.1.2. International operation of the gold standard

The gold standard is a fixed exchange rate regime. If the USA sets the price of dollars for gold at \$35/ounce and France does the same at FF 210/ounce, then triangular arbitrage will prevent the exchange rate of dollars for francs from deviating very far from FF6/\$. If it rose above this figure, say to 6.2, it would make sense to purchase gold in France with francs, transport it to the USA, tender it to the central bank in exchange for US dollars, and, finally, convert these dollars into

---

[1] The special drawing rights (SDR) are described below in S. 20.3.2.

BOX 20.1. BIMETALLISM AND GRESHAM'S LAW

It was only at the end of the nineteenth century that gold became the premier international medium of exchange. For centuries, silver and gold had competed against each other. **Bimetallism**, as the system was called, established a fixed parity between gold and silver, and coins in both metals were usually accepted for all transactions, both nationally and internationally. The relative value of gold and silver was set by international agreements, which were occasionally called into question as new discoveries of either metal threatened to upset the parity. Troubled times then followed with the operation of **Gresham's law**. This principle states that the currency (metal) that is more valuable (in non-monetary markets) than its official rate stops circulating: 'bad money chases out good'.[2]

Partly because silver became more plentiful, bimetallism ceased to exist in Europe in the 1870s. The last major countries to defend bimetallism formed the Latin Monetary Union in 1865, setting a parity of 15.5 ounces of silver for 1 ounce of gold. This union consisted of Belgium, France, Italy, and Switzerland. (For this reason all save Italy use the 'franc' as the name of their national money.) In the USA, where a central monetary authority was absent, bimetallism survived for a longer time. The final blow occurred when the newly created German state switched to gold and unloaded large amounts of silver on the free market. The risk of complete gold loss in a world under a gold standard forced the remaining countries to abandon bimetallism entirely.

---

francs in France. For every franc tendered in France for gold, the transaction would yield $FF(1/210)(35)(6.2) = 1.03\overset{.}{3}$, a profit of 3.3%. This example ignores transaction costs, which include the bid–ask spread and the cost of transporting the gold across the ocean.[3] Once these are accounted for, there will generally be a band within which the exchange rate will move without triggering arbitrage activity.

A second feature of the gold standard was the free flow of gold as the counterpart of balance of payment imbalances. A country running a trade deficit would lose gold to its trading partners; the metal was physically shipped abroad to pay for the excess of imports over exports. The exported gold coins were then minted and coined in the currency of the surplus country. A trade deficit implied a shrinking money supply, a surplus an expanding money supply. This had two consequences. First, the reduction of the money supply in the deficit country led to higher interest rates and to a capital inflow; a capital account surplus financed the trade deficit, but higher interest rates tended to slow economic activity. Second, declining money supply translated into falling prices (and contracting economic activity), which improved the country's competitiveness and restored the trade balance. In the surplus country the process went in the oppo-

site direction: balance of payment surpluses led to gold inflows, which raised the money supply and depressed interest rates. In the medium run, higher inflation would tend to reduce the surplus. This symmetric process is often called the **Hume mechanism**, after the Scottish economist and philosopher David Hume who first described it.

20.2.1.3. The main benefits of the gold standard

The world has never seen, and probably never will see, a true pure gold standard. As will be discussed below, this is not necessarily a regrettable circumstance! Chapter 8 stressed that virtually anything can serve as money—including paper, bank ledger entries, and large stones in the South Pacific—as long as it is generally accepted as a means of payment.

Why do some observers regret the passing of the gold standard? First, the Hume mechanism had the virtue of credibility. Under a gold standard, monetary policy is entirely determined by the stock of gold. In principle, it is out of the politicians' hands. Second, with the money supply naturally constrained, inflation is not likely to emerge on any significant scale. This is documented in Table 20.2. Third, it does not require that a particular country be at the centre of the world monetary system, avoiding conflicts on which country that should be.

20.2.1.4. Limits of automatism

The gold standard did not operate without its problems. It was regulated by the central country of the time, the UK. Sterling was the main currency, backed by the most developed financial centre, London.

---

[2] The principle bears the name of its 16th c. discoverer. Sir Thomas Gresham had been in charge of royal finances, then became a foreign exchange trader in Antwerp until he created the Royal Exchange, better known today as the London Stock Exchange. It is sometimes argued that the gold standard in the UK was an artefact of Isaac Newton's decision in 1717 to undervalue silver in terms of gold; within little time, Sir Isaac had only gold on his hands.

[3] These transport costs are unnecessary as long as participating countries are willing to serve as custodial agents for each other's gold—as was often the case in the heyday of the gold standard period.

Table 20.2. Inflation Rates in Five Countries, 1900–1913 (annual average rate of increase in GDP deflator, %)

France	Japan	USA	Germany	UK
0.9	2.8	1.3	1.3	0.9

Source: Maddison (1989)

Britain had been on the gold standard since 1819, when the Bank of England received its key statutes (Peel's Act). Furthermore, Britain was the largest creditor country, thus providing the rest of the world with sterling balances, which often ended up as reserve currency held by other central banks.[4] If the Bank of England was setting the interest rate for the world, it was doing so with an eye to British economic conditions. In principle, liabilities issued by the Bank of England (banknotes and bank reserves) should have automatically increased and the interest rate should have declined whenever Britain ran balance of payments deficits. In fact, the Bank of England maintained a ratio of reserves to deposits—known as the Proportion—that was well below 100%; at the height of the gold standard late in the nineteenth century, the Proportion fluctuated between 30% and 50%. To the extent that the Proportion could vary, the Bank of England possessed considerable leeway in setting its discount rate and shielding the money supply from external influences.

Other countries also tinkered with the tight theoretical link between trade imbalances and the money supply. Some actually imposed limits on gold exports and imports, as well as on minting and coinage. Furthermore, gold was not the only asset backing national banknotes. Many central banks accumulated sizeable reserves in the form of foreign currencies: first and foremost the pound sterling, but also French francs and German marks. It is reported that, when the gold standard is assumed to have established its dominance in the early 1880s, Belgium, Finland, and Sweden were holding more foreign exchange than gold as backing. Thus, the gold standard never relied on gold primarily, and the assumed link between metal and money supply was less than fully automatic. Furthermore, the gold reserves of the Bank of England quickly fell below the value of the Bank's liabilities towards other central banks, leading to an 'overhang' of unbacked British debt. It is somewhat surprising that the overhang never threatened the credibility of external sterling liabilities.

20.2.1.5. Problems with a metallic standard

While the gold standard may have been mismanaged, there are a number of inherent problems with any metallic—or commodity—standard. Table 20.3 provides a comparison of macroeconomic conditions in the USA and the UK between the gold standard and postwar periods. While average growth was comparable to the postwar experience and inflation was lower, the table also shows that both measures were more variable under the gold standard. Unstable economic conditions imposed serious costs on individuals at the time, as is made clear by the unemployment rates displayed in Figure 20.1. Was it just a coincidence? In fact, the very automatic mechanisms that are often considered the main advantage of the gold standard imply such an outcome. It may well be that many countries did not fully abide by the automatisms precisely because of these costs.

This is precisely the conflict between rules and discretion addressed in Chapter 16. Automatism means that a choice is made in favour of rules—very strict ones, if actually observed—under the gold standard. With the money supply largely a function of external balance, macroeconomic adjustments were necessarily mediated by nominal price changes. If prices adjust slowly—that is a central message of Chapters 11 and 12—this process may take a long time. In the meantime, the economy 'goes through the wringer' of unemployment and economic distress. Output, unemployment, and in the medium run price variability most likely reflect the presence of nominal rigidities.

Another problem is that the national supply of gold depends on natural discoveries, private tenders of hoarded gold[5] to the central bank, and sales by foreign central banks. During the late nineteenth century, rapid economic growth brought with it a rapidly expanding demand for real balances. If the gold supply is limited, an increase in the real money supply can occur only if the price level declines—the price of gold in terms of other goods must rise. This may induce an increase in the supply of hoarded gold tendered to the central bank, and thereby in the money supply, but the process takes time, and liquidity shortages invari-

---

[4] During the 40 years preceding the First World War, an average of some 20% of British savings were invested abroad.

[5] By 'hoarded gold' is meant not only gold bars (bullion) in private hands, but also industrial and cosmetic gold which could be melted down into bullion form.

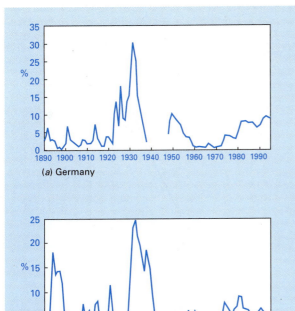

(a) Germany

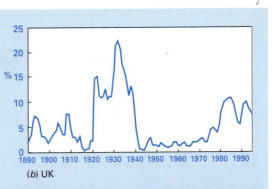

(b) UK

(c) USA

Figure 20.1. Unemployment Rates since 1890: Germany, the UK, and the USA

Although each country reveals its own particular movements in the unemployment rate, there are important coincidences. These are associated with the years following the First World War, the Great Depression, and the 1980s. In contrast to European countries, the US unemployment rate has returned recently to levels roughly consistent with the experience of the past century.

Sources: Mitchell (1978); *US Dept of Commerce*; OECD, *Main Economic Indicators*

Table 20.3. Macroeconomic Conditions in the USA and the UK: Gold Standard (1870–1913) and Postwar Periods (1946–1979)

	UK		USA	
	Gold standard	Postwar	Gold standard	Postwar
Growth rates				
Average	1.4	2.4	1.9	2.1
Standard deviation	2.5	1.4	3.5	1.6
Inflation				
Average	−0.7	5.6	0.1	2.8
Variability	4.6	6.2	5.4	4.8
Money supply growth				
Average	1.5	5.9	6.1	5.7
Variability	1.6	1.0	0.8	0.5

Notes: Growth is measured by the rate of growth of per capita income. Inflation is the rate of growth of the wholesale price index. Variability is the coefficient of variation.

Source: Cooper (1982)

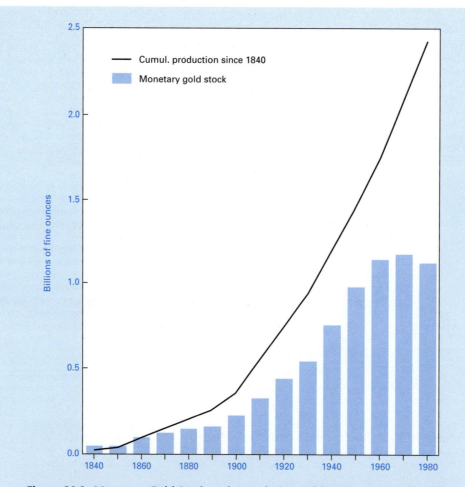

Figure 20.2. Monetary Gold Stock and Cumulative Gold Production, 1840–1980

Although gold production has continued over time, its rate of increase has tapered off. At the same time, the demand for gold for industrial purposes has increased over the past hundred years. Perhaps not coincidentally, gold stocks held by central banks have remained flat for several decades.

Source: Cooper (1982)

ably lead to an economic slowdown. Figure 20.2 shows that the gold supply did not increase in a regular way over this time interval, and was subject to long periods of scarcity followed by the great discoveries in California, Alaska, and South Africa, as well as technological advances in mining and mineral processing. As these shocks were largely random, the money supply and the price level were hardly stable. In fact, during periods of extreme liquidity shortage, banks were quick to introduce financial innovation to substitute for gold.

20.2.2. The Interwar Period

Three sub-periods can be identified in the history of interwar monetary arrangements. The first ranges from the end of the First World War to the return to the gold standard in 1926. The gold standard was then maintained until 1931, and was followed by a period of managed float marked by competitive devaluations and a collapse of world trade as a consequence of the Great Depression.

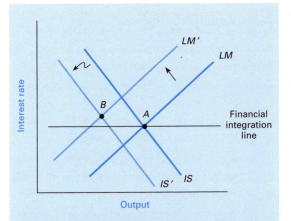

Figure 20.3. The British Deflation Illustrated

Tight monetary and fiscal policies move the economy from point *A* to point *B*. The high interest rate leads to an overvaluation. The output contraction is followed by a deflation.

20.2.2.1. The free float period (1919–1926)

After the First World War, costly reconstruction prevented any country from challenging British–American supremacy in monetary affairs. Except for a gold embargo, the USA had never left the gold standard during the war. The UK, under the leadership of Chancellor of the Exchequer Winston Churchill, quickly pledged a return to the gold standard at the prewar parity of $4.86.[6] In the aftermath of an expensive conflict financed by central bank credit and accompanied by high inflation, the pound reached a low of $3.40 in 1920. Strongly deflationary policies were required, and implemented, to accomplish Mr Churchill's objective. In Figure 20.3, these policies are represented by leftward shifts of both the *LM* (tight money) and *IS* curves (budgetary restraint). At point *B*, the interest rate rises above the world level, the currency is overvalued, and the economy is in recession. Sustaining a below-trend GDP long enough, inflation fell below the rest of the world rate, which alleviated the over-valuation. By 1921 the pound had regained its prewar parity, but was still considered significantly overvalued in real terms. Simply fixing a parity was not enough: a central feature of the gold standard is that exports and imports of gold are free, a step that could be taken by the UK only in 1925.

Germany and a number of other central European countries returned to the gold standard only after experiencing and vanquishing their celebrated hyper-inflations. France devalued the franc immediately after the war but underwent rapid inflation in the years 1922–6. Its return to the gold standard in 1926 after the Poincaré stabilization marked the return to the prewar situation.[7]

20.2.2.2. Ephemeral gold standard (1927–1931)

The newly restored gold standard had two competing centres: London and New York. Britain had an overvalued currency; the periphery included countries such as France with undervalued currencies. Gold holdings became an ever smaller part of the periphery reserves as most central banks were accumulating dollar and pound balances and sterilizing changes in their foreign exchange reserves. Free convertibility between bank notes and gold was suspended, and most central banks actively discouraged or prohibited the circulation of gold coins.[8] The Hume mechanism, the key automatism behind the success of the prewar gold standard, was circumvented. The vestiges of the system were the principle of currency convertibility[9] and fixed exchange rates.

When the Great Depression hit the world after 1929, the gold standard was weak. With its overvalued currency, Britain was particularly vulnerable. Its gold reserves shrank quickly while France, with an undervalued currency, was accumulating gold and selling off its sterling balances. Soon Britain's official liabilities exceeded its gold reserves. When it suspended external convertibility in September 1931 and let sterling float, the gold standard was over.

20.2.2.3. The managed float (1931–1939)

After Britain allowed the pound to depreciate sharply to about $3.3/£, a number of countries holding large sterling balances followed suit (Table 20.4). Overnight, formerly overvalued currencies became undervalued. At a time when all countries were struggling against the Great Depression, these devaluations were seen as

---

[6] The USA had not changed its gold parity, so returning to a dollar price of $4.86 per pound was identical to restoring the old gold sterling parity. Box 13.4 recounts this episode.

[7] For more on the Poincaré stabilization, see Box 16.6.

[8] In some cases, e.g. Britain, convertibility was possible only for large denominations, since the Bank of England restricted its conversion to bullion (as opposed to coins). The system is sometimes referred to as the 'gold bullion standard'.

[9] A currency is declared convertible when holders, both private and official, may exchange it without restriction. Convertibility does not necessarily imply a fixed exchange rate, since a floating rate system also allows participants freely to purchase and sell foreign exchange as

Table 20.4. Beggar-thy-Neighbour Depreciations, Various Countries, 1931–1938 (value of currencies as a % of their 1929 gold parity)

	1931	1932	1933	1934	1935	1936	1937	1938
Belgium	100.1	100.2	100.1	99.9	78.6	72.0	71.7	71.8
Denmark	93.5	70.3	55.8	50.0	48.5	49.0	48.6	48.1
France	100.1	100.3	100.0	100.0	100.0	92.4	61.0	43.4
Germany	99.2	99.7	99.6	98.6	100.3	100.1	99.7	99.6
Italy	98.9	97.4	99.0	97.0	93.0	82.0	59.0	59.0
Norway	93.5	67.2	62.7	56.3	54.5	55.2	54.7	54.1
Netherlands	100.1	100.3	100.1	100.0	100.0	94.9	80.9	88.8
Switzerland	100.6	100.6	100.2	100.1	100.0	92.6	70.2	70.0
UK	93.2	72.0	68.1	61.8	59.8	60.5	60.0	59.3
USA	100.0	100.0	80.7	59.6	59.4	59.2	59.1	59.1

Source: League of Nations, *Statistical Bulletins*

tools to export the recession. A gold bloc, including France, Belgium, the Netherlands, Italy, Switzerland, and Poland, was established to resist the temptation of retaliatory depreciations. The situation worsened seriously in 1933 when the USA, the remaining centre of the gold standard, imposed an embargo on gold exports, introduced exchange controls, and depreciated the dollar from $20.67 to $35 per ounce of pure gold. The *coup de grâce* was the dissolution of the gold bloc following the devaluation of the Belgian franc in 1935.

'Beggar-thy-neighbour' policies (competitive devaluations) were soon followed by tariffs designed to restrict imports. Table 20.5 provides some examples of the forces that led to a marked slowdown of international trade as shown in the spiral of Figure 20.4.

20.2.2.4. Lessons from the interwar period

This period profoundly influenced those who were responsible for the reconstruction of the international monetary system after the Second World War. The first lesson was that freely floating exchange rates are subject to inherently high levels of volatility, as suggested by the overshooting principle (Chapter 19). Second, competitive devaluations inevitably trigger self-defeating retaliations. Third, an international monetary system is stable only if it relies on a single

Table 20.5. Steps in the Tariff War, 1929–1932

1929		
March	USA imposes special tariffs to protect farmers	
	France and Italy increase tariffs on motor cars	
1930		
April	Australia increases tariffs across the board	
June	USA sets wide-ranging tariffs (Smoot–Hawley Act)	
	Italy increases tariffs on motor cars	
July	Spain increases tariffs across the board	
	Switzerland imposes boycott of US products	
1931		
	Exchange controls set in Germany and Austria, followed by much of Eastern Europe	
1932		
August	Canada raises tariffs three times	

Source: Kindleberger (1973)

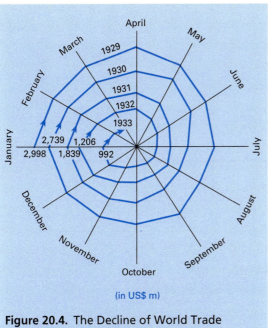

Figure 20.4. The Decline of World Trade during the Great Depression

During the period 1929–33, the enormous increases in world trade that had been accomplished in the previous three decades were wiped out by a spiral of protectionist measures. This famous illustration by Professor Kindleberger of MIT shows just how quickly trade wars can get out of hand.

Source: Kindleberger (1973)

centre, a variant of the $N-1$ problem presented later in Chapter 21. The dual British–American leadership was seen as a source of instability contributing to the collapse of the gold standard. Furthermore, leadership imposes strict responsibilities for the country at the centre: its policies must be sound, its currency must be neither overvalued nor undervalued, and its international assets must be consistent with its external liabilities. Finally, a point that was stressed in the 1920s but quickly forgotten, central banks must be shielded from political pressures such as those discussed in Chapter 16.

20.2.3. The Bretton Woods System of Fixed Exchange Rates

20.2.3.1. The principles

Preparations for the Bretton Woods conference of July 1944 started long before the end of the Second

World War.[10] The conference led to the creation of the International Monetary Fund (IMF), an international institution set up to help manage and monitor international payments. The new world monetary order was to stand in sharp contrast to the interwar situation.

First and foremost, exchange rates were to be fixed. Realignments without IMF approval were prohibited. The IMF was endowed with financial resources to help provide an alternative to devaluation for countries facing balance of payments difficulties. Exchange rate fixity implied the official declaration of a fixed **par** or **central value** (*vis-à-vis* gold or the US dollar: see next section), and each country was committed to maintaining the market value of its currency within a band of fluctuation of 1% around the par value. Exchange controls and tariffs were allowed only as temporary measures for the immediate postwar period.[11] Actually, full currency convertibility was achieved by European currencies only in 1958, and most of the less developed countries (LDCs) still have non-convertible currencies and capital controls. With the exception of Greece, EU countries have removed most significant forms of capital controls.

20.2.3.2. Gold and the dollar

While the Bretton Woods agreements were vague, practice set a definitive hierarchy among currencies. Officially, all currencies were defined in terms of gold. Yet, at the end of the Second World War, the USA held about 70% of all gold reserves and was the only country credible enough to set a gold parity. The best that the other countries could do, with the US Marshall Plan providing them with dollar balances,[12] was to declare a parity *vis-à-vis* the US currency. The outcome was a *de facto* two-layer system, represented in Figure 20.5. Gold remained the fundamental standard of value, but for all currencies this was mediated by the dollar, hence the name **gold exchange standard** given to the Bretton Woods system. The system thus relied on the ability of the USA to maintain the declared parity of $35 per ounce of gold.

Here an important lesson of the interwar experience

---

[10] The celebrated conference that gave birth to the postwar international monetary system was held at Bretton Woods, a ski resort in the US state of New Hampshire. The US and British plans, published in 1943, bore the imprints of the US Treasury Secretary Harry White and of John Maynard Keynes, respectively.

[11] Keynes was in favour of controls on short-term capital flows. The rolling back of tariffs was later entrusted to the GATT (General Agreement on Tariffs and Trade).

[12] The Marshall Plan was a massive aid programme for post-war Western Europe funded by the USA.

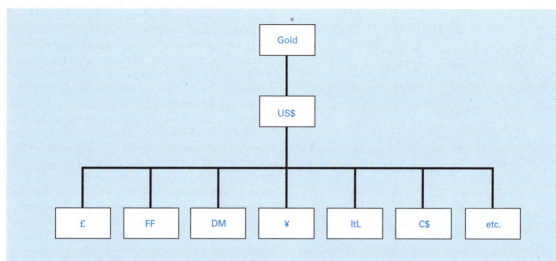

Figure 20.5. The Three Layers of Bretton Woods

The three layers of the Bretton Woods system consisted of gold, the US dollar, and the other participating currencies. The USA declared a gold parity for the dollar, thereby pegging to gold. Intervention took place mostly in dollars, but implicit was the understanding that gold stood behind the dollars.

was ignored. The use of the dollar as the world currency meant that the USA would need to run persistent balance of payments deficits in order to supply the world with liquidity. Since the USA ran current account surpluses during the 1950s, the concern was widespread that the rest of the world would experience a dollar shortage, with a contractionary influence, much as with the limited gold supply under the gold standard.

20.2.3.3. The International Monetary Fund

The initial experience of the Bretton Woods system was positive. After a rash of postwar parity adjustments—including an unauthorized devaluation of the French franc in 1948—exchange rate stability prevailed. Trade expanded quickly and was easily financed by dollar balances, provided initially within the framework of the Marshall Plan for European reconstruction, then by US trade deficits and capital flows.

The International Monetary Fund became the much respected watch-dog of the fixed exchange rate system. It developed an elaborate system of loans to countries suffering balance of payments difficulties. The Fund's resources were provided by member-country deposits. These deposits are made 25% in gold or US dollars—depending on the country's gold stock—and 75% in the country's own currency. The size of a coun-

try's deposit, based on its size in international trade, determines its **quota**.[13] Quotas determine each member-country's voting weight and its borrowing rights.

The IMF holds a large stock of resources—gold, dollars, and a mix of all the currencies of member-countries. Most of these currencies, being nonconvertible, are not usable at all. Devaluations were in principle restricted to cases of 'fundamental disequilibria', a concept apparently never formally spelled out so as to give the IMF flexibility in reviewing proposed parity changes. In order to help member-nations avoid devaluation, the IMF made, and still makes, resources available for immediate lending—called 'purchase agreements' when effected and 'repurchase' when reimbursed. In practice, each member-country is eligible for immediate lending in convertible currency up to 25% of its quota, the so-called *gold tranche*. Beyond that, lending becomes conditional: the IMF grants loans in exchange for a formal agreement on specific policy steps and results designed to solve the 'non-fundamental' part of external disequilibria. The rationale is that temporary disturbances are optimally dealt with through current account imbalances. This **conditionality** has become the central source of power of the

[13] The complex formula used to determine the quota also accounts for the country's size and is flexible enough to be agreed upon in negotiations.

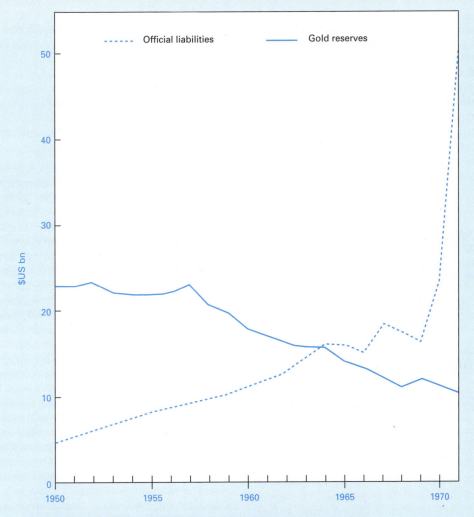

Figure 20.6. US Official Liabilities and Gold Reserves, 1950–1970

As long as foreigners were willing to hold dollars, the USA could finance its large balance of payments deficits by increases in foreign holdings of official assets (dollars held by central banks). Yet the gold reserve of the USA declined over the entire period shown, as foreign central banks occasionally tendered their dollars for gold. Sometime in 1964, the stock of external official claims against the US gold exceeded the dollar's gold backing. In that instant, the credibility of the gold exchange standard was called into question.

Sources: Dam (1982); IMF

IMF, and has survived the collapse of the Bretton Woods system.

20.2.3.4. Squaring the circle: the Triffin problem

The growth of international trade meant that more 'international money' would be needed. Since the US dollar was the international money, it became clear that somehow more dollars would have to be made available to the world economy. The **Triffin paradox**[14] holds that, in order for internationally held dollar balances to grow, the USA must run balance of payments deficits. Eventually, US official liabilities must outgrow the country's gold reserves. Figure 20.6 shows that this happened in 1964. But then, how could the USA

---

[14] It is named after Belgian-born and Yale-based economist Robert Triffin, who first identified the 'fundamental flaw' of the Bretton Woods system.

simultaneously guarantee the gold value of the US dollar, the fundament of the Bretton Woods system?

The Triffin problem is a reflection of a deeper question: what should the world monetary standard be? Precious metals, with their fluctuating supply unrelated to international money needs, do not fit the bill. At the same time, no single country can supply the world's reserve money. If it is backed by gold it is likely to fail, because its gold reserves are unlikely to keep up with the growth in world trade and the demand for international reserves. If it is not backed by gold, it represents a seigniorage windfall to the country at the centre, which other member-countries will find objectionable. One solution would be to have an international organization issue the international money; this was the Bancor proposal of Keynes at the Bretton Woods conference. The alternative, to drop gold backing entirely, was adopted *de facto*.

20.2.3.5. The collapse of the Bretton Woods system

A conjunction of events brought the situation to a climax. An increase in US public spending, arising from the Vietnam War and domestic social programmes, accelerated growth and deepened current account deficits. At the same time, countries critical of the system, which they had been unable to shape at Bretton Woods, began to protest loudly. The French President de Gaulle publicly complained about the US '*privilège exorbitant*', allowing the USA to finance through seigniorage its political activities (the Vietnam War) and economic power (the acquisition of European corporations by US companies). In a dramatic gesture, France began to swap dollars for gold in the mid-1960s, increasing its precious metal stock from $3.7 to $5.2 billion between 1964 and 1966.

The markets took notice and forced a number of monetary authorities comprising the Gold Pool (Belgium, Italy, the Netherlands, Switzerland, West Germany, the UK, and the USA, with France inactive after 1967) to sell gold to maintain the $35/ounce parity. As the drain on official gold holdings accelerated, these countries pulled out of the gold market and declared that they would trade gold only among themselves—would neither sell to nor buy from private parties—at the official price. The market started to trade gold at a price substantially higher. Tensions within the Gold Pool grew until President Nixon's historic decision to suspend the gold parity of the US dollar on 15 August 1971, a date that marked the end of the Bretton Woods system.

20.2.4. After Bretton Woods

20.2.4.1. From the Smithsonian Agreement to Jamaica

The severing of the gold–dollar link wrecked a key component of the Bretton Woods arrangement, but the gold crisis was not the sole factor in its demise. Inflation had been rising in most countries in the late 1960s, but at increasingly different rates (Figure 20.7). Even a simple application of the PPP rule was enough to call into question a number of parities that had remained unchanged since the late 1940s.[15] Speculative capital movements started to challenge the old order. Britain and Italy came under IMF conditionality in 1969. The pound was devalued in 1967, followed by the French franc in 1969, a year that also witnessed a revaluation of the Deutschmark.

In a last effort to salvage the system, an agreement was reached in December 1971 at a meeting held at the Smithsonian Institution in Washington, DC. The dollar was devalued *vis-à-vis* gold to $38 per ounce, yet it remained inconvertible into gold even among central banks. Some currencies were revalued, others devalued; the margins of fluctuations enlarged from 1% to 2.25% around par value; and it was hoped that the revamped system of fixed exchange rates could survive. The EC countries decided to stick to a reduced (half) margin: this was the '**Snake**' arrangement. By the end of 1972, the pound was floating, soon to be followed by the Swiss franc, the Italian lira, and the Japanese yen. In March 1973, the remaining 'Snake' members decided to float jointly *vis-à-vis* all other currencies including the dollar within a wider 2.25% margin. France left, then re-entered, as did Italy; then both left again. Sweden and Norway joined informally. By 1975 the principle of fixed exchange rates was dead, at least for the convertible currencies of the industrialized countries. In January 1976, the Jamaica agreement made official the new role of the IMF: from then on, it would be in charge of overseeing a world monetary system of possibly flexible exchange rates.

---

[15] The French franc had been devalued in 1958 and the Deutschmark and Dutch guilder revalued in 1961.

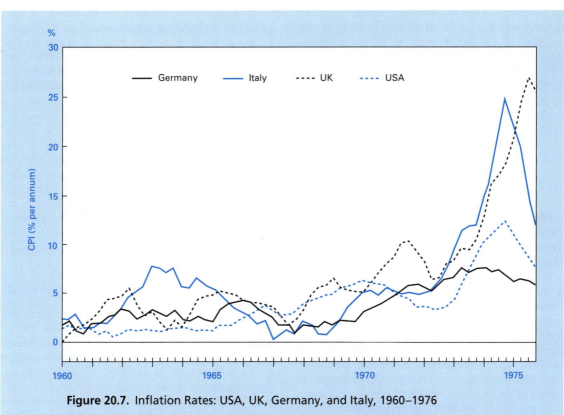

Figure 20.7. Inflation Rates: USA, UK, Germany, and Italy, 1960–1976

Inflation rates during the Bretton Woods era moved closely together, which is characteristic of a fixed exchange rate regime. As soon as the system collapsed in 1971, inflation rates diverged sharply.

Source: IMF

20.3. The International Monetary Fund and its Role Today

The influence of the IMF is probably stronger today than in the heyday of the Bretton Woods system, if only because it is now in charge of a system that is not fraught with internal inconsistencies. The current situation is often described as a non-system, because each country is free to choose its own exchange rate regime, the status of gold is in limbo, and there is no agreed-upon international currency. On the other hand, it is a flexible arrangement, able to weather disturbances in a pragmatic way, under the umbrella of the IMF.

20.3.1. IMF Assistance

In a world of perfectly free exchange rates, external imbalances are only temporary. Eventually, the exchange rate moves to eliminate external disequilibria. The overshooting principle and the arguments presented in Chapter 19 suggest that this is not likely to be the preferred solution for most countries. To the extent that exchange rates are managed, external imbalances remain a potential problem. Deficits and surpluses are an appropriate response to temporary disturbances, but the size of negative imbalances may occasionally exceed the financial means of many countries. The IMF has retained the resources deposited by its member-countries and continues to lend them under the conditionality principle. In fact, at the time of the oil shocks, its resources were in such great demand that the IMF enlarged them through a variety of 'facilities'.

20.3.2. Special Drawing Rights

An unresolved issue continues to cause problems for the world economic order: what should be the international means of payment? The US dollar continues to serve as the key currency for international trade and as a foreign exchange reserve of central banks, although it has been challenged in recent years by the Deutschmark and the yen. In the late 1960s, many countries pushed for the creation of a new world currency. If the IMF could be transformed into the world central bank, it was thought, it could issue its own currency which could be used by all central banks to settle their payments and borrow from each other to intervene on exchange markets. Two difficult questions arose. First, would it displace completely the US dollar? Second, would it be linked to gold, the ultimate source of monetary respectability, and if so, how?

The outcome was the creation of **special drawing rights (SDRs)**, decided at the Rio conference in 1967. Like a bank credit, a given amount of SDRs are allocated to each country, in proportion to its quota defined above. These are credit positions with the IMF, which can be used by member-countries to obtain convertible currencies. Each SDR was valued at the rate of SDR 35/ounce of gold, thus making it worth exactly US$1. Importantly, though, there was never any pretence that the SDRs were backed by gold or dollars: SDRs are valued simply because they are accepted by central banks and the IMF, just like money.[16] All the same, this 'legal tender' aspect of SDRs is limited: central banks are required by IMF rules only to accept them up to a fixed multiple of their quota in exchange for their own currency.

After gold convertibility was suspended, a basket definition replaced the previous one: one SDR is now valued as the sum of given amounts of five currencies.[17] In order to persuade countries to hold them, SDRs yield an interest rate—the weighted average of interest available on the respective currencies. The SDR has become the IMF's unit of account. As a basket, it is less volatile than any of its components, which has made it a convenient unit for other purposes. Some countries peg their exchange rate to the SDR. Private debt issues have been denominated in SDRs, although technically they are just a basket of the constituent currencies. Its official status is still unclear, however. Some 9 billion SDRs were created by the Fund in the late 1970s. Since then, no new allocation has been decided.

20.3.3. Surveillance

The IMF looks into individual countries' affairs, and not just those of borrowing countries. Each year an annual review takes place where IMF staff members present their confidential assessment, including policy advice, to each member-country. Clearly, such advice carries more weight with smaller countries and countries in need of assistance.[18] Yet, each government knows that its policies are monitored and that the conclusions are presented to the Executive Board of the Fund in a procedure described in Box 20.2. In view of the dramatic deterioration of monetary relations in the interwar years, surveillance is seen as a way of avoiding a return to disruptive policies. When countries pursue economic policies that are criticized by the IMF, it is highly likely that this disapproval will filter through to the outside world and result in political pressure which may make all the difference between an unruly and a better policed world.

20.3.4. An Unpleasant Recipe

The IMF is despised in many countries. It is known to come with ready-made recipes which it imposes on cash-strapped governments, inflaming nationalist sentiments and sometimes clashing with political realities. More often than not, countries are subjected

---

[16] Hence the following quote by the economist Fritz Machlup: 'Now the forward-looking experts of the Fund and the negotiating governments have proved that their reputation for backwardness in economic thinking had been undeserved. All that matters for the acceptability of anything as a medium of exchange is the expectation that others will accept it. . . . Money needs takers, not backers'. (quoted by Dam 1989: 152).

[17] The five currencies are the US dollar, the DM, the French franc, the yen, and the pound.

[18] In recent years the IMF has actively assisted the new market economies of Central and Eastern Europe in establishing their financial systems and stabilizing their currencies.

BOX 20.2. HOW THE IMF IS MANAGED

The ultimate authority is exercised by the IMF's Board of Governors which meets, in principle, once a year. The governors are the finance ministers of all member-countries. Voting is in proportion to each country's quota. The Board delegates managing authority to the Board of Executive Directors. There are twenty-two executive directors. The largest-quota countries (the USA, the UK, Germany, France, Japan, and Saudi Arabia) have one executive director each, while the other executive directors represent several countries, grouped along regional lines. The executive directors select a managing director to run the professional staff. All decisions are taken by the Board of Executive Directors who cast votes in the name of each country according to its quota. In this way the executive directors represent the interests of their countries, while the staff and the managing director represent the institution. Table 20.6 displays the quotas of some countries.

Table 20.6. IMF Quotas in 1995 (%)

	Quota	Holdings of SDRs
USA	18.3	37.4
UK	5.1	1.3
Germany	5.7	6.8
France	5.1	3.2
Japan	5.7	9.9
Saudi Arabia[a]	3.5	2.1
Italy	3.2	0.2
Canada	2.9	4.0
Netherlands	2.3	2.9
Belgium	2.1	1.7
Spain	1.3	1.4
Sweden	1.1	1.4
Industrial countries	61.0	75.6
Africa	5.7	0.8
Asia	15.0	13.9

[a] 1994

Source: IMF

to conditionality because of their own gross policy mistakes or even malfeasance.

A standard source of friction is the exchange rate. For good reasons (upholding their terms of trade) and bad (national pride), many countries attempt to maintain overvalued exchange rates. Forcing a devaluation is seen as an infringement to sovereignty. Yet, if these same countries had convertible currencies, the market would have long ago imposed more realistic rates, overshooting notwithstanding.[19] Another source of

friction concerns the primary source of overvaluation: ongoing inflation. Quite often, inflation is traced back to seigniorage, and the need to finance gaping budget deficits. The IMF recipe—sometimes called orthodox—is just what economic principles would prescribe: cut spending, raise taxes, reduce monetary growth. These recommendations are unpopular. Instances of civil unrest and even riots following IMF-imposed cuts in subsidies on food and transport are not uncommon.

20.4. The Choice of an Exchange Rate Regime

20.4.1. The Case for Flexible Exchange Rates

In the late 1960s, as the Bretton Woods system was unravelling, the conventional wisdom shifted away

from fixity and in favour of exchange rate flexibility. The case was put forward most eloquently by Nobel Prize laureate Milton Friedman. First, if the only justification for exchange rate changes is inflation differentials, flexibility is needed to maintain PPP. In this case, Friedman foresaw smoothly adjusting exchange rates, not overshooting responses. Second, if real disturbances require a shift away from PPP, he noted that a fixed exchange rate regime would require all prices

---

[19] In fact, most often under these conditions, a black market thrives and sets the exchange rate at a less favourable rate. The IMF often uses the black market rate as a guide to its policy proposals.

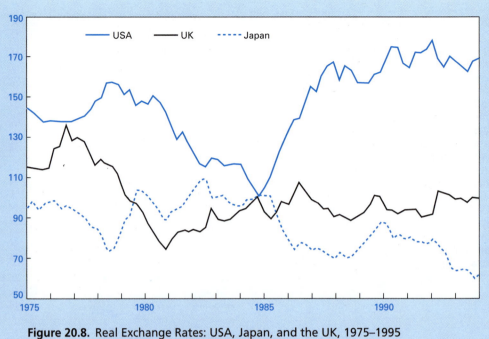

Figure 20.8. Real Exchange Rates: USA, Japan, and the UK, 1975–1995
Index 100 = average over 1975–95

Whether it is indicative of overshooting or of a change in the real equilibrium exchange rate, the post-Bretton Woods era has been characterized by a sharp increase in real exchange rate variability.
Source: IMF

to adjust. Acknowledging price rigidity as a fact of life, he argued that such extensive adjustments could be protracted and painful, possibly requiring pressure on wages and prices to be brought about by the Phillips curve mechanism.[20]

20.4.2. The Case against Flexible Exchange Rates

The shift to flexibility, which occurred in 1973, produced a degree of exchange rate instability unforeseen by its proponents. Figure 20.8 exhibits the real ex-

change rates for the three main floaters, the USA, Japan, and the UK. If PPP were to hold, and exchange rate changes were to make up smoothly for inflation differentials, then we should have relatively constant or at least smooth real exchange rates. In fact, this is not what we see: PPP is not an inexorable law, and real exchange rate changes often accompany fundamental changes in competitiveness. A key lesson from Chapter 7 was that the equilibrium real exchange rate can change; however, one would expect these changes to take place occasionally, and not to be reversed within a few years. What we observe is that real exchange rates have swings—periods of, say, appreciation followed by a return to the initial (PPP) position. It is this tendency of real exchange rates to return to PPP that is troublesome. It indicates that real exchange rate changes over long periods may not always correspond to changes in fundamentals. It is tempting to interpret misalignments as a product of monetary forces and overshooting. In this case, floating rates may cause unnecessary damage to economies.

---

[20] In a famous metaphor, Friedman noted that the shift to summer time can be achieved by having everyone adapt behaviour and do the same things an hour earlier, or by moving the clock ahead by one hour. The latter is much easier, he argued, than changing habits of millions of people. Similarly, changing the exchange rate is easier than changing millions of prices.

20.4.3. The Case against Fixed Exchange Rates

The case against fixed exchange rates often starts with the view that we do not know with much precision what the equilibrium value of the exchange rate should be. The implication is that those who manage the exchange rates do not have much basis for setting and defending a particular parity. Policy mistakes arise from ignorance. Critics of fixed exchange rates also believe that mistakes arise from political pressure; they reason that, in the absence of a clear and agreed-upon rule for setting parities, monetary authorities are likely to base their judgements on political expediency. Their list of examples is impressive. It starts with Britain's painful return to an obviously overvalued pre-First World War gold parity in 1925, to the dollar overvaluation that preceded the collapse of the Bretton Woods system, to numerous cases where thriving black markets indicate that the official parity is off the mark. Most recently it was reflected in the decisions of Italy and the UK to leave the European fixed exchange rate mechanism.

20.5. The Current Non-System

20.5.1. Issues and Proposals

The current non-system has survived for almost as long as the Bretton Woods system. Its durability is the result partly of its flexibility, partly of the lack of agreement on alternatives. Extreme solutions—Bretton Woods-type fixity or full flexibility—are unappealing for reasons presented in the previous section. We are left with two strong cases: the case against flexible exchange rates—they are too volatile, especially in the medium run—and the case against fixed exchange rates—they tend to be set at the wrong level. The current tendency seems to be to let each country find what is best suited for it, including regional arrangements like the European Monetary System (EMS). In the meantime, more fundamental issues are simply ignored. While many central banks still own gold, most have discontinued metallic transactions. The US dollar is very much the most widely used international currency, but its influence has diminished in the past two decades. SDRs are transacted, but there is currently no plan to resume new issues.

The price of gold is now freely determined by the markets, the most important role being played by London. Since 1972 this price has fluctuated widely, as is shown in Figure 20.9. Its tenfold increase has naturally led monetary authorities to seek ways of cashing in on their enormous capital gains. The USA argued in the late 1970s that gold should be demonetized, i.e. that central bank holdings should be sold to the private sector. It actually sold some of its own gold stock between 1975 and 1978, even managing to force a majority in the IMF to sell 50 million ounces from its stock in 1976. France strongly opposed removing the monetary role of gold. Then, in the early 1980s, President Reagan appointed a committee to report on the desirability of a return to the gold standard. The committee recommendation was negative, very much for the reasons outlined in Section 20.2. Since then, the issue has not been raised again, and a considerable amount of gold is frozen in central banks' vaults.

While the post-Bretton Woods era has been devoid of major crises, the large fluctuations of some of the world's major currencies (see Figure 20.8) have created discomfort. There is only limited pressure to undertake a major overhaul of the international monetary system. To the widespread agnosticism about radical changes there corresponds a tendency to adapt the system at the margin whenever problems arise. Two reform proposals are presented in Box 20.3.

20.5.2. Summitry and Economic Co-operation

Starting in 1975, heads of state of the largest industrialized countries have met annually each summer to discuss economic issues. It started as a G-5 (Group of Five) meeting, bringing together leaders of the USA, Japan, France, Germany, and the UK. The next year Italy and Canada joined the group, now referred to as the G-7. Together the G-7 countries represent 80% of OECD GDP. Occasionally, consultation takes place

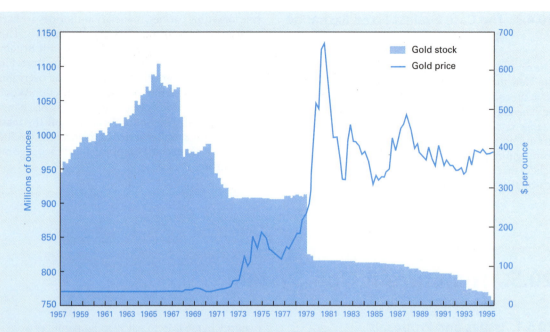

Figure 20.9. Gold Stock and Gold Prices, 1957–1994

Over the past twenty years gold has been largely demonetized. The price of gold in terms of currencies has been allowed to fluctuate widely on world markets. The monetary gold stocks of central banks have declined in physical terms.

Source: IMF

BOX 20.3. TARGET ZONES VERSUS FIXED RATES, AGAIN

One conclusion from the debate on fixed versus flexible rates is that no system is best and that the optimum may lie somewhere in between. One proposal is to have 'flexible fixed rates': the target zone idea is to declare fixed parities but to allow for large margins of fluctuations, say 10%. Its proponents, Marcus Miller and John Williamson,[21] claim that the fixed parity offers an anchor to market expectations while the wide bands prevent harmful overshooting. Critics of one kind see the bands as being so wide as to be useless, while critics of the other kind worry about misjudgements about the par value. Many policy-makers consider that this is the way the post-Bretton Woods system works informally and see no benefit in formalizing it.

A more ambitious and elaborate proposal has been advanced for years by Ronald McKinnon, from Stanford University. His reasoning is based on two principles. First, in the long run inflation is determined by money growth. Second, PPP is a good starting point for setting exchange rates. His proposal is for the USA, Germany, and Japan to fix once and for all their respective exchange rates according to PPP, i.e. such that internationally traded good prices are equalized. Thereafter, the three major countries would agree on a binding growth rate for their aggregate money supply. This growth rate would be set to achieve near-zero inflation. Through frequent consultations, the three central banks would decide how to allocate to each country its share of money growth. This proposal faces several criticisms. First, relying on price changes to affect the real exchange rate is seen as doing the hard work with the least effective instrument. This is the Friedman argument again, that it is easier to change one exchange rate than all prices. Second, it not only denies monetary policy independence—as is the case with any fixed exchange rate system—but also makes independent fiscal policy difficult. Indeed, fiscal policy actions normally affect the exchange rate. Fixing the exchange rate in the face of divergent fiscal policies amounts to transmitting disturbances from one country to the other.

within the G-3—the USA, Germany, and Japan, the three largest economies. Much more discreet consultations occur routinely between central bankers within the highly secretive framework of the Basel-based Bank for International Settlements (BIS).[22]

The industrial countries have mostly undertaken to keep exchange markets 'orderly'. Their co-operation became most visible in the mid-1980s, when the US dollar was overvalued, was at a forward discount, and yet continued to appreciate in bubble-like fashion. Two meetings were called, one in New York and one in Paris, leading to the so-called Plaza and Louvre Accords. Little is known of these agreements except that the monetary authorities stated a renewed willingness to limit exchange rate fluctuations.

Three principles have been stated publicly. First, there are no target exchange rates, PPP or otherwise. There is little indication that a return to some degree of fixity is being contemplated, at least within this framework. Second, co-operation is designed to slow down exchange rate changes, not to counter them. Some observers believe that these two agreements imply a target zone approach, but this would conflict with the stated view that there is no central parity objective. Others interpret the agreements as implying a maximum rate of exchange rate change per period (day, week, or month), i.e. that the monetary authorities will accept any long-run exchange rate that the markets consider appropriate, but prefer to move there 'slowly'.

The third, and more important, agreement is that the central banks of industrial countries are committed to intervene on exchange markets in a co-ordinated fashion when necessary. Previously, the USA and the UK had both stated the view that the exchange rate is not something that governments should care about. Thus the agreements represent an important shift towards managed floating. Indeed there have been numerous instances since the Plaza and Louvre meetings when central banks have intervened massively and simultaneously. In some cases they have been able to slow down, or even stop, sharp movements in exchange rates.

---

[21] Marcus Miller, from the University of Warwick, and John Williamson, from Washington's Institute of International Economics, have proposed 'fuzzy margins', i.e. margins that are meant to be respected but not defended at all costs. Some claim that this is in fact the way the European Monetary System has been functioning after the crisis of 1993 (see Ch. 21).

[22] Larger consultative groups have also been observed in action, but for obvious reasons are less ambitious. The G-10 (G-7 plus Belgium, the Netherlands, and Sweden, with Switzerland invited) is active within the IMF. As a counterweight, 24 Third World countries make up the G-24, comprising 8 countries each from Africa, South and Central America, and Asia. The G-24 acts on behalf of a larger grouping of Third World countries, the G-77.

20.6. Summary

1. International monetary arrangements initially arose from the need to provide international trade with easy means of settling trans-border payments. For centuries, both domestic and international trade was carried out using gold and silver. On the other hand, the famed gold standard lasted less than forty years, from 1879 to 1914.

2. Taken literally, the gold standard implied a rigid monetary rule and a fixed exchange rate regime. By the Hume mechanism, a trade deficit caused a shrinking money supply, while a surplus meant an expanding money supply. Both processes act to equilibrate trade imbalances.

3. The gold standard did not function as well in practice as in theory. Countries on the gold standard also circumvented the tight theoretical link between gold tenders and sales at the central bank, trade balances, and changes in the money supply.

4. The evolution of the monetary system after the First World War can be seen as a series of *ad hoc* responses to international crises and system inadequacies. In particular, the Bretton Woods system was designed to avoid the competitive devaluations of

the interwar period by establishing a system of fixed exchange rates based on the US dollar's link to gold. Nevertheless, it was not a gold standard in the strict sense.

5. The collapse of the Bretton Woods system was due to the internal inconsistency of a system that required increasing amounts of international reserves to be provided by the USA, reserves that were in theory convertible into gold. The large US balance of payment deficits that emerged in the late 1960s created a dollar overhang of official external liabilities which far exceeded the USA's gold assets.

6. The current system is a mosaic of systems, ranging from groups of economies that peg their exchange rates to each other, to countries whose exchange rates are determined primarily by economic forces, with a wide range of 'managed floaters' in between.

7. The advantages of fixing and floating are still contested today. Floating exchange rates may subject countries to large and costly short-run swings in nominal, and thus real, exchange rates. Fixing the exchange rate not only requires knowledge of the appropriate real exchange rate, but also presupposes the ability to discern changes in underlying fundamentals—real shocks to competitiveness and wealth, among other things—that would require changes in the real exchange rate.

8. Economic policies of countries have external effects on their neighbours. Summitry is a rational economic response to this problem, and demonstrates the potential value of economic co-operation.

Key Concepts

- International Monetary Fund (IMF)
- gold standard
- Gresham's law
- bimetallism
- Hume mechanism
- par or central value
- band of fluctuation
- dollar shortage
- Bretton Woods conference
- quota
- gold exchange standard
- conditionality
- Triffin paradox
- special drawing rights (SDRs)
- Plaza and Louvre Accords

Exercises

1. The choice of an exchange regime is not black or white. Evaluate the pros and the cons of fixed and flexible exchange rate regimes.

2. Consider a small country which is specialized in exporting one crop-good such as coffee or peanuts, or a primary commodity like tin or oil. This country imports industrial goods like machines or cars. Prices of crop-goods and primary commodities tend to fluctuate widely. What exchange rate regime would you recommend, and why?

3. A currency board system (adopted in the early 1990s in Argentina, Estonia, Lithuania) works as follows: when its net reserves of foreign exchange rises, the central bank automatically creates the same amount of monetary base; inversely, it reduces the monetary base when foreign exchange reserves decline. Represent this system using the central bank's balance sheet. Explain its logic, its advantages and drawbacks.

4. The poorer countries regularly ask that the IMF issue more of its SDRs and distribute them to support their development. The richer countries refuse, contending that this would be inflationary. What do you think of this plan?

5. In the winter of 1994–5 Mexico suffered a violent attack on its foreign exchange reserves and was forced to let the peso float. The peso immediately depreciated by more than 100%. The IMF and the USA quickly provided the Mexican authorities with a support of about $50 billion, the largest amount ever offered a country under stress. Critics contended that taxpayers offered a free insurance to private investors in Mexico and an incentive to the Mexican authorities to mismanage their economy. The IMF and the US authorities claimed that the attack was unjustified and was making matters worse for a country that needed only a 20%–30% devaluation. Evaluate this debate.

Suggested Further Reading

A general purpose text is:

Yeager, Leland B. (1976), *International Monetary Relations: Theory, History, and Policy*, Harper and Row, New York.

For accounts of the gold standard see:

Bloomfield, Arthur (1959), *Monetary Policy under the International Gold Standard*, Federal Reserve Bank, New York.

Cooper, Richard (1982), 'The Gold Standard: Historical Facts and Future Prospects', *Brookings Papers on Economic Activity*, 1: 1–56.

Dam, Kenneth D. (1982), *The Rules of the Game*, University of Chicago Press.

Eichengreen, B. (1992) *Golden Fetters: the Gold Standard and the Great Depression, 1919–39*, Oxford University Press.

The interwar experience is described in:

Cairncross, Alec, and Eichengreen, Barry (1983), *Sterling in Decline*, Basil Blackwell, Oxford.

Kindleberger, Charles (1973), *The World in Depression*, University of California Press.

Robert Triffin's influential statement of the Bretton Woods dilemma is:

Triffin, Robert (1960), *Gold and the Dollar Crisis*, Yale University Press, New Haven.

On the Bretton Woods system, see:

Bordo, Michael, and Eichengreen, Barry (eds.) (1993), *A Retrospective on the Bretton Woods System*, University of Chicago Press.

Horsefield, J. Keith (ed.) (1969), *The International Monetary Fund 1945–65: Twenty Years of International Monetary Cooperation*, IMF, Washington.

On the post-Bretton Woods era, see:

Funabashi, Yoichi (1988), *Managing the Dollar: From the Plaza to the Louvre*, Institute for International Economics, Washington.

McKinnon, Ronald (1993), 'The Rules of the Game: International Money in Historical Perspective', *Journal of Economic Literature*, 31: 1–44.

Williamson, John and Miller, Marcus (1987), *Targets and Indicators: a Blueprint for the International Coordination of Economic Policy*, Institute for International Economics, Washington.

21

Policy Co-ordination and Exchange Rate Crises: the EMS and the EMU

21.1. Overview

The European Monetary System (EMS) is the most prominent example of exchange rate co-operation since the demise of the Bretton Woods system. Although it can be seen as the successor to the 'Snake' arrangements of the early 1970s, from the outset it was more cohesive and ambitious. The *raison d'être* of the EMS goes to the heart of the issue of economic policy co-ordination. Co-ordination among nations is called for when one country's actions affect other countries' well-being. 'Beggar-thy-neighbour' policies (discussed in the previous chapter) that result in competitive devaluations can be avoided through economic consultation. The more closely integrated the countries are, the greater is the need for consultation and co-operation.

These facts were evident to the writers of the Treaty of Rome. When they created the European Common Market in 1957, they envisioned monetary co-operation all the way to a monetary union. Indeed, the success of the Common Market has carried over into an ever increasing degree of real and financial integration among member-countries. The EMS is therefore a useful case study for understanding the notion of international co-ordination of economic policies, both its successes and its failures. Under proper conditions,

co-ordination works, but it is a never ending challenge. When conditions change and success breeds ever higher expectations, co-ordination becomes elusive, even within tight monetary arrangements. The recession of the early 1990s, coupled with audacious plans to move towards **European Monetary Union**, have resulted in spectacular exchange crises, which have led to the disintegration of the EMS as we knew it.

Emboldened by the positive performance of the Common Market and the EMS, by the mid-1980s policy-makers had started to design new steps towards closer integration. The Single Act aimed at achieving integration at its highest degree by removing obstacles to the movement of goods, people, and capital. In particular, it mandated the elimination of restriction to capital flows by July 1990, with few exceptions. Then came the Treaty of Maastricht, signed in late 1991 and ratified the following year, which mandates the shift towards the ideal of a European Union, implying closer monetary and political integration. The adoption of a single currency throughout Europe has proved difficult for many countries to accept. It raises new issues of co-ordination linked to the principle of **optimum currency areas**.

21.2. The European Monetary System in Theory

21.2.1. Brief History

The **European Monetary System (EMS)** was the brainchild of French President Valery Giscard d'Estaing and German Chancellor Helmut Schmidt in April 1978. Having set the stage for the agreement, they then extended an invitation to all other EC members to join. The idea was formally approved at the Bremen European summit meeting in June 1978, and the operating principles were established a few months later in Brussels. The initial declaration cited the creation of a 'zone of monetary stability in Europe' as a primary objective of the EMS. It was a time of major upheaval on world exchange markets: the US dollar appeared unable to serve as a reliable numeraire for international transactions, and the European 'Snake' had been only a mixed success since several members, including France, Italy,

and Sweden, were unable to participate for more than brief periods.

All nine European Community (EC) members at the time formally joined the EMS, agreeing in principle to fixed exchange rates and the accompanying measures. The UK initially postponed its participation in the **Exchange Rate Mechanism (ERM)**, which stipulates the fixing of exchange rates; after many years of hesitation, it began full participation in the ERM in October 1990. When Greece in 1981, and Spain and Portugal in 1986, became members of the EC, they too pledged to join the EMS; Spain did so in July 1989 as an active member of the ERM, and Portugal followed in April 1992. Following violent speculative attacks, Italy and the UK 'temporarily' left in September 1992. A new crisis in 1993 led to a looser system. Of the new members entering the EU in 1995—Austria, Fin-

BOX 21.1. JOINING THE ERM: THE CASE OF BRITAIN

In October 1990, the UK entered the Exchange Rate Mechanism (ERM) of the European Monetary System. The Bank of England committed itself to maintain the value of sterling within a 6% band around the central parity of £0.7/ECU. In doing so, it ended nearly twelve years of ambivalence towards the EMS. As a member of the EMS, Britain could boast that the ECU contained about 9p of sterling—roughly 10%–15% of its total value—but it refused actually to fix the value of sterling in terms of the ECU, and thus did not participate in the Exchange Rate Mechanism.

Why did the UK straddle the fence for such a long time? The struggle over joining highlights the arguments for and against fixed exchange rates. First, apart from considerations of national sovereignty, joining a fixed exchange rate regime means losing much, if not all, monetary autonomy. As a full member of the EMS, Britain cannot change its parity without the agreement of all other EMS countries. Second, there is the petro-currency argument. In the late 1970s, oil from the North Sea came on line, and for reasons discussed in Chapter 7 sterling appreciated considerably until the early 1980s. Future oil price changes or oil discoveries may require further adjustments in the value of sterling. A more Machiavellian viewpoint holds that, while industry is bound to profit

from a fixed rate of exchange to the Continent, banking and finance are likely to lose, since they thrive on trading in and insuring against turbulent markets. In effect, a stable £/FF or £/DM rate reduces the need for exchange rate instruments such as options, futures, and swaps; moreover, it would eliminate currency trading, an important profit source for banks. Some opponents to EMS membership even claimed that the City of London would lose its pre-eminence in world finance to Paris or Frankfurt in the aftermath of Britain's full participation in the EMS.

The crisis of September 1992 may have been the outcome of a mistaken choice for the peg: consistent with their desire to use the ERM as a tool to fight inflation, the British authorities may have chosen to err on the side of overvaluation, inadvertently inviting the subsequent attack. The end of ERM membership has led to a deep re-examination of Britain's monetary future. The consequence of renewed floating was a deep depreciation of sterling, which boosted exports and helped lift Britain out of the recession. Soon thereafter, having lost its exchange rate anchor, the Bank of England launched a new strategy of targeting inflation. The success of this policy remains to be fully assessed.

---

land, and Sweden—only Austria has joined the ERM. The differences between EMS and ERM membership are made clear in the case of the UK in Box 21.1.

21.2.2. Key Operating Features of the EMS

21.2.2.1. The parity grid

The EMS shares many features with its direct predecessor, the European 'Snake', not to mention the defunct Bretton Woods system which both the 'Snake' and the EMS sought to replace within Europe. It is a system of fixed but adjustable rates. Fixity is defined as an official central parity between any pair of member-currencies: it implies a central rate, and a band of fluctuation within which the exchange rate is allowed to move around the fixed parity. For example, the official FF/DM central parity in 1995 was 3.354; the actual exchange rate could vary freely between 2.851 and 3.857, corresponding to the wide margins of ±15%. These margins were adopted in the middle of a major exchange rate crisis in August 1993. Before that, the normal margins were of ±2.25%, for example constraining the FF/DM around the same central parity but within a range of 3.279–3.431.[1] The complete set of central parities and margins of fluctuation, often called the **parity grid**, is displayed in Table 21.1. For each pair of currencies, the grid specifies the central parity and the upper and lower limits of fluctuation.

21.2.2.2. The ECU

The establishment of the EMS was accompanied by the creation of a new unit of account, the **European Currency Unit** or, more commonly, the **ECU**. Technically, the ECU serves for all EC official transactions and is an easy way of defining the central parities from which all bilateral rates can be computed. It is a basket of member-currencies, worth its official content of fractions of all member-countries' currencies. Table 21.2 shows that to make up 1 ECU we need DM 0.6242 + FF 1.332 + ... The second column shows the relative weights of each currency in the total basket.

---

[1] There is one exception in the current arrangement: Germany and the Netherlands have separately agreed to maintain between themselves the old narrow ±2.25% band. In the previous arrangement, some countries maintained a wider band of ±6%: Spain, Portugal, and the UK. Until January 1990, the Italian lira enjoyed a similar status.

Table 21.1. Bilateral Central Rates and Intervention Points, March 1995 (Units of national currency)

	BFr	Fl	DKr	DM	FFr	I£	Pta	Es	Sch
Belgium	100	6.34340	21.4747	5.63000	18.8800	2.33503	478.944	577.090	39.6089
	—	5.46286	18.4938	4.84837	16.2608	2.01090	412.461	496.984	34.1107
		4.70454	15.9266	4.17500	14.0050*	1.73176	355.206	428.000	29.3757
Netherlands	2125.60		393.105	103.058[1]	345.650	42.7439	8767.30	10564.0	725.065
	1830.54	100	338.537	88.7526	297.661	36.8105	7550.30	9097.55	624.417
	1576.45		291.544	76.4326[2]	256.350	31.7007	6502.20	7834.70	537.740
Denmark	627.880	34.3002		30.4450	102.100	12.6261	2589.90	3120.50	214.174
	540.723	29.5389	100	26.2162	87.9257	10.8734	2230.27	2687.31	184.444
	465.665	25.4385		22.5750	75.7200	9.36403	1920.70	2314.30	158.841
Germany	2395.20	130.834[3]	442.968		389.480	48.1696	9878.50	11903.3	816.927
	2062.55	112.673	381.443	100	335.386	41.4757	8507.18	10250.5	703.550
	1776.20	97.0325[4]	328.461		288.810	35.7143	7326.00	8827.70	605.877
France	714.030	39.0091	132.066	34.6250		14.3599	2945.40	3549.00	243.586
	614.977	33.5953	113.732	29.8164	100	12.3666	2536.54	3056.35	209.773
	529.660	28.9381	97.9430	25.6750		10.6500	2184.40	2632.10	180.654
Ireland	5774.45	315.450	1067.92	280.000	938.950		23817.5	28698.3	1969.71
	4972.89	271.662	919.676	241.105	808.631	100	20511.3	24714.5	1696.29
	4282.60	233.952	792.014	207.600	696.400		17664.1	21283.8	1460.82
Spain	28.1525	1.53793	5.20640	1.36500	4.57780	0.566120		139.920	9.60338
	24.2447	1.32445	4.48376	1.17548	3.94237	0.487537	100	120.493	8.27008
	20.8795	1.14060	3.86140	1.01230	3.39510	0.419859		103.770	7.12200
Portugal	23.3645	1.27637	4.32100	1.13280	3.79920	0.469841	96.3670		7.97000
	20.1214	1.09920	3.72119	0.975561	3.27188	0.404620	82.9927	100	6.86356
	17.3285	0.946611	3.20460	0.840100	2.81770	0.348453	71.4690		5.91086
Austria	340.420	18.5963	62.9561	16.5050	55.3545	6.84544	1404.10	1691.80	
	293.163	16.0149	54.2170	14.2136	47.6706	5.89521	1209.18	1456.97	100
	252.470	13.7918	46.6910	12.2410	41.0533	5.07688	1041.30	1254.70	

Notes: For each currency pair, the second line is the central parity, the first and third lines being the upper and lower bounds. These bounds are 15% above and below the central parity. Germany and the Netherlands bilaterally agreed to lower bounds.
[1] 90.7700   [2] 86.7800   [3] 115.2350   [4] 110.1675

These weights are decided on the basis of the relative size of each country (measured by GDPs and trade, mainly) and are renegotiated every five years. The last column gives the central parity ECU exchange rate for the countries participating in the ERM.

All bilateral central parities can be recovered from the ECU exchange rates shown in Table 21.2. But the margins of fluctuation around the ECU parities are not the same for every country. The reason is that the ECU is a weighted average of all EMS currencies: when the value of a currency changes, the value of the ECU vis à vis all other currencies also changes. A currency with a large weight will drag the ECU behind. This is why a 'heavyweight' currency can fluctuate more widely around its ECU parity while staying within its official bilateral band than a currency with a small weight.[2]

The ECU is the official unit of account for transac-

[2] This was initially perceived as a potential problem. To deal with it, an 'indicator of divergence' was established, at 75% of the margin of fluctuation vis à vis the ECU. Countries that triggered this signal, in either direction, were meant to take corrective action. The indicator was never actually used.

Table 21.2. The ECU: Central Parities and Weights, March 1995

	Amount in 1 ECU	Weight (%)	Central rate (national currency per ECU)
Belgian franc	3.43100	8.71	39.396
Danish krone	0.19760	2.71	7.2858
Deutschmark	0.62420	32.68	1.91007
Dutch guilder	0.21980	10.21	2.15214
French franc	1.33200	20.79	6.40608
Greek drachma	1.44000	0.49	
Italian lira	151.80000	7.21	
Irish punt	0.00855	1.08	0.792214
Portuguese escudo	1.39300	0.71	195.792
Spanish peseta	6.88500	4.24	162.493
UK sterling pound	0.08784	11.17	

Source: Bulletin de la Banque Nationale de Belgique

tions involving the EMS central banks, as well as the European Community. One intention behind the creation of the ECU was to go further, to move one step in the direction of a genuine European currency. Yet the monetary authorities have been careful not to give the ECU any of the attributes of a true currency: it was not meant to circulate publicly, and is not exchanged between central banks and the public. On the other hand, it has been adopted by financial markets. Bonds have been issued directly in ECUs, first by private corporations, then by some governments. These bonds, traded on several markets, have given the ECU a life of its own. By 1991, the year when the Maastricht Treaty was signed, ECU bond issues had exceeded in volume issues in sterling or Deutschmarks, as is shown in Table 21.3. The difficulties encountered in ratifying the Treaty and the ensuing crises, however, have led to considerable suspicion of the ECU.

Table 21.3. The ECU Markets: International Bond Issues by Currency Denomination

	(in billions of US $) US dollar	Deutschmark	ECU	Sterling
1983	39.21	4.04	2.19	2.15
1984	65.33	4.32	2.94	3.96
1985	96.80	9.60	6.90	6.10
1986	118.10	17.10	7.10	10.60
1987	58.10	15.00	7.40	15.00
1988	74.50	23.70	11.20	23.60
1989	117.50	16.40	12.60	18.50
1990	70.00	18.30	17.90	20.90
1991	76.90	19.90	31.60	25.70
1992	103.20	33.80	21.30	23.30
1993	147.70	54.70	7.10	42.70
1994	149.40	31.60	7.60	30.40

Source: OECD Financial Market Trends

The emergence of private ECUs is closely associated with the eventual launch of a single currency in Europe. The difficulties encountered since 1992 have reduced the private ECU market. For the ECU to become a real currency, a number of practical and legal steps are required.[3] For example, private dealings in ECUs are expensive because, technically, an ECU is a bundle of currencies, so converting it into, say, Dutch guilders is done formally by converting each component; since each transaction has a cost, dealings in ECUs are prohibitively expensive. More importantly, the private sector would need to conduct a significant share of its transactions in ECU bank accounts. This requires enabling legislation in many EC countries.

21.2.2.3. Borrowing facilities

The EMS exhibits a number of unique features which distinguish it from other existing systems. First, in theory at least, there is no special-status currency, like the US dollar under Bretton Woods: all parities are defined on a pairwise basis. Second, there exist a number of borrowing facilities among member central banks. This system allows any member-bank to borrow virtually unlimited amounts from another member-bank at very short notice. Prompt repayment is required—normally within forty-five days—but revolving credits are also possible. Third, all members have deposited with the European Monetary Cooperation Fund 20% of their gold and dollar holdings. In return, central banks hold ECU deposits with the Fund which they can use to settle accounts among themselves. So far, this facility has been used only infrequently.

21.2.2.4. Collective decision-making on exchange rates

Finally, the EMS is characterized by collective decision-making. A country cannot unilaterally alter its ECU parity within the system, which determines its parity *vis-à-vis* all other member-currencies in the ERM. (Whereas a similar rule existed under the Bretton Woods system, in practice, the IMF was informed of a parity change at the last minute.) Realignment decisions are made on a unanimous basis. They usually occur over weekends when exchange markets are closed, which gives time for negotiations. The discussion covers both the appropriateness of the requested parity changes and their sizes. Despite the apparent restrictiveness of this rule, realignments are not at all infrequent. Table 21.4 provides a complete history of realignments.

21.2.3. The Exchange Rate Mechanism (ERM)

In joining the **Exchange Rate Mechanism (ERM)**, a country undertakes to maintain the value of its currency *vis-à-vis* all other participating currencies. Practically, this means that central banks must undertake unlimited interventions in their home markets to defend the agreed-upon parity. Arbitrage between markets guarantees that, when two currencies reach their common bilateral limit of fluctuation, both central banks will intervene to prevent any further deviation. Figure 21.1 shows how two bilateral exchange rates have moved around their central parities within narrow and large bands, and the effect of realignments. Typically, a currency wanders within its band until some disturbance pushes it to its floor or ceiling. At that stage the central banks must intervene to keep the exchange rate within the band. If the monetary authorities decide that a particular parity cannot be defended, a new parity can be decided, along with the corresponding new margins of fluctuation. Figure 21.1 shows that the French franc and the Italian lira have been devalued several times.

While exchange market interventions are compulsory at the endpoints, central banks often intervene well within the bands. The purpose of such **intramarginal interventions** is to dissuade markets that a realignment is under consideration. For obvious reasons, data on interventions are closely guarded by central banks. From a few rare central bank studies,[4] a few facts are known. First, the Bundesbank executes most of its interventions in US dollars, whereas the other members have increasingly used EMS currencies and their ECU accounts. Second, Germany intervenes mostly to manage its exchange rate *vis à vis* the US dollar, leaving it to the other central banks to intervene to manage their exchange rate *vis à vis* the Deutsch-mark. By intervening frequently before their currencies reach the limits of their margins of

---

[3] Several countries have issued coins, usually of precious metals, denominated in ECUs, but these are not legal tender. More likely, they represent a clever way for governments to raise seigniorage, since they are generally hoarded or collected for numismatic reasons.

[4] Notably the work of Mastropasqua *et al.* (1988).

Table 21.4. Dates and Sizes of EMS Realignments to the ECU, 1979–1995 (%)

Currency	Date of realignment								
	1979 24 Sept.	1979 30 Nov.	1981 22 Mar.	1981 5 Oct.	1982 22 Feb.	1982 14 Jun.	1983 21 Mar.	1985 21 Jul.	1986 7 Apr.
Belgian franc					−8.50		1.50	2.00	1.00
Danish krone	−2.90	−4.80			−3.00		2.50	2.00	1.00
German mark	2.00			5.50		4.25	5.50	2.00	3.00
French franc				−3.00		−5.75	−2.50	2.00	−3.00
Irish punt							−3.50	2.00	
Italian lira			−6.00	−3.00		−2.75	−2.50	−6.00	
Dutch guilder				5.50		4.25	3.50	2.00	3.00
Spanish peseta	n.m.	n.m.	n.m.	n.m.	n.m.	n.m.	n.m.	n.m.	n.m.
Portuguese escudo	n.m.	n.m.	n.m.	n.m.	n.m.	n.m.	n.m.	n.m.	n.m.
UK pound	n.m.	n.m.	n.m.	n.m.	n.m.	n.m.	n.m.	n.m.	n.m.

Table 21.4. (cont.)

Currency	Date of realignment								
	1986 4 Aug.	1987 12 Jan.	1990 7 Jan.	1992 14 Sept.	1992 17 Sept.	1992 23 Nov.	1993 1 Feb.	1993 14 May	1995 6 Mar.
Belgian franc		2.00							
Danish krone									
German mark		3.00							
French franc									
Irish punt	−8.00						−10.00		
Italian lira			−3.80	−7.00	susp.	susp.	susp.	susp.	susp.
Dutch guilder		3.00							
Spanish peseta	n.m.	n.m.			−5.00	−6.00		−8.00	−7.00
Portuguese escudo	n.m.	n.m.	n.m.	n.m.		−6.00		−6.50	−3.50
UK pound	n.m.	n.m.	n.m.		susp.	susp.	susp.	susp	susp.

Note: n.m.: not a member of ERM.
susp.: suspended participation in ERM

fluctuation, the other central banks rarely put the Bundesbank in a situation where it is forced to intervene. Such glimpses into the secret world of interventions reveal that by the late 1980s the Bundesbank had assumed a special role, effectively managing the relationship between the EMS currencies and the rest of the world, while the other central banks were taking care of their respective positions *vis-à-vis* the Deutschmark. The potential for asymmetry in the ERM is discussed in Section 21.3.2.

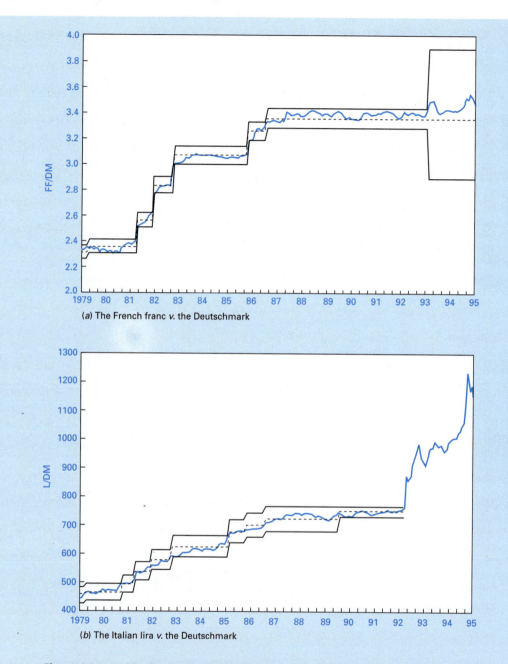

(a) The French franc v. the Deutschmark

(b) The Italian lira v. the Deutschmark

Figure 21.1. Inside the Bands of Fluctuations

Each pair of currencies has an official central parity and margins which defines the allowable band of fluctuation. The French franc operated within the narrow (±2.25%) band until August 1993, when it was 'temporarily' suspended and replaced with the wider band of ±15%). Italy first operated within the ±6% band—also adopted by the UK, Spain, and Portugal—and then shifted to the narrow band in January 1990, until it left the Exchange Rate Mechanism in September 1992. Realignments—here shown as devaluations *vis à vis* the Deutschmark —take the form of a new central parity and new associated margins of fluctuations.

21.2.4. Monetary Policy Independence

A country that pegs its currency and maintains capital mobility gives up the effective control of its money supply. Any attempt to expand the stock of money lowers the interest rate and prompts outflows of short-term financial funds. As the central bank defends the parity, it sells its foreign exchange reserves, which reduces the monetary base and brings the aggregate money stock back to its initial level. The final outcome is simply a swap of domestic credit—defined as the total credit of the central bank and the commer-cial banking system to the non-banking sector—for foreign exchange reserves. How does this work in practice?

When foreign exchange reserves decline, the monetary base contracts only if the central bank's domestic credit remains unchanged. However, the central bank may attempt to offset the effect on the monetary base of the reduction in its foreign exchange reserves through open market purchases of domestic assets. This procedure, described in Chapter 9 as sterilization, can effectively shield the monetary base and the aggregate money supply from exchange market inter-

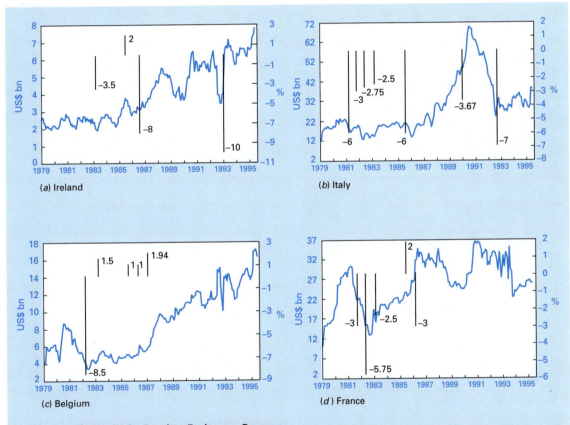

(a) Ireland   (b) Italy   (c) Belgium   (d) France

Figure 21.2. Foreign Exchange Reserves

When the foreign exchange markets expect a realignment, speculative attacks can occur. During such periods, a central bank experiences sudden changes in its reserves over a few days' time. A large foreign exchange reserve outflow is usually the immediate cause of a devaluation. Here such movements can be identified in some but not all realignments. Notice the contagion in the autumn of 1992, after Italy left the ERM: Ireland was forced to devalue, while Belgium and France managed to repel attacks.

Note: A + indicates a revaluation *vis-à-vis* the ECU; a − indicates a devaluation.

Sources: IMF; Banque de Belgique

BOX 21.2. SPECULATIVE ATTACKS

Speculative attacks arise when market participants perceive that the central bank would rather devalue or exit the fixed exchange rate system than let its foreign exchange reserves fall below some level, say $\bar{F}$. Because speculative currency profits can be very substantial when the parity is abandoned, traders attempt to anticipate the central bank's action well before reserves reach their critical level. The consolidated accounts of the central and private banking sectors establish that the money supply M is equal to foreign exchange reserves F plus domestic credit DC (Chapter 9):

$$M = F + DC.$$

Under a fixed exchange rate regime, the money supply is endogenous and is given by the public's demand for it. A central bank that increases DC faster than the demand for M simply sees its foreign exchange reserves F decline. Expecting that this process may end up in the exhaustion of foreign exchange reserves, rational markets will anticipate that a realignment—or the abandonment of the fixed exchange rate regime—is unavoidable. This provides an urgent incentive to sell the currency and triggers a speculative attack in which every trader tries to avoid being left with a devalued currency in his books. The last moment for selling the domestic currency is when the inventory of foreign exchange reserves is just enough to buy back what the market wants to sell, which is represented by the jump from point A to point C in Figure 21.3. The fixed exchange rate is abandoned in advance of the date at which reserves would have reached the minimum level $\bar{F}$ if simply decumulated to match the rise

in domestic credit (point B). After the speculative attack, the currency floats and the money supply—equal to $\bar{F} + DC$—grows, as does domestic credit.

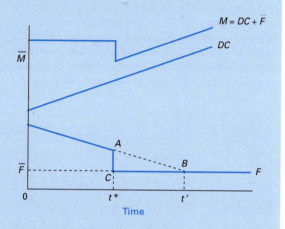

Figure 21.3. Speculative Attack

If reserves fall below level $\bar{R}$, the central bank abandons the fixed exchange rate. As long as the monetary authorities peg the exchange rate, the money supply M is beyond the control of the central bank (here assumed fixed at $\bar{M}$). If domestic credit grows there will be some point (t') at which the foreign exchange reserves will fall below the critical level $\bar{R}$. The speculative attack will occur before this point, however, because a jump depreciation at t' could be anticipated. The attack occurs at t^*.

ventions, and is known to be the standard operating procedure of most central banks. So, is monetary independence preserved?

The hitch is that sterilization cannot go on for ever. If, for example, the monetary authorities reduce the interest rate, capital will flow out and foreign exchange reserves will decline. As the central bank creates a new monetary base to replace what it buys on the exchange market—that is, what it withdraws from circulation—the interest rate remains depressed and capital outflow continues: it is as if the central bank were trying to fill a punctured wine cask. As long as the process continues, foreign exchange reserves keep declining. Sooner or later, sterilization must come to an end. As long as foreign exchange reserves last, monetary independence is preserved, but this must be short-lived. Indeed, daily

exchange market transactions generally exceed the combined reserve stocks of all central banks.[5]

A central bank that attempts to pursue policies widely at variance with the other EMS countries is often subject to a **speculative attack**, in which its reserves are quickly exhausted. Some of these instances can be spotted in Figure 21.2, which shows the behaviour of reserves in EMS countries around realignment dates. Speculative attacks occur when market participants anticipate either an imminent change in the parity or the adoption of a floating-rate regime. Box 21.2 provides some detail on how such attacks occur. The figure reveals the severity of the attacks that occurred in Au-

[5] The opposite also holds with capital inflows. It is a good exercise to ask yourself why central banks cannot sterilize in this case either.

gust and September 1992. According to some reports, the Banca d'Italia lost an amount greater than its gross reserves; two hours were enough for the Bank of England to spend half its reserves. Much the same happened again in July 1993, when the Banque de France also lost all its reserves in a few hours. Section 21.3.3 notes the role of capital controls, or their absence, in periods of speculative attacks.

21.3. The European Monetary System in Practice

21.3.1. Performance

21.3.1.1. Disinflation

The EMS was created shortly before the second oil shock. At that time most advanced countries had concluded that the high rates of inflation inherited from the first oil shock were unacceptable. The second oil shock triggered an almost universal contractionary policy response.[6] Inflation did indeed decline in the following years throughout the EMS countries. Yet, Figure 21.4 shows that the reduction of inflation was not a feature specific to the EMS member-countries. In fact, the EMS countries have disinflated more slowly, on average, than the non-EMS advanced countries. On the other hand, once achieved, low inflation has been better maintained within the EMS than outside.

21.3.1.2. Monetary policy

Low inflation requires an uncompromising monetary policy. One gauge of monetary policy is the real interest rate. Figure 21.5 confirms the evidence on disinflation. Real interest rates have been slow to rise among the EMS countries during the deflationary period of the early 1980s, but then have stayed higher than outside the EMS zone. This is an indication that monetary policy has been gradually tightened up and has remained tight. The behaviour of real interest rates is interesting because, as can be seen in Figure 15.6, Germany has traditionally kept its real rate fairly high while many EMS countries (France, Italy, the Netherlands, and the UK) have had low, sometimes even negative, real rates. The shift from the mid-1980s onwards signals a convergence of real interest rates towards German levels.

21.3.1.3. Exchange rate stability

The 'island of stability' objective set for the EMS was really meant to prevent intra-European exchange rates from fluctuating too widely and possibly disrupting trade among increasingly integrated countries. What matters therefore is the stabilization of relative prices. Figure 21.6 presents real effective exchange rates in two representative EMS countries (Denmark and Germany), and compares them with the real effective exchange rate of the US dollar and the pound sterling, which stayed in the ERM only briefly, from October 1990 to September 1992. There is little doubt that EMS exchange rates have been successfully stabilized.

21.3.1.4. Convergence of interest rates

Figure 21.7 displays the behaviour of nominal interest rates in several EMS countries. The interest parity condition states that, in the absence of an expected realignment, nominal interest rates should be the same. Clearly they are not, which suggests that markets expect a change in the exchange rate to occur over the period, with some probability.

The figure reveals three important periods. Until the late 1980s, realignments were always expected, and indeed occurred frequently. During that early period, fairly large differences in the rate of inflation were maintained. Germany and the Netherlands achieved generally low inflation rates, with a limited and temporary rise at the time of the 1980 oil shock. Other countries, like France, Denmark, or Italy, allowed double-digit rates of inflation for several years running. Fisher's equations (see Chapter 19), along with the expectation that realignments would be based on PPP, predict that interest rates will reflect these differences in inflation. It is not surprising, therefore, to observe interest rates that remain far apart.

In the late 1980s, the picture changes. All nominal interest rates seem to enter into a funnel, moving increasingly together. This phase was temporary, however. In the early 1990s, while one group of countries

---

[6] Ch. 13 explains the lessons drawn for dealing with supply shocks.

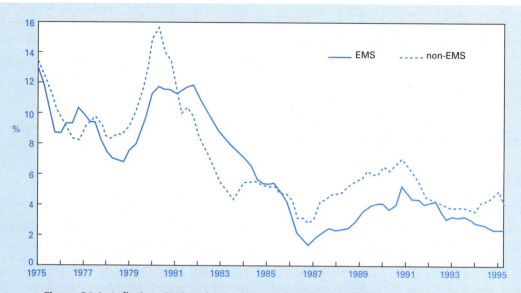

Figure 21.4. Inflation: EMS and Non-EMS Countries: 1975–1995

Being a participating member of the Exchange Rate Mechanism is not a necessary condition for reducing inflation. Other economies in the OECD area were able to wring inflation out of their systems as well. The decisive factor seems to have been the election of anti-inflation governments throughout the OECD starting in 1978.

Sources: Summers and Heston (1989); IMF

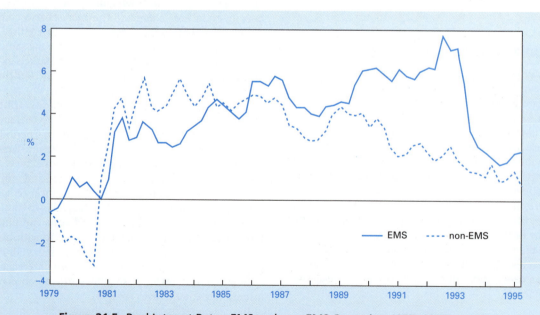

Figure 21.5. Real Interest Rates: EMS and non-EMS Countries: 1975–1995

Real interest rates rose throughout the OECD in the 1980s. One consequence of the EMS is that real interest rates have remained at persistently higher levels than the non-EMS OECD in the latter half of the decade.

Sources: Summers and Heston (1989); IMF

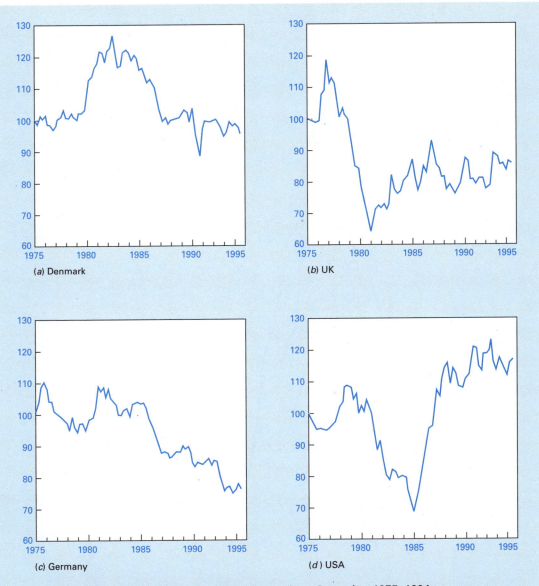

Figure 21.6. Real Effective Exchange Rates, Four Countries, 1975–1994

The effective exchange rates of EMS currencies—here, the Danish krone and the Deutschmark—exhibit significantly less variability than those of non-EMS currencies such as sterling (which, while formally part of the EMS, only briefly operated within the Exchange Rate Mechanism).

Source: IMF

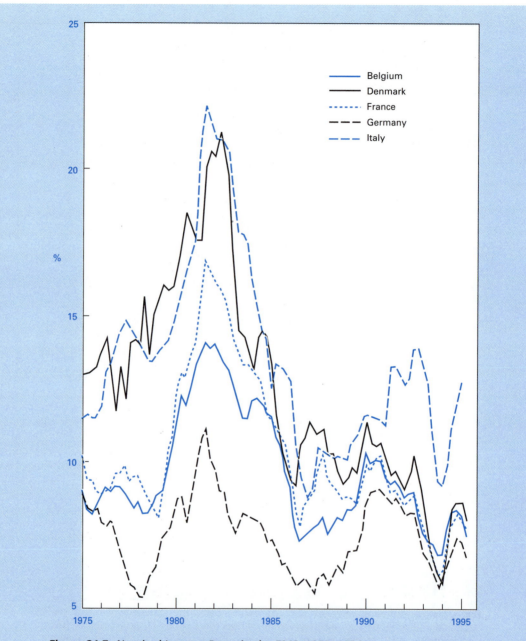

Figure 21.7. Nominal Interest Rates in the EMS, 1975–1994

Despite many realignments over the period 1979–87, a 'core' group of countries have seen their nominal interest rates converge, reflecting a similar behaviour of inflation rates. Italy, which failed to converge by the end of the 1980s, was forced to leave during the crisis of 1992.

Source: IMF

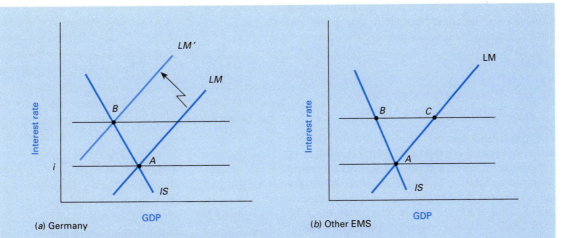

Figure 21.8. The Asymmetry Hypothesis

Initially at point *A* the interest rate is identical in Germany and elsewhere, bearing out the expectation that no realignment is contemplated. Then a contractionary monetary policy in Germany is shown by the move to point *B* in panel (*a*). To maintain the parity, the other EMS countries must allow their interest rates to rise, hence must follow Germany's policy stance: the *LM* curve in panel (*b*) rises until it passes through point *B*. An alternative is to depreciate *vis-à-vis* the DM: the *IS* curve shifts to go through point *C*. (In fact, Germany's *IS* curve would shift left, meeting the other EMS countries somewhere in between.)

continues to operate within a tight tunnel, others (the figure shows Italy, but the same is true of Spain and Portugal) again move away, ending the period of generalized convergence of interest rates.

21.3.2. The Four Phases of the EMS

The previous analysis may be summarized by dividing the EMS experience into four phases.

During the first phase, from its establishment until the mid-1980s, the EMS operated as a fairly loose system, tolerant of countries' diverse tastes for inflation. Realignments were frequent and undramatic, aimed at correcting deviations from purchasing power parity (PPP) resulting from persistent differences in inflation rates between participating countries.

The second phase, from the mid-1980s to 1992, was marked by the gradual emergence of the Deutschmark as the system's anchor currency. Realignments were successfully avoided from January 1987 to September 1992. All countries tried to emulate the mark's strong currency status and identified low inflation as the main objective of monetary policy. With this aim in mind, Spain, the UK, and Portugal joined the ERM. Figures

21.4 and 21.5 confirm this generalized toughening of monetary policy and of inflation. During this time the EMS came to be perceived as a major success: the absence of any realignment for nearly six years was attributed to adroit policy co-ordination.[7] Emboldened by success, the authorities proceeded to prepare a shift to a single currency: the result was the Maastricht Treaty adopted by the heads of states late in 1991.

The second phase came to an abrupt end in the summer of 1992. Over the following twelve months, continuous upheaval rocked the ERM ship, and it nearly sank. Not only did several realignments occur in quick succession, but two currencies left the ERM to float on their own. In the end, in August 1993, the margins of fluctuation were widened to the point where the fixed exchange rate differed little from free floating. This fourth, and latest, phase, an 'ERM without teeth', was hastily designed in the wake of speculative attacks. With 15% wide bands, the situation has calmed somewhat, but the EMS has lost credibility and reputation in the aftermath. This phase is characterized by

---

[7] The change in the Italian lira in January 1990 was purely technical: as the band of fluctuation was narrowed from ±6% to ±2.25%, it was decided to keep the upper band unchanged, which required an upward adjustment of the central parity, as seen in Fig. 21.1.

divergence among the EMS countries, with renewed monetary and inflation rectitude in one group and some relaxation of monetary policy in the other.

21.3.3. Convergence and the Asymmetry Hypothesis

The convergence process of the mid-1980s, exemplified by Figure 21.7, is important for three reasons. First, it has been interpreted as the outcome of successful policy co-ordination to the point where monetary union appeared as a reasonable, if not easy-to-achieve, goal. Second, it has led to a re-interpretation of the EMS. The initial objective was to protect Europe from international monetary disturbances; now, the goal has shifted to the task of achieving low and similar inflation rates to the point where realignments would become unnecessary. Third, the EMS seems to be evolving into a system in which Germany exerts *de facto* leadership. All three of these aspects are inter-related: given Germany's uncompromising stance on inflation, co-operation and internal stability could be achieved only on that country's terms.

Yet, the emergence of a German monetary leadership, the so-called **asymmetry hypothesis**, is surprising in light of the structural symmetry of EMS institutions. As previous sections have shown, intervention should occur in both the relevant countries, and both monetary authorities should lose their ability to conduct monetary policy. The asymmetry hypothesis implies that Germany has retained independence of its monetary policy. Figure 21.8 illustrates the case: if Germany decides to tighten up its monetary policy, the other EMS countries must decide whether they want to maintain their DM parities—and tighten up their own monetary policies—or devalue *vis à vis* the DM. The asymmetry hypothesis states that the choice has increasingly been that of upholding the DM parity and adopting the Bundesbank's stance, no matter what.

The issue of asymmetry points to a shortcoming of EMS statutes, the failure to address the so-called **N − 1 problem** illustrated by the following example. Consider an EMS consisting of just two countries. There is only one bilateral exchange rate to fix, but there are two central banks. They must agree not only on a given parity, but also on how to defend it, in order to avoid interventions at cross purposes. They can try to develop tight co-ordination and share the burden of interventions. Alternatively, it can be agreed

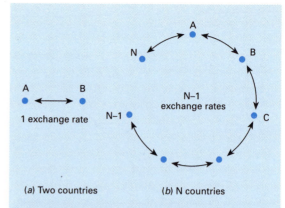

Figure 21.9. The N − 1 problem

Two countries which decide to fix their exchange rate lose one degree of freedom. When *N* countries form a fixed exchange rate system, they commit *N* − 1 exchange rates, or *N* − 1 degrees of freedom. (All the bilateral exchange rates can be calculated from just the *N* − 1 rates shown in panel *b*: all the missing arrows can be drawn using triangular arbitrage as in Figure 18.3.)

that one of the two central banks will devote itself to upholding the exchange rate parity; in that case, the other one remains free to do whatever it likes.[8]

For more than two countries, the argument can be generalized as follows. In a system of *N* fixed parities, there are *N* − 1 independent bilateral exchange rates, as Figure 21.9 illustrates. (All the other bilateral rates can be retrieved from these *N* − 1 rates via triangular arbitrage.) This implies that *N* − 1 central banks lose their independence, and the *N*th remains free of policy constraints. In the Bretton Woods system, all central banks were pegging to the US dollar, leaving the Fed with the task of pegging the dollar to gold. According to the asymmetry hypothesis, all EMS countries have given up monetary policy independence to maintain their parities *vis à vis* the DM, so that Germany has captured the last or *N*th degree of freedom.

In formulating the rules of the fixed rate system, the founders of the EMS neglected to address the *N* − 1 problem. In an oversight that may have had great diplomatic wisdom, they left it to history to allocate the *N*th degree of freedom of the system, officially relying on co-ordination. Two hypotheses, which are not nec-

---

[8] Put differently, if both central banks focus on the same bilateral exchange rate, the money supply in *both* countries is indeterminate!

essarily exclusive, explain how Germany acquired the Nth degree of freedom.[9]

21.3.3.1. Borrowing the Bundesbank's Credibility

One hypothesis maintains that the Nth degree of freedom was spontaneously given to the most reliable central bank. Joining a fixed exchange rate system—more generally, entering into co-operative agreements—implies the willingness to give up some independence. In return, this commitment is expected to bring credibility. (The concept of credibility is presented in Chapter 16.) If monetary authorities are known to be keen to surprise the public with devaluations designed to expand the economy, wages and prices will anticipate this possibility, and will reflect these expectations ahead of the next devaluation. Rather than eliciting economic expansion, the devaluations will simply cause inflation. Inflation will be higher because of the central bank's perceived temptation to inflate, i.e. its lack of credibility. In order to restore or establish credibility, the central bank usually must prove itself by pursuing tough monetary policies, even if this means enduring a depressed level of output for some time until inflation and inflationary expectations are beaten down.

A way to make this 'learning period' as brief as possible is for the central bank to tie its own hands. Pegging the exchange rate to a strong currency represents a highly visible commitment, easy for all to understand and monitor. Tying to the DM is thus a way of 'borrowing' the Bundesbank's credibility. By adopting the Bundesbank's strict stance, EMS countries can impose discipline upon themselves.

21.3.3.2. Systemic asymmetry

The second interpretation stresses the role of sterilization operations by a central bank which tries to retain control of the money supply while conducting foreign exchange market interventions to defend a parity. Imagine two central banks, both committed to uphold their common fixed-but-adjustable exchange rate, but one of them aiming at a lower rate of money growth than the other. If interest rates are such that capital flows from the country with the less restrictive monetary policy to the country with the more restrictive monetary policy, both central banks must intervene to keep their joint parity. If both of them sterilize to keep the money supply on target, the more expansionary country loses reserves and increases its domestic lending while the less expansionary country accumulates foreign exchange reserves. Even if they co-operate, the expanding country loses foreign exchange reserves, or borrows at cost, and is obviously in a more delicate situation than the other one. The situation is clearly asymmetric.

The asymmetry is not due to any rule: it is a fundamental aspect of any fixed exchange rate arrangement when policies diverge. It is, however, related to the $N-1$ problem. In the absence of a declared anchor currency to which other EMS members peg, all member-countries initially attempt to give up as little as possible of their monetary independence, hoping to capture the Nth degree of freedom. The struggle, however, is uneven. Eventually, the central bank that pursues the most restrictive money growth target must prevail. Seen in this light, the first eight years of the EMS, with recurrent crises and realignments, was a period of struggle to be the Nth country. Under this interpretation, the shift to a DM zone, with a long period of exchange rate stability, corresponds to the Bundesbank's domination, not to perfect co-ordination.

21.3.4. Crises and Divergence

In two steps, the EMS has been transformed beyond recognition: (1) it lost two important members when the lira and the pound sterling left the ERM in September 1992; (2) the bands of fluctuation were broadened from ±2.25% to ±15% in August 1993. The story of the crisis that forced these changes is briefly told in Box 21.3. The result has been the emergence of a 'two-speed Europe', with a core of countries that were able to resist the attacks and a 'periphery' struggling to contain the inflationary effects of the devaluations. Many lessons have been learned from the crises of 1992–3.

First, capital flows can be fatal to a system of fixed exchange rates. With daily intervention volumes of the order of ECU 20 billion or more, central banks fighting speculative attacks have learned how powerful unregulated markets are. Figure 21.10 shows the evolution of the foreign exchange reserves of the Banque de France over the month preceding the move to the wide band. This issue is further studied in the next section.

---

[9] A third hypothesis, which is not considered here, attributes German dominance to its hegemonic position in Europe—i.e. its sheer size. Given the size of Italy, UK, and France as counterweights in economic and political matters, this view seems somewhat implausible.

BOX 21.3. FOREIGN EXCHANGE CRISES IN 1992–1993

The worst foreign exchange rate crisis of the postwar period in Europe started the day after Denmark voted against the Treaty of Maastricht on 3 June 1992. This vote, which was eventually reversed in another referendum, sent a powerful signal to the markets: maybe there would not be a single currency, and therefore maybe the EMS would have to survive as a system under the exclusive control of the Bundesbank. What might have succeeded as a transition arrangement appeared untenable for the long run.

Inconsistent policies played a role too. At that time Germany was facing inflationary pressure resulting from unification with East Germany and had decided to tighten monetary policy. The other EMS countries were entering a recession, following a fall in private spending, and needed easier monetary policy conditions. The decoupling of monetary policies was impossible without realignments

vis à vis the DM. This approach was favoured by Germany but vetoed by other countries eager to preserve a strong currency status. The self-imposed pain of tight monetary policy during a recession—reminiscent of Britain's return to gold in 1925—led the exchange markets to wonder how serious their commitment to follow the German leadership really was. First the lira and the pound, both considered overvalued, were attacked. The prompt ousting of these two currencies from the EMS revealed the markets' new power in an era of full capital mobility. Like dominoes, one currency after another discovered that it was not perceived quite as strong as the Deutschmark: by May 1993 the Spanish peseta had been devalued three times, the Portuguese escudo twice, and the Irish punt once. Then in July the markets attacked the Belgian and French francs and the Danish krone, until the margins of fluctuations were finally widened to ±15%.

Second, the long period without realignment was merely the eye of the storm. The strategy of using the exchange rate as an anchor to borrow the Bundesbank's credibility and speed up inflation convergence was working, but could be upheld temporarily only as

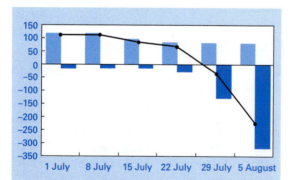

Figure 21.10. Attack on the Foreign Exchange Reserves of France, July 1993

Net foreign exchange reserves are the difference between foreign currency assets held by the central bank and its borrowing in foreign currency, from commercial banks or other central banks. During the month of July 1993, the Banque de France first spent some its holdings and then resorted to wide-scale borrowing. By the time the margins of fluctuations were widened, the Banque de France's reserves were effectively negative.

Source: Banque de France

long as inflation rates had not fully converged to German levels. Competitiveness was constantly altered, and would eventually require a nominal exchange rate correction. When this is the case, corrections should be more frequent and of a smaller magnitude.

Third, real shocks—in contrast to nominal shocks which affect money, prices, and nominal wages—require real exchange rate adjustments. Germany's unification was such a shock, it had to be accompanied by a real appreciation of the mark. This real appreciation could be achieved either through a nominal appreciation of the DM, or through higher inflation in Germany, or else through lower inflation among Germany's partners.[10] In the end, all three happened. It would have been easier simply to adjust the nominal exchange rate. The cost of that policy mistake was disinflation throughout Europe, with a recession and rising unemployment, as predicted by the short-run Phillips curve, while the Bundesbank had to tighten up monetary policy to moderate the inflationary impact.

Fourth, a number currencies that faced attacks were not obviously overvalued: the Danish krone, the French franc, even the Irish punt, had not been quoted by market participants as candidates for a devaluation until the crisis erupted. Why then did they also fall victim? One explanation is **contagion**: once one country devalues, the others lose competitiveness and become candidates for devaluation, even if they were not

---

[10] The real exchange rate EP^*/P can be appreciated, i.e. reduced, either through a decrease in E, an increase in P, or a decline in P^*.

candidates initially. As long as prices in the devaluing country are sticky, the more currencies depreciate, the stronger is the pressure on the others. In this way, financial markets imposed the real appreciation of the DM.

A fifth lesson is the possibility of **self-fulfilling attacks**. These attacks are not justified by the exchange rate fundamentals, strictly seen from the perspective of Chapters 7 and 19. Self-fulfilling attacks occur because, if they succeed, the authorities will relax monetary policy, proving the attack to be rational *ex post*. For example, in 1992–3 the French franc was generally considered strong, based on past inflation and monetary policy. Yet, unemployment was rising, as was political pressure towards lower interest rates. If however the franc were to be forced out the ERM, there would be little political reason to maintain the high interest rates required by the defence of the parity. Self-fulfilling attacks are particularly worrisome. They imply that an exchange rate attack can be triggered by the markets' assessment that monetary policy will be changed by the attack itself.

Finally, the Bundesbank discovered that it was not immune from exchange market pressure either. Indeed, when the other currencies hit the limit of their margins of fluctuation, the Bundesbank was bound to intervene with—or, equivalently, to lend—unlimited amounts, and the German money supply surged temporarily as a result of the 1992–3 crises. Unlimited borrowing rights is a particularly strong commitment rarely seen in exchange rate systems, since it could mean a considerable increase in the money supply. Under pressure, this agreement has not worked fully up to its promises. The floating of the lira and the pound, the succession of devaluations, and the shift to the wider bands of fluctuation in August 1993 can be viewed as ways of weakening an untenable open-ended commitment.

21.3.5. Capital Controls and the EMS

The EMS has evolved from a loose arrangement among countries pursuing different inflation objectives to a more cohesive system in which inflation is low and differs relatively little from one country to another. This has been achieved through the adoption of monetary policies similar to those traditionally pursued by the Bundesbank. As Germany emerged as *primus inter pares*, the centre of an EMS committed to low inflation, the other countries have gradually abandoned

their monetary independence. The loss of monetary independence was hastened by the decision to eliminate capital controls by July 1990 as a part of the Single European Act,[11] an overall effort to remove restrictions on the mobility of goods, people, and capital within the EC implemented on 1 January 1993.

21.3.5.1. The role of capital controls

During the Bretton Woods era, and in the EMS until the late 1980s, a large number of countries maintained various restrictions to the movement of assets across their borders, as explained in Box 21.4. Capital controls represent one way of recovering some form of monetary policy independence: the choice of the trend inflation rate. Indeed, any inflation rate is compatible with membership to a fixed-but-adjustable exchange rate system provided that realignments occur frequently enough. Countries with less than average inflation revalue their currencies, while high-inflation countries re-establish competitiveness through recurrent depreciations. The problem is that markets can easily guess which currency will be revalued and which will be devalued. What is called a 'one-way bet' is an irresistible temptation for speculators to sell the devaluation-prone currency and buy the revaluation-prone one, with no risk: either the expected realignment occurs and great profits are pocketed, or it does not and little is lost.

21.3.5.2. The impossible trilogy

The coexistence of fixed exchange regimes and capital controls may be more than coincidental. Capital controls enable countries participating in fixed exchange rate arrangements to preserve some monetary autonomy. The countries that use capital controls are also those that tend to have higher inflation. Indeed, controls may be essential to organize orderly realignments in the face of market attacks. The **impossible trilogy** principle states that, while pairwise compatible, the following three characteristics are jointly incompatible: (1) full capital mobility; (2) fixed exchange rates; (3) monetary policy independence. This principle is a direct implication of the Mundell–Fleming (*IS–LM*) framework: if capital is fully mobile, the interest rate is given exogenously by the foreign rate i^*, and the *LM* curve is given by cumulated net capital inflow.

This principle offers a powerful way to review the

---

[11] Greece and Portugal have obtained a grace period.

BOX 21.4. CAPITAL CONTROLS

Capital controls are designed to limit or eliminate movements of assets across countries. Many reasons, mostly bad ones, have been invoked to limit capital mobility. The nationalistic viewpoint is that our savings should stay at home to finance our investments and create jobs for our workers. Another view is that capital outflows often conceal illegal business or tax avoidance. One effect of controls is to separate, at least temporarily, domestic and foreign financial markets. This physical separation invalidates the interest parity principle and weakens the link among national interest rates. It represents one means of restoring some degree of monetary independence, by allowing national authorities to affect the domestic interest rate.

Capital or exchange controls can take a number of forms. The more direct procedure is to ban (some categories of) international financial transactions. For example, residents may be forbidden to send money abroad or to buy foreign assets. More subtle procedures include taxing international financial transactions: if the tax is high enough, many transactions cease to be rewarding and do not take place.[12] Thus, in the early 1970s, facing massive capital inflows, Germany and Switzerland imposed negative returns on bank deposits by non-residents.

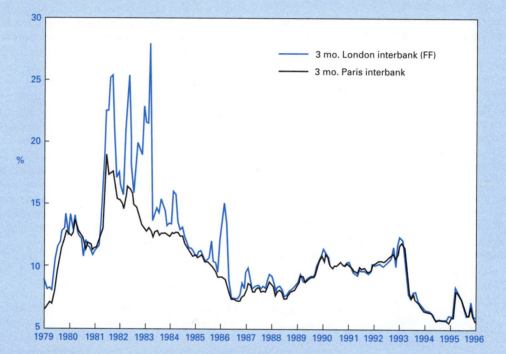

Figure 21.11. French Interest Rates, Onshore and Offshore

The interest parity condition implies that when speculators expect the franc to be devalued they require a higher interest rate. At times of speculative attacks, interest rates on the franc in London rise sharply relative to identical rates in Paris. French authorities used capital controls until 1988 and were able to insulate Paris interest rates from the interest parity condition. But the market in London is not subject to controls and reflects the traders' expectations. Over time, leakages between the two markets occur and the two interest rates are brought back into line. The figure shows the interbank rate—the interest rate that banks charge each other for three months' deposits—in January of each year.

Source: IMF

---

[12] Taxes on exchange rate transactions are often called Tobin taxes, in reference to James Tobin, Nobel Prize winner, who once suggested that governments 'throw sand in the wheels of international finance'. The view that international capital flow can be excessively volatile and a source of concern was endorsed earlier by Keynes.

BOX 21.4. (cont.)

Another possibility is to treat current and capital account transactions differently: dual exchange rate markets have existed, for example, in Belgium (until 1990 there existed a commercial franc for current account transactions and a financial franc for capital account transactions) and in South Africa until 1995. Another approach to deterring capital outflows is to impose deposit requirements on foreign assets: any purchase of foreign assets must be matched by a zero-interest one-year deposit at the central bank. (This has been done e.g. in Italy and, briefly, Spain.) To deter outflows, deposit requirements can be imposed on foreign liabilities to non-residents (as in Chile and Colombia, which escaped unscathed the crisis that followed the December 1994 collapse of the Mexican peso). The problem with capital controls is that they can eas-ily be circumvented. This does not prevent them, how-ever, from slowing down speculative attacks. Because of the costs involved in complying with, or circumventing, controls, reactions to fleeting expectations of realignment are dampened. This gives monetary authorities room for manoeuvre: as long as they 'bite', controls separate domestic and foreign financial markets. Figure 21.11 shows interest rates on French francs in Paris and in London. Because French legislation does not apply there, movements on the franc in London are completely free and interest parity applies. The fact that the interest rates on identical assets (here, franc interbank deposits) can differ from one financial centre to another is a proof that controls work, at least for a while.

EMS experience and outlook. The early EMS was able to survive because of the presence of capital controls. It permitted, during the first phase, the co-existence of fixed exchange rates and some degree of monetary independence, mainly the coexistence of different inflation rates compensated for by periodic realignments. The second phase was an attempt to adopt the same monetary policy everywhere under German leadership. As long as economic conditions did not call for different policies, this was a relatively costless way to cope with the impossible trilogy. It is during that period that capital controls were dismantled. However, the shock of German unification and a worldwide recession in the early 1990s, which raised the costs of the loss of monetary policy independence, changed all that. The crises that followed correspond to the travails imposed by attempts to ignore the impossible trilogy. The solutions adopted—free floating in Italy and the UK, wide bands elsewhere—correspond to the abandonment of the fixed exchange rate.

21.3.5.3. The logic of the European Monetary Union without capital controls

Once capital controls are removed, the choice boils down to either a single monetary authority or a free float. The experience of 1992–3 shows that the temptation of monetary independence—including the risk of self-fulfilling attacks—plays havoc with a fixed exchange rate arrangement. It was probably unavoidable that countries that had lost their monetary independence, but supported fixed exchange rates, would question the wisdom of following the Bundesbank leadership. It is not surprising that the countries that pledged in the mid-1980s to abandon capital controls —Belgium, France, Italy, and Spain—soon thereafter proposed the creation of a European Monetary Union. Nor is it surprising that the Bundesbank expressed doubts about the urgency of taking a step which amounts to sharing its undisputed control over European monetary policy.

21.4. European Monetary Union

At the Rome Council[13] in 1989, the EC countries formally pledged to move towards monetary union. The Treaty of Rome, the Act that gave birth to the EC in 1957, contained provisions that the eventual objective of the signatory countries was full economic and monetary integration. This was amended in 1992 to incorporate the decision reached in Maastricht to adopt a single currency by January 1999 at the latest. In the following sections we examine the argument for having a single currency throughout Europe, beginning with a discussion of the theory of optimum currency areas.

[13] The European Council is the name given to meetings of heads of states.

21.4.1. The Theory of Optimum Currency Areas

A region is an **optimum currency area** when its use of a common currency implies no loss of welfare.[14] To grasp this point, it is useful to consider two extreme examples. Surely, a city—even a large one like London or Paris—is a currency area. Its citizens move about all the time, and Parisians would find it cumbersome, to say the least, to change 6th Arrondissement francs for 17th Arrondissement currency whenever importing newspapers or *baguettes* from across town. At the other extreme, few would consider the world as a whole to be an optimum currency area.[15] When disturbances of one form or another arise in some part of the world, it has proven practical to adjust the relevant exchange rate. These two examples suggest that an optimum currency area (a geographical area wherein a single currency is used) lies somewhere in between, say, a city and the whole world. But this statement is not very helpful, because it leaves us with too vague a conclusion. What is clear is that, for the most part, actual currency areas generally match national boundaries.[16] This is probably because, as stressed in Chapters 8 and 9, national governments are best suited for internalizing the information externality that having a common currency entails, which they do by declaring money to be legal tender. Which key characteristics, then, define an optimum currency area? Two main criteria have been suggested.

21.4.1.1. Mobility of factors production

The first criterion emphasizes factor mobility, or the rapidity with which capital, labour, and other factors of production can move to other locations. Barring restrictions on its ownership, physical capital is quite mobile. Over time, investments accumulate in the right place, and the success of the 1992 programme of the EC is testimony to this fact. In contrast, labour may not be so mobile. Language is the most often cited barrier to migration, but differing customs, traditions, and preferences matter as well. As noted in Chapters 6 and 17, governments may even implement policies that inhibit labour mobility, by regulating house prices and rents, subsidizing declining industries, or providing unemployment benefits. Inefficient property markets may make moving an expensive proposition if it means selling and refinancing property and business assets.

Suppose that the southern part of London were struck by an earthquake. Factories and residents would be able to relocate with little difficulty to the northern part of the city, at least until the southern half was rebuilt. However, if the earthquake were to hit all of the UK instead, it is doubtful whether relocation to neighbouring France or Denmark would be as easy, for either the Britons, or the French and Danes. The UK might prefer to depreciate its currency, in order to make it easier to quickly export what can still be produced and also to attract foreign capital with low labour costs. Note that a real depreciation is warranted, since the wealth and competitiveness of the UK economy will have suffered. The nominal depreciation would simply provide a less painful means of achieving this end.

On this criterion, even some nation-states would not qualify as optimum currency areas. Labour mobility is notoriously limited between the south and the north of Italy, for example, or between northern and southern England, or between Schleswig-Holstein and Bavaria. Indeed, it may well be that a single currency for all of the UK or Italy or Germany is not economically desirable, but has been adopted for political reasons. The German monetary union between East and West Germany makes this aspect quite evident.

21.4.1.2. Common shocks

A second criterion for optimum currency areas concerns the disturbances that may threaten a city, region, or nation. Earthquakes are just one illustration. Others are more likely to be important. For example, if a region exports some natural resource the price of which is quite variable, exchange rate changes are an efficient way of weathering such price fluctuations. A typical example is the state of Texas, which relies on oil exports for much of its economic fortunes; coal-dependent areas such as Lorraine in France or the Ruhr in Germany share the same problem. Other examples of potentially important disturbances include different patterns of productivity advances or local cost increases arising from labour unrest or ecological restrictions.[17] On this basis, an optimum currency area

---

[14] The seminal work on optimum currency areas is by Robert Mundell, the same economist who shaped the Mundell–Fleming *IS–LM* framework presented in Ch. 11.

[15] Some economists, like Keynes, supported a world currency, as we were reminded by Alistair Milne from the University of Surrey.

[16] There are some exceptions. Luxemburg and Belgium share the same currency; Liberia and Panama use the US dollar; many former French colonies in Africa use a version of the French franc, although apparently with growing discomfort.

---

[17] Such disturbances must be quantitatively large—the oil price increase is probably insufficient to justify excluding Scotland from the British currency area—and sufficiently long-lasting—a bad grape harvest in the Bordeaux region has little persistence over time—to require more than temporary borrowing.

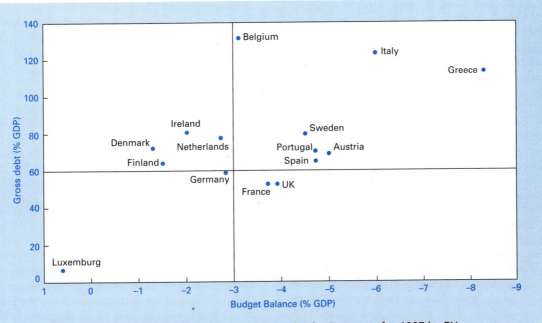

Figure 21.12. The Budgetary Convergence Criteria: Forecasts for 1997 by EU Commission

The decision on which countries are eligible for monetary union membership will be made in early 1998 based on the performance on 1997. The two budgetary criteria are described on the vertical (gross public debt not in excess of 60%, or at least significant progress) and horizontal (budget deficit not in excess of 3% of GDP) axes. Eligible countries must be inside the lower left rectangle. Forecasts made late in 1995 indicate that only two countries would meet both criteria in 1996: Luxemburg and Germany.

Source: European Economy

extends over a region which, on average, faces roughly similar economic disturbances. For example, if wages frequently follow dissimilar patterns in two regions, say because trade unions are organized along regional lines, at least one of these regions may lose from sharing currency with the other.

21.4.2. Is Europe an Optimum Currency Area?

Both arguments are suggestive of what may define an optimum currency area, especially with respect to Europe. Yet it is difficult to make this definition operational. Labour mobility, for example, may be endogenous to the existence of a currency area and some of its accompanying features. Workers will relocate more readily to regions sharing the same currency (e.g. in order to remit their earnings) if legal institutions

are similar, and if retirement benefits are transferable. Similarly, unions tend to organize on a national level, but why not at the currency-area level? In the end, the two criteria help us understand better why a city is an optimum currency area and the world as a whole is not. When it comes to finer segmentation, however, they do not provide a clear answer. If North and South Germany—or East and West Germany—can form a successful currency area, why not the EMS countries?

21.4.3. Towards a Monetary Union

The Treaty of Maastricht, signed in December 1991 and ratified by all EU members, lays the groundwork for the process leading to the European Monetary Union (EMU). The Treaty defines three stages. The first stage began with the removal of the remaining capital controls in July 1990. The increased integration of financial markets was meant to usher in an enhanced commitment to fixed parities within the EMS and possibly the further limitation of allowed margins of fluctuations. The second stage began in 1994 with the setting up of the **European Monetary Institute (EMI)** in Frankfurt. The EMI is preparing the practical steps required to establish an integrated system of European central banks, including the partial pooling of foreign exchange reserves and the development of common operating procedures. Along with the Commission of Brussels, the EMI will propose to the heads of state in the spring of 1998, the list of countries deemed ready for entering the EMU on 1 January 1999.[18] The third stage, the last, is to start with the irrevocable fixing of exchange rates among the countries admitted to Monetary Union. It will be accompanied by the creation of a **European System of Central Banks (ESCB)**. At the centre of this system will lie the **European Central Bank**, a new institution which will determine monetary policy across the EMU. National central banks are to survive as local subsidiaries, mostly in charge of bank supervision and operational aspects. At this stage the common currency is to begin circulating, gradually replacing the national currencies.

21.4.4. Convergence Criteria

The adoption of a common currency by independent states raises a number of fears. Will the countries see eye-to-eye on what should be the proper conduct of monetary policy? In particular, Germany, which stands to lose one of the world's strongest currencies, has insisted all along that the new European currency must

be as strong as the DM, and that inflation in the EMU must never be allowed. The response is the adoption of **convergence criteria** which must be met by any country before it enters the Monetary Union. The five main criteria are: (1) the member-country's inflation may not exceed the average of the three lowest inflation rates in the EMS by more than 1.5%; (2) its long-term interest rate must not exceed the average of the interest rates in the three countries with the lowest inflation rates by more than 2%; (3) its exchange rate must have been in the 'normal' band of the ERM without devaluation for at least two years;[19] (4) its public debt cannot exceed 60% of its GDP; (5) the budget deficit must not exceed 3% of its GDP.

These criteria are meant to guarantee that the countries that join the EMU will have achieved, and will be able to sustain, a low rate of inflation. The first three criteria are directed at achieving low inflation: not only must inflation be low, and have been low long enough for the country to have been in the ERM at an unchanged rate, but the markets, which use the Fisher principle when setting long-term rates, must believe that inflation will remain low in the distant future. The last two criteria refer to the risk of debt monetization: EMU member-countries should solve their budgetary problems through non-inflationary means.

At the time of the Maastricht agreement, only three countries satisfied all five criteria: Denmark, France, and Luxemburg (which does not have its own currency). Figure 21.12 shows the situation concerning the budgetary criteria. Some countries have an excessive debt and cannot hope to bring it below 60%. The Treaty allows for some flexibility, as it considers that substantial progress towards that objective is acceptable. In 1995, Ireland was officially recognized as having achieved sufficient progress.

---

[18] In principle, a country declared admitted to the Union must join the EMI. Denmark and the UK have obtained an 'opt-out clause'. In addition, the German Supreme Court has ruled that the final decision must be ratified by the European Parliament. Of course, a country can always willingly miss the convergence criteria (see next section) and be rejected.

[19] When the Treaty was adopted, the normal bands unambiguously refered to the ±2.25% bands, in contrast to the ±6% bands. The adoption, officially 'provisional', of the ±15% bands in 1993 leaves open the issue of what is 'normal'.

21.5. Summary

1. The European Monetary System is a system of fixed but adjustable exchange rates. Via a set of central rates with respect to the ECU, the EMS parities are declared pairwise for all currencies in the grid.

2. The European Currency Unit (ECU) is a unit of account determined as a weighted average of EC currencies. The actual fixing of exchange rate parities is implied only by participation in the Exchange Rate Mechanism (ERM).

3. The EMS is strengthened by an agreement that allows central banks to borrow freely from each other in order to defend existing parities. Parity changes must be agreed by all ERM members.

4. Any fixed exchange rate system with N participating countries gives up $N-1$ degrees of freedom (the $N-1$ exchange rates sufficient to determine the entire set of bilateral rates). As a result, one central bank can target the money supply and retain monetary policy independence; the others are committed to their exchange rate targets and lose monetary policy independence.

5. In principle, the ERM requires all participating countries to intervene in a symmetric way. In practice, sterilization can be sustained for a longer period for a country with an appreciating currency than for one with a depreciating currency.

6. Speculative attacks represent the markets' effort at correcting imbalances. They occur when the markets expect that a change of parity is approaching: in order to avoid losses, and to make gains, traders must act before the authorities change the parity. Speculative attacks may also be self-fulfilling.

7. The Treaty of Maastricht sets forth convergence criteria which must be met for admission to the EMU. These criteria, which encompass inflation, long-term interest rates, deficits, and debt levels, are designed to achieve harmony in economic policies in member countries.

Key Concepts

- economic policy co-ordination
- European Monetary System (EMS)
- Exchange Rate Mechanism (ERM)
- central parity; parity
- band of fluctuation
- parity grid
- European Currency Unit (ECU)
- intramarginal interventions
- speculative attacks

- asymmetry hypothesis
- N – 1 problem
- contagion
- self-fulfilling attacks
- impossible trilogy
- optimum currency area
- European Monetary Union (EMU)
- European Monetary Institute (EMI)
- European System of Central Banks

Questions for Discussion

1. 'By providing an island of stability, the EMS has fostered trade among its members at the expense of trade with non-EMS countries.' Comment.

2. The Italian lira has been devalued several times since the creation of the EMS. After each devaluation, Italian interest rates remain higher than in Germany. How can this be explained?

3. Membership in the EMS has resulted in inflationary pressure in Germany. True or false?

4. An argument in favour of Britain's full EMS membership has been that it would then be easier to fight inflation. Evaluate this argument.

5. When there is a single currency in Europe and yet different states, how might the gains from seigniorage by distributed?

6. Some proposals for the future European Central Bank envisaged the non-voting presence of European Community officials on the central bank's governing board. What are the implications of such a presence?

7. The absence of realignment within the EMS is equivalent to the existence of a monetary union, so what can Germany gain from joining a monetary union?

8. Critics assert that the EMS is an engine of recession. What could their arguments be? Do you agree? (You are encouraged to turn to evidence presented elsewhere in this book.)

9. It is said that Germany's unification required a real appreciation of the DM. Others maintain that a depreciation was necessary. What could be the arguments?

10. If only some EU countries enter the EMU, what will happen to monetary relations with those that stay out? What do you predict will happen to monetary and exchange rate policy for the 'outsiders'?

Suggested Further Reading

The EMS is presented and analysed in:

Giavazzi, Francesco, and Giovannini, Alberto (1989), *Limiting Exchange Rate Flexibility: the European Monetary System*, MIT Press, Cambridge, Mass.

Giavazzi, F., Micossi, S., and Miller, M. (eds.) (1988), *European Monetary System*, Cambridge University Press.

Weber, Axel (1991), 'Reputation and Credibility in the European Monetary System', *Economic Policy*, 12: 57–102.

The 1992–3 attacks have been studied in:

Eichengreen, Barry, and Wyplosz, Charles (1993), 'The Unstable EMS', *Brookings Papers on Economic Activity*, 1:51–124.

Obstfeld, Maurice (1995), 'International Currency Experience: New Lessons and Lessons Relearned', *Brookings Papers on Economic Activity*, 1:119–220.

Svensson, Lars E. O. (1994), 'Fixed Exchange Rates as a Means to Price Stability: What Have We Learned?' *European Economic Review*, 38:447–68.

The classic reference for the European Monetary Union is the Treaty of Maastricht itself. For analyses, see:

Bean, Charles (1992), 'Economic and Monetary Union in Europe', *Journal of Economic Perspectives*, 6(4): 31–52.

Begg, David, Giavazzi, Francesco, Spaventa, Luigi, and Wyplosz, Charles (1991), 'European Monetary Union: the Macro Issues', *Monitoring European Integration: the Making of Monetary Union*, Centre for Economic Policy Research, London.

Buiter, Willem, Corsetti, Giancarlo, and Roubini, Nouriel (1993), 'Excessive Deficits: Sense and Nonsense in the Treaty of Maastricht', *Economic Policy*, 16:57–100.

De Cecco, Mario, and Giovannini, Alberto (eds.) (1989), *A European Central Bank*? Cambridge University Press.

De Grauwe, Paul (1992), *The Economics of Monetary Integration*, Oxford University Press.

Eichengreen, Barry (1990), 'One Money for Europe? Lessons from the US Currency Union', *Economic Policy*, 10: 117–88.

Fratianni, Michele, and von Hagen, Jurgen (1992), *The European Monetary System and European Monetary Union*, Westview Press, Boulder, Colo.

Fratianni, Michele and Peters, Theo (eds.) (1978), *One Money for Europe*, Macmillan, London.

For a good presentation of alternative fixed exchange rate regimes (crawling bands), see:

Helpman, Elhanan, Leiderman, Leo, and Bufman, Gil (1994), 'A New Breed of Exchange Rates: Chile, Israel and Mexico', *Economic Policy*, 19:259–306.

References

Abel, Andrew (1982), 'Dynamic Effects of Permanent and Temporary Tax Policies in a q Model of Investment', *Journal of Monetary Economics*, 9: 353–74.

Adelman, Irma and Adelman, Frank (1959), 'The Dynamic Properties of the Klein-Goldberger Model', *Econometrica*, 27: 596–625.

Akerlof, Georges, Rose, Andrew, Yellen, Janet, and Hessenius, Helga (1991), 'East Germany in from the Cold: the Economic Aftermath of Currency Union', *Brookings Papers on Economic Activity*, 1: 1–106.

Alesina, Alberto (1988a), 'The End of Large Public Debts', in L. Spaventa (ed.), *High Public Debt: the Experience in Italy*, Cambridge University Press.

—— (1988b), 'Macroeconomics and Politics', *NBER Macroeconomics Annual*, 3: 13–62.

—— (1989), 'Politics and Business Cycles in Industrial Democracies', *Economic Policy*, 8: 55–98.

—— and Perotti, Roberto (1995), 'Fiscal Adjustments: Fiscal Expansions and Adjustments in OECD Countries', *Economic Policy*, 21: 205–48.

—— and Summers, Lawrence (1993), 'Central Bank Independence and Macroeconomic Performance', *Journal of Money Credit and Banking*, 25: 151–62.

Ashenfelter, Orley, and Layard, Richard (1986), *The Handbook of Labor Economics*, North-Holland, Amsterdam.

Baltensperger, Ernst, and Dermine, Jean (1987), 'Banking Deregulation in Europe', *Economic Policy*, 4: 63–110.

Barnouin, Barbara (1986), *The European Labour Movement and European Integration*, Francis Pinter, London.

Barro, Robert (1989), 'The Ricardian Approach to Budget Deficits', *Journal of Economic Perspectives*, 3: 37–54.

—— (1991), 'Economic Growth in a Cross Section of Countries', *Quarterly Journal of Economics*, 106: 407–44.

—— and Gordon, David (1983), 'Rules, Discretion, and Reputation in a Model of Monetary Policy', *Journal of Monetary Economics*, 12: 101–22.

—— and Sala-i-Martin, Xavier (1995), *Economic Growth*, McGraw-Hill, New York.

—— and Wolf, Holger (1989), 'Data Appendix for Economic Growth in a Cross-Section of Countries', unpublished.

Bartolini, Leonardo, Symansky, Steven and Razin, Assaf (1995), 'G7 Fiscal Restructuring in the 1990s: Macroeconomic Effects', *Economic Policy*, 20: 109–46.

Baumol, William (1952), 'The Transactions Demand for Cash: an Inventory Theoretic Approach', *Quarterly Journal of Economics*, 66: 545–56.

Bean, Charles (1994), 'European Unemployment: a Survey', *Journal of Economic Literature*, 32: 620–39.

—— and Symons, James (1989), 'Ten Years of Mrs. T', *NBER Macroeconomics Annual*, MIT Press, Cambridge, Mass., 4: 13–60.

Bean, Charles, Danthine, Jean-Pierre, Giavazzi, Francesco, and Wyplosz, Charles

(1990), 'The East, the Deutschmark, and EMU', in *Monitoring European Integration: the Impact of Eastern Europe*, Centre for Economic Policy Research, London.

Bean, Charles, Giavazzi, Francesco, Spaventa, Luigi, and Wyplosz, Charles (1991), 'European Monetary Union: the Macro Issues', *Monitoring European Integration: the Making of Monetary Union*, Centre for Economic Policy Research, London.

Berg, Andrew, and Sachs, Jeffrey (1992), 'Structural Adjustment and International Trade in Eastern Europe: the Case of Poland', *Economic Policy*, 14: 117–73.

Bertola, Guiseppe (1990), 'Job Security, Employment and Wages', *European Economic Review*, 34: 851–86.

Blanchard, Olivier J. (1987), 'Reaganomics', *Economic Policy*, 5: 15–56.

—— and Bentolila, Samuel (1990), 'Spanish Unemployment', *Economic Policy*, 10: 233–81.

Bloch, Laurence, and Coeuré, Benoit (1994), '*q* de Tobin marginal et transmission des chocs financiers', *Annales d'Economie et de Statistique*, 36: 133–67.

Bloomfield, Arthur (1959), *Monetary Policy under the International Gold Standard*, Federal Reserve Bank, New York.

Booth, Alison L. (1995), *The Economics of the Trade Union*, Cambridge University Press.

Bulow, Jeremy, and Rogoff, Kenneth (1990), 'Cleaning Up Third World Debt without Getting Taken to the Cleaners', *Journal of Economic Perspectives*, Winter: 31–42.

Burda, Michael (1988), 'Wait Unemployment in Europe', *Economic Policy*, 7: 391–426.

—— and Gerlach, Stefan (1990), 'Exchange Rate Dynamics and Currency Unification: the Ostmark–DM Rate', INSEAD Working Paper no. 90/78/EP.

—— and Wyplosz, Charles (1994), 'Gross Job and Worker Flows in Europe', *European Economic Review*, 38: 1287–1315.

Burmeister, Edwin, and Dobell, A. Rodney (1970), *Mathematical Theories of Economic Growth*, Macmillan, New York.

de Caires, Brian (1988), *The GT Guide to World Equity Markets 1988*, Euromoney.

Cairncross, Alec, and Eichengreen, Barry (1983), *Sterling in Decline*, Basil Blackwell, Oxford.

Calmfors, Lars, and Driffill, John (1988), 'Bargaining Structure, Corporatism, and Macroeconomic Performance', *Economic Policy*, 6: 13–62.

—— and Nymoen, Ragnar (1990), 'Real Wage Adjustment and Employment Policies in the Nordic Countries', *Economic Policy*, 11: 397–448.

Cardoso, Eliana, and Dornbusch, Rudiger (1989), 'Brazilian Debt Crises: Past and Present', in Barry Eichengreen and Peter Lindert (eds.), *The International Debt Crisis in Historical Perspective*, MIT Press, Cambridge, Mass.

Chadha, Bankim and Eswar Prasad (1994), 'Are Prices Countercyclical? Evidence from the G-7', IMF Working Paper WP 94/91, August.

Chan-Lee, James H. (1986), 'Pure Profit and Tobin's *q* in Nine OECD Countries', *OECD Economic Studies*, 7: 205–32.

Chiappori, Pierre-Andre, Mayer, Colin, Neven, Damien, and Vives, Xavier (1991), 'The Microeconomics of Monetary Union', in *Monitoring European Integration*, Centre for Economic Policy Research, London.

Cline, William (1984), *International Debt*, MIT Press, Cambridge, Mass.

Cooper, Richard N. (1982), 'The Gold Standard: Historical Facts and Future Prospects', *Brookings Papers on Economic Activity*, 1: 1–56.

Dam, Kenneth W. (1982), *The Rules of the Game*, University of Chicago Press.

Danthine, Jean-Pierre and Donaldson, John (1993), 'Methodological and Empirical Issues in Real Business Cycle Theory', *European Economic Review*, 31: 1–36.

Davis, Phil (1990), 'The Financial Sector and the UK Economy', unpublished paper.

Dean, Andrew, Durand, Martine, Fallon, John, and Hoeller, Peter (1989), 'Saving Trends and Behaviour in OECD Countries', OECD Working Paper no. 67, June.

Dornbusch, Rudiger (1976), 'Expectations and Exchange Rate Dynamics', *Journal of Political Economy*, 84, 1161–76.

—— (1988), 'Stabilization, Debt, and Growth', *Economic Policy*, 7: 231–84.

—— and Fischer, Stanley (1986), 'Stopping Hyperinflations Past and Present', *Weltwirtschaftliches Archiv*, 122: 1–47.

Dreze, Jacques, Wyplosz, Charles, Bean, Charles, Giavazzi, Francesco, and Giersch, Herbert (1987), *The Two-Handed Growth Strategy for Europe: Autonomy through Flexible Cooperation*, Centre for European Policy Studies, Brussels.

Ehrenberg, Ronald, and Smith, Robert, (1988), *Modern Labor Economics*, 3rd edn., Scott Foresman, London.

Eichengreen, Barry (1990*a*), 'Trends and Cycles in Foreign Lending', Discussion Paper, Centre for Economic Policy Research, London.

—— (1990*b*) 'One Money for Europe? Lessons from the US Currency Union', *Economic Policy*, 10: 117–87.

Emerson, Michael (1988), 'Regulation or Deregulation of the Labour Market', *European Economic Review*, 32: 775–818.

Engel, Charles, and Hamilton, James D. (1990), 'Long Swings in the Dollar: Are They in the Data and Do Markets Know It?', *American Economic Review*, 80: 689–713.

Fair, Ray C. (1987), 'International Evidence on the Demand for Money', *Review of Economics and Statistics*, 69: 473–80.

Feldstein, Martin, and Horioka, Charles (1980), 'Domestic Saving and International Capital Flows', *Economic Journal*, 90: 314–29.

Fischer, Stanley (1977), 'Long term Contracts, Rational Expectations, and the Optimal Money Supply Rule', *Journal of Political Economy*, 85: 163–90.

Flood, Robert, and Garber, Peter (1984), 'Collapsing Exchange Rate Regimes: Some Linear Examples', *Journal of International Economics*, 17: 1–13.

Frankel, Jeffrey A. (1990), 'Quantifying International Capital Mobility in the 1980s', in D. Bernheim and J. Shoven (eds.), *Saving*, University of Chicago Press.

Frenkel, Jacob, and Assaf, Razin (1987), *Fiscal Policies and the World Economy*, MIT Press, Cambridge, Mass.

Friedman, Milton (1953), 'The Effect of Full Employment Policy on Economic Stability: a Formal Analysis', in *Essays in Positive Economics*, University of Chicago Press.

—— (1968), 'The Role of Monetary Policy', *American Economic Review*, 58: 1–17.

Froot, Kenneth, and Frankel, Jeffrey (1989), 'Forward Discount Bias: Is it an Exchange Risk Premium?', *Quarterly Journal of Economics*, 104: 139–61.

Garber, Peter (1990), 'The Dollar as a Bubble', in S. Gerlach and P. Petri (eds.), *The Economics of the Dollar Cycle*, MIT Press, Cambridge, Mass.

Gerlach, Stefan, and Smets, Frank (1995), 'The Monetary Transmission Mechanism: Evidence from the G-7 Countries', CEPR Discussion Paper No 1219, July.

Giavazzi, Francesco, and Giovannini, Alberto (1989), *Limiting Exchange Rate Flexibility: the European Monetary System*, MIT Press, Cambridge, Mass.

—— and Pagano, Marco (1990), 'Can Severe Fiscal Policy Contractions be Expansionary? Tales of Two Small European Countries', CEPR Discussion Paper no. 417.

Gilder, George (1981), *Wealth and Poverty*, Basic Books, New York.

Goodhart, Charles A. E. (1988), *The Evolution of Central Banks*, MIT Press, Cambridge, Mass.

Gordon, Robert J. (1990), 'What is the New Keynesian Economics?' *Journal of Economic Literature*, 28: 1115–71.

Grilli, Alberto, Masciandaro, Donato, and Tabellini, Guido (1991), 'Political and Monetary Institutions and Public Financial Policies in the Industrial Countries', *Economic Policy*, 13: 341–92.

Gros, Daniel (1991), 'A Note on Seigniorage in the EC', *European Journal of Political Economy*.

Hagemann, Robert P., Jones, Brian R., and Montador, R. Bruce (1988), 'Tax Reform in OECD Countries: Motives, Constraints and Practice', *OECD Economic Studies*, 10: 185–226.

Hamilton, Carl, Neven, Damien, Norman, Victor, Sapir, André, Smith, Alasdair, and Winters, L. Alan (1990), 'Trade Patterns and Trade Policies', CEPR Report on *Monitoring European Integration: the Impact of Eastern Europe*, Centre for Economic Policy Research, London.

Hellwig, Martin, and Neumann, Manfred (1987), 'Economic Policy in Germany: Was There a Turnaround?' *Economic Policy*, 5: 103–46.

Homer, Sydney (1963), *A History of Interest Rates*, Rutgers University Press, New Brunswick, NJ.

Hughes, Gordon, and Smith, Stephen (1991), 'Economic Aspects of Decentralized Government: Structure, Functions and Finance', *Economic Policy*, 13: 425–59.

Issing, Otmar (1994), 'Experience Gained with Monetary Policy Instruments in Germany', in Jachmich (ed.), *Monetary Policy Instruments: National Experiences and European Perspectives*, Vol. 27 of *Bankhistorisches Archiv*, Fritz Knapp Verlag, Frankfurt.

Jevons, William (1875), *Money and the Mechanism of Exchange*, Routledge & Kegan Paul, London.

Kaldor, Nicholas (1961), 'Capital Accumulation and Economic Growth', in F. Lutz and V. Hague (eds.), *The Theory of Capital*, St Martin's Press, New York, pp. 177–222.

Keynes, John Maynard (1930), *A Treatise on Money*, Macmillan, London.

—— (1936), *The General Theory of Employment, Interest and Money*, Macmillan, London.

Kindleberger, Charles (1973), *The World in Depression*, University of California Press.

Kydland, Finn E., and Prescott, Edward (1977), 'Rules Rather than Discretion: the Time Inconsistency of Optimal Plans', *Journal of Political Economy*, 85: 473–90.

Lackó, Maria (1996), 'Hungarian Hidden Economy in International Comparisons: Estimation Method Based on Household Electricity Consumption and Currency Ratio', unpublished, Institute of Economics, Hungarian Academy of Sciences.

Lasheras, Miguel (1991), 'Reflexiones en torno a un sistema fiscal alternativo', *Moneda y Credito*, 192: 163–98.

Layard, Richard, Nickell, Stephen, and Jackman, Richard (1991), *Unemployment*, Oxford University Press.

Levich, Richard (1978), 'Tests of Forecasting Models and Market Efficiency in the International Money Market', in Jacob A. Frenkel and H. G. Johnson (eds.), *The Economics of Exchange Rates*, Addison-Wesley, Reading, Mass., pp. 129–58.

Lindbeck, Assar, *et al.* (1993), 'Options for Economic and Political Reform in Sweden', *Economic Policy*, 17, 220–63.

Lipton, David, and Sachs, Jeffrey (1990), 'Creating a Market Economy in Eastern Europe: the Case of Poland', *Brookings Papers on Economic Activity*, 1: 75–133.

Lucas, Robert, E. Jr. (1966), 'Optimal Investment with Rational Expectations', reprinted in R. E. Lucas and T. J. Sargent (eds.), *Rational Expectations and Econometric Practice*, University of Minnesota Press, Minneapolis, 1981.

——— (1976), 'Econometric Policy Evaluation: a Critique', in K. Brunner and A. Meltzer (eds.), *The Phillips Curve and Labor Markets*, Vol. 1 of *Carnegie-Rochester Conference Series on Public Policy*, North-Holland, Amsterdam, 19–46.

——— (1988), 'On the Mechanics of Economic Development', *Journal of Monetary Economics*, 22: 3–42.

——— (1990), 'Why Doesn't Capital Flow from Rich to Poor Countries?' *American Economic Review Papers and Proceedings*, 80: 92–6.

Machin, Stephen and Manning, Alan (1994), 'The Effects of Minimum Wages on Wage Dispersion and Employment: Evidence from the UK Wages Councils', *Industrial and Labor Relations Review*, 47(2): 319–29.

Maddison, Angus (1982), *Phases of Economic Development*, Oxford University Press.

——— (1989), *The World Economy in the 20th Century*, OECD, Paris.

——— (1991), *'Dynamic Forces in Capital Development*, Oxford University Press.

Mankiw, N. Gregory, Romer, David, and Weil, David N. (1990), 'A Contribution to the Empirics of Economic Growth', *Quarterly Journal of Economics*, 57: 407–38.

Marx, Karl (1867), *Das Kapital*, Vol. I. Dietz Verlag, Berlin.

Mastropasqua, Cristina, Micossi, Stefano, and Rinaldi, Roberto (1988), 'Interventions, Sterilization, and Monetary Policy in European Monetary System Countries, 1979–87', in F. Giavazzi, S. Micossi, and M. Miller (eds.), *European Monetary System*, Cambridge University Press.

Matthews, Kent, and Minford, Patrick (1987), 'Mrs Thatcher's Economic Policies', *Economic Policy*, 5: 59–101.

Miller, Merton and Orr, Daniel (1966), 'A Model of the Demand for Money by Firms', *Quarterly Journal of Economics*, 80: 413–35.

Missale, Alessandro (1991), *Debt Maturity: the Evidence*, Ph.D. dissertation, MIT.

Mitchell, Brian R. (1978), *European Historical Statistics*, Columbia University Press, New York.

——— (1983), *International Historical Statistics*, Macmillan, London.

——— (1988), *British Historical Statistics*, Cambridge University Press.

Mussa, Michael (1979), 'Empirical Regularities in the Behavior of Exchange Rates and Theories of the Foreign Exchange Market', in K. Brunner and A. Meltzer (eds.), *Carnegie-Rochester Conference Series*, 11: 9–58.

Pagano, Marco, and Roëll, Ailsa (1990), 'Trading Systems in European Exchanges', *Economic Policy*, 10: 63–115.

Phelps, Edmund, S. (1968), 'Money-Wage Dynamics and Labor Market Equilibrium', *Journal of Political Economy*, 76: 687–711.

Phillips, A. W. (1958), 'The Relationship between Unemployment and the Rate of Change of Money Wage Rates in the United Kingdom, 1861–1957', *Economica*, 25: 283–99.

Repullo, Rafael (1991), 'Financing Budget Deficits by Seigniorage and Explicit Taxation: the Cases of Spain and Portugal', CEPR Discussion Paper no. 583, October.

Roberts, Benjamin C. (1985), *Industrial Relations in Europe*, Croom Helm, London.

Rogoff, Kenneth (1990), 'Symposium on New Institutions for Developing Country Debt', *Journal of Economic Perspectives*, 4: 3–6.

Roll, Eric *et al.* (1993), *Independent and Accountable: a New Mandate for the Bank of England*, Report of an independent panel, CEPR, London.

Romer, David (1996), *Advanced Macroeconomics*, McGraw-Hill, New York.

Sachs, Jeffrey D. (1980), 'Wages, Flexible Exchange Rates and Macroeconomic Policy', *Quarterly Journal of Economics*, 94: 731–47.

—— and Wyplosz, Charles (1986), 'The Economic Consequences of President Mitterrand', *Economic Policy*, 2: 261–322.

Sahay, Ratna and Végh, Carlos (1994), 'Dollarization in Transition Economies: Evidence and Policy Implications', International Monetary Fund, unpublished.

Sargent, Thomas J. (1979), *Macroeconomic Theory*, Academic Press, New York.

—— (1982), 'The End of Four Big Inflations', in R. E. Hall (ed.), *Inflation*, University of Chicago Press, pp. 41–110.

Sharpe, William, and Alexander, Gordon (1990), *Investments*, 4th edn., Prentice-Hall, Englewood Cliffs, NJ.

Siebert, Horst (1991), 'German Unification: the Economics of Transition', *Economic Policy*, 13: 287–340.

Sinn, Gerlinde and Hans-Werner (1992), *Jumpstart: the Economic Unification of Germany*, MIT Press, Cambridge, Mass.

Sinn, Stefan (1990), *Net External Asset Positions of 145 Countries*, Kieler Studien no. 234, J.C.B. Mohr, Tübingen.

Solow, Robert M. (1970), *Growth Theory: an Exposition*, Oxford University Press.

—— (1976), 'Down the Phillips Curve with Gun and Camera', in D. Belsey *et al.* (eds.), *Inflation, Trade, and Taxes*, Ohio State University Press, Columbus, Ohio.

Spencer, Grant H. (1984), 'The World Trade Model: Revised Estimates', *IMF Staff Papers*, 31: 469–98.

Summers, Lawrence H. (1981), 'Taxation and Corporate Investment: a G-theory Approach', *Bookings Papers on Economic Activity*, 1: 67–127.

Summers, Robert, and Heston, Alan (1988), 'A New Set of International Comparisons of Real Product and Price Levels: Estimates for 130 Countries, 1950–1985', *Review of Income and Wealth Series*, 34: 1–25.

—— (1991), 'The Penn World Table (Mark 5): an Expanded Set of International Comparisons, 1950–1988', *Quarterly Journal of Economics*, 106: 327–68.

Tobin, James (1956), 'The Interest Elasticity of the Transactions Demand for Cash', *Review of Economics and Statistics*, 38: 241–7.

—— (1958), 'Liquidity Preference as Behavior towards Risk', *Review of Economic Studies*, 25: 65–86.

—— (1963), 'Commercial Banks as Creators of "Money"', in D. Carson (ed.), *Banking and Monetary Studies*, Richard D. Irwin, Homewood, Ill., pp. 408–19.

—— (1969), 'A General Equilibrium Approach to Monetary Theory', *Journal of Money Credit and Banking*, 1: 15–29.

—— (1972), 'Inflation and Unemployment', *American Economic Review*, 62: 1–18.

—— (1974), *The New Economics: One Decade Older*, Princeton University Press.

Triffin, Robert (1960), *Gold and the Dollar Crisis*, Yale University Press.

US Department of Commerce (1975), *Historical Statistics of the United States*, US Government Printing Office, Washington, DC.

Weber, Axel (1991), 'Reputation and Credibility in the European Monetary System', *Economic Policy*, 12: 57–102.

van Wijnbergen, Sweder (1991), 'Mexico and the Brady Plan', *Economic Policy*, 12: 14–56.

Wyplosz, Charles (1989), 'EMS Puzzles', *Revista Espanola de Economia*, 7: 33–66.

Miscellaneous Publications

Annual Abstract of Statistics, Central Statistics Office, London

Bank of England Quarterly Bulletin

Bulletin de la Banque de Belgique

Bulletin Trimestriel de la Banque de France

Economie et Statistiques, Institut National de la Statistique et des Etudes Economiques, Paris

Employment Outlook, OECD, Paris

European Economy, Commission of the European Communities, Brussels

Historical Statistics, OECD, Paris

International Financial Statistics, International Monetary Fund, Washington, DC

Main Economic Indicators, OECD, Paris

Monthly Report of the Deutsche Bundesbank

National Accounts, OECD

World Debt Tables, World Bank

World Economic Outlook, International Monetary Fund, Washington, DC

Glossary

This glossary presents brief definitions of the key concepts listed at the end of each chapter. Numbers refer to the corresponding chapter(s).

absolute purchasing power parity (8): theory asserting that price levels are equalized across countries once they are converted into a common currency

absorption (2): total national (private and public) spending on goods and services

accelerator (4): the positive effect of an increase in GDP on the rate of investment

accounting identities (2): relationships linking macroeconomic magnitudes to each other by definition

active labour market policies (17): programmes involving direct job creation, targeted job securities, retraining, relocation of families from distressed regions, or special programmes to get young people started in the job market

activist policies (16): government policies which try to improve market outcomes by correcting market dysfunctions

acyclical (14): an economic variable is acyclical when it does not move systematically with aggregate output over the business cycle

aggregate demand (1, 11, 12, 13): the sum of planned consumption, investment, government purchases of goods and services, plus net export of goods and services (the primary current account)

aggregate demand curve (13): downward-sloping curve relating aggregate demand negatively to the rate of inflation

aggregate production function (5): a relationship linking total output to employed resources such as capital, labour, and other factors of production

aggregate supply (12): total volume of goods and services brought to market by producers at a given price level

aggregate supply curve (12): upward-sloping curve linking inflation to aggregate output supplied by firms

animal spirits (4): term referring to entrepreneurs' optimism and willingness to undertake risky investment projects

appreciation (exchange rate) (7, 8, 13, 18, 19): a market-determined increase in the value of a currency (less of that currency must be relinquished to buy one unit of foreign currency); *see*: depreciation; revaluation

arbitrage (11, 13, 18): the simultaneous purchase and sale of assets of identical characteristics to earn a profit without risk-taking: **spatial arbitrage** responds to diverging asset prices across different market locations, **yield arbitrage** responds to differing asset returns, and **triangular arbitrage** to three asset prices that are not mutually consistent

asymmetry hypothesis (21): the hypothesis that the German Bundesbank posesses a dominant role in the operation of EMS

augmented Phillips curve (12): a Phillips curve incorporating core inflation and allowing for supply shocks

autarky (3): the state in which a country operates when it does not trade with the rest of the world

automatic stabilizer (15): the economic mechanism that automatically cushions the impact of exogenous changes in aggregate demand, via the effect of income on saving decisions

average or unit costs (12): production costs per unit of output

balance of payments (2): a summary of all real and financial transactions of a country with the rest of the world

balance sheet (8): a statement of the financial position of a firm or other entity at a particular point in time, indicating its assets, liabilities, and net worth

balanced growth (5): term describing a steadily growing economy where certain key ratios remain constant, for example the capital–output ratio

Balassa–Samuelson effect (7): the observation that price levels in richer nations are systematically higher than in poor ones; attributed to higher nontraded goods price inflation in fast growing countries

band of fluctuation (20): the range within which the market value of a national currency is permitted to fluctuate by international agreements, or by unilateral decision by the central bank

bank reserves (9): the central bank liabilities (cash or central bank deposits) that commercial banks choose or are required to hold to meet demands of depositors and/or the requirements of regulators

beggar-thy-neighbour policies (11): policies, especially exchange rate policies, designed to divert domestic demand away from foreign goods and towards domestically produced goods

Beveridge curve (17): downward-sloping curve relating the unemployment rate to the vacancy rate; the position of this curve measures the efficiency of the job-matching process

bid–ask spread (18): in the foreign exchange market, the bid is the price at which one can sell foreign exchange (to some market maker); the ask is the price at which one can buy it on the market. The spread is the difference—usually quoted as a percentage—between the two prices

bimetallism (20): the use of both gold and silver as a commodity money standard

boom/recession (14): period of expanding/contracting aggregate economic activity

borrowing constraint (3): restrictions on borrowing arising from uncertainty about future incomes, which prevent agents from taking advantage of their intertemporal allocation of resources

Bretton Woods Conference (20): meeting held in 1944 and attended by officials from 45 nations to shape a new international money order after the Second World War

British terms (7): one of two ways of quoting the exchange rate, here in units of the foreign currency per one unit of domestic currency (e.g. US$1.52 for $1 for UK residents); *see also* European terms

bubbles (18): persistent deviations of asset prices from their fundamental values, or from widely held views about their fundamental values

Burns–Mitchell diagram (14): a diagram displaying the behaviour of macroeconomic variables over the typical business cycle as a deviation from their values at the cyclical peak

business cycles (1, 11, 12, 14): succession of periods of rapid growth and slowdown or decline in which output fluctuates around its long-run trend

capacity utilization (rate) (1): the proportion of installed equipment currently employed; higher rates occur during booms, lower rates correspond to recessions

capital (2): one of the factors of production; usually refers to plant, equipment, inventories, and structures

capital account (2): component of the balance of payments accounts that records financial transactions with the rest of the world

capital accumulation (5): the increase of the stock of capital, sometimes called net investment or net formation of capital. It differs from gross investment, which also includes the capital put in place to replace depreciated equipment

capital adequacy (9): minimum net worth banks are required to have as a fraction of total risky assets

capital control premium (19): the deviation from the covered interest parity arising from restrictions on capital movements

capital controls (11, 17, 21): restrictions on the movement of assets into and out of a country

capital–labour ratio (5): the ratio of the stock of capital to the use of labour

central bank (9): a public or quasi-public agency with an explicit legal mandate to issue banknotes and other liabilities as legal tender

classical dichotomy (10): the situation pertaining when equilibrium values of nominal variables can be determined independently of real variables; the real side of economic activity (growth, unemployment, etc.) is affected only by technology and tastes

closed economy (10): an economy that does not trade with, borrow from, or lend to other countries

Cobb–Douglas production function (5): a particular form of the general production function linking output Y to capital K and labour L: $Y = AK^{\alpha}L^{1-\alpha}$

coefficient of variation (1): a measure of variability expressed as the standard deviation divided by the mean

coincident indicator (14): a macroeconomic variable which coincides with aggregate output over the cycle

collective labour supply curve (6): the link between the amount of man-hours that workers supply collectively (via wage negotiations or through their unions) and the real wage

collectively voluntary/individually involuntary unemployment (6): unemployment that is undesirable from the point of view of individual workers but accepted by them collectively as they trade off higher wages for fewer jobs

commodity money (8): forms of money that have intrinsic value in other uses, or derive their value from the commodity out of which they are made, chiefly gold or silver

competition policy (16): policies aimed at decreasing monopoly power and increasing rivalry among sellers in markets

conditionality (20): requirements imposed by the IMF on member-countries' macroeconomic policies for obtaining certain types of loans

constant returns to scale (5): term describing a production function in which simultaneous equiproportional increases in the factors of production result in an equiproportional increase in output

consumer price index (1, 2, 12): an index of prices of a basket of goods representative of the consumption pattern of the 'average consumer', using fixed quantity weights in some base year

consumer surplus (17): the difference between the maximum amount that a consumer would be willing to pay for a specified quantity of good and what she must actually pay for it

consumption (2): goods and services produced and sold to households for the satisfaction of wants

consumption function (4): a symbolic way of stating that the aggregate consumption is positively related to aggregate wealth and, if a significant proportion of households is constrained in credit markets, to disposable income

consumption–leisure trade-off (6): the fundamental determinant of the labour supply decision: in order to consume, we need income and therefore we need to work, which means giving up leisure time

consumption smoothing (4, 15): optimal choice by households to smooth out the impact of temporary disturbances to income on consumption plans by either borrowing (in the case of a negative shock) or saving (in the case of a positive shock)

contagion (21): situation arising when one country devalues in a fixed exchange rate system, causing others to lose competitiveness and become candidates for devaluation, even if this was not initially justified

convergence criteria (21): set of conditions that must be met by countries wishing to join the European Monetary Union

convergence hypothesis (5): the hypothesis of a negative association between per capita growth and initial per capita GDP

co-ordination failure (1): situation occuring when agents (households, firms) fail to realize that their actions are interdependent, and that acting jointly might benefit all

core or underlying inflation rate (12): the inflation rate taken into account during wage bargaining to anticipate future inflation or to recuperate losses from past inflation

corporatism (6): the degree to which trade unions, management, and governments work together to achieve macroeconomic objectives

correlation coefficient (1): a statistical measure, ranging from −1 to 1, which shows how closely two variables move together: a value of zero indicates the absence of correlation; a value of 1 indicates perfect positive correlation; a value of −1 indicates perfect negative correlation

countercyclical (14): term used to describe an economic variable when it is negatively correlated with the state of the economy; that is, it moves in the opposite direction to aggregate output over the business cycle

countercyclical fiscal policy (15): corrective device intended to keep the economy near its equilibrium level by increasing or decreasing aggregate demand via public spending or tax policies

covered interest parity (19): a no-arbitrage condition equating the difference between domestic and foreign interest rates to the forward exchange discount

credibility (16, 21): the degree to which authorities are believed by the public to take specific actions in response to disturbances; e.g. credible central bank is known not to tolerate inflation; *see*: reputation

credit rationing (4): a condition in loan markets in which there is excess demand for loans at the market interest rate

crowding out (11): mechanism by which an expansionary fiscal policy may in the end have little, no, or even a negative effect on aggregate output and income because other components of demand decline

current account (2, 3, 7): the sum of a country's trade in goods, services, and unilateral transfers with the rest of the world

cyclically adjusted budgets (15): budgets adjusted for the effect of the business cycle on tax revenues

damped, explosive and oscillating cycles (14): a time series is denoted to be damped (explosive, oscillating) if it displays diminishing (increasing, steady) cycles

debt stabilization (15): the process of arresting explosive growth in the debt–GDP ratio, usually achieved by cutting government expenditures and raising taxes

decision lag (16): time lag in policy effectiveness needed by government to formulate policy

decreasing returns to scale (5): describes a production function for which an equiproportional increase in the factors of production results in a less than equiproportional increase in output; *see also* constant and increasing returns to scale

deflation (1, 13): a period of sustained decrease in the general price level, or more generally a sustained decline in the inflation rate

demand determined output (10): when suppliers produce whatever is demanded at a given price level

demand management (16): policy to keep the economy at its equilibrium level by correcting aggregate demand

demand shock (14): sudden increase or decrease in aggregate demand

demand side (1, 12): the analysis of spending decisions by economic agents

depreciation (capital) (2, 4); the loss of original value of a physical asset owing to use, age, and economic obsolescence

depreciation (exchange rate) (7, 8, 13, 18, 19): a market-determined decrease in the value of a currency (more of that currency must be relinquished to buy one unit of foreign currency); *see:* appreciation, revaluation

derivatives (18): securities that derive their value from the behaviour of other underlying securities

desired demand function (10): total planned spending given the interest rate and real GDP

detrending (14): removing the trend in economic time series

devaluation (11, 13, 20): decision by the monetary authority to reduce the value of the currency; *see:* revaluation, appreciation, depreciation

diminishing marginal productivity (3, 5): the tendency that, as the inputs into production are increased, the increments of output will decline

discount lending or rediscounting (9): instrument of monetary control employed by the central bank when it lends reserves directly to commercial banks at the discount rate

discount rate (9): interest rate at which the central bank lends reserves to a commercial bank by discount lending or rediscounting

discounting (3): valuing future goods or money in terms of goods or money today; *see also* intertemporal price

disequilibrium (10): situation occuring when, at given output or interest levels, desired demand is not equal to supply

distortionary taxation (17): *see* tax distortions

diversification (18): purchasing several different assets to reduce risk to wealth caused by fluctuations in the value of any single asset

dollar shortage (20): a situation that was feared within member-countries of the Bretton Woods system in the 1950s, because the USA ran current account surpluses

dominated asset (8): an asset that bears a lower rate of return than assets of comparable riskiness

double coincidence of wants (8): a condition required for barter to take place, in which the type and quantity of goods offered by one trader match those desired by the other

durable goods (4): goods that yield a flow of services into the future

Dutch disease (7): the loss of competitiveness arising from a real exchange appreciation as a result of the discovery of natural resources

dynamic inefficiency/efficiency (5): an economy is dynamically inefficient when a reduction of current savings can make all generations better off; it is dynamically efficient when future generations can be made better off only by reducing consumption (i.e. increasing savings) today

economic agents (1): term used to denote decision-makers in an economy

economic growth (1, 5): secular increases in the output of an economy, usually measured by the annual growth in GDP per capita

economic rents (17): returns to factors of production that exceed the minimum amount necessary to keep those factors of production in operation

effective exchange rate (7): an index consisting of a weighted average of a country's exchange rates *vis-à-vis* its main trading partners

effectiveness lag (16): time lag resulting from a slow or delayed impact of economic policies on real activity

efficiency wages (6): wages paid in excess of the marginal productivity of labour in order to induce sufficient effort on the part of the workers

endogenous and exogenous variables (1): endogenous variables are explained by economic principles; exogenous variables, in contrast, are determined outside the system under study

endogenous growth (5): an explanation of growth as the result of decisions taken by private agents in response to economic conditions, rather than in response to the exogenous evolution of technical progress

endowment (3, 4): the exogenous resources that economic agents expect to have in the present and in the future

equilibrium rate of unemployment (6, 11): the unemployment rate that occurs when employment and unemployment stabilize, i.e. when aggregate demand for labour is met by aggregate supply. Because labour supply may not perfectly reflect individuals' preferences, this unemployment may be in part involuntary (structural unemployment), but it may also reflect the efficiency of the labour market (frictional unemployment)

equity–efficiency trade-off (15): the fact that improving equity among society's members often has a negative impact on the economy's efficiency

European Central Bank (21): centre of a planned new European System of Central Banks

European Currency Unit (ECU) (21): the unit of account of the European Monetary System and the European Community, and the basis for defining the parities in the Exchange Rate Mechanism (ERM); consists of a basket of the EC currencies; *see* Exchange Rate Mechanism

European Monetary Institute (EMI) (21): body located in Frankfurt which prepares the practical steps required to establish an integrated system of European central banks

European Monetary System (EMS) (21): international agreement set up in 1979 to stabilize the exchange rates between the currencies of some EC countries

European Monetary Union (EMU) (21): the planned-for achievement, by 1999 at the latest, of a single common currency for the European Community

European System of Central Banks (21): system including the European Central Bank and national subsidiaries in an integrated system of European central banks

European terms (7, 18): one of two ways of quoting the exchange rate, here in units of domestic currency per one unit of the foreign currency (e.g. DM1.5 for US$1 for German residents); *see also* British terms

excess supply (10): a market situation in which the quantity supplied exceeds desired demand at prevailing prices

Exchange Rate Mechanism (ERM) (21): the fixed exchange rate system of the European Monetary System

exchange rate regime (11): description of the exchange rate system adopted by a country: the exchange rate may be fixed, so that the central bank maintains the value of the domestic money in terms of another currency or group of currencies or it may be freely floating

export function (11): function representing part of a country's foreign spending and therefore following its fluctuations—the greater the foreign spending, the greater will be exports

externalities (5, 15, 17): activities that affect the welfare of economic agents not undertaking them directly

factors of production (1, 2): inputs in the production process, such as labour, capital, or land, which create value added (in contrast to intermediary inputs)

fiat money (8): money which the state declares to be legal tender although its intrinsic value may be little or nothing

final and intermediate sales (2): final sales refer to sales of goods and services to the consumer or firm that will ultimately use them; intermediate sales refer to producers who use and transform these goods or services as part of their own production of goods and services

financial integration line (11): the line in the IS–LM diagram defining the domestic interest rate level consistent with financial integration in the world economy with full capital mobility

financial intermediaries (9): economic entities that collect funds from depositors and lend them to borrowers

financial intermediation (2, 18): activity of bringing together borrowers and lenders; usually conducted by banks and other financial intermediaries, which collect savings and then lend them out to those willing to pay for their use

finding rate (6): the rate at which unemployed workers find a job, calculated as a ratio of job finds (per month or per year) to total unemployment

fiscal policy (13, 15, 16): the use of the government budget to affect the volume of national spending, or more generally to provide public goods and services, as well as to redistribute income

Fisher principle (8): the decomposition of the nominal interest rate (i) into the sum of the real interest rate (r) and the expected rate of inflation (π^e)

fixed capital formation (3): *see* investment

flows and stocks (1): a flow is an economic variable measured between two periods of time; a stock is a magnitude measured at a given time

foreign exchange interventions (2, 9): purchases and sales of foreign money in exchange for domestic money undertaken by monetary authorities

foreign exchange reserves (2): foreign currencies held by the monetary authority for the purpose of intervening in the exchange markets

forward bias (19): the difference between the expected future spot exchange rate and the corresponding forward rate

forward market (18): the market for foreign exchange delivered and paid for at some point in the future but at a price agreed upon today

forward forecast error (19): the deviation of the forward rate from the realized spot exchange rate

forward premium or discount (18): price of a forward contract with respect to the spot price

frictional unemployment (6): unemployment resulting from individuals' changing jobs or entering the labour force

fundamentals (7, 18, 19): factors driving the exchange rate; the net external position, and determinants of the primary current account as well as monetary conditions and the degree of price rigidity: in general, the underlying real factors that determine the value of an asset

futures (18): contracts for future delivery of goods or financial assets, including **foreign exchange general equilibrium** (1, 6, 7, 10); a characterization of an economy that considers all markets and heirs impact on each other rather than a single market in isolation

general equilibrium (10, 11): condition of equilibrium applying simultaneously to several markets at the same time, recognizing the interdependencies between markets

GNP or GDP deflator (2): the ratio of nominal to real GNP or GDP, the rate of increase of which is a frequently used measure of inflation

gold exchange standard (20): the system established at the Bretton Woods conference in 1944 whereby gold was the fundamental standard of value, but for all currencies the gold parity was mediated by the dollar

gold standard (20): a system whereby a country defines its monetary unit in terms of gold

golden rule (5): proposition that per capita consumption is maximized in a growing economy at the point at which the marginal product of capital is equal to the growth rate

goods market equilibrium (10): is the situation in which the desired demand equals supply

Gresham's Law (20): the proposition that a money which is more valuable than its official exchange rate will disappear from circulation: 'bad money chases out the good'

gross domestic product (GDP (2): a location-based measure of a country's productive activity, corresponding to the value added generated by factors of production, both local and foreign-owned, within a country

gross national product (GNP) (2): a measure of the productive activity of a country computed on the basis of the ownership of the factors of production

hedging (18): techniques used to protect oneself against foreign exchange fluctuations; more generally, any trading techniques used to eliminate risk

human capital (5, 6, 17): the education, training, and work experience acquired by individuals

Hume mechanism (20): the process by which trade imbalances were equilibrated under the gold standard system: a trade deficit (surplus) implies a reduction (increase) in gold and money supply, which leads to higher (lower) interest rates, to capital inflows (outflows), and to falling (rising) prices improving (worsening) the country's competitiveness

hyperinflation (1, 8, 13, 16): term used to describe periods of extremely high inflation, usually when the monthly rate exceeds 50%

hysteresis (6): the failure of certain macroeconomic variables to return to their original values after the cause of the change is removed; temporary changes in certain variables lead to permanent changes in others

implementation lag (16): time lag in policy effectiveness as a result of the time taken by parliaments and ministries to pass and originate legislation

import function (11): function representing part of domestic spending and therefore following its fluctuations: the greater domestic spending, the greater will be imports

impossible trilogy (21): principle stating that, while pairwise compatible, full capital mobility, fixed exchange rates, and monetary policy independence are jointly incompatible

impulse-propagation mechanism (14): mechanism that transforms shocks (impulses) into irregular oscillations like the business cycle

income effect (4, 6): the portion of change in quantity demanded which is attributed to the change in real income that results from the price change

increasing returns to scale (5): a characteristic of the production function which occurs when a simultaneous equiproportional increase in the factors of production results in a more than equiproportional increase in output.

index (1): a number that has no dimension (i.e. is not expressed in units such as DM, tons, hours, etc.); it is usually set to take a simple value like 1 or 100 at a specific date

indexation (12): a provision in wage or other contracts by which nominal values are adjusted frequently to reflect changes in some price index and to maintain the real value of the contract's provisions

indifference curves (4): a graphic representation of all possible combinations of two items that will yield equivalent utility (satisfaction)

industrial policies (17): these amount to official backing of national corporations or whole industries, taking on the form of subsidies, public orders, or trade policies

inflation differential (8, 16): the difference between the domestic and foreign inflation rates

inflation rate (1, 8): the rate of change of the level of prices, measured by some price index or deflator

inflation tax (9, 15): real revenue that the government obtains by inflation. Inflation erodes the real value of nominal assets and therefore may improve financial condition of the government, reducing the value of its nominal liabilities

information asymmetry (8): a situation in which one party has better information than the other/s about the probability of an outcome, and all parties know it

installation costs (4): the costs of installing new productive equipment

interbank market (9): a wholesale market for money, which brings commercial banks together

interest rate (3): payment for use of funds over a period of time; equivalently, the price of future income or goods in terms of present income or goods

interest rate parity (11, 13): the condition that interest rates are equalized across countries taking account of expected exchange rate changes

internal terms of trade (7): the ratio of traded to nontraded goods prices

international Fisher equation (19): uncovered interest parity and purchasing power parity imply that the real interest rates are equal across countries *ex ante*

International Monetary Fund (IMF) (20): an institution set up at the Bretton Woods conference in 1944 to promote international monetary co-operation and exchange rate stability, to establish a multilateral system of payments for current transactions, and to assist members facing balance of payments difficulties

intertemporal budget constraint (3): the relationship summarizing resources and opportunities available in the present and the future to a household for consumption; the present value of spending must be less than, or equal to, wealth

intertemporal price (3): the price of goods tomorrow in terms of goods today; how much we would be willing to pay for—or sell for—the good today for delivery at some future date

intertemporal trade (3): trade conducted by households and firms across time

interventionism (1): policy whereby a government supports, co-ordinates, and even controls certain aspects of private activity; *see*: *laissez-faire*

intramarginal interventions (21): interventions by central banks within the bands of fluctuation to try to dissuade markets that a realignment is under consideration

investment (3): the acquisition of productive equipment for later use in production; also called fixed capital formation

investment function (4): relationship between investment and its fundamental determinants: aggregate investment depends positively upon Tobin's q and GDP growth, and negatively upon the real interest rate

investment, gross and net (1, 2, 3, 4, 5): the acquisition of new productive equipment: gross investment comprises the total expenditure on new capital goods, including replacement of worn-out equipment; net investment represents addition to the capital stock

invisibles (2): trade in services between a country and the rest of the world

involuntary unemployment (6): unemployment that occurs when individuals are willing and able to work at the going wage rates but cannot find a job

IS curve (10): for given values of exogenous variables, the combinations of nominal interest rate i and real output (GDP) that are consistent with goods market equilibrium

job finding rate (6): the rate at which workers move from the state of unemployment to that of employment; *see*: separation rate

job matching (17): the matching of job offers of firms' and unemployed workers

job separation rate (6): the rate at which workers move from being employed to being unemployed, because of quits, redundancies, or for other reasons

Keynesian assumption (10, 11): the assumption that the evolution of the price level is insensitive to aggregate demand in the short run

Keynesian model (11): model based on the assumption that prices are sticky, at least in the short run

Keynesian revolution (1): the development of ideas and policies to deal with situations where price and/or wage rigidities lead to recessions; these ideas stand in opposition to (neo)classical economics, which holds that markets are able to take care of themselves

(Keynesian) demand multiplier (11): a ratio indicating the effect of increases in exogenous components of aggregate demand on total aggregate demand

Keynesianism (16): the view that government demand management policy should play a key role in macroeconomic policy: Keynesians hold that markets suffer from imperfections—for example slow clearing of labour and product markets—which are responsible for the occasional underutilization of resources

labour (1): factor of production, usually measured in man-hours, i.e. the total number of hours worked in a firm, an industry, or a country

labour and profit shares (1, 5): the labour or wage share is the fraction of total income paid to workers; the profit share is that going to the owners of capital

labour demand (6): the relationship linking the number of man-hours that firms wish to hire and the cost of labour

labour force (6): the total number of individuals who are either working or actively looking for a job

labour force participation (1, 6): the proportion of working-age people who are in the labour force

labour supply, individual and aggregate (6): the relationship linking the wage rate and the number of hours that employees are ready to work: aggregate supply refers to the overall behaviour of the labour force, while establishing that workers are interested in providing more working hours, and firms will want to use fewer man-hours, when the real hourly wage rate increases

labour tax wedge (17): the difference between labour's cost to firms and wages actually received by workers

Laffer curve (17): the relationship between government tax revenues and the average tax rate: beyond some point, increases in tax rates are associated with decreases in tax revenues, because the distortionary effects outweigh the revenue gained

laissez-faire **(1):** term used to describe the view that properly functioning markets will deliver the best possible social outcome, and that intervention by the government in economic affairs should be rejected; *see:* interventionism

leading and lagging indicator (14): a macroeconomic variable which systematically leads (lags) aggregate output over the cycle

leakages (11): part of income not respent in the circular flow of income and expenditure, either as private savings, taxes, or imports

legal tender (8, 9): money that is mandated by law to be accepted in the payment for goods and services

leisure (6): time spent not working

lender of last resort (9): the central bank, in its implicit commitment to protect bank customers by providing failing banks with sufficient monetary base to prevent collapse

life-cycle theory (4): theory that consumption choices are made with a planning horizon equal to the individual's expected remaining lifetime; that an individual will build up savings during working years and exhaust them during retirement years

LM curve (10): for given values of the exogenous variables and the price level, the combinations of real output (GDP) and interest rates for which the money market is in equilibrium

long-run aggregate supply (12): the vertical line in inflation–output space, showing that real and nominal variables do not influence each other in the long run

Lucas critique (16): the hypothesis that households and firms incorporate perceptions of the policy regime in their behaviour; as a result, shifts in the policy regime can have fundamental effects on behaviour

Lundberg lag (14): assumption that output responds to spending with a lag, on the hypothesis that firms react initially to sudden changes in demand not by changing production, but by running down inventories

man-hours (6): a measure of labour input which is equal to the number of people employed times the average number of hours spent working

marginal cost of capital (4): the cost of an additional increment to productive capacity

marginal productivity of capital (4): additional output produced by employing an additional unit of capital in the production·process

marginal productivity of labour (6, 12): additional output produced by employing an additional unit of labour in the production process

marginal rate of substitution (4): the rate at which one commodity can be substituted for another without changing the level of utility

market-clearing (16): term describing a market that works perfectly by equalling demand and supply at every instant

market efficiency (18): the property that asset prices reflect all the available information and risks attached to any single asset

market maker (18): traders or institutions that stand ready to deal in a particular asset

markup pricing (12): the percentage by which a firm increases the selling price of goods above the average or unit costs of production

mathematical model (1): a list of equations formalizing postulated linkages between exogenous and endogenous variables

median voter theorem (16): if voters' preferences are evenly spread along some dimension, then a political party's maximizing election strategy is to advocate policies that are most favoured by the median ('middle') voter

medium of exchange (8): currency or other objects used to pay for goods

menu costs (10, 11, 12): lump-sum costs incurred when adjusting a nominal price or wage

merchandise trade balance (2): the sum of exports less imports of merchandise goods for a country *vis-à-vis* the rest of the world over some time period

minimum wages (6): the lower bound set on wage rates that may be paid to workers, usually but not always by law

misalignment (19): a persistent deviation of the real exchange rates from its equilibrium value

misery index (1): the sum of the unemployment and inflation rates

mismatch (6): situation arising when the labour market doesn't clear because workers and vacancies are of such different industrial, occupational, or location nature that not enough job matches can take place

model (1): a set of economic linkages, including the assumptions made in drawing up the list of endogenous and exogenous variables

monetarism (16): ranging from the view that the quantity of money has the major influence on economic activity and the price level to the view that money affects only nominal—not real—variables, this multi-faceted school of thought concludes that monetary policy is best used by targeting the rate of growth of the money supply; monetarists reject activist policies because of uncertainty, lags, and government incompetence

monetary aggregates (8): various definitions of the money stock, differing largely by their degree of liquidity

monetary approach (19): the view that, under stable-equilibrium exchange rates, all long-run movements of the nominal exchange rate are due to changes in the nominal money supply

monetary base (9): the sum of currency in the hands of the public and bank reserves

monetary economy (1, 10, 11, 12, 13): the part of the economy dealing with monetary and financial, nominal phenomena

monetary interdependence (11): term referring to the fact that, under fixed exchange rates, foreign monetary policy changes impact on domestic monetary conditions

monetary neutrality (8, 10): term used to describe the fact that money does not affect the real side of the economy

monetary policy (9): actions taken by central banks to affect monetary and financial conditions in an economy

monetary union (21): an agreement among sovereign countries to use a common currency

monetization (9, 15): open market purchases of Treasury bills by the central bank, or, more generally, the lending of the central bank to the government to cover its deficit

money demand function (9): the relationship between real money demand and its determinants: real GNP, the nominal interest rate, and the cost of bank transactions

money growth line (13): is a horizontal line corresponding to the rate of inflation controlled by the domestic monetary authorities under flexible exchange rates

money illusion (12): term used to describe the failure to distinguish monetary from real magnitudes

money market equilibrium (10): equality of the exogenous and the central-bank-controlled money supply and the money demand that corresponds to a particular output level and exogenous transaction costs

money multiplier (9): the link between the monetary base and wider monetary aggregates

multiplier–accelerator model (14): model of the business cycle developed by Paul Samuelson in which the interaction of the accelerator principle of investment and the multiplier leads to cyclical behaviour

Mundell–Fleming model (11): the open economy version of the IS–LM model

N – 1 problem (21): in a fixed exchange rate system with N countries, the fact that $N - 1$ bilateral rates can be sufficient to determine all, leaving one degree of (monetary) independence

neoclassical assumptions (10): the view that prices adjust even in the short run, so that the economy is always dichotomized

neoclassical approach (10): model claiming that flexible prices clear all markets even in the short run

net exports (2): difference between the flow of domestic goods and services sold to foreigners and the flow of imported goods and services

net national product (2): a measure of national output which nets out the depreciation of productive equipment

net taxes (2): the government's tax income from households and firms after transfers have been subtracted

net worth (8): the difference between assets and liabilities listed in an institution's balance sheet, representing its value to the owners

neutrality of money/monetary neutrality (8, 10): the principle that the money supply does not affect real variables such as real output or unemployment, but rather the price level

no-arbitrage condition (18): the condition imposed on a model that arbitrage profits must be absent

noise traders (18): irrational or misinformed traders who cause deviations of stock prices from their fundamental value for a long time

nominal (1): a variable expressed in value or money terms, as opposed to 'real' terms (i.e. terms of goods)

nominal anchors (16): in stabilization programmes, the practice of setting or targeting one or more nominal variable—such as the exchange rate or nominal wages—

in order to hasten return to the equilibrium level of output and to influence expectations

nominal exchange rate (7): the value of foreign currency in terms of domestic money

nominal interest rate (8): the interest rate as quoted on financial markets or by banks

nominal wage and price rigidity (12): the fact that, owing to menu costs, contracts, or customer relations, prices denominated in money do not react immediately to changes in demand, and thereby prevent output and employment from reaching their equilibrium levels in the short run

non-traded goods (7): goods that are not easily traded

normative economics (1): economics that passes judgement or provides advice on policy actions; *see*: positive economics

numeraire (7): a benchmark good in terms of which all other goods are priced

offshore markets (18): markets for assets denominated in a country's currency but located outside that country

Okun's law (1, 12, 13): the observed inverse relationship between fluctuations of real GDP around its trend growth path and fluctuations of the unemployment rate around its equilibrium level

open market operations (9): transactions undertaken by a central bank which exchanges securities for its own liabilities; these operations have the effect of supplying reserves to, or draining them from, the banking system

opportunity cost (3, 4, 8): the value of a resource in its best alternative use

optimal capital stock (4): the stock of physical capital that maximizes the value of the firm, for which the marginal productivity of capital is equal to the marginal cost of investment

optimal currency area (21): a region for which no welfare loss is implied by the use of a common currency

option (call and put) (18): a contract that allows the owner to purchase (call) or sell (put) an asset at some predetermined price at or before some specified point in time

out-of-equilibrium conditions (5): conditions when a market is not equilibrium

output cost of disinflation (13): the sacrifice ratio, which compares the cumulated increase in the rate of unemployment with the reduction in inflation achieved over some period of time

output gap (12): temporary deviations of GDP from its trend or equilibrium level

output–labour ratio (5): the ratio of output to the labour used to produce that output

overshooting (17): situation arising when, in response to a disturbance that modifies its long-run level, the nominal exchange rate moves in the short run in the same direction but by a larger amount, to be eventually reversed

par or central value (20): the fixed official exchange rate declared by the monetary authority of a country

parallel currencies (8): currencies issued by private institutions or foreign countries that are used alongside domestic money

parity/central parity (21): defined as a fixed but adjustable exchange rate between any pair of countries; *see also* par or central value

parity grid (21): the complete set of central parities and margins of fluctuation in the EMS

partial equilibrium (5): the analysis of the determinants of equilibrium in a particular market, ignoring whether other markets are in simultaneous equilibrium

partial market equilibrium condition (1, 6): the equality of demand and supply in a particular market under study

partisan business cycles (16): business cycles resulting from the succession in power of parties with different economic priorities and preferred policies; *see:* political business cycles

PCA function (11): function given by the difference between exports and imports and determined by domestic spending, foreign spending, and the real exchange rate

peak/trough (14): upper/lower turning point of a cyclical economic time series

pecuniary/non-pecuniary externalities (17): externalities that are/are not transmitted by the market's price mechanism

permanent income (4): the flow of income which, if constant, would deliver the same present value as the actual expected income path

persistence (14): long-lasting effect of a shock hitting the economy

personal income/personal disposable income (2): total household income after income taxes and fines and fees have been paid; the amount that can be used for consumption or savings

Phillips curve (12): an empirical relationship linking the inflation rate negatively to the unemployment rate

Plaza and Louvre Accords (20): agreements from the mid-1980s between industrial countries on limiting exchange rate fluctuations

policy lags (16): the delays (recognition, decision, implementation, and effectiveness) between the occurrence of a situation calling for policy action and the ultimate effect of that action; may actually exacerbate rather than smooth economic fluctuations

policy mix (11): the joint use of monetary and fiscal policies

policy regime (11, 16): explicitly or implicitly established set of rules of governments

political business cycles (16): business cycles resulting from the use of macroeconomic policies to improve the state of the economy just before elections; *see:* partisan business cycles

position (long or short) (18): a trader is long in a given currency when she owns, or has contracted to receive, that currency in the future; similarly, a trader is short when she has contracted to make payment in a foreign currency at some future time

positive economics (1): the description and explanation of economic phenomena; *see:* normative economics

poverty trap (5): a situation where a country cannot enter a phase of sustained growth

PPP (purchasing power parity) line (13): a horizontal line corresponding to the foreign inflation rate, because at fixed exchange rates purchasing power parity rules out permanent differences between domestic and foreign inflation

preferences (5): the way we describe an individual's behaviour when faced with alternative spending opportunities

present discounted value (3): the value of a stream of income or spending spread over time and valued at today's price; *see also* intertemporal price

price level (1): the average level of prices in an economy

price line (7): graphic description of the relative price of two goods

primary budget deficit (3): the budget deficit net of debt service (i.e. net of the payment of interest on the public debt)

primary current account (3): the current account less net interest payments (net investment income); alternatively, the difference between gross domestic product output and aggregate domestic spending when unilateral transfers are equal to zero

primary current account function (4, 7): the relationship linking the primary current account positively to the real exchange rate and negatively to the level of GDP or income

primary government budget surplus (3): the excess of government tax revenues over non-interest expenditures, or, equivalently, the excess of net taxes plus interest payments over government purchases of goods and services

privatization (1, 17): the sale or transfer of part or all of state-owned enterprises to the private sector

procyclical (14): an economic variable that it is positively correlated with the state of the economy; that is, it moves in the same direction as aggregate output

producer surplus (17): difference between the price that a producer actually receives for a given quantity of goods and the amount corresponding to the minimum price at which he would be willing to supply the same quantity

production function (3, 5, 6): theoretical relationship linking aggregate output to inputs of factors of production

productive efficiency (15): the optimal use of available productive resources

productivity growth slow-down (5): the downturn of total factor productivity growth observed since the mid-1970s despite the developments of new technologies

profit share (6): the proportion of GDP paid out to shareholders

progressive tax (17): tax system in which the tax rate is increasing with the (pre-tax) income level

public goods (8, 15, 17): goods and services that are provided free of charge and the consumption of which by one person does not prevent the consumption by another person (characterized by non-excludability and non-rivalry)

purchasing power parity (PPP) (7, 8, 13): principle asserting that the rate of nominal exchange rate depreciation is equal to the difference between the domestic and foreign inflation rates; a stronger (and less plausible) absolute form of PPP equates price levels across countries when expressed in a common currency

q-theory of investment (4): theory linking investment to Tobin's q, the ratio of firms' market value to the replacement cost of installed capital

quits (6): voluntary separations from jobs on the part of the employee

quota (IMF) (20): a country's voting and borrowing rights in the IMF, based on its initial deposit upon joining

Ramsey principle of public finance (17): principle that, for a given amount of revenue to be raised, goods with the most inelastic demands and supplies should be taxed most heavily in order to minimize overall loss of consumer and producer surplus in an economy

random walk (19): a variable that changes randomly from period to period, where the only change between its value today and its value tomorrow will be white noise and can be positive or negative

rate of capacity utilization (1): measure of the degree to which firms employ their plants and equipment; one indicator of cyclical conditions

rational expectations hypothesis (3): hypothesis asserting that agents evaluate future events using all available information efficiently so that they do not make systematic forecasting errors

real (1): a variable expressed in volume, adjusted from its nominal counterpart to take account of inflation

real business cycle theory (14): theory of the business cycle which explains economic fluctuations primarily as a consequence of technology shocks assuming price flexibility

real consumption wage (6): the ratio of nominal wages to the consumer price index; a measure of the price of leisure (or the return to work) in terms of consumption goods

real economy (1, 10, 11, 12, 13): term referring to the production and consumption of goods and services, and the incomes associated with productive activities; *see*: monetary economy

real exchange rate (7): the cost of foreign goods in terms of domestic goods, defined as the nominal exchange rate adjusted by prices at home and abroad

real interest parity (19): the difference between domestic and foreign real interest rates, which is equal to the corresponding nominal differential less the expected inflation differential

real interest rate (8): the difference between the nominal interest rate and the expected rate of inflation

real wage rigidity (6, 12): rigidity arising when unemployment fails to cause real wages to decline

recognition lag (16): time lag in discovering that policy intervention is called for

relative price (7): the price of one good in terms of another, usually computed as the ratio of two nominal prices

relative purchasing power parity (8): situation occurring when the cost of the same basket of goods in different countries increases at the same rate once converted into a common currency

reputation (16): the effect on the public of self-imposed rules by the government to refrain from some actions, even if at some point such actions are highly desirable

reserves ratio (9): the ratio of a commercial bank's reserves (vault cash or deposits at the central bank) to the total demand deposits it has issued

returns to scale (5): the impact on output of an increase in all inputs by the same proportion: if output increases equiproportionally, the production function is said to exhibit constant returns to scale; if output increases more or less than proportionally, we have respectively increasing or decreasing returns to scale

revaluation (11, 13, 20): decision by the monetary authority to increase the value of the currency; *see*: devaluation, appreciation, depreciation

Ricardian equivalence (3): hypothesis that the time profile of taxes needed to finance a given stream of government purchases has no effect on agents' intertemporal budget constraint and therefore on real spending and saving decisions; then public debt is not considered as private wealth

risk averse (18): behaviour characterized by a preference to avoid risk

risk neutral (18): behaviour characterized by an indifference to risk

risk premium (18, 19): compensation above and beyond the expected rate of return on an asset required by agents to hold it

Robertson lag (14): assumption that current spending is related to past income

rules vs. discretion (16): legal rules are established to rule out time-inconsistent discretionary government policies

saving (2): postponement of consumption using some part of disposable personal income

seigniorage (9, 15, 20): exploitation by the government of the monopoly power of the central bank to create money as a means of raising real resources

self-fulfilling attacks (21): exchange rate attacks that are not justified by the exchange rate fundamentals, but occur because, if they succeed, the authorities will relax monetary policy, proving the attack to be rational *ex post*

separation rate (6): the rate at which employed workers become unemployed per unit of time; *see*: job-finding rate

severance payments (6): compensation, usually in the form of lump-sum cash payments, paid by employers to workers who are made redundant for economic reasons

small-country assumption (11): working assumption that real and financial conditions abroad are unaffected by domestic economic developments and that the 'foreign' rate of return is exogenous

'Snake' (20): arrangement between EC countries during the final years of the Bretton Woods System to stick to a reduced (half) margin

soft budget constraint (15): expression used to describe the situation of state-owned firms whose losses are automatically covered by the government budget

Solow decomposition (5): the three-way decomposition of the sources of economic growth into capital accumulation, increase in labour utilization, and the Solow residual capturing technological progress

Solow growth model (5): a theory that analyses growth as being driven by exogenous technological change and the accumulation of factors of production

Solow residual (5): the part of GDP growth unexplained by the increase in factors of production and conventionally ascribed to technological progress

spatial arbitrage (18): arbitrage that occurs when investors identify a divergence of prices of identical assets in different market locations; *see* arbitrage

special drawing rights (SDRs) (20): a reserve money created by the IMF in 1967 and allocated on the basis of quotas; used among central banks as an additional source of liquidity

speculative attacks (21): sudden loss of foreign exchange reserves of central banks, arising when exchange market participants anticipate an imminent devaluation

speculative bubbles (18): persistent deviations of market prices from their fundamental values

spot market (18): market in which transactions are for immediate delivery of good or asset purchased

stabilization policies (15): policies designed to stabilize aggregate income and spending as well as unemployment

stagflation (12, 13): periods when both inflation and unemployment increase

stationary GDP (14): the level of GDP that would in theory result after full adjustment occurs, in the absence of further shocks to the economy

steady state (6): a hypothetical state in which all variables have responded fully to exogenous changes in the environment

sterilization (9): actions undertaken by central banks to offset the impact of a foreign exchange intervention on the domestic money supply, usually a money market purchase or sale of securities in the same amount as the foreign exchange market intervention

sticky price business cycle theory (14): class of theories of the business cycle in which the rigidity of prices are of central importance

structural unemployment (6): unemployment arising as the result of a mismatch of demand and supply of labour; *see*: mismatch

substitution effect (4, 6): the component of the total change in quantity demanded that is attributable to the change in relative prices

supply determined output (10): when the price level adjusts freely, so that general equilibrium is always found at the intersection of the IS and the goods supply schedule, then output is supply determined

supply shocks (12, 13, 14, 17): exogenous increases in non-labour production costs

supply side (1, 12, 17): the productive potential of an economy and the factors that determine its overall efficiency

swap transactions (18): exchange of sums of money of the same currency but on different terms, for instance selling francs for delivery now while simultaneously buying them back for delivery in three months' time

systemic risk (9): the risk of a generalized collapse of the banking system, arising because banks and financial institutions hold large amounts of each other's liabilities

tax distortions (15): effects on real behaviour arising from the wedge that taxes introduce between the price received by the provider of a good or service and the price paid by its consumer

tax smoothing (15): the proposition that a government should not change tax rates in response to temporary causes of budget deficits, but should borrow instead

technological progress (5): the contribution to economic growth of technological change, usually captured by the rate of increase of total factor productivity

terms of trade (7): the ratio between the price of exportables and the price of imports; measures how many foreign goods can be purchased with one unit of domestic output

time inconsistency (16): characterizes policies which, although optimal today, become less desirable at a later stage, especially after agents have adjusted their behaviour accordingly

Tobin's q (4): the ratio of the present value of the return from new investment to the cost of installed capital; often approximated as the ratio of share prices to the replacement price of equipment

total factor productivity (5): productivity in the production process that is attributable not to any particular factor of production, but to all; growth in total factor productivity is often measured as a weighted average of growth in average productivities of all factors of production

tradable goods (7): goods actually traded or potentially tradable with foreign countries

trade policies (17): policies designed to support a domestic product's sales through tariffs on foreign goods, or quotas on imports

trade union voluntary/involuntary unemployment (6): unemployment resulting from the fact that trade unions ask for higher real wages than if the market were perfectly competitive, which may be involuntary from the perspective of individuals

trade unions (6): organizations of workers formed for the purpose of taking collective action against their employers to obtain improvements of pay and other working conditions

transaction costs (8, 17): costs arising from transactions, especially financial transactions

transfers (2): direct payments by the government to individuals or firms not related to the provision of goods and services, e.g. subsidies, unemployment benefits, pensions

trend (1, 13): long-term tendency in a time series

triangular arbitrage (18): arbitrage requiring that the relative prices of three or more assets are consistent with each other; *see* arbitrage

Triffin paradox (20): the inconsistency of the US dollar (a national currency) as a world reserve currency with its gold backing: in order for internationally held dollar balances to grow with the world economy, the USA had to run balance of payment deficits over time which eventually outstripped its gold reserves

turning points (14): times when economic cycles reach a peak or a trough

uncovered interest parity (UIP) (19): the condition that rates of return on assets of comparable risk are equalized across countries once expected exchange rate changes are taken into account

underground economy (2): economic activities from which income earned is not reported and therefore is untaxed

undervaluation/overvaluation (7, 19): a currency is undervalued/overvalued when its exchange is below/above its long-run equilibrium value, or the level consistent with its long-run fundamentals

undiversifiable risk (18): a risk that cannot be reduced by holding a mix of several different assets

unemployment (6): individuals without a job who are actively seeking work

unemployment benefit (6): financial assistance to those seeking a job but unable to find suitable employment

unemployment rate (6): the ratio of the number of unemployed workers to total labour force

unemployment stocks and flows (6): the stock of unemployment is the number of people willing to work but unemployed at a moment in time; flows refer to workers coming into unemployment (inflows) or to previously unemployed workers finding a job or leaving the labour force (outflows)

utility (4): the satisfaction that a consumer derives from the consumption of goods and services

value added (2): increase in the market value of a product at a particular stage of production; calculated by subtracting the value of all inputs bought from other firms from the value of the firm's output

velocity of money (8): the number of times on average that a unit of money is spent during the measurement period (usually a year)

voluntary unemployment (6): the difference between total labour availability and the employment that would result from labour market equilibrium; reflects the fact that some people who are in the labour force do not wish to work at the current wage level

wage inflation (12): the annual rate of growth of nominal wages

wage share (6): the proportion of GDP paid out as wages

wealth (2, 3, 4): the sum of inherited assets or debts and the present value of current and future incomes

yield arbitrage (18): arbitrage which applies to assets that are equivalent in terms of their risk characteristics; *see* arbitrage

Index

Words and phrases in blue are defined in the glossary and also appear as key concepts which are listed at the end of each chapter.